ART APPLIED   IN

DE OUTSIDE/PETRA BLAISSE

ART APPLIED

INSIDE OUTSIDE/PETRA BLAI

EDITED BY FREDI FISCHLI & N

GTA EXHIBITIONS

INSTITUTE FOR THE

HISTORY AND THEORY OF AR

ETH ZURICH

MACK

SE

LS OLSEN

HITECTURE (GTA)

"AFTER MATERNITY LEAVE, LATE JUNE 1981, THE APPLIED ARTS DEPA

GAVE ME PERMISSION TO TAKE MY BABY DAUGHTER ANNA, THEN

WE MADE A SOFT BABY BED INSIDE ONE OF THE WICKER COLLEC

HAD THE RIETVELD BUFFET BROUGHT UP TO OUR DEPA

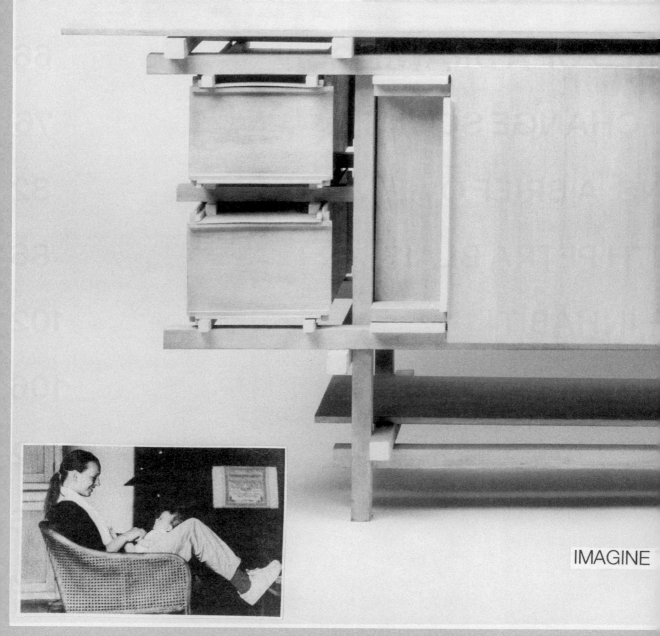

IMAGINE

MENT OF THE STEDELIJK MUSEUM IN AMSTERDAM, WHERE I WORKED,

HT WEEKS OLD AND BREAST FEEDING, WITH ME TO WORK.

BASKETS, AND MY BOSS WIL BERTHEUX (1916-2004),

MENT SO THAT I COULD CHANGE ANNA'S NAPPIES ON IT.

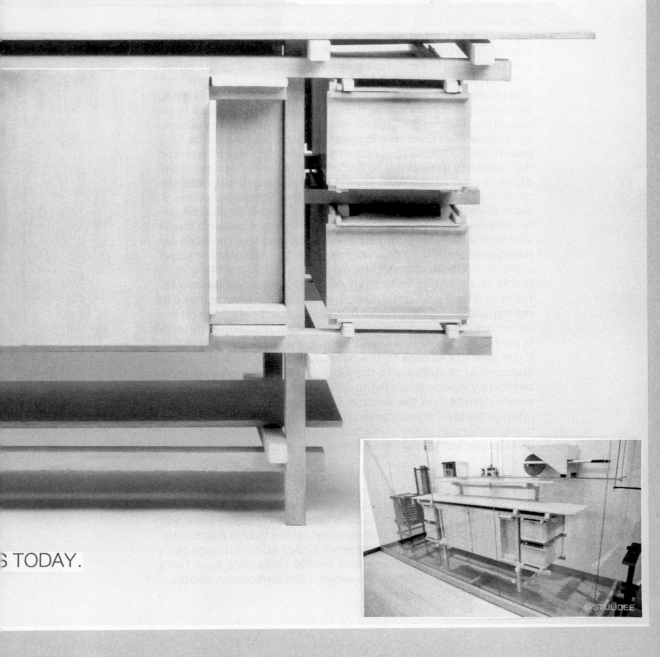

S TODAY.

INCOMPLETE OEUVRE

Untold volumes are dedicated to architects. In format, layout and chronology, they all follow the same conventions of canonical historisation. They ignore anything related to the social or economic context, the background of the clients, the team of people who devote their time to a single author, or the impact on an architect's personal life. In short, the reality of life is excised from the clean layouts, the professional photography and the meticulous technical drawings framed between hard covers. The rigid format of an *oeuvre complète* suggests the clear and finite work of an architect and promises a permanent place in cultural memory.

It is with these reservations in mind that we chose to apply this burdened term – *oeuvre complète* – to the work of Inside Outside. We visited the studio's archive where we met with the three partners, Petra Blaisse, Aura Luz Melis, Jana Crepon and their team in Amsterdam. We were intrigued by the difference between Inside Outside's oeuvre and that of an architect. The studio's practice over more than three decades has led to outcomes that defy conventional definition and refuse to be classified, from "recipe" drawings to skewed treatments of scale to creative malapropisms in space, material and presence. This oeuvre, being harder to capture than that of architects, sparked our curiosity in seeking to trace, identify and document the studio's past works with almost forensic exactitude. Blaisse challenges the concept of singular authorship; she prefers to work collectively. In fact, Inside Outside's work is never singular inasmuch as it takes shape as one element within a larger whole; it unfolds in subtle interventions that react to both existing environments and newly designed architecture. Instead of solid products of concrete, metal, or glass, the work is malleable and responsive to change, for which reason Blaisse returns to it time and again, keeping track of its development. In retrospect, this *softness* can be read as a tactical attack on the supremacy of male-dominated architecture. Blaisse's early work in scenography, interiors and gardens did not pose a threat, but it did give her access to the field of architecture. Acting as a supporting contributor to the work of architects, she played a seemingly innocent role in the discourse and gradually, subversively intruded on the architectural canon. Yet, although her interventions ultimately entered the domain of architecture, her contributions to many iconic buildings are often ignored, much like the work of earlier female practitioners of modernism.

This publication plays with the paradox of historicising a practice based on conceptual schemes, impermanent propositions and collaborative processes. As a survey of both materialised and non-materialised projects, it takes a subjective view and presents a collection of propositions rather than a chronological documentation of finite works. Our editorial approach corresponds with Blaisse and Inside Outside's own form of representation. Recipe drawings – like cartoonish scores –

communicate works and studies as manuals for a wide-ranging audience, as production guidelines, or as a means of sharing methods with interested colleagues.

THE POLITICS OF INSIDE

Blaisse's choice of name for her studio – Inside Outside – implies a fundamental critique of architectural basics. Inside Outside do not escape the confines of architecture nor do they abandon the building as such, but they do remain ambiguous, possessed with the intersection of *inside* and *outside*. In the architectural discourse, the term *inside* is fraught with sexual politics.[1] In the fifteenth century, Leon Battista Alberti's foundational treatise *On the Art of Building* (1443–1452) already observed the complicity of patriarchal authority in the design of private houses since spatial order is tantamount to a form of surveillance. The house situates men closest to the outside world while women are relegated to chambers in the back of the house, a spatial confinement that restricts access to exchange and thus knowledge. In her essay *The Architect & the Housewife* (1999), the artist Frances Stark examines this binary discrimination and the shortcomings of modernism's designs for living and public settings. One of her examples is Rudolph Schindler's residence, which he planned for himself and his wife plus another couple. They had private bedrooms but shared other areas. The architect's alternative to conventional domesticity failed; the other couple moved out and his marriage with Pauline G. Schindler deteriorated. They tried to divide the house and live separately but failed again, partly because she was so bold as to decorate her section of the house with her own choice of wallpaper and carpeting. Schindler was incensed: "I am sure you are familiar with the reasoning for my choice of materials and that what you have done is completely incongruent with my design and destroys the integrity of the structure."[2] Inside Outside transcend these entrenched conventional orders; they challenge the normative boundaries and spatial layouts inscribed in the profession of architecture.

The studio's trademark softness also unmasks another issue inscribed in architecture's founding myths. Textiles have always been a salient feature of their work, with curtains essentially becoming structural elements of the architecture in the form of soft walls. The contrast between the softness of textiles and the hardness of stone draws attention to gender-specific connotations that persist in the history of architecture; the low decorative arts are traditionally associated with femininity. In *The Four Elements of Architecture* (1851), Gottfried Semper argues that textiles were the original building material, in the form of twisted and knotted threads instead of layered stones. Even so, a firm distinction is made between architecture and textiles, for the soft material not only poses a threat to the hegemony of architecture, it also smacks of arts and crafts, which is clearly incompatible with the perceived status of the architectural arts. This battle of high art versus craft persisted into the twentieth century. While modern and contemporary art challenged the autonomy of high art, there still remains a classed, raced and gendered distinction between "high craft" meant for institutional display and the "low craft" of hobbyists that is not meant to "travel beyond the living room and remains stained by 'bad taste.'"[3]

The Bauhaus specifically excluded textile work from the professional sphere of architecture. Although the movement proclaimed equality of the sexes in its founding manifesto, female students were denied participation in architecture workshops and were required to study weaving instead. Walter Gropius's brutal gender division reflected his outspoken belief that women only had the capacity to work in two dimensions, whereas men could master three. Architecture commissions remained rare and provided limited income to the school, but the women's weaving workshop – along with the carpentry workshop that included both male and female students – became the most successful, providing the largest financial contribution to the school. Nonetheless, history is still reluctant to recognise the fact that the women at the Bauhaus rescued the school from bankruptcy.[4]

It is no coincidence that we decided to stage Inside Outside's retrospective (2018), a precursor to this publication, in the central hall of the ETH's building originally designed by Gottfried Semper. Inside Outside's intervention consisted of two immense, white curtains of a filmy fabric that could well have been used for a night gown. Gracefully and sensuously swaying in the circulating air, they literally flew in the face of the monumental hall that marks the heart of the institution. Does such an ephemeral, seductive presentation belong in the hallowed halls of the renowned Federal Institute of Technology?

THE FEAR OF APPLIED ARTS

Art Applied, the title of this book, zeroes in on this sore spot – on the uneasy role of architecture within the arts. Having argued that architecture is based on low decorative arts and borrows from crafts such as pleating and weaving, Semper challenged the hierarchical division between high and low art. In consequence, his theory unsurprisingly met with resistance and repression. He even went so far as to repudiate the traditional claim that crafts are applied art, declaring that the first craft – weaving – is not applied or dependent on other structures, as proven by the distinction between *Wand* (wall) and *Gewand* (dress), which underscores the principle of dressing as the origin of architecture. In her first major project, the curtain for the Nederlands Dans Theater (1987), Blaisse devised a spatial element that evokes a dress. The golden curtain with a dotted pattern creates the effect of a screen animated by the bodies of dancers. It is transformed from a functional device into a fleeting, temporal surface, expressing delicacy, artifice, frivolity, ornament and charm.

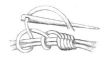

We read Inside Outside's work as a renaissance of the applied arts, as a practice that opposes the increasingly dominant domain of design. Interiors and their fittings have become increasingly capitalised, subverting the integrity of any modernist ideology that was once embedded in twentieth-century design: cantilevered steel tubular chairs can be perceived as a new Biedermeier. Despite the growing prevalence of this form of design, Inside Outside's work is consistently site-specific, ensuring a unique response to each individual context. In contrast to many design products, their works cannot be multiplied and distributed; they are, in fact, often made of impermanent materials and means, as best illustrated by the characteristic use of cable-binders to attach curtains to garage door tracks. Gone is the status of a fixed, finite form as a factor of value. The interventions are designed to function in their own specific site, and although they undoubtedly evoke desire and beauty, their materiality is in most cases raw and does not rely on precious textiles. Industrial PVC and packaging materials are, in fact, some of the studio's preferred materials.

Inside Outside's development is contemporaneous with the global expansion of signature architecture, and while contributing monumental icons to this period of cultural production, Blaisse takes an entirely anachronistic approach. Her team is small; they work closely together; they draw by hand, sew and produce crude, tactile objects of an entirely different economic and aesthetic order within the built environment of late capitalism. A far cry from the alienation of producers from what they produce, their craft blithely bypasses the pitfall of luxurious, exclusive production and instead takes a turn towards the ephemeral design of stage sets and the improvisation of found objects.

CARE VS THE ART OF DISPLAY

The point of departure for Blaisse is the museum where she learned about two very different concerns: care and the art of display. When she recounts her experience of working as an assistant in Stedelijk Museum's Department of Applied Arts, one would think she were reenacting Lea Lublin's *Mon Fils (My Son)*. In 1968 at the Salon de Mai in Paris, the Argentinian artist placed a crib in the museum and took care of her seven-month-old son for the duration of the show. In 1981, Blaisse took her eight-week-old daughter along to the museum and used a Rietvelt sideboard from the collection – the same one on view in a protective vitrine at the museum today – to change the baby's diapers, and repurposed one of the department's wicker baskets, in which sensitive collection pieces are transported throughout the building, as a crib. A collage of text banners in the style of Barbara Kruger posters, showing a blend of the language of propaganda and billboards, became Blaisse's manifesto on introducing the notion of care into the realm of the museum.[5] Lublin's artwork and Blaisse's anecdote reveal the reality of working as a mother within the patriarchal art system.

The approach of Inside Outside embodies care in many ways, as seen, for instance, in the studio and its work culture. The team not only share work on objects, drawings and plantings; they also collectively cook lunches and cultivate a garden on the studio's roof terrace: an intimate atmosphere prevails despite the challenges of a global economy and difficult working conditions.

Blaisse's early introduction to the art of display and exhibition making by working as a curator and scenographer would become integral to the studio's later practice. The experiences decisively influenced her understanding of scenarios and the distinctive message she developed of staging them without relying on convention. One of her first exhibition designs as an independent practitioner was devoted to the work of OMA: *The First Decade* at Rotterdam's Boijmans van Beuningen museum in 1986. Study of the archival photographs reveals several elements that would become iconic ingredients of her work. The project not only marked the beginning of her longtime collaboration with Rem Koolhaas and OMA, but also made a strong contribution to the niche domain of exhibiting architecture. Architecture is often considered paradoxical and indeed impossible to present in a museum. Eeva-Liisa Pelkonen aptly wonders how one can "exhibit something as large and complex as a building or a city, and [...] communicate something as elusive as an architectural experience that unfolds in space and time?"[6] Every architectural curator struggles to find alternatives to simply displaying models, photographs and drawings of buildings. Blaisse's displays mark a paradigm shift in this field. She does not represent built work but a scenography that enhances collective processes, showcases *how to work* and, most importantly, encapsulates the attitude of the exhibited authors.

At OMA's early travelling shows, she did not place artifacts on normative plinths but instead made tree-shaped columns out of rebars from constructions sites. And instead of didactic wall texts, she put up wild, associative wallpapers that she describes as collages with which a teenage girl might plaster the walls of her room. These function as mind-maps, revealing the architect's diverse sources, from poetry to porn. It is as if Blaisse were appropriating Independent Group's *accrochages* of the 1950s but without the educational mission of modernism. Using a form of display that resembles the walls of a teenager's bedroom is far removed from their 1955 exhibition *Man, Machine and Motion* and also offers a more inclusive, subjective and sexualised gaze on cultural production.

The use of textiles and curtains as well as of deconstructed walls, as in the readymade rebars in *The First Decade*, relate to modernist visions of exhibitions and museums. New prototypes for exhibition halls in the 1930s staged the traditional typology of the enfilade almost like a skeleton, where each plane becomes a light-weight screen and thus deconstructs the solid nineteenth-century museum. For our exhibition *Theft is Vision*

(2017), Inside Outside proposed an enfilade that was even more deconstructed and phantom-like. Translucent walls, made of plastic wrapping used for shipping containers, act as partitions suggesting individual wing-like galleries in which the artworks are displayed.

Lilly Reich and Mies van der Rohe's soft architecture of large-scale velvet curtains for the exhibition *Die Mode der Dame* (1927), staged in Berlin's Funkturmhalle and two years later at the International Exposition in Barcelona, proved to be a model for Blaisse. There, curtains of black, orange and red velvet, as well as black and lemon-yellow silk suspended from curved metal tracks, created a small group of spaces that flow into each other.[7] This novel concept of flexible, soft and moving displays evolved into permanent projects, such as LocHal (2018) in Tilburg. There she transformed a vast, repurposed locomotive repair factory by introducing semi-translucent curtains, creating changeable divisions and dispensing with static architecture that relies on walled interiors. Lino Bo Bardi's *Bahia no Ibirapuera* design for the Fifth Sao Paolo Biennale (1959) was nothing but a shell of wavy blue curtains. Bo Bardi's lively spatial choreography added other dimensions to design, such as a performative involvement of sound. She covered the floors with leaves, a ritual practiced by local Brazilians during festivities; the rustling sound of visitors walking on them enlivened the exhibition. The notion of sound or sonic landscapes has not been addressed in the documentation of Inside Outside, although it does exist, as in the Sound Curtain in the Kunsthal in Rotterdam (1992), where high tones were transmitted through integrated speakers, in the mechanical noise of the moving curtains in the Dutch Pavilion at the Venice Biennale (2012), or in the crackling sound of walking on paths covered with mussel shells in the landscape of State Detention Center (1997).

IN PLACE OF ARCHITECTURE

Initially designed for theatres and the domestic context, Inside Outside's curtains changed dramatically in scale and function over the years, as in the above-mentioned LocHal. Their landscape design has also grown so much in scale that it belies the connotation of a "garden." The Biblioteca degli Alberi (2018), located in the midst of urban Milan and spanning almost ten hectares, has revitalised a raw site surrounded by a maze of traffic arteries, trains and metro stations and framed by invasive real estate development. Significantly, the increase in scale has not affected the spirit of the studio with its emphasis on personal contact, collaboration and hands-on practice. The landscape for the gigantic Shenzhen Stock Exchange Headquarters (2013) eminently illustrates the studio's resistance to corporate production. On the patio of the high-rise, Inside Outside's garden becomes a romantic collage on top of the implacable world of finance; it is like an absurd layering of two incompatible realities. Based on medieval floral drawings, Inside Outside's proposal consists quite simply of a surrealist expansion of scale, from tiny drawing to XL-landscape. This playful act of enlargement causes ruptures and the built garden appears pixelated, resulting in an unexpected beauty that stands in great contrast to the generic, so-called refined productions encountered in real estate developments all over the world. In short, despite embarking on such ambitious projects in architecture's global economy, Inside Ouside creates designs that are still driven by experimental applied art.

In this regard, their work has always struck us as paradoxical. On the one hand, we note a kind of "corporate" aesthetic in the use of industrial materials, yet on the other, the work is pure craft. Almost everything is a one-off and has the quality of a prototype. Industrial materials like PVC are not ordinarily associated with arts and craft, but a closer look reveals the human, handmade involvement: someone did the stitching, cut the holes and laid the unusual stones or mirrors in the grass of the landscape architecture. We would argue that this is both the quality and the challenge of the work. For a client who wants a professional solution for a special situation, the result might be too quirky, too self-made, too intimate, while the choice of material might seem too corporate for those who seek creative and artistic authorship. This ambiguity is among the many things that makes Blaisse's oeuvre so fascinating.

The mature work of commercially successful architects is often said to lose the charm of their earlier work. The original handwriting is wiped out by the system. Some try to deal with the almost inevitable transformation that attends commercial growth by distancing themselves from the early days of their practice and transitioning from a hand-knit to a machine-knit approach. Significantly, when Inside Outside were invited to produce a display for the newly opened Prada store in New York, designed as an "epicenter" by OMA, they eschewed the serial, high-tech production methods taken for granted in this context of high-end fashion meeting high-end architecture. Instead they locked themselves into a hotel room and used hand-torn strips of silver organza to knit a gigantic sock, essentially an abstract garment made out of "Lasergewebe CS." The high-tech sheen of the synthetic material collided with the housework domesticity of the production; the tiny hotel room-cum-factory stood in great contrast to the imposing destination of its output. Never would one expect the intimacy, sacrifice and devotion of the hours, indeed days of manual labour that went into creating the final product. The difference between art and architecture, design and applied arts might perhaps be negotiated somewhere between these extremes. But why is this relevant for production today? For one thing, the studio addresses users directly by taking such an undogmatic approach. When SANAA architects completed the Toledo Museum of Art, Inside Outside was commissioned to make a contribution that would underscore intimacy and care. Their curtains softened the space, screened it from light and sound, and gave it a human scale. This was not a top-down masterplan imposed on a space but a set of propositions. Working with applied arts adds a human trace; it challenges architectural grandeur and encourages interaction with the space.

The countless means of intervention detailed in this monographic publication as well as the collection of Inside Outside's recipes (manuals available to any user) offer manifold possibilities for engaging with art, architecture and design. At a time when the building and design industry is in disrepute and the profession of architecture is being questioned, we can learn from the "art applied" of Inside Outside. Their trajectory could prove useful in modifying or adding to existing structures with accessible, light-weight methods and materials, and most helpful in discovering unprecedented means of reusing, reseeing and contributing to our built environment.

Fredi Fischli and Niels Olsen

Illustrations for Gottfried Semper's "Stil in den technischen und tektonischen Künsten, oder Praktische Aesthetik" (1860/63) in gta Archives, ETH Zurich

1   For a reading of sexuality and space and the spatial politics of "inside" in architectural discourse, see Mark Wigley, "Untitled: The Housing of Gender," in *Sexuality and Space*, Beatriz Colomina (ed.), New Jersey: Princeton Architectural Press, 1992.
2   Schindler is quoted in: Frances Stark, *The Architect & the Housewife*, London: Open House/Book Works, 1999, p. 16.
3   Julia Bryan-Wilson, *Fray: Art and Textile Politics*, Chicago: University of Chicago Press, 2017, pp. 13–14.
4   For more on the Bauhaus women as spatial producers, see Harriet Harriss, "Blocks Versus Knots. Bauhaus Women Weavers Contribution to Architecture's Canon," in *The Routledge Companion to Women in Architecture*, Anna Sokolina (ed.), New York: Routeledge, 2021, pp. 112–28.
5   See pp. 8–9 in this publication.
6   Eeva-Liisa Pelkonen, Carson Chan, David Andrew Tason, *Exhibiting Architecture. A Paradox?*, New Haven: Actar/Yale School of Architecture, 2015, p. 10.
7   Matilda McQuaid, *Lilly Reich. Designer and Architect*, New York: The Museum of Modern Art, 1996, p. 25.

OMA City Hall Presentation, Haags Gemeente Museum
LOCATION The Hague, the Netherlands
CLIENT Municipality of the Hague
YEAR 1986
STATUS Completed
SCOPE Design and installation of OMA City Hall presentation in one gallery of the Haags Gemeente Museum
SCALE ca. 20 m²
COLLABORATORS OMA team, Hans Werlemann, Vincent de Rijk

→ p. 866
Liquid Gold, Nederlands Dans Theater
LOCATION The Hague, the Netherlands
CLIENT Nederlands Dans Theater/OMA
YEAR 1985–1987
STATUS Completed
SCOPE Design of stage curtain and interior interventions, seating for auditorium, sound reflectors, underside of "flying" champagne foyer; vintage furniture for dancers' lounge and dressing rooms, restaurant
SCALE ca. 4,000 m², auditorium and seating for 1,001 persons; stage curtain, 22 × 11 m; six sound reflectors; gold foil column, 100 × 50 cm
COLLABORATORS OMA, Hans Werlemann, Utopia, Theatex, Texoprint

Restaurant Christophe
LOCATION Amsterdam, the Netherlands
CLIENT Christophe Royer
YEAR 1987
STATUS Completed
SCOPE Design of textile, acoustic wall covering in restaurant; design and implementation of shaded garden on (below street-) kitchen level, including dog-house and garbage area
SCALE ca. 40 m²
COLLABORATORS Paul van den Berg

→ p. 856
Villa Kralingen
LOCATION Kralingen, Rotterdam, the Netherlands
CLIENT Private owner
YEAR 1986–1988
STATUS Completed
SCOPE Interior finishes, curtains and garden (for one of the twin houses)
SCALE Curtains, 266 m²; garden, 500 m²
COLLABORATORS OMA

→ p. 864
Rotterdam '88, Cultural Year
LOCATION Holland America Line, Kop van Zuid, Rotterdam, the Netherlands
CLIENT Rotterdamse Kunststichting
YEAR 1987–1988
STATUS Completed
SCOPE Selection and preparation of location, organisation and design of a series of fine and applied arts exhibitions throughout 1988
SCALE ca. 4,500 m²
COLLABORATORS OMA, Rotterdamse Kunststichting team

→ p. 862
Office for Metropolitan Architecture. Arbeiten 1972–1988, Architekturmuseum Basel
LOCATION Basel, Switzerland
CLIENT Architekturmuseum Basel – director Ulrike Jehle Schulte-Strathaus
YEAR 1988
STATUS Completed
SCOPE Exhibition design and installation
COLLABORATORS OMA, Hans Werlemann/ Hectic Pictures, Claudi Cornaz, Herman Helle, Parthesius & de Rijk, Ron Steiner

→ p. 848
OMA The First Decade, Museum Boijmans van Beuningen
LOCATION Rotterdam, the Netherlands
CLIENT Museum Boijmans van Beuningen – director Wim Crouwel
YEAR 1989
STATUS Completed
SCOPE Exhibition design and installation
SCALE 450 m²
COLLABORATORS OMA, Hans Werlemann/ Hectic Pictures, Claudi Cornaz, Herman Helle, Parthesius & de Rijk, Ron Steiner

Energieen, Stedelijk Museum
LOCATION Stedelijk Museum, Amsterdam, the Netherlands
CLIENT Stedelijk Museum – director Wim Beeren
YEAR 1990
STATUS Completed
SCOPE Co-design of OMA's "Tres Grande Bibliotheque" installation at *Energieen* group exhibit
SCALE 1 room 5 × 10 m
COLLABORATORS Hans Werlemann/ Hectic Pictures, Vincent de Rijk, OMA

Poetry International Festival
LOCATION De Doelen, Rotterdam, the Netherlands
CLIENT Poetry International Festival
YEAR 1990
STATUS Completed
SCOPE Site-specific installation *Sand Mountain* at entrance hall for the Poetry International Festival
COLLABORATORS Paul van den Berg

→ p. 840
OMA Fin de Siècle, L'Institut français d'architecture (IFA)
LOCATION Paris, France
CLIENT L'Institut Français d'Architecture (IFA) – Patrice Goulet, Luciana Ravanel
YEAR 1990
STATUS Completed
SCOPE Exhibition design and installation
COLLABORATORS OMA, Hans Werlemann/ Hectic Pictures, Jennifer Sigler, Herman Helle, Parthesius & de Rijk, Chiel van Stelt, Het Paleis van Boem, Hard Werken

Rem Koolhaas. 9 Projets d'OMA à Lille, Musée des Beaux Arts
LOCATION Musée des Beaux Arts, Lille, France
CLIENT Rem Koolhaas, OMA
YEAR 1990
STATUS Completed
SCOPE Exhibition design
COLLABORATORS OMA team, Hans Werlemann, Jennifer Sigler, Herman Helle, Frans Parthesius, Vincent de Rijk, Chiel van Stelt, Het Paleis van Boem, Hard Werken

Music Garden
LOCATION Amsterdam, the Netherlands
CLIENT Private owner
YEAR 1990
STATUS Completed
SCOPE Concepts for private north-oriented city garden
SCALE ca. 50 m²

→ p. 832
Villa Dall'Ava
LOCATION Saint Cloud, Paris, France
CLIENT Private owner
YEAR 1987–1991
STATUS Completed
SCOPE Interior finishes and furnishing advisory, curtains for living room and bed rooms, photoshoot production Hectic Pictures
SCALE Interior and curtains, 1,350 m²
COLLABORATORS OMA, Maarten van Severen, Yves Brunier, Hans Werlemann/Hectic Pictures, Marc Mimram, Loic Richalet, Robert Coulon

→ p. 830
Typical Home, Nexus World Housing
LOCATION Fukuoka, Japan
CLIENT Fukuoka Jisho
YEAR 1988–1991
STATUS Completed
SCOPE Interior finishes and furnishing for model home; curtains for living and bedrooms; general patio and green roof design for the OMA housing complex
SCALE Living room curtain, ca. 35 m²; bedroom 1, 12.5 m²; bedroom 2, 8.75 m² roof gardens, 18 m² each; patio gardens, 20 m² each
COLLABORATORS OMA, Keiko Hoshino, Fred Bosschaert, local seamstresses

→ p. 824
OMA – Barcelona, Collegi d'Arquitectes de Catalunya
LOCATION Barcelona, Spain
CLIENT Collegi d'Arquitectes de Catalunya
YEAR 1991
STATUS Completed
SCOPE Exhibition & lighting design and installation
SCALE ca. 250 m²
COLLABORATORS OMA, Groszstadt/Donald van Dansik, Parthesius & De Rijk, Ron Steiner, Herman Helle, Hans Werlemann/ Hectic Pictures, Claudi Cornaz, Jos Stoopman

→ p. 820
Private Estate De Putter
LOCATION Olst, the Netherlands
CLIENT Private owner
YEAR 1990–1992
STATUS Completed
SCOPE Gardening education, including ground preparation; clearing and general layout of land; creation of nursery; soil, plant and root basics; botanical names; planting techniques; tool care; moon calendar
SCALE ca. 2.5 ha
COLLABORATORS Lily Terkuile, Rosemarijn Nitzsche, farmer De Jong and son

Dune Garden
LOCATION Bloemendaal, the Netherlands
CLIENT Private owner
YEAR 1992
STATUS Schematic design
SCOPE Design of private sand garden in dune-area; including planting and maintenance plan

→ p. 814
Multiple Choice, Two Gardens for the Stedelijk Extension
LOCATION Amsterdam, the Netherlands
CLIENT Stedelijk Museum Amsterdam
YEAR 1992
STATUS Competition, 2nd prize
SCOPE Design for general landscape, including two alternative inner gardens, a sloping sculpture field and a sculpture garden on the curator's office roof
SCALE approx. 1 ha
COLLABORATORS OMA, Rosemarijn Nitzsche

→ p. 804
Noise Dress and Flower Field, Kunsthal Rotterdam
LOCATION Rotterdam, The Netherlands
CLIENT Municipality of Rotterdam
YEAR 1987–1993
STATUS Completed
SCOPE Advisory on interior finishes and furniture, auditorium curtain, restaurant sofa, design and implementation of sloping roof garden
SCALE Curtain, ca. 240 m²; roof garden, 500 m²
COLLABORATORS OMA, James Rubery, Mostert De Winter, Hans Werlemann/ Hectic Pictures, Theatex

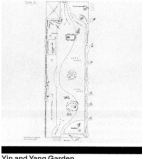

Yin and Yang Garden
LOCATION Hilversum, the Netherlands
CLIENT Private owner
YEAR 1993
STATUS Concept design
SCOPE Private garden design, planting plan
SCALE ca. 120 m²

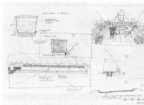

Canal House
LOCATION Amsterdam, the Netherlands
CLIENT Private owner
YEAR 1993
STATUS Completed
SCOPE Roof garden and living room curtains for an eighteenth-century monument along Amsterdam canal
SCALE ca. 30 m²
COLLABORATORS Owners

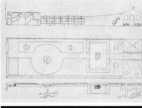

Classic Garden
LOCATION Rotterdam, the Netherlands
CLIENT Private owner
YEAR 1993
STATUS Schematic Design
SCOPE Private garden design; planting plan.
SCALE ca. 160 m²

→ p. 798
Museumpark with Yves Brunier
LOCATION Rotterdam, the Netherlands
CLIENT Municipality of Rotterdam
YEAR 1988–1994
STATUS Completed
SCOPE Assisting landscape architect Yves Brunier during the design of a public park as "living art piece"
SCALE 4 ha
COLLABORATORS Yves Brunier, OMA/ Rem Koolhaas, Fuminori Hoshino, Chris van Duijn, Ank van Peski

→ p. 784
Milky Way, Lille Grand Palais
LOCATION Lille, France
CLIENT City of Lille, SAEM Euralille, Association Lille Grand Palais
YEAR 1992–1994
STATUS Completed
SCOPE Research and advisory on furniture, materials and colours, design of curtains, acoustic walls, restaurant, terrace floors
SCALE Main auditorium, 37 × 11 m; small auditorium, 16.8 × 12.3 m; entrance hall, 39 × 10 m
COLLABORATORS OMA, François Delhay Architectes, Julie Sfez

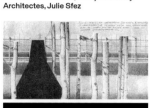

Greenhouse Zone
LOCATION Harmelerwaard, The Netherlands
CLIENT Vinex Nederland, Municipality of Utrecht
YEAR 1994
STATUS Commissioned Study
SCOPE Landscape design for large, relocated greenhouse zone, with focus on opportunities for nightlife and day-tourism (dance/music clubs; cycling and hiking paths); including soil studies and planting plan
SCALE ca. 40 ha
COLLABORATORS Maxwan Architects and Urbanists

Miami Performing Arts Center
LOCATION Miami, Florida, USA
CLIENT Metropolitan Dade County, Performing Arts Center Trust
YEAR 1994
STATUS Competition
SCOPE Interior design, stage curtain
COLLABORATORS OMA

Boutique Nathalie Vincent
LOCATION Antwerp, Belgium
CLIENT Nathalie Vincent
YEAR 1995
STATUS Completed
SCOPE Ceiling-high curtain defining two dressing rooms and a storage space, back-lit by fluorescent lamps, spread over back wall (illusion of endless space)
SCALE ca. 4 × 6 m
COLLABORATORS Wim de Vos

MoMA The Museum of Modern Art
LOCATION New York, USA
CLIENT Museum of Modern Art, New York
YEAR 1995
STATUS Schematic Design
SCOPE Transparent screen between reception and restaurant area on second floor of museum: 2 holed curtains, winter and summer version
SCALE 2 mock ups, each 1.4 × 3.5 m

Qingshui Service Area
LOCATION Chinsuei, Taiwan
CLIENT Developer
YEAR 1996
STATUS Completed
SCOPE Landscape design for service area along new highway, including car and bus parking, playgrounds, gardens, grey-water cleansing water feature, shaded picnic area
COLLABORATORS Aaron Tan, SWA Lanscape Architects

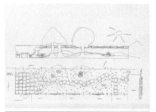

→ p. 812
Kids' Garden
LOCATION Blaricum, the Netherlands
CLIENT Private owner
YEAR 1992
STATUS Schematic Design
SCOPE Design for a family garden, including planting and maintenance plan
SCALE ca. 300 m²

→ p. 766
Connective Green, H-Project
LOCATION Seoul, South Korea
CLIENT Samsung Cultural Foundation
YEAR 1995–1997
STATUS Completed
SCOPE Landscape and infrastructure in the heart of the city, connecting three separate museum buildings by Botta, Nouvel and OMA and the clinic building by Terry Farrell
SCALE 4 ha
COLLABORATORS Irene Curulli, Andrew McNair; Mario Botta, Jean Nouvel, OMA and Terry Farrell, Samoo Architects & Engineers, Sacha Curiel

→ p.778
Shade Honey, Dutch House
LOCATION Holten, the Netherlands
CLIENT Private owners
YEAR 1995–1997
STATUS Completed
SCOPE Steel mesh and black voile exterior curtain, shading screens for terrace, design and installation of "butterfly" garden and "Persian carpet"
SCALE Curtain, 35 m²; garden works, ca. 400 m²
COLLABORATORS OMA, West 8, Liesbeth Sillem & partner

Artillerie Terrein
LOCATION Arnhem, The Netherlands
CLIENT Geerlings Vastgoed Developers
YEAR 1997
STATUS Schematic Design
SCOPE Landscape design for new residential area on former military site
SCALE ca. 2 ha

→ p.754
Maison Bordeaux 1.0
LOCATION Floirac, France
CLIENT Private owners
YEAR 1994–1998
STATUS Completed
SCOPE Garden interventions, interior finishes, kitchen flooring, design of all curtains
SCALE Various
COLLABORATORS OMA, Maarten van Severen, Vincent de Rijk

Office Building
LOCATION Rijswijk, the Netherlands
CLIENT Geerlings Vastgoed Developers
YEAR 1998
STATUS Schematic Design
SCOPE Design for roof garden with integrated parking for staff
SCALE ca. 300 m²

→ p.732
Universal Headquarters
LOCATION Hollywood, Los Angeles, USA
CLIENT Universal Studios
YEAR 1996–1999
STATUS Definitive Design
SCOPE Interior and terrace gardens, surrounding landscape and infrastructure
SCALE 3 ha
COLLABORATORS OMA, Nancy Goslee Power, Mia Lehrer & Associates

→ p.744
The Path as Spatial Tool, State Detention Centre
LOCATION Nieuwegein, the Netherlands
CLIENT Rijksgebouwendienst (Dutch State Building Department)
YEAR 1997–1999
STATUS Completed
SCOPE Landscape design of six gardens for female and male prisoners, entrance and parking areas; (separate) shelters for prisoners and guards; lighting and maintenance plan
SCALE 2.5 ha
COLLABORATORS Archivolt Architecten, DS Landschapsarchitecten

Second Stage Theater
LOCATION Off-Broadway, New York, USA
CLIENT Second Stage Theater
YEAR 1998–1999
STATUS Completed
SCOPE Darkening and 'showcase' curtains along main facade windows that line the busy Off Broadway street
SCALE 25 × 7.2 m
COLLABORATORS OMA, Gluckman Mayner Architects

Mick Jagger Centre
LOCATION Dartford, Kent, United Kingdom
CLIENT Dartford Grammar School for Boys, Kent
YEAR 1999–2000
STATUS Completed
SCOPE Interior colour advisory, darkening curtains and light filtering veils for main auditorium / concert hall
SCALE 4 curtains, 24.34 × 6.44 m
COLLABORATORS Tim Ronalds Architects

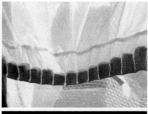

Holiday House
LOCATION Harbour Island, Bahamas
CLIENT Private client
YEAR 2000
STATUS Definitive Design
SCOPE Curtains for inside and outside; landscape design
SCALE Landscape, ca. 3 ha; curtains, various sizes
COLLABORATORS OMA

Parking Lot, Het Oosten Traffic
LOCATION Amsterdam, The Netherlands
CLIENT Max1
YEAR 2000
STATUS Commissioned Study
SCOPE Research project for traffic and parking strategy; design concept for street and parking lot layout and graphics
COLLABORATORS Max1

Tree City, Downsview Park
LOCATION Toronto, Ontario, Canada
CLIENT Canada Lands Company, Federal Government
YEAR 2000
STATUS Competition, 1st prize
SCOPE Site research and landscape design concept
SCALE 240 ha
COLLABORATORS David W. Oleson – Oleson Worland arch., Bruce Mau Design, Rem Koolhaas

→ p.724
Movements: Introduction to a Working Process, Storefront for Art and Architecture
LOCATION Soho, New York, USA
CLIENT Storefront for Art and Architecture – director Sarah Herda
YEAR 2000
STATUS Completed
SCOPE Design for retrospective exhibition including printed matters and site-specific installation
SCALE Curtain, 15 × 10 m; (3×) grass cushions 1 × 1.2 m; et al
COLLABORATORS Frans Parthesius, 2×4, Frits Veenis, Helena Kierulf

→ p.730
Movements 25%, Introduction to a Working Process
LOCATION Amsterdam, the Netherlands
CLIENT Storefront for Art and Architecture / Sarah Herda
YEAR 2000
STATUS Completed
SCOPE Exhibition catalogue, *Movements 25%: Introduction to a Working Process*
SCALE 236 pages / 10 × 14.5 cm
COLLABORATORS Irma Boom

→ p.696
Prada Epicenter New York
LOCATION New York, USA
CLIENT Prada
YEAR 1999–2001
STATUS Completed
SCOPE Curtains for VIP dressing rooms, knitted audio sock for main shop; advisory on interior "landscape" and materials
SCALE VIP (2×), 12 × 3.5 m; Sock, 5 × 4.75 m
COLLABORATORS OMA, Helene Kierulf

Chassé-Terrein
LOCATION Breda, the Netherlands
CLIENT Joint Venture Chassé c.v.
YEAR 1999–2001
STATUS Completed
SCOPE Landscape in between five residential towers, continuing into the different entrance lobbies, including bicycle parking, furniture and lighting plan
SCALE 4,500 m²
COLLABORATORS XDGA – Xaveer de Geyter Architects, Johan Jumelet, Van Kemenade Tuinen

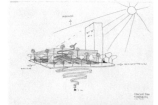

→ p.718
Hammer Museum Landscape
LOCATION Los Angeles, California, USA
CLIENT UCLA Hammer Museum
YEAR 2000-2001
STATUS Partially realised
SCOPE Landscape design for museum courtyard and streetscape
SCALE Courtyard, 960 m²; streetscape, 2,500 m²
COLLABORATORS Michael Maltzan Architects, Studio MLA

Linear Garden
LOCATION Chelsea, New York, USA
CLIENT Private owner
YEAR 2000-2001
STATUS Schematic design
SCOPE Design for a private city garden
SCALE ca. 60 m²

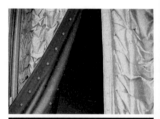

Lensvelt Headquarters
LOCATION Breda, the Netherlands
CLIENT Lensvelt BV
YEAR 2000-2001
STATUS Completed
SCOPE 1 darkening and 1 separate, translucent privacy curtain for main meeting room
SCALE 8.95 × 3.28 m, 7.69 × 3.28 m

Wedding Curtain
LOCATION Rotterdam, the Netherlands/ New York, USA
CLIENT private
YEAR 2001
STATUS Completed
SCOPE Wedding gift curtain
SCALE 3 × 4 m

Computer History Museum
LOCATION Silicon Valley, California, USA
CLIENT Computer History Museum
YEAR 2001
STATUS Competition
SCOPE Theme-related landscape around, under and through the museum
SCALE ca. 12,200 m²
COLLABORATORS Michael Maltzan Architects

Maharam Textiles
LOCATION New York, Chicago, USA
CLIENT Michael Maharam
YEAR 2001
STATUS Concept
SCOPE Textile series

Skin, Cooper Hewitt, Smithsonian Design Museum
LOCATION New York, USA
CLIENT Cooper Hewitt, Smithsonian Design Museum
YEAR 2001
STATUS Completed
SCOPE Garden carpets for Green Room & video films on IO works
SCALE 19.4 × 4 m/77.6 m²

→ p.716
Radial Views, Penthouse
LOCATION Cinnabar Wharf, London, United Kingdom
CLIENT Private owners
YEAR 1999-2002
STATUS Completed
SCOPE Roof garden and all curtains for this round, two-floor penthouse with sloping ceiling, including stainless steel mesh curtain for golf room
SCALE Curtains: lower floor, 19 × 3.1 m, 82.8 × 3.3 m, 4 × 3.2 m; top floor, 17.5 × 1.4 m; roof garden, ca. 80 m²
COLLABORATORS Bushe Associates, Master Gardeners

→ p.580
Swamp Garden, Public/Private Parking
LOCATION Almere Stad, the Netherlands
CLIENT Municipality of Almere
YEAR 1999-2007
STATUS Completed
SCOPE Underground linear garden to separate public from private parking
SCALE 2,000 m²
COLLABORATORS Pieters Projectbureau, Bureau Bouwkunde, Kleinjan Advies – en ingenieursbureau/Team Groen, Water en Natuur

→ p.708
Garage Door Curtain, Lehmann Maupin Gallery
LOCATION Meat Packing District, New York, USA
CLIENT Lehmann Maupin Gallery
YEAR 2001-2002 (addition in 2004)
STATUS Completed
SCOPE Space-defining and darkening curtain for art gallery, track and storage configuration, studies for other space-dividing interventions
SCALE 12.5 × 4.35 m (2×)
COLLABORATORS OMA, Irene Curulli

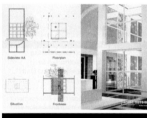

Das Geheimnis des Schattens: Licht und Schatten in der Architektur, Deutsches Architekturmuseum (DAM)
LOCATION Frankfurt, Germany
CLIENT Deutsches Architekturmuseum (DAM)
YEAR 2002
STATUS Completed
SCOPE Participation in group exhibtion with "Light and Shadow" curtain
SCALE 3.6 × 6 m, 2.6 × 6 m

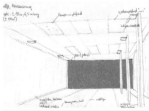

Tennispark De Delftse Hout
LOCATION Delft, the Netherlands
YEAR 2002
STATUS Concept/Recipe
SCOPE Commission for "artistic" textile division wall
SCALE Curtain wall, ca. 18 × 6.5 m

Holiday Home
LOCATION Celerina, Switzerland
CLIENT Private owner
YEAR 2002
STATUS Completed
SCOPE Interior interventions
SCALE 200 m²

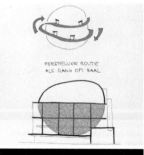

Luxor Theatre
LOCATION Rotterdam, the Netherlands
CLIENT Luxor Theatre
YEAR 2002
STATUS Commissioned Study
SCOPE Theatre refurbishment; interiors, routing, textiles

UnA Hotel Vittoria Firenze
LOCATION Florence, Italy
CLIENT UNA Hotels and Resorts/ Fabio Novembre
YEAR 2002
STATUS Concept
SCOPE Outdoor facade curtain for a historic facade
SCALE 33 × 16 m
COLLABORATORS Studio Fabio Novembre

→ p.438
Mobile HIV Clinic
LOCATION Sub-Saharan Africa
CLIENT Architecture for Humanity, San Francisco
YEAR 2002
STATUS International competition
SCOPE Design for a mobile HIV clinic for the Sub-Saharan countries
SCALE Multiple units of each 1.2 × 2.4 m
COLLABORATORS Irene Curulli, Rebecca Gomperts

→ p. 714
Curtain for a Lover
LOCATION Rotterdam, the Netherlands
CLIENT Private
YEAR 2002
STATUS Completed
SCOPE Birthday present
SCALE 2.88 × 1.76 m

Artist's House
LOCATION Amsterdam, The Netherlands
CLIENT Private owner
YEAR 2002
STATUS Completed
SCOPE Wall replacing curtain, protecting living/dining from cold and draught and improving the acoustics
SCALE 5.4 × 2.8 m

→ p. 676
Angelica, The Embassy of the Netherlands
LOCATION Berlin, Germany
CLIENT Ministry of Foreign Affairs of The Netherlands
YEAR 2000–2003
STATUS Completed
SCOPE Two darkening curtains for main reception room with track and storage configuration; glare control curtain concepts for all offices along the facade (tulip printed Tervira CS voile – not realised); interior finishes advisory; concept for adjacent public parkland faacing the Spree River
SCALE 2 darkening curtains, 17.4 × 5.1 m, 9.3 × 3.7 m
COLLABORATORS OMA, TextielLab Tilburg, Frits Veenis, De Ploeg, Theatex

→ p. 712
TOUCH, Wallpaper Series for Wolf Gordon
LOCATION New York/Long Island, USA
CLIENT Wolf Gordon Inc.
YEAR 2001–2003
STATUS Completed
SCOPE Designer wallpaper series TOUCH for the US market (based on Inside Outside textile samples)
SCALE (8×) 54" wallpaper
COLLABORATORS Four Color BV (technical photography)

Student Apartment
LOCATION Maastricht, the Netherlands
CLIENT Private owner
YEAR 2002–2003
STATUS Completed
SCOPE Foulard for sofa
SCALE Foulard, 2.5 × 1.6 m

Private House
LOCATION Maastricht, the Netherlands
CLIENT Private owner
YEAR 2002–2003
STATUS Completed
SCOPE Space-defining, darkening curtain
SCALE Curtain, 4.5 × 3 m

Faculty of Aerospace Engineering
LOCATION Delft, the Netherlands
CLIENT Faculty of Aerospace, TU Delft
YEAR 2002–2003
STATUS Completed
SCOPE Art commission for a floor finish in the faculty's main restaurant space and adjacent corridors
SCALE Polyurethane art flooring, 124 m²
COLLABORATORS Rudy Uytenhaak

Vienna International Airport
LOCATION Vienna, Austria
CLIENT Flughafen Wien Aktiengesellschaft/FWAG
YEAR 2003
STATUS Competition
SCOPE Contribution to landscape, streetscape, parking plan and traffic logistics
COLLABORATORS Buro Kiefer Berlin

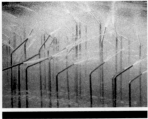

Walsall Waterfront
LOCATION Walsall, United Kingdom
CLIENT Walsall Metropolitan Borough Council
YEAR 2003
STATUS Competition
SCOPE Waterfront revitalisation strategies
SCALE 6.9 ha
COLLABORATORS S333 architecture + urbanism

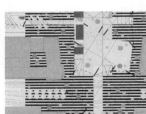

Earth Bluff
LOCATION Trautmanndorff, Italy
CLIENT Estate Management Laimburg, the Gardens of Trauttmansdorff Castle
YEAR 2003
STATUS Competition
SCOPE International artistic competition for the (re-)design of the large earth bluff that reinforces the steep hill-flanks of the Castle
SCALE ca. 2 ha

Central Station
LOCATION Rotterdam, the Netherlands
CLIENT Municipality of Rotterdam
YEAR 2003
STATUS Competition
SCOPE Design for "shared" public plaza, including a "flexible" tree plan with trees from the Trompenburg Arboretum collection Rotterdam
SCALE ca. 2 ha
COLLABORATORS OMA

→ p. 608
McCormick Tribune Campus Center
LOCATION Chicago, Illinois, USA
CLIENT IIT Illinois Institute of Technology
YEAR 1998–2004
STATUS Competition, 1st prize/Completed
SCOPE Darkening and blackout curtains for entire west facade, interior finishes, patio and "flying" gardens, surrounding landscape
SCALE Curtains, 17.2 × 8.4 m, 19.4 × 8.4 m, 18.9 × 6.4 m; carpets, various sizes; landscape, 1.6 ha
COLLABORATORS OMA, 2×4; Peter Lindsay Schaudt, Kate Orff

→ p. 684
Undoing Boundaries, Seattle Central Library
LOCATION Seattle, Washington, USA
CLIENT Library Foundation Seattle
YEAR 2000–2004
STATUS Competition, 1st prize/Completed
SCOPE Landscape design for surrounding streetscape, entrance plazas and transitional areas; concept designs and colour scheme for all spaces; advisory on interior finishes, carpets and furniture; designs for acoustic ceilings and walls; double-faced curtain for auditorium, track configuration (S-shape to turn curtain from stage curtain to backdrop); project carpet design, ten patterns in three colours for the "Garden Carpets"
SCALE Landscape, 3,320 m²; curtain, 24.75 × 8.75 m; green carpets, 19.75 × 10.7 m, 7.9 × 5.35 m, 1.7 × 6.9 m, 13.82 × 9.3 m; red carpet, 11.85 × 11.7 m; mauve carpet, 11.85 × 18.3 m
COLLABORATORS OMA, LMN, Jones & Jones, Kate Orff, Renz van Luxemburg, Mathew Stadler, Tony Oursler, Ann Hamilton

→ p. 696
Prada Epicenter Beverly Hills
LOCATION Beverly Hills, Los Angeles, USA
CLIENT Prada
YEAR 2003–2004
STATUS Completed
SCOPE Curtains for VIP dressing rooms, taking acoustic privacy and sprinkler system into account
SCALE 12.4 × 2.9 m, 14.7 × 2.9 m
COLLABORATORS OMA, Gerriets GmbH

→ p. 348
Giardini di Porta Nuova/Biblioteca degli Alberi, Milan
LOCATION Porta Nuova, Milan, Italy
CLIENT Municipality of Milano, INGRE
YEAR 2003–2004
STATUS Competition, 1st prize
SCOPE Urban park design
SCALE 10 ha
COLLABORATORS Mirko Zardini, Michael Maltzan Architecture, Ro d'Or/Rob Kuster, Irma Boom, Piet Oudolf.

Les Halles
LOCATION Paris, France
CLIENT SEM Paris Centre
YEAR 2003–2004
STATUS Competition
SCOPE Landscape advisory
SCALE 27.9 ha
COLLABORATORS OMA, XDGA, One Architecture, Agence Ter, Partenaire Development, Alterra, Tom Matton

Museumdagen 2004, Installation at Museumpark
LOCATION Rotterdam, the Netherlands
CLIENT NAi (Netherlands Architecture Institute)
YEAR 2004
STATUS Completed
SCOPE Informative/connective routing (red "museum rope" with attached information signs about Yves Brunier's Museum park design) between NAi and Kunsthal buildings during Museumdagen 2004
SCALE 200 poles; 570 m red cord

→ p. 706
Blue Moon Hotel
LOCATION Groningen, the Netherlands
CLIENT Toyo Ito & Associates
YEAR 2004
STATUS Completed
SCOPE Multipurpose curtains for two hotel rooms
SCALE Floor 1, 3.63 × 2.7 m (2×); floor 2, 3.63 × 2.4 m (2×)
COLLABORATORS Hosoya & Schäfer Architects

→ p. 680
Art Intervention with Berend Strik, Embassy of the Netherlands
LOCATION Berlin, Germany
CLIENT Ministry of Foreign Affairs of The Netherlands
YEAR 2004
STATUS Art Competition
SCOPE Proposal for art intervention linking the Embassy's entrance plaza to its interior world
COLLABORATORS Berend Strik

Privacy Screens for Vitra
LOCATION Birsfelden, Switzerland
CLIENT Vitra/Rolf Fehlbaum
YEAR 2004
STATUS Concept
SCOPE Conceptual designs for transportable, stowable and foldable textile privacy screens for office interiors

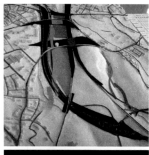

Luxopolis, Porte de Hollerich
LOCATION Porte de Hollerich, Luxemburg
CLIENT Ville de Luxembourg
YEAR 2004
STATUS Competition
SCOPE Collaboration on a visionary urban design by extending and intensifying the existing landscapes and traffic flows, instigating a high level of urbanity for a new urban quarter centred around the new train station for the Capital of the Grand Duchy
SCALE 120 ha
COLLABORATORS S333/Burton Hamfelt, Arup

Car Collector's Garden
LOCATION Eindhoven, the Netherlands
CLIENT Private owner
YEAR 2004
STATUS Concept
SCOPE Garden and car park design for lifted private villa with in-house car collection
SCALE 3,040 m²
COLLABORATORS MVRDV

→ p. 660
Casa da Música
LOCATION Porto, Portugal
CLIENT Porto 2001, Casa da Música
YEAR 1999–2005
STATUS Competition, 1st prize/Completed
SCOPE 11 acoustic, blackout and view-filtering curtains and sunscreens; interior and exterior finishes consultant; concept for public square
SCALE Sala I: 3 curtains, 22 × 15 m, and 3 curtains, 22 × 13 m; Sala II: 2 curtains, 14 × 12 m, and 1 curtain, 14 × 7 m; rehearsal rooms: 65 × 8 m, 55 × 8 m
COLLABORATORS OMA, Renz van Luxemburg, Gerriets GmbH

→ p. 654
Restoration Revised, Curtains for Hackney Empire Theatre
LOCATION Hackney, London, United Kingdom
CLIENT Hackney Empire Theatre, The Heritage Lottery Fund, The London Arts Council
YEAR 1999–2005
STATUS Completed
SCOPE Guillotine house curtain and acoustic drapes for main auditorium; blackout and space-defining curtains for studios; darkening, acoustic and backdrop curtains for café; concept for wallpapers
SCALE Main auditorium, 10.4 × 10.6 m; 9 × 5.6 m (2×); studios, 35.8 × 3.9 m, 15.3 × 4.75 m; Pepys pub, 20 × 4.5 m, 11.3 × 4.5 m
COLLABORATORS Tim Ronalds Architects, Ken Creasy Ltd

Congress Centre
LOCATION Cordoba, Spain
CLIENT Gerencia Municipal de Urbanismo de Cordoba
YEAR 2002–2005
STATUS Competition, 1st prize/schematic design
SCOPE Landscape design, auditorium curtains and exterior weather-resistant shading curtains
SCALE Landscape, 16,700 m²; curtains, 3,440 m²
COLLABORATORS OMA, dUCKS scéno

→ p. 630
Invisible Presence, Glass Pavilion, Toledo Museum of Art
LOCATION Toledo, Ohio, USA
CLIENT Toledo Museum of Art
YEAR 2002–2005
STATUS Partially realised
SCOPE Space-defining, acoustic and darkening curtains for multipurpose room; sun and UV screening voiles for exhibition spaces; washable view-filter curtain for canteen; shading plan for interior spaces through plantings in surrounding museum garden (not realised); rack and storage configurations and all test samples (realised)
SCALE Space 1, 75.3 × 4 m; space 2, 34 × 4 m; space 3, 60.4 × 4 m; space 4, 95 × 4 m
COLLABORATORS SANAA, TRANSSOLAR Energietechnik GmbH/Matthias Schuler

→ p. 652
Window Windows, Architectura & Natura Bookstore
LOCATION Amsterdam, the Netherlands
CLIENT Architectura & Natura bookstore/ Gaston Bekkers
YEAR 2003–2005
STATUS Completed
SCOPE Shading curtain for south-facing shop window and backdrop for book showcase; showcase lamp
SCALE 4.75 × 3.55 m
COLLABORATORS Johan Jumelet (lamp)

Seoul National University Museum of Art
LOCATION Seoul, South Korea
CLIENT Seoul National University Museum
YEAR 2003–2005
STATUS Completed
SCOPE General landscape and planting plan (realised); curtain design for auditorium (not realised)
SCALE ca. 2,000 m²
COLLABORATORS OMA, Samoo Architects & Engineers

→ p. 672
Sun and Moon, Villa Leefdaal
LOCATION Leefdaal, Belgium
CLIENT Private owner
YEAR 2003–2005
STATUS Completed
SCOPE Design of multiple curtains to organise light, space and sound, in bedrooms, living room, study
SCALE 20 × 2.75 m, 13 × 2.75 m, 8 × 3 m, 7 × 3 m, 7.65 × 2.2 m
COLLABORATORS Macken & Macken, Theatex

Palazzo del Cinema di Venezia
LOCATION Venice, Italy
CLIENT Biennale di Venezia
YEAR 2005
STATUS Competition
SCOPE International competition for Nuovo Palazzo del Cinema and neighbouring areas: landscape design that takes the various yearly programming into account, while acting as connector between buildings on different levels
SCALE ca. 1.5 ha
COLLABORATORS Stefano Boeri Architetti

Ceramica Bardelli
LOCATION the Netherlands
CLIENT Art on Tiles Distributions
YEAR 2005
STATUS Concept
SCOPE Designs for tile series "Buttons" and "Tulips"
SCALE 20 × 20 cm wall tiles, 40 × 40 cm floor tiles

→ p. 644
Rifletutti, Villa Manin
LOCATION Villa Manin Contemporary Art Centre, Codroipo, Italy
CLIENT Francesco Bonami (curator)
YEAR 2005
STATUS Completed
SCOPE Art commission to create a temporary pavilion in the gardens of the estate
SCALE 50 "private pavilions" (translucent/mirroring parasols); 18 mirroring discs (polished stainless steel, 5 mm thick), (10×) 0.25 m; (5×) 0.5 m; (3×) 1 m diameter

Rothschild's London Headquarters
LOCATION New Court, London, United Kingdom
CLIENT NM Rothschild & Sons
YEAR 2005
STATUS Completed
SCOPE Designs for various roof gardens and outside entrance area
SCALE 882 m²
COLLABORATORS OMA

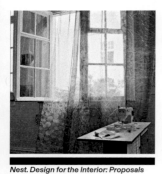

Nest. Design for the Interior: Proposals for Municipal Art Acquisitions 2004, Stedelijk Museum Amsterdam
LOCATION Amsterdam, the Netherlands
CLIENT Stedelijk Museum
YEAR 2005
STATUS Completed
SCOPE Installation in group exhibition; IO Garden Carpet and Garden Voile (both acquired for SM textile collection)
SCALE Carpet, 5.4 × 2.54 m; curtain, 2.4 × 4 m

De Plussenburgh
LOCATION Rotterdam, the Netherlands
CLIENT Stichting Ouderenhuisvesting Rotterdam
YEAR 2002–2006
STATUS Completed
SCOPE Landscape and parking entrance, fishing balcony and guard-rail designs; wall-to-wall "water-plant" carpet for communal living room
SCALE Landscape: 2,500 m²; carpets, 200 m²
COLLABORATORS Arons en Gelauff Architecten

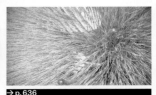

→ p. 636
Hairs, Fins, Sauerkraut and Furs, Mercedes-Benz Museum
LOCATION Stuttgart, Germany
CLIENT DaimlerChrysler Immobilien, Berlin
YEAR 2004–2006
STATUS Completed
SCOPE Three space defining, darkening, sun-/view-filtering curtains; acoustic wall for the upstairs café; advisory on security curtains for shops
SCALE 6 curtains: 35 × 4.25 m, 32.6 × 4.25 m, 27.8 × 4.25 m, 11.25 × 5–4.2 m, 13.6 × 3.7 m, 33.3 × 2.03 m; acoustic wall, 32 × 2.72 m
COLLABORATORS UN Studio, Concrete Amsterdam, Mink Bürsten, Lammerts en Van Bueren, Gerriets GmbH, Seilemaaker

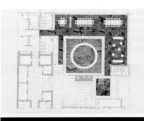

TPG Post Headquarters
LOCATION The Hague, the Netherlands
CLIENT TPG Post (PostNL)
YEAR 2004–2006
STATUS Schematic design
SCOPE Interior interventions to improve the routing through the public areas, from entrance lobby along all floors, and the recognisability of the different departments per floor
SCALE "Stamp" carpet, 4,755 m²; "Colour" curtain, 120 m²

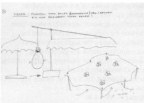

Oudolf Parasol
LOCATION Hummelo, the Netherlands
CLIENT Private owners
YEAR 2005–2006
STATUS Concept design
SCOPE "Artistic" shading device for outside dining
SCALE 3 × 4 m

Terminal F, Schiphol Airport
LOCATION Schiphol Airport, Amsterdam, the Netherlands
CLIENT Amsterdam Airport Schiphol
YEAR 2005–2006 (additional installation in 2010)
STATUS Completed
SCOPE "Dutch Landscape" Bathroom Tiles for washrooms Terminal F
SCALE Walls covered with printed ceramic tiles, 300 m²
COLLABORATORS Art on Tiles

ARTEM Campus
LOCATION Nancy, France
CLIENT ARTEM
YEAR 2006
STATUS Competition
SCOPE Landscape, interiors
SCALE 4.45 ha
COLLABORATORS OMA

Jebel Al Jais Mountain Resort
LOCATION Ras al Khaimah, United Arab Emirates
YEAR 2006
STATUS Schematic Design
SCOPE General landscaping, sports and play areas, patio gardens
SCALE 90 ha
COLLABORATORS OMA

Textiel Museum Tilburg
LOCATION Tilburg, the Netherlands
CLIENT Municipality of Tillburg
YEAR 2006
STATUS Schematic Design
SCOPE Commission for the re-design of all exterior spaces around old and new museum buildings
SCALE ca. 1 ha

Al-Rai Development
LOCATION Kuwait City, Kuwait
CLIENT Mabanee
YEAR 2006
STATUS Schematic Design
SCOPE Landscape masterplan and shading concepts for patio gardens and open-air market areas
SCALE ca. 33 ha
COLLABORATORS OM

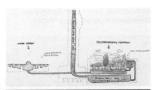

→ p. 648
Cool Inlays Landscape, Dubai Renaissance Tower
LOCATION Dubai, United Arab Emirates
CLIENT Dubai Properties
YEAR 2006
STATUS Competition
SCOPE Sustainable landscape design in connection to the high rise building's energy and water management ambitions
SCALE 3.8 ha
COLLABORATORS OMA, Arup, Vincent de Rijk, Frans Parthesius, Hans Werlemann, Irma Boom

Young Family Apartment
LOCATION Amsterdam, the Netherlands
CLIENT Private owner
YEAR 2006
STATUS Completed
SCOPE Curtains, cushions, wallpapers
SCALE curtains: 4 × 2.5 m; IO "Knit" wallpaper, 4 × 2.5 m

Workshop Tourism for Lisi Lake
LOCATION Lisi lake, Tbilisi, Georgia
CLIENT Georgian Reconstruction & Development Company (GRDC)
YEAR 2006
STATUS Workshop
SCOPE Redevelopment strategies to attract (health) tourism to the Lisi lakes – Lake Lisi territory development project
SCALE 400 ha
COLLABORATORS One Architecture/Matthijs Bouw

Villa S
LOCATION Mexico City, Mexico
CLIENT Private owners, LAR
YEAR 2006
STATUS Completed
SCOPE Concept designs for interior finishes, light and colour use, connection inside-outside, cooling green roof and the general landscape of Villa S
SCALE Interior, 357 m²; garden, 500 m²
COLLABORATORS LAR team/Fernando Romero

Dubai Land Park
LOCATION Dubai, United Arab Emirates
CLIENT Dubai City
YEAR 2006
STATUS Commissioned Study
SCOPE Landscape masterplan, central park design and general planting plan
SCALE Open space/central park, 534,000 m²; 2,725 residential plots, 464 m² each
COLLABORATORS OMA

→ p. 624
African Institution of Science and Technology (AIST)
LOCATION Abuja, Nigeria
CLIENT Nelson Mandela Institution
YEAR 2006
STATUS Competition, 2nd prize
SCOPE Landscape design for campus and surroundings
SCALE 112 ha
COLLABORATORS OMA, Arup

→ p. 622
Textile Works, Vlaams Nederlands Huis De Buren
LOCATION Brussels, Belgium
CLIENT Vlaams-Nederlands Huis de Buren, director Dorian van der Brempt
YEAR 2006
STATUS Completed
SCOPE Solo exhibition on the textile works by Inside Outside
SCALE 2 carpets; 6 curtains; 13 digitally printed panels; 2 banners; video loop; sound installation
COLLABORATORS Stephan Willenborg, Frans Parthesius

CCTV Media Park
LOCATION Beijing, China
CLIENT China Central Television (CCTV)
YEAR 2006
STATUS Competition, 1st prize/Completed
SCOPE International bidding for the design of CCTV new site media park
SCALE 3 ha
COLLABORATORS EDSA; competition team: Arup, Atelier Markgraph, Brian Eno, Piet Oudolf, Charles Waldheim.

Spoorzone
LOCATION Amsterdam, the Nertherlands
CLIENT Arons en Gelauff Architecten
YEAR 2006
STATUS Concept Design
SCOPE Landscape design for housing development
SCALE ca. 1 ha
COLLABORATORS Arons en Gelauff Architecten

→ p. 604
Riga Port City
LOCATION Riga, Latvia
CLIENT New Riga Development Company
YEAR 2006
STATUS Commissioned study
SCOPE Landscape development strategy (re-use of materials, introduction of temporary nurseries, playgrounds and recreation areas and phasing plan) and landscape masterplan for the transformation of former harbour and waterfront of Riga, into a new commercial, cultural and residential area
SCALE Daugava riverfront, 4.5 km; project surface, 100 ha
COLLABORATORS OMA

→ p. 596
Shifted Room, Haus der Kunst
LOCATION Munich, Germany
CLIENT Haus der Kunst – director Chris Dercon
YEAR 2004–2007
STATUS Completed
SCOPE Sound regulating and film projection curtains, encircling the main hall
SCALE 38.2 × 9.1 m; 39 × 9.1 m; 20.7 × 9.1 m
COLLABORATORS Boesel Stahlbau, Hespe & Woelm GmbH, Theatex

Villa Haaksbergen
LOCATION Haaksbergen, the Netherlands
CLIENT Private owner
YEAR 2005–2007
STATUS Completed
SCOPE Facade curtains, darkening and sun-reflecting, for entire circular inner facade of living, dining and bedrooms facing central garden
SCALE 7 curtains: voile, 21.38 × 2.3 m, 6.59 × 2.3 m, 1.92 × 2.3 m, 6.41 × 2.3 m; velour: 3.83 × 2.3 m, 3.78 × 2.3 m, 3.75 × 2.3 m
COLLABORATORS Architecten Cie

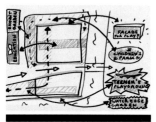

BLOX – DAC/Danish Architecture Center
LOCATION Copenhagen, Denmark
CLIENT Realdania By og Byg
YEAR 2006–2007
STATUS Concept Design
SCOPE Landscape concept for all areas around and inside the building and along the quay leading to the building and down to the river
SCALE City Plaza, 1,780 m²; water plaza, 2,870 m²; roof terraces and playground, 5,702 m²
COLLABORATORS OMA, Kragh & Berglund

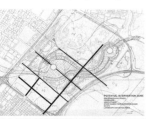

→ p. 592
Central Business District Bay
LOCATION Dubai, United Arab Emirates
CLIENT Dubai City
YEAR 2006–2007
STATUS Schematic Design
SCOPE Landscape masterplan for a large new urban area, including a new salt-water waterline, streetscapes and green
SCALE 5.7 ha
COLLABORATORS OMA

→ p. 588
Urban Oasis, City in the Desert
LOCATION Ras Al Khaimah, United Arab Emirates
CLIENT RAK Gateway Authority
YEAR 2006–2007
STATUS Competition, 2nd prize
SCOPE Landscape masterplan for a new city in the desert, with biodiverse shaded green zones and cooling airflows as major focus; includes sports and play areas, intimate patio gardens; outside the city's defined boundaries, tree and shrub formations protect against wind and sand storms
SCALE Total city of approx. 120 ha
COLLABORATORS OMA

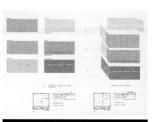

OMA Offices
LOCATION New York City, New York, USA
CLIENT OMA
YEAR 2006–2007 (+ additions in 2017)
STATUS Completed
SCOPE Space-defining darkening curtains for meeting rooms and work spaces
SCALE Curtain 1, 5.7 × 2.5 m; curtain 2, 7.9 × 2.5 m; curtain 3, 4.85 × 2.5 m; curtain 4, 6 × 2.5 m; carpet: 4 × 5 m

Private Apartment
LOCATION New York, USA
CLIENT Private owner
YEAR 2006–2007
STATUS Completed
SCOPE Art commission for 2 curtains to closed-off closets on both sides of the bed in master bedroom (silk and brass)
SCALE 4.12 × 2.99 m
COLLABORATORS Christian Hubert Studio

Museum of the Moving Image
LOCATION Museum of the Moving Image, New York, USA
CLIENT Leeser Architecture
YEAR 2006–2007
STATUS Concept Design
SCOPE Landscape, interior and curtain concepts
SCALE 5 carpets, total 669 m²; 3 curtains 39 × 3.6 m, 4.6 × 7.6 m, 13 × 7.6 m; terrace 247 m²; courtyard, 524 m²
COLLABORATORS Leeser Architecture

Saudi Aramco Cultural Center
LOCATION Dhahran, Saudi Arabia
CLIENT Saudi Aramco
YEAR 2007
STATUS Competition
SCOPE Landscape as integral part of the architecture
SCALE 10 ha
COLLABORATORS OMA

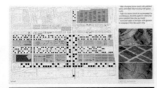

Satwa District
LOCATION Dubai, United Arab Emirates
CLIENT Dubai Municipality
YEAR 2007
STATUS Commissioned Study
SCOPE Preservation research on Satwa District: the protective role of living greenery and mapping of original/maintained gardens
COLLABORATORS OMA*AMO

→ p. 586
Genesis. Life at the End of the Information Age, Centraal Museum Utrecht
LOCATION Utrecht, the Netherlands
CLIENT Centraal Museum Utrecht – director Pauline Terreehorst
YEAR 2007
STATUS Completed
SCOPE Exhibition design in which the overlap between science and art is addressed in a series of rooms that each contain (art) installations and active technological and biological experiments
SCALE 1,011 m²
COLLABORATORS Dr Emilie Gomart

→ p. 578
Inside Outside Petra Blaisse, Monograph
LOCATION Amsterdam, the Netherlands
CLIENT NAi Publishers/Birkhauser; Monacelli Press/NAi Publishers
YEAR 2002–2007; 2009 reprint
STATUS Completed
SCOPE Monograph published by NAi Publishers/Birkhauser (2007) and Monacelli Press (2009)
SCALE 18 × 25 × 4.3 cm
COLLABORATORS Irma Boom, Kayoko Ota; authors: Cecil Balmond, Bernd Baumeister, Gaston Bekkers, Chris Dercon, Tijs Goldschmidt, Dirk van den Heuvel, Sanford Kwinter, Helene Lemoine, Renz van Luxemburg, Tim Ronalds, Michael Shermer

→ p. 576
Mexico City Workshops
LOCATION Museo Soumaya, Mexico City, Mexico
CLIENT LAR, Fernando Romero
YEAR 2006–2008
STATUS Completed
SCOPE Workshops on ideas for interiors and landscaping; logistics of movement around and through the buildings; facade and interior surface treatment; colour scope for each floor; site visits and studies
COLLABORATORS LAR, Fernando Romero

KIVI – Koninklijk Instituut Van Ingenieurs
LOCATION The Hague, the Netherlands
CLIENT Royal Netherlands Society of Engineers (KIVI)
YEAR 2007
STATUS Completed
SCOPE Darkening and privacy curtains facing inner garden and neighboring building at main conference room
SCALE 2 items: darkening curtain, 13.5 × 5 m (double layered); privacy curtain, 13.5 × 5 m
COLLABORATORS AAArchitects

Kamer van Koophandel
LOCATION Rotterdam, the Netherlands
CLIENT Chamber of Commerce, Rotterdam
YEAR 2007
STATUS Concept Design
SCOPE Analysis and conceptual ideas for acoustic, light and climate improvements to conference and meeting rooms
COLLABORATORS Kraaijvanger Urbis

Movements 25%. Film Screenings
LOCATION The Hague, Breda, Rotterdam, Almere, Porto, Lille, Bordeaux, Paris, Munich
YEAR 2000–2008
STATUS Completed
SCOPE Initiative, introduction and assistance to filmmaker FP before and during film takes to realise the documentary video of selected Inside Outside curtains and landscape projects
SCALE 18 Inside Outside projects
COLLABORATORS Phosfor/Frans Parthesius

Edificio Roentgen, Università Commerciale Luigi Bocconi
LOCATION Milan, Italy
CLIENT Bocconi University, Milan
YEAR 2006–2008
STATUS Design Development
SCOPE Design commission for large curtains along the street-level glazing of Auditorium Undercroft (light filtering and privacy) and for a pendant ceiling lamp, both for the high theatre/cinema foyer
SCALE 2 curtains, 46.15 × 6.5 m, 14.2 × 6.5 – 0.3 m (triangular); 1 light object, 2 × 3.5 m
COLLABORATORS Grafton Architects

VIP Center, Schiphol Airport
LOCATION Schiphol Airport VIP Center, Amsterdam, the Netherlands
CLIENT Schiphol Airport
YEAR 2007–2008
STATUS Completed
SCOPE Welcoming intervention for door and entrance, security check area and elevator lobby of VIP Center, Schiphol Airport
SCALE 2 carpets, 23 × 4 m, 10 × 4 m
COLLABORATORS Irma Boom (glass entrance door decoration)

→ p. 572
Crescent Island
LOCATION Dubai Waterfront, United Arab Emirates
CLIENT Nakheel Properties
YEAR 2007–2008
STATUS Definitive Design
SCOPE Landscape masterplan and design of all green areas
SCALE 171 ha
COLLABORATORS OMA, Verdaus

Grandeur, Kunsttentoonstelling, Park Sonsbeek
LOCATION Arnhem, the Netherlands
CLIENT "Sonsbeek 2008" – Anna Tilroe
YEAR 2007–2008
STATUS Completed
SCOPE Way-finding installation for sculpture exhibition in the forested park: each work to be "announced" in a very visible manner
SCALE Park site, 100 ha; IO's pin objects spread throughout.

→ p. 570
Music Wall, Art Commission for Muziekgebouw en Wilminktheater
LOCATION Enschede, the Netherlands
CLIENT Municipality of Enschede
YEAR 2007–2008
STATUS Competition, 1st prize/Completed
SCOPE Art commission for the continuous wall that connects all venues/theatres of the music hall with the shared entrance and foyers
SCALE Length, 150 m; height, 5–12 m; total surface, 1,234 m²

Ein Hawd
LOCATION Ein Hawd, Israel
CLIENT FAST (Foundation of Achieving Seamless Territory) – Malkit Shoshan
YEAR 2008
STATUS Full recognition of the village by Israeli state and reconnection to Israel's electric grid in same year
SCOPE One Land Two Systems – a new Masterplan for Ein Hawd. Activist gathering of international artists, architects, designers and scientists to contribute to a new masterplan and site-specific activities and interventions to draw press attention to this typical Palestinian village where Israel's bureau-cratic protocols, imposed restrictions and discriminatory policy that undermined the village's chances of survival (case example); IO's contributions: workshop, lecture, concept design for central square
SCALE 766 m²
COLLABORATORS FAST/Malkit Shoshan; The Association of Forty (human rights organisation representing the unrec-ognised Palestinian villages), Muhammad Abu el-Hayja (Mayor of Ein Hawd), Matthijs Bouw (Architect), Yona Friedman (artist, architect), Raneen Garis (Feminist activist), Dan Graham (artist), Ali Kazma (artist), Alexander "Sandy" Kedar (land law scholar), Rassem Khamaissi (geographer), MAP Office (artists), Multiplicity (artists), Tomás Saraceno (Artist) and Museo Aerosolar (artists), Debra Solomon (artist), Berend Strik (artist), Sharif Waked (artist, designer)

Private Apartment
LOCATION Amsterdam, the Netherlands
CLIENT Private owner
YEAR 2008
STATUS Completed
SCOPE Refurbishment of apartment, design for garden and curtains
SCALE Apartment, 42 m²; garden, 42 m²; curtain, 3.2 × 2.7 cm
COLLABORATORS Van Kenemade Tuinen, Aura Melis

Wilminktheater
LOCATION Enschede, the Netherlands
CLIENT Municipality of Enschede,
Reyn van der Lugt
YEAR 2008
STATUS Completed
SCOPE Art commission for the stage
curtain of the main concert hall
SCALE Stage curtain, 22 × 11.5 m
COLLABORATORS Koninklijke Ten Cate

De Singel
LOCATION Antwerp, Belgium
CLIENT De Singel, director Moritz Kung
YEAR 2008
STATUS Completed
SCOPE Inside Outside temporary
installation throughout building and
garden
SCALE Site, 25,000 m²; installations,
1,000 m²

International Criminal Court (ICC)
LOCATION The Hague, the Netherlands
CLIENT Ministry of Justice
YEAR 2008
STATUS Competition
SCOPE Landscape design and planting
plan for the sand dune site
SCALE 7.2 ha
COLLABORATORS OMA

Diana und Aktaion, Kunstpalast
Düsseldorf
LOCATION Düsseldorf, Germany
CLIENT Museum Kunstpalast Düsseldorf
YEAR 2008
STATUS Completed
SCOPE Two sinuous curtains meander
through the entire installation to
emphasise and symbolise the *Diana und
Aktaion* exhibition on sensual art through
the ages
SCALE 2 items: hall 2, 56 × 4.4 m (double
layered); hall 3, 29 × 4.42 m (3 layers)
COLLABORATORS Tijs Visser

Karstadt Boulevard
LOCATION Berlin, Germany
CLIENT Multi Veste Berlin GmbH
YEAR 2008
STATUS Schematic Design
SCOPE Textile art objects for large-scale
vitrines, to catch the attention of
passers-by during the day and when lit
after dark
SCALE Textile objects, (3×) 10 × 25.9 m
COLLABORATORS Ortner and Ortner
Baukunst

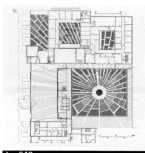

→ p. 642
Gezondheidscentrum Sint Jozef
LOCATION Former Catholic monastery by
Van der Laan, Deventer, the Netherlands
CLIENT Deventer Health Center
YEAR 2008
STATUS 2 Concept Design
SCOPE Landscape design for 4 enclosed
gardens
SCALE 1,447 m²
COLLABORATORS One Architecture

→ p. 568
Flower Circle Garden
LOCATION Haarlem, the Netherlands
CLIENT Private owner
YEAR 2007–2009
STATUS Completed
SCOPE Garden design and realisation
SCALE 20 × 100 m
COLLABORATORS Van Kemenade Tuinen,
Johan Jumelet

**Seminar, "Landscaping, Architecture and
performance: Crisis and possibilities for
landscaping in Lima"**
LOCATION Lima, Peru
CLIENT The Association for Theatre
Investigation La Otra Orilla (LOT) and
the non-profit citizen activism group
Tierra Viva
YEAR 2009
STATUS Completed
SCOPE One-week seminar in which social,
artistic, historic and environmental
investigations were exchanged and
continued with the focus on the public
spaces, parks and monuments in the city
of Lima. The occasion rose from the fact
that the second largest desert city of the
world suffered from lack of municipal/
regional landscaping policies, leading to
privatisation of land by developers. This
resulted in poorly maintained public
spaces versus thriving, fenced, private
parks and the appropriation of historic
sites. Our seminar focused on the role
that artistic expression and historic/
ecologic education can play to influence
the political perspective on the value of
the urban public space and the protection
of monuments for all citizens.
COLLABORATORS Manuel de Rivero, Jeroen
van der Zalm/La Otra Orilla, Tierra Viva,
Roberto Dias/Sitio Roberto Burle Marx

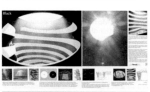

Solomon R. Guggenheim Museum
LOCATION New York City, New York, USA
CLIENT Guggenheim Museum
YEAR 2009
STATUS Competition
SCOPE Request for "Contemplating the
Void: Interventions in the Guggenheim
Museum Rotunda," "deleting" the
background/muting sound, opening the
roof for day- and moonlight, enhancing
the spiral
COLLABORATORS Level Acoustics/
Renz van Luxemburg

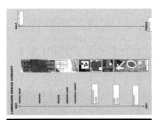

Al-Shamal
LOCATION Al-shamal, Qatar
CLIENT OMA
YEAR 2009
STATUS Concept
SCOPE Landscape masterplan
SCALE 240 × 3,250 m/78 ha
COLLABORATORS OMA

Building Facade
LOCATION Nieuwegein, the Netherlands
CLIENT Municipality of Nieuwegein
YEAR 2009
STATUS Competition
SCOPE Art commision for facade
treatment of the residential building "The
Edge," located next to a busy motorway
SCALE 2,900 m²

→ p. 562
Arbor Garden
LOCATION Amsterdam, the Netherlands
CLIENT Private owner
YEAR 1984–2010
STATUS Completed
SCOPE Design of private garden,
installation and maintenance
SCALE 8 × 10 m

→ p. 494
Walled Garden
LOCATION Wassenaar, the Netherlands
CLIENT Private owner
YEAR 1985–2010
STATUS Completed
SCOPE Private garden installation and
maintenance
SCALE 4,000 m²
COLLABORATORS Owner

Liberal Jewish Community Synagogue
LOCATION Amsterdam, the Netherlands
CLIENT Reform Jewish Congregation
Amsterdam
YEAR 2007–2010
STATUS Completed
SCOPE Shading and privacy curtains for
east and west facades of the Sjul
(imagery east, ancient tree; west, young
twigs; with 12 tribes of Israel on second,
transparent layer)
SCALE 57.3 × 12.47 m (2×)
COLLABORATORS SeARCH

Swarovski Headquarters
LOCATION Zurich-Männedorf, Switzerland
CLIENT Swarovski Immobilien AG, Männedorf
YEAR 2008–2010
STATUS Completed
SCOPE Entrance zone and landscaping of surrounding hill (realised); design and track configuration for sun-reflective division curtains (not realised)
SCALE 1.4 ha
COLLABORATORS Ingenhoven Architects

→ p. 564
State Detention Centre, Dendermonde
LOCATION Dendermonde, Belgium
CLIENT Regie der Gebouwen/ Jan de Nul Group
YEAR 2009–2010
STATUS Competition
SCOPE Landscape masterplans and designs of all prison gardens, walls and exterior entrance and parking areas
SCALE 13 ha
COLLABORATORS 51N4E, Hootsmans Architectuurbureau

MedAustron
LOCATION Vienna, Austria
CLIENT Moser Architects; EBG GmbH MedAustron
YEAR 2010
STATUS Concept design
SCOPE Proposals for privacy/division curtains, Cancer Centre for lon beam therapy and research

Experimentarium
LOCATION Tuborg nord, Gentofte, Denmark
CLIENT Experimentarium – (nonprofit foundation), Municipality of Gentofte
YEAR 2010
STATUS Competition
SCOPE Co-designing the requested interior program and layout
SCALE 16,200 m² of exhibition area
COLLABORATORS Adept Architects

→ p. 558
Con los Ojos Abiertos, La Casa Encendida
LOCATION Madrid, Spain
CLIENT Fundación Montemadrid
YEAR 2008–2010
STATUS Completed
SCOPE Site-specific installation
SCALE Facade, 34 "bird" sunshades, 2.38 × 1.8 m; one continuous ribbon carpet over five flights of stairs, 102 × 0.6 m; roof curtain, 51.5 × 4.5 m; interactive poster, 2 × 2 m
COLLABORATORS Ariadna Cantis, Sociedad Española de Ornitilogîa, La Casa Encendida team

→ p. 544
Park of the New Horizon, West Kowloon Cultural City
LOCATION West Kowloon, Hong Kong
CLIENT WKCD Authorities
YEAR 2009–2010
STATUS Competition, 2nd prize
SCOPE Landscape masterplan, including all infrastructure above and below ground: "Park of the New Horizon"
SCALE 42 ha
COLLABORATORS OMA, Atelier Urbanus Shenzhen, Mc Kinsey & Company, Michael Schindhelm, Hou Hanru a.o.

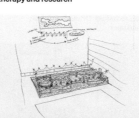

New Royal London Children's Hospital
LOCATION Whitechapel, London, United Kingdom
CLIENT Vital Arts – the Arts Organisation within Barts Health NHS Trust
YEAR 2010
STATUS Competition
SCOPE Landscape concepts for roof garden; interior advisory
COLLABORATORS John Cooper Architecture

Sabhā Oasis city
LOCATION Sabha, Sabha District, Libya
CLIENT Wahat, developers and architects
YEAR 2010
STATUS Schematic Design
SCOPE Large central park on the edge of the city centre; focus on tourism, culture and native planting
SCALE 140 ha
COLLABORATORS OMA

Rabobank Headquarters
LOCATION Utrecht, the Netherlands
CLIENT Rabobank Utrecht
YEAR 2009–2010
STATUS Schematic Design
SCOPE Art commission for two sound absorbing wall objects in the entrance area of the bank's main hall
SCALE 2 atrium wall covers, each 23.6 m × 7.5 m
COLLABORATORS Kraaijvanger Urbis

→ p. 552
Desert City, Masterplan for Ghadames
LOCATION Ghadames (World Heritage Site), Nalut district, Libya
CLIENT Wahat, developers and architects
YEAR 2009–2010
STATUS Schematic Design
SCOPE Landscape masterplan and phasing plan for the abandoned ancient desert town; landscape design for a new film festival and tourist spa on a former military site nearby; gardens for a planned hotel on the former airplane landing strip
SCALE 268 ha
COLLABORATORS OMA

→ p. 542
Workshop Freiflächen im Kunstareal München
LOCATION Munich, Germany
CLIENT Bayerischen Staatministerium fuer Wissenschaft, Forschung und Kunst und der Landeshauptstadt Muenchen
YEAR 2010
STATUS Completed
SCOPE 3-day workshop organised by the city of Munich to identify and define the potential of the open spaces in the Kunstareal, Munich
SCALE ca. 10 ha
COLLABORATORS Hager, Gross.Max, Studio Urban Catalyst, Atelier Le Balto

→ p. 538
Hans Vredeman de Vries Curtains, Cornell University College of Architecture
LOCATION Ithaca, New York, USA
CLIENT Cornell University, College of Architecture, Art and Planning
YEAR 2007–2011
STATUS Completed
SCOPE Darkening curtains for Milstein Hall auditorium; view filter and glare control curtains for AAP forum
SCALE Auditorium curtain, 47.4 × 3.7 m; AAP forum curtain, 31 × 3.7 m
COLLABORATORS OMA

Penthouse
LOCATION Paris, France
CLIENT Private owner
YEAR 2010
STATUS Completed
SCOPE Terrace and roof gardens; shading device for outside living for triple-floor penthouse in the centre of Paris
SCALE 670 m²
COLLABORATORS HAR ÉTUDES

Museumpark
LOCATION Rotterdam, the Netherlands
CLIENT Municipality of Rotterdam
YEAR 2008–2011
STATUS Completed
SCOPE Readjustment of room 1 and cultural podium
SCALE ca. 1.7 ha
COLLABORATORS OMA, Department of Green, Municipality of Rotterdam

→ p. 564
State Detention Centre, Beveren
LOCATION Beveren, Belgium
CLIENT Regie der Gebouwen/ Jan de Nul Group
YEAR 2009–2010
STATUS Competition
SCOPE Landscape masterplans and designs of all prison gardens, walls and exterior entrance and parking areas
SCALE 12 ha
COLLABORATORS 51N4E, Hootsmans Architectuurbureau

Kromhout Kazerne
LOCATION Utrecht, the Netherlands
CLIENT Art Olive/Ministry of Defence
YEAR 2009–2010
STATUS Completed
SCOPE Art commission for officer's villas: privacy and darkening curtains
SCALE 3 curtain installations, 510 m²
COLLABORATORS Meyer en van Schooten Architecten

→ p. 536
Chazen Museum of Art
LOCATION Madison, Wisconsin, USA
CLIENT Chazen Museum of Art – director Russell Panczenko
YEAR 2008–2011
STATUS Completed
SCOPE Translucent curtain for privacy and acoustic absorbance in the lobby of the new annex; motorised track and storage configuration; stage curtain for auditorium; lamp
SCALE Lobby curtain, 20 × 6.94 m; auditorium curtain, 14 × 5.5 m; lamp: 6.94 × 0.15 m
COLLABORATORS Machado and Silvetti Associates

De Rotterdam
LOCATION Kop van Zuid, Rotterdam, the Netherlands
CLIENT OMA
YEAR 2009–2011
STATUS Completed
SCOPE Study of interior finishes, furnishings and curtains
SCALE 162,000 m²
COLLABORATORS OMA

→ p. 528
Rothschild's London Headquarters
LOCATION New Court, London, United Kingdom
CLIENT NM Rothschild & Sons
YEAR 2009–2011
STATUS Completed
SCOPE Acoustic, space-defining and view-filtering curtain for the entrance lobby; advisory on interior finishes; colour and furnishing concepts
SCALE lobby curtain, 54.4 × 5.2 m; interiors, 13,000 m²
COLLABORATORS OMA, Ken Creasey Ltd

→ p. 524
Piper Auditorium, Harvard GSD
LOCATION Cambridge, MA, USA
CLIENT Harvard University Graduate School of Design
YEAR 2010–2011
STATUS Completed
SCOPE Space dividing curtain for the Piper Auditorium
SCALE 33.5 × 5.8 m (double-layered)

National Museum of Syria
LOCATION Damascus, Syria
CLIENT National Museum Damascus
YEAR 2010–2011
STATUS Competition, project cancelled in 2011
SCOPE Landscape design for museum gardens and consultancy on exhibition layout in combination with garden concept
SCALE ca. 3 ha
COLLABORATORS OMA

Snapshot, Van Gogh Museum
LOCATION Amsterdam, the Netherlands
CLIENT Van Gogh Museum
YEAR 2010–2011
STATUS Completed
SCOPE Exhibition design showing the influence of the Kodak camera on late-nineteenth-century and early-twentieth-century painting
SCALE 1,583 m²
COLLABORATORS Museum team

Bedroom Curtain
LOCATION Amsterdam, the Netherlands
CLIENT Private owners
YEAR 2011 (Restoration in 2020)
STATUS Completed
SCOPE Blackout curtain for bedroom
SCALE 3.50 × 3.15 m

J + J apartment
LOCATION Amsterdam, the Netherlands
CLIENT Private owner
YEAR 2011
STATUS Concept
SCOPE Sun-filtering curtain
SCALE 4.93 × 2.57 m

UPC (now Ziggo) Headquarters Schiphol Rijk
LOCATION Schiphol Rijk, Amsterdam, the Netherlands
CLIENT UPC
YEAR 2011
STATUS Completed
SCOPE Wall-to-wall "project" carpets (i.e., desk-chair resistant, cleanable, anti-static) for office spaces
SCALE Polder Carpets, 118.8 m²/129.6 m²/ 129.6 m²
COLLABORATORS Concern / Gilian Schrofer

High Court of The Netherlands
LOCATION The Hague, the Netherlands
CLIENT Ministerie van Justitie en Veiligheid
YEAR 2011
STATUS Competition
SCOPE Landscape design and interior interventions
SCALE 15,000 m² + sidewalk and back garden
COLLABORATORS Paul de Ruiter, Hootsmans Architectuurbureau

Administrative Centre / Social Housing
LOCATION Sint-Niklaas, Belgium
CLIENT Municipality of Sint-Niklaas
YEAR 2011
STATUS Competition
SCOPE Landscape design, pedestrian flow and traffic logistics
SCALE 33,168 m²
COLLABORATORS Hootsmans Architectuurbureau

Piranesi Pixel, Landscape CCTV Headquarters and TVCC Conference Centre
LOCATION Beijing, China
CLIENT China Central Television (CCTV)
YEAR 2002–2012
STATUS Completed
SCOPE Landscape design for streetscape, security zones, roof gardens, public garden and entrance areas; street and path pavings; floor and wall finishes of entrance halls
SCALE 10 ha + interior spaces
COLLABORATORS OMA, ECADI

UPC (now Ziggo) Offices
LOCATION Leeuwarden, the Netherlands
CLIENT UPC
YEAR 2010–2012
STATUS Completed
SCOPE Wall-to-wall "project" carpets for staff restaurant and offices; curtain to define staff coffee shop / bar area; atrium garden
SCALE Restaurant curtain, 38.44 × 2.8 m; Polder Carpets, 575 m²
COLLABORATORS Paul de Ruiter, Concern, Hollandse Nieuwe

→ p. 496
Re-Set, new wings for architecture, Dutch Pavilion – Venice Architecture Biennale
LOCATION Giardini della Biennale, Venice, Italy
CLIENT NAi (Netherlands Architecture Institute)
YEAR 2012
STATUS Completed
SCOPE Installation representing economical and flexible use of vacant buildings inside the Dutch Pavilion
SCALE Curtains, 21 × 5.4 m (2×); track length, 148 m; loop of 12 configurations, 90 seconds per stop; speed, 4 sec / m; total duration, ca. 22 minutes
COLLABORATORS Gerrit Rietveld 1950s, Gerriets GmbH, Rob Nijsse, Hans Jansen, Landstra & deVries

→ p. 510
Damask Tapestry, Stedelijk Museum
LOCATION Amsterdam, the Netherlands
CLIENT Stedelijk Museum Amsterdam – director Ann Goldstein
YEAR 2011–2012
STATUS Completed
SCOPE Tapestry in restaurant and on walls of the entrance hall to improve acoustics
SCALE Tapestry foyer, 14 × 10.4 m; tapestry restaurant, 20.5 × 3.15 m; total, 210 m²
COLLABORATORS Desso Tarkett, Aura Melis

→ p. 754

Maison Bordeaux 2.0
LOCATION Floirac, France
CLIENT Private owners
YEAR 2011–2012 (revision)
STATUS Completed
SCOPE Re-design of all existing curtains in 2012, two additional red carpets
SCALE Seven curtains, 8.44 × 2.33 m, 12.96 × 2.28 m, 4.84 × 2.28 m, 5.76 × 2.38 m, 9.61 × 2.38 m, 20.74 × 2.4 m, 25 × 2.4 m; two carpets, 3.4 × 2.18 m, 5.97 × 2.5 m

Movements 25%, Introduction to a Working Process
LOCATION Amsterdam, the Netherlands
CLIENT Architectura & Natura (publisher 2012)
YEAR 2012
STATUS Completed
SCOPE Re-Publishing of exhibition catalogue *Movements 25%, Introduction to a Working Process*, including DVD of works filmed by Frans Parthesius and plastic cover by Irma Boom,on the occasion of the 13th Architecture Biennial Venice, 2012
SCALE 236 pages/10 × 14.5 cm
COLLABORATORS Irma Boom, Frans Parthesius

Penthouse
LOCATION Amsterdam, the Netherlands
CLIENT Private owner
YEAR 2012
STATUS Completed
SCOPE Major refurbishment of loft; roof terrace; curtains
SCALE Loft, 200 m²; roof terrace, 35 m²; curtain, (1×) 2.7 × 3.5 m, (2×) 2 × 1 m
COLLABORATORS Heike Löhmann

→ p. 490

Pink!, Private Apartment
LOCATION Byzantium building, Amsterdam, the Netherlands
CLIENT Private Owner
YEAR 2012
STATUS Completed
SCOPE Create darkening and cooling curtain along glazed south facade
SCALE 9.8 × 2.4 m

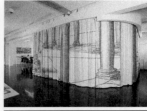

Gerriets GmbH Headquarters
LOCATION Umkirch, Germany
CLIENT Gerriets GmbH
YEAR 2012
STATUS Completed
SCOPE Acoustic curtain to define and isolate Gerriets main meeting room
SCALE 12.52 × 2.57 m, 6.87 m × 2.57 m

De Schipperskaai, Oude Dokken
LOCATION Ghent, Belgium
CLIENT Municipality of Ghent, Dienst Stedelijke Vernieuwing
YEAR 2012
STATUS Competition
SCOPE Landscape contribution to new "housing+" development plan
COLLABORATORS MVRDV, MVV, DKV, Lustarchitecten, Dierendonckblancke architecten

Qatar Foundation Headquarters
LOCATION Education City, Doha, Qatar
CLIENT Qatar Foundation
YEAR 2012
STATUS Completed
SCOPE Recipes (track typology and shape, materials, sewing techniques) for darkening curtains for the two main auditoriums inside the building
SCALE 4 curtains, all double-layered; auditorium, 55.3 × 7.7 – 3.59 m, 28.73 × 7.01 – 3.59; visitors' centre, 24.2 × 6.51 – 3.16 m, 24.2 × 6.51 – 3.16 m
COLLABORATORS OMA

Ruten Park
LOCATION Sandnes, Norway
CLIENT Sandnes Kommune
YEAR 2012
STATUS Competition, 1st prize/completed
SCOPE Landscape advisory, conceptual ideas during competition
SCALE ca. 2 ha
COLLABORATORS Spacegroup, Superunion Arch., Atelier Ten, Anne B. Hovind Curator, Ljusarkitektur

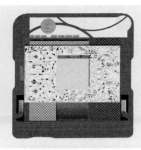

→ p. 474

Sino-European Gardens, Shenzen Stock Exchange Headquarters
LOCATION Futian District, Shenzhen Shi, China
CLIENT Shenzhen Stock Exchange
YEAR 2007–2013
STATUS Competition, 1st prize/Completed
SCOPE Landscape design, public park, entrance areas and plazas; vertical, interior and patio gardens; floor patterns for entrance halls and restaurant; roof garden
SCALE ca. 6 ha
COLLABORATORS OMA, SADI Engineers, SED, Verte Asia

Tencent Beijing Headquarters
LOCATION Zhonguancun Software Park, Beijing, China
CLIENT Tencent
YEAR 2011–2013
STATUS Completed
SCOPE Landscape design for the corporate building's surrounding park, interior patios and large-scale food production roof garden (for a staff of 10,000)
SCALE Site, 7.6 ha; courtyards, 226 m²; food production and relaxation roof, 7,300 m²
COLLABORATORS OMA, Maya Lin Studio, Margie Ruddick Landscape

Caen la Mer
LOCATION Caen la Mer, préfecture Calvados, France
CLIENT Mairie de Caen
YEAR 2011–2013
STATUS Competition
SCOPE Landscape masterplan for the former industrial half-island Caen-la-Mer
SCALE 10 ha
COLLABORATORS OMA

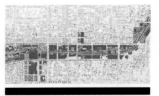

Regeneration of downtown Lexington
LOCATION Lexington, Kentucky, USA
CLIENT Lexington-Fayette Urban-County Government
YEAR 2011–2013
STATUS Competition 2011: Landscape Masterplan Srts and Entertainment district, 1st prize; Competition 2013: Regeneration of downtown Lexington, 2nd prize
SCOPE Landscape plan for the improvement of the landscape and environmental conditions in downtown Lexington; traffic and parking re-organisation
SCALE 19 ha
COLLABORATORS Phase 1 – Spacegroup architects, Omni, Adams Kara Taylor, Atelier Ten; Phase 2 – Carman, Omni, Tetra Tech, Rick Darke, 2×4

Private Villa
LOCATION Oslo, Norway
CLIENT Private owners
YEAR 2011–2013
STATUS Completed
SCOPE All curtains and "curtain wall" for sound room; dining-room carpet
SCALE 5 curtains, 13 × 5.5 m, 7 × 2.5 m, 5.45 × 2.5 m, 7.27 × 2.47 m, 16.8 × 2.32 m; 1 carpet, 2.7 × 4 m
COLLABORATORS SpaceGroup

Walker Art Center
LOCATION Minneapolis, Minnesota, USA
CLIENT Walker Art Center
YEAR 2012–2013
STATUS Schematic Design
SCOPE Meandering curtain for Cargill Hall, to form various rooms for different kinds of use
SCALE Track, 51 m; curtain 19.92 × 7.4 m
COLLABORATORS HGA Architects, Olga Viso & Andrew Blauveld

Sandridge Energy Parkside Building
LOCATION Oklahoma, USA
CLIENT Rogers Marvel Architects
YEAR 2012–2013
STATUS Concept Design
SCOPE Street and roof landscape and curtain designs
SCALE Curtain, 49 × 11.4 m

Narcissus Flying Curtain
→ p.472
LOCATION Several theatres in the Netherlands: Hervormde Kerk, Den Bosch; Muziekgebouw aan het Ij, Amsterdam; Korzo Theater, The Hague; De Vereeniging, Nijmegen
CLIENT Nieuw Amsterdams Peil, Calliope Tsoupaki
YEAR 2013
STATUS Completed
SCOPE Scenography for a chamber music performance
SCALE Floor, 7 × 6.4 m; curtain, 36 × 7 m; approx. 40 helium balloons
COLLABORATORS Tanja Durloo (scent expert), Calliope Tsoupaki (composer)

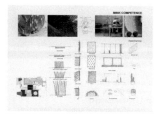

Mink Bürsten Headquarters
LOCATION Göppingen, Germany
CLIENT Mink-Bürsten KG, Göppingen
YEAR 2013
STATUS Concept Design
SCOPE Visitors' routing, running from the entrance gate through the building to the exhibition spaces.

Stedelijk Museum Shop
LOCATION Amsterdam, the Netherlands
CLIENT Stedelijk museum shop
YEAR 2013
STATUS Completed
SCOPE Inside Outside product installation and public lecture at Walther König museum bookstore, in line with the realisation of the "Damask" tapestry in Stedelijk's entrance hall and restaurant
SCALE "Damask" mouse pads (A4 size), "Damask" tapestry pieces (ca. 3 m²), Riflettuti parasols, Seattle Library carpet samples (1 × 1 m), IO books (2000 and 2007 editions)
COLLABORATORS König bookstore team

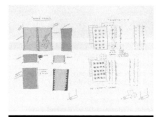

Knoll Textiles
LOCATION New York, USA
CLIENT Knoll Textiles
YEAR 2013
STATUS Concept
SCOPE Invitation to present an Inside Outside textile series for the Knoll curtain and upholstery collection.

Mobile curtain, Inside Outside Studio
LOCATION Amsterdam, the Netherlands
CLIENT Own production/Original request: Chamber Gallery, NYC
YEAR 2013
STATUS Completed
SCOPE A mobile, independent curtain
SCALE 1.4 × 2.1 × 0.6 m
COLLABORATORS Wouter de Baan, sculptor

Private House
LOCATION Amsterdam, the Netherlands
CLIENT Private owners
YEAR 2013
STATUS Completed
SCOPE Interior design and curtains
SCALE 3 items: (1×) 1.8 × 2.7 m; (1×) 6 × 3.2 m; (1×) 9 × 3.2 m

Rabobank
LOCATION Sittard, the Netherlands
CLIENT Rabobank Westelijke Mijnstreek
YEAR 2012–2014
STATUS Completed
SCOPE Monumental curtain and two side-curtains to define, enclose and organise an auditorium and workplaces inside the bank's spacious entrance lobby
SCALE 3 items: 29.6 × 10.5 m; 12.39 × 8.88 m; 11.35 × 6.2 m
COLLABORATORS Mecanoo

Hamilton College of Art
LOCATION Clinton, New York, USA
CLIENT Machado and Silvetti Associates
YEAR 2013–2014
STATUS Completed
SCOPE Double-layered curtain to close off gallery space from entrance lobby while improving light and sound situation of both entrance area and gallery, allowing a view down from the studio space on level 2
SCALE 20 × 6.5 m
COLLABORATORS Machado and Silvetti Associates

Espace public (Limites), AGORA 2014 Biennale de Bordeaux
→ p.466
LOCATION Hangar 14, Bordeaux, France
CLIENT Municipality of Bordeaux
YEAR 2013–2014
STATUS Completed
SCOPE Exhibition design for the 6th edition of the AGORA Biennale
SCALE Scenography, 5,400 m², including 212 gabion exhibition panels on the ground floor and a large curtain (195 × 3.62 m) on the first floor
COLLABORATORS Youssef Tohmé and team, Studio DB

Inside Outside installation at Inflatable Gallery
→ p.470
LOCATION Bordeaux, France
CLIENT Arc en Rêve Centre d'Architecture
YEAR 2013–2014
STATUS Completed
SCOPE Exhibition design and installation of Inside Outside works
SCALE ca. 75 m²
COLLABORATORS AVD Productions/ Anna van Dorp, Frans Parthesius, Hans-Walter Müller

Schiphol Airport VIP Entrance
LOCATION Schiphol, Amsterdam
CLIENT Schiphol Airport
YEAR 2014
STATUS Completed
SCOPE Design for glass screen in VIP luggage check area to create privacy without loosing sense of space and light
SCALE 11.3 × 2.75 m
COLLABORATORS Benthem Crouwel Architekten

Heilig Hart College Campus
LOCATION Heilig Hart College campus, Waregem, Belgium
CLIENT vzw Katholiek Secundair Onderwijs Waregem-Anzegem-Avelgem
YEAR 2014
STATUS Competition
SCOPE Design for the school's walled play- and sportsground
SCALE 12,660 m²
COLLABORATORS ZAmpone Architects

Joli Cœur-Süd
→ p.306
LOCATION Berlin-Charlottenburg, Germany
CLIENT Home Center Management GmbH
YEAR 2014
STATUS Schematic Design
SCOPE Landscape design for the new housing development area behind the Joli Cœur (former hospital) building
SCALE 21,100 m²
COLLABORATORS Carlos Zwick Architekten BDA

Résidence l'Etoile
LOCATION Amsterdam, the Netherlands
CLIENT Kroonenberg Groep
YEAR 2014
STATUS Completed
SCOPE Darkening and privacy-generating curtains for entrance lobby of high-end residential apartment building
SCALE Entrance, 4.94 × 5.4 m; reception curtain 1, 13.81 × 5.4 m, curtain 2, 1.1 × 5.4 m
COLLABORATORS Bureau Veenendaal & Associates

HOPE Boutique Hartenstraat
LOCATION Amsterdam, the Netherlands
CLIENT HOPE by Ringstrand Soderberg Stockholm – Sweden
YEAR 2014
STATUS Completed
SCOPE Interior intervention for the walls of the fashion boutique, working with given paper-based, stiff panels
SCALE 18 Minerite plates of 200 × 120 × 0.12 cm

Private Residence
LOCATION Buenos Aires, Argentina
CLIENT Private owners
YEAR 2014
STATUS Completed
SCOPE Space dividing acoustic curtain to close off open office space in private loft's living room area
SCALE Curtain 1, 16.65 × 2.16 m; curtain 2, 18.92 × 2.16 m
COLLABORATORS Estudio Maliar Bonardo

Municipal (Olympic) Swimming Pool
LOCATION Satd Oostende, Belgium
CLIENT TMVW, Municipality of Oostende
YEAR 2014
STATUS Competition, 1st prize
SCOPE Landscape plan, roof gardens and interior advisory for the restoration of 1970s buidling by architects P. Felix and J. Thanghe & new expansion by BEL Architecten
SCALE ca. 2 ha
COLLABORATORS BEL Architecten, NEY & Partners

→ p. 458
Knoll Showcase, Salone del Mobile
LOCATION Milan, Italy
CLIENT Knoll International
YEAR 2013–2015
STATUS Completed
SCOPE Space-defining curtains
SCALE 2013–2014, 153 m × 4.75 m; 2015, 2 curtains (exterior, 180 × 4.75 m; interior, 195 × 4.75 m)
COLLABORATORS OMA

→ p. 438
Solar Curtain Research
LOCATION Case study sites: Textile Museum, Tilburg (northern European climate) and Qatar National Library, Doha (desert climate)
CLIENT TextielMuseum Tilburg
YEAR 2013–2015
STATUS Commissioned research
SCOPE "Develop a test of something you have wanted to test for a long time…"
SCALE Varied
COLLABORATORS TextielLab Tilburg, Solar Fiber, Eindhoven University of Technology

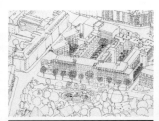

Metropol Park
LOCATION Berlin, Germany
CLIENT Home Center Management GmbH
YEAR 2014–2015
STATUS Schematic design
SCOPE Garden design for each courtyard; interior design for main entrance lobby and staircases
COLLABORATORS Axthelm Rolvien Architekten

Garage Museum of Contemporary Art
LOCATION Gorky Park, Moscow, Russia
CLIENT Garage Center of Contemporary Culture
YEAR 2014–2015
STATUS Completed
SCOPE Landscape design for the Garage public square
SCALE ca. 2 ha
COLLABORATORS OMA

Vlaamse Radio- en Televisieomroeporganisatie (VRT) Headquarters
LOCATION Brussels, Belgium
CLIENT Flemish Radio and Television Organisation (VRT)
YEAR 2014–2015
STATUS Competition
SCOPE Landscape design, including a green plan for the building's terraces
SCALE 72,000 m²
COLLABORATORS OMA

Bella Donna Offices
LOCATION Amstelveen, the Netherlands
CLIENT ProWinko Nederlands B.V.
YEAR 2014–2015
STATUS Completed
SCOPE Stainless steel-and-voile embellishment of narrow entrance situation of high-end, art-collecting, commercial development company to improve spatial experience of entrance situation
SCALE Mirroring stainless steel wall, 10.34 × 3.95 m; curtain, 11.37 × 3.95 m
COLLABORATORS Anything is Possible, Benthem Crouwel Architekten

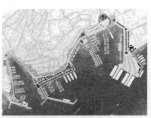

Waterfront La Maddalena
LOCATION La Maddalena, Sardinia, Italy
CLIENT Municipality of La Maddalena
YEAR 2014–2015
STATUS Commissioned Study and Concept Design
SCOPE Study for the improvement of the town's sailboat harbor, ticket offices, quay edges, ferry docks, traffic flow and car parking situation, including a greening plan for all areas
SCALE ca. 4 ha
COLLABORATORS Stefano Boeri Architetti, Marina Perot, Rem Koolhaas

→ p. 450
Huis Sonneveld
LOCATION Rotterdam, the Netherlands
CLIENT Het Nieuwe Instituut
YEAR 2014–2015
STATUS Completed
SCOPE Temporary art installation in the museum Huis Sonneveld
SCALE Ground floor, 33 m²; first floor, 167 m²; second floor, 61 m²; roof, 22 m²
COLLABORATORS Brinkman en Van der Vlugt (1933), Herman Pols / Castano Xylos, HNI team

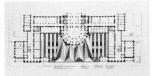

ETH Zurich Zentrum
LOCATION Zurich, Switzerland
CLIENT ETH Zurich
YEAR 2015
STATUS Competition
SCOPE Landscape design of entrance plaza and edge areas
SCALE 1,620 m²
COLLABORATORS Baukuh

Osumi Island
LOCATION Osumi Island (UNESCO World Heritage Site), Berat, Albania
CLIENT Atelier Albania, City of Berat
YEAR 2015
STATUS Competition
SCOPE Landscape study and design to improve the town's river edge and its river-island situation in view of regular floods; landscape design for the river-island in connection to the new outdoor public swimming pool
SCALE 0.3 km²
COLLABORATORS BEL architecten

Het Nieuwe Instituut
LOCATION Rotterdam, the Netherlands
CLIENT Het Nieuwe Instituut, Rotterdam
YEAR 2015
STATUS Completed
SCOPE Transformation of Re-Set curtains made for the Dutch Pavilion at the Venice Architecture Biennale 2012: darkening, acoustic and privacy curtains for the HNI auditorium; included in the architecture collection of the Institute
SCALE 18 × 5.26 m

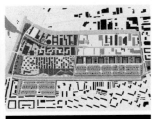

Garden Island Wilhelmsburg
LOCATION Hamburg, Germany
CLIENT IBA Hamburg
YEAR 2015
STATUS Competition
SCOPE Landscape plan in connection to urban development plan with inclusion of existing allotments on both sides of the river
SCALE ca. 111 ha
COLLABORATORS BeL Societät für Architektur, NL Architects

Solid Nature
LOCATION Paris & Monaco, France
CLIENT Solid Nature
YEAR 2015
STATUS Completed
SCOPE Monumental space defining and dividing curtains for Solid Nature (natural stone) product stand in Paris and Monaco.
SCALE Paris: exposition area, 294 m²; 4 curtains, 24.5 × 4.87 m, 11.4 × 4.87 m, 8.2 × 4.87 m, 5.6 × 4.87 m; Monaco: screens, 2 × 2 m
COLLABORATORS OMA

→ p. 444
Doha Art Mill
LOCATION Doha, Qatar
CLIENT Qatar Museums
YEAR 2015
STATUS Competition
SCOPE Convert the flour mill into an Art Mill, with gallery and studio spaces, screening rooms, classrooms, gardens, restaurants, terraces, parking lots
SCALE 9.4 ha with 3.2 ha of gardens
COLLABORATORS Lacaton & Vassal Architects

→ p. 424
Water Recipe Garden, Qatar Foundation Headquarters
LOCATION Education city, Doha, Qatar
CLIENT Qatar Foundation
YEAR 2007–2016
STATUS Completed
SCOPE Experimental ecological semi-public garden on concrete plate above parking lot; street furniture and lighting plan; design of darkening curtains for the building's two auditoriums
SCALE 3.8 ha
COLLABORATORS OMA, Dr. Ekhlas M. M. Abdel Bari, Prof. Dr. Kamal Batanouny

Bibliothèque Alexis de Tocqueville
LOCATION Caen, France
CLIENT Bibliothèque Alexis de Tocqueville
YEAR 2010–2016
STATUS Completed
SCOPE Design and realisation of a curtain that darkens the glazed upper halves of the auditorium walls on 3 sides and that acts as light object over the blind wall, covering all wall surfaces with the exception of entrance and emergency doors while improving the room's acoustic quality
SCALE 80 × 4.1 m (double-layered)
COLLABORATORS OMA, Francisco Martinez

→ p. 442
Zuiderdokken
LOCATION Zuiderdokken, Antwerp, Belgium
CLIENT Municipality of Antwerp
YEAR 2015–2016
STATUS Competition, 2nd prize
SCOPE Design flexible, multipurpose public park in the historical heart of Antwerp
SCALE 3.4 ha
COLLABORATORS BEL architecten, Landschaap, Witteveen & Bos, Roel Huisman

→ p. 400
Pierre Paulin, Centre Pompidou
LOCATION Paris, France
CLIENT Centre Pompidou
YEAR 2015–2016
STATUS Completed
SCOPE A timeline and backdrop curtain for the retrospective exhibition *Pierre Paulin*
SCALE 77 × 3.6 m

Consulate of Saudi Arabia
LOCATION The Hague, the Netherlands
CLIENT Consulate of Saudi Arabia
YEAR 2015–2016
STATUS Completed
SCOPE Curtains in all office and meeting spaces cover all windows of this classic, free-standing building; darkening curtains block light in the auditorium on top floor; screens create privacy for functional spaces on street level
SCALE 31 curtains
COLLABORATORS AAArchitects

Family Garden
LOCATION St John's Wood, London, United Kingdom
CLIENT Private owner
YEAR 2016
STATUS Concept Design
SCOPE Multi-faceted garden design for car and family life outdoors
SCALE 380 m²

Citta vecchia Taranto
LOCATION Taranto Old Town, Taranto, Puglia, Italy
CLIENT Invitalia
YEAR 2016
STATUS Competition
SCOPE Urban regeneration, landscape plan
SCALE Study area, 27 ha; landscape interventions along the waterfront, 4.9 ha
COLLABORATORS Alvisi Kirimoto Architects

Extreme Climate Workshop
LOCATION Yakutsk, Federal Republic of Sakha, Siberia
CLIENT MARCH Architecture School / Irina Alexeeva, City architect of Yakutsk
YEAR 2016
STATUS Completed
SCOPE Workshop with young architecture professionals; lectures; keynote speaker at conference
SCALE 3 ha

Afval Energie Centrale
LOCATION Antwerp, Belgium
CLIENT ISVAG
YEAR 2016
STATUS Competition, 1st prize
SCOPE Design for a cleansing landscape that surrounds and interacts with the waste-to-energy plant
COLLABORATORS BEL Architecten

Wedding Foulard
LOCATION Amsterdam, the Netherlands
YEAR 2016
STATUS Completed
SCOPE Wedding gift bed spread
SCALE 2.5 × 2.5 m

→ p. 390
Textile City Park
LOCATION Prato, Italy
CLIENT Municipality of Prato
YEAR 2016
STATUS Competition
SCOPE Landscape design for a new park in the heart of the old city
SCALE 3.3 ha
COLLABORATORS Alvisi Kirimoto Architects

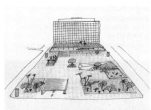

Rabin Square
LOCATION Tel Aviv, Israel
CLIENT Tel Aviv Municipality
YEAR 2016
STATUS Competition
SCOPE Re-design of Rabin Square to improve conditions of existing building and its connections to the square and underground parking lots, with additional new program (inside and outside).
SCALE 2.25 ha
COLLABORATORS Efrat-Kowalsky Architects, Heide & Von Beckerath

→ p. 392
Wings for the Gallery
LOCATION Zurich, Switzerland
CLIENT Institute for the History and Theory of Architecture (gta), ETH Zurich
YEAR 2016
STATUS Completed
SCOPE Flexible screens for gta Exhibitions gallery space
SCALE 3.13 × 18.86 m; 3.13 × 21.72 m; 3.13 × 21.98 m; 3.13 × 26.14 m; 3.13 × 11.77 m
COLLABORATORS gta Exhibitions

→ p. 396
Das Museum des 20. Jahrhunderts
LOCATION Berlin, Germany
CLIENT Stiftung Preußischer Kulturbesitz
YEAR 2016
STATUS Competition, 2nd prize, honorable mention
SCOPE Landscape design for the new museum's surroundings, streetscape and plazas, and its roof and inner gardens
SCALE ca. 1 ha
COLLABORATORS OMA

Roshen, Kyiv Confectionery Factory
LOCATION Kyiv, Ukraine
CLIENT ROSHEN International Confectionery Corporation
YEAR 2016
STATUS Competition, 2nd prize
SCOPE Child-friendly, inviting landscape design for the sunken, walled area around the Roshen sweets and chocolate factory that opened its doors for sight-seeing, with an emphasis on its main entrance and its active, inviting presence
SCALE 25,500 m²
COLLABORATORS Artgeo Ukraine

→ p. 406
Two Family Tales and Heritage Gardens, Qatar National Library
LOCATION Education City, Doha, Qatar
CLIENT Qatar Foundation
YEAR 2008–2017
STATUS Completed
SCOPE Landscape design for the surrounding garden, patios and heritage garden
SCALE Total area, 4.3 ha; gardens, 2.3 ha
COLLABORATORS OMA, Sergio Roland, Solid Nature

→ p. 378
Walker Art Landscape
LOCATION Minneapolis, Minnesota, USA
CLIENT Walker Art Center
YEAR 2011–2017
STATUS Completed
SCOPE Landscape design, enhancing visibility of existing entrance on Hennepin Avenue and integrating new entrance wing on Vineland (HGA); advisory on interior and exterior circulation
SCALE 2.1 ha
COLLABORATORS HGA / J. Sorrano, J. Cook, Olga Viso, Andrew Blauveld; Research phase: David Adjaye, Ai Wei Wei

→ p. 386
Roeterseiland Campus, University of Amsterdam
LOCATION Amsterdam, the Netherlands
CLIENT UvA Universiteit van Amsterdam
YEAR 2011–2017
STATUS Completed
SCOPE Design of all public spaces and inner courtyards
SCALE Landscape, 2.2 ha; total surface, 4.5 ha
COLLABORATORS Arcadis, AHMM Architects

→ p. 416
Cosmic Curtain, Qatar National Library
LOCATION Education City, Doha, Qatar
CLIENT Qatar Foundation
YEAR 2012–2017
STATUS Completed
SCOPE Art commission for a monumental curtain that creates a deployable auditorium in the main hall
SCALE 700 m²; 100 × 4.9–6.4 m
COLLABORATORS OMA, J&C Joel, TextielLab Tilburg, Arup

Super Models, travelling exhibition
LOCATION Travelling exhibition, shown (among others) in Eindhoven, Amsterdam, Tbilisi, Bogota and Jakarta
CLIENT Gilian Schrofer / Concern
YEAR 2014–2017
STATUS Completed
SCOPE "DD Doll House" – a dolls house wall, built up of 60 models of "typical" rooms, by 40 different Dutch designers and architects; part of the larger Dutch Design promotion project *Super Models*
SCALE (60×) 1:12 scale rooms; (6×) 1:20 scale houses; (120×) 1:6 scale chairs
COLLABORATORS Concern team

→ p. 374
Europa, Banco Popular Headquarters
LOCATION Madrid, Spain
CLIENT Banco Popular Inc.
YEAR 2015–2017
STATUS Completed
SCOPE View filtering and acoustic curtains with patterns based on the Euro paper money, and vertical black / white, darkening screens; both for the main glazed auditorium, "Europa"
SCALE 645 m² – 68.42 × 9.42 m (double-layered)
COLLABORATORS Arquitectos Ayala

Black Rhino Academy
LOCATION Karatu, Tanzania
CLIENT Black Rhino Academy
YEAR 2016–2017
STATUS First phase completed
SCOPE Shaded play and educational food garden and natural edge conditions to prevent wild animals from tresspassing
SCALE 7 ha
COLLABORATORS NLÉ Architects

Barkow Leibinger Offices
LOCATION Berlin, Germany
CLIENT B-L Barkow Leibinger Architekten
YEAR 2016–2017
STATUS Completed
SCOPE Multi-layered curtains for privacy and acoustic improvement of main meeting room
SCALE 3 items: 9.1 × 3.73 m, 7.7 × 3.72 m, 9.8 × 3.73 m
COLLABORATORS Barkow Leibinger team

Maggie's Oldham
LOCATION The Royal Oldham Hospital, Oldham, United Kingdom
CLIENT Maggie's Cancer Centre
YEAR 2016–2017
STATUS Completed
SCOPE Thick, acoustic flexible wall to create an intimate room for meetings and therapy sessions
SCALE 29.53 × 2.68 m
COLLABORATORS dRMM / Alex de Rijke

Solar Curtain Prototype
LOCATION Wolfsburg, Germany
CLIENT Autostadt Wolfsburg
YEAR 2016–2017
STATUS Completed
SCOPE Installation with a research prototype of the solar curtain at the show *Design on Display* at Volkswagen's exhibition space
SCALE Prototype, 2 × 3.5 m, incl. other tests, yarns and measuring objects
COLLABORATORS TextielLab, Konstantin Grcic, Friedrich von Borries

Workshop at Bezalel Academy of Arts and Design
LOCATION Jerusalem, Israel
CLIENT Bezalel Academy of Arts and Design
YEAR 2017
STATUS Completed
SCOPE Workshop on "The curtain as architectural tool"; and lecture at Bezalel Academy of Arts and Design
COLLABORATORS Students

Terrarium, Nazarbayev University
LOCATION Astana, Kazakhstan
CLIENT Nazarbayev University
YEAR 2017
STATUS Schematic Design
SCOPE Design for the monumental climatised atrium of the campus: Paving, gardens, performance areas, terraces and main plaza, including facade finishes and colour compositions
SCALE Atrium: 330 × 48 m (× 26.5 m height)
COLLABORATORS Tasmim Architects

Workshop Woodbury University, San Diego
LOCATION San Diego, USA
CLIENT Woodbury University, School of Architecture
YEAR 2017
STATUS Completed
SCOPE Workshop on the regeneration of urban leftover spaces

Rechts / Averechts. Textiel tussen Kunst en Design, Design Museum Gent
LOCATION Ghent, Belgium
CLIENT Koninklijke Academie voor Schone Kunsten (KASK)
YEAR 2017
STATUS Completed
SCOPE Participation in group exhibition with contribution on Damask tapestry at Stedelijk Museum Amsterdam
SCALE 1 tapestry panel, 3.58 × 1.63 m; video film

Academy of Architecture
LOCATION Amsterdam, the Netherlands
CLIENT Academie van Bouwkunst
YEAR 2017
STATUS Completed
SCOPE "Garden" tapestry for visual effect and acoustic improvement of reception / secretary area next to main entrance
SCALE Tapestry, 2.7 × 4 m

House Rogers
LOCATION Parkside Wimbledon, London, United Kingdom
CLIENT Harvard Graduate School of Design (GSD)
YEAR 2017
STATUS Completed
SCOPE Carpet design for guesthouse
SCALE Garden carpet, 4 × 2.7 m

Phaeno Science Centre
LOCATION Wolfsburg, Germany
CLIENT Phaeno Science Center
YEAR 2017
STATUS Completed
SCOPE Acoustic velvet and stainless steel curtain inside public workshop space
SCALE 13.5 × 2.8 m

Restaurant Dauphine
LOCATION Restaurant Dauphine, Amsterdam, the Netherlands
CLIENT Private owner
YEAR 2017
STATUS Completed
SCOPE Thick grey velvet and silver faux leather curtain with window to visually separate restaurant from next-door news centre and to improve the acoustics of the restaurant space
SCALE 13 × 6.18 m

→ p.372
One Line Workshop, Domaine de Boisbuchet
LOCATION Lessac, France
CLIENT Alexander von Vegesack, Mathias Schwartz-Clauss
YEAR 2017
STATUS Completed
SCOPE Week-long workshop on the French estate with 12 international interior architecture students of varied ages and levels of experience
SCALE Line, 830 m × 2.8 m in an area of 150 ha

→ p.370
Jubilee in Gold, 50 years gta Institute
LOCATION Zurich, Switzerland
CLIENT Institute for the History & Theory of Architecture (gta), ETH Zurich
YEAR 2017
STATUS Completed
SCOPE Jubilee curtains for the exhibition
SCALE 2 curtains, 3.12 × 10.4 m
COLLABORATORS gta Exhibitions

ArcelorMittal Headquarters
LOCATION Luxembourg City, Luxembourg
CLIENT ArcelorMittal
YEAR 2017
STATUS Competition
SCOPE Roof and stair landscape
SCALE 7,300 m²
COLLABORATORS OMA

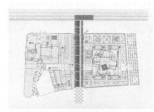

Citroën Cultural Centre
LOCATION Brussels, Belgium
CLIENT Fondation KANAL, SAU-MSI
YEAR 2017
STATUS Competition
SCOPE Introducing living green and ever-changing, space-dividing curtains to the interior; landscape design for surrounding public space, connection to adjacent park and quai, floating garden installation along the river bank
SCALE Landscape, 2.1 ha; curtain, 40 × 10 m
COLLABORATORS OMA*AMO, Wessel de Jonge Architects

→ p.348
Biblioteca degli Alberi
LOCATION Giardini di Porta Nuova, Milan, Italy
CLIENT Municipality of Milan/INGRE
YEAR 2003-2018
STATUS Competition, 1st prize 2003-2004; completed 2018
SCOPE Urban park design, planting plans, infrastructure, furnishings, lighting plan; fences around site of Fondazione Riccardo Catella
SCALE 9.5 ha
COLLABORATORS Mirko Zardini, Michael Maltzan Architecture, Piet Oudolf, Irma Boom, Ro d'Or/Rob Kuster (competition team); Franco e Simona Giorgetta (local landscape architects); Piet Oudolf (plant recipe for Piet Garden); Irma Boom (graphic interventions); Carve (advisory on fence detailing)

→ p.342
X-Y-Z, King Abdulaziz Center for World Culture
LOCATION Dhahran, Saudi Arabia
CLIENT Saudi Aramco
YEAR 2012-2018
STATUS Completed
SCOPE Art commission for guillotine stage curtain
SCALE 210 m²; 20 × 10.5 m
COLLABORATORS Arup, Octatube, Showtex Middle East

→ p.330
LocHal
LOCATION Spoorzone Tilburg, the Netherlands
CLIENT Municipality of Tilburg, Library Midden-Brabant, Seats2Meet, BKKC
YEAR 2014-2018
STATUS Competition, 1st prize/Completed
SCOPE Flexible textile architecture, interior landscape, "style rooms," moving furniture, interior moving garden
SCALE Interior, 4,125 m²; curtains A1, A2, each 47.3 × 14.85 m; curtains B1, B2, each 32 × 10.8 m; curtains C1, C2, each 57.8 × 11.16 m
COLLABORATORS Civic Architects, Braaksma & Roos Architecten, Arup, TextielLab Tilburg, LevTec, Seilemaaker, Theatex

Société Vêtements Weill
LOCATION Paris, France
CLIENT Société Vêtements Weill
YEAR 2016-2018
STATUS Completed
SCOPE Sunshading screens and curtains for entrance hall, studios and offices
SCALE 57 screens (148 m²), 3 curtains 2.96 × 2.45 m, 6.6 × 2.45 m, 1.5 × 2.45 m
COLLABORATORS Arnaud Puel/APAR Architecture, Seilemaaker

→ p.322
Intercity Next Generation, Dutch Railways
LOCATION The Netherlands, Belgium
CLIENT Dutch Railways
YEAR 2016-2018
STATUS Competition, 2016, 1st prize; train in use, 2023
SCOPE Artistic application on all interior glass and wall partitions and toilet units
SCALE 30 glass partitions per train, 222 m²; foil prints, 21 m² per train; total trains, 99 for the Netherlands, 22 for Belgium
COLLABORATORS Alstom Paris, Frans Parthesius, Jesse Koolhaas

→ p.320
Waste no Waste
LOCATION Groningen, the Netherlands
CLIENT Municipality of Groningen, Claudi Jongstra
YEAR 2017-2018
STATUS Completed
SCOPE Space-defining, acoustic curtains and textile walls for a temporary educational building
SCALE Carpet, 2.7 × 2 m; curtains, 4.6 × 2.87 m, 2.31 × 2.5 m
COLLABORATORS Claudy Jongstra team, Jeroen Kooistra

→ p.314
Theft is Vision, Luma Westbau
LOCATION Zurich, Switzerland
CLIENT Luma Westbau
YEAR 2017-2018
STATUS Completed
SCOPE Exhibition design
SCALE 4 screens of 218 m² in a space of 267 m²
COLLABORATORS Niels Olsen, Fredi Fischli (curators)

Renault Design Workshop, Domaine de Boisbuchet
LOCATION Lessac, France
CLIENT Renault Group
YEAR 2018
STATUS Completed
SCOPE Workshop: analysing 1 × 1 × 1 m in the landscape and visualisation of the findings (individually) and realising a curtain from found objects in one day (collectively)
SCALE 8 × 4 m

Scalo Farini
LOCATION Milan, Italy
CLIENT Municipality of Milan
YEAR 2018
STATUS Competition
SCOPE Landscape masterplan that connects two city areas
SCALE ca. 10 ha
COLLABORATORS Hosoya Schaefer Architects, I T E R Studio Associato, S.C.E. PROJECTS Srl, IBV Hüsler Traffic Planning, Transsolar

Gallery Vitrina
LOCATION Mexico City, Mexico
CLIENT MEXTROPOLI 2018, Vitrina
YEAR 2018
STATUS Completed
SCOPE Miniature Inside Outside exhibition in gallery storefront, parallel to architecture conference Mextrópoli 2018
SCALE 1 Garden Carpet, 5.4 × 4 m; 3 Rifletutti parasols

Workshop Strelka Institute
LOCATION Moscow, Russia
CLIENT Strelka Institute
YEAR 2018
STATUS Completed
SCOPE Workshop: Discovering silence spaces within the Metropolitan region of Moscow and visualising the findings
SCALE Metrolopolitan region of Moscow: 2,600,000 ha

Geluidsschermkunst A27
LOCATION Highway A27, Blaricum, the Netherlands
CLIENT Municipality of Blaricum
YEAR 2018
STATUS Competition, shared 1st prize
SCOPE Artistic design for sound barrier walls along highway
SCALE ca. 2 km

Restaurant Sous
LOCATION Amsterdam, the Netherlands
CLIENT Sous Bar-Bistro
YEAR 2018
STATUS Completed
SCOPE Cold isolating curtain at the restaurant entrance
SCALE 3.6 × 2.6 m
COLLABORATORS Bram van Leeuwen

→ p. 134
Inside Outside/Petra Blaisse. A Retrospective, gta Exhibitions, ETH Zurich
LOCATION Zurich, Switzerland
CLIENT Institute for the History and Theory of Architecture (gta), ETH Zurich
YEAR 2018
STATUS Completed
SCOPE Design for traveling retrospective exhibition, including site-specific installation with films, curtains samples, models and grass cushions
SCALE 2 curtains, each 30 × 12.2 m with print of 70 projects and 28 IO items (curtain samples, grass cushions, Rifletutti parasols, models, brushes, films)
COLLABORATORS Niels Olsen, Fredi Fischli, gta Exhibitions, Teo Schifferli, Frans Parthesius, AVD productions

Axel Springer Security Line
LOCATION Berlin, Germany
CLIENT Axel Springer SE
YEAR 2018
STATUS Competition
SCOPE Design of security barrier around new Axel Springer Media Campus
SCALE 400 m
COLLABORATORS OMA

Kasbah Colonial, Jardin El Mechouar
LOCATION Tiznit, Royame du Maroc
CLIENT Municipality of Tiznit
YEAR 2018
STATUS Competition
SCOPE Opening up the colonial gardens to the public in a community-involved process
SCALE 4 ha
COLLABORATORS Agence Salima Naji and David Goeury, Nika Jazaei, AIR-Architects in Rabat

→ p. 312
READYMADES BELONG TO EVERYONE, Swiss Institute
LOCATION New York, USA
CLIENT Swiss Institute New York
YEAR 2018
STATUS Completed
SCOPE Production of a ready-made curtain for the exhibition
SCALE 6.48 × 4.79 m
COLLABORATORS Niels Olsen, Fredi Fischli (curators)

Amstel III – Molenwetering Development
LOCATION Amsterdam-Zuidoost, the Netherlands
CLIENT Municipality of Amsterdam
YEAR 2018
STATUS Commissioned Study
SCOPE Rethinking a uniform water channel as a backbone for ecological and recreational connections in Amsterdam South East
SCALE 7 ha

→ p. 298
Irma Boom Library
LOCATION Amsterdam, the Netherlands
CLIENT Private owner
YEAR 2017–2019
STATUS Completed
SCOPE Darkening curtain for the library's meeting and (re-)presentation room facing south
SCALE 8.5 × 4 m – in three parts
COLLABORATORS Owners

Charity Monument
LOCATION Jumeirah Beach, Dubai, United Arab Emirates
CLIENT Ethar Foundation
YEAR 2017–2019
STATUS Schematic Design
SCOPE Monument for charity: large-scale sculptural installation to celebrate the culture of charitable giving in the UAE
SCALE Site, 200 × 122 m; 1,680 triangular columns (recycled aluminium)
COLLABORATORS OMA

Collection Museum De Lakenhal
LOCATION Leiden, the Netherlands
CLIENT Museum De Lakenhal
YEAR 2018–2019
STATUS Completed
SCOPE Design for a 50 linear meter roll of "Laken" – a woolen, woven then felted cloth for the museum collection and sales, with fitting shoulder bag and folder with DIY recipe
SCALE 1 roll of 50 × 1.5 m; 1 handbag 0.6 × 0.7 m

→ p. 132
Inside Outside/Petra Blaisse. A Retrospective, La Triennale di Milano
LOCATION Milan, Italy
CLIENT La Triennale di Milano
YEAR 2018–2019
STATUS Completed
SCOPE Design for traveling retrospective exhibition, including site-specific installation with films, curtains samples, models and grass cushions
SCALE 2 curtains, each 30 × 8.5 m with print of 70 projects & 28 IO items (curtain samples, models, brushes, films)
COLLABORATORS Frans Parthesius, AVD productions, Triennale team

Bakemapark Zuid
LOCATION Amsterdam, the Netherlands
CLIENT Municipality of Amsterdam
YEAR 2019
STATUS Tender
SCOPE Biodiverse landscape for housing development, entering the entrance lobby on ground floor and connecting front to back garden.
SCALE 4,132 m²
COLLABORATORS Space Encounters

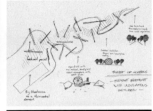

Berlin-Grunewald
LOCATION Berlin-Grunewald, Germany
CLIENT Home Center Management GmbH
YEAR 2019
STATUS Concept Design
SCOPE Flexible landscape masterplan and phasing strategy for art- and food-production-related temporary hub
SCALE 3.4 ha
COLLABORATORS Barcode architects

→ p. 164
Radura della Memoria
LOCATION Genova, Italy
CLIENT Municipality of Genova
YEAR 2019
STATUS Completed
SCOPE Design for temporary circular "memorial square" under the new bridge by Renzo Piano, implementing 43 different trees and names of the deceased
SCALE 8,326 m²
COLLABORATORS Stefano Boeri Architetti, Studio Laura Gatti

Casa de Vidro Lina Bo Bardi
LOCATION São Paulo, Brasil
CLIENT Architecture Biennale of São Paulo
YEAR 2019
STATUS Concept Design
SCOPE Applied art intervention connecting inside and outside
SCALE 15 curtains, total 50 × 3 m, balcony on scaffold structure 3.2 × 4.7 m

Biekorf Bibliotheek
LOCATION Brugge, Belgium
CLIENT Municipality of Brugge
YEAR 2019
STATUS Concept Design
SCOPE Courtyard gardens, interiors, division screens for reading room
SCALE 2 courtyards, 241 m², 320 m²; interior, 3,400 m²
COLLABORATORS Dertien12

Villa Heverlee
LOCATION Heverlee, Belgium
CLIENT Private owners
YEAR 2019 (+2022 additional planting plan)
STATUS Completed
SCOPE Multi-faceted garden design, including a sloping greened roof and patio garden at the heart of the circular house
SCALE 1,630 m²
COLLABORATORS guerrilla office architects/ geert de neuter

Aesop Store Brera
LOCATION Milan, Italy
CLIENT Aesop Skincare
YEAR 2019
STATUS Completed
SCOPE Interior garden installation for the store's shop windows during Milan Design Week 2019, showing soil sections based on the Biblioteca degli Alberi park's soil stratification
SCALE 3 shop windows: 30 young trees; 2 m³ soil of various sources and colour
COLLABORATORS Matteo Brioni – Terra per l'architettura

Sportanlagen Uitikon
LOCATION Uitikon, Zurich, Switzerland
CLIENT Gemeinde Uitikon, Schule Uitikon
YEAR 2019
STATUS Competition
SCOPE Landscape design for sports park
SCALE ca. 4 ha
COLLABORATORS NL architects, Lukas Haller

Design Museum Gent
LOCATION Ghent, Belgium
CLIENT Municipality of Ghent
YEAR 2019
STATUS Competition
SCOPE Exterior and interior spaces and logistics
SCALE Landscape, ca. 370 m²; interior: 2,725 m²
COLLABORATORS BEL Architecten

→ p. 306
Joli Cœur Attic
LOCATION Berlin-Charlottenburg, Germany
CLIENT Home Center Management GmbH
YEAR 2014–2020
STATUS Unrealised
SCOPE Private house in the attic of the former hospital Joli Cœur
SCALE Attic, 374 m²; glass house, 15 × 7 × 4 m in height; landscape masterplan, ca. 6 ha
COLLABORATORS Paul Friedrich Bratring, 1900; Arup Engineers; Reinier Suurenbroek

→ p. 200
Axel Springer Media Campus, Berlin
LOCATION Berlin, Germany
CLIENT Axel Springer SE
YEAR 2014–2020
STATUS Landscape masterplan commission: Schematic Design, on hold; Building Competition, 1st prize: Completed
SCOPE Landscape masterplan, streetscape connecting outdoor and interior spaces on groundfloor, entrance plaza flooring, roof garden
SCALE Masterplan: 1.9 ha; realised landscape design: ground floor, 5,000 m²; roof garden 7,000 m²
COLLABORATORS OMA, Simons und Hinze Landschaftsarchitekten

Sun Apartment
LOCATION Beirut, Lebanon
CLIENT Private owners
YEAR 2016–2020
STATUS Completed
SCOPE All curtains for the house, filtering sun and daylight and solving acoustic, climate and spatial issues
SCALE 316 m²
COLLABORATORS Studio Khachatryan

→ p. 302
Hudson Valley Estate
LOCATION Piermont, Hudson Valley, New York, USA
CLIENT Private owners
YEAR 2016–2020
STATUS Completed
SCOPE Landscape strategy for the estate, garden design, restoration of pool
SCALE 2 ha
COLLABORATORS James Sullivan

→ p. 284
Düsseldorfer Schauspielhaus Curtains
LOCATION Düsseldorf, Germany
CLIENT Düsseldorfer Schauspielhaus
YEAR 2018–2020
STATUS Completed
SCOPE Curtain design, advisory on interior of foyers and restaurant for the restoration of the Düsseldorfer Schauspielhaus
SCALE Restaurant, 36.9 × 3.6 m; foyer: curtain 1, 20.5 × 3.6 m, curtain 2, 32.8 × 3.6 m; gallery: curtain 1, 50.9 × 2.45–2.93 m (sloping ceiling), curtain 2, 85.9 × 2.46–2.96 m (sloping ceiling); foyer Kleines Haus, two curtains, 21 × 2.32 m each
COLLABORATORS Ingenhoven Architects, Professor Schmuck, EE Exclusives

→ p. 274
DAWN, Wall Piece for Private Apartment
LOCATION Manhattan, New York, USA
CLIENT Private owner
YEAR 2018–2020
STATUS Completed
SCOPE Design of a flexible, space-defining wall
SCALE Wallpaper, 2.96 × 3.28 m; screen, 2.96 × 3.25 m; curtain, 6.69 × 3.24 m
COLLABORATORS LUCE et studio

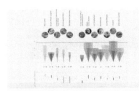

Lecture Hall, University of Amsterdam
LOCATION Roeterseiland campus, Amsterdam, the Netherlands
CLIENT UvA-Universiteit van Amsterdam
YEAR 2018–2020
STATUS Schematic design
SCOPE Vertical greening, roof garden and water management to improve interior climate and attract biodiversity
SCALE 1,500 m²
COLLABORATORS OIII

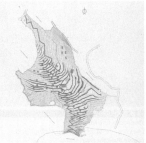

→ p. 278
Santorini Red Beach
LOCATION Santorini, Greece
CLIENT Home Center Management GmbH
YEAR 2020
STATUS Commissioned Study
SCOPE Site study and landscape concept for agro-tourism development
SCALE 6.38 ha

→ p. 276
Confinement Cadavres Exquis
LOCATION Zurich, Switzerland
CLIENT gta Exhibitions, ETH Zurich
YEAR 2020
STATUS Completed
SCOPE Drawing(s) for digital and physical exhibition on the subject of confinement (Covid-19)
SCALE 3 sheets of A4 paper
COLLABORATORS The three IO partners

Hebrew Language Academy & Hebrew Museum
LOCATION Kiryat Leum, Jerusalem, Israel
CLIENT Hebrew Language Academy
YEAR 2020
STATUS Competition
SCOPE Landscape plan, both inside and outside the buildings' boundaries
SCALE 5,500 m²
COLLABORATORS Efrat-Kowalsky Architects, Lieber Gal Architects

University of Tiznit Campus
LOCATION Tiznit, Royaume du Maroc
CLIENT Ministère de l'Education Nationale, de la Formation professionnelle, de l'Enseignement Supérieur et de la Recherche Scientifique
YEAR 2020
STATUS Competition
SCOPE Resilient and drought-resistent landscape design improving local biodiversity, integrating energy production and shaded routings between faculty and service buildings with effective vegetal and textile devices
COLLABORATORS Agence Salima Naji and David Goeury, Driss Ketami Architecte

→ p. 282
Bedroom Curtain
LOCATION Amsterdam, the Netherlands
CLIENT Private owners
YEAR 2020
STATUS Completed
SCOPE Darkening curtain for master bedroom
SCALE 3.5 × 3.87 m

Andre Losch Auditorium
LOCATION Luxembourg-City, Luxembourg
CLIENT André Losch Fondation
YEAR 2020
STATUS Competition
SCOPE Landscape advisory and design concept
COLLABORATORS OMA

Makerstoren Sloterdijk
LOCATION Amsterdam, the Netherlands
CLIENT RW54 (Ian Gray, Henk van der Lely)
YEAR 2020
STATUS Completed
SCOPE Greening and shading advisory to improve interior climate and allow for healthy growth on terraces and roof
SCALE 1,500 m²
COLLABORATORS Allard Architecture

→ p. 258
Nach der Natur, Humboldt Labor Exhibition at Humboldt Forum
LOCATION Berlin, Germany
CLIENT Humboldt University
YEAR 2018–2021
STATUS Competition, 1st prize/Completed
SCOPE Exhibition design, technical detailing and tender documents for the three-year+ installation Nach der Natur
SCALE 735 m²
COLLABORATORS Cookies, Arup, Jens Casper, Julia Neller, Schnellebuntebilder

Private Apartment
LOCATION Faubourg Saint Germain, Paris, France
CLIENT Private owner
YEAR 2018–2021
STATUS 1st phase completed/new interior works activated
SCOPE Light and sun filtering curtains & screens
SCALE 3 items: living room, 14.48 × 2.65 m; bedroom, 6.5 × 2.65 m, 6.3 × 2.63 m
COLLABORATORS Arnaud Puel – APAR Architecture

→ p. 270
Sessions Auditorium Curtain, Mingei International Museum
LOCATION San Diego, USA
CLIENT Mingei International Museum
YEAR 2018–2021
STATUS Completed
SCOPE Textile art object (darkening, cooling, filtering)
SCALE 15.5 × 3.85 m
COLLABORATORS LUCE et studio

De Nieuwe Kern
LOCATION Ouder-Amstel, Amsterdam-Zuidoost, the Netherlands
CLIENT Municipality of Amsterdam
YEAR 2018–2021
STATUS Commissioned study
SCOPE Analysis of urban plan and traffic & parking logistics, advisory on water management, strategic landscape design
SCALE ca. 80 ha (4,500 houses, offices, restaurants, shops, sports fields)
COLLABORATORS Municipality of Amsterdam

→ p. 250
A Story for the Future. MAXXI's First Decade, MAXXI
LOCATION Rome, Italy
CLIENT MAXXI – Museo Nazionale delle Arti del XXI Secolo
YEAR 2019–2021
STATUS Completed
SCOPE Exhibition design
SCALE 586 m²
COLLABORATORS Hou Hanru, Elena Motes, Sylvia La Pergola, Etaoin Shrdlu Studio

→ p. 246
Grand Café Vooruit
LOCATION Ghent, Belgium
CLIENT Grand Café Vooruit
YEAR 2019–2021
STATUS Completed
SCOPE Acoustic and darkening curtains for music performances and events, integration of the curtains to the historic facade, interior and planting advisory
SCALE 4 curtains, 3.95 × 5.88, 7.87 × 5.87 m, 3.42 × 5.89 m, 9.94 × 5.92 m
COLLABORATORS B-ILD, Chris Pype lighting, Kahle Acoustics

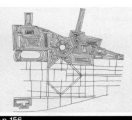

→ p. 156
Garage Campus, Gorky Park
LOCATION Moscow, Russia
CLIENT Garage Museum of Contemporary Art
YEAR 2020–2021
STATUS Concept Design
SCOPE Landscape masterplan for gardens, trajectories and wayfinding to connect the Garage buildings within Gorky Park
SCALE 12.6 ha

Ex Macello
LOCATION Milan, Italy
CLIENT Brioschi Developers
YEAR 2020–2021
STATUS Competition
SCOPE Landscape masterplan and planting plan for school, creative hub and urban agriculture as part of the redevelopment of the former slaughterhouse area
SCALE 15 ha
COLLABORATORS Femia Ateliers, Cino Zucchi Architetti, Studio Laura Gatti

Watertorenberaad
LOCATION the Netherlands
CLIENT Watertorenberaad, Breda
YEAR 2020–2021
STATUS Commissioned Study
SCOPE Advisory on high density, urban developments in various cities in the Netherlands, with CO_2 absorbency, strategic water management, vital soil and biodiverse planting schemes as key subjects of attention

→ p. 148
European Parliament, Paul-Henri SPAAK Building
LOCATION Brussels, Belgium
CLIENT European Parliament
YEAR 2020–2021
STATUS Competition/Honorable mention
SCOPE Resilient landscape design for the esplanade entrance, drop-off and natural security line, 3 roof gardens and outdoor loggia, large sloping roofed garden with work spaces connecting the Leopold park to the interior – all designed as biodiverse, water-retaining and -cleaning biotopes
SCALE 17,000 m²
COLLABORATORS OMA, Boydens, Transsolar, dUCKS scéno, Irma Boom

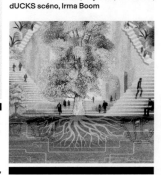

De Knoop, New Development Area
LOCATION Utrecht, the Netherlands
CLIENT Rijksvastgoeddienst and Atelier Rijksbouwmeester
YEAR 2020–2021
STATUS Commissioned study
SCOPE Advisory on the urban development of the high density urban environment of Utrecht Central station; establishing a competition brief from landscape and "vital soil" perspective
SCALE 1.3 ha

Slachthuis
LOCATION Hasselt, Belgium
CLIENT ION, Steps Real Estate
YEAR 2021
STATUS Competition, 2nd prize
SCOPE Landscape design for a new housing development, referring to the site's slaughterhouse history with "releasing the livestock" as theme
SCALE 14,052 m²
COLLABORATORS Seppe Claes, Stefaan Jamaer, Jaspers-Eyers

Two Friends' Apartments
LOCATION Zurich, Switzerland
CLIENT Private owners
YEAR 2021
STATUS Completed
SCOPE Material advisory and sewing recipe; sun-reflective and light filtering curtains
SCALE 3 curtains, each 4 × 2.3 m

Setun Park
LOCATION Moscow, Russia
CLIENT APEX project bureau
YEAR 2021
STATUS Competition, 3rd prize
SCOPE Landscape design for residential development along the Setun river, with focus on colourful, local planting, play, sports and routing
SCALE 7.57 ha
COLLABORATORS Hadi Teherani Architects

→ **p. 248**
Porta Romana
LOCATION Milan, Italy
CLIENT Coima, Covivio, Prada
YEAR 2021
STATUS Competition
SCOPE Landscape masterplan around Olympic city; commercial and residential towers, including large, circular wildernesses
SCALE 16 ha
COLLABORATORS Studio Paola Vigano, Office KGDVS, Piovenefabi, TPS pro Srl, Ambiante Italia, F&M Ingeneria Spa

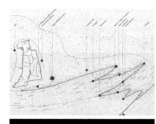

Kasbah Agadir Oufla
LOCATION Kasbah Agadir Oufla, Royame du Maroc
CLIENT Agence Salima Naji and David Goeury
YEAR 2021
STATUS Concept Design
SCOPE Landscape design to connect the city to the Kasbah of Agadir Oufella with sightseeing trajectory through indigenous planting communities
SCALE 100 ha
COLLABORATORS Agence Salima Naji and David Goeury

Institut Méditerranéen de la Ville et des Territoires
LOCATION Marseille, France
CLIENT Oppic
YEAR 2021
STATUS Competition
SCOPE Art commission for an intervention with functional charateristics (shade, wind break) on the architecture institution's roof terrace
SCALE 480 m²
COLLABORATORS Arup

Maritiem Operatiecentrum Kustwacht
LOCATION Den Helder, the Netherlands
CLIENT Rijksvastgoedbedrijf and Kustwacht
YEAR 2021
STATUS Competition
SCOPE Biodiverse lanscape, patio and roof gardens
SCALE Building, 800 m²; training area, 1,500 m²
COLLABORATORS Prototype, Antea Group

Den Bell
LOCATION Antwerp, Belgium
CLIENT Municipality of Antwerp
YEAR 2021
STATUS Competition
SCOPE Re-design of public plaza and greening of roofs and facades with focus on CO_2 absorbency, biodiversity, re-use of materials, water management, multi-faceted forms and times of use, acoustics, way-finding
SCALE Courtyard, 4,000 m²; roofscape, 7,300 m²
COLLABORATORS Gevelinzicht, Urban Roofscape, Commons lab

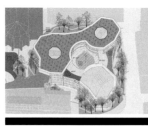

Algemene Rekenkamer
LOCATION The Hague, the Netherlands
CLIENT Rijksvastgoedbedrijf and Algemene Rekenkamer
YEAR 2021
STATUS Competition
SCOPE Shaded entrance gardens and roof gardens for meetings and silent working, both adressing water management and climate issues, taking the original intentions of Aldo van Eyck's early '90s monument into account
SCALE Ground floor landscape, 1,278 m²; roof gardens, 826 m²
COLLABORATORS Braaksma & Roos Architects, Prototype, Antea Group

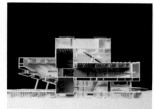

→ **p. 222**
Taipei Performing Arts Center
LOCATION Shilin District, Taipei City, Taiwan
CLIENT Department of Cultural Affairs Taipei, Taipei City Government
YEAR 2009–2022
STATUS Competition, 1st prize / Completed
SCOPE Landscape design, including a public square for food markets and fairs, public garden areas, streetscape as well as roof, terrace and interior gardens; colour and material concept for entire building; upholstery for seating in three auditoriums; consultant for all wall, floor and ceiling finishes; stage curtains for two main auditoriums
SCALE Landscape, 4.6 ha; grand theatre curtain, 20.3 × 14.45 m; proscenium play stage membrane, 20 × 12.15 m
COLLABORATORS OMA, Artech, dUCKS scéno, Gerriets GmbH

→ **p. 198**
Facade Curtains
LOCATION Le Marais, Paris, France
CLIENT Moussafir Architectes
YEAR 2016–2022
STATUS Completed
SCOPE Facade curtain (shading / glare control) for fashion / office / residential building
SCALE Curtain, 131 m²: (3×) 12 × 2.8 m, (1×) 12 × 2.5 m
COLLABORATORS Moussafir Architects, Lenco Zonwering

→ **p. 158**
Zeller Haus
LOCATION Zell am See, Austria
CLIENT Private owner
YEAR 2019–2022
STATUS Completed
SCOPE Double-layered, darkening curtain for the bedroom and garden design (ongoing)
SCALE Curtains, (2×) 5.85 × 3.5 m; garden, ca. 900 m²
COLLABORATORS OMA, 7478 / Federico Pompignoli

→ **p. 200**
Axel Springer Media Campus
LOCATION Berlin, Germany
CLIENT Axel Springer SE
YEAR 2019–2022
STATUS Completed
SCOPE Curtain and track design
SCALE 102 curtains, 1,955 m²; 76 office curtains, 1,279 m²; 17 furniture pods, 190 m²; one visitors' lounge curtain, 53 m²; two campus curtains, 157 m²; four Forum curtains, 180 m²; two Idealo curtains, 96 m²
COLLABORATORS OMA, Gerriets GmbH

Q Residences Amsterdam
LOCATION Amsterdam, the Netherlands
CLIENT Kroonenberg Group
YEAR 2020–2022
STATUS Art commission / Completed
SCOPE Curtain as art object for lobby
SCALE 3 items: 11.52 × 5.22 m; 17.28 × 5.22 m; 14.04 × 5.22 m
COLLABORATORS Studio Gang, Rijnboutt Architecten

Sluisbuurt Kavel 4a
LOCATION Amsterdam, the Netherlands
CLIENT Municipality of Amsterdam
YEAR 2021–2022
STATUS Tender
SCOPE Landscape design for a nature-inclusive residential tower / vertical ecological infrastructure and horizontal stepping stones
SCALE Full soil park, 140 m²; natural roof landscapes, 1,361 m²; green facades, 3,147 m²; green quai walls, 25 × 4 m; ecological (canal) banks, 45 × 6.5 m; floating islands with underwater habitats, 66 m²
COLLABORATORS Dura Vermeer, Dok Architecten, Ronald Buiting, Marco Roos / Naturalis Biodiversity Center, Koninklijke Ginkel Groep, Merosch, Reef Systems, Respyre, Vogelbescherming

Alipa Hill
LOCATION Paleokastritsa, Corfu, Greece
CLIENT Home Center Management
YEAR 2021–2022
STATUS Schematic Design
SCOPE Landscape masterplan and planting design for a holiday "glamping" garden embedded in nature
SCALE 30,000 m²
COLLABORATORS Nomadic Resorts

→ p. 128
*Inside/Outside Petra Blaisse.
A Retrospective*, MAXXI Rome
LOCATION Rome, Italy
CLIENT MAXXI – Museo Nazionale delle Arti del XXI Secolo
YEAR 2021–2022
STATUS Completed
SCOPE Design for traveling retrospective exhibition including outdoor, indoor site, specific installations and models
SCALE 2 curtains, each 25 × 12 m; floor treatment (380 m white tape, 640 m black tape, 25 silver disks and brushes), 10 films and models
COLLABORATORS Frans Parthesius, AVD productions, MAXXI Exhibitions team

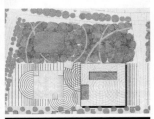

Vltava Philharmonic Hall
LOCATION Vltavská, Prague, Czech Republic
CLIENT Capital City of Prague & Prague Institute of Planning and Development
YEAR 2021–2022
STATUS Competition
SCOPE Landscape design for entrance plaza, traversable wilderness and connective riverfront
SCALE Plaza, 8,500 m²; wilderness forest, 10,600 m²; riverfront, 5,650 m²
COLLABORATORS OFFICE Kersten Geers David Van Severen, Christ & Gantenbein, Kolmo-Martin Hejl

→ p. 196
Euroflora
LOCATION Parchi di Nervi, Genoa, Italy
CLIENT Municipality of Genoa
YEAR 2021–2022
STATUS Completed
SCOPE Garden installation at Euroflora Genova 2022 based on linear Parco del Polcevera design
SCALE 940 m²
COLLABORATORS Studio Laura Gatti

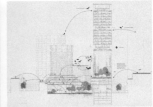

Bank for International Settlements
LOCATION Basel, Switzerland
CLIENT Bank for International Settlements
YEAR 2022
STATUS Competition
SCOPE Nature inclusive landscape design for park, terrace and roof gardens as ecological stepping stones between the old and new tower; interior advisory, carpets and curtains
SCALE Park, 2,760 m²; roof gardens, 4,740 m²; carpets-curtains, 700 m²
COLLABORATORS HHF architects, Tatiana Bilbao Estudio, André Rey

Volkswagen Trinity
LOCATION Wolfsburg-Warmenau, Germany
CLIENT Volkswagen AG
YEAR 2022
STATUS Competition, ongoing
SCOPE Landscape Masterplan taking into account surrouding villages and sustainable solution for planting and water management and design of outdoor spaces for factory staff
SCALE 130 ha
COLLABORATORS OMA

Workshop
LOCATION Formignano, Italy
CLIENT Faculty of Architecture, University of Bologna, Cesena
YEAR 2022
STATUS Completed
SCOPE Workshop "Designing the Void" at the former Sulphur mine landscape of Formignano
SCALE 800 ha
COLLABORATORS Marta Agueda, architect; Anagoor, theatre collective; Guido Guidi, photographer; Anupama Kundoo, Architect; Enrico Malatesta, percussionist and sound researcher; Anton Roca, artist

Temple Works Library
LOCATION Leeds, United Kingdom
CLIENT The British Library
YEAR 2022
STATUS Competition
SCOPE Landscape design, interior advisory and a series of multifunctional, space-defining curtains
SCALE Northern yard, 3,000 m²; roof, biodiverse meadow 7,825 m²; interior, 8,000 m²; 6 curtains, 2,500 m²
COLLABORATORS Hawkins/Brown

Daskalopoulos Arts Building
LOCATION Athens, Greece
CLIENT Athens College & SYNNEON Civil Non-Profit Association
YEAR 2022
STATUS Competition
SCOPE Landscape design for a sports and events plaza and outdoor auditorium; interior advisory and space defining curtain for exhibition space
SCALE Masterplan area, ca. 7 ha; landscape, 5,100 m²; curtain, 25 × 6 m
COLLABORATORS Point Supreme, BEL Architecten

Artist's Studio
LOCATION Zurich, Switzerland
CLIENT Private client
YEAR 2022
STATUS Completed
SCOPE Space defining & sound and light regulating curtain
SCALE 10.35 × 2.39 m

Aviation Museum Riyadh
LOCATION Riyadh, Saudi Arabia
CLIENT King Salman Park Foundation
YEAR 2022
STATUS Competition
SCOPE Landscape design for the Aviation Museum, representing the ecosystems of the Arabian peninsula
SCALE 5.2 ha
COLLABORATORS O+C | Oualalou+Choi

→ p. 140
Curtains for a Polder House
LOCATION Ankeveen, the Netherlands
CLIENT Private owners
YEAR 2022–2023
STATUS Completed
SCOPE Multi-functional curtains for living space and kitchen
SCALE Curtain 1, 12.8 × 2.75 m; curtain 2, 5.4 × 2.75 m
COLLABORATORS Dirk Jan Postel/ Kraaijvanger Architects

Inside Outside Objects
LOCATION Amsterdam, the Netherlands
CLIENT Self-initiated
YEAR 1999– ongoing
STATUS Ongoing
SCOPE Design & in-house production of cushions, curtains, bags, grass, cushions, tables, flexible room-divider, mirror-corners, foulards
SCALE Various

Garden Carpets
LOCATION Private houses, offices, cultural and commercial spaces
CLIENT Various
YEAR 2000–ongoing
STATUS Production on demand
SCOPE Various designs for project carpets with garden theme
SCALE 2.7 × 2 m; 2.7 × 4 m; 2 × 5.4 m
COLLABORATORS Various

→ p. 188
Protected Landscape
LOCATION Sardinia, Italy
CLIENT Private owner
YEAR 2008–ongoing
STATUS Ongoing
SCOPE Landscape restoration, maintenance of protected estate
SCALE 10 ha
COLLABORATORS Marina Perot, Sergio Rolland, Carlo del Bene, Aura Melis, Gianluca Tramultono

→ p. 242
Mirror Garden
LOCATION Amsterdam, the Netherlands
CLIENT Private owner
YEAR 2010–2022
STATUS Ongoing
SCOPE Private garden installation and maintenance
SCALE 18 × 11 m

→ p. 192
Bait La Ivrit / House of Hebrew
LOCATION Rishon LeZion, Israel
CLIENT Municipality of Rishon LeZion
YEAR 2015–ongoing
STATUS First phase completed in 2019, second phase ongoing
SCOPE Connective landscape for the International Center for the Hebrew Language, Haviv elementary School, Museum of Hebrew and Medalya Coffee House; a continuous greened pergola as security fence and inhabitable shaded space
SCALE 1.3 ha
COLLABORATORS Efrat-Kowalski Architects, Moria Architects / Studio MA

→ p. 186
Papirøen Island – Københavns Haller
LOCATION Christiansholm, Copenhagen, Denmark
CLIENT CPH City & Port Development, CØ P/S (Danica Ejendomsselskab, Unionkul Ejendomme, Nordkranen), NCC
YEAR 2015 – ongoing
STATUS Competition, 1st prize, under construction since 2020
SCOPE Landscape design for entire island, including public and private roof gardens, traffic logistics and a continuous, folded wooden boardwalk encircling the island
SCALE 2.4 ha
COLLABORATORS COBE, Via Trafik, Transsolar

Penthouse
LOCATION Halvemaansteeg, Amsterdam, the Netherlands
CLIENT Private owner
YEAR 2017–ongoing
STATUS Ongoing
SCOPE Design of a roof garden, shading curtains for the penthouse
SCALE 175 m²
COLLABORATORS XML, Koninklijke Ginkel Groep

→ p. 294
Vakantiepark De Klepperstee
LOCATION Ouddorp, the Netherlands
CLIENT Vakantiepark de Klepperstee
YEAR 2017–ongoing
STATUS Ongoing
SCOPE New, sustainable landscape concept for holiday park; design and realisation of natural swimming pond and club house terraces
SCALE 2 ha; masterplan, 28 ha
COLLABORATORS Suzanne Loen, Vakwerk Architecten, De Bomenconsulent

→ p. 184
Het Marktkwartier
LOCATION Amsterdam, the Netherlands
CLIENT Volker Wessels Vastgoed & Ballast Nedam Development
YEAR 2017–ongoing
STATUS Ongoing (Definitive Design)
SCOPE Landscape masterplan and design for the transformation of the Foodcenter from a restricted-access wholesale area to an urban residential area: "Het Marktkwartier"
SCALE 9.35 ha
COLLABORATORS Mecanoo

AFC Ajax soccer fields
LOCATION Amsterdam, the Netherlands
CLIENT AFC Ajax
YEAR 2017–ongoing
STATUS Competition 1st prize / Ongoing
SCOPE Landscape masterplan for the professional trainingscomplex, new competition areas and public spaces of Amsterdam's main soccer club Ajax
SCALE 30 ha
COLLABORATORS NL Architects

SPOT Amsterdam
LOCATION Hondsrugpark, Amstel III, Amsterdam-Zuidoost, the Netherlands
CLIENT COD + Duqer developers
YEAR 2017–ongoing
STATUS Under Construction (to be completed in 2025)
SCOPE Landscape design for a dense, mixed-use area of ten high rise towers including entrance zones, bicycle parkings, sports- & playgrounds and richly planted gardens on all levels, solving wind and water retention issues
SCALE 1.4 ha
COLLABORATORS KAAN Architecten

Trailer Park
LOCATION Amstel III, Amsterdam-Zuidoost, the Netherlands
CLIENT Municipality of Amsterdam
YEAR 2018–ongoing
STATUS Ongoing
Scope: Interchangeable truck parking, sports park with improved water managment
SCALE 1.25 ha

Artist House
LOCATION Geneva, Switzerland
CLIENT Private owner
YEAR 2019–ongoing
STATUS Concept design
SCOPE Curtains for living room, interior advisory
SCALE 6 × 3.25 m

Waterfront Morcote
LOCATION Morcote, Canton Ticino, Switzerland
CLIENT Municipality of Morcote
YEAR 2019–ongoing
STATUS Competition, shared 1st prize, on hold
SCOPE Landscape, pedestrian flow and traffic logistics
SCALE 10 ha
COLLABORATORS XDGA – Xaveer de Geyter Architects

→ p. 164
Il Parco Del Polcevera e il Cerchio Rosso
LOCATION Valpolcevera, Genoa, Italy
CLIENT Municipality of Genoa
YEAR 2019–ongoing
STATUS Competition, 1st prize / Ongoing
SCOPE Richly programed, biodiverse public park under the collapsed Morandi bridge that addresses soil health and sustainable water management, including memorial gardens for the deceased of august 2018
SCALE Competition masterplan, 24 ha; preliminary landscape design, 13 ha
COLLABORATORS Stefano Boeri Architetti, Metrogramma, Studio Laura Gatti, MIC / Mobility in chain, Transsolar, H&A Architetti, Antonio Secondo Accotto, Tempo Riuso, Luca Vitone

→ p. 176
Vallée de l'Oued Yissi
LOCATION Ait Mansour, Province de Tiznit, Région Souss Massa, Morocco
CLIENT Société de Développement Touristique Souss Massa
YEAR 2019–ongoing
STATUS Ongoing
SCOPE Development strategies and landscape design for 6 hubs along a 14 km road that crosses the semi-abandoned valley
SCALE 140 ha
COLLABORATORS Agence Salima Naji and David Goeury

→ p. 154
Soil Biodiversity Studies
LOCATION Amsterdam, the Netherlands
CLIENT Self-initiated Research (with support from the Creative Industries Fund NL)
YEAR 2019–ongoing
STATUS Ongoing
SCOPE Research on how to introduce biodiversity and living soil in the urban realm
COLLABORATORS Municipality of Amsterdam, Naturalis Biodiversity Center, Vrije Universiteit Amsterdam, Wageningen University, Koninklijke Ginkel Groep, Bodemzicht, Flock Theatre and others

Sustainable Textile Research
LOCATION Amsterdam, the Netherlands
CLIENT Self-initiated research
YEAR 2020–ongoing
STATUS Ongoing
SCOPE Sustainable textile research for archive and use

De Omval
LOCATION Weespertrekvaart, Amsterdam, the Netherlands
CLIENT Municipality of Amsterdam
YEAR 2021–ongoing
STATUS Competition, 1st prize / Under construction
SCOPE Landscape design for plaza, quay-side, streetscape and 1st floor public terrace of sustainable and mixed-use building in which the existing 1938 café building is integrated
SCALE Public space, 1,780 m²; roof gardens, 180 m², 750 m²; curtain, 42 × 6.85 m
COLLABORATORS Space & Matter. Barend Koolhaas

1

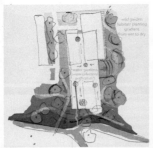

Campo

LOCATION Neuhegi, Winterthur, Switzerland
CLIENT SKKG-Stiftung für Kunst, Kultur und Geschichte, Terresta
YEAR 2021–ongoing
STATUS Test planning/Competition
SCOPE Landscape design for a combined urban campus that contains an art collection, offices, housing and creative industries
SCALE 5,000 m²
COLLABORATORS 51N4E, TEN Studio, Studio Urbane Strategien

Josef Hotel

LOCATION Prague, Czech Republic
CLIENT Ploberger
YEAR 2021–ongoing
STATUS Ongoing
SCOPE Design of 2 courtyard gardens and interior advisory
SCALE Courtyard 245 m², sunken garden 60 m²
COLLABORATORS Marc Paulin, Partero

→ p. 150

Iconische Stadskerken

LOCATION Domkerk, Utrecht; Sint Bavo cathedral, Haarlem; Sint Jan Cathedral's Hertogenbosch
CLIENT Chief Government Architect and the National Office for Cultural Heritage
YEAR 2021–ongoing
STATUS Competition, 1st prize/Ongoing
SCOPE Landscape, sustainability, programming and maintenance vision for the re-integration of iconic city churches in the day-to-day life of (local) society
COLLABORATORS Braaksma & Roos Architects, Antea Group, Johanna van Doorn

→ p. 152

Bioreceptive Textile Nurseries

LOCATION Amsterdam, the Netherlands
CLIENT Self-initiated research (with support from the Creative Industries Fund NL)
YEAR 2021–ongoing
STATUS Research/Ongoing
SCOPE Research by design on textile circularity and bioreceptivity, biomaterial prototyping, and experiments of plant biocolonisation on textiles for interior and exterior applications
COLLABORATORS HKRITA – Hong Kong Research Institute of Textiles and Apparel, Jacqueline Baar/Soil Best, Officina Corpuscoli, Margherita Soldati

→ p. 142

Ujiri Court

LOCATION Kigali, Rwanda
CLIENT RINO GLOBAL, LLC
YEAR 2021–ongoing
STATUS Ongoing
SCOPE Landscape design for an urban sports campus as part of the "Giants of Africa" project initiated by NBA basketball player and coach Masai Ujiri; site program contains sports-, events and recreational facilities, hotel, shops and bars, all embedded in a green landscape
SCALE 2.5 ha
COLLABORATORS NLÉ, Afrilandscapes

Rijksmuseum Twenthe Enschede

LOCATION Enschede, the Netherlands
CLIENT Rijksmuseum Twenthe
YEAR 2021–ongoing
STATUS Ongoing
SCOPE Landscape for a new Museumpark wrapping the introvert museum building and creating a public zone of interaction, inviting passers-by into the museum
SCALE 1.3 ha
COLLABORATORS Bureau SLA

Paestum Città Unesco e Parcheggi dell' Area Archeologica

LOCATION Salerno, Italy
CLIENT Municipality of Paestum
YEAR 2022–ongoing
STATUS Competition/Ongoing
SCOPE Landscape masterplan to improve accessibility and interrconnection between arcaeological sites and surroundings
SCALE 1.2 ha
COLLABORATORS Demogo Architetti

→ p. 146

Nature-inclusive architecture? A study

LOCATION Europe
CLIENT Self-initiated studies
YEAR 2022–ongoing
STATUS ongoing
SCOPE Nature inclusive architecture
SCALE Various
COLLABORATORS Specialists on the fields of ecology, soil biology, organisations for nature protection, nature-inclusive material innovators, specialised landscape contractors

Public Library Reykjavik

LOCATION Reykjavik, Iceland
CLIENT City of Reykjavik's Environment and Planning Department
YEAR 2022–ongoing
STATUS Competition, 1st prize, ongoing
SCOPE Tapestry, curtains, carpets, interior advice and landscape design (renovation project)
SCALE Landscape, 1,860 m²; curtains, 680 m²; interiors, 6,150 m²
COLLABORATORS JVST, Hanrath Architects, Kreativa

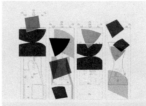

→ p. 144

Venetian Islands Villa

LOCATION Miami, Florida, USA
CLIENT Private owner
YEAR 2022–ongoing
STATUS Ongoing
SCOPE Landscape design for private garden and curtains, interior advisory
SCALE Landscape, 970 m²; interior, 600 m²
COLLABORATORS OMA, Christopher Cawley, CLF Architects

De Gashouder Westerpark

LOCATION Westerpark, Amsterdam, the Netherlands
CLIENT Millten Developers
YEAR 2022–ongoing
STATUS Ongoing
SCOPE Conversion of the gasholder into an event venue: landscape and interior design, circulation and acoustic advisory
SCALE Landscape, 7,400 m²; interior, 3,600 m²
COLLABORATORS Buro Van Stigt, Westergas

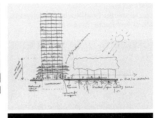

Multigenerations' Highrise

LOCATION Winterthur, Switzerland
CLIENT OASE Gruppe
YEAR 2022–ongoing
STATUS Competition, 1st prize, ongoing
SCOPE Nature inclusive landscape design for park and "skygardens" for a mixed-use, senior housing tower; interior advisory, "garden carpets" and curtains
SCALE Park and public spaces on the ground, ca. 6,000 m²; tower skygardens and common spaces distributed over 18 floors, ca. 2,000 m²
COLLABORATORS TEN Studio, Dürig AG, André Rey

Casa de las Bellas Artes

LOCATION Tijuana, Mexico
CLIENT Promotora de las Bellas Artes, CETYS Universidad
YEAR 2022–ongoing
STATUS Ongoing
SCOPE Landscape (both in- and outside), interior advisory and curtain design for shading, spatial organisation and acoustic absorbance
SCALE Landscape, 2,400 m²; curtains, 1,520 m²
COLLABORATORS Studio Huerta

Schiphol-Oost

LOCATION Schiphol-Oost, the Netherlands
CLIENT Schiphol
YEAR 2022–ongoing
STATUS Ongoing
SCOPE Landscape for new business campus with multiple traffic connections
SCALE 26.2 ha
COLLABORATORS Goudappel

Slimme Schakels/Smart Links
LOCATION Antwerp, Belgium
CLIENT Municipality of Antwerp
YEAR 2022–ongoing
STATUS Competition, Ongoing
SCOPE Artistic proposals for bus and tram "canopies" reusing port structures
SCALE 3 prototypes: Pointer (S), Liner (M), Shelter (L)
COLLABORATORS AJDVIV, Kosmos

Musikhuspark
LOCATION Aarhus, Denmark
CLIENT Municipality of Aarhus
YEAR 2022–ongoing
STATUS Competition, Ongoing
SCOPE Re-design of existing park into an ecological, biodiverse, multifunctional, cultural public space that connects all surrounding cultural institutions, the city hall and the adjacent areas
SCALE 2.4 ha
COLLABORATORS Sleth, MeMe/Metropolitan Metaculture

Demi Lune, La Défense
LOCATION La Défense Paris, France
CLIENT Paris La Défense, Linkcity
YEAR 2022–ongoing
STATUS Tender, Ongoing
SCOPE Landscape for repurposed traffic knot in the heart of La Défense
SCALE Site, 9,700 m²; program, 110,000m²
COLLABORATORS XDGA, L'AUC

Spoorzone/Railzone
LOCATION Apeldoorn, the Netherlands
CLIENT Grehamer & Company
YEAR 2023–ongoing
STATUS Ongoing
SCOPE Landscape for new high-rise residential area along the city's main train tracks
SCALE 1.3 ha
COLLABORATORS DAM en partners

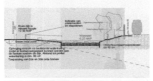

Noise barrier
LOCATION Sloterdijk, Amsterdam, the Netherlands
CLIENT Prorail
YEAR 2023–ongoing
STATUS Ongoing
SCOPE Sound-absorbing and aesthetic interface between new residential and park development and the existing train track
SCALE 1 km × 4 m
COLLABORATORS Movares, Gemeente Amsterdam

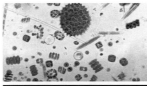

Art Competition
LOCATION Not to be disclosed
CLIENT Not to be disclosed
YEAR 2023–ongoing
STATUS Competiion, Ongoing
SCOPE Art installation in metro station
SCALE 630 m²
COLLABORATORS Hou Hanru

Maggie's Centre
LOCATION Royal Free Hospital, London, UK
CLIENT Maggie's Cancer Centre
YEAR 2023–ongoing
STATUS Ongoing
SCOPE 5 curtains for acoustic improvement and intimacy
SCALE 80 m²
COLLABORATORS Maggie's Cancer Centre team

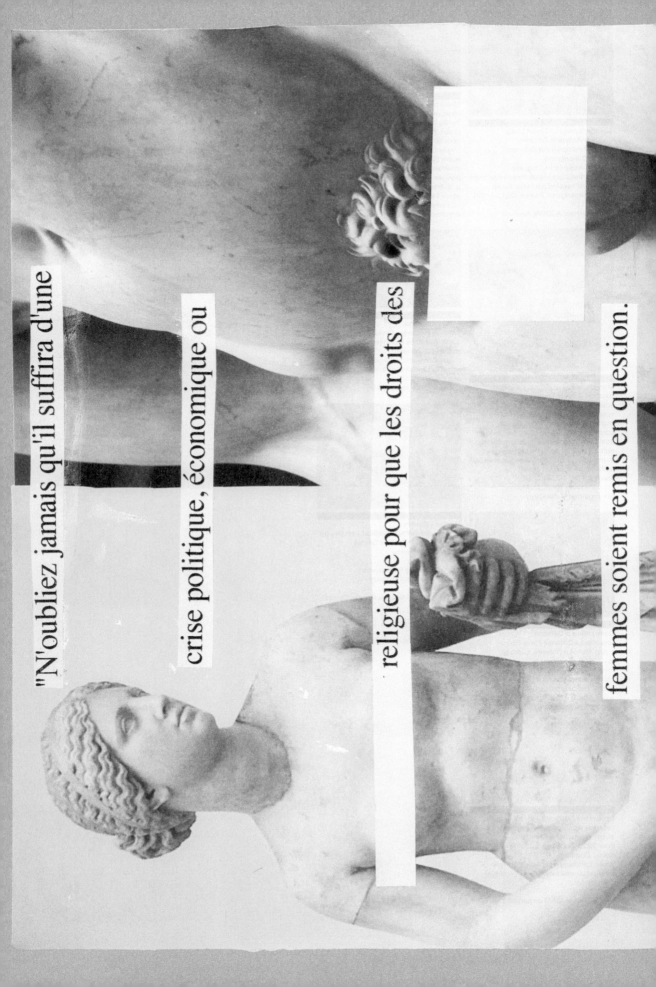

"N'oubliez jamais qu'il suffira d'une

crise politique, économique ou

religieuse pour que les droits des

femmes soient remis en question.

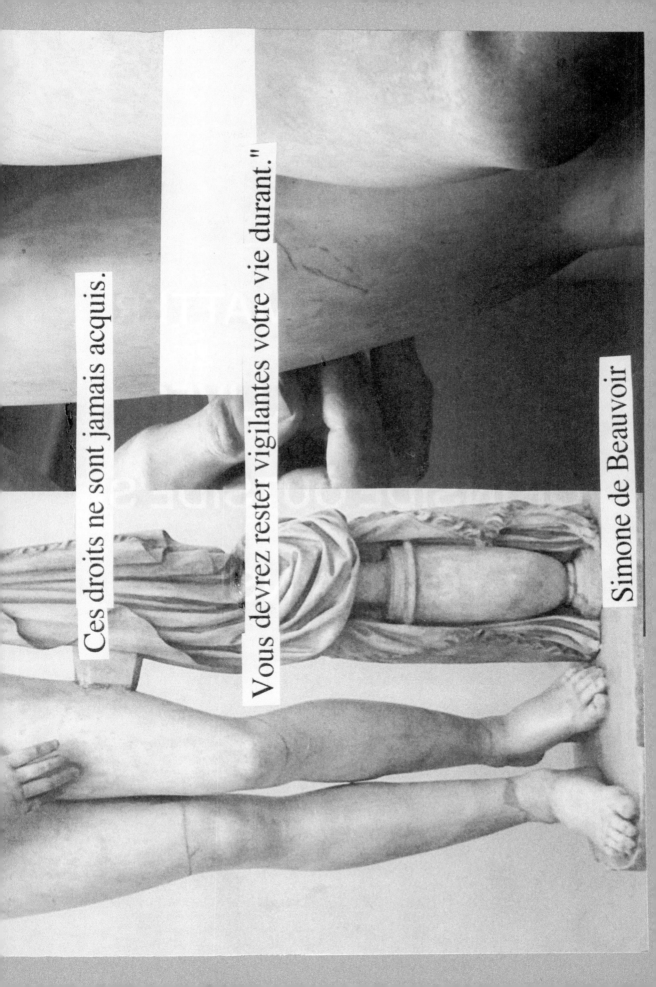

Ces droits ne sont jamais acquis.

Vous devrez rester vigilantes votre vie durant. "

Simone de Beauvoir

CHARLOTTE MATTER

THE SEXUAL LIVES OF INSIDE OUTSIDE'S CURTAINS

[1] Pink silk curtain encircles bath, runs along bathroom windows, then enters husband's bedroom, Maison à Bordeaux, Floirac

[2] Fontainebleau school, *Presumed Portrait of Gabrielle d'Estrées and Her Sister, the Duchess of Villars*, ca. 1594, oil on wood, 96 × 125 cm, Paris, Musée du Louvre

[1]

When architecture is discussed through the prism of sexuality, we are often told of phallic skyscrapers, womb-like amphitheatres and penetrating (or penetrated) tunnels. The entire repertoire of heteronormative sexuality is grafted onto architecture, as if the ultimate goal – both in buildings and desire – was always, and exclusively, procreation. But it gets interesting when architecture complicates such hegemonic conceptions and explores other forms of sexual practice and identities. Against the figure of the ever erect high-rise, Eva Díaz has, for instance, delightfully discussed a single-family home completed in 1969 by Mark Mills for the widowed sculptor June Foster Hass, which the architect referred to, on several occasions, as the Limp Penis House.[1] Expounding how this house "refuses to 'get hard,'" Díaz points out how the phallus, "culturally imagined in a patriarchy to be perpetually in its virile, priapic hard-cock state," challenges images of masculinity in its flaccid state.[2] There is something unsettling about softness in architecture, troubling our idea of (and need for) solid, protective walls. Yet – or precisely because of this uneasiness – there is also something highly sensual, libidinous about it, which is exactly what Petra Blaisse and her studio Inside Outside explore, in the curtains they have produced for public and private spaces since 1987.

SOFT AND HARD

In 1968, Reyner Banham juxtaposed the "responsive environment"[3] in *Barbarella* (as in much radical architecture of the 1960s) with the rigidity of "hardware" oriented structures.[4] The epitome of the latter, for Banham, was another science-fiction film released the same year, Stanley Kubrick's *2001: A Space Odyssey*, whose stern aesthetics he considered obsolete and positively disgusting: "All that grey plastic and crackle-finish metal, and knobs and switches, all that … yech … *hardware*!"[5] In contrast, Banham described the libidinous sets in *Barbarella*, with its transparent plastic bubbles and other soft membranes, as "an ambiance of curved, pliable, continuous, breathing, adaptable surfaces."[6]

Banham's description of "responsive environments" could just as well apply to Inside Outside's practice in interior architecture. The properties of softness and flexibility reverberate in Inside Outside's own descriptions of their curtains, as being "flexible, textile architecture" or "flexible, soft walls." Their choice of words – reconciling the conventionally antithetical qualities of "soft" and "hard" – sabotages the macho claim to architecture as enduring and conclusive. Inside Outside's curtains might be read as a manifesto against predetermined rooms that seek to condition our movements and experiences. Their flowing, soft walls respond to different needs and show unpredicted versatility. Sometimes they even act as subversive agents that wreak havoc with the spatial program and introduce new rules of play or, rather, "escape" the architecture, as Inside Outside so delicately put it in reference to their re-design of the curtains for the Maison à Bordeaux (2011–2012). This emancipatory approach is saturated in sensuality because it stimulates the desire to explore the spaces and find new uses for them.

Since it is the essence of curtains to veil and reveal, they are by nature subliminally lascivious. Shower curtains in particular lend themselves to frivolous compositions, as illustrated by the light-pink curtain in the Maison à Bordeaux, voluptuously draped around the bathtub, not only concealing but potentially displaying the naked bodies bathing there. This potential was already exploited in the art of the Renaissance, for instance in the presumed portrait of Gabrielle d'Estrées bathing with her sister, an anonymous work of the Fontainebleau School (ca. 1594). The delicate pinching of the nipple has been interpreted as an indication of the pregnancy, and subsequent lactation, of Henry IV's mistress, yet it remains a suggestive gesture. It is no coincidence that the erotic touch at the centre of the composition is framed by curtains. As the theatre scholar Georges Banu puts it, curtains are sensual devices that foster tactility, and are perhaps therefore so frequently pictured in combination with naked bodies in the history of art.[7] The haptic factor is also a strong presence in Inside Outside's curtains, since they are specifically conceived to be moved and rearranged in ever-changing configurations. Their curtains thus encourage

[2]

[3]

[3] White veils connect to printed plastic 4 m-high seams with cable belts, (2×) 12 × 25 m, Semper/Triennale/MAXXI

[4] View under the skirt of the privacy curtain for the entrance lobby of the Chasen Museum, with upright lamp in its centre

[5] Extremely reflective and darkening bedroom curtain for private house, Amsterdam

50

[4]

hands to touch them and glide over them. Sometimes they even suggest auto-erogenous moments, when the curtain rolls up as in a snail shell and their two sides rub against each other, as they do, for instance, in the Kunsthal Rotterdam, at the Chazen Museum of Art and at the Maggie Keswick Jencks Cancer Caring Centre.

Inside Outside is highly inventive in exploiting the erotic potential of curtains, as in the use of flexible textile walls that restructure rooms with niches for more privacy, a device that was already common in antiquity, where curtains were hung to subdivide the rooms of private homes.[8] Moreover, illuminated manuscripts of the Middle Ages testify to the fact that they enclosed not only doors and windows, but beds as well.[9] For centuries, canopy beds were an indispensable item among the affluent and, to this day, they are closely associated with intimacy and sensuality in the collective imaginary. Bed curtains not only keep out drafts and cold air; they also make it possible to indulge in private pleasures, screened off from inquisitive intruders. Among the many bed curtains created by Inside Outside are those for the Maison à Bordeaux as well as homes in London (2002), Leefdaal (2003–2004), Haaksbergen (2005–2008), Amsterdam (2011) and Oslo (2013). Other designs, not necessarily for private spaces, sometimes generate similarly intimate situations, when a curtain for instance offers glimpses to the outside but shields from inside views, as in the lobby of the Résidence L'Étoile in Amsterdam (2014). Inside Outside occasionally couple these newly created places of intimacy with another pleasure principle, namely the secret hideaway. Depending on how they are arranged, the curtains may become a maze and, as such, an invitation to get lost within them. The textile walls then entice users (if only in their imagination) to engage in frivolous games of hide and seek, transforming chaste halls into pleasurable, labyrinthine sites.

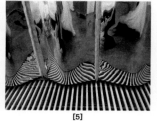

[5]

EROTIC PLASTICS

Another factor that makes for the sensuality of Inside Outside's curtains is their choice of unexpected, often challenging materials, as in their persistent use of synthetic fabrics. Although their curtains have an opulent effect – generated not least by their often substantial dimensions – they frequently consist of materials ordinarily written off as cheap and ugly, such as faux leather and other plastics originally developed to replace more precious or rare resources. The invention of celluloid was driven, for example, by the search for a substitute for ivory in billiard balls. For this reason, plastics were long considered inferior, ersatz materials. In fact, cultural historian Jeffrey Meikle quotes a thesaurus entry for the word "plastic" listing the following, not exactly flattering synonyms: "sham, meretricious, counterfeit, substitute, factitious, spurious, synthetic, artificial, specious, bogus, factoidal."[10]

Yet Inside Outside do not employ plastics ashamedly. Rather, they exploit and indeed celebrate their artificiality. A conspicuous case in point is the curtain for the auditorium of the Seattle Public Library, which consists of polyvinyl chloride (commonly abbreviated as PVC and also referred to as vinyl) printed with a bearskin pattern. Neither material nor motif lay any claim to factual mimesis; on the contrary, the camp eccentricity of this fake fur is gleefully overstated through the shiny surface and the enlarged scale of the photographic print reproduction. Sometimes an entire curtain is made of plastic. Sometimes a synthetic fabric is irreverently combined with precious textiles, when, for example, a layer of shiny, transparent plastic is placed between heavy velour and ethereal silk for the Barkow Leibinger architecture office in Berlin (2017). Similarly, the curtain for the Maggie Keswick Jencks Cancer Caring Centre (2017) consists of yellow cotton velour on one side, and reflective silver faux leather on the other. Front and back can be reversed thanks to a sophisticated system of ceiling tracks, so that warm and cold, matte and glossy can be juxtaposed in many different ways. Compositions of this kind highlight the singular characteristics of each fabric, emphasising the importance of materiality for Inside Outside. For the Harvard University's Piper Auditorium (2010–2012), a grey exterior of heavy-duty PVC is pitted against a gold interior. In this case, the curtain plays with ostensible worthlessness (industrial "chic") and presumed preciousness (faux

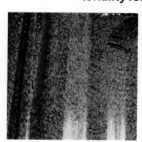

[6]

[7] Curtain with "earring seam" for the golden brocade, Piper Auditorium, Harvard, 2010–2011

[8] Black-and-white, ringed veils dim the "snapped" yellow and "stitched" pink velvet curtains of the auditorium curtains, Mick Jagger Centre, Dartford

51

[7]

gold). Surfaces that deceive, concealment that flirts with abstinence, revealing the hidden: these are all motifs of an erotic repertoire.

Synthetics are in fact historically charged with eroticism because their development was also a byproduct of the sex industry (besides, obviously, the military industry). In the 1970s, Gosnell Duncan, a former mechanic who had become paralysed from the waist down after a work accident, teamed up with a chemist at General Electric to develop a new silicone formula for dildos to make them supple, hypoallergenic and easy to disinfect. Duncan's contribution was revolutionary, as Hallie Lieberman observes, because he designed dildos and developed a safe material specifically for a disabled audience, whose sexual needs had always been ignored.[11] Furthermore, Duncan made sex toys more diverse, supplementing the then standard "skin-colored" pink with three darker tones.[12] Duncan would also make dildos acceptable in feminist circles by developing more abstract models in creamy vanilla and pale lavender in collaboration with feminist sex shops in the late 1970s.[13]

The development of new synthetics also boosted the fetish for rubber clothing.[14] Inside Outside's curtains of pitch-black lacquered plastic in Zurich and Milan conjure this wet and smooth look, its emphatically artificial, hyper-glossy surface evoking kink aesthetics. Other materials add to the references to BDSM, such as steel-mesh curtains (for a private home in Holten, 1995, and for the Hackney Empire Theatre in London, 2005) or the piercing of delicate textiles with coarse links. To produce the gigantic portions required for curtains in such unusual settings as a former locomotive depot (LocHal, three pairs of curtains measuring a total of 4,125 m²), Inside Outside drilled holes into the fabric, reinforced them with metal rings, and connected the sections with heavy-duty carabiners, resulting in crude, seductive seams à la Frankenstein. And the curtains at the Mick Jagger Centre in Dartford (London, 2000) are linked with snaps, yielding the striptease effect of being able to rip them apart.

[8]

PEEP

The curtain as a device to construct pictorial lust presumably enjoyed its heyday in the eighteenth century, when motifs of concealment and secrecy became the preferred means of erotic stimulation. Jean-Honoré Fragonard's painting, *Curiosity* (ca. 1775–1780), exemplifies this form of entertainment. Two young women have gently drawn a curtain aside with the tips of the fingers and are peeking through the gap. One of them is almost entirely hidden behind the curtain while the other is a bit more audacious. We see her blushing cheeks, her half-open mouth, and, below left, her bared breast. The eroticism of this small wooden panel in powdery hues lies in the very fact that it does not show the conventional voyeuristic composition of a female subject reduced to the passive object of unilateral visual pleasure.[15] Instead, we are confronted with a complex reciprocity in which the two girls are quite as actively voyeuristic as we the viewers are. The curtain plays a crucial role and dominates the composition, its undulating curves and dark slit no less suggestive than the gaze of the two women and their unabashedly bare skin. At the same time, the curtain acts as a border that maintains distance. However, since hiding always goes hand in glove with the possibility of revealing, the curtain – ambiguously pictured in a suspended state between opening and closing – enhances the seductive nature of what we see, for it may introduce the transition from a purely visual to a physical act or, conversely, suddenly block the view.

For the changing rooms of the Prada Beverly Hills store, Inside Outside created opulently pleated, cream-coloured curtains instead of walls and doors, conjuring a powdery boudoir atmosphere comparable to Fragonard's painting. The folds are deliberately designed to muffle sounds and ensure complete privacy for customers. But transparent plastic inserts in the lower part provide the frivolous thrill of potential exposure of presumably naked bodies getting dressed or undressed behind. While such designs merely hint at sensuality, other curtains by Inside Outside ooze sexuality. Take, for instance, those designed for the exhibition space of the archi-

[9]

[9] Jean-Honoré Fragonard, *Curiosity*, ca. 1775–1780, oil on wood, 16 × 13 cm, Paris, Musée du Louvre

[10] Heavy plissé inside, transparent plastic outside and "peep" windows in the seams of the two VIP shaping curtains at Prada Epicenter, New York

[11] 'Wings' for the gta gallery: Bed sheets and black lacquer divide the large space into several galleries, Zurich

52

[10]

tecture department at ETH Zurich (2016). Made of white fabric and glossy, deep black PVC, they are each pierced in the middle with a hole from transparent plastic. Given their use in a museum context, this sexualised display, which invites to sneak a peek, heightens the pleasure of the gaze that lies in the nature of an exhibition. Along these lines, the curtains for commercial viewing – for example, for Knoll International at the Salone del Mobile in Milan (2015) – could almost be described as pornographic. The seductive, solid black plastic conceals the objects of desire (the furniture on sale) from view, but Inside Outside give the aroused visitors scopophilic satisfaction through their voyeuristically sparing insertion of transparent horizontal slits.

Inside Outside have created numerous variations on the peephole motif (Lehmann Maupin Gallery, New York, 2003; Private House, Oslo, 2011–2013; UPC Leeuwarden, 2012; Immeuble Weill, Paris, 2018, to name but a few), lending even greater weight to the above-mentioned principle of concealment and revelation that underpins the sexual nature of curtains. The erotic nature of the peephole looks back on a long tradition over space and time. It features in a seventeenth-century Chinese novel of the Ming Dynasty, in which we read that holes

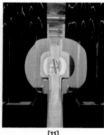

[11]

were drilled into the walls of brothels, enabling potential customers to watch nude sex workers.[16] Such devices became a regular fixture in many nineteenth- century *maisons closes* that adapted to the increasingly visual needs of their customers, staging erotic *tableaux vivants* of naked bodies in suggestive poses.[17] The appeal of looking without being seen would later also define the visual aesthetics of *Playboy*, characterised by pictures taken through a hole, a crack, or the frame of a window, thus turning the reader into a voyeur peering into a private room, as Paul B. Preciado has brilliantly analysed.[18]

Yet in contrast to the "pornotopia" of *Playboy*,[19] which made use of semi-transparent mirrors, secret passages, adjustable sofas and rotating beds to subordinate the invariably female body as a passive object to the male gaze, Inside Outside's curtains draw their eroticism from an entirely different mechanism.

Their interventions are "soft" as they are pliable and responsive, adapting to their surroundings and needs, and at the same time can subtly turn inside out a given architecture program. But they are also "hard" in being made of unexpected, erotically charged materials, such as plastics and their slick, wet-look surfaces favored in queer erotic practices centered around pleasure instead of procreation. In addition, Inside Outside create lustful dispositives, availing themselves of holes to peep through and inviting bodies to hide and seek between the layers and folds of their curtains. Their flexible walls do not cater to the construction of heteronormative spaces of seduction. Rather, they explore non-binary queerness, being both soft and hard, conflating smooth environments and hardcore innuendos.

[12]

[12] Cover of *Atomage* no. 13, Supplement no. 1, 1976

1   Eva Díaz, "Soft Architecture," in: *Harvard Design Magazine*, Family Planning, no. 41, Fall/Winter 2015, pp. 36–37, p. 36.

2   Accordingly, she also notes how the house is emphatically described as "shell-like" by a real estate agent in a promotional video, the metaphor of the limp penis probably not stimulating sales. Ibid., p. 37.

3   Reyner Banham, "Triumph of Software," in: *New Society*, vol. 12, no. 318, October 31, 1968, pp. 629–30, p. 629.

4   The idea of a flexible, soft, plastic architecture that combines hippie nomadism with hypertechnology is already present in an earlier essay by Banham, in which he posits a transparent "Environment-Bubble" as a counter-model to "the persistence of architecture-as-monumental-space" in a time shaped by social and personal mobility. Reyner Banham, "A Home is Not a House," illustrated by François Dallegret, in: *Art in America*, April 1965, pp. 70–79, p. 79.

5   Banham, "Triumph of Software," p. 629.

6   Ibid.

7   Georges Banu, *Le Rideau ou la fêlure du monde*, Paris: Adam Biro, 1997, p. 70.

8   James Yates, "Velum," in: William Smith (ed.) *Dictionary of Greek and Roman Antiquities*, 2nd edition, improved and enlarged, Boston: Little, Brown, and Company, 1870, pp. 1185–86, p. 1185.

9   The use of bed curtains was in fact so prevalent in the Middle Ages that they came to signify the bed itself. Thus, the idiom "under the curtain" meant being in bed. Thomas Wright, *The Homes of Other Days: A History of Domestic Manners and Sentiments in England from the Earliest Known Period to Modern Times*, New York: D. Appleton, 1871, p. 268.

10   Jeffrey L. Meikle, *American Plastic: A Cultural History*, New Brunswick, New Jersey: Rutgers University Press, p. 7.

11   Hallie Lieberman, *Buzz: A Stimulating History of the Sex Toy*, New York: Pegasus Books, 2017, pp. 93–101.

12   Ibid., p. 100.

13   While vibrators were considered symbols of sexual emancipation, dildos were extremely controversial in feminist circles. The debate focused particularly on whether they represented the penis, and if they did, whether their use represented submission to the patriarchal order or, on the contrary, could be reinterpreted as a subversive act. See the chapter "Dildo Debates" (ibid., pp. 199–214).

14   This predilection can be traced back to the 1920s and 1930s, with sources testifying to the erotic enthusiasm for rubberised Mackintosh raincoats. Valerie Steele, *Fetish: Fashion, Sex and Power*, New York/Oxford: Oxford University Press, 1996, p. 149. As Steele remarks, "the invention of PVC was especially important because it made the 'wet look' possible, adding a new twist to the old enthusiasm for raincoats." Ibid., pp. 152–53.

15   For a discussion of the passive/female connotation of "to-be-looked-at-ness," see Laura Mulvey, "Visual Pleasure and Narrative Cinema," in: *Screen*, vol. 16, no. 3, October 1, 1975, pp. 6–18.

16   *Du Rouge au gynécée, roman érotique de la dynastie Ming*, trans. from the Chinese by Martin Maurey, Paris: Philippe Picquier, 1990, pp. 53–4 and p. 67.

17   Laure Adler, La vie quotidienne dans les maisons closes, 1830–1930, Paris: Hachette, 1990, p. 130.

18   [Paul B.] Preciado, *Pornotopía: Arquitectura y sexualidad en "Playboy" durante la guerra fría*, Barcelona: Editorial Anagrama, 2010, p. 54.

19   Preciado derives this term from Foucault's concept of heterotopia and uses it to describe the sexualised variation in a late capitalist, technology-oriented society of hyper consensus. Ibid., pp. 118–21.

CHRISTOPHE GIROT

TWINE & GARDEN

I met Petra Blaisse and her two partners at Inside Outside, Jana Crepon and Aura Luz Melis, on the roof of their office compound in Amsterdam West. On this soft, breezy, sunny late August day, we sat in the shade of a parasol at a table around simple cups of tea. A few potted plants strewn irregularly around the open roof and a grassy train dike served as our backdrop. The chirp of birds mixed with the whisper of the trains passing by, as we talked for almost two hours about the evolving place of landscape in society and the philosophy of their design office.

Our discussion took us to many places. We reflected on how landscapes can help shape different urban contexts and came to the conclusion that a garden offers a different glimpse of our place and time in the world – always. For that reason alone, it has never really been fully ecological nor fully natural, but rather cultural. It embodies a modified form of nature akin to a living embroidery of plants and materials that reflect cultural values and the way we live. A landscape plays a vital role in society; the natural ingredients that go with it are essential to life: animals, insects, worms, microorganisms, bacteria, fungi, droppings, decomposing matter and blossoms. It is a biotope of sorts, an important place for biological and chemical exchange between plants, living organisms and soil. Awareness of the soil and its invisible below-ground ecosystem is a leitmotif of all projects by Inside Outside. The discussion converged into a soft manifesto: a landscape is meant to bring coherence and legibility to a place, as well as mystery and complexity to human behaviour. The design must focus on simplicity through the use of quality elements such as water and soil, materials and plants, placed in progressive rhythms to produce a vividness of life and form. Even in the most difficult locations, like an exposed roof, it is always a challenge for the landscape architect to bring it to life, to make it vibrant.

The scope of the work produced by Petra Blaisse and her two associates over the past decade is impressive. The personalities of the three partners seem quite different, yet complementary – as it should be in any successful partnership. Inside Outside is the product of a highly intuitive and curious designer, Petra Blaisse, whose impressive green gaze captures the essence of what the imaginary of a garden can offer. This green gaze is nurtured by the fact that she regularly does gardening at her home in Amsterdam. Her gardener's

experience has significantly enriched her knowledge of the soil, life cycles and seasonal processes; it also plays a fundamental role in her ability to respond creatively to a situation: "This part of my life – gardening and witnessing and experiencing nature on a daily basis – makes me extremely happy," she says with a smile. According to landscape architect Jana Crepon, it is part of the experience that the office strives to achieve wherever possible for the public at large. Jana brings resolve and a solid ability to design and implement landscapes even in the most extreme and challenging conditions. She and the office have learned how to perfect a style that is both resilient and identifiable even in the most difficult climates. Aura Luz Melis, architect, gives projects shape and form through conscientious constructive rigour, long-standing experience and accumulated landscape know-how. Her contributions range in scale from highly detailed single projects to master plans stretching over vast territories in different latitudes.

It is this unusual mix of proficiencies that makes the team of Inside Outside distinct from any other practice that I know. It appears that Petra Blaisse has, slowly but surely, been able to spin her years of experience in curtain design into the creative realm of landscape investigation and design. She understands the curtain as a tangible threshold between cool and warm, a diaphanous membrane operating between lightness and darkness. It is the shroud of life to be overcome through what Petra calls the "emancipation of the curtain."

With only your thought, I was mad and blind,
Curtains pulled away, spellbound is my mind!
If in my whole life, one day is spent with thee,
This is my harvest, the rest sinks in the sea.
– Saadi Shirazi

As can be gathered from this quote by the twelfth-century Persian poet Saadi, nothing is new. The curtain has been an integral part of garden culture since the most ancient times. Its fabric, while reacting to the realms of inside and out, is interlaced with all the scents, colours and transparencies of a garden. A curtain reacts to the slightest atmospheric variations in light and air, depending on the time of night or day. Persian culture has always shown numerous examples of vertical awnings – so-called *talar* curtains that mediate between garden, patio and house. When raised on poles in front of the portico, the heavy cloth helps the cool air flow into the privacy of the home at night.

In daytime the heavy curtains are drawn down to keep out the sun's blistering heat. The cloth of the *talar* curtains is a garden mediator of sorts. As it flaps in the wind, it carries sounds that sweep across the cypress grove over a moonlit mirror pool and conveys the heady fragrance of damask roses amidst babbling waters and nightingales. The heavy veil acts as a diaphanous membrane, with time set to unwind like countless threads caught in the breeze. The curtain acts as a poet revealing a garden; it is a scenographic device capable of unravelling countless scenes and mysteries for the visitor. As an operative tool that draws out the wonder of a garden, the curtain is intrinsic to the landscape approach of Inside Outside.

The young French landscape architect Yves Brunier, who designed the Museum Park in Rotterdam with Rem Koolhaas in the early 1990s, was assisted in the years before his death by Blaisse who helped him translate his design thoughts from French into Dutch. She executed his project with great mastery over the next decade. The highly expressive and poetic plan for the Museum Park describes four quadrants with different atmospheres that are left open to interpretation. The original photo montage shows a blossoming white orchard, which was initially planted with species of old Dutch apple trees. They were placed in a bed of white seashells to be mirrored on the wall of the Cultural Podium. Because of poor soil conditions and after consulting with Rotterdam's Green department, Blaisse had to replace the apple trees with a grove of white flowering honey locusts. A new, diagonal and more architectural organisation of the trees was drawn up with colleague Rosetta Elkin. The quadrant with the romantic garden became the place for a vibrant display of garden colours throughout the seasons. Until recently, the park was not only a landmark for the city but a reference for creative landscape design in more ways than one. The Cultural Podium had become a place where people gathered, were entertained, and with which they strongly identified. The elaboration of this park early in her career undeniably influenced the subsequent landscape styling of Petra Blaisse and Inside Outside.

The word "garden" comes from the old German *Garto* signifying a fenced-in space. The history of palisades, where natural materials such as reeds and branches were interwoven and braided across vertical wooden posts, tells us a lot about some of our oldest customs rooted in the elementary shaping of space. Back then, palisades were raised because nature threatened and defensive shelters around settlements were a necessity. The protective membrane of the palisade defined an inside and an outside. The clearly defined spatial perimeter of a fence gave birth not only to the garden, but also to the prototypical town. Etymology continued to chart a capricious path: the old German word *Zaun* or "fence" became the English word "town," while the Dutch *tuin* came to mean "garden." Sitting there and chatting, we wondered how town and garden could be so readily confused, so that one culture could name it and understand it in opposition to the other. The woven twigs and branches of palisades, like the woven rattan of baskets, followed the same rules as the yarn and twine of a canvas weave. It is beautiful to believe that such a practical feature as a fence helped define and support one of the most fundamental spatial parameters of dwelling, both inside and out.

It is no accident that Blaisse, along with Crepon and Melis, works knowingly and precisely at the threshold of town and garden. The recently completed project for the Bait La Ivrit School in Rishon LeZion, Israel, is a good example that plays on a series of variations on the theme of enclosure and the fence. By extension, it becomes a pergola, a table, a vertical garden, or a bench as it evolves and wraps around the longitudinal school yard, sometimes opening to the interior of the school building, allowing rooms to communicate freely with the outside. The fence plays skilfully with the notion of a safe haven; on the inside, it opens generously towards the garden, while separating and protecting the school from the outside. The Belgian poet Henri Michaux often referred to the notion of *lointain intérieur* in his poems and that is exactly what the involuted spatial configuration of the Bait La Ivrit School has achieved.

The Roeterseiland project for the University of Amsterdam further exemplifies the play of interweaving elements throughout an urban site. It stands out among other projects for its particular, careful approach to an historic site. The use of a strong serial graphic element, namely the pattern made by the white brick "ribbon" set into the brick paving, is meant to help unite disparate areas of the campus. What appears as a whimsical graphic feature on the plan, somewhat akin to the bright orange ribbon of the Windy Zero roof garden project at the Plussenbugh in Rotterdam, translates into a series of highly coherent and recognizable spaces. The campus ribbon of the Roeterseiland transforms space as it wraps around the buildings, twirling and twining into something apparently nonsensical and convoluted until it is finally met by traditional, mixed-border beds. It is the simplicity in the materialisation of this ribbon that makes this project unique and remarkable. Winding around, it may become a bench or a surface where students can meet to work or dream of a whirlwind of other possibilities.

The work of Petra Blaisse and Inside Outside brings two seemingly opposite aspects closer together. One can sense that the yarn of textiles and the intertwined paths of a garden repeatedly fuse in the work process. By carefully weaving a particular kind of canvas, the two seemingly distinct realms of indoors and outdoors are bound at the seams leading to a particular kind of creative interaction. Following the thread of the unbuilt park project in Prato, Tuscany, we discover the extraordinary convergence of knowledge and experience that could have come about had it been implemented. Each area of the park was thought of as an expression of a fibre or a plant dye, the mulberry tree for silk, the hemp field for jute and rope, and linen and wool for drapery and cloth. In this case it is less the matrix set in the landscape plan than the association of plants brought together that really matters.

What lies behind the relationship between textile and landscape design? In the case of Inside Outside, the key is to understand how textile can be seen as a landscape canvas that interacts with the development of a garden. A garden always tries to weave its plants into place in a coherent spatial pattern and framework; the question remains how finely, accurately and appropriately this canvas can react to context. Plants compete with each other in nature; they relentlessly seek light, water and nutrients from the forest floor to the highest tree canopies. Each plant can be considered a phenotype that expresses its form and place by reacting to different degrees of dryness and humidity.

Inside Outside's collaborations with the plant physiologist Rosetta Elkin from 2003 to 2005 shed light on the particular tack the office took regarding the potential of adaptive horticulture. By focusing more particularly on plant adaptation and anatomy, the projects created first in Dubai and then Qatar are quite exemplary, because they appear at first sight like a neatly woven tapestry on canvas. In Qatar, the vegetation in each plant location presents a different size, colour and texture. The garden is thus understood as a microcosm that relates back to the bigger picture of the plant world, where each patch tells a story of its own. Many other projects by the office, set in other locations, show a similarly playful treatment of plant life, which is clearly a product of in-depth research and great rigour. The Qatar National Library and the Qatar Foundation play with the theme of the garden matrix, on a roof garden and in full soil, respectively. The plants in these examples are set either in circles or in squares. The patterns follow repetitive geometric rules and patterns reminiscent of the serial art trend of the 1970s and 1980s. Each plant was chosen for its ability to withstand exposure to the extremely arid climate of the Gulf. Each microgarden thus exposed tells a story about its degree of humidity, dryness and depth of soil. It adds a strong narrative touch to the project, inspired by Joseph Cornell's *Cabinets of Curiosities*. The garden becomes an open partition to create one's own landscape narrative, where visitor and gardener share their knowledge of plants and watch each specimen tell its evolutionary story.

The garden in the work of Inside Outside is like a sounding board for experimentation. The creation of gardens stems from years of experience and knowledge acquired through practice with textiles, curtains, spatial thinking and topographic design. Similarly, every garden requires a clear order and structure to enable things to fall into place as planned. Like the patterns woven on a loom, or twine on a rug, the motifs that emerge in a garden are often borrowed from other cultures. In ancient nomadic carpets from Central Asia, the floral motifs often represent paradise. Travelling via Persia, archaic floral patterns were adapted to suit the techniques of silk brocade and subsequently perfected as damask paisley patterns in Byzantium. Exported to Europe via Genoa and Venice, the richly embroidered silk textiles in turn influenced the style of late Renaissance and early Baroque gardens with their *parterres de broderies* set along a *tapis vert*. The original silk textile motifs literally merged into the highest forms of garden art, which helped propagate the style of the time and brought about an unprecedented degree of horticultural refinement, diversity and colour to the *parterres*. Blaisse's early Inside Outside projects, like the Shenzhen Stock Exchange, incorporate this history and quite literally play on floral pattern-making and mapping. The plants work as ornamental inlays embossed on the surface of the entire roof and despite a tendency towards bilateral symmetry in the floral motifs, the project is, in fact, more akin to a Brazilian garden in the style of Roberto Burle Marx than some neo-Baroque garden.

Each epoch understands the meaning of nature and its trajectories differently. We live in an age where respect towards nature and the need for balance is, more often than not, wanting and without form. The Biblioteca degli Alberi is not a library but a botanical park in which a rigorously stylised form of nature contributes knowledge, vitality and pride to a bustling neighbourhood in Milan. It is a place of many paths where a broad collection of trees have now been planted. It will be interesting to see how these trees evolve and adapt to city life over time. Through variations in the size and shape of the different species, the park will gradually be transformed into a variegated urban forest. What might be interpreted at first sight as a formal geometric frame, containing a mosaic of paths and trapezoidal surfaces, can also be understood as a canvas for many gardens to come. The park exposes or rather juxtaposes various aspects of the same thing: the garden is a place for both the dreams and realities of a city. A garden will emerge that reflects the potential and spirit of a given public realm. In time, the sun and shade in the Biblioteca degli Alberi will weave patterns through the stems and branches of the garden, showing us how things can change, grow and mingle differently.

Some gardens exclude exotic rarities, preferring the play of indigenous plants with a palette of local species and recycled materials. Back in the 1970s, the Dutch landscape architect Louis Leroy already praised a humble approach to "native" vernacular design. In this respect, the Vakantiepark de Klepperstee located in the Kop van Goeree identifies with a vein of historic vernacular landscapes that are quite specific to the Netherlands. A vast landscape quadrant of Dutch elm trees helps frame large open "green rooms" for various activities, each defined and set apart from each other by a microtopography of small dikes and dunes. Crepon tells us that this holiday park by the North Sea represents a very personal interpretation of ecology, local factors and history by accentuating the adaptive reuse of existing structures in the surrounding landscape. One could call this project a subtle mix of ecological and cultural palimpsests that reads very much like a patchwork of green cells on a leaf.

The recently developed Parco del Polcevera in Genoa, including the Radura della Memoria, epitomises the skill with which Blaisse and Inside Outside resolve the dilemma between a site's recent memory and civic use. The 22-hectare park created in collaboration with Stefano Boeri and Metrogramma is located underneath the place where a highway bridge collapsed, killing many drivers and inhabitants. Inside Outside responded to this tragedy in the form of serial gardens placed like ribbons running parallel to each other on the valley floor. Each garden tells the story of rebirth and hope, with multiple approaches to planting that actively engage contemporary methods of water management and conservation. But the project is not only about ecology; most importantly, it is about the immensity of human grief. As the plants grow, grouped together in lines, they act like many threads of a loom that form the life and pulse of the park.

If there is a credo that resonates at Inside Outside, it is the fact that town and park, and house and garden, are inseparable and cannot exist in isolation. They interact and complete each other, steadily nurturing the senses throughout the day. The oscillation between inside and out strikes me not only as significant, but essential to this approach. I visited the home that Petra Blaisse shares with her partner in Amsterdam. There, to my surprise, I experienced an entirely open and seamless physical relationship between the rooms of the house and the garden, in which she has invested so much time and reflection. A fairly traditional Amsterdam School-style brick, turn-of-the-century townhouse, as seen from the outside, is transformed inside into a play of mirrors, reflecting surfaces and materials such as glass, cloth, wood and polycarbonate ceilings, creating a kaleidoscope of colours and textures as one moves from the garden into the house and back out again towards the street. The curtains, gently swaying veils, dance nonchalantly beside the large open windows of their home; they manifest how both realms interact in a continuous biome through the interplay of light, lush garden textures and reflections. There is no distinction whatsoever between house and garden; they have delicately, unobtrusively merged and intertwined into one. For an instant, the illusion that the rear access to the garden had vanished and been replaced by a thin veil of light has become a tangible reality.

This essay on twine and garden juxtaposes two aspects of the same thing: the garden is a place that produces dreams and reality. The production of a garden reflects a specific human investment within a given cultural realm. It is meant to weave a place of comfort out of sun and shade. The designer in Petra is always thinking about how a garden might change and grow into something extraordinary, triggering through the slightest impulse an infinite combination of textures, heights and colours. There is a thread in the history of twine that binds dream and reality, from linen and silk to cotton and wool, from jute and hemp to raffia and rope: everything hints at how things come together in a garden quite naturally, transcending time and cultures, towns and countries. The garden interweaves fibres from distinct realms, sowing the seeds of different horizons into so many layers of feeling and meaning. Inside Outside produce gardens that are giant, animate canvases; they are vibrant cultural constructs that interweave pure novelty with tradition, conferring the ultimate meaning to a place in the present.

FATMA AL SEHLAWI

REDEFINING

LANDSCAPE

IN QATAR

[1] Natural desert landscape of Northern Qatar: *Ziziphus spina-christi* trees in Al Shaffallahiya desert depressions, 2023

[2] Seasonal plants nursery, Al Khor, Qatar, 2022

61

[1]

When asked by Petra Blaisse to write an article on her work in Doha – the gardens at Qatar National Library and Qatar Foundation Headquarters – I saw this as an opportunity to suggest a broader observation. There have recently been attempts in Qatar and the surrounding region to define an alternative to prevailing garden design, which usually consists of importing foreign plant species to serve a specific visual appetite of evergreen lushness. The concept of a garden has largely been reduced to an aesthetic value that is almost synthetic in character, challenging the soil, water and climatic factors.

The few alternative attempts are mostly mutual in their proposition to host palettes of local plants, or those tolerant to the climate in this region. To understand the need for such an alternative, one must reassess native practices adapted to the specific social and geographic conditions, and the diversion towards alternative foreign practices. I here briefly outline how we, the inhabitants of this land, might have neglected the most fitting means of introducing plants and coexisting with them in the way earlier generations did.

[2]

Currently, garden design in the public realm usually involves creating surfaces of high maintenance grassed lawns, evergreen trees, shaped bushes and ephemeral flowering plants replaced every season. Residential gardens incorporate a similar selection of plants. Nurseries, which all stock a similar range of imported plants, are the source of both public and private gardens. Commercial gardening companies are usually hired to maintain such gardens and since this proves costly, hardscape landscaping became increasingly common, with an obvious decrease in greenery within residential boundary walls and public areas. In gardens and along the streets, trees were planted at regular intervals as standalone landscape features. Such mono-planting has created the need for even higher maintenance, as the plants are prevented from coexisting within symbiotic plant communities which help them thrive.

This was not always the case.

In Qatar, a desert peninsula without any rivers or lakes, settlements his-

torically flourished where alternative freshwater bodies were found providing access not only to water but also to vegetation. Inland, tribes settled around *rawda*s (seasonally flooded depressions with plant communities), along *wadi*s (rainwater valleys lined with vegetation), and where the groundwater table was high enough to access through wells known as *ain*. The people depended on the natural resources, coexisting with nature through seasonal understanding and sustainable reaping. The inland desert carried an array of native plants, which the settlers had learned to sustainably exploit through long experience. Some plants were edible, others could be used as slow-burning wood and oils, and still others tempered the climate with the shade of their canopies.

In coastal settlements, most households dug groundwater wells. The inhabitants depended on the same group of desert plants, but also reaped the benefits of salt-tolerant coastal mangroves and the influx of plant species from merchant ships. These imported plants were selected sensibly; most were fruit-bearing and able to withstand the Qatari environment.

Later, domestic gardens emerged in the traditional courtyard houses of the 1920s. As an extension of the indoor living space, the courtyard was an outdoor area with the desired privacy where the women prepared and cooked the food, gathering with neighbours in the mornings and later with the family. The courtyards typically had towering date palms (*Phoenix dactylifera*) and sheltering trees, with canopies extending over the house shading public alleyways. Simplicity was key, with a sophisticated appreciation for each species and its derivatives. The usual plant palette was limited, yet rich in purpose and benefits. Each plant's presence was felt, appreciated and respected.

The *Loz* (Indian Almond / *Terminalia catappa*) is one example, which was imported from India in the first half of the 1900s and became popular in courtyards for its shading canopy, low maintenance, drought tolerance and summer fruits. Gradually a naturalised plant palette developed from species that had been introduced from elsewhere.

[3]

[4] *Avicennia marina* plants of the Al
Thakhira Mangroves, North-Eastern
coast of Qatar, 2022

[5] Trees and traditional courtyard
houses, Doha, 1960s

62

[4]

A new garden in the desert typology emerged in the late 1950s by farming the desert. The Qatari government initiated a multifaceted project to commercialise and modernise agriculture, distributing plots of land in the desert at no cost to the citizens, each plot with a water well. The vertical proximity of fresh groundwater indicated areas of more fertile soil. Here foreign expertise, mostly from Sudan and Pakistan, helped inform on new methods of agriculture. These farms were fast transformed into human-made oases of palm groves, native trees and shrubs, as well as climatically tolerant imported species. A new form of green agglomerations in the desert emerged.

The desert continued to provide medicinal products; the farmlands provided crops, and the domestic plants provided seasonal fruits and environmental moderations. Plants continued to be fundamental in the livelihood of society, sustaining a personal and binary relationship between human and nature.

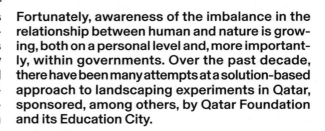

[5]

The 1970s introduced modern means of town planning, orchestrated by a new planning ministry and foreign planning firms. The aim was to alter the formation of settlements and modernise the country's capital city in order to accommodate an established state and a growing society. The character of streets changed, from a network of alleyways to a radial ring road system. Vegetation was introduced to alter the streetscape character, not as an extension of the desert but rather as a visually developed capital city, with Washingtonia lined streets. Instead of courtyard houses, a new typology of single-family villas emerged with externalised gardens. This altered the use and perception of domestic gardens. Being more exposed to outside view, they were no longer treated as an extension to indoor living spaces. Moreover, within the larger context, aesthetic taste began to change, fuelled by imported practices, television and cinema, residents of various nationalities and backgrounds residing in Qatar, as well as increase in travel. This aesthetic shift also affected garden design and the choice of vegetation, leading to the abovementioned practices in landscaping. In many aspects and not limited to the character of gardens, the binary

relationship between human and nature was reduced and altered, as in many areas of the world.

The change in the appreciation and treatment of desert landscapes was as rapid as urban development. Many scholars recognised the importance of keeping a record of the desert landscape. One such specialist Kamal El Deen Batanouny documented the native landscape and flora of Qatar and different countries of the Gulf and Egypt, among others. He was appointed by Qatar University in the early 1980s as a Professor of Environmental Sciences, conducting numerous specialised research projects with his students to study the flora of the country and publish the outcomes. One of his many substantial publications, *The Environment and Plant Life in the State of Qatar* (1986), has become a standard reference work today in understanding the diverse natural landscape phenomena of the Qatari desert as well as its rich palette of plants, their habitats and uses. Batanouny later created a set of six botanical drawings of native flora as stamps for the Qatar Post Office. Another valuable resource, *A Guide to Wild Plants of Qatar* by Muhanna Al Asiri Al Muadheed, documents the indigenous knowledge of Qatar's flora with an emphasis on recollections in Qatari and Arab poetry.

Fortunately, awareness of the imbalance in the relationship between human and nature is growing, both on a personal level and, more importantly, within governments. Over the past decade, there have been many attempts at a solution-based approach to landscaping experiments in Qatar, sponsored, among others, by Qatar Foundation and its Education City.

The growing interest among landscape architects in featuring local plant palettes rooted in their context's ecology is epitomised by Inside Outside with the completion of two experimental gardens for Education City in 2016. The gardens are the result of in-depth research into the naturally occurring native vegetation of inland Qatar. Both projects attempt to adopt existing formulas that respond to the peninsula's climatic conditions consisting of lengthy hot and humid summers, salty North winds known as

[6]

[7] Emergence of Washingtonia robusta
and imported seasonal flowers in public
spaces, Doha, 1970s

[8] *The Environment & Plant Life in the
State of Qatar* book cover, by Kamal El
Deen Batanouny, 1986

63

[7]

Shammal, short cold winters and long periods of drought. The gardens also respond to the architecture of the three buildings they surround, designed by OMA for Education City, with different operational requirements and user conditions.

The larger of the two, the Water Recipe Garden, serves two neighbouring buildings: the Qatar Foundation Headquarters (QFHQ) and the Think Bay, in essence, the epicentre of Education City's administration. The garden's core notion is to showcase a series of plant habitats, performing under varied conditions as trials to be studied rather than perceived as a finished garden.

Structurally, the garden is an elevated travertine platform. It conceals a concrete car park underneath and shades the underground entrances into both buildings. A perforated roof garden is created with multiple, framed moments of unique botanical scenarios.

[8]

Consistent with the parametric varying pattern of the QFHQ's facades, the garden is populated with a grid of square elements, transforming into a gradient of dimensions, depths and purposes. A pattern of planted and hollow squares creates a functional garden to be studied while also forming a rich and decorative carpet-like layout. This pattern enlivens the views from the upper floors of the surrounding buildings, most strikingly from the panoramic balcony of the QFHQ. I have recently learned that employees of the QFHQ even have favourites among the plant families in "their" garden. One member of the Qatar National Library team, Dr. Alwaleed Alkhaja, has been using a full spectrum camera that detects infrared with a filter that allows anything reflecting light (chlorophyll in plants) to become red in colour, to study each species in the Water Recipe Garden.

Most of the square elements are planters hosting different plant communities, in a manner that mimics the layered vegetation found naturally coexisting here in Qatar's deserts. In nature the native plant communities have been formed due to interdependencies, the natural water conditions and the subterranean soil composition. The Water Recipe Garden imitates

these naturally layered communities in their entirety, then gradually and systematically excludes certain species to allow a smaller selection of plants to be the focus of the showcase. This is where the particular water and soil recipes prescribed by Inside Outside come into play.

The grid of planters varies systematically along two axes: from wet to dry habitats, and from complete communities to dominant species. The dimensions vary from large to small and deep to shallow, gradually shifting from the garden's northern to southern ends. As the number of species decreases, so does the size of the planter. As the height of the plants decreases, so does the depth of the planters. Another correlation is the change in the planter's depth relative to the change in irrigation levels. The calculated amount of irrigation creates layered lush green groups, sculptural dry groups and states in-between, varying from sufficient irrigation to no irrigation.

Native trees, shrubs, flowering plants and bulbs dominate the introduced plant communities. Occasional interruptions and instances of foreign yet tolerant species from the same hardiness zones as Qatar are integrated to add varying visual and sensory effects.

At systematic intervals within the garden, some squares act as punctured light wells or stairs for vertical access to and from the basement. In both cases, the square openings illuminate and aerate the car parking structure underneath. Walking through the Water Recipe Garden, I recall seeing staff and visitors landing at different parts of the "roof garden" depending on where they have parked on the level below, animating the grid of squares further and allowing for moments of new discoveries. From the light wells, lush canopies of trees planted in the basement level rise above the garden, providing more shade and instants of surprise while in bloom.

The square elements are utilised further to form two security stations, while all others host bins, lighting, irrigation and drainage systems, as well as air exhausts. A well-ordered garden is created without the usual

[9]

[10]

clutter of functional elements found in landscaping projects.

The Water Recipe Garden is an investigative garden showcasing an experiment towards testing the plants' performance in an urban human-made setting and prescribing the optimum recipe for their success.

Walking eastwards from the Water Recipe Garden, one passes by the wild gardens of Weill Cornel University designed by Arata Isozaki, with its high Sidra (*Ziziphus spina-christi*) trees and varied grasses, and thereafter arrives at the Garden of Two Family Tales. This second garden designed by Inside Outside is a garden reminiscent of a forgotten simplicity felt in earlier landscaping, and suggestive of the patches of green intermittently grouped in the desert where water collects. It receives the library's visitors, and leads them towards the set-back entrance, under the building's raised concrete volume.

The garden's recipe is simple: a landscape of multiple circular concave imprints, hosting only two groups of drought-tolerant plants, as well as occasional groups of seats and one special water feature, a golden fountain celebrating the value of water. The imprints stand out minimally within a vast plane of local beige limestone. The hardscape hints at the local *froosh*, planes used in traditional Qatari architecture made with coral stones collected along the shores at low tide.

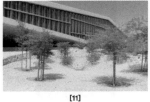

[11]

After sunset, each concave garden is softly lit, creating silhouettes of the plants. The entrance fountain, shaded by the folded library building, is transformed from its daytime golden sheen to a coloured light show, becoming a beautiful sight for the library's visitors, especially on their way out.

The two exhibited xerotolerant plant groups are *Acacia* and the succulent *Agave*. Unlike *Acacia*, *Agave* is not native to Qatar, but both are climatically tolerant and here presented in a diversity of forms and colours. The imported agave plants were acclimatised at the plant nurseries of Education City, where multiple landscape trials take place.

The imprints dotted with acacia trees provide shade for those strolling

under the trees or sitting on the crescent shaped seating bordering the round garden. The circles vary in size and depth, creating moments of visual change and interest. The smaller and shallower circles host fewer plants of the same species, while the larger, deeper ones contain more vegetation, creating denser gardens.

The *Agave* plants are the garden's evergreens, and when they bloom after maturity, they add hues of yellow and orange to the gardens with blossom stalks towering high above the plant. Their leaf texture and structure allow for a water management system that reduces the evaporation of water. Moreover, the plant itself produces rooted offspring at its base that will gradually increase the density of the garden.

The *Acacias* enjoy the warm and dry climate of Qatar. While they pass through periods of leaf loss, they do create two moments of surprise during the year with their yellow pom-pom-like blooms, exceptionally scented and attractive to pollinators. I have spotted wild beehives in them.

Inside Outside's experimental design theories are present in the irrigation system of the library garden. The two plant families are chosen for their tolerance to drought and are only watered sparsely for the first two years. The choice of plants and concave planters is a considered step towards the goal of gradually establishing a self-watering system, where irrigation is not required. The Two Family Tales Garden is an opportunity to study the potential of two specific plant species and one system of water management that is alien to the maintenance workers, accustomed to copiously watering thirsty "immigrant" plants. It is another example of an urbanised local botany that also serves as a place of research, complementing and advancing the overall landscaping approach of Education City – like Inside Outside's Water Recipe Garden around the QFHQ building.

Inside Outside has created a living experiment that raises questions and requires patience and observation. Not only students of botanical environment programs in Qatar but also the public, residents and employees

[12]

[13]

are invited to study and analyse the garden as it develops.

The contextual architecture in Education City has proven a laudable alternative to conventional construction. Education City has now gone a step further by fostering experimental alternatives to garden design that are better suited to the climate, culture and context of Qatar. This could prove a much-needed move towards mitigating the depletion of Qatar's groundwater and slowing the steadily growing demand for desalinated water, caused in part by non-native landscaping. Measuring and analysing the successes and failures of the two gardens created by Inside Outside is a fruitful opportunity to develop more effective measures.

Ultimately, the goal would be to promote garden design of this kind among the resident population and to revive the time-honoured practices of the local inhabitants. Ideally, the gardens at Education City should be perceived not as completed projects, but as works in progress, for study, improvement and potential future implementation.

[14]

[15]

[15] Infrared imagery of the Water Recipe Garden, Education City, 2022

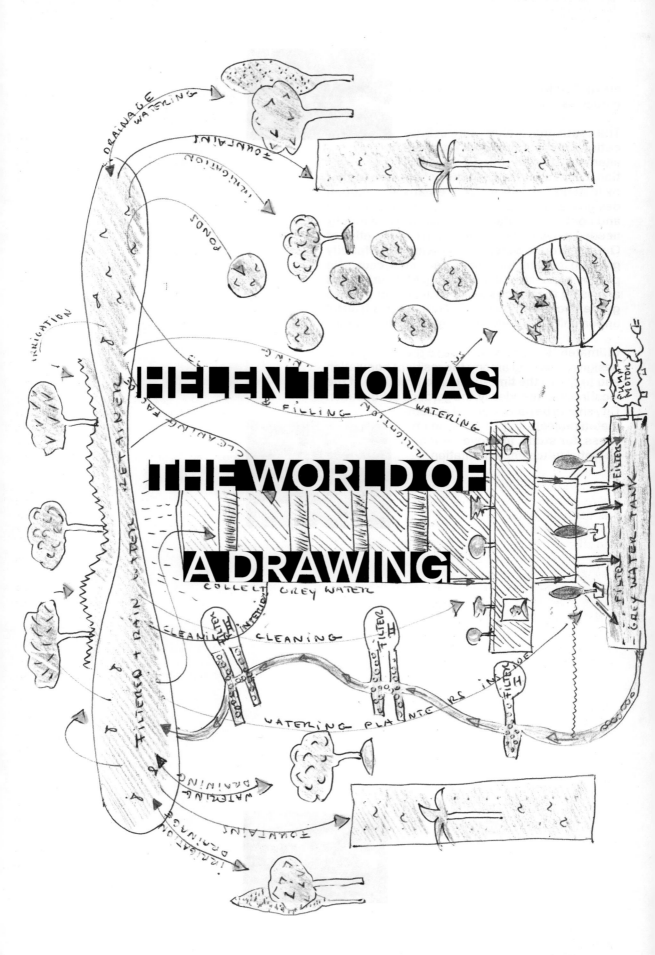

HELEN THOMAS

THE WORLD OF

A DRAWING

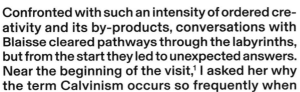

[1]

I never saw the studio of Petra Blaisse that she had left behind, although I had heard a lot about its atmosphere and character, much of which seemed to have been translated in her new place. There, downstairs, the walls of the workroom are lined with drawings and fabrics, printouts and photographs. A cutting table fills the space next door, surrounded by shelves of swatches, samples and overflowing haberdashery in abundant order, which finds its counterpart upstairs in a library densely stacked with archive boxes and books, adjacent to Blaisse's own glass-walled office. In front of the vast windows and even hanging from special frames on wheels are experiments and prototypes for multi-layered textile planes – curtains, moving walls and screens; removable clothing for the buildings that the finished pieces will one day inhabit. In the work of Blaisse, many of these objects could be construed as drawings in some form or another.

Confronted with such an intensity of ordered creativity and its by-products, conversations with Blaisse cleared pathways through the labyrinths, but from the start they led to unexpected answers. Near the beginning of the visit,[1] I asked her why the term Calvinism occurs so frequently when Dutch designers and artists talk about their cultural background. Blaisse herself has mentioned it in previous interviews with other people, in relation to sobriety, modesty and a strong work ethic.[2] She began to tell me, in an ironic way, about her love of libraries and categories, and then suddenly stopped. "Actually, I was brought up Catholic," she said.

[3]

Her one step remove from the intellectualised cultural production of her peers transforms their world into a Platonic cave for her to rifle. In response to this setting, Blaisse has her own intuitions that draw from life within the different European homelands of her childhood – England, Portugal, Austria, Sweden and finally the Netherlands. Lifting large sheets from a plan chest downstairs, we came across a number of her handmade collages from the '80s and '90s. [FIG. 1] In the distance is Hong Kong's colourful waterfront.

Bound to it by a turquoise field, the foreground is dominated by the cut edges of a black-and-white reproduction of a rocky promontory. This embraces an image of Álvaro Siza's tidal swimming pools of Leiça de Palmeira at the western edge of Europe. "I remember swimming there as a child," Blaisse told me.

The overlapping of motifs from different times and places occurs frequently in Inside Outside's work, sometimes stemming from what they call scale studies in the studio. An archive box from the upstairs library revealed delicate leaves of preparatory drawings for their designs for the four gardens of the Shenzhen Stock Exchange, an OMA project completed in 2013. One of the now-planted landscapes is laid over the roof scape of a rectangular podium around the tower, raised high above the ground. A square shape on an early sketch plan shows the location of the tower at the centre of the garden, whose detailed layout as it rises upwards is a ghostly presence beneath a layer of drafting paper [FIG. 2]. The skein of fine lines traced over this surface reveals an intricate pattern that defines a strategy for the planting, clearings and pathways of this communal place. Scattered with clear intention across the pink-brown ground, small irregular fields of green, pale blue and teal are coded to mark the territories of deep perimeter hedges, beds of grasses and trimmed shrubs. Their shapes recall the trefoil outlines of medieval motifs, and from somewhere deep within the archive box a colour photocopy of a page from a book emerged to explain this design. "That pattern came from a book that a friend gave me for my birthday," said Blaisse, and so we lifted the volume down from the top shelf in her office. Leafing through a rare and fragile early French edition of Owen Jones's *The Grammar of Ornament,* the page soon turned up, labelled "Middle Ages I."

Edges are tended to in Blaisse's work, and the drawings always have a keen sense of the frame – sometimes it is deliberately acknowledged, often it is transgressed. In the landscape designs, the edge permits a transition

[4]

from one state to another. The most obvious is the boundary of ownership, but the effective transitions are more atmospheric, and concerned with the modification, but also exploitation, of often harsh external conditions. In the case of the Shenzhen Stock Exchange Podium Garden, there is the obvious danger of a large drop, but its unnatural presence also has to be addressed. The informal blue-pen and coloured-pencil sketch section of the Stock Exchange [FIG. 3] shows her proposal for the recycling of rain and grey water for irrigation. This magic-realist image shows the filtered rainwater reservoir as a wooded island cloud floating above the tower; small ponds and trees rain down around it, connected together by labelled arrows and wriggling pipes. Again, a medieval worldview is evoked [FIG. 4], one that precedes and is unfettered by the requirements of perspective to show the mathematical relationships between objects. These hand-made drawings are the opposite of a BIM model, although their intention is prosaic and practical – to describe effectively and clearly the systems of plumbing and the economies of supply and demand within a large and complex compound of buildings.

RECEPES/RECIPES

"I am not an artist, although I started art school," says Blaisse. "That way of being, the work coming out of the individual ego, is not how I am. I don't work alone, I collaborate." Blaisse's recipes[3] are evidence of how this communal labour plays out. They are made to communicate with collaborators, but also with an outside audience; the stage at which the drawing is made in the design process decides its primary role. The first recipe, for example [FIG. 13], was invented in retrospect to explain and summarise an experimental process, one that had involved the many questions and conversations, false starts and blind alleys of such a venture. At the bottom of the page, ex-voto style, a note mentions a recipient and identifies the maker of the drawing – Blaisse – who is also its narrator.

Blaisse's storytelling presence in the recipe is essential, and in this way her will permeates the design but also the process of making, while at the same time allowing for inventive dialogue and interpretation. The consecutive scenes depicted in the recipes are uninhabited: there is no one carrying out the tasks; the imagination of the viewer can transcend the picture plane to place them right there, in an active role among the arrows and the sewing machines, scissors and other tools. Instead of people, the elements of production become the characters in the story – the glue pot and the ink pot vie with each other for a job, the floating sheets of foil and cloth swoop around like magic carpets.

The technique of the drawing creates uniformity – the line width is always the same, a single pen is used to make the recipe and annotate it. This establishes a non-hierarchical clarity; each moment of the process being described is as important as the next. The drawing communicates the order of things, but it also gives a strong sense of their nature and character. In the Dance Theater Curtain recipe this includes the impromptu specification at the top right hand corner, and is evident in the details that Blaisse has chosen to draw – the short tufts of the "stiff mohairs" and the "flat hairs," for example, or the sketch-sections giving the sense of the thin cloth and the three-dimensional objects that have a corporeal weight, especially effective in the "metal pressing plate with circles sticking out." The energy of individual actions animates the story, often through an economical use of small marks: the hovering gold plastic foil glows, the effort of pressing and tearing off of the foil sheet is apparent.

A later group of seven drawings – "an original recepe" – provide instructions for seamsters assembling the two curtains for the VIP dressing rooms in the New York Prada Epicenter [FIGS. 5–12]. Although preceding the outcome and not summarising it, the same technique is used as in the earlier recipe. Characters such as the sewing machine, a busy little animal, the curtain like a jolly ghost and the rushing waterfall of cloth inhabit the pages alongside details of corners and complex seams. Again, Blaisse the narrator is present, supervising the production. From the swish of the first page to the popping cap of a beer bottle on the last, she is encouraging the reader through each step.

The process of cutting, folding and stitching unfolds over five pages in a practical and precise way, the quality and the order clearly explained. These are not architectural working documents drawn to scale; the dimensions and proportions are annotated in the manner of written instructions. Comparisons could be made with sewing patterns or flat-pack guidelines, but these are directives for making generic objects. A sewing

[5–12] Petra Blaisse, "How to go about
the 2 VIP curtains for the New York Prada
Clinic: an original recepe," sketches, 2001

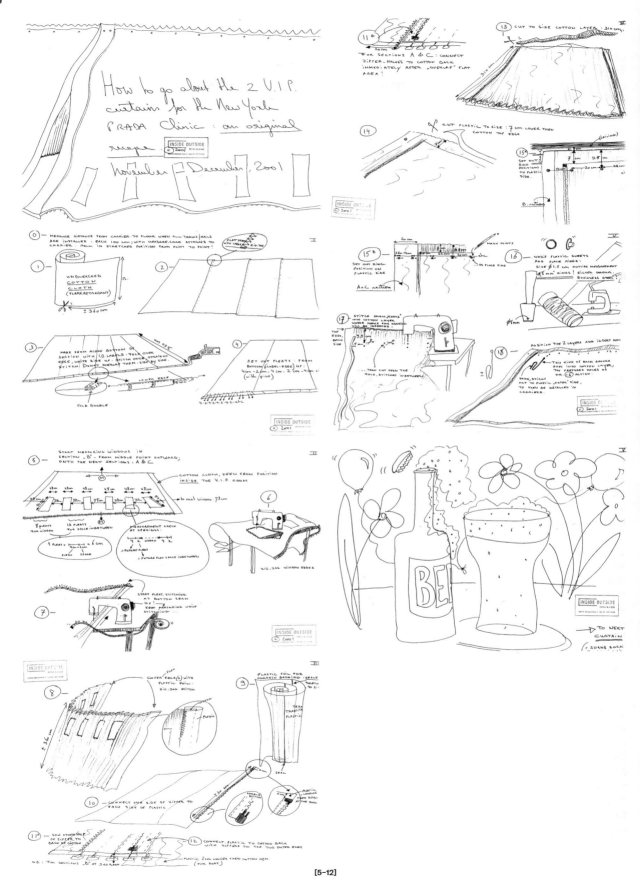

[13] Petra Blaisse, the first recipe drawing: *The Making of Dance Theater Curtain* (1987)

[14] Sol LeWitt, diagram for *Wall Drawing #459*, Asymmetrical pyramid with colour ink washes superimposed, first drawn 1985

70

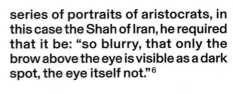

[13]

pattern comes with the arcs of different sizes to fit all body shapes overlapping each other at every seam. A flat-pack kit is devised to fit into almost any room. The Inside Outside recipes, on the other hand, describe how to make luxurious bespoke objects, custom- made for a specific time and site. Even though the drawing and its outcome persist in the world, the recipe's magic is spent; as an instruction it requires its outcome to be a fantasy, which cannot occur twice.

"Color ink wash
The apex is center. The background
is yellow, yellow, red, yellow. Three
sides.
1 – yellow, blue, yellow; 2 – red,
blue, gray (1:16); 3 – yellow, red,
gray, yellow
134 × 128" (335 × 320 cm)"[4]

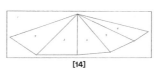

[14]

Sol LeWitt made drawings, called *Wall Drawings*, at single (but potentially consecutive) sites, completed by a hand usually not his own, but that of an assistant. This draftsperson followed a set of instructions composed of a diagram with written directions on how to make it [FIG. 14]. These specific instructions were followed within the context of more generic guidelines, such as "All drawings are on white walls unless otherwise indicated" and "Pencil lines are drawn with hard (8H or 9H) graphite."[5] As instructions, the diagrams and their notes are analogous to the Inside Outside recipes, but unlike the Blaisse curtains, the *Wall Drawings* can be sold and resold as works of art, and be reincarnated in a different place. Layers of white latex paint annul the superseded manifestation. Whether the identity of the work of art resides in the *Wall Drawing* on site or exists within the instructions was resolved by a certificate of authenticity. This included the diagram, written instructions and site and date of the first installation, and was signed by LeWitt, but which was a solution that did not allow for his death in 2007. Another illustration of the communication of concept made tangible, in which the source of authenticity is located, is that of Gerhard Richter's instructions to his printer, August Haseke. Directing remotely the offset prints of a

[15]

series of portraits of aristocrats, in this case the Shah of Iran, he required that it be: "so blurry, that only the brow above the eye is visible as a dark spot, the eye itself not."[6]

Another drawing describing an intervention into a single site is Gordon Matta-Clark's *Directive for Day's End Pier 52* (1975) [FIG. 15]. As a description of the nature of the work and the means to effect it – by cutting out portions of the walls and ceiling of a derelict warehouse on the Hudson River near Greenwich Village – the directive is similar to a Blaisse recipe, but far more spare in its communication, and also simply a diagram and not a story. The equivalent to the narrative element of Blaisse's drawings is enacted in the 23-minute long film that Matta-Clark and his team made of the process of selective demolition and reconfiguration of the warehouse.[7] The camera pans the existing structure before filming different people climbing, hanging, measuring and cutting, as the work comes into being. It shows the fact of the work and reveals its idea, but at no time does it dwell on the experience of the outcome. This has to be formed in the imagination of the viewer in response to the drawing, using what is implied in the film. The wielding of the tools, the action, is the artwork and not the outcome. In this way, the intention of the *Day's End Pier 52* film is different to those commissioned to show Blaisse's work, such as *Liquid Gold* (2012) by Frans Parthesius, which shows the Nederlands Dans Theater curtain. It revels in the sensuous quality of the finished product in action – its surfaces shown in detail and in movement as the curtain opens and closes, the folds like a glittering chorus line. Sound animates this movement – swishing, silence, clapping; and in another of Parthesius's films, *Bordeaux Revisited*, the noise of sliding panels, chirping birds and a gentle breeze as it disturbs the fluid surface of various curtains animate scenes of the house and its permeable boundaries. Human presence is incidental; it is the viewer outside the film to whom the experience is given.

The timing of Blaisse's recipes determines their character in different

[16]

[15] Gordon Matta-Clark, *Schematic for Day's End Pier 52* (1975), black felt-tip pen and graphite on paper, sheet: 19 × 25 cm, frame: 29 × 35 × 2.8 cm

[16] Petra Blaisse, fax concerning planters in the living room/5th Avenue, 2001

[17] Inside Outside/Petra Blaisse and Franco Giorgetta, Giardini di Porta Nuova: Parco "Biblioteca degli Alberi" Impianto di Irrigazione generale – 1° Fase. Plan, sections and specification, 1:500, 2013, print of CAD drawing, 594 × 841 mm

[18] Anonymous, fan-shaped radial muqarnas quarter vault, overlay drawing for Plate 15 of Topkapi Scroll, late fifteenth century. Un-inked radial grid lines of concentric quarter circles shown as black lines superimposed over the plate fifteenth scroll segment, 257 × 350 mm

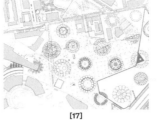

[17]

ways, and sometimes the drawing is made rapidly at a moment of negotiation. When this happens it is more a notation than a recipe, closer to the Matta-Clark drawing or a conventional architectural detail, but with a provisional role and quality. This is the case with the fax sent from the Inside Outside Studio in Amsterdam to Joshua Ramus at the OMA office in New York [FIG. 16]. The Tippex applied thickly onto the paper shows that the drawing was modified in the making, coming straight out of the imagination and not planned beforehand. Filling the lower two thirds of the sheet, the image splits into two horizontal zones, the lower one repeating and extending the upper to include both the inside and the outside. The scale is hard to read, and only a note in the top drawing gives a clue to the gigantic size of the planter and the space surrounding it, which shows that its frame is a "metal seat edge." More than the vertical lines depicting the plane of glass dividing the two sides, it is the whipped-up energy that beats against it that gives a sense of its presence. The reality of the planter remains enigmatic, but the atmosphere of the encounter between inside and outside is plain to see.

UNDERLYING GEOMETRIES

"the sleeves beneath were like a flowered tapestry spread against the evergreen pines" [8]

At first glance, the plan showing the *Impianto di Irrigazione generale*, or general irrigation system, of the Biblioteca degli Alberi [FIG. 17] – a new, rare garden park in the Garibaldi-Repubblica district on the borders of Milan's historic centre – is both straightforward and mystifying. In other words, it is a typical architectural production drawing whose authorship is revealed in the official stamps and signatures of Petra Blaisse, the designer, and Franco Giorgetta, the local architect, but the identities of those who made it are hidden in the detail. This same thicket hides a secret world of unexplained possibilities that the hard, precise lines of the CAD drawing seek to clarify.

With time, motivation and knowledge of the codes and conventions of architectural drawing, uncovering their intentions is not too hard. Different parts of the sheet reveal distinct aspects and kinds of information. A column on the left-hand side is half-filled with words and numbers. These are lists of quantities – pipe sizes, numbers of irrigation points but also shrubs and trees, lengths of water arcs and the identity of sector coordinates. Alongside are types of planted field, or Irregular Fields [9] – wild meadows, smooth lawns and woody copses – which, unlike the quantified elements, resist control, except in their naming. The imaginative realm between the name and the potential reality is vast; the big plan in the middle makes a bridge.

[18]

Constructed in many layers within a computer file, the drawing shown here is only one version from a vast range of possibilities, each one of which reveals a different aspect of the garden's manufacture. Just a few layers have been activated in this plan to show the irrigation scheme for the Circular Forests that are dispersed over the park, and the drawing's subjects are delineated in colours – blue, red, orange, green and yellow. These are coded to represent specific elements, such as the trunk and the canopy extent of each tree, the network of water pipes, and the location and reach of sprinklers, the symbols of which are explained in a caption in the right-hand column. Beneath the vibrant geometrical patterns made by the trees and pipes, a ghostly drawing defines the physical context. Grey shapes represent the buildings around the edge, and the pale criss-crossing pathways that link them across the open ground are embroidered with the fine black lines of ramps and steps that provide clues to the complex layering of the park's surface.

[19]

"their long, flowing sleeves brought the scent of plum blossoms in from the veranda, and as always it took on a kind of mysterious depth as it drifted past" [10]

The layering of the drawing functions metaphorically too, evoking the strata of the park's artificial ground, but

[20]

[19] Anonymous, Plate 15 of Topkapi Scroll, late fifteenth century, red and black ink on paper

[20] Inside Outside/Petra Blaisse, Design Frame and (Underground) Infrastructure plan, CAD Drawing, 2011

[21] Inside Outside/Petra Blaisse, Site Sections from competition entry, CAD Drawing, 2003–2004

[22] Petra Blaisse, sketch plan of a Circular Forest (Acer Griseum), pen and coloured pencil on paper, 2013.

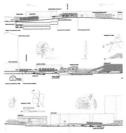

[21]

also the interdependent geometrical systems that the plan reveals. Like the late medieval patterns of the *Topkapi Scroll* from Iran, the visible geometry is the product of an intimate juxtaposition with a hidden design, the Islamic equivalent of which was called a *dead drawing*.[11] This was composed of un-inked, incised construction lines. The visible pattern emerged from their intersection points, in that the lines connecting them defined the boundaries of its dart- and star-shaped and polygonal fields. This can been seen in the examples shown in [FIG. 18], the dead drawing, where the incised lines are shown in black, and [FIG. 19], the resultant pattern. Unlike the design from the *Topkapi Scroll* shown here, however, the visible geometry of the park's surface reproduces the diverse morphology of the living city surrounding it, and not the ideal spatial continuum of Islamic art. An irregular grid of overlapping pathways connects surrounding governmental, residential and commercial centres with two metro stations and the Porta Garibaldi train station, for example. The organisation of the pathways creates the Irregular Fields,[12] with which the Circular Forests engage in different ways – some are located in the middle of a field, but most often they embrace a junction of paths. The composition of the Circular Forests – both as an irregular grouping, but also in the controlled geometry of concentric circles that organises each individual copse – maintains an intimate relationship with a hidden equivalent of the "dead drawing." In the *Impianto di Irrigazione generale* this is the fine network of blue lines showing the routes of water pipes and the arc circumferences of sprinklers. These too are concealed, but physically rather than conceptually – they still exist below the ground's surface, and become apparent at certain times of the day, when water sprays over the fields and pathways.

"Wisteria is like the sleeve of a maiden, Lovelier when someone cares for it"[13]

Although plants predominate over the surface of the park, the ground into which their roots penetrate is far from natural. In addition to the network of water pipes and sprinklers, the earth contains a myriad of different kinds of conduits that serve the surrounding city. In another site plan [FIG. 20], this time showing the underground transport tunnels winding their way in giant arabesques below the park, the presence of the Circular Forests is reduced to thin black lines, and the ramped paths between them in an even fainter grey. In the sections through the site [FIG. 21], the interface between the open-air realm of human occupation and the constructed ground beneath is delineated as a thick red line.

Humans occupy this underground realm too – there are car parks, train tunnels, metro stations; there is room for bridges, elevated platforms for buildings and accommodation for canals.[14] In the sections, vividly coloured trees balance on top of this line; they have trunks and crowns, but no roots. Fine drawings of selected tree species depict their skeletons and shapes, the nature of their fruits and flowers, and hand-written notes with their names and other details. The secrets of underground life are not included in these drawings – the roots and the huge systems of mycorrhizal fungi that connect the trees together underground, and through which they communicate.[15] These are the non-built, uncontrolled elements of the terrain that have to work around the apparatus of the city; their presence is unseen and they cannot be designed, and so no drawing needs to show them.

The forests of the park are wholly idealised, their beauty is as artificial as that of a neo-classical temple, or the perfect idea of nature embodied in the *Topkapi Scroll*. Belonging to this idealised world, a new Enlightenment, is the overt system of naming and taxonomical inclination of this Library of Trees. This is manifest in various ways – as drawings made onto the ground as lists of botanical names, for example, and in the self-contained concentric groves of trees, each of which is composed of a single species.

"Narrow these sleeves, now lodging for the moonlight.
Would they might keep a light which I do not tire of."[16]

[22]

[23]

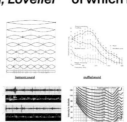

[24]

[23] Victor Vasarely, *Supernovae*, 1959–61, oil paint on canvas, 2419 × 1524 mm, Tate Modern, London

[24] Inside Outside, sample sheet: Sound Visualisation Techniques, 2018

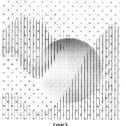

[25]

Despite the efficient practicality of the drawings, the idealised quality of the park's beauty, and the materialist classification of its parts, the hidden and spontaneous part of the garden is important to Blaisse. She remembers that, as a child, she "loved sleeping outdoors, wide awake, listening to the sounds and watching snails, night owls and bats by moon- or torchlight." Some of this feeling is captured in the hand-drawn plan and legend for one of the Circular Forests [FIG. 22] – Acer Griseum – which shows the relationship of the trees to covering of the ground. Each tree has its own character, evident in the curly circumference of its crown, as has each layer of the concentric circles in the plan, which are labelled Field A, Field B and Field C and accompanied by delicate and evocative symbols. The earth and moss of the muddy ground seeps over the path that cuts through to one side, making dirty streaks on its pristine surface. These little clues intimate a conviction that Blaisse has already articulated: "It has now become clear," she said, "that it is necessary for us to reconsider the invisible, the subconscious, the action–reaction: the sheer biology of things."[17]

BETWEEN INSIDE OUTSIDE

"The train came out of the long tunnel into the snow country."[18]

"Landscape is ultimately uncontrollable, so you need to start with a strong state, a graphic presence. For me, Op-Art reminds of contour lines, and that is a good beginning," explained Blaisse. Looking at *Supernovae* by Vasarely [FIG. 23], for example, the viewer is invited to explore the relationship between perception and movement. As the painting is viewed from different positions, the patterns alter and the separate points appear to ebb and flow, mimicking the pulsing luminosity of supernova stars. The relationship between pattern and movement has formed the basis of a recent Inside Outside art implementation project called "Intercity New Generation," commissioned by the Netherlands Railway. Proposals for a series of drawings made onto the surfaces of specific sites within a new fleet of trains – glass screens, lavatory enclosures, sliding doors and various other thresholds – use techniques like ceramic print and lenticular glass profiles to create visual effects that represent and exploit both the interior landscape and that through which the train passes. The result, a conflation of inside and outside, assimilates the graphic and the sensual aspects of Inside Outside's work played out over time.

"Visualisation techniques differ, from simple simulation or oscilloscope display to more elaborate ones with a plurality of composed effects."[19]

[26]

Taking different conventions of representing sound [FIG. 24], the Inside Outside team developed a visual language that could be interpreted to relate to specific situations. These had already been organised into spatial, sound-defined categories, such as "Meet and Greet," "Work and Quiet" and "Silence." The proposal for *Circular and Wave Sound Combination* [FIG. 25] overlays techniques of image-making; the ridges of the glass with the optical effects of applied tones at different scales occurs on the screens at the boundary between "Work and Quiet" and "Silence." Two systems collide; the wave-like pattern that evokes a mountain landscape at a large scale from "Work and Quiet" underlies a scattering of moon-like elements that are used to conjure the floating daydreams of "Silence."

Photographic images cover the surfaces of enclosed spaces within the train. Their interiors are Dutch landscapes, while the walls facing into the circulation spaces present as curtains replicated from previous projects – the Dance Theater Curtain, for example, and one from the Rothschild Bank in London, now pressed flat into static two dimensions. It is not possible to pass through these rigid planes by brushing past a fold of fabric, so a hard threshold, which Blaisse has chosen to accentuate and celebrate, is required.

The doorway [FIG. 26], with its frame, is a place of confrontation, meeting, transgression, and invitation that curtains with their soft negation of rigid thresholds circumvent. The tangible boundary between inside and outside is hard to ignore. This brings to mind Simon Schama's reflections on inside outside, to which a chapter in his book *The Embarrassment of Riches: An Interpretation of Dutch Culture in the Golden Age* (1987) is devoted. In his discussion, the social realm is introduced, and with it the possibility that the name "Inside Outside" transcends the spatial and atmospheric divergence of the interior and the garden to evoke a Dutch means of dealing with the confrontation of different social as well as physical realms.

Schama chooses a series of paintings through which to discuss the theme. These depict the opened front doors of *burgerlijk* dwellings that explore the delicate quality of that boundary between the street and the *voorhuis*. On either side and sometimes transgressing the doorstep are the women of the house and the vendors and travelling musicians of the street. Here Schama says, "Insiders and outsiders, then, are united within the picture frame but divided by the domestic threshold. . . . That distinction between home and world, between safety within and unknowns without, is sharply emphasised by the prominence of the door frame."[20] He selects another painting, Jan van der Heyden's *An Architectural Fantasy*, ca. 1670, to examine the nature of this boundary further, for seeing what distinguishes insiders from outsiders is one way of defining the limiting perimeter of the culture itself. The fantasy is in the distance – a grand Palladian villa, but in the foreground, "at the estate gateway – the very boundary between aristocratic fantasy and common reality – a beggar woman stands in confronting accusation. But the reaction of the embarrassed patrician is to hesitate before two equally reprehensible actions: indifference before the claims of the poor, and their indiscriminate (as distinct from institutionalised) relief."[21]

Coming full circle, the question of Calvinism recurs. Addressing a period of Dutch culture several centuries later than Schama's history, Ed Soja reports on his time spent in Amsterdam during 1990. A mixture of gentrification and dishevelled potential, which at that time was being enjoyed by the squatter movement, defined the character of the Centrum where he lived. "From my vantage point on Spuitstraat a moving picture of contemporary life in the vital centre of Amsterdam visually unfolded, opening my eyes to much more than I ever expected to see. The view from the window affirmed what I continue to believe is the most extraordinary quality of this city, its unheralded achievement of highly regulated urban anarchism, another of those creative paradoxes like 'repressive tolerance,' 'flexible inflexibility,' 'squatter-renters' and indeed the 'strangely familiar' that two-sidedly filter through the geohistory of Amsterdam."[22] Together, Schama and Soja confirm what Blaisse's work implies: that boundaries – between landscapes, people, expectations, rooms and perspectives – are inescapable. In order to be transgressed, whether socially, spatially, or conceptually, they must first be acknowledged, and in this sense they are not fixed but ephemeral situations whose conditions can alter in the most unexpected ways.

1   All the quotes from Petra Blaisse, unless otherwise stated, come from conversations with the author during a visit to the Inside Outside Studio, 9–10 May 2019.

2   See, for example, the dutchDesign infield interview with Blaisse from 2011: available at http://2011.sfudutchdesign.ca/2011/petra-blaisse (2:40 min and 5:05 min).

3   This name occurs with two different spellings – sometimes the drawing is called a Recepe, sometimes a Recipe. This type of drawing has developed within the working process of the Inside Outside Studio, and is now more often drafted by curtain designer Peter Niessen.

4   *Sol LeWitt Wall Drawing* (Bern: Kunsthalle Bern, 1992), p. 126. The caption also details who it was first drawn by (Andrea Marescalchi, Luigi Morrone, Anthony Sansotta), and where it was first installed (Galleria Mario Pieroni, Rome, Italy, December 1985).

5   Ibid., p. 215.

6   Caption for *Elisabeth I, 1966* in the exhibition notes for *Gerhard Richter. Editionen, Entwürfe, Briefe, Materialien* 29 June – 22 September 2019, Staatliche Kunstsammlungen Dresden. In addition to stipulating the quality of the blurring of the image, to be judged subjectively, Richter also "formulated precise specifications for the size of the print ('50 × 50 is the minimum?')."

7   See http://ubu.com/film/gmc_day send.html or https://www.youtube.com/watch?v=N91f03XDOJw.

8   Murasaki Shikibu, *The Tale of Genji* (translated by Edward G. Seidensticker, 1921), https://ebooks.adelaide.edu.au/m/murasaki-shikibu/tale-of-genji/index.html, chapter 35 "New Herbs," n.p.

9   These terms for the elements in the drawing – Irregular Fields, Circular Forests, Library of Trees – are taken from a magazine produced in the Inside Outside Studio, 2018, and were invented for and perpetuate from the original competition design in 1992.

10   Murasaki, *The Tale of Genji*, chapter 42, "His Perfumed Highness."

11   Ibid., p. 10. Located in the Topkapi Palace Museum Library, the *Topkapi Scroll* is a collection of workshop drawings and patterns for wall surfaces and vaults made as instructional documents. It is 29.5 m long and 33–34 cm high, and contains 114 drawings pasted together at an unknown date (see p. 29). Necipoğlu points out in her preface (p. ix) that "the scroll's geometric language parallels that of late Gothic architectural drawings, a parallel informed by a shared late antique cultural heritage that often engendered similar design methods and aesthetic sensibilities."

12   The Irregular Fields themselves contain a variety of geometrical patterns that belong to a different layer of the drawing, not shown here. Sometimes these ripple out concentrically from the Forest Circles to fill the fields, with the disruptions of their overlapping spheres creating further pattern structures on the ground.

13   Murasaki, *The Tale of Genji*, chapter 33, "Wisteria Leaves."

14   In the project description for the Giardini di Porta Nuova, Petra Blaisse describes how "the train tunnel underneath the park creates a long topographical hump that divides the park in two." Petra Blaisse, Inside Outside, Basel: Birkhäuser, 2007, p. 128.

15   Various sources suggest that these are also the means by which trees communicate with each other – by means of chemical and electrical signals, in addition to using airborne scents. See, Colin Tudge, *The Secret Life of Trees* (London: Penguin, 2005) especially pp. 259–261, the discussion on secondary metabolites p. 267, and the sharing of airborne hormones on p. 272. Peter Wohlleben, *The Hidden Life of Trees* (London: Harper Collins, 2017; first published in German, 2015), especially the chapter "United We Stand, Divided We Fall" pp. 49–55, which discusses the role of fungi.

16   Murasaki, *The Tale of Genji*, chapter 12, "Suma."

17   Petra Blaisse, "The Instinctive Sense of Space and Boundary" in *Energies, New Material Boundaries: Architectural Design*, May / June 2009, p. 97.

18   Yasunari Kawabata, the first line of *The Snow Country* (London: Penguin, 2011, translated by Edward G. Seidensticker, first published 1937), p. 1.

19   These are the accompanying notes for *Sound Visualisation Techniques* and *Circular and Wave Sound Combination* in Inside Outside's project booklet: *InterCity New Generation*, August 2018, p. 5.

20   Simon Schama, "Inside, Outside" in *The Embarrassment of Riches: An Interpretation of Dutch Culture in the Golden Age* (London: Collins, 1987), p. 570.

21   Ibid., p. 573.

22   Ed Soja, "The Stimulus of a little Confusion" in *Strangely Familiar* (London: Routledge, 1996), p. 30.

JACK SELF

CHANGE LIFE!

CHANGE SOCIETY!

Over the last decade, European interior design has become aspirationally normative and increasingly conservative. People seem to want domestic and public spaces that are either generic, familiar, "traditional," or a combination – which is to say, there is a trend towards the predictable, non-confrontational and uncontroversial. Such conventionalism is both aesthetic and conceptual, and it (perhaps predictably) mirrors a period of social regression and economic stagnation across the continent. This trend is a product of our era's dominant paradigm, an obsession with the elimination and management of risk in all its forms. Our economies are fuelled by the sale of future labour (the very definition of debt), which means that tomorrow must not deviate substantially from yesterday. No event can be allowed to be unanticipated, a paradigm that is directly linked to this popular aversion to all things provocative or challenging. Of course, the mask has slipped several times. There is an almost black humour to the paradox of a continent trying to de-risk its interiors at the very same time it has allowed risk to balloon existentially in our relationship with the natural world.

Within this context, the work of Petra Blaisse appears increasingly timely, relevant and urgent – standing in clear opposition to any idea of comfortable predictability. Blaisse's designs are startling, indefinable and progressive. But they also contain their own contradiction; underpinning a sense of artistic virtuosity is a painstaking precision, a negotiation between an extreme open-endedness of use and a highly calculated concept of design.

"I am compelled by contradiction," Blaisse says. "I might intend to create a surprise, or evoke physical discomfort. But in every case, my aim is to encourage people to see "normal' life in a different way, and so to expose normality as a construction … Public situational awareness tends to be quite low, but contradiction can wake them from their reveries. Whether moving through a landscape or an interior, most people ignore the design of what is around them. Everything blends into a smooth background. The point is to jolt that smoothness … I aim to challenge by contradiction."

At the core of Blaisse's work is a profound interrogation of everyday life, and a critique of how social dynamics are formed and perform in the built environment. In this sense, one entry point to Blaisse's oeuvre might be through Henri Lefebvre. He argued that ideology does not exist in the abstract, but is firmly embedded within human objects and our relations to them. Concepts like nationality, family, or individuality do not exist outside the material world, but rather inside reality. To sustain these relations requires a constant performance of faith. By means of example, Lefebvre outlines how capitalism is inseparable from its financial artefacts, which is to say money. Accordingly, if you could intervene at the precise moment that a particular coin is exchanged by two people for goods or services, and convince those people that the coin was in fact worthless, you would fatally weaken the entire underpinning of capitalism.

To sustain any ideology requires the production of its supporting objects, spaces and procedures. And precisely by producing these things, their very existence aids their reproduction. This is the danger of conservatism – a regressive feedback loop that closes off alternative visions of reality. From within the network of material culture, the particular ideology will increasingly appear like "common sense," although it is nothing of the kind. To escape from normality, Lefebvre instructs us in *The Production of Space* to: "Change life! Change society! Ideas completely lose their meaning [if they do not have] an appropriate space."

All designers are implicated in sustaining normality, since they either directly or indirectly shape the fabrication of reality. This is the source of their agency, but also their weakness; mostly, the dominant social class (manifest through the client) instrumentalises designers to serve and perpetuate their particular ideology. An intelligent designer – especially one committed to socially progressive ideals – will not be capable of uncritically executing the instructions of the dominant social class. But nor can they reject the values of their client outright – no matter how blindly they might accept the assumptions of their ruling paradigm – as it will most likely cause the designer to lose the project. Resisting the brutality of "common sense," and so finding ways to reshape normality, thus demands great sensitivity.

This type of counter-normal design is a subversive act, and one that hides in plain sight. It must exist without need for its own justification. It cannot be speculation, but fact – in the literal sense of *factum* (a thing that self-evidently exists). The power of Blaisse's work lies in its directness, employing very real material devices to create unexpected and fluid spatial conditions. These devices or elements produce new types of relationships between beings and objects in time, which in turn make possible alternative social ideologies.

Modernism correctly understood that the role of design in the production of space is causative: any intentional input creates a measurable output. Indeed, groups like CIAM were founded on ideological principles of social engineering, and specific spatial forms were developed whose express intention was to produce transformative social outcomes. Modernists believed they could use design to improve human morality and influence the basic structures of power. Pattern books, manifestos, manuals and standardised models – from Le Corbusier and Schütte-Lihotzky to Herzberger, Christopher Alexander or Neufert – were all driven by functionalist precepts. The fatal mistake of modernism was thinking that the production of space is predictable and repeatable, and that the effects of their interventions were non-volitional. In reality, the results of design are highly contingent on factors far beyond the designer's control.

Petra Blaisse departs from the exact opposite assumption of the modernists: design should avoid prescriptive logic. "You cannot foresee how people will occupy and use a space," she says, "and to some extent, as designers, we should not try." This absence of moralism is important for the sense of inclusivity and acceptance that Inside Outside tries to foster in their work. Open-ended spatiotemporal designs do not prejudge the values of their inhabitants – which in itself is an important liberal value (although this principle can be a source of some difficulty when it collides with illiberal or orthodox societies). Blaisse's "recipes" are therefore wholly unlike those of the modernist tradition: "Recipes are not dictatorial instructions, they are gestures – they set out a direction, or a general ambition. They might be quite clear about a method, but they do not force an outcome. The recipes of Inside Outside acknowledge that design is dependent on human interaction, including how a textile, a space or a landscape is being maintained over time."

By embracing the relationship between space and power relations as non-linear, it no longer becomes necessary to develop templates driven to produce certain relationships. Rather, what we see in so many of Blaisse's projects – including the Forum at Tillburg's LocHal, Harvard's Piper Auditorium or Maggie's Centre in Oldham – is the concentration of intention within the architecture of the curtain itself. Certainly, the curtain is used as a way to frame space for programmatic purposes, and so it strongly shapes the parameters of possible use. However, the Inside Outside curtain is also a uniquely technical object, pushed to unprecedented levels of precision. It is a kind of self-contained architecture, and its details are carefully engineered to produce a scope of environmental effects. Its contingencies are not only spatiotemporal, but also psychological, emotional, cultural, auditory and haptic.

For example, the selection of a wheeled, hooked or ball-bearing track significantly influences the curtain's sound, and thus the scope of emotional responses from its subjects. Does it resemble a sudden rush of rain or downpour, the shuffling of mah-jong tiles or the gliding stealth of a cloaked assassin? By focusing design into the control of these technical aspects, Blaisse evokes intentional, but not prescriptive, responses. As she says herself: "I want to challenge every aspect of its design. Why should a curtain go up and down or from side-to-side? What speed should it have and what consequence does this have on the airflow of the room? What is the visual effect of the person pushing and pulling, and the choreography of its use? Or if it is motorised, how do we perceive its movement, perhaps as magic or somehow as the figure of a passing body? What is the significance of the trajectory and shape of the track? Does the curtain assume a dramatic character or is it subtle, elegant, even shy – a character that hardly wants to be there? What is behind the curtain and what is inside it?" Blaisse's textiles contain their own instructions, as invitations to generate ever-shifting conditions. While finite objects, they also represent a time-released form which is never finished but nearly infinitely adaptable. Significantly, they remain constantly open to interpretation and appropriation by their occupants.

What Blaisse referred to above as "gestures" could be understood as pointing towards a very different concept of how space is formed. Amongst the best examples of this corporeal space is the Rotterdam Kunsthal. The project includes an insulating curtain for an auditorium space. It is a technically complex object, with spiral rails set flush and cast in-situ into the concrete slab ceiling. The curtain is wired to include speakers so that, when extended, it functions as a surround-sound environment.

Due to the building envelope, it is obliged to follow the sloping window of the auditorium, but this hasn't constrained its expressive qualities. "It is not placed between the spectators and the stage or as a curtain lining the glass facade, but it rolls itself out into the space to create a separate, rounded auditorium – independent of the given architectural form." When it is closed, the spiral assumes the form of a taut body, resembling a sculptural evening gown.

The Rotterdam Kunsthal curtain performs similarly to those in the Prada New York Epicentre, where a sock-like column of fabric is mounted on motorised rails that rove the store. In both cases, the cloth has no body to carry it. As Blaisse says: "It is not that the curtain represents the body. It is not metaphorical. Its presence replaces the body and is an extension of it." For Inside Outside, the production of space is closely tied to physicality. And like the body, it is not infinitely flexible or adaptable; there is no universal model for humans. Nonetheless, every instance falls within a defined field of parameters. The body has a fixed form and restricted possibilities for acting: there are limitations to the scope of its movement (determined by the structure of the bones, organs, tissue and muscles) and its operational range (associated with metabolism, thermal comfort and exertion). In spite of these very real limitations, the body has nearly infinite possibility for gesture: the precision of its form in fact enhances its applications, and does not decrease them. There are endless nuances of physical movements, each of which is attached to a semiotic carrier, cultural signifiers, modes of communication, vague associations, connotations and allusions. These are contingent on culture, language, subjectivity, community. The ideal state for this corporeal space exists at the boundary of abstraction. It must both communicate certain universal relationships with space, while remaining sufficiently non-realistic. This is perhaps what Blaisse means when she says the curtain is not representational.

If a layperson only knows one thing about contemporary architecture, there is a good chance it will be the principal of "inside-outside flow." This mysterious notion appears to be a folk distillation of modernism since it does not originate from within the architectural discipline itself. Inside-outside flow values the dissolution of a building's envelope, the "blurring" of its thresholds, and often refers to any extensive use of glass in a warmer climate. For Blaisse, the name Inside Outside quite simply describes the scope of her work: she designs interiors and landscapes. And yet, unlike "flow," Blaisse is not at all concerned with resolving dichotomies. It would be a mistake to think that her use of textile, transparency and materiality are somehow linked to concepts of unification. Her ambition is not to reconcile the conflict between interior and exterior. Quite the opposite: inside and outside are stable realms with their own discrete qualities. Blaisse's design strategy frequently repurposes these specific qualities in each other's service, through juxtaposition and estrangement.

We can understand the interior as the human environment *par excellence*, and the only realm in which we can simulate conditions of absolute control. Interiors are defined by what they exclude, or protect their inhabitants from – they are a sign of retreat and shelter. The objects they contain always carry a double sense, first as real object and second as symbolic object. This duplicity stems from the role of interior objects in producing the space of everyday life. The life of interiors is therefore linear and entropic, as soon as they are finished they begin to decay. The continued existence of an interior depends on its maintenance, which is the endless process of concealing the reality of its decomposition. When Blaisse transfers aspects of the inside into the outside, she is projecting notions of control, security, care, attention and identity onto a realm that is intrinsically wild and chaotic.

The term outside necessarily implies a relation with an interior, and this is quite different from the idea of "landscape," which has no opposite. Blaisse's use of outside is defined by cyclical renewal, an outside that does not fear decay since it contains its own creation and destruction. Most of all, this outside is robust – every organism working to thrive in concert with its ecosystem. When Blaisse brings the outside into the inside, she harnesses durability, hardiness, indeterminacy and vast scale. In both instances, the effect is détournement. Explaining the difference, Blaisse says: "You expect that textiles degrade. The beauty of a textile is that it can be finished, you are able to see the work as you intended it. You witness it as an author, and you're happy. But from that moment, it slowly disintegrates, it will wear, it will get dirty, be mistreated and perhaps eventually restored. With landscape and the outside…of course, you work towards a vision, but you cannot control it, not entirely. You plant, and seed, and hope that maintenance will shape it. But the vision you have today exists fifty years or a hundred years into the future, by which time we, the creators, can no longer witness its development."

When the studio appropriates a material used for external application and puts it into the interior, the effect is one of détournement. "For example, in an interior project we might work with sailboat linen, scaffolding mesh, woven nylon from sports or agriculture or camouflage netting. When you change the context, you give a material or object a whole new life," she has said. "I might try to achieve contradiction in another way. When you weave a cheap material in a complex, precise manner, you create unique effects that cannot be purchased. In an era of standardised architectural products, you are demonstrating the value of labour and time of manufacture."

In practice, this process of challenging normality through contradiction assumes many forms, not only related to the qualities of the textile itself. In OMA's Maison Bordeaux, for example, we see a bathroom dematerialised into a loose pink curtain, an open spiral that is at once translucent and satin. In the master bedroom, an identical textile stretches the length of the facade, confusing the boundary of its bathroom altogether – the interior curtain wall is indistinguishable from that parallel to the exterior windows. The uncanny quality of the space comes from this ambiguity, as well as the overturning of expectation. The bathroom is one of the most functionally deterministic spaces in the house, and traditionally also one of the most enclosed domestic rooms. It is the origin of privacy, and one of the last truly private spaces within the home. The expectation of a boundary, a lock on the door, or a door *tout court*, is contradicted by the pink fabric, which only loosely defines this wet space.

At Casa da Musica in Porto, the contradiction is different again. One of Blaisse's interventions in the main hall is a vast curtain acting as a sunscreen. At more than 300 m², its surface area is truly impressive, and from a distance it resembles a fishing net. On closer inspection it is indeed a simple tied cable structure, with a thin voile hand-knotted at every junction. The incredible amount of labour needed to create this curtain is diametrically opposed to the low cost of its materials – pointing to an idea of value that is not economic, but affective and tied to human investment. In the context of such a high-tech, expensive building, this strategy is even more extreme; the curtain descends to cover amongst the most technically advanced soundproof glass partitions ever realised.

The scale of the project does not prevent Inside Outside from making equally strong design statements. *Theft is Vision* was an exhibition held at the Luma Foundation in 2018, which examined questions of citation and appropriation in art. It presented the idea of theft as one of adulation, subversion and appropriation. Blaisse's exhibition design used recycled metal structures and industrial Saran wrap to create entirely transparent walls. From one side, the artworks appeared normally. But from the adjacent space, it became possible to see the backside of the paintings, a part of the artworks always concealed. Suddenly the institutional and gallery details of the art were revealed, speaking of a literal and conceptual transparency. By using materials associated with the transport and mobility of art, Blaisse also pointed to the role of copying in the establishment of art as a commodity. These three brief examples demonstrate just three different means by which Blaisse uses contradiction in her work to weaken convention: to dissolve functionalist predetermination in space; to challenge a conception of value in cultural production as it relates to time; and to expose the problematics of the institutionalisation and financialisation of art.

All traditions are intergenerational reinventions, sustained by the will of individuals and society driven by an idea of stability. Against the will of global neoliberalism, our era is already one that is defined by increasing instability. Rather than resist this change, the work of Inside Outside demonstrates how we can benefit from embracing indeterminacy and rupture with tradition. For decades, she has shown us the way forward, using strategies of détournement, contradiction and juxtaposition to break convention and so challenge the ideologies produced by the spaces we occupy.

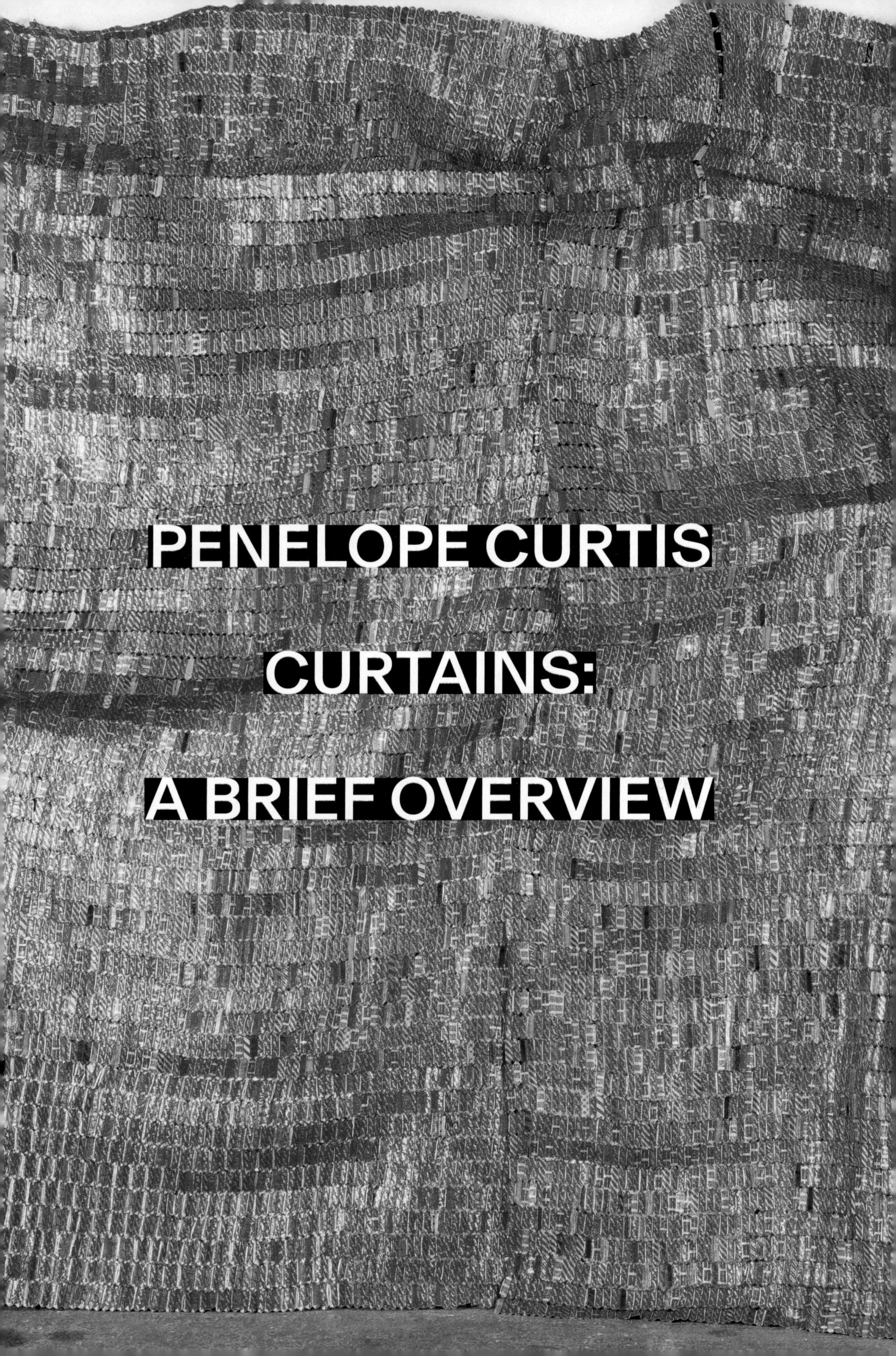

PENELOPE CURTIS

CURTAINS:

A BRIEF OVERVIEW

[1] Ludwig Mies van der Rohe and Lilly Reich, Tugendhat House, Brno, Czech Republic, 1928–1930, living room with curtains drawn and Lehmbruck's sculpture "Torso of a Young Woman," gelatin silver print, 16.8 × 22.9 cm

[2] Lilly Reich, View of the *Café Same und Seide*, at the exhibition *Die Mode der Dame*, Berlin, 1927, gelatin silver print, 20.3 × 25.4 cm

[1]

Curtains have interestingly ambivalent associations. Once used to enclose a bed (the earliest use in the English language), to keep out draughts and to assert privacy, they have gradually accrued equally public, even monumental associations.

Petra Blaisse's sites of production include the private and the public. She has worked on many private houses, but also in theatres, museums, libraries and other kinds of public auditoria. Curtains have been a key feature of her work since 1987.

Curtains can be, and increasingly are, used to signal status at the same time as they suggest its absence. They can glamourise even as they suggest a kind of modest functionality. They can protect and shield objects of high worth or vulnerability, and yet are themselves inherently impermanent.

The manoeuvrability of the curtain makes it very suitable for a world concerned not only with performativity, but also with ambivalence. This kind of reticence may usefully seem to decline self-importance. It may also be read as feminine.

[2]

Curtains denote time; they are opened at the beginning and drawn (or dropped) at the close; they mark the length of the day, or of the act. This temporal quality is matched by their purportedly transitional nature, but we need only think of a fire curtain, a safety curtain or a curtain wall, to correct any superficial links with lightness.

The theatrical associations of the curtain were deployed by Mies van der Rohe and Lilly Reich in a natural way, using the notion of the stage set (backdrop and stage) to arrange their characters (the furniture substituting the future inhabitants). Our reliance on black-and-white photographs, staged for posterity, only increases the sense of theatre we see in their projects (such as the German pavilion and the Tugendhat House). Mobile objects are stilled and set in position.

Mies and Reich met the silk manufacturer Hermann Lange in early 1927, and later that year made a Velvet and Silk Café in order to represent the Verein deutscher Seidenwebereien

(the Krefeld-based Silk Manufacturers' Association, of which Lange was Chairman) at *Die Mode der Dame* show in Berlin. It used hanging drapery at different heights (2 to 6 metres) to differentiate areas within the vast spaces of the trade fair. Its novelty lay principally in the curved spaces and their ambiguous functions. The product on show thus became the backdrop, self-effacing yet all-encompassing. Huge swathes (ca. 850 square metres) of fabric hung in mid-air: there was absolutely no need for economy, quite the opposite. Viewed from above, the ground plan clearly resembled an abstract composition (like contemporary painting or the sculpture of Kobro) and its mix of curved and rectilinear angles echoed the shapes of the tubular steel furniture which it housed.

Two years later, Mies and Reich were again commissioned by the Association to represent them, this time at the International Exhibition in Barcelona. The following year they completed the Krefeld houses for Lange[1] and his business associate Esters, in which their experience with textile promotion (Reich would also work independently on the Kunstseide Verkaufsbüro or Rayon sales office in Berlin) allowed them to develop the use of fabric "walls" set against large "panels" of daylight. This was another version of Mies's all-important transitional zone between indoors and out.

Famous as the interiors designed by Mies and Reich are, they are not unique. Contemporary projects by members of the Wiener Werkstätte, such as E. A. Plischke, and also by the Luckhardt brothers, show both the ways in which photography helped to condense a set of receding chiaroscuro planes, and how cinema must have helped develop that look. Here, curtains both frame the scene and provide its backdrop.

Mies and Reich might be characterised by their placement of "domestic" fittings in public spaces: enlarging the scale, obviously, but also unsettling the reading of a space by making it private and public at the same time. Petra Blaisse, by contrast, has been more consistently public in her use of the curtain. Even when a curtain project has deliberately tackled

[3] Alexander Michailowitsch Rodchenko, *Worker's Club Installation* at the 1925 at the Exposition Internationale des Arts Décoratifs et Industriels Modernes, Paris 1925 (Exhibition of Decorative Arts and Modern Industry), photo: Henri Manuel, gelatin silver print, sheet: 29.05 × 21.91 cm

[3]

[4]

troublingly monumental space, as in the Haus der Kunst, it has retained the public scale and function.

The age of temporary exhibitions and trade fairs, which might be seen to have commenced in 1851, has familiarised us with a panoply of similar solutions to the division of space and the promulgation of information. Fictive interiors were created to convey diverse national environments; more overtly commercial spaces were designed to showcase new materials and techniques.

The ingenuity of exhibition-making may be seen to have reached an apogee with the national and international propaganda displays developed by totalitarian regimes in the inter-war period. Mies and Reich were of this generation, which included brilliant designers such as Rodchenko in the Soviet Union and Persico in Italy. Convincing solutions included the communication of subliminal messages within a distinctive environment which overcame its merely temporary status. Petra Blaisse's designs for exhibitions are within this line – primarily informative – rather than in the creation of permanent solutions for the presentation of art.

The Italian designers who came of age in the era of Fascist-sponsored exhibitions moved beyond the temporary showcasing of information to create long-lasting museum interiors. Scarpa, Albini, BBPR, Gardella and their contemporaries were those who both benefited from and created the post-war museum renaissance in Italy, and by inference, more widely. They used "temporary" solutions – which included curtains, panels, easels and other kinds of innovative non-wall based supports first essayed in temporary venues – to assert new kinds of art galleries. Their singling out of objects and pictures, displayed at mid-range, at an indeterminate depth, has come to characterise a new museum language of seeing. Whereas this grammar is one of accentuation and rhythm, that of Blaisse is more uniform, more all-encompassing. Hers is not so much an environment for art, as an environment for being and absorbing. Less about object-based appraisal, and more properly about immersion.

Female architects play an interesting role in post-war exhibition design. Ostensibly working alongside their male partners, a closer reading of their archives shows that they often played the lead role. Lilly Reich has been steadily rehabilitated since the 1980s, allowing her earlier contribution to emerge from under Mies's American shadow. From the early 1950s, Franco Albini carried out all his museum projects with Franca Helg, and Alison Smithson, it appears, was the more active partner in the Smithsons' exhibition designs. Their innovative approach to the museum space – like that of the Eames – might be characterised as domestic, or it might be characterised as private. In any case, they bring a wider vocabulary of material and treatment into the public space, allowing the visitor to think of it as a place which can be inhabited.

While curtains have featured in exhibition design since at least the 1930s, it is only more recently that artists have taken them up as a way of inserting a simple architectural presence into their own exhibitions. Felix Gonzalez-Torres, Goshka Macuga, Charlotte Moth, Ulla von Brandenburg and Celine Condorelli are among those artists who have put curtains into their shows in recent years. This is often more than just an homage to Lilly Reich. Curtains fill space very effectively without claiming too much. They can add opulence (with gold, silver, pink, as well as black and white, being favourite colours, and not just for Blaisse) without real expense. They are theatrical, cinematic and sculptural. They can act as the support for paintings or words: El Anatsui uses curtain-like drops for his fabric pieces; in *Certain*, Bethan Huws used the curtain as if it were a whiteboard. Curtains can also involve others in an easily managed communal project, and Blaisse has talked of this aspect as important.

At worst (which isn't bad) curtains are inoffensive. At best they are transformative. Curtains are relatively cheap, they can be seen as temporary and they deal with problems left over or unforeseen: lack of colour, texture or security; surplus of light, sound, draughts. Blaisse has capitalised on some of these perceived problems and her early (ca. 1990–1998) contributions to OMA's villas (Paris, Bordeaux, Holten) use

[5]

[6]

[7] Felix Gonzalez-Torres,
Untitled (Golden) (1995), strands of beads
and hanging device, plastic and string,
dimensions vary with installation

[8] Goshka Macuga, *Haus der Frau 2*,
2007, glass, fabric, steel, fabrics,
designed by Eva Berendes, Bernd Ribbeck,
Klaus Weber

[7]

the wind, the weather and the time
to give unexpected dynamism to the
architecture. Set in nature, it is as if
the curtains here are the almost uncanny force which animates the villa.
Far from being quiescent, curtains
like these give movement and mutability to the
stillness of architecture.

In this respect we might see Blaisse, consciously
or not, as responding to a suggestion set up by
Anni Albers when she wrote "The Pliable Plane;
Textile in Architecture," published in 1957.[2] Tracing
the historic journey made by textiles from the exterior to the interior, and thus from a mobile to a
static state, she proposed that in this new habitat
curtains can take on more aesthetic functions,
while we, when "we revert to nomadism [...] are
open to textile behaviour"

1   Christiane Lange, the great grand-
daughter of Hermann Lange, published
her study of the Lange commissions to
coincide with an exhibition in the Lange
House in Krefeld in 2007. It coincided with
my own exhibition, *Figuring Space: Sculpture / Furniture from Mies to Moore* at the
Henry Moore Institute in Leeds. Her book
has added to my own research in this area.
2   Anni Albers, "The Pliable Plane; Textile
in Architecture," *Perspecta*, vol. 4 (1957),
p. 39. Thanks to Eliana Sousa Santos for
mentioning this essay in conversation.

[8]

[9] El Anatsui, Red Block, 2010, Aluminum and copper wire, two pieces, each
200 ¾ × 131 ½ in. (509.9 × 334 cm)

[9]

LAURENT STALDER

IN CONVERSATION

WITH PETRA BLAISSE

[1] Petra at 18, Hammersmith College of Art, London

87

[2] Biba was one of the fashion greats at the time, together with Punk and Laura Ashley – three totally opposite currents! I liked to mix-and-match. (Captions by Petra Blaisse.)

[1]

Petra Blaisse has not been trained as a textile designer, an architect or a landscape architect; nor has she been trained as a stage designer or a dressmaker. She never finished her education as an artist. She is none of these and all of them at the same time.

Her studio is a space where projects are designed, models built, textiles produced and printed; where people cook, eat and discuss – all at the same time. But it is also a repository of materials and samples, an archive that holds the memory of her work and informs her present activity. It extends to the intimacy of her private garden, which is a place of rest, but similarly operates as a laboratory to observe and investigate plants and trees, and it even extends to building sites, where mock-ups that are sometimes required in the course of construction are made on location.

[2]

Her designs elude all that has been theoretically defined, delimited and circumscribed as architecture; her designs challenge the confined boundaries of what is deemed architecturally relevant, important or even visionary. Sound, smell, temperature, colours or simply a gaze matter as much to Blaisse as do structures or materials. Her designs are about life and not vice versa.

Her work defies existing conceptions of architecture not because she rejects them, like the avant-garde, or neglects them, like the contractor, or despises them, like professionals, but because she lends architecture an excess of meaning: a curtain can be a thermal device and a visual one at the same time (as in Toledo), an article of clothing and an enclosure (as in Bordeaux), a three-dimensional body and a delimitation (as in Saint Cloud); a flowerbed can be a carpet or vice versa (as in Seattle or Rotterdam); a path can be a street, a ramp or even a wall (as in Milan); a knitted sock can be a piece of furniture (as in New York); and a fishing net a curtain (as in Porto).

The work is systematic, not because it follows a given theoretical frame, but because it revolves around a deep, coherent engagement with the task at hand. Design becomes a form

of knowledge – knowledge of material, construction, climate, intimacy, comfort, behaviour, usage, history – which repeatedly manifests itself in each new project. It is aesthetic, not only because of her mastery of materials, shapes and spaces but because her approach is at the crossroads of different interests and thus, in the etymological sense of the word, a shared experience.

The work is historical, not because it is dated or has been surpassed, but because it is already part of history. To understand the immediate past, it is more fruitful to look at her works and less at those of her collaborations, because it is a precise comment on today's condition. In her work, architecture is more than a building and its construction; it encompasses the entire environment from the interior and its climate to the territory and its boundaries. Her work turns the hierarchy of architecture upside-down and demonstrates that the building – an object long considered to be the ultimate and sole goal of the architect – is actually just an interface between the infinitely small and the infinitely large.

This is what this interview with Petra Blaisse is about.

[3]

LAURENT STALDER By education at least, you are an artist. You started studying Fine Arts, Graphic and Textile Design at an art school in London in 1973, but left for Holland halfway through your studies.

PETRA BLAISSE This was typical of my generation, I think. We felt pretty free. I stayed for less than two years at the Hammersmith College of Art in London – it was the time of punk and Biba, and the introduction of Bob Marley and reggae culture – but soon had the desire to return to the Netherlands to study at the Rietveld Academie in Amsterdam. I didn't fit into the mentality there, though. I had come from London with big platform shoes, completely dressed in black, wearing a hat with black feathers. My eyes were completely framed in black makeup and I had some dark mauve lipstick, as Biba prescribed. Even the portfolio

[3] Meeting a lot of artists, musicians and theatre people, I dated (Native and African American) guitarist Al Anderson for a while. He performed with different Black musicians at first but joined Bob Marley, who was brought to London by Chris Blackwell of Island Studios with The Wailers in the early '70s

[4]

[4] From 1979 to 1986 I worked at the Stedelijk Museum in Amsterdam as assistant at the Applied Arts Department, where architecture, industrial design, arts and crafts, graphic design and photography were collected and exhibited

[5] Fortunately I got more and more involved in the department's installations, from which I learned a lot about light, colour, scale and spatial effects

[6] Living in Lisbon between my first and fourth year, I remember sounds, smells and music very well.

88

[5]

for my work was a beautiful black. But the teachers at the Rietveld were into knitting their own clothes and rolling their own cigarettes, and were more interested in my political opinions than in my work. I declined their offer to attend night classes and went to Groningen instead, only to leave that city after six months. The cultural gap between London and Groningen was a bit too big. Tractors were driving through town!

I think things didn't really get started for me until I came back to Amsterdam. I first worked at a fashion agency where I met wonderful photographers and film-makers and became their assistant, mainly in the areas of publicity, advertisement and fashion. I was asked to assist them technically, and learned a lot about the use of light, materials and colours for photography and film; but I was also sent out to find props and suitable locations for shoots and asked to "style" places and models. The work was interdisciplinary, not theoretical, as in the academies, but really hands-on.

LS   After four years you applied for a job at the Stedelijk Museum.

PB   Yes, I applied for the job of assistant to the Department of Applied Arts in 1978. They chose me out of 200 applications. This was an incredible honour as I had not completed any of my studies, and only had some work experience. But I have always been interested in modern art, and the Stedelijk became my second home.

LS   And what did you do at the Department of Applied Arts?

PB   The work changed over the course of the time as I assisted five curators, all of whom had their own specific specialty. But the work consisted of what you usually do in a museum, being an assistant when mounting the exhibition and more of a clerk when archiving the collection. The latter was especially interesting training for me. There were of course no computers yet, so you would work with an archiving system of cards, all properly organised in

[6]

[7]

drawers. You had to describe the object in question with great precision: whether it was a glass, a huge tapestry or a very small architectural model. You had to do it in such a way that it could be identified without a photo – and in just a few words. I love language so I really enjoyed doing it.

LS   Did you also start designing exhibitions at the Stedelijk?

PB   I did only two on my own. One was about a new municipal trash bin – haha! – whose designer, Bas Pruyser, won the Kho Liang Ie Design Prize. The bin was connected to steel tubing for people to lean against at the tram station and, since the exhibit was in the glass corridor that connected the Stedelijk building to Sandberg's New Wing, it was possible to place the structure half inside and half outside. I had the tube system sawn in half and glued to the glass facade on two sides. Thus, the trash bin was visible from the inside and from its romantic location in the museum garden.

The second "exhibition" actually refers to all the installations I made in display cases over the years: placing small objects in spaces of various sizes and levels of transparency (with 4, 3 or 2 sides open to the eye). These installations taught me about the qualities and challenges of limitation: limited space, limited view and visibility, limited distance, limited height, limited object size; the effect of scale and size, the effect of light intensity, direction and colour (how to accentuate or change a material quality or level of importance) and reflection; the effect of material structure, of positioning: high, low, suspended, standing, lying on one side, individually or in combination with other objects, distance between objects, position in relation to the viewer, the right space and place for text, the influence of letter font, size and readability; the effect of text boards regardless of size and colour.

In short, while doing those "finger exercises" at the Stedelijk, I learned to understand the qualities and possibilities of a given space; how to make

[8]

[7] I lived in Vienna when John F. Kennedy and Nikita Khrushchev met during the Cold War era. This was, of course, big news that was discussed at length by the grow-ups that surrounded us as children

[8] As my parents were Catholic, we went to (Latin spoken) church every Sunday, where the music, the heavy smell of incense, the light through stained glass windows and the dramatic imagery of biblical paintings and sculptures made a huge impression

[9] The first installation I was asked to co-design as a freelancer was the competition presentation of the City Hall by OMA at the Gemeente Museum in The Hague – a beautiful building by Berlage

[10] In 1987 and 1988 I worked for the Rotterdamse Kunststichting where I managed the exhibitions inside the Holland Amerika Lijn building during the Rotterdam '88 cultural year

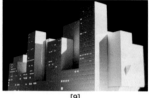

[9]

use of and influence it with specific or even strategic effects. But these were the only installations I was ever made responsible for. At the Stedelijk Museum, a public institution where you are a civil servant, job descriptions are very strict. In a Calvinist country like the Netherlands, you are only supposed to do what is asked of you and what you are paid for, nothing more.

LS   Where did you gain experience as a designer then, since you left the Stedelijk precisely in order to become one?

PB   Of course, I learned a lot at the Stedelijk and in all my various jobs before that. For instance, I got experience in teamwork, and also in light, placement, composition, lettering and text writing. But I have always wanted to create my own environments. I think it has to do with my personal history. We moved a lot, from one country to another when I was a child, so maybe that's why shaping my own environment is so important to me. My mother was a potter and later a painter, very much interested in the "modern" lifestyle, in music, design and the arts, so we used to live in carefully arranged surroundings.

[10]

In addition to certain comforting souvenirs, I have intense memories of particular environments from my childhood. I remember listening to the melancholic voice of Amália Rodrigues and the guitar sounds that accompanied her in a café in Lisbon when I was three, surrounded by people smelling of garlic; later the rhythmical whining of Hungarian violins in Vienna; the Catholic churches in Lisbon and Vienna with their colourful, dramatic biblical decorations and sculptures, the stained glass windows that projected patches of colour on visitors, the Latin mass, the choirs and the classical music, the light and smells of the wide-open landscapes in Scandinavia. In a totally different vein, there were all the museums, galleries and fashion shows our mother took us to in order to acquaint us with painters such as Klimt, Hundertwasser, Schiele, Wunderlich, Kandinsky, Klee and others, along with works of the

Wiener Werkstätte and the architecture of Hoffman and Hundertwasser. She introduced us to the fashion designs of Yves Saint Laurent, Cardin, Courrèges and Marimekko, not to forget the modern music and films we were exposed to on a daily basis, the black-and-white TV that informed us about Eastern European politics, winter sports, boxing and wrestling matches, horse shows and pop culture, like The Beatles – I became a fan when I was eight. We lived in Lisbon, Vienna and Stockholm between 1956 and 1964. Later my father treated us to foreign cuisines, modern architecture and the latest shows in New York, London and Paris – like *Equus* with Richard Burton, or the musicals *Hair* and *Jesus Christ Super Star*. These intense impressions and experiences make such an impact when you are young; they affect you deeply and stay with you all your life.

LS   Seen from the outside at least, the year 1986 seems to have brought a lot of changes: you began to work at the Nederlands Dans Theater in The Hague and on the Patio Villa project with OMA. When reading your somehow very reserved biography, one is struck by the difference between the understatement of your recordings in contrast with the maturity of these first public

[11]

works. The powerful design of your first exhibition, *A First Decade*, about OMA in the Museum Boijmans van Beuningen, challenged every conceivable notion of a monographic architectural exhibition.

PB   It was very important for me to represent the mental maps of the architects. I knew the OMA team in Rotterdam very well as it was still quite small then. They had moved from London in 1981, I think, and had only been in Holland for six years. We were in touch from the beginning. I had access to every note, even scribble, and all of the models from the studio. I plunged right in. I could also exchange thoughts on each project – like a curator, I suppose, at least that was how it felt – carefully working through each sketch and model, following the whole process for coming up with a design, which I thought was more interesting than just the end result.

[12]

[11] In the 80's I started to collect and archive OMA Rotterdam's architectural materials – sketches, study models, drawings, sources of inspiration to serve as material for the upcoming traveling exhibitions, to be held between 1989 and 1992

[12] The first OMA exhibit we installed was at the Museum Boymans van Beuningen in Rotterdam, where Wim Crouwel was director and where he appointed the best spaces of the museum: two large, daylit rooms designed by architect Alexander Bodon

[13] During the development of the Nederlands Dans Theater in The Hague, Koolhaas invited his wife Madelon Vriesendorp to propose a mural for the stage tower of the building, and introduced me to the OMA team to work on the interior finishes and furniture; later to design the stage curtain

[14] My first stage curtain was for the Nederlands Dans Theater in 1986: heavy grey wool velvet with rows of golden dots that picked up every ray of light

[13]

LS   Yet your exhibition design goes well beyond this: you worked very meticulously with light, textiles, rebars and even wind.

PB   Yes, creating a mind map also entailed symbolising – or illustrating – the mentality and energy of the architect: the constant search for the right design, the path towards a solution for a specific commission, but also the diverse sources of inspiration. I chose the technique of collage to represent this path. I called the mind maps the girl's room collages, where all sources of inspiration come together, both in images and in words: poetry, recipes, quotes, portraits of heroes, pornographic images (especially Japanese ones where private parts were "censored"), film stills, etc. I think it is important to address physical sensations and theatricality when exhibiting stark objects like building models and technical drawings. With light effects one can communicate vibrant energy, optimism, doom, deep thought or even the fun of funky, aimless experimentation. Sound effects help to create illusions of space and scale, and using different scales to play with the imagery or models triggers the viewer's awareness of a project's potential. Textiles help spread or filter light, mute sound, introduce sensuality, temporality and change; wind introduces movement, a breeze, a breath of fresh air, the billowing of a skirt or curtain.

LS   Was the work with OMA the first time you worked freelance?

PB   Yes. But the first thing they asked me to do was to help them create an installation for a presentation of their competition at the Gemeente Museum for the city hall in The Hague. I had already been in touch with Rem Koolhaas about the Dans Theater building in Scheveningen, near the sea just outside The Hague, when it was still in the planning stages. We corresponded over fax and discussed, for instance, the colour and character of the auditorium: why shouldn't an auditorium be purple or pink instead of a black box or why should it have a certain height and the roof a certain shape? The collaborations went

[14]

smoothly because these projects were still in their preliminary stages.

LS   The centrepiece of the theatre in The Hague is the curtain. This appears to be another crucial step in your work, as it is not anymore the visitor who is moving, but the architecture itself is in movement.

PB   This was around 1986 or 1987. OMA asked me to collaborate on the interior of the Nederlands Dans Theater, now located in The Hague, on a square with other cultural buildings and the new city hall (won by Richard Meier), part of an urban plan by the Dutch architect Carel Weber. I proposed a colour and material scheme for the whole building. A key aspect of the proposal was conceiving the auditorium, stage and the stage tower as a black box. The auditorium was to focus entirely on the stage and the art of dancing. I proposed dark blue velvet chairs as a classic, very subtle addition. We decided on gold-powdered wooden reflective sound panels and strategically positioned them along the side walls. Sound experts later placed tiny mirrors in their centres to reflect the laser beams that simulated the sound waves through the auditorium. We left the mirrors in place. Once all this had been decided, the only missing element was the stage curtain. Who would design it? I offered to do it even though I had never done anything like that before – nobody knew this, of course. Somehow, it is easier to take such a daring step when everything is a collaborative effort. I had a clear idea of what this curtain should be: a flood of interconnected round or rectangular gold metal plates that would reflect the faintest light source… a bit Courrèges! For the implementation, however, I relied on a theatre textile company called Theatex, run by three sisters. They taught me what a stage curtain needs to be: not just any composition of loose elements or any piece of textile, but a heavy fire-, light- and soundproof drape, thick and strong enough to withstand intense use for many years, to absorb all sounds during set changes and to block the tiniest light source at all times.

From the very beginning I envisioned a gold curtain, but it took an on-site

[15]

[15] I also proposed and hand-painted the six wooden, gold-coloured sound panels of the dance theatre

[16]

[16] Lack of money made us cover half of the smallest concrete column of the building – in the outer and lowest corner of the oyster-shaped foyer – with gold leaf. The simple construction lamp on the floor transforms the column into a Mayan sun god

[17]

presentation of 1:1 samples of the design to convince Rem Koolhaas, Jiří Kylián and Karel Birnie, the creative and managing directors of the Dans Theater at the time, to accept this idea. The description of the design reminded Jiri of the kitschy interiors of East European theatres. Actually, the curtain, with its mat grey velvet base and its "rain" of golden dots, represents the opposite. Its presence and character changes with each movement and with each variation in light intensity or colour: it can be ice cold with blue light, burn like the sun when lit with warm light or smoulder like the softest sunset if subtly touched by faint light. In its various movements and speeds, it can act like a can-can dancer, slither in like a snake or enter in grandeur like a queen at her coronation.

[18]

LS   At the Dans Theater, you worked closely with Rem Koolhaas and also with the photographer Hans Werlemann.

PB   Yes, obviously with Koolhaas, as he was greatly involved in every detail. He takes the final decision on all matters large and small. Hans and I had been working together since the installation for the city hall competition. He was an extremely important partner in all the exhibition projects before and after the Dans Theater. There he was responsible for the lighting but he helped out everywhere and worked on everything. He has a particular eye for light and composition, and like Rem, he is allergic to overdoing things. The collaboration with Hans and other creative people (film-makers, designers, sound artists) was symptomatic for the way OMA used to work. Somehow we were not just professional partners; we became a group of friends, working together all the time, even if not earning much – I actually earned almost nothing for years! Nerds, crazy people, nomads! Discussing, creating, cooking, eating, improvising, inventing, experimenting. We fixed ceiling lamps, painted walls, upholstered second-hand furniture, printed textiles, spotted and transported found objects to use for interiors and found specialists as needed – all by ourselves. The budget for this project,

[19]

one of OMA's first buildings, was incredibly low because the money came from what the Dans Theater had saved itself over many years. This was challenging; the architect had to be extremely inventive and smart. We covered half of the smallest concrete column in the Dans Theater foyer (the "muscle" of the oyster) with gold leaf, a symbolic gesture because we couldn't afford to cover it entirely. Perched on ladders, we rubbed gold powder into the wooden acoustic panels in the auditorium. We were really into communal creation and hands-on work, and Koolhaas was the driving force through all of it.

LS   The garden for the Linthorst patio house in Rotterdam from 1988 is another collaborative work, again with OMA, but this time with Yves Brunier.

PB   No, not with Yves Brunier. There is some confusion about this. While I was working on the house, he was working on the Museum Park in Rotterdam. I helped him out occasionally as an interpreter because he only spoke French, and he helped me make one drawing for the Villa Kralingen garden because I couldn't do it: a perspective drawing of the willow hedge on the western side of the site with the golden glow of the setting sun, which I wanted to show to the client. Somehow the drawing got lost, or maybe it's in the archives of OMA, who knows. But I designed this little garden as an extension of the house's interior, starting with a terrace as a continuation of its wooden floor. Then the owners made it clear that they had no affinity with plants and gardening, so I sank the garden level a bit, with the wooden floor hovering above it. It became a wooden boardwalk that led straight to the brook, which formed one of the boundaries of the garden. The garden, then, was seen from above. At first, I designed a meditative garden, very simple and Japanese-like, with a perfect round mound at the end of the property and bamboo hedges flanking both sides. The mound became a problem for the owners because it partially blocked their view of the brook with ducks and geese swimming by. I therefore modified the design. The mound became a large

[20]

[21] The Villa Kralingen actually consists of two villas under one roof. The colours of the facade counter-act the sub-division

[22] It was clear to me that I didn't want a designer's role when applying for this gardener's apprenticeship. Learning by doing has always been my motto

92

[21]

circle of plants that dives under the boardwalk: a curving box hedge filled with perennials with their characteristic leaves and seasonal colour. The surrounding field was covered with ivy, and contained one large tuft of high ornamental grass and a twin apple tree, willow branches, stuck into the moist ground, formed a living screen to the west and bamboo plants provided privacy from the next-door neighbours to the east.

LS   But Brunier was an important reference for you, wasn't he?

PB   Definitely! Everyone learned from Yves's way of representing and designing landscapes and gardens, not being afraid to be "weird" and abstract at the same time. Painting with plants, as it were, visualising his ideas in collages, often photocopies of photographs topped with paint, ink, Tippex, scraps of paper – graphic, artistic and full of energy! Building models with found objects, earplugs, sponges, torn paper, blobs of paint. Choosing plants and shrubs with extreme forms, thorns, fruit, flowers, autumn colours, winter profiles! This approach was just plain fun for me, so much creative freedom… It was such a relief, in a way that you can just be yourself and do it. Coming from an art school background in the seventies, it felt very natural to work in that way, but I realised I had never really dared to play like he did. In their early years, Koolhaas and his team also had this playfulness. They weren't self-conscious and they challenged ideas in a way that was very liberating to a control freak like myself! Yves's representations were not precise but

[22]

beautiful and effective, which was still possible at that time: people still believed in conceptual thought, in beauty without logic or restraints. It wasn't all about safety, efficiency and economics. But although arty in representation, his visions were still accurate and realistic. The landscapes he was able to create, for instance with Jean Nouvel in Bordeaux and with Rem Koolhaas in Rotterdam, remained stunningly original. So sad he left our world so soon. And so sad that the Museum Park has been changed, completely different from the original intent of the park as

a connective "art piece" or "painting" embedded between four important cultural buildings.

LS   Did you also do the curtains and the wall painting on the front side of the Villa Linthorst?

PB   Yes, the curtain and the material choices for the house were mine, but not the painted facade. That was typical Rem, although we all participated in the discussions about it and in the process of creating endless collages and try-outs: should the facade be divided in three or four colour planes, should they be black, white and grey or should they have colour, etc. But for Rem, the essence was that the composition should camouflage the actual division of the house, as it was a two-villas-under-one-roof situation. But the facade looked like one abstract painting with a few rectangular cut-outs for doors and slits for windows.

LS   You wrote somewhere that you then went to work with Lily Terkuile for two and a half years, learning how to create nursery beds, transplant plants, take cuttings, start seeds in the greenhouse, etc. Did you feel a lack of practical knowledge after this first landscape project?

PB   I was collaborating part-time with OMA and working part-time with Lily on their newly bought estate in Overijssel. It was a wonderful time, and I was completely isolated from the outside world for two to three days a week. No mobile phones at the time, remember, and I slept in a wagon in the woods, as the couple still lived in the tiny house of the previous owner. I could hear every sound of the night, the wind, the animals. It was hard work: waking up at six thirty, breakfast at seven with coarse organic bread topped with dry peanut butter, cheese or homemade jam. Really, organic food was inedible at that time – then field work until the bell rang at eleven for a coffee break, at quarter past one for lunch, at five for tea and at half past six for dinner. At nine in the evening we were so tired that we just fell into bed – after checking one another for ticks.

[24]

[25] Part of our landscape seen through the round window of CCTV's overhang

[26] The first name for my one-man studio was Binnen Buiten, and Andrew MacNair designed my first business card – with holes of course. Here the last specimen left

93

[25]

Lily and her husband had just bought three hectares of land behind a dike that runs along the Ijssel River. The land was densely overgrown with old pine trees – basically, a former Christmas tree nursery. With the help of neighbouring farmers we strategically cleared some areas, letting light in again, creating open, transparent and more opaque areas. We ground the trees down to wood chips, composted the leaves, heaped the twigs and branches into piles and wove them into open structures that meandered through the woods, marking boundaries, lining the driveway and becoming living quarters and hiding places for many animals. Lily would recycle and upcycle everything, an important lesson I took from her. She was – even if I did not fully realise it at the time – a dedicated Rudolf Steiner anthroposophist.

LS   But her convictions went well beyond questions of reuse. Didn't you have to plant the seeds depending on lunar cycles?

PB   Yes, exactly. We had to work according to the lunar calendar. Lily and her husband, a judge in The Hague, also believed in little dwarves, in elves, living in the woods. It was a continually surprising world: they would speak of dwarves while I was learning plant names from piles of garden books in the evenings. But in spite of all that, it really worked. It was truly miraculous how well everything grew, how healthy everything was and how little was eaten by the rabbits and deer that lived on the land – thanks to our positive energy and the help of dwarves, of course.

LS   Once again, you acquired basic knowledge through practical work, as you did at the Stedelijk.

PB   Yes, knowledge about gardening and plants, but also developing an eye for space and scale as well as the effect of light, colour, movement and levels of transparency. I also learned how to take the most basic decisions in uncontrolled conditions. There was nothing on the plot: no house, no garden – just neglected nature, overgrown woods. So, we started by measuring out the plot, opening it up, creating views,

[26]

BINNEN BUITEN
PETRA BLAISSE INC.
INTERIORS/EXTERIORS
BILDERDIJKKADE 16A
1052 RW AMSTERDAM
NETHERLANDS
TEL. & FAX: 31 - 20.6125246

[27]

inviting the sun to give life to the soil and all that was hidden underneath. We discovered the riches and secrets of the land along the way! Next we worked on the nursery, multiplying, growing, naming. Then we traced the flower beds and paths (with long water hoses), slowly giving form to a garden. Only then did the proper location for the house arise.

LS   From a historical perspective and in relation to your work, the name of your studio Inside Outside, seems obvious today. But how did the name pop up in 1991, just after this anthroposophical experience?

PB   The idea came from my work, such as the Villa Linthorst project. But also from a personal perspective. Gardens as attractive living environments were always important for me. My mother was a painter but also a passionate gardener; in fact her sisters and her mother are all artists and gardeners. But the name itself came up while I was working on the so-called H-Project in Seoul, Korea. The director of Samsung owned a plot of land and wanted to turn it into a space for culture and fitness with buildings by different architects. I was brought in to design the connective landscape, the green that would unite the buildings and spaces and reinforce the area's unique character. I think Andrew MacNair (from New York, architect and editor of *Zapp Urbanism*) and I thought of the Dutch name Binnen Buiten first. But later when I was in France, working on the interiors and curtains of Lille Grand Palais, nobody understood Binnen Buiten so the name became Inside Outside.

LS   Inside Outside is more than a studio. It is also a hands-on workshop where people build, saw, cut, stitch and knit.

PB   Yes, experimenting, discovering, observing and understanding – all are key. I like to stimulate our team to draw by hand and to test what we design one-to-one and in detail as much as possible: if you draw a path that is 150 or 500 cm wide, you need to check how wide it is inside, here in this room or outside

[28]

[27] For years I worked from home and from the back of my car, until I finally found a 'real' work space in an old brick building – a former school. This moving announcement aka business card was carefully designed by (now visual artist) Paul Ouwerkerk

[28] Detail image of our current studio

[29] This is our treasure corner where all our hundreds of curtain and carpet tests are stored around the cutting table and sewing machines

[30] Of course all our curtain ideas are first tested and sometimes entirely made true-to-scale in our studio – first by Anky and since 2002 by our curtain specialist Peter Niessen, who also makes the most amazing IO pillowcases for departing colleagues

94

[29]

on the street. Please take tape and mark off the path. Then mark the flowerbed or building beside it and imagine the plants you would plant there growing larger, the building being approached, entered, used. What do you see? What needs to improve? Or: we want to use this specific material but ten times the size of the sample we are holding; how does that affect the material and what is the effect of the material's colour (or shape) on its environment? Well… this kind of thing, very basic actually. I also want our team to look for materials in person, not only online: visit the companies that produce, print, sew, construct because we all need to understand each other's profession, the ins-and-outs of a process or a specific technique. Otherwise you cannot realise a product's full potential, how to apply it and broaden its possibilities; how it behaves through time, in various climates and forms of use, and what the effect of scale and weight are, etc. Go into the city, into nature, visit gardens, go to performances, watch films, read the newspaper, document your travels and what impresses, disturbs or frightens you. Ask questions, note how others live, what drives people, drives all living things. Bring it back into your work, integrate it somehow, and tell us about it so we can all learn from these experiences.

[31]

LS   The studio is also a very well-organised repository, an archive of all the knowledge you have accumulated over the years.

PB   Yes, we try to be as precise as we can but time is an issue. We are pretty fanatic collectors; once you start looking at things that attract you, like stones, textiles, plants, art, objects, souvenirs, pictures, books and other printed material, you soon find yourself collecting everything. So, we have pots with sand and granulates from beaches and glaciers from all over the world (now illegal), we have stones, seeds and shells (also banned) and pieces of glass and tools from building sites, but mostly we have an archive of textiles and prints from various countries and cultures, in different weavings and colours, thick and thin. To be more precise, we have two collections:

one of material samples that we are constantly renewing because industrial products – especially the ones we like – are often taken off the market. And then we have a collection of our own curtain samples, all tests and mock-ups we made in the process of searching for a final design. This collection is a source of inspiration for later designs.

LS   You have a lot of mock-ups.

PB   Yes, and these are very important to us so we organise them carefully with names and dates. We can't weave, but we can sew, knot, knit, crochet, tear, glue, print, sample, hang, plant, seed, build and cook. And so together we build models, worlds and prototypes to measure and experience things in their true scale, taste and materiality.

LS   So, every project physically goes through your studio?

PB   Yes, definitely.

LS   Is the same true of your garden?

PB   Yes, my garden is similarly a place of experimentation and collecting! It is a place where I have a lot of flowering and fruit-bearing plants that attract insects and birds, a compost heap, areas with different soil types and exposures to the sun (created with mirrors) and a few little ponds that attract animal life. I observe how things develop and behave. It is a kind of ecological microcosm in the city. You can find me there every day of the year.

LS   The boundaries between work and leisure are pretty fluid in your office. You not only work together but have lunch together as well. This sense of community seems crucial to your work.

PB   Absolutely. We used to take turns cooking – myself included in the beginning. This is unusual in Holland, where lunch generally consists of bread and cheese and a glass of milk. In the office, we all like the communal cooked lunch as it allows us to come

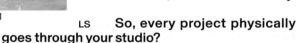

[32]

[31] Typical for our studio, we have warm lunch around the round table each day and celebrate the yearly Sinterklaas and Christmas feasts together

[32] The old studio in the former school building also had its charm

[33]

together, to relax a bit, to exchange thoughts and experiences, to share what we are working on, or just reflect on the movies we have watched, on politics and the news. These exchanges are particularly important as the team is very diverse and constantly changing. The different cultures and generations work together and learn from one another, an opportunity we wouldn't want to miss. Only a very few people have been at the office for the longer term, such as my current partners, the landscape architect Jana Crepon, who is in charge of the landscape team and the architect Aura Melis, who heads up the interior and exhibition team. Both have worked with me for many years and became partners in September 2016. And Peter Niessen, a former is fashion and costume designer, who responsible for all curtain tests and production processes and manages the track and motor systems as well as the materials archive: he has been key in almost all curtain projects since 2001, I think – both as critic and experienced seamstress – though he did leave Inside Outside for a few years at one point. And then there is Loes Gieles, our business manager at the head of the team.

[34]

LS   How do you manage, in your daily work, to combine such disparate fields as landscape and interior design?

PB   That has a lot to do with the brief of each project and how our task is specified in the contract. This greatly influences the way in which projects are conducted. Normally, the landscape team is completely absorbed in its own work, and the same is true for the interior and exhibition design team. Ideally, the landscape architect Jana should be able to jump in and sew one of the curtains, but unfortunately this is not the case. Yet, I do try to involve the landscape team in manual work such as hammering holes and squeezing metal studs or rings into cloth – haha! More often, though, the interior team, consisting mainly of architects, helps out on large-scale landscape projects, drawing up plans, building scale models and creating collages. The other way around is more difficult. I don't have the answer yet. Do you?

[35]

LS   Perhaps it is more difficult to formally organise collaborations in a studio, but you, yourself, seem to do it quite naturally. A striking example is the big sock for the Prada Epicenter by OMA in New York that you knitted in a hotel room.

PB   Yes, it can be hands-on, and that is so much fun. In 2001, I knitted the Sound Sock together with Anky, my assistant at the time, in the Gramercy Park Hotel. OMA had planned a track system for the Epicenter on which elongated, metal-mesh cages, open on one side and displaying dressed mannequins with clothes storage underneath, were suspended from the ceiling. In the evening, the cages were pushed together to form a closed, secure block, a spectacular idea. I was involved in the interior design and came up with the idea of covering the suspended loudspeaker system with a knitted silver voile – forming a "soft cage" as part of the hanging system. We knitted this with enormous wooden needles that we made ourselves and connected with a piece of green garden hose, which is necessary if you want to knit in continuous circles. We ordered rolls of flame-retardant silver voile from Germany to be sent to the Gramercy Park Hotel. The rolls were very large and we tried to get them into the elevator, but they didn't fit. So we had to unroll them in front of the big Christmas tree in the lobby, and put this mountain of silver into the elevator to transport it to our suite on the 11th floor. There we started to tear the voile into ten-centimetre strips, and began to knit in opposite directions. We were literally sitting on each other's lap for the first few rows, but as the length of the sock grew, the farther apart we got. It took us seven days to finish this 5 × 10-meter sock. The cleaning lady went bananas, not only because we were knitting all the time, but because the sock kept growing in size, crawling up the walls. We had a very tight schedule, knitting two hours, then taking a short break outside. The salt-treatment of the textile filled the air of our room, which made us extremely thirsty and made our skin dry and red. So we needed to drink a lot, and kept bringing back huge containers full of water. After

[36]

[35] For the House in Bordeaux we also designed the soft green polyurethane floor on the lower floor: monochrome for the kitchen, marbled with various colours for the ironing room

[36] For the main bathroom, Vincent de Rijk developed this amazing transparent washbasin

[37]

seven days, we finished the sock, and we knew more about each other than anyone else in our lives. We put our creation into one of the hotel's large blue garbage bags, threw it out of the window onto the sidewalk, pushed it into the back of the taxi, and finally hung it at the Epicenter. That's the story.

LS   Your main activity over these years and since the late eighties, though, has been a series of houses: The Villa dall'Ava in Saint-Cloud (1984–1991), the House in Holten (1995), the Villa Floirac in Bordeaux (1996–1998/2011–2012). In these projects, you worked on the interior, which entailed engaging with the most intimate aspects of clients' lives.

[38]

PB   Well I'm not sure about "the most" intimate part, but yes, you're right, a private house is an intimate process. You need to understand people's lives, tastes, needs, allergies. It is not always easy to engage so deeply at first, but you often become friends along the way. I think we were particularly lucky with the clients that you mention, as they were not interested in showing off. Their taste was both critical and dignified. They were more concerned with culture and art, and were active participants throughout the process.

Again, these projects were collaborations with friends and architects. Maarten van Severen was very much involved, as were Xaveer de Geyter, Julien Montfort, Gro Bonesmo, Jeroen Thomas from OMA and Cecil Balmond from Arup on Rem's side; and Hans Werlemann, Vincent de Rijk, Joep van Lieshout and myself for interior interventions; for the gardens Yves Brunier, Adriaan Geuze and me – so, architects, photographers, artists, designers, landscapists and clients working together.

LS   In the villa in Saint-Cloud, you also worked on the photo shoot of the giraffe with Hans Werlemann. There's also a rumour that you brought Jean Nouvel in as a mannequin. Is that true?

PB   Yes, I knew Jean from some previous encounters and thought it

[39]

would be fun to invite a so-called "competitor" of the architect to introduce his newly finished building! I was of course teasing Rem a bit, or rather questioning the notion of authorship. As Rem and Jean were friends, Jean happily agreed and appeared in his then "signature" black cape. He was a great model, a sort of handsome Dracula inhabiting the house and the garden in turns as thinker, worker, man, sculpture, ghost, conscience… We also had the giraffe, indeed, and the cleaning lady and the Olympic swimmers on the roof, a poorly composed quote from *Delirious New York*, remember? The Russian Olympic swimmers leaving Russia for Manhattan in a rectangular pool the size of a city block, swimming towards Russia but moving backwards towards the west. These other scenarios were Hans Werlemann's ideas. He loved the work of Rem Koolhaas and OMA. In assignments for magazines and other publications, Hans usually worked in a polite manner, but he wanted to respond boldly to this crazy Villa dall'Ava.

LS   In Saint Cloud, Yves Brunier designed the garden, but for the Villa Floirac your studio did both the interior and the landscape, right?

PB   Well, we didn't really design the landscape; we just cut away the most invasive wilderness and opened up views towards the river Garonne and the old city of Bordeaux.

LS   But the earth mound on the south side, with its opening to the valley, seems to be quite thoughtfully designed.

PB   This was indeed a crucial part of the landscaping at Floirac: leaving the territory as is, but shaping and manicuring it here and there, for instance the driveway with its circular lawn in the centre. For the interior, I only did the curtains and helped select materials and furniture, just like in Saint Cloud, for the Villa dall'Ava and for the Villa Kralingen.

LS   You speak very humbly about your interventions, but they do seem to radically question the traditional relationship between architecture

[40]

[41]

and interior design. The curtains, even the furniture, have become actual spatial devices of the house. They do not merely reinforce or embellish the architecture; they actually shape the life of its inhabitants and guide their movement. The structural frame of the architecture becomes secondary to the so-called interior design, which influences the habits, behaviour and imagination of its inhabitants.

PB   Yes, that might be true. My experience has been that the proprietors realise along the way that this new, custom-made architecture requires special furniture to complement it. Like curtains, each piece of furniture has its own personality and effect on space and the way it is used. Interior design influences your daily life and habits; it articulates social relations and writes scenarios much like architecture does, but in a different manner. At the Villa dall'Ava the curtain interventions were still quite rudimentary, with a crazily decorated and colourful seventeenth-century textile design for the daughter's room (sewn together in an irregular pattern). A yellow silk curtain defined and enclosed the living room, although it would suddenly billow out into the garden when the glass facade was opened. This intervention was of course based on the Lilly Reich curtains in Mies's buildings and exhibition designs. I came to realise that the difference from modernist design is the importance of movement and change in my work. In addition to envisioning a curtain's possible trajectories and placements, it is essential to think about how it moves. This movement can be influenced by the manipulation of the user, by the behaviour of the curtain itself due to draughts and wind, by the effects of the time of day, lightness and darkness, but also by the characteristics of the cloth itself: heavy, light, thick, thin, open, massive, etc.

LS   In Bordeaux, the whole house seems to be under the spell of the curtains. Even the structure, as described by Cecil Balmond, or the office space on the elevator platform, designed by OMA, are in movement, or at least in equilibrium. After you refurbished it in

[42]

[43]

2011, this becomes even more evident, as the architecture of the house is reduced to the floors and ceilings.

PB   I didn't mean to ignore the architecture. The whole point was to accentuate the idea behind the architectural concept, its contradictory structure and build-up. There might be a lot of curtains, but they all serve a purpose, depending on the place they inhabit.

LS   One of them is the pink curtain in the bathroom and adjoining bedroom.

PB   I think. Although Monsieur Lemoine initially had some hesitations about a pink curtain in a man's bedroom, he was eventually convinced that it was not actually a real "pink pink," but a beautiful warm pink that enhances the body and softens the harshness of daily life. The cloth, the two layers, the stitching technique and the combination with concrete, mirrors, water and beds – it is consoling for mind and body alike. They came to enjoy it.

LS   In the renovation of the house in 2011, it becomes even more evident that the curtains are not only a background for its inhabitants, but that they also strongly shape their daily routine: a curtain with a hole, which directs the gaze or a carpet on the floor that divides different zones.

PB   When we designed the interior of Maison Bordeaux in 1998, the kids were still in the house. The curtains that we chose were much thinner and commercially available, except for the pink silk curtains enclosing the parents' intimate quarters. Then, the children grew up and left and Monsieur Lemoine passed away. After a couple of years Madame Lemoine asked me to rethink the interior, to give it the necessary comfort, but also some protection. Especially the glass-enclosed living room which turns into a cold box after dark with a black, reflecting surface. You couldn't see outside, but outside can see in, and this is uncomfortable. She also felt the living room needed some direction to create distinct places, to define more intimate seating areas. This was a challenge we

[44]

[45] The luxury of a 1:1 (true-to-scale) mock up, here for the Glass Pavilion in Toledo Ohio, taught us the value of such test where all building elements come together for inspection and criticism

[46] These (blackout) tests for the future multipurpose space of the pavilion were appreciated but not approved by the architects

[45]

had encountered in Seattle some years before. In the library, there is this beautiful endless, open floor surface, but one didn't know where to sit or where to read. With a simple carpet, you can organise a space, indicate a place, trigger direction and provide a soft surface for touch and acoustics.

In the house in Bordeaux it was, of course, important to include the "elevator" platform, Monsieur Lemoine's former room, into the new carpet composition and to connect it to the living room more clearly. This moving plateau was initially created for Monsieur Lemoine to allow him to move from the kitchen to the living room to the bedroom, passing the elegant transparent shelves with all the things he needed within his reach. It had now become the dining area. So you can set the table downstairs in the kitchen while looking after the pots and pans on the stove, then (possibly with your company of friends) you can hop onto the platform and be elevated, together with table, chairs, food, up to the first floor. There you can enjoy your meal in a space integrated into the living room, with a view of the garden and the "mosquito curtain" over which salamanders climb up and down!

But where was I: the curtains. What is crucial for the curtain concept is that their tracks are integrated in the architecture, literally poured during construction into the concrete. This was already the case at the Kunsthal in Rotterdam.

LS   If the Kunsthal is thus the ideal of integration, the Toledo Glass Museum, designed by SANAA, would be quite the opposite, as the interior of the glass box as proposed by the architects had to be modified after the design had been finalised to protect the precious exhibits from UV rays, heat, light and acoustics.

PB   A beautiful building. SANAA's lead architects, Kazuyo Sejima and Ryue Nishizawa, arrived one day at my office, straight from the airport, suitcases in hand. They wanted a Petra curtain for the multipurpose

room of the museum, a space that is partly auditorium, partly meeting room, partly venue hire etc. In other words, they wanted a decorative object with a strong presence. I was greatly honoured and we started working on the project. Along the way, priorities shifted and we were put to work on the other rooms where the glass collection was to be exhibited. The climate engineer, the lighting engineer and the curators of the museum asked us to help them solve the UV and temperature problems in these rooms with the help of curtains.

[46]

The challenges were immense as the building has a glass facade with glass structures inside it and an air space between two glass facades. If you were to hang a pleated curtain between these glass layers, you would create air pockets that heat up. But not only that: if you have a really small object made out of glass on display and a curtain that pleats, even if accidentally, you get vertical shadows. This is, of course, not good at all!

This was a very interesting challenge from a scientific point of view as all our proposals had to be tested by different engineers. We were experienced with textiles and had a battery of ideas about what to use and how. There are, for instance, very thin and transparent textiles with an aluminium powder coating on one side that reflects the sun; there are all kind of thicknesses that influence both the transmittance of light and the temperature. Still, all of the proposals had to undergo feasibility studies. Another challenge was the aesthetic quality, as the curtains were not to detract attention away from the exhibits in any way!

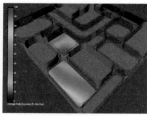

[47]

LS   The tests were run on a one-to-one scale, is that right?

PB   Yes, that was a great luxury in this project: a full-scale mock-up was made on site in which all typical conditions were recreated. Later I would experience the same situation in Doha, with OMA's Qatar National Library project. I think that a one-to-one mock-up of

[47] In the end, our task was to develop all track systems and numerous "invisible" technical curtains to cool and shade the galleries, in close collaboration with light and climate engineers

[48]

[48] All spaces' maximum temperatures and light conditions were analysed, and all materials carefully screened for effectiveness

[49] One of my design drawings for the section of the park Biblioteca degli Alberi in Milan that was to be developed in the first phase of the building works: the Fondazione Riccardo Catella site that we managed to regain as crucial component of the park.

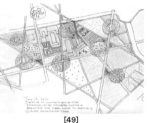

[49]

[50] Our team having lunch in our former studio kitchen on Eerste Nassaustraat, Amsterdam.

a building should always be done; one corner at least, where all the components come together and can be tested, the roof, glass facades, ceilings, floors and walls, along with the curtains, air conditioning, electricity, light, sprinklers and sunken rail details, and the acoustic and air movements… all in one mock-up.

LS   Were light and temperature for the Glass Museum tested in the lab?

PB   Yes. We sent all proposals to a university lab in Germany. They would test them and send us the results, with advice on how we should, for example, let the air move through the weave and how we should organise the pleats to prevent closed air tunnels from heating up. It took almost two and a half years to do all the research. We designed the tracks and the motors, and figured out how to make everything work. Unfortunately, we weren't able to complete the project because the new museum director thought that there were too many foreign designers involved. An American party was chosen to take over. So that was that.

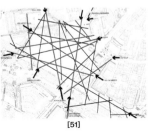

[50]

LS   The organisation of the team for the Giardini di Porto Nuova was completely different. At first sight, this project appears to be a continuation of your numerous previous landscape designs for prisons, universities and corporations all over the world. Yet, you repeatedly describe it as a critical project, because it is the first time that you were the lead architects. What did you mean when you wrote: "We were the invited party with the accompanying burden and responsibility, or on the contrary, the complete independence from "lead architects"?

PB   I don't think, I would put it that way now. We have obviously matured over the years and have also learned with whom we work best. If we are invited to participate in a competition for a landscape project, then we obviously have the lead role. But if the architect asks us to join a competition for a building or master plan, the opposite is true.

[51]

As for the Giardini, the invitation to participate to the competition came to us from the municipality of Milan. It was a closed competition, by invitation only. We formed a team with very strong professionals from other disciplines. So, while we were clearly the principals, it was the intense collaboration that enabled us to win the competition and realise the public park.

LS   Interior design and exterior design, from curtains to entire areas, the changes of scale do not seem to bother you. How do you deal with this on a practical level? Or to ask this in another way, is your approach to these different scales the same?

PB   Yes, I think so. Especially if you understand the lines in the landscape, as we did in Milan, not only as arbitrary geometric design, but as lines of life that allow different scenarios and forms of experience to unfold. Of course, initially and on a rational level, it seems to make sense to draw straight lines to physically and mentally connect different points of interest in that area to places farther away, to the monuments and mountains of Milano. Yet, the web of paths and the irregular fields we created transformed the way one experiences and walks through that area, the manner in which one now connects to all of the places and streets nearby, the way in which one can slow down, visit and enjoy the park on the way to work or use it as a social or an athletic destination close to one's home.

Certain decisions, of course, can only be made by landscape designers, for instance, the idea of the botanic garden. Mirko Zardini's proposition to give Milan a new botanic garden, as the one in Brera was completely abandoned at the time, resonated with our passion for systematising, archiving, collecting. Thus, the irregular fields became different kinds of gardens – a collection of typologies. Finally, to give the park scale but of course also for shade, we proposed a series of circular tree formations, which we called the "confetti of bosques." These were sprinkled over the web of paths and the

[51] The essential component of our park design for the Biblioteca degli Alberi: the "web of paths" that connects all important points and areas in the most efficient way

[52]

[52] The "web of paths" creates irregular fields that each represent a different garden typology

fields, creating vegetal pavilions which, when they are fully grown, will form covered public spaces. So, it was about imagining different ways of experiencing the park, with your children or your elderly mother, or as business person hurrying off to a meeting; imagining how you want to move from one point to the next through different "rooms" that trigger sensations like smell, temperature, enclosure, intimacy, darkness, light, seasons, colour, sound. In that sense, I think that exterior design is similar to interior design.

LS   In your texts, you like to compare the tracks of your curtains with the paths of your gardens.

PB   Both curtain tracks and garden paths create places and choreograph movement depending on how lines are drawn. Tracks, like paths, create a choreography in the space they traverse. The garden path is a line or a surface on the ground on which you walk up or down, straight, diagonally or in curves, while the track sets a curtain and its user in motion. Both landscape and curtains organise views and spaces and affect the way they are used. Working with the landscape team as well as the interior design team, we always first look at what composition and effects and sensations we want to achieve before we start to take any decision on curtains or planting. That's where things come together.

Inside Outside

WORKS

986-ongoing

by Petra Blaisse &

PHILIP URSPRUNG

EXHIBIT – INHABIT

In spring 2021, I held a seminar under the title "Exhibit – Inhabit" with the architecture students at ETH Zurich. The title suggests a tension between two verbs – to exhibit and to inhabit. The aim was not to define concepts and pin down meaning. Rather, we intended to make this tension productive. We wanted to allow it to resonate with associations, like a chord resonating on a musical instrument. We wished to find out more about the relation between exhibition and habitation, between exposure and introversion, display and privacy, the homely and the uncanny, the exorcised and the haunted.

This tension between exhibiting and inhabiting also resonates with the architectural work of Petra Blaisse. Since the early 1990s, her studio Inside Outside deals with the connections between displaying and living, small and large scale, introversion and extroversion. While architectural education still differentiates between architecture, interior design, product design, scenography and landscape architecture, Blaisse absorbs them all into her design. While most of today's architectural practices adhere to distinct categories, Inside Outside moves within the disciplines with ease and elegance.

The curtain is the most emblematic element in Blaisse's formal universe. More than other elements it marks the transition between the inside and the outside, the private and the public, the static and the dynamic, the rigid and the flexible. Curtains interact more directly with the environment, change their form with the air currents, can be drawn, opened and closed. From an ephemeral accessory of architectural design, Blaisse has transformed the curtain into a driving force of spatial production. I was thinking of Blaisse's curtains – or rather their absence – while we met in the course of our seminar on "hybrid" mode during the regime of social distancing. Some students were scattered in tiny images on the screens. We could see into their rooms like miniature stages. Others were sitting, masked and far apart, in the exhibition space of our campus.

The space we used was the very space that Blaisse had transformed in 2016 with *Wings*, an enfilade of black and white curtains which altered the way we thought about the display of objects. We liked this playful scenography and invited her to design the exhibition of the 50th anniversary of our Institute for the History and Theory of Architecture, the gta. In 2017 she designed golden-coloured Jubilee Curtains for the celebratory exhibition *Phantom Theory*. Her interventions blurred the distinction between the prolonged existence of the 1970s building, which houses the Department of Architecture, and the exhibition space, which changes fundamentally from one show to the next. They blurred the distinction between solid objects and ideas, which are the main product of the institute. And they blurred the distinction between the realm of a public institution and a quasi-private interior. While many visitors feel intimidated by exhibitions, for once everyone felt at home. Even after the curtains were taken down, the room kept its lightness.

As I was looking out of the window during our meetings, I recalled how the golden-coloured curtain had also altered the way we perceived the environment. By blocking the frontal view towards the busy campus centre and directing the gaze towards a small garden, Blaisse drew attention to one of the rare examples of landscape architecture within our university. I had spent much time in this space, yet I had never seen it like this before.

A year later, in 2018, Blaisse installed the retrospective of Inside Outside in the central hall of ETH's main building. Now even larger curtains activated the space. The main hall of the building, designed by Gottfried Semper and substantially altered during the twentieth century, expresses the authority of institutions of higher education. Originally conceived as an exhibition space for plaster casts, it was modified and is now a passageway for students on the way to classes. Hardly anyone comes to a halt in this hall.

Blaisse's curtains reoriented the movement. The space became an area to contemplate and reflect – not only on the history of Inside Outside, but also on Semper's building. The presence of textile heightened awareness of the building's textile qualities. The exhibition by Blaisse helped to see the surfaces and patterns in a new light. It reminded us that Semper's ambitions were theatre and opera and that his architecture functions like a succession of scenographies. Blaisse made us see our environment with new eyes.

Architectural change happens not within but between the traditional categories. In the last two decades, vague terms such as atmosphere, presence and performativity indicate a transformation of space. The presence of digital technologies in everyday life, the segregation within societies and the privatisation of public space are forces which have led to the transformation of space. The pandemic has heightened our awareness of this change. Blaisse's design happens in a zone which is affected by these changes, and which enables us to perceive them more clearly. Is it architecture, interior design, landscape architecture, product design, performance, scenography? The fact that we cannot answer this question adequately is proof of the vitality of Blaisse's work.

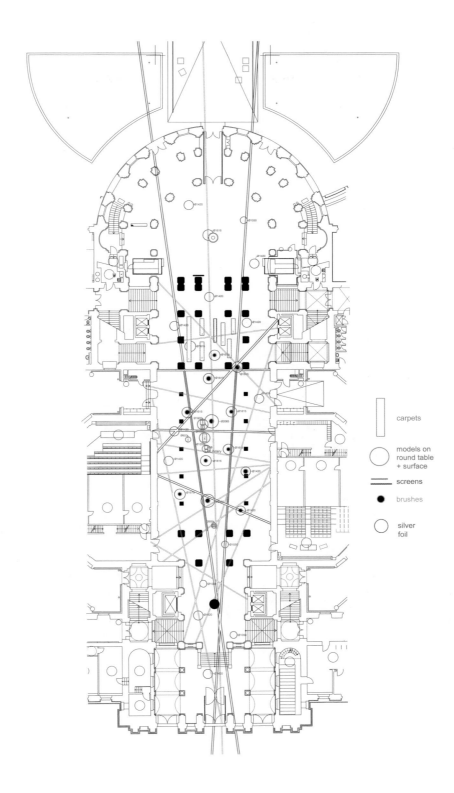

legend:

carpets

models on
round table
+ surface

screens

brushes

silver
foil

Drawing for Inside Outside's exhibition
(2018) at ETH Zurich's main hall, originally
designed by Gottfried Semper

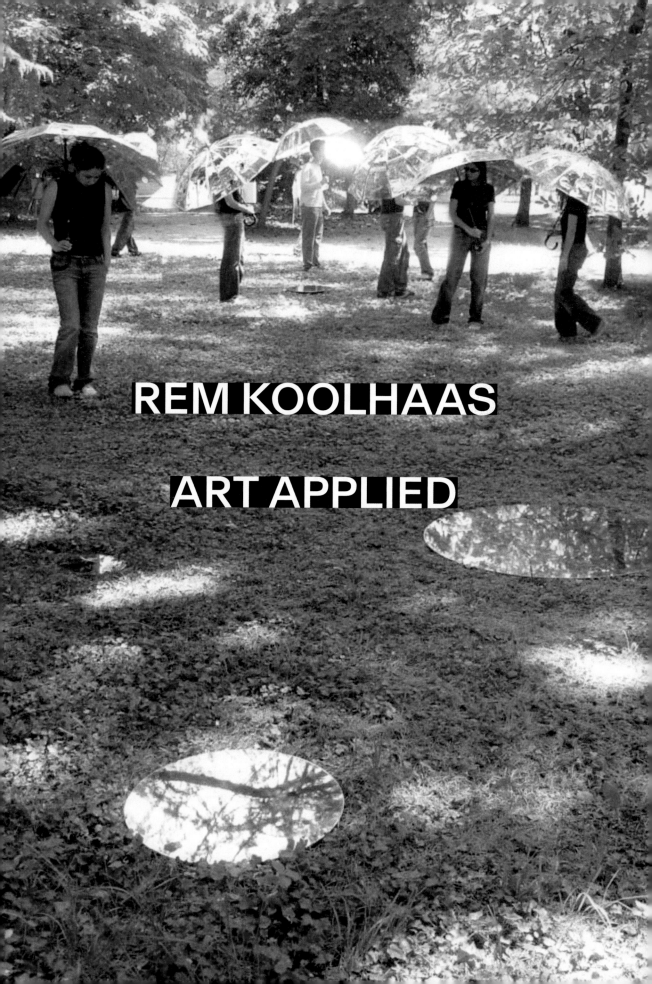

REM KOOLHAAS

ART APPLIED

Abridged text of lecture by Rem Koolhaas on the occasion of *Inside Outside / Petra Blaisse: A Retrospective* at ETH Zurich, 18 October 2018.

It is obviously risky to talk about someone you are involved with in real life and also in work. It is also complicated because we are both a "we." There is very little we do without collaborators. The names of our offices both sound neutral: Office for Metropolitan Architecture and Inside Outside. For that reason, this presentation will make the minimum of personal declarations and personal references but simply try to talk about the work of Petra on her own and the work of Inside Outside.

I met Petra in the '80s when she was working as an assistant curator at the Stedelijk Museum. She talked to me about the possibility of doing a show of our work. Curator is a beautiful word because it implies care. It soon became very evident that Petra had an incredible ability to care and to make things look extremely good, almost independent of their quality. Working with her on exhibitions here in Barcelona, I experienced her ability to engineer an aesthetic vision. And maybe she, in turn, learned about space. I use the word *learning* because it is key to understanding Inside Outside. We soon began collaborating with her and the first thing she did was a curtain for a dance theatre in Den Haag, OMA's first public building.

In buildings such as the Seattle Central Library (1999–2004), it is almost impossible to separate what they did from what we did. Although Petra is typically very aware of her contribution, I am more vague. But the contribution of Inside Outside is crucial in key images like this one. Here is a typical "Petra Drawing," which illustrates that one of the central elements of the Seattle building is the infiltration of nature, an urban garden outside that enters each part of the interior. In this photograph you see very nicely how two realities merge: the reality of the plants outside and the printed reality of the carpets inside.

Dinner at Restaurant Zinc, Rotterdam, 1988

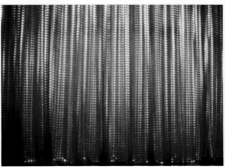

Installation view of *Rem Koolhaas: OMA. Fin de Siècle* with an exhibition design by Petra Blaisse, 1990, Collegi D'Arquitectes de Catalunya, Barcelona

Petra Blaisse, Liquid Gold, Curtain for Nederlands Dans Theater, 1985–1987, Den Haag

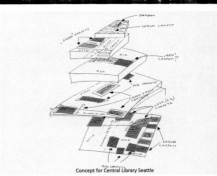

Inside Outside, drawing for the gardens and interiors of Central Library by OMA in Seattle, 1999–2004

Central Library by OMA in Seattle, 1999–2004, with Garden Carpets by Inside Outside

Curtains by Inside Outside in the Casa da Musica by OMA in Porto, 1999–2005

Drawing for Piranesi Pixel landscape for CCTV Headquarters by OMA in Beijing, 2004–2012

View from CCTV Headquarters interior to the landscape designed by Inside Outside, 2004–2012

Inside Outside, source material for Taipei Performing Arts Center, 2009–2022

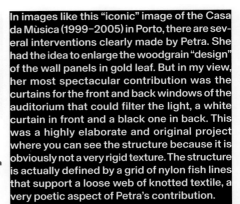

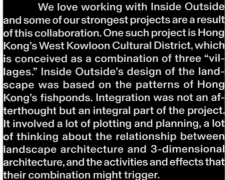

Inside Outside, collage for Taipei Performing Arts Center, 2009–2022

In images like this "iconic" image of the Casa da Mùsica (1999–2005) in Porto, there are several interventions clearly made by Petra. She had the idea to enlarge the woodgrain "design" of the wall panels in gold leaf. But in my view, her most spectacular contribution was the curtains for the front and back windows of the auditorium that could filter the light, a white curtain in front and a black one in back. This was a highly elaborate and original project where you can see the structure because it is obviously not a very rigid texture. The structure is actually defined by a grid of nylon fish lines that support a loose web of knotted textile, a very poetic aspect of Petra's contribution.

Here we see how the CCTV Headquarters (2002–2012) is imbedded in a landscape. That landscape copies Piranesi's plans of the Roman forum and gives the heart of Beijing a sense of urban density. Exactly what CCTV really needed. It produces its own context.

In a building we are currently doing in Taipei, the Taipei Performing Arts Center (2009–2022), her interesting contribution was to correct OMA's habit of "diversifying" and to consider that it could be more interesting to repeat one colour and to play with a single identity for three very different theatres, and to then play with textures such as the curtain, upholstery and wall treatments so that one single colour became a kind of leitmotif for the entire building. The difficulty in architecture is that it takes such a long time: over eleven years for this one and there are two more years to come. You have to think in advance of fashion, in advance of everything that can go wrong in terms of redundancy or other aesthetic developments. But I think it will be exciting.

We love working with Inside Outside and some of our strongest projects are a result of this collaboration. One such project is Hong Kong's West Kowloon Cultural District, which is conceived as a combination of three "villages." Inside Outside's design of the landscape was based on the patterns of Hong Kong's fishponds. Integration was not an afterthought but an integral part of the project. It involved a lot of plotting and planning, a lot of thinking about the relationship between landscape architecture and 3-dimensional architecture, and the activities and effects that their combination might trigger.

The great thing about this long-term collaboration, which also applies to our structural collaboration with Arup and Cecil Balmond, is that when two such different domains work intimately together, they each learn about the other's profession and therefore it makes both sides more confident in the other's fields – not always easy.

This is the Axel Spring Campus (2013–2020) which we are doing in Berlin. The challenge is how to not only integrate a very large structure into the very dense centre of Berlin, but how to introduce something that is connected to work but also to pleasure. The idea was to generate a landscape pattern that is rolled out over the entire site to give intensities and irregularities, to generate appealing "exceptions" outside and inside as well.

Renderings of OMA's Project of West Kowloon Cultural District, Hong Kong, Park of the New Horizon, landscapes designed by Inside Outside, 2009–2010

OMA completed two buildings in Qatar. You see here the landscape by Inside Outside that surrounds the National Library in Doha (2008–2017), almost an inventory of drought-tolerant plants. The library is surrounded by sunken bowls of vegetation, but perhaps the most important feature is the curtain inside. From the outside white and from inside dark blue, it offers the possibility of creating an enclosure within a wide-open space. The patterns on the curtain come from Arabic measuring devices developed before Pythagoras. Here you see the exit from the inside and how it works as a single "room." The space doesn't just accommodate lectures; it is also used for theatre, music, etc.

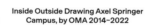

Inside Outside Drawing Axel Springer Campus, by OMA 2014–2022

Landscapes by Inside Out for National Gallery in Qatar, 2008–2016

But actually, that's not what I'm here to tell you about. I'm here to talk about Petra Blaisse and Inside Outside. I want to put her work in context and explain how it is different from design. For the past maybe 10, 15, or 20 years the world has been inundated with design. It has become an enormous commercial force and sustains a large part of the Dutch economy. It is now defining "Dutchness" as creative, sustainable and "funny." Holland is at risk of becoming the central theme of Dutch design. But the word "designer" does not apply to Blaisse. When I first met her at the Stedelijk, people still talked about "applied arts." I think this is the key to understanding her work. "Applied artist" is the opposite of designer. The term is not about pragmatically solving certain kinds of issues in the world and it's not about pleasing a certain audience. "Applied arts" essentially boils down to art that engages with the world outside the museum and maybe that is the most precise way of describing what Inside Outside does.

Inside Outside, Cosmic Curtain, National Library, Doha, 2008–2016

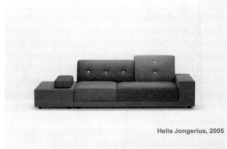

Hella Jongerius, 2005

Hella Jongerius, Polder Couch, 2005

For me there is no project that shows the quality of Inside Outside or Blaisse more than this one: Blaisse was invited to contribute to an art show in a mansion near Venice. What was extremely beautiful in my view were the two devices that Blaisse and her team thought of. One was a mirroring umbrella. Even if it did not rain, you saw grass and trees reflected above you as you walked around the beautiful park. The umbrella became a portable park. The second device was circular mirrors that looked as if they had been randomly thrown on the ground all over the estate. They made you feel as if you could walk over the sky. The key experience here was to walk with an umbrella over this incredibly poetic landscape that – with only two devices – had been converted into a radical experience. It takes an extremely sensitive and artistic approach to generate such a profound effect through the involvement of the visitors. The work couldn't exist without them and that is perhaps where the word "applied" comes in.

Here we have a similar effect but more brutal and more powerful. I use these two words despite the stereotypical male connotation. Brutal and powerful are rarely applied to women, but I think here and in Petra's case, these words are occasionally deserved. This is a relatively bourgeois interior in a classical kind of modern villa in Rotterdam. And this is what Petra turned it into simply by covering all the floors with mirrors. Again, I think this was less subtle and perhaps more Dutch. But it was also deeply critical and profound. You could even say it turned visitors into researchers. Research is an overused word these days. But I have never looked so carefully at the underside of a chair, a bed or a chest. So what is unique about this simple act of mirroring is that it zooms in on parts of daily life that you never ordinarily perceive, let alone think about.

Moool, 2006

Moooi, Horse Lamp, 2006

Inside Outside, Rifletutti mirroring umbrellas, Villa Manin, 2005

Inside Outside, Rifletutti mirroring umbrellas, Villa Manin, 2005

Inside Outside, Huis Sonneveld, Rotterdam, 2014–2015

Inside Outside, Huis Sonneveld, Rotterdam, 2014–2015

What I actually would like to explain in this lecture is the connection – complex as it is – between inside and outside. How can you claim, as Petra does, a role in the world inside and a role in the world outside? You can talk about landscapes and interiors, but I think the connection is "planes," horizontal and vertical planes. The former is typically landscape, the latter typically curtains. If you look at it in this way, you may see a connection between the two.

Inside Outside, Huis Sonneveld, Rotterdam, 2014–2015

This is the courtyard of a prison in the Netherlands, an early project by Inside Outside. It is a very daring project because it introduces a path, a path that ends in the centre and is laid out in a strange, almost crude, childlike way. Very irregular. But that is exactly what I think it takes for a prisoner – even if he is in this prison for a short time – to appreciate a difference between the daily rigidity of his existence and the irregularity of the garden.

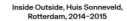

Inside Outside, The Path as a Spatial Tool, State Detention Centre, 1997–1999, Nieuwegein, the Netherlands

6 prison gardens, Nieuwegein prison (Utrecht) 1997-1999

Inside Outside, The Path as a Spatial Tool, State Detention Centre, 1997–1999, Nieuwegein, the Netherlands

Here you see a curtain, so you see the difference in approach. If you look beyond park and interior and focus on horizontal and vertical planes, you can see Petra or Inside Outside as an artist that does applied art for these two conditions, horizontal and vertical. I will start with a number of horizontal planes. This is the entire prison garden. You see that there is a labyrinth, a path of continuity that kind of wraps around the building and that at every point generates an alternative that is more frivolous, more alive and therefore perhaps a more eloquent representation of a "different" condition.

Inside Outside, making of Cosmic Curtain for Qatar National Library, 2008–2016

Here we have the University of Amsterdam on Roeterseiland. The drawing itself ranges from total confusion to absolute clarity, suggesting many different conditions; it's a script of a very high calibre written for a horizontal plane.

Inside Outside, drawing for Roeterseiland Campus, University of Amsterdam, 2010–2017

Roeterseiland University Campus paths, Amsterdam

The garden on the roof of the Shenzhen Stock Exchange tower. It almost looks absurd, a layer of beauty on top of a money-making – or losing – machine, but that absurdity is exactly the point here: we see one of the most rigid, rigorous and powerful economies of the current world deliberately covered, even cancelled with an extremely "girlish" quotation from the seventeenth century.

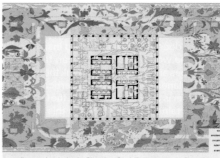

podium garden design for Shenzhen Stock Exchange tower, Shenzhen

Inside Outside, drawing and collage for Sino-European Gardens, Shenzen Stock Exchange, 2007–2013

The headquarters of the Qatar Foundation are just a few hundred feet away from the National Library that I showed earlier. Inside Outside created a landscape – a horizontal plane – with an unbelievably intricate composition of the actual species that are necessary to bring a structure like that to life; it's seemingly simple but actually a very complex entity. And scientific in the sense that it means developing deep knowledge to make entire planes – of over a hectare – grow and generate the density of emotion that does justice to their scale.

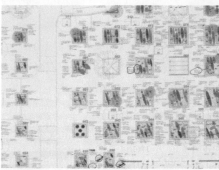

Inside Outside, technical drawing with planting scheme for Water Recipe Garden, Qatar Foundation Headquarters, Doha, Qatar

Inside Outside, Water Recipe Garden, Qatar Foundation Headquarters, Doha, Qatar

Perhaps the provisional culmination of these horizontal plans is the public park that will open in a few days in Milan, where the key objective is to connect arbitrary points in the centre of Milan that previously had no connection. By connecting these points, a grid of irregular fields is created that contains a number of Circular Forests. The outcome looks very simple, as it so often does after such a long process of planning and deliberation, but while this drawing may look playful, it is actually a gesture so compelling that it is paradoxically compatible with the brutality of the city itself. I think this field shows the essence of what I mean when I talk about applied arts. And here you see the layering that defines the aesthetics as a whole.

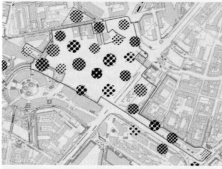

Inside Outside, conceptual drawing for Biblioteca degli Alberi, Giardini di Porta Nuova, Milan, Italy, 2003–2018

So far I have spoken about horizontal planes. Now let's take a look at some vertical ones. This curtain acts as a wall in a home in Amsterdam. I would say here this is not a curtain, it seems more like a work closer to the architecture of the Italian '60s perhaps, but still it's a curtain.

wall-replacing curtain for private house, Amsterdam, 2002

Curtain wall, artist residence, Amsterdam, 2002

One of the early curtains that I was confronted with – that is maybe the word – was for the Kunsthal in Rotterdam (1987–1992). It creates a space for the audience inside the open architecture. For the rails Petra insisted on a presence integrated in the concrete ceiling. The curtains are not decorative elements but rather architectural incisions. Here you see the curtain in its 'stored' position, when it is not used as an auditorium wall: a spiral that wraps around a column where it becomes almost a sculpture. The curtain began to play games with the architecture and render certain parts of it invisible.

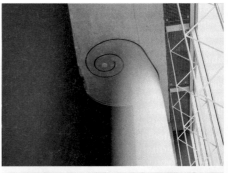

Petra Blaisse, spiraling curtain for the
Kunsthal Rotterdam, 1992

Petra Blaisse, spiraling curtain for the
Kunsthal Rotterdam, 1992

Here you see a very traditional curtain in this early picture of a villa in Paris (Villa dall'Ava, 1984–1991). I already mentioned the word "discovery." The curtain looks kind of classical and pleasant here, but as soon as you open the windows, you discover that it behaves very unpredictably. A single presence turns into a double presence. So, Petra or Inside Outside or Blaisse – I think Blaisse is the best term – realised here that curtains have a secret life apart from what was planned for them. If you are attuned to that, you can vastly expand the potential of a curtain. Not only did Blaisse become more emancipated, she in turn emancipated curtains.

Petra Blaisse, curtain for living room of
Villa Dall'Ava by OMA Rem Koolhaas, 1991

Petra Blaisse, curtain for living room of
Villa Dall'Ava by OMA Rem Koolhaas, 1991

Here we see the program for the villa in Bordeaux. Again, the traces of future behaviour carved out from the concrete ceiling. Then you see the behaviour of that curtain itself, completely spontaneously. Simply through drafts or open parts of the building, the curtains escape from the living room and engage with nature, making movements and spaces that are completely unfeasible in architecture. Therefore, the curtain can have a potential and a power that have rarely been seen before.

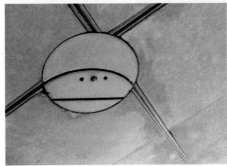

Petra Blaisse, track for living room
curtain of Villa Dall'Ava by OMA
Rem Koolhaas, 1991

Two factors in Blaisse's biography are of significance. She was educated in Catholic schools, something ordinarily presented as a traumatic experience, but I think it has given her an enviable amount of discipline that she has been careful to use and nurture. And she is an autodidact, a term which is currently not very much in vogue. We all study, you all study and the idea that we are not going to study almost seems like an aberration. The beautiful thing about being an autodidact is that you do not occupy a defined territory. You can define your territory the way you want. Plus the fact that autodidacts have not received a specific amount of knowledge but begin and end by creating their own body of knowledge. Therefore, they are not complacent because they are never finished with learning. I think these are really important elements that influence how Blaisse works.

For instance, she has discovered that what curtains can do is vastly more sophisticated that what architecture can do. Architects have to use the extreme sophistication of the digital world; curtains just need a bit of wind to assume countless identities in a single moment. So it is easier, more sophisticated, more complex in terms of result, less stable and therefore continuously more exciting and wonderful. I think it would be hard to identify when or how Blaisse began to work on more rigorous, challenging and ambitious entities; maybe it was when she became Inside Outside – or simply when she discovered there are things she could do better than any architect.

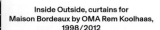

Inside Outside, curtains for
Maison Bordeaux by OMA Rem Koolhaas,
1998/2012

Inside Outside, curtains for
Maison Bordeaux by OMA Rem Koolhaas,
1998/2012

Curtain in the former studio of Inside
Ouside in Amsterdam

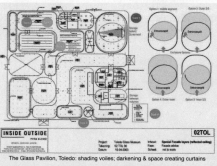

Inside Outside, schematic drawings,
curtains for the The Glass Pavilion at
Toledo Museum of Art by SANAA, 2006

An important moment is the glass pavilion for the Toledo Museum of Art in Ohio by the Japanese architect Sejima (SANAA). The museum is like a glass box with smaller glass boxes inside, which create lots of reflections in between a boomerang-shaped public space. It's absolutely wonderful. But when you look at it in terms of air or heat and all the technical specifications to which a museum has to conform, it is a beautiful structure architecturally, but a nightmare to make it "work." That's where Blaisse comes in. I saw how she almost systematically dismantled the typical approach of architecture by introducing lighter elements as solutions for issues that architecture could barely resolve. Here you see the almost scientific rigour of that work. Inside Outside was able to propose a number of details and insights, which was deeply intimidating.

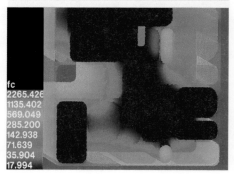

Inside Outside, source image, curtains for
The Glass Pavilion at Toledo Museum of
Art by SANAA, 2006

Another project from about the same time shows once again how Blaisse benefits from being an autodidact, and also how passionate and ambitious she is about everything she does. It was for the Haus der Kunst in Munich – a building practically crushed by its associations with the Nazi regime. It survived the war and became a state-run art gallery. Here you can see a piece of modern art inside the great hall, formerly one of the key spaces of Nazism. Chris Dercon, the director of the museum, asked Blaisse to do something with that hall and with the memory of its past. She came up with a solution that cost a fraction of what an architect would have had to invest to achieve a similarly striking and extremely efficient result. She introduced asymmetry to this hyper symmetrical domain, a gesture that in itself undoes its evil spirit. And then, being able to use her intervention as a projection screen adds not only an aesthetic, but also a programmatic dimension.

We have seen her almost scientific approach with Sejima, and the ideological approach here. Now Inside Outside begins to work on the curtain in itself, denying that it is a kind of flat sheet or vertical plane.

The curtain in the Hackney Empire Theatre – in red velvet – shows this obsession with depth and structure that is beginning to take over and define many of Blaisse's curtains: a softer version of the elements that play a big role in architecture, a more appealing aesthetic. In America at the Chazen Museum of Art (Madison Wisconsin, 2008–2011), it is almost not clear anymore whether it is a curtain or a kind of a portable wall or a proto-facade.

As I said, Blaisse and Inside Outside are very ambitious. You notice a relentless advance; they are becoming architecture or displacing architecture or matching it. In this case, architecture is actually a portable wall; what's even more amazing is that the curtain floats, gravity is temporarily suspended (Narcissus, 2013). It was developed for concerts at various locations, so the membrane just becomes a portable facade. Thousands of architects for thousands of years have looked for this Holy Grail – overcoming gravity, achieving weightlessness. And here it's been done almost casually.

Hitler's inaugural speech in the Mittelhalle at Haus der Kunst, 1937

Inside Outside, curtains for the Mittelhalle at Haus der Kunst, 2004–2007, Munich

Inside Outside, curtains for Haus der Kunst, 2004–2007, Munich

Inside Outside, detail view of curtain for Hackney Empire Theatre in London, 1999–2005

Inside Outside, detail view of curtain for Hackney Empire Theatre in London, 1999–2005

In a recent project, a theatre curtain in Saudi Arabia, the curtain becomes a three-dimensional event. It reaches into the auditorium and also protrudes backstage. So, it is no longer satisfied with merely separating stage and audience, but it actually invades both sides. A curtain has to be light and using the principle of "tensegrity," a term coined by Buckminster Fuller, it can be lightweight and still rigid. Here we see it used in the King Abdulaziz Center for World Culture in Saudi Arabia.

Inside Outside, curtain for King Abdaluaziz Center for World Culture, 2012–2018, Dharan, Saudi Arabia

A project in the Netherlands illustrates Inside Outside's ambition to equal or even replace architecture. A former maintenance shed of the Dutch Railways, still largely intact, has been transformed into a public library, art and workspace. The blue indicates the architecture required so that it can be used for an entirely different purpose and it demonstrates my theory: the incredible economy and elegance of this kind of intervention compared to conventional architecture. The total cost of about €600,000 is so little in comparison to the effect that has been achieved. That is a daunting challenge to architecture. Here you see the scale, the nature and the effect of the curtains. I almost feel professional envy to see the efficiency and playfulness of these unstable entities that would be horribly formalistic and heavy-handed if they were built... And there's more to it – the way these vertical planes act in space and the way they occupy it. In this sequence of slides we also see Blaisse's increasing monumentality. That's something to be careful about. But Blaisse gives it a human face and sensitively combines seriousness with fun and pleasure. That also applies to the main hall of the ETH Zurich, which we have all seen together.

LocHal train repair workshop, 1939

Inside Outside, collage for LocHal Library, Tilburg, 2014–2018

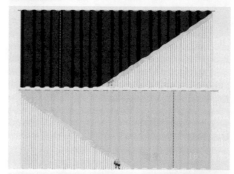

Inside Outside, drawing for LocHal Library, Tilburg, 2014–2018

Now, it is time to show that the curtains created by Inside Outside are no longer curtains and that the vertical planes have become walls. This is the crucial thing that has been happening in the past two years and you can see that Inside Outside has reached a point where they probably have to decide whether to stay in this domain which they have themselves defined or go further and become architects too.

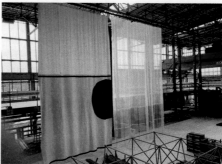

Inside Outside, making of curtains for LocHal Library, Tilburg, 2014–2018

At the Luma Foundation in Zurich, Inside Outside has now actually made walls that are rigid and fixed. In this case they separate four sections of a single exhibition through the placement of very elegant frames wrapped in plastic foil. The beauty of this wrapping is that it is by definition irregular and, as the transparent walls recede, the view becomes more and more blurred, the work more and more mysterious and the space itself more and more enigmatic. Once again, this is a very smart and powerful way of thinking about walls. The curtain has now definitely become a facade.

Inside Outside, making of the exhibition architecture for *Theft is Vision* (2018), Luma Westbau, Zurich

Inside Outside, making of the exhibition architecture for *Theft is Vision* (2018), Luma Westbau, Zurich

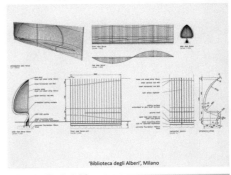

Inside Outside, exhibition architecture for *Theft is Vision* (2018), Luma Westbau, Zurich

Screens for exhibition Theft is Vision, Luma Foundation, Zurich, 2017

Inside Outside, drawing for a fence, Giardini di Porta Nuova, Milan, 2003–2018

'Biblioteca degli Alberi', Milano

Another example in the park in Milan is an enclosure of private property within the park, basically a fence but the fence is warped, curved in such a way that it generates program. Even though it is made of iron, it doesn't only separate, it also connects by generating seating both inside and outside the closure. In a way, this is another example of where the curtain has become a facade but – as so often – a permanent and permeable one.

Inside Outside, fence in the Giardini di Porta Nuova, Milan 2003–2018

The final project I want to talk about is in Berlin where Inside Outside has clearly taken the next step in becoming architects. It's an attic in a former hospital in Berlin, almost a cathedral structure with very little light originally, but of course you can always increase light. Here are some sketches of how architecture could exist inside this attic, the rectangular box positioned strategically inside the attic, breaking through the roof to appear on the outside. This plan is actually a copy of Philip Johnson's Glass House, placed to also create the oligarch's sleeping quarters. Inside Outside has landed in the field of architecture but of course with a daunting range of abilities that go far beyond that. Interestingly, the darkness of the attic is challenged and therefore they make openings in the attic that reveal sections of the Berlin skyline – without curtains.

In conclusion, I hope that with this lecture I have shown many aspects of Blaisse and Inside Outside and given you a kind of sense of their "Werdegang," their growth and development, what their ambition has been, how they have systematically worked on this ambition and how this systematic work could not have happened without discipline, without a sense of discovery and without infinite curiosity.

Inside Outside, collage for "Glass House," Joli Cœur, Berlin-Charlottenburg, 2015–2019

Inside Outside, sketch for "Glass House," Joli Cœur, Berlin-Charlottenburg, 2015–2019

Inside Outside, drawing for "Glass House," Joli Cœur, Berlin-Charlottenburg, 2015–2019

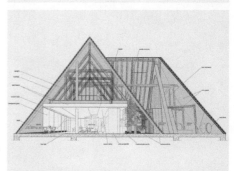

Inside Outside, rendering of the interior of "Glass House," Joli Cœur, Berlin-Charlottenburg, 2015–2019

Inside Outside, photograph during construction "Glass House," Joli Cœur, Berlin-Charlottenburg, 2015–2019

SELECTED PROJECTS 2023-1

PB Petra Blaisse
JC Jana Crepon
NE Nafsika Efklidou
AM Aura Luz Melis
PN Peter Niessen

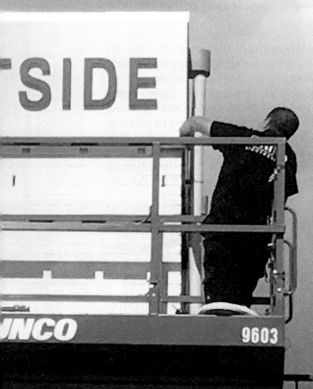

Inside Outside / Petra Blaisse:
A Retrospective

"Fredi and Niels's challenging and humorous invitation led to the production of two retrospective curtains, where the medium and the (selected) content together communicate the essence of our work: an overview of many years of lively teamwork and conceptual thinking – about seventy examples of our curtains, interiors, exhibitions and landscaping. This 'retrospective' installation, pliable and flexible as it is, has since travelled from place to place, temporarily transforming each location (ETH Zurich, Triennale di Milano, MAXXI Rome) on the way – most recently billowing in the wind outside and within Hadid's impressive feminine monumentality."

"The exhibition in 2018 ignited the curators' interest in a comprehensive publication, an overview of our creative work from A to Z in the form of a printed paper object with a soft cover and many thin pages that follow each other in narrative succession, telling stories in written language and colourful images – just like the one you have in your hands right now – presenting my work from my first years as an independent, when I still worked alone from my house and the back of my car, then with persons that I invited to join me per project, then through to the collaborative teamwork of Inside Outside up until today. So exciting. So confrontational. So complex. So rich. So simplistic, naïve at times. So infuriating. So exhausting. So uplifting. So fulfilling. So challenging. So educational. So much fun. So moving and surprising to see it all together now. Thank you ETH Zurich. It's a real pleasure." PB

LOCATION	Zurich, Switzerland; Milan, Italy; Rome, Italy
CLIENT	Institute for the History and Theory of Architecture (gta), ETH Zurich 2018; Triennale di Milano 2019–2020; MAXXI – Museo Nazionale delle Arti del XXI Secolo, Rome 2022.
STATUS	Completed
SCOPE	"Design a retrospective exhibition on your own work (1986–2018) in three months"
SIZE	Two curtains, 25 × 8–12 m each, floor treatment (380 m white tape, 640 m black tape, 25 silver disks and brushes), IO films and models
MATERIALS	Trevira CS voile and PVC, models of various materials, brushes, foam, stickers, tape, paint; video films, textile curtain samples, Rifletutti mobile pavilions, printed matter such as posters, folders, books
COLLABORATORS	Niels Olsen, Fredi Fischli, gta Exhibitions, Triennale team, Maxxi Exhibitions team, Teo Schifferli, Frans Parthesius, AVD Productions
DESCRIPTION	After we had collaborated on several projects for a few years, Niels Olsen and Fredi Fischli quite naturally took the initiative, in the name of the Institute for the History and Theory of Architecture (gta), to mount an Inside Outside retrospective exhibition in the Semper Building in Zurich (constructed in 1864 by Gottfried Semper and extended by Gustav Gull between 1914 and 1925), and to realise this 35-year retrospective within three months.

The curtain seemed to descend from the sky. The contrast between the curtain, transparent and billowing in the wind, and the building's static, muscular concrete structure was stunning.

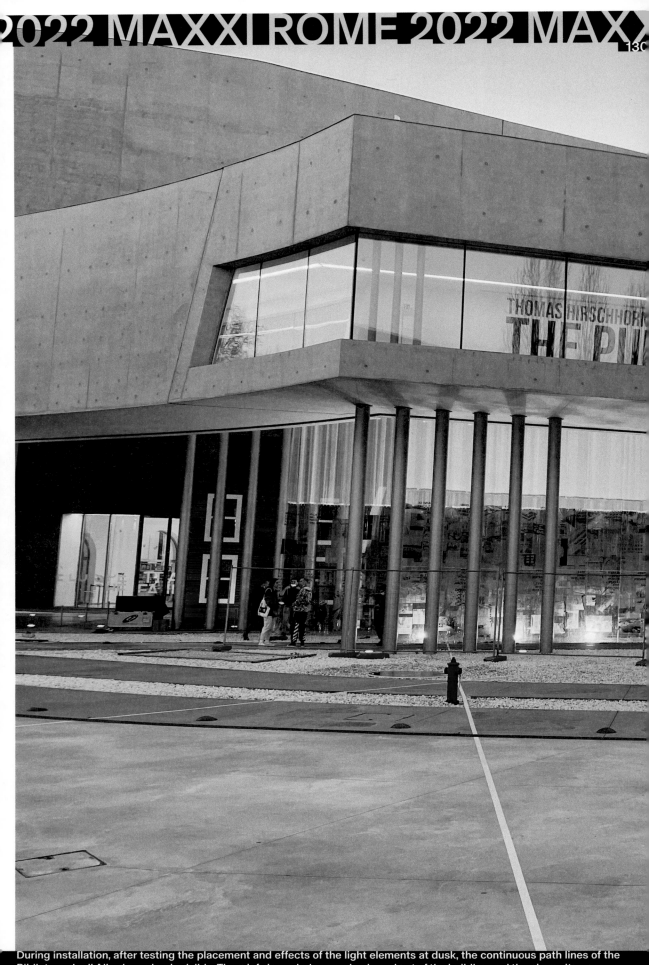

During installation, after testing the placement and effects of the light elements at dusk, the continuous path lines of the Biblioteca degli Alberi are clearly visible. They defy boundaries, moving in and out of the building and the given site.

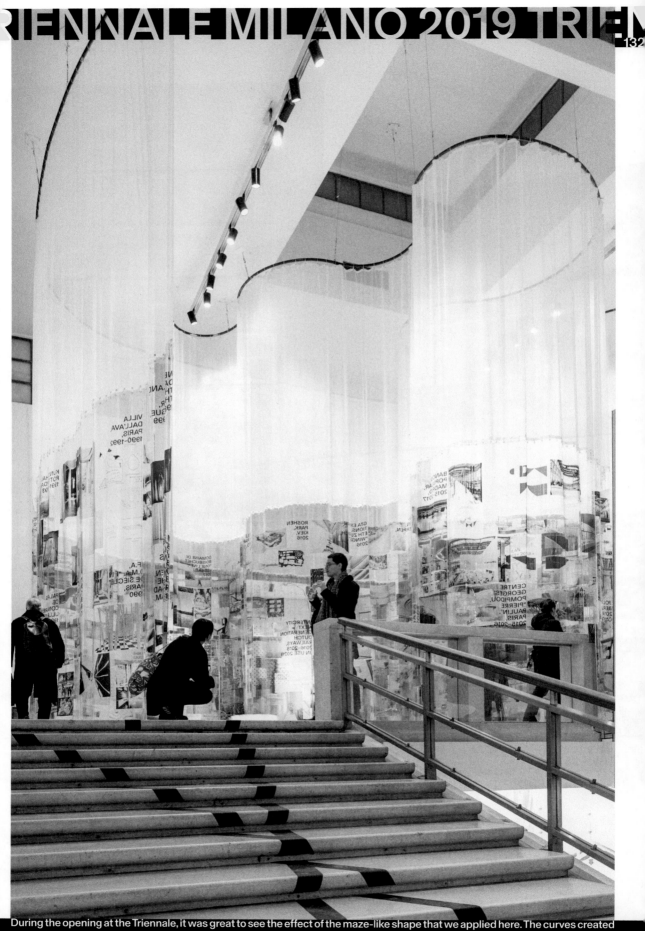

During the opening at the Triennale, it was great to see the effect of the maze-like shape that we applied here. The curves created small niches where models were placed, and the meandering of the curtain made the walk-through feel like strolling through a garden. As always, the Biblioteca path composition was represented by continuous lines on the floor, and the Circular Forests by our favourite brushes. Out of view, just around the corner to the left, video films and curtain samples were on display.

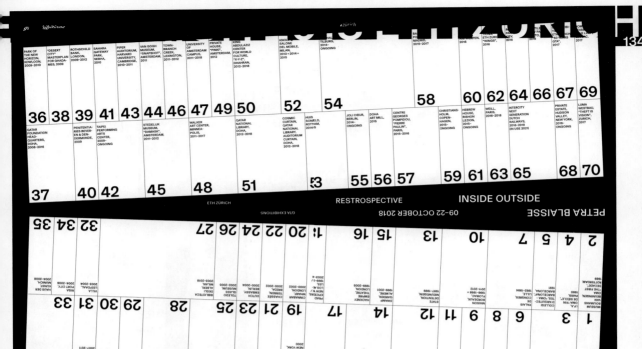

Exhibition booklet and poster

The initiative to design and install our retrospective in the Semper Building's main hall within a few months and exhibit it for a very short period of time was demanding and energising! As always, we challenged the architecture and its maker(s) with our intervention while telling our own story at the same time.

Seventy selected projects printed on the transparent plastic seam. 4 metres high and twice 25 metres long.

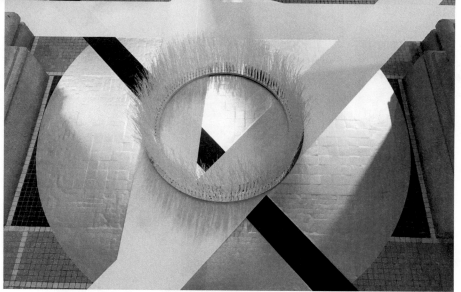

The endless lines of black and white tape represent the path structure of the Biblioteca degli Alberi in Milan. Escaping the building, these lines ignore all boundaries.

Wait till the evening sun enters through that glazed door in the back...!

"The owners, a young couple with two teenage children, visited our studio to meet and to understand more about our work and mentality. They were introduced by the architect. All went well. The Farnsworth-like villa is built on a sliver of extremely green land in the Dutch polders, covered by grasses, herbs and beautiful trees, surrounded by water with swaying reeds along its banks. Birds fly overhead, endless skies are reflected in the still waters and tree branches filter the light differently each season. Traditionally farmers would have their farmhouse, sheds and livestock on this land, but now the plots are bought by city dwellers who prefer open space and silence; a life seamlessly connected to nature. Lots of Nile geese quickly took possession of the surrounding terraces, their acidic excrement damaging the wooden surface. Local farmers taught the new owner to use a strong laser-pointer to scare them away instead of reaching for a broom or gun. This works."   PB

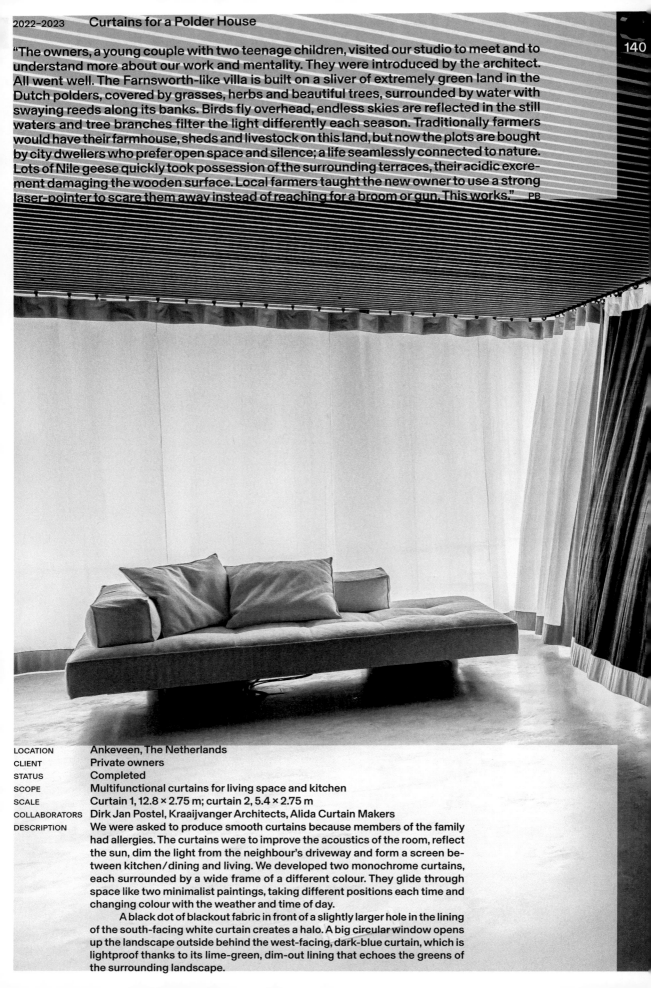

LOCATION	Ankeveen, The Netherlands
CLIENT	Private owners
STATUS	Completed
SCOPE	Multifunctional curtains for living space and kitchen
SCALE	Curtain 1, 12.8 × 2.75 m; curtain 2, 5.4 × 2.75 m
COLLABORATORS	Dirk Jan Postel, Kraaijvanger Architects, Alida Curtain Makers
DESCRIPTION	We were asked to produce smooth curtains because members of the family had allergies. The curtains were to improve the acoustics of the room, reflect the sun, dim the light from the neighbour's driveway and form a screen between kitchen/dining and living. We developed two monochrome curtains, each surrounded by a wide frame of a different colour. They glide through space like two minimalist paintings, taking different positions each time and changing colour with the weather and time of day.

A black dot of blackout fabric in front of a slightly larger hole in the lining of the south-facing white curtain creates a halo. A big circular window opens up the landscape outside behind the west-facing, dark-blue curtain, which is lightproof thanks to its lime-green, dim-out lining that echoes the greens of the surrounding landscape.

Landscape masterplan
Ujiri Court

"Masai Ujiri, Vice-Chairman and President of the NBA's Toronto Raptors and his non-profit, Giants of Africa, have announced a multi-year, 100-court investment in the infrastructure of basketball throughout Africa. This physical investment in the continent continues the foundation's commitment to creating opportunity for youth in Africa through sports, and harnessing the power of the next generation to propel the continent forward.

Nigerian-Canadian Ujiri founded Giants of Africa in 2003 to improve the lives of African boys and girls through sport. Since launching in Nigeria, it has its footprint and programming across the continent, prioritising skills training and personal development through basketball, health and wellness, leadership and social impact initiatives.

'Since we began investing in the future of sports in Africa over the last two decades, it became clear that camps and programming were not enough to create long-term opportunities for growth in sports,' said Ujiri. 'These public spaces have the power to unite communities, build togetherness and improve quality of life for all people.'

'Sports are one of the best ways that we can help our young people achieve their goals and I look forward to hearing the stories of the thousands of young people who will be able to utilize these courts to help make their communities stronger over the next ten years and beyond,' said Ujiri.

Ujiri Court is an urban lifestyle, real estate, hospitality, sports and entertainment brand that caters to the booming African middle and millennial class. Ujiri Court embraces the cool depths of African tradition while maintaining an unyielding commitment to innovative development." EXCERPTS FROM THE OFFICIAL ASSIGNMENT INTRODUCTION

LOCATION	Kigali, Rwanda
CLIENT	Rino Global, LLC
STATUS	Ongoing
SCOPE	Landscape design for an urban sports campus as part of the "Giants of Africa" project initiated by NBA basketball player and coach Masai Ujiri; site program contains sports-, events and recreational facilities, hotel, shops and bars, all embedded in a green landscape
SCALE	2.5 ha
COLLABORATORS	NLE, Afrilandscapes
DESCRIPTION	Kigali lies in a region of rolling hills with a series of valleys and ridges joined by steep slopes. Our landscape concept for this triangular site refers to the description of Rwanda as "the country of a thousand hills." The basketball court and the seating stairs that surround it lie sheltered under a large, wing-shaped canopy. Next to it, a large plaza welcomes play, gatherings and festivities, with, at its centre, a café with a large, shaded terrace. The landscape surrounds the square and basketball field on a slightly higher level. It is composed of soft green hills that gently rise from the spacious and inviting grass carpet that connects all areas. Through their positioning and varied heights, the hills, each covered with local plants of different leaf, bloom and volume, create a diversity of intimate, scented spaces between them. Hollows form ponds and skate bowls that, during the rainy season, act as basins for excess rainwater. Tall-stemmed trees shelter the garden under their wide crowns, creating a cool and lush oasis within the city. Meandering paths run through this landscape, their porous red brick surfaces, laid in reinforced earth, ensuring the absorbance of rainwater. The entire landscape's porous soil substance allows for enough oxygen and a well-managed water system for a vital underground root- and ecosystem.

Ujiri Court is located in a vibrant and central area of Kigali and designed to become the new gateway to the Sports City in the Remera district. All people are welcome to join matches and make free use of the garden with its playgrounds, soccer fields and callisthenics park, while enjoying the hotel with its landscaped roof to one side, and the new retail area, cafés and bars on the other side of the gardens. Housed in second-hand shipping containers, these spaces are cooled by a recycled rainwater system, the shade of trees and the natural breeze. From here, people can go on to Amahoro Stadium, Kigali Arena or the Petit Stade.

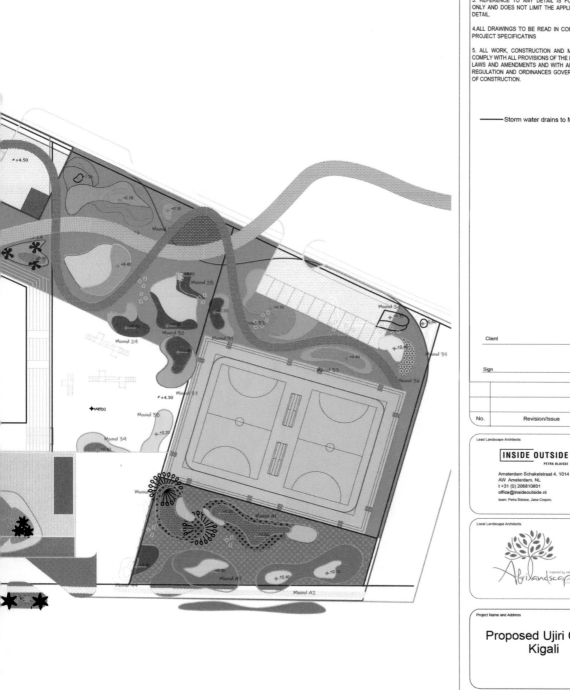

Client

Sign

No.	Revision/Issue	Date

Lead Landscape Architects:

INSIDE OUTSIDE
PETRA BLAISSE

Amsterdam Schakelstraat 4, 1014
AW Amsterdam, NL
t +31 (0) 206810801
office@insideoutside.nl
team: Petra Blaisse, Jana Crepon,

Local Landscape Architects:

Project Name and Address

Proposed Ujiri Court, Kigali

Drawing	Sheet
WALKWAY LAYOUT	
Date 01.11.2022	**W02**
Scale AS SHOWN	

"The house is elevated and therefore protected from the extreme weather conditions and rising sea levels that can occur in Miami. Gardens and terraces on different levels respond to the narrow site and yet augment the qualities of the surroundings. The different garden areas, carefully composed, turn into sculptural green expressions. Distorted rectangular carpets of airy grasses or lime-green succulents float on top of one single ground-cover surface; a circular pool is sliced by and becomes part of a protective sea wall; a row of lime-green palms form a privacy fence; a composition of small trees, grasses and agaves inhabits two elevated podiums. The rooftop with its relaxing lawn landscape affords a beautiful, ocean-side view, while a flowering cushion in shades of pink forms the transition between roof terrace and interior."   AM

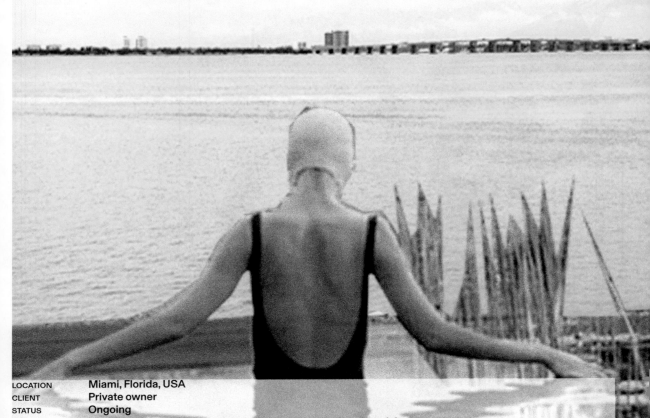

LOCATION   Miami, Florida, USA
CLIENT   Private owner
STATUS   Ongoing
SCOPE   Landscape design for private garden and curtains; interior advisory
SCALE   Landscape, 970 m²; interior, 600 m²
COLLABORATORS   OMA, Christopher Cawley, CLF Architects
DESCRIPTION   One continuous diagonal movement crosses the entire section of the private house, from the Biscayne Bay to the natural pool, through the gardens and fitness area, up towards the bedrooms, kitchen, living space and roof landscape. This results in a dynamic sequence of spaces that are interconnected in unexpected ways.

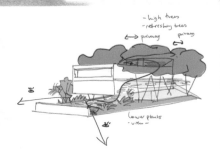

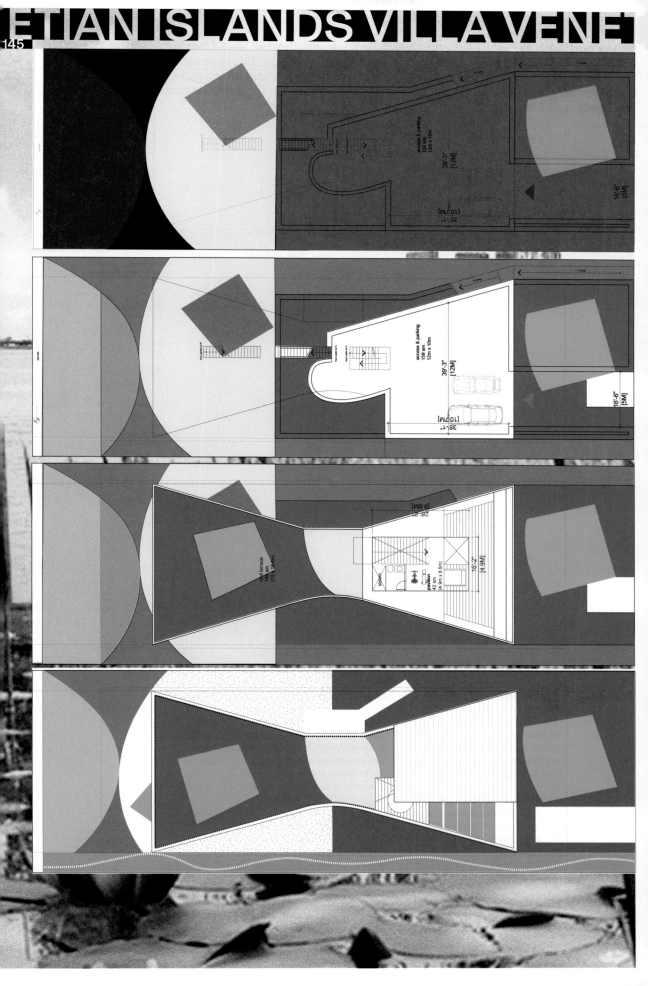

Nature-inclusive architecture?
A study

"In the end I wonder, with all these good intentions, whether we are, in fact, introducing puzzling new issues: Will human beings actually benefit from this fabricated intimacy with nature, right outside their apartment windows? What about allergies, hygiene and possible health issues? And is not the key to enjoying nature the contrast between city and landscape? And what about beauty…?" PB

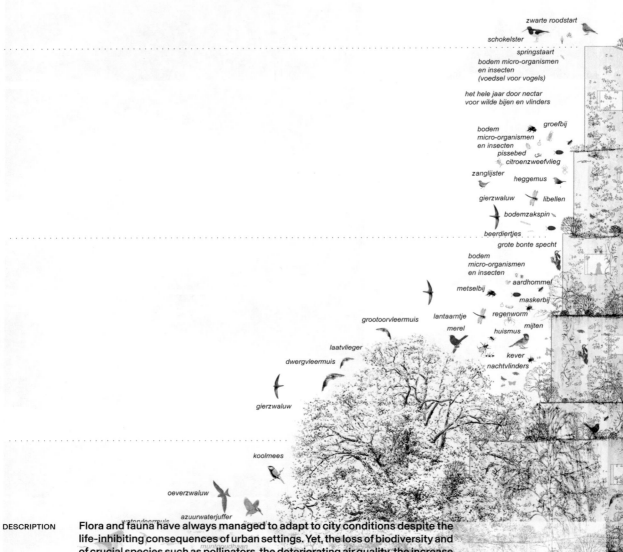

DESCRIPTION

Flora and fauna have always managed to adapt to city conditions despite the life-inhibiting consequences of urban settings. Yet, the loss of biodiversity and of crucial species such as pollinators, the deteriorating air quality, the increase of allergies among humans due to mono-planting, the warming of the globe and the psychological effects of little contact with nature in our daily lives, all contribute to a pervasive state of alarm and sense of urgency. It is imperative for interdisciplinary teams such as ours to take immediate action to help living organisms thrive in our built environment and to ensure that all species can reclaim their space.

Following Alexander von Humboldt's observations on the gradual change of vegetation and fauna as the logical effect of successive contour lines, we propose a residential tower typology that integrates flora and fauna on its stepped, bioreceptive surfaces, according to that same logic.

Local plants can settle in vital soil on alternating horizontal "stepping stones," while herbaceous vegetation, young shrubs and trees can grow from street level upward, letting wind and sun define their shape. Climbing plants growing on the vertical, porous facades give shelter to birds, lizards and insects, while bird and bat houses strategically installed at different heights provide nesting facilities.

Instead of designing the perfect, readymade landscape that needs to be carefully maintained, we create conditions that permit nature to settle, prevail and evolve on its own terms within the urban realm.

zwarte roodstart
schokelster
regenworm
spinnen
beerdiertjes
bodem micro-organismen
en insecten
(voedsel voor vogels)
kleine vos
kleine vuurvlinder
citroenvlinder
icarusblauwtje
hoibeestje
wilde bijen
merel
zanglijster
heggemus
libellen
gierzwaluw
grote veldhommel
koolmees
dagvlinders
sprinkhanen
pissebed
spinnen
regenworm
aardhommel
springstaart
spreeuw
huismus
mijten
nachtvlinders
libellen
zwarte wegmier
homo urbanus

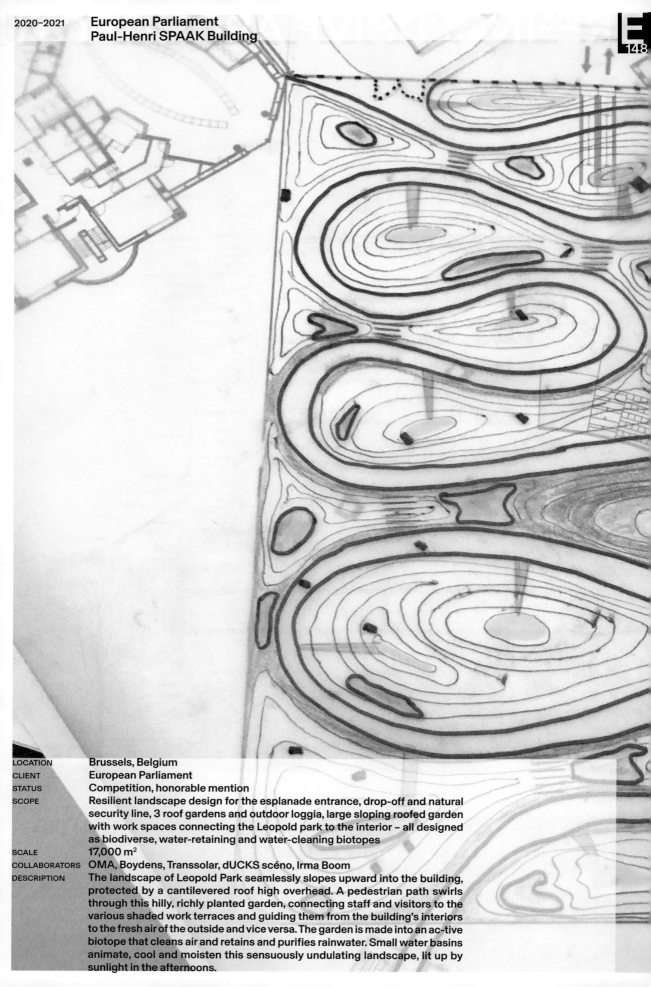

LOCATION	**Brussels, Belgium**
CLIENT	**European Parliament**
STATUS	**Competition, honorable mention**
SCOPE	**Resilient landscape design for the esplanade entrance, drop-off and natural security line, 3 roof gardens and outdoor loggia, large sloping roofed garden with work spaces connecting the Leopold park to the interior – all designed as biodiverse, water-retaining and water-cleaning biotopes**
SCALE	**17,000 m²**
COLLABORATORS	**OMA, Boydens, Transsolar, dUCKS scéno, Irma Boom**
DESCRIPTION	**The landscape of Leopold Park seamlessly slopes upward into the building, protected by a cantilevered roof high overhead. A pedestrian path swirls through this hilly, richly planted garden, connecting staff and visitors to the various shaded work terraces and guiding them from the building's interiors to the fresh air of the outside and vice versa. The garden is made into an ac-tive biotope that cleans air and retains and purifies rainwater. Small water basins animate, cool and moisten this sensuously undulating landscape, lit up by sunlight in the afternoons.**

Petra's drawing for the building's main garden, which is a continuation of Parc Leopold. It flows into the building and slopes up to the third floor, where the garden then connects to office and meeting spaces.

"We made a universal diagram to represent everything that a place of prayer and meditation originally stood for – churches, temples, synagogues and mosques, and we suggested filling the churches' gardens with plantings that play a role in the writings and myths of all religions and philosophies – gardens without fences, where everybody is welcome any time of day or night; gardens in which wondrous stories are told, where music is played and plays are performed."

"After having been briefed on all the ins and outs of two of the three impressive churches, we visited the manager of the third church, the gothic St Jan Cathedral in 's-Hertogenbosch. We discussed important issues such as the church's relation to the local community, the connection of its garden to the surrounding restaurants as a place for consumption and relaxation, the implications of its position next to the large public square where the yearly cultural parade takes place, the importance of sharing its sculpture collection with the public by exhibiting it on the church grounds, the church's weakened historic position globally and the rich iconography of the architecture, especially the dense array of figurative, expressive sculptures on the roof. These subjects were addressed in that sequence, each subject more interesting than the next. Then the church representative ended our working day confessing that, actually, his largest, practical concern was public urination against the church's facade. The three-dimensional exterior along the main nave creates small niches, which have become outdoor pissoirs. This has become one of the most intriguing subjects for which we have to find an effective solution."   AM

LOCATION	Domkerk, Utrecht; Sint Bavo cathedral, Haarlem; Sint Jan cathedral, 's-Hertogenbosch
CLIENT	Chief Government Architect and the National Office for Cultural Heritage
STATUS	Competition, 1st prize/ongoing
SCOPE	Landscape, sustainability, programming and maintenance vision for the re-integration of iconic city churches in the day-to-day life of (local) society
COLLABORATORS	Braaksma & Roos Architects, Antea Group, Johanna van Doorn
DESCRIPTION	The former chief government architect of the Netherlands, Floris Alkemade, launched an open competition for interdisciplinary teams to collaborate on a vision for the future of nine iconic churches in the Netherlands. We teamed up with restoration architects Braaksma & Roos, Antea engineers and cultural history professor Johanna van Doorn and were selected as one of three parties to each address three iconic churches in our country. The brief specified the need for a sustainable and economic way to maintain and heat the buildings, plus creative solutions to bring them back into the heart of society – not only as Christian institutions but as active social, educational and cultural meeting places – not least in order to generate income and cover costs. They have become too detached and disconnected from city life and its multicultural, multigenerational inhabitants. To foster active life and mutual involvement, they need to open their doors to all people, regardless of nationality, religion or belief.

Our team suggested opening up the facades and doors of the churches, reinserting former windows and restoring existing ones for literal transparency, dismantling gates, installing gardens and creating public routings through the buildings and up to their attics and roofs to activate spaces both inside and out. The architectural qualities can be made accessible to a larger audience and the gardens can be enjoyed by the community as places for encounters, play and learning (using plants mentioned in the Bible/Koran/Tenach/Holy Book/Shruti/Smriti/Vedas/etc!).

We see great opportunities for generating sustainable energy by using the buildings' large roof surfaces and the surrounding gardens. Fields with solar cells and small wind turbines can be integrated into roofs and gardens to cool the buildings; and strategically placed plantings can shield spaces from wind and cold. By improving the soil conditions of the different gardens and plazas, large porous surfaces that absorb CO_2 can be created, while better water management can store and filter water to be recycled and used for irrigation and cleaning.

Take away the fences! Open your gates, doors and windows! Step aside and invite everyone in, people of all ages and from all social strata, of any religion or belief, to visit, study, read, recite, produce, cook, grow, co-create, share, play, build, help, repair, maintain, teach, learn, relax, sing and speak in every possible language – and this all year round! Goodwill and grants will follow, hurrah!

Bioreceptive Textile Nurseries

"Imagine a scaffolding net around a construction site, growing with moss, lichen and epiphytic ferns, able to grow in soilless conditions. Through the chemical composition of its yarns and the three-dimensional, microgeometry of its knitted or knotted surface, this textile substrate encourages the growth of plants with minimum external influence. It not only protects the building and workers, but also purifies the air around it. Once construction is complete, this plant-textile ecosystem finds a new placement as a living, green, flexible space-divider, a lightweight green shading facade or a living canopy. The passing of time does not necessarily degrade a textile but transforms it. Experimenting in outdoor and indoor trials, we are now testing different textile prototypes, morphologies, porosities and chemical compositions in interaction with carefully selected epiphytic plant organisms, observing and learning how to engage in multispecies interactions." NE

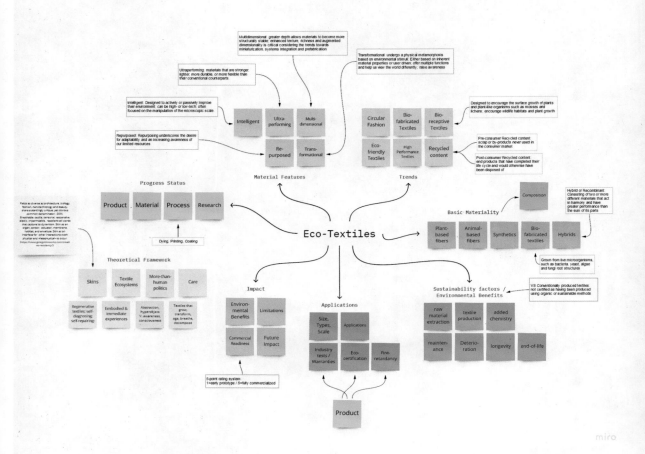

LOCATION	Amsterdam, the Netherlands
CLIENT	Self-initiated research, supported by the Creative Industries Fund NL
STATUS	Research, ongoing
SCOPE	Research by design on textile circularity and bioreceptivity, biomaterial prototyping and experiments of plant biocolonisation on textiles for interior and exterior applications
COLLABORATORS	HKRITA (Hong Kong Research Institute of Textiles and Apparel Ltd), Jacqueline Baar / Soil Best, Officina Corpuscoli, Margherita Soldati
DESCRIPTION	This research was born of our passion for textiles and the desire to take active responsibility for the environment as the core of our practice and to influence our choice of materials. Scanning the horizon of what (textile) sustainability really means, we came across a novel set of bioreceptive concrete and ceramic materials. In 1995 the bioengineer Guillitte identified bioreceptivity "as the aptitude of a material to be colonised by one or several groups of living organisms without necessarily undergoing any biodeterioration." It gripped us instantly!

Greentecstyle
by Sioen Industries

- Flame composite
- Pre-cut pockets for plants and sensors
- Pre-manufacturing sleeves
- ...

greentecstyle.eco
GreenTecStyle

San Telmo Museum
by Nieto Sobejano

Living wall systems

Waterproof layer | Steel frame | Irrigation | Geotextile layer | Plants
Fig 1.3b: LWS facade system

Green facades

Breathing textiles

Bioreceptive Concrete
by biologist Sandra Manso Blanco

A significant step was made by the Spanish biologist Sandra Manso Blanco who tested and developed a new type of bioreceptive concrete that provides a biological substratum for growth of photosynthetic systems to proliferate without affecting structural concrete.

Living, Water-Recycling Building Wrapped in a Network of Tubes
inhabitat.com

A metropolis becomes green

Harmonia 57
by Triptyque

Harmonia 57
by Triptyque

Composite green facade

Photo.Synth.Etica
by Ecologic Studio

:: photo.Synthetica ::
EcoLogicStudio ::

Conceived as an "urban curtain", Photo.Synth.Etica, conceived in partnership with Climate-KIC, EU's most prominent climate innovation initiative, captures CO2 from the atmosphere and stores it in real-time: approximately one kilo of CO2 per day, equivalent to that of 20 large trees.
Composed of 16, 2 x 7 meter modules, the unique curtain prototype envelopes the first and second floor of the main façade of the Printworks building at Dublin Castle. Each module functions as a photobioreactor, a digitally designed and custom-made bioplastic container that utilizes daylight to feed the living micro-algal cultures and releases luminescent shades at night.

Bioreceptive Concrete
by Marineterrein Amsterdam Living Lab

At Marineterrein Amsterdam Living Lab we will start with the proof of concept from stage one, whereby the experiment will be functionally integrated combining the setup with the public showers. This will create more green and a solution that uses natural capital (ecosystem services provided by a thick layer of moss) which is spontaneous, virtually maintenance-free and therefore very cost-effective for the owner or manager in the form of prefab elements or applied as layer (stucco) to existing bare and often unattractive concrete surfaces.

www.ams-institute.org

Bio-receptive concret for liveable cities

At AMS institute we design solutions urban challenges, and educate tomorrow's engineers. We develop a deep understanding of the city and research & explore interdisciplinary metropolitan soluti to integrate these into the city of Amsterdam.

Curtain
oop.pH

Biogarmentry
by Roya Aghighi

Project biogarmentry is designed to address the drastic increase to the environmental impact of textile waste and air pollution. The project employs the fields of synthetic biology and design. With the help of a group of scientists at the University of British Columbia, we created the first proof of concept for the survival of photosynthetic living cells on natural fabrics--such as different kinds of cellulose and protein based fibers.
Since the life cycle of the living photosynthetic textile, is directly dependent on how it is taken care of, the work challenges our current relationship to clothing, while acting as a catalyst for towards a more healthy environment. This bioreceptive material has the power to make our future interiors grow and evolve to become alive, regenerative and interactive spaces.

www.theatlantic.com

The Future of Architecture: Moss, Not Mirrors

Plants and lichens on a concrete wall used to be a sign of decay, but soon ...

Bioreceptive Facade studies
by TU Delft

Biocrete
by Material Evolution

Material Evolution, is developing plant-friendly concrete panels, known as 'biocrete' with an open cell structure to allow for plant and water ingression while providing protection for waterproof membranes and insulation behind

Bioreceptive concrete

arq

Bio Responsive Bloom – materiality

Marcos Cruz Architect
Bioreceptive Facades Design research - 2015-17 BiotA Lab EPSRC funded research: Computational Seeding of Bioreceptive Materia...

BiotA Lab wins EPSRC funding to develop bio receptive materials

www.ucl.ac.uk

Labs
by studio S. Boon

LABS: Future Interiors
A healthy and sustainable interior functions as a living ecosystem in balance. How can we design interiors as ecosystems? Our interiors consist for the most part of an invisible, but very essential 'mass' air. As several studies from the World Health Organisation (WHO) and the United Nations (UN) show, the air quality of the built environment is one of today's crucial challenges, and poor air quality can become a threat to our health.
LABS: Future Interiors takes kombucha scoby biofilm as its raw material and conducts research into bacteria grown textiles as 100% biodegradable interior elements and as substrate for air-purifying plants. During LABS: Future Interiors research process we developed the material KOMBUTEX. The material offers smart opportunities to tackle the challenges of indoor air quality ...

architecture is the grounded, the fixed, then textiles are its very antithesis.
Textiles in Architecture, 1957)

being transformed from passive into active technological tools.

Inside Outside, 2000
Storefront for Art and Architecture

The creation of diverse microbial communities that are in competition and/or synergy with each other on the surfaces of materials is only recently being understood

Case studies
Bioreceptive Concrete

Bioreceptive Concrete facades
by BiotA Lab, Bartlett UCL

Bioreceptive Stations, NS
by Scape Agency

Scape Agency

Bioreceptive glass tiles

Warm glass

- scale of impact on environment?
- aesthetics?
- long term material performance?

limitations

bioreceptivity is an inherently time-based, yet self-regulating condition in sustainable design.

Fig i.xx: Types of Bio-receptivity (Guillitte, 1995)

Lightweight
Flexible, Movable
Adaptable to weather

More-than-human perspectives

Caring
Gardening
Engendering
Resurgence
Nurture
Contingency
Knots
Assemblages
Terrestrial
Interdependence
Precarity
The Dithering

Bioreceptive Textiles

Bioreceptive Materials

Bioreceptivity

Bioreceptive Design

Definitions

ecological benefits

Bio-fabricated

Bio-compatibility

Bio-colonization

Surface growth of plants upon a material is known as biocolonization.
(Cruz & Beckett, 2016)

Bio-deterioration

'aesthetic of cleanliness' / pseudo 'health' of the architectural skin

Impure Aesthetics

Possible applications

- Living, biodegradable scaffolding net (outdoor/temporary use)
- Living canopy
- Textile green walls in atriums for air purification, sun glare control, noise absorption (indoor/long term installation)

rn(s) or a certain (3d?) weave
ometry and material qualities for
?
extile substrate change
metry etc.) from an outdoor to an
?
nisms can grow? What are the
, water, soil, light etc.)

g Biological Interfaces
tile, sensorial, responsive, elastic, impermeable, repellent

Walls are gaining a sense of "inhabitable flesh". (Cruz & Beckett, 2016)

The material design in all these projects creates a sense of scaffolding which aims to provide surface roughness, pH levels and optimised porosity values along with water absorption, distribution and retention properties to provide optimal conditions favourable for microorganisms, algae, lichens and bryophytes to establish and grow.

Cryptogams

how much biomass can such bioreceptive components really produce in a large scale?

what plants are the most suitable? for which microclimate?

Bioreceptivity Parameters

how or how to create hydrophilic conditions?

what are different geometry types that influence self-sustaining moss growth?

Cryptogams / poikilohydric plants (algae, mosses, lichens)

Plants

skin > bark

Tortula muralis
Bryum agenteum
Grimmia pulvinate
Tortula ruralis

Substrate

Scale

morphology
geometry

porosity

water permeability, absorption & storage

CaCO3 presence

low pH values

Environmental factors

orientation of 'green wall' | local climate/ microclimate | rain, moisture, temperature, exposure to water | dust, pollution levels | diaspores propagation through wind

epiphytes plants

Bio-scaffolds can be biodegradable or rigid (non-degradable). When biodegradable (in some cases working as implants), they can work as temporary scaffolds; temporary barriers; or multifunctional scaffolds.

Vertension Sands by Matthew Soules Architecture

Interwoven

"Let's make gardening more than a hobby and roll up our collective sleeves. Let's take urban roof gardens seriously as potential biotopes and make all forms of landscapes a public concern: it is necessary, urgent and incredibly inspiring at the same time. Unfortunately, gardening doesn't solve famine, discrimination and inequality or prevent wars, but we at Inside Outside can contribute to the environment through our field of work and, hopefully, beyond – even if on a modest scale. The world seems ready for it – and God knows we are." PB

LOCATION	Amsterdam, the Netherlands
CLIENT	Self-initiated research, with support from the Creative Industries Fund NL
STATUS	Ongoing
SCOPE	Research on how to introduce biodiversity and living soil in the urban realm
COLLABORATORS	Municipality of Amsterdam, Naturalis Biodiversity Center, Vrije Universiteit Amsterdam, Wageningen University, Koninklijke Ginkel Groep, Bodemzicht, Flock Theatre and others
DESCRIPTION	Impossible not to dive into the issue of soil, plant life and everything in and around it if you're a gardener, landscape architect, biophile, human being. As 90% of our landscape work consists of roof gardens and landscaping on roof-like structures, we are constantly faced with the difficulty of convincing developers, municipalities, architects, engineers, investors and owners to invest in a structure and infrastructure that allows for a fruitful ground build-up and a sustainable water management system. We want more than a thin green layer that merely symbolises green, we need to create a living environment for natural, thriving growth and for many years, giving it time to mature so it can start to coalesce underground and multiply above. Attracting bird and insect life and stimulating soil life – even in the urban context in which so many of us live. A porous, planted surface absorbs CO_2, produces oxygen, helps plants and trees grow and cools the environment. We decided to make our ambition official, to write about the topic, to talk about it, read about it and to actively get acquainted with as much knowledge and establish as many connections with specialists in the fields as possible, nationally and internationally. That is our study field for the coming years, which started two years ago.

Groeibevorderende en beschermende micro-organismen

Wortelknolletjes met Rhizobium-bacteriën

Vraatinsect belaagd door aaltjes en schimmels

Wortelwond scheidt chemische stoffen uit; aantrekking micro-organismen

INSIDE OUTSIDE

Garage Campus
Gorky Park

"Petra and I had visited the Gorky Park and Garage Museum in the summer of 2018 when we gave a week-long workshop at the Strelka School of Architecture. While there, we went to the exhibitions and the garage plaza, which we had designed in collaboration with OMA a few years earlier. After that we took a stroll and explored the park, not knowing that we would get the chance to develop a masterplan for it a few years later.

But then Covid hit for two years and now there's a war going on between Russia and Ukraine – so no chance to visit the park again, leaving us in limbo, trying to figure out all sorts of details about the complex site conditions and not wanting to let go. The Garage team and local landscape architects did their best to provide us with information at the time, but to not physically experience the place remains a handicap. One day during Covid we "took a walk" via a WhatsApp call with Dimitri from the Garage team. Dimitri didn't speak English, so our colleague and friend Katja joined us from Milan, translating for us and directing Dimitri's walk: "Turn around please. What is behind those shrubs? Where are those people going?" Etc.

It answered a lot of questions, though not all. Still, it felt pretty cool to be able to do that. Today, of course, the whole project lies frozen in our cupboard … symbol of the frightening fate that hit Russia and the Ukraine – leaving us wondering about the well-being of our dear colleagues and friends who live and work to the east of us." JC

LOCATION	Moscow, Russia
CLIENT	Garage Museum of Contemporary Art
STATUS	Concept design
SCOPE	Landscape masterplan for gardens, trajectories and wayfinding to connect the Garage buildings within Gorky Park
SCALE	12.6 ha
DESCRIPTION	In 2015, we co-designed with OMA the outside space of the then newly built Garage Museum of Modern Art (embedded in Gorky Park) as an extension of the museum. We composed a large square inlaid with angular carpets of stone cobbles, wooden blocks and in-situ concrete with a rounded garden island in the centre. The whole was framed by a slightly elevated, concrete edge of generous width and large meadows with numerous fruit and berry trees and a plaza hosting temporary programs such as cinema and sculpture exhibitions. The site has since become one of the city's best-known public spaces.

In the meantime, the owners of the museum are carefully expanding their campus within Gorky Park by acquiring and restoring other existing buildings such as the Hexagon by SANAA and the film building by Chipperfield. In 2020, Inside Outside was asked to develop a connective landscape masterplan that subtly defines the campus visually, so as to link the different buildings owned and managed by Garage to each other. Visitors should easily recognise the language of the campus and find their way from one building or art installation to the next. The future landscape should also include more specific gardens and outdoor areas around each building to announce their program. The now restored and enlarged Hexagon building, with its integrated garden by local landscape architects, is one such example. In collaboration with the Garage team and local landscape architects MOX, we will work towards an overall masterplan as a springboard for zooming in on specific areas.

"The site is narrow and steep and has a fantastic view onto the lake, the mountains and the village of Zell am See. OMA created a sculptural, white concrete volume both above and below ground, with interconnected floorplans and exciting viewpoints. The whole thing is custom-made for the owner and his family.

 To define and separate the master bedroom from the adjacent spaces, we developed a curtain wall in two layers, consisting of a furry surface and a shiny blue membrane with a large circular opening. Next, we will look at the very steep garden slivers of this very narrow site and see what we can contribute there."   PB

LOCATION	Zell am See, Austria
CLIENT	Private owner
STATUS	Completed
SCOPE	Double-layered, darkening curtain for the bedroom and garden design (ongoing)
MATERIALS	Blue high-gloss PVC lacquer, soft grey heavy mohair velour, gold dupion silk
SCALE	curtains, (2×) 5.85 × 3.5 m; garden, ca. 900 m^2
COLLABORATORS	OMA, 7478 / Federico Pompignoli
DESCRIPTION	This residence of white concrete looks as if it had been carved right out of the snow-white mountain behind it. With its back against the mountain, the floors of the home are staggered like a staircase, partially cutting into the mountain to follow its contours.

 On the highest floor the bedroom curtain separates the bedroom from the staircase and foldable bathroom. As a reference to Adolf Loos's bedroom and a nod to classic Austrian culture and cold winters, we thought it an interesting idea to use a fur-like material for the bedroom curtain in contrast to the smooth modern materials of the architecture.

 The side facing the stairs shows a separate layer of icy blue, high-gloss lacquer. A circle, 1.9 m in diameter, is cut out to serve as an entrance, reminiscent of the classic James Bond gun barrel sequence. Both layers run parallel on independent tracks until their paths separate to each seek their own storage space. The positioning of the tracks was a challenge because of the sloping roof, folded in two directions. In order to make the tracks level they "float" under the ceiling, attached to transparent spacers – a fine invention by the architects.

How exciting it is to step through a hole! To close and open up a space in one go. To feel the fresh air flow through! To see the world outside, crisp and clear, without leaving bed...

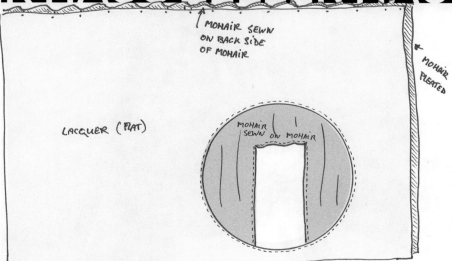

MOHAIR SEWN
ON BACK SIDE
OF MOHAIR

MOHAIR
PLEATED

LACQUER (FLAT)

MOHAIR
SEWN ON MOHAIR

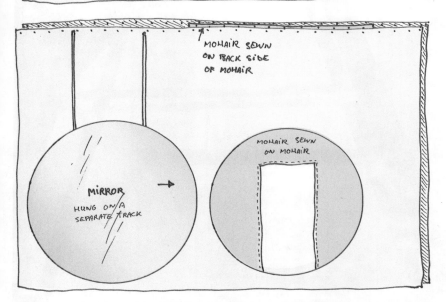

MOHAIR SEWN
ON BACK SIDE
OF MOHAIR

MOHAIR SEWN
ON MOHAIR

MIRROR
HUNG ON A
SEPARATE TRACK

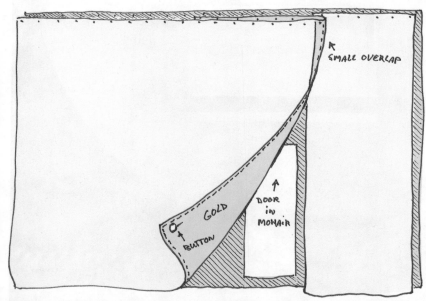

SMALL OVERLAP

GOLD

DOOR
IN
MOHAIR

BUTTON

A four-poster bed made of wood?! No! Let's make it of Plexiglas, printed with traditional Austrian decorations and shapes. When visitors come, let's cover the bed with an inflatable silver cover… no, with blue lacquer plastic… no… let's think.

"While visualising a fairy tale-like botanical garden with wonderful collections of trees, plants, water features and attractive conditions for play, sports, technology and the arts, we are also taking the responsibility to improve the current industrial site's ground conditions to address the acute problems of inundation and a worn sewage system, and to transform the existing, polluted soil into a healthy, living one. This is a huge undertaking that will take many years to accomplish as the site is in the hands of many different owners and stakeholders, and budgets and ownerships are, understandably, managed and acquired step by step."

"The Parco Del Polcevera will not just revitalise the area and create jobs, but also offer local workers and residents a new place of repose at walking distance from the sites where their daily rhythms and routines unravel, with flowers blossoming in the midst of a plethora of scents, a rich array of trees providing shelter and shade and a capable soil structure as the backbone that sustains the ever-changing site. The park will include a new train station, residential housing, offices and workshops. Thus, the reconfigured landscape will not just connect the two ends of the valley but will also connect visitors, workers and the people of Genoa to one another." PB

LOCATION	Valpolcevera, Genoa, Italy
CLIENT	Municipality of Genoa
STATUS	Competition, 1st prize / ongoing
STATUS	Competition, 2019, 1st prize / ongoing
SCOPE	Richly programed, biodiverse public park under the collapsed Morandi bridge that addresses soil health and sustainable water management, including memorial gardens for the deceased of August 2018
SCALE	Competition masterplan, 24 ha; preliminary landscape design, 13 ha
COLLABORATORS	Stefano Boeri Architetti, Metrogramma, Studio Laura Gatti, MIC Mobility in Chain, Transsolar, H&A Architetti, Antonio Secondo Accotto, Temporiuso, Tempo Riuso, Luca Vitone
DESCRIPTION	Together with the architects, Inside Outside / Petra Blaisse won an international competition initiated by the municipality of Genoa that intends to breathe new life into the *Val Polcevera*, the valley directly underneath the new San Giorgio bridge by Renzo Piano, where the former Ponte Morandi tragically collapsed in August 2018. The reconstruction project is a crucial turning point in the area's road to recovery.

Genoa's public botanical park in combination with the red circular walkway will ultimately connect the disjointed landscape. Currently, the valley is mercilessly cut through by the *Torrente Polcevera*, a series of highways and two impassable train tracks that run from north to south – but the park fastens each of these fragmented areas to each other by making them an integral part of the whole.

The new park area is squeezed in between the mounds of Cornigliano and Garbo. The design consists of a series of linear fields – with a width that ranges from 7 to 20 metres – with their appertaining paths placed parallel to each other. Each field displays an entirely different garden typology in soil, topography and planting, so that the botanical park is brimming with biodiversity. A variety of tree species, most of which can also be found in the forested mounds next to the valley, are systematically positioned across the park.

A zigzagging path, running perpendicular to the fields, creates a passage from the eastern to the western edge of the valley, and merges with Stefano Boeri Architetti's *Cerchio Rosso*, the red circular walkway. The intricate maze of paths provides efficiency but also creates aesthetically immersive experiences that lead visitors along a multitude of vantage points and heights. The circular red walkway meant for pedestrians and cyclists and functioning as sun and wind energy collecting machine – gently floats over the landscape but also directly permeates it at times, making it into an always-active participant. Together, the public park and the red circle ensure that all edges of the valley are connected, allowing local inhabitants to travel from both ends of the river and valley with unprecedented ease.

All green areas, plazas and retaining walls along the riverbed are constructed so as to absorb and store superfluous water. All excess water will find a purpose in the drier periods and ensure a consistent, favourable water balance for the underground root systems. Solar panels will be interspersed across the park – wherever roofs and open fields allow – to distribute green energy to the area. The park's terms of existence are resilient. Its graphic composition displays a sophisticated structure that each and every garden contributes to. Over time, the park's plantation will develop, grow and prosper on its own terms, but without affecting the essence proposed in the overall design.

the romantic interplay between magnificent, landscaped nature and harsh, rigid urbanity

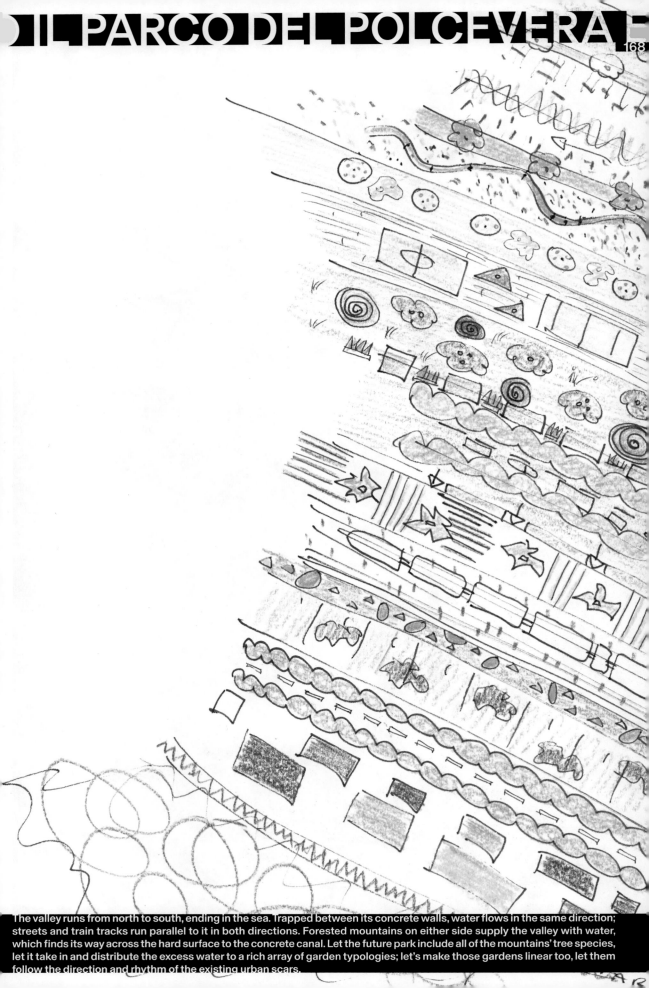

The valley runs from north to south, ending in the sea. Trapped between its concrete walls, water flows in the same direction; streets and train tracks run parallel to it in both directions. Forested mountains on either side supply the valley with water, which finds its way across the hard surface to the concrete canal. Let the future park include all of the mountains' tree species, let it take in and distribute the excess water to a rich array of garden typologies; let's make those gardens linear too, let them follow the direction and rhythm of the existing urban scars.

SALIX/WET PARK

CIPRES PARK

CITRUS PARK

EVERGREEN PARK

BLOSSOM PARK

WATER PARK

BLOSSOM PARK

SPORTS + FLOWERPARK

NUT- & FRUITPARK (EDIBLE PARK)

SPORTSPARK

FRUIT- & PLAYPARK

HOUSING/VEGETABLE PARK

TRAFFIC PARK

VERTICAL PARK

PARKING PARK

TRAINPARK

COLOUR PARK

OLIVE

TILIE DV PARK

STREETPARK

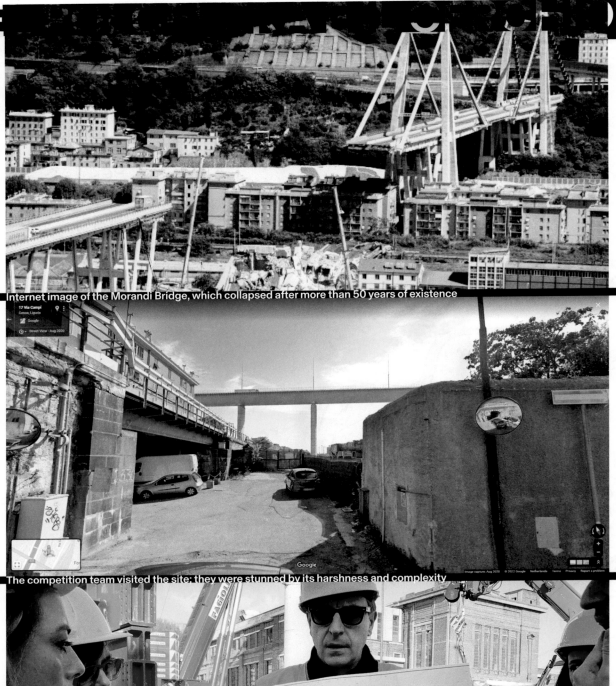

Internet image of the Morandi Bridge, which collapsed after more than 50 years of existence

The competition team visited the site; they were stunned by its harshness and complexity

Andrea Boschetti and the competition team reviewing the effects of the frequent flooding in the various valleys of Genoa

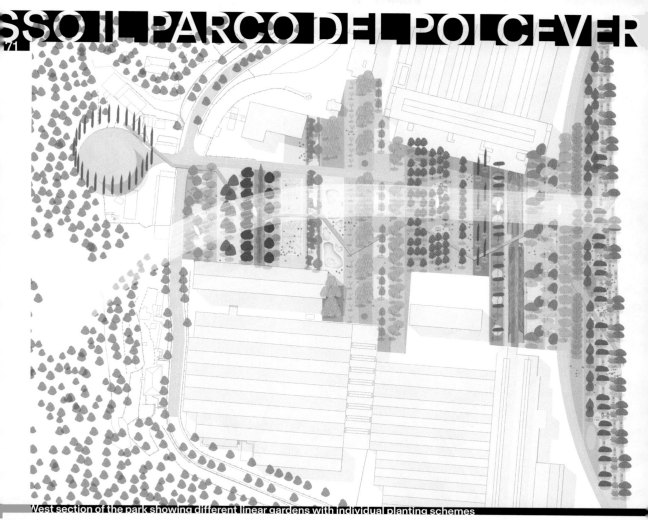

West section of the park showing different linear gardens with individual planting schemes

East–west sections of park site showing water management ambition

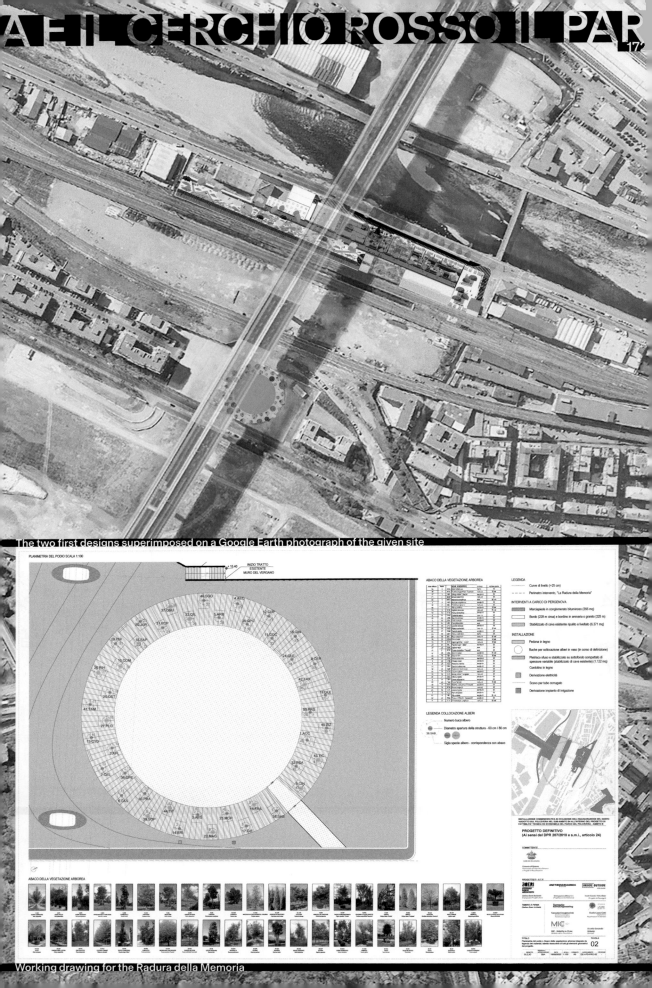

The two first designs superimposed on a Google Earth photograph of the given site

Working drawing for the Radura della Memoria

The first intervention we were able to realise on site was a temporary memorial for the 43 deceased. Together with our colleagues Laura Gatti, Luca Vitone and the team of Stefano Boeri Architetti, we detailed this circular memorial, Radura della Memoria, with 43 different trees and integrated the names of the deceased into the wooden platform.

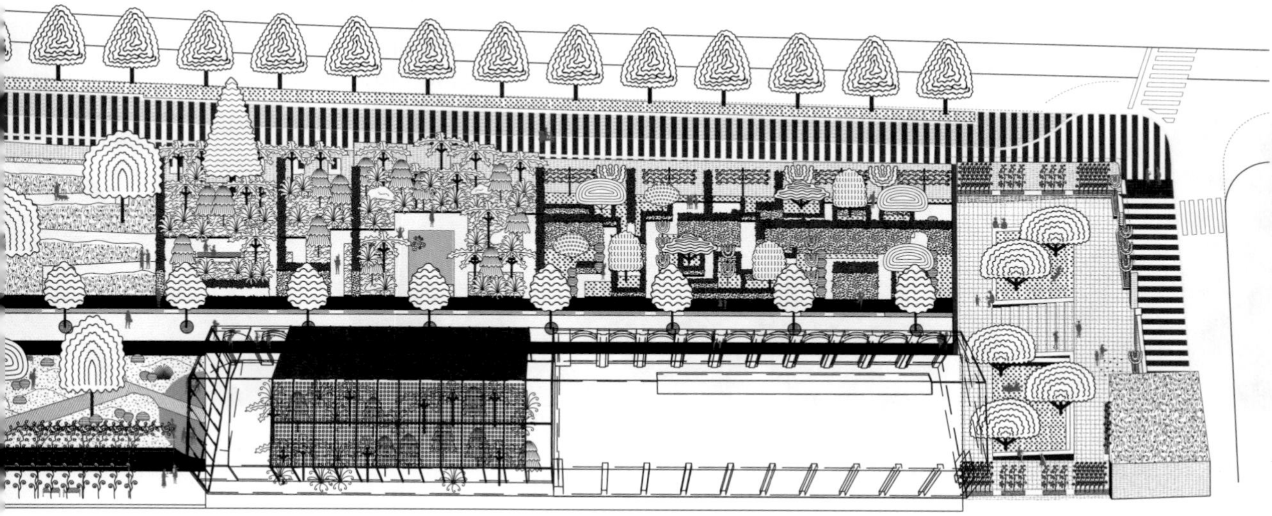

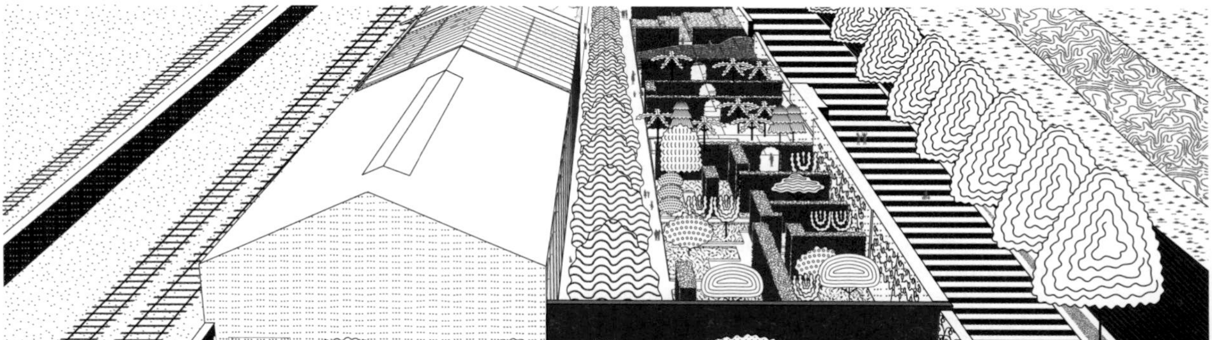

After the delivery of the feasibility studies for the complete park project (leaving the Cerchio Rosso and the buildings aside for this phase), we started to develop the design for the Giardino della Memoria, the permanent replacement of the temporary memorial. After IO delivered the definitive design in 2021, we created these images as a more narrative and entertaining way to present the design; the style of the images was based on old Genovese etchings and paintings (see figures and background of lower-left drawing).

"The 'hubs' should be seen as 1:1 mock-ups for the valley's future development as a sustainable tourist destination – a form of tourism that does not offer wellness and luxury, but a simple and economic form of tourism with an almost anthropological interest in and respect for the local culture and history, and for the day-to-day needs of inhabitants and their visions for their future. The more the local community experiences the social and economic benefits of such sustainable tourism, the more they will care for and invest in the landscape and environment of their own accord. There will be more room for incentives, new possibilities to set up cooperatives for and by the residents of the valley's many villages. Ultimately, the local communities will be the paramount force in driving change."

"We wonder, of course, whether the appreciation from outside – ours and that of future tourists – can persuade the local people to treasure their own agricultural and architectural heritage. Can community-based, rural tourism create an economically attractive alternative to the major tourist cities? How can we even start making this remote 14 km valley interesting and accessible for tourists if not with the help of the local community?"

"A site visit in the blazing heat: getting in and out of the car in different places, walking down to the oasis over rocky hills, in between crumbling mud houses. The cool shade of the tall date palms, the discovery of ancient ruins of mosques, fortresses, watchtowers and graveyards; the hospitality of locals offering us an improvised lunch at their house, with dates, almonds, melon and mint tea… Moving on in the intense afternoon heat, David almost passing out. But then, suddenly, the stunning coolness of a draught blowing through one of the narrow alleys of the village – bringing us back to life. Nothing like traditional cooling techniques!"   JC

LOCATION	Ait Mansour, Province de Tiznit, Région Souss Massa, Morocco
CLIENT	Société de Développement Touristique Souss Massa
STATUS	Ongoing; shortlisted for the Aga Kahn Award
SCOPE	Development strategies and landscape design for 6 hubs along a 14 km road that crosses the semi-abandoned valley
SCALE	140 ha
COLLABORATORS	Agence Salima Naji and David Goeury
DESCRIPTION	Valley de l'Yissy is 14 km long and located in the Sous-Massa region in the province of Tiznit. It is one of the lush valley oases of the Anti-Atlas mountain region of Morocco and was once a place of vitality and abundance: endless date palm groves dotted with almonds, figs, apricots and argan trees against the background of red-granite mountains with mud villages invisibly inlaid along their flanks. This rich rural area has gradually been undercut by the socio-economic and cultural stagnation which have become common in small rural villages globally. Like so many others, this valley has witnessed a gradual exodus of its inhabitants to live and work in urban areas. The inhabitants of Valley de l'Yissy have been unable to maintain their steady agricultural production and preserve their architectural heritage.

The Moroccan public sector has set out to redirect tourism from the densely occupied coastal areas and major touristic cities towards the country's rural areas, with its almost untouched and often undervalued cultural heritage. Our team visited all villages and spots of possible "touristic" value along the 14 km-long valley. We defined six small "hubs," one per village, each with a thematic and functional purpose, to make the valley accessible and attractive to passing visitors and at the same time useful places for the local communities. All six connect to the main road, offering rest stops with drinking water and WC, information and signposts, space for social gatherings, fresh drinking water and rainwater and spring water pools for swimming (upgrading traditional irrigation basins). The hubs' presence emphasises the surroundings, pointing out moments of beauty and objects of historic value, natural and man-made. They create awareness of the local culture and natural environments that otherwise run the risk of being overlooked.

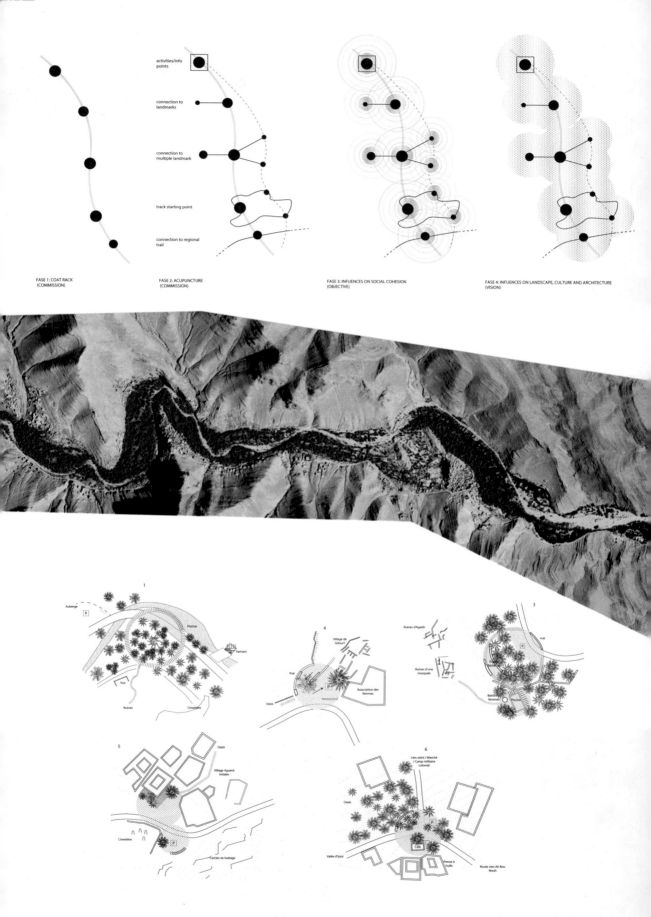

FASE 1: COAT RACK
(COMMISSION)

FASE 2: ACUPUNCTURE
(COMMISSION)

FASE 3: INFUENCES ON SOCIAL COHESION
(OBJECTIVE)

FASE 4: INFUENCES ON LANDSCAPE, CULTURE AND ARCHITECTURE
(VISION)

activities/info
points

connection to
landmarks

connection to
multiple landmark

track starting point

connection to regional
trail

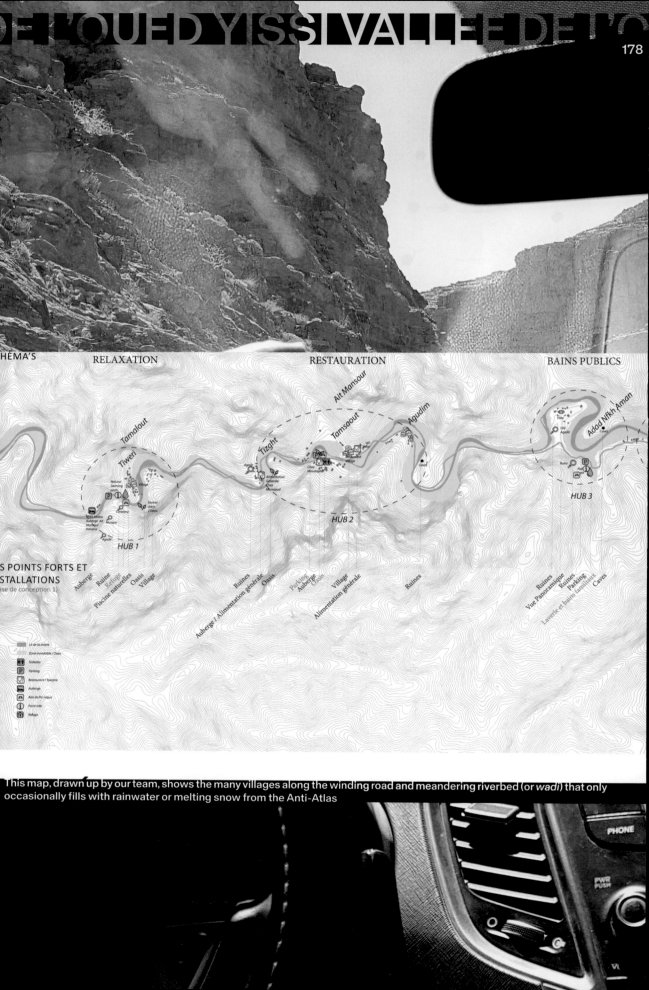

HÉMA'S   RELAXATION   RESTAURATION   BAINS PUBLICS

Ait Mansour

Tamalout

Tamsaout

Agudim

Adad N'Ikh Aman

Tiwerl

Tizght

HUB 1

HUB 2

HUB 3

S POINTS FORTS ET
STALLATIONS
ase de conception 1)

Auberge   Ruine   Refuge   Oasis   Village   Ruines   Oasis   Parking   Village   Ruines
Piscine naturelles   Auberge   Oasis
Auberge / Alimentation générale   Alimentation générale   Ruines
Vue Panoramique   Ruines   Parking   Caves
Laverie et bains (publics)

Lit de la rivière
Zone inondable / Oasis
Toilettes
Parking
Restaurant / Épicerie
Auberge
Aire de Pic-nique
Point info
Refuge

This map, drawn up by our team, shows the many villages along the winding road and meandering riverbed (or *wadi*) that only occasionally fills with rainwater or melting snow from the Anti-Atlas

PHONE

PWR
PUSH

ARCHITECTURE   AGRICULTURE   TRANSIT

Reparties selon la distance entre les différents villages et lieux d'intérêt, nous avons sélectionné sept zone d'intérêts, chacun ayant un objectif thématique et fonctionnel. Les différents thèmes offrent un accès global à la vallée. Bien que les zone sélectionnées présentent plusieurs aspects intéressants, il est souhaitable qu'un concept touristique clair permette de répartir les informations et les installations de manière uniforme.

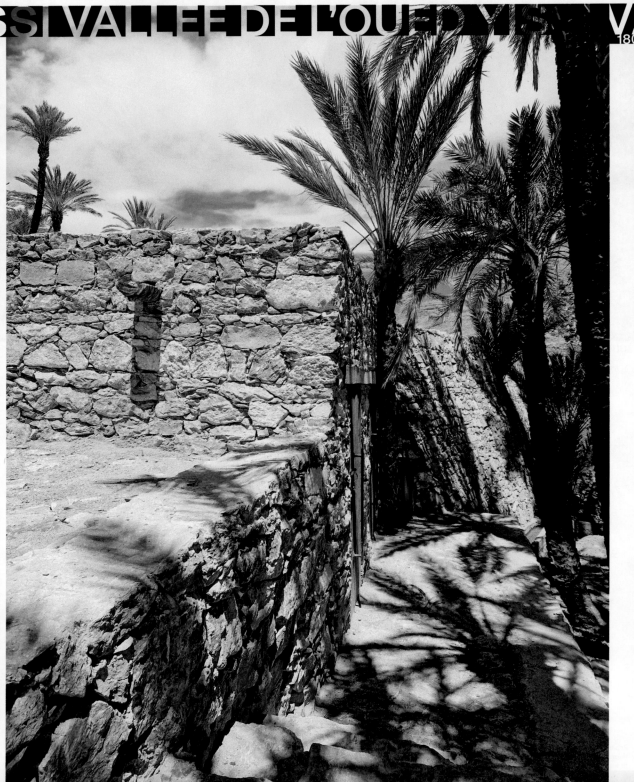

Here you see the first restoration works of (partly) existing structures that mark the rest stops along the road, which crosses the entire valley. All materials used are local and applied according to traditional methods.

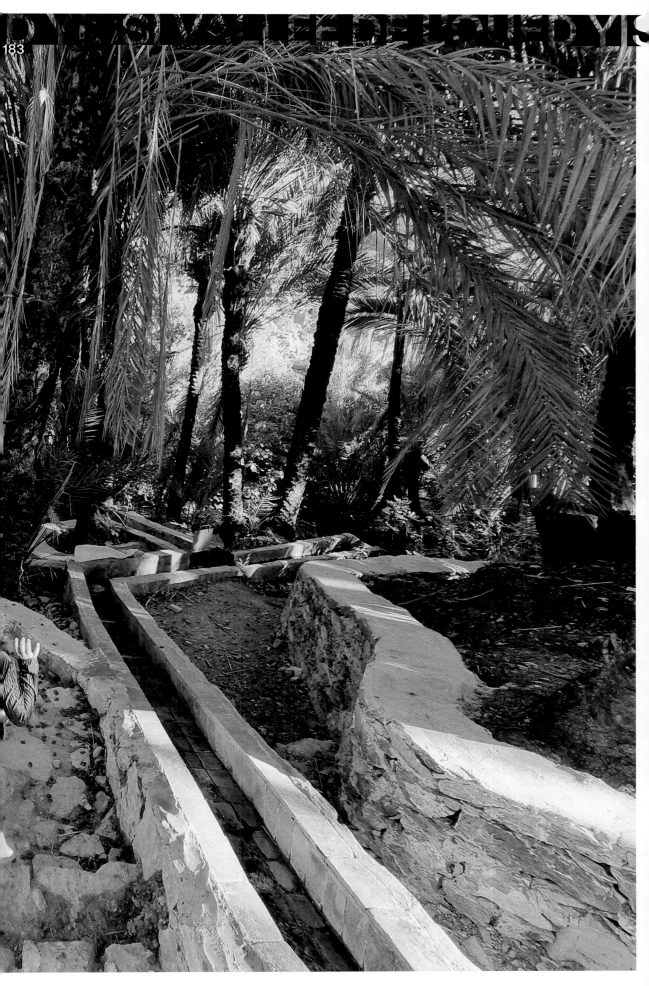

"This project has been a test of perseverance and the ability to anticipate ever-changing conditions. Four years after starting this project, we are the only survivors. Other than the urban planners (Mecanoo), all of the consultants and key figures on the client's and municipality's side have been replaced, and often it is up to us to remind the team of the project's history and initial ideas. Again, like in so many other projects, we feel like bulldogs fighting for our goals... Recently, we introduced this project as test case for a 'research by design' commission, subsidised by the Dutch Stimuleringsfonds. Our aim is to develop a visual language with which to communicate, in a simple manner, the fascinating world below ground, that is, to visualise all living organisms that together form 'vital soil,' one of the most essential bases for life on earth." JC

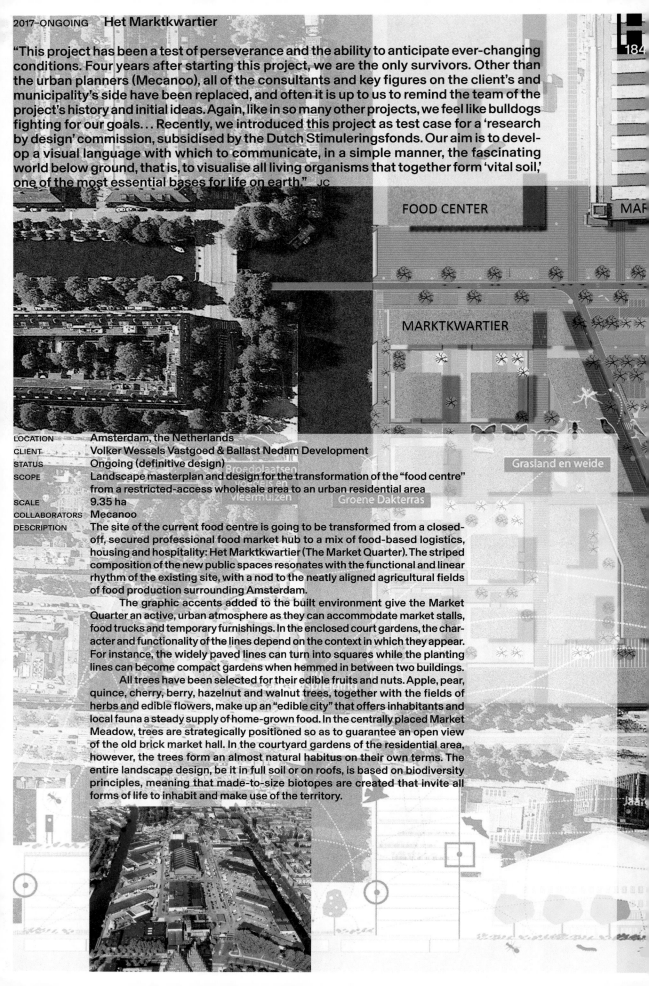

FOOD CENTER

MAR

MARKTKWARTIER

Broedplaatsen

Grasland en weide

vleermuizen   Groene Dakterras

LOCATION	Amsterdam, the Netherlands
CLIENT	Volker Wessels Vastgoed & Ballast Nedam Development
STATUS	Ongoing (definitive design)
SCOPE	Landscape masterplan and design for the transformation of the "food centre" from a restricted-access wholesale area to an urban residential area
SCALE	9.35 ha
COLLABORATORS	Mecanoo
DESCRIPTION	The site of the current food centre is going to be transformed from a closed-off, secured professional food market hub to a mix of food-based logistics, housing and hospitality: Het Marktkwartier (The Market Quarter). The striped composition of the new public spaces resonates with the functional and linear rhythm of the existing site, with a nod to the neatly aligned agricultural fields of food production surrounding Amsterdam.

The graphic accents added to the built environment give the Market Quarter an active, urban atmosphere as they can accommodate market stalls, food trucks and temporary furnishings. In the enclosed court gardens, the character and functionality of the lines depend on the context in which they appear. For instance, the widely paved lines can turn into squares while the planting lines can become compact gardens when hemmed in between two buildings.

All trees have been selected for their edible fruits and nuts. Apple, pear, quince, cherry, berry, hazelnut and walnut trees, together with the fields of herbs and edible flowers, make up an "edible city" that offers inhabitants and local fauna a steady supply of home-grown food. In the centrally placed Market Meadow, trees are strategically positioned so as to guarantee an open view of the old brick market hall. In the courtyard gardens of the residential area, however, the trees form an almost natural habitus on their own terms. The entire landscape design, be it in full soil or on roofs, is based on biodiversity principles, meaning that made-to-size biotopes are created that invite all forms of life to inhabit and make use of the territory.

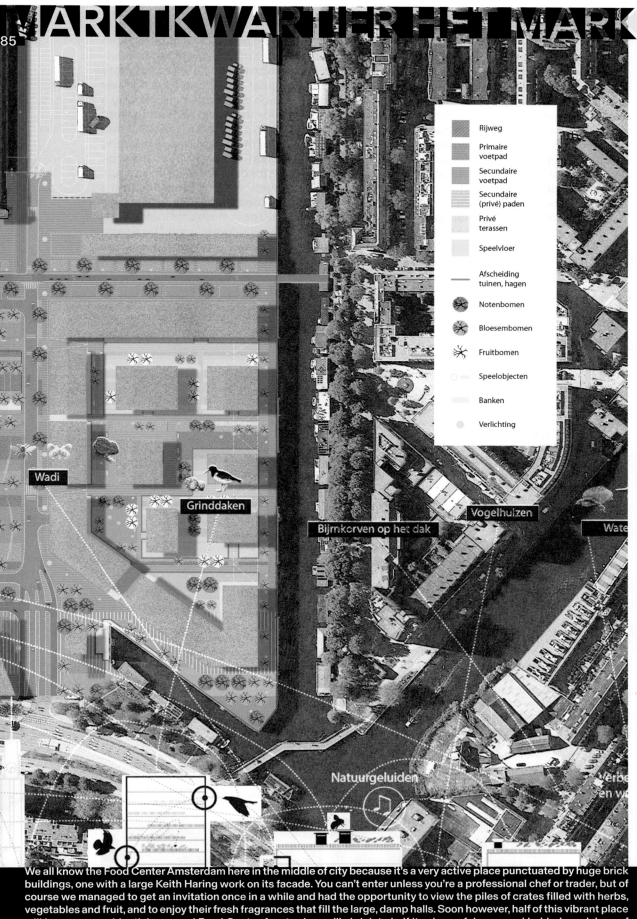

Rijweg

Primaire voetpad

Secundaire voetpad

Secundaire (privé) paden

Privé terassen

Speelvloer

Afscheiding tuinen, hagen

Notenbomen

Bloesembomen

Fruitbomen

Speelobjecten

Banken

Verlichting

Wadi

Grinddaken

Bijrnkorven op het dak

Vogelhuizen

Wate

Natuurgeluiden

We all know the Food Center Amsterdam here in the middle of city because it's a very active place punctuated by huge brick buildings, one with a large Keith Haring work on its facade. You can't enter unless you're a professional chef or trader, but of course we managed to get an invitation once in a while and had the opportunity to view the piles of crates filled with herbs, vegetables and fruit, and to enjoy their fresh fragrances that fill the large, damp halls. Soon however, half of this vibrant place will become a residential area and Food Center Amsterdam will shrink to half its size, safely secured behind vandal-proof fences. We were invited to supplement Mecanoo's urban plan with a general landscape design, which we enthusiastically developed into an all-encompassing food garden that attracts all forms of animal life – much to the disapproval of the still active Food Center on the other side of the fence.

"Kengo Kuma was commissioned to design a public swimming pool in an appointed area that takes up a quarter of the island – a whole corner. By that time, however, we had further developed our initial, linear boardwalk of the competition phase into a much more exciting, erratic zigzag version, referring to COBE's triangular roofscape casting their shadows onto the quays between dawn and midday – which we discovered making a model for sun-studies. The irony was that Kuma's design for the quay, with integrated outdoor pools, was based on our original winning proposal. This caused a deadlock that seemed insoluble, until one day we were locked up in one of the glass-walled meeting rooms in COBE's office and were instructed to figure out a way to synchronise the mismatch without making any substantial changes to either part for the sake of saving design costs. The clients were watching us from the other 'aquarium' waiting for us to send a 'white smoke' signal. Within minutes, our teams reached a consensus; not necessarily our preferred one, but we had to admit that the most realistic option was for Inside Outside to revert their design to the earlier scheme, so that the 'newcomer' could be seamlessly integrated. What a loss! Yet that is how it was done. Just for the fun of it, our teams took an hour before announcing the positive outcome, ensuring that we had given it enough time to call it a careful deliberation."   JC

LOCATION	Christiansholm, Copenhagen, Denmark
CLIENT	CPH City & Port Development, CØ P/S (Danica Ejendomsselskab, Unionkul Ejendomme, Nordkranen), NCC
STATUS	Competition, 2015, 1st prize; under construction since 2020
SCOPE	Landscape design for entire island, including public and private roof gardens, traffic logistics and a continuous, folded wooden boardwalk encircling the island
SCALE	2.4 ha
COLLABORATORS	COBE, Via Trafik, Transsolar
DESCRIPTION	A papercutting by Hans Christian Andersen forms the base of the landscape concept for this island, once used to store paper. A spacious boardwalk surrounds the island on three sides, bringing the visitor close to the saltwater and providing ample terrace space. Ground and roof plantings, parking for bicycles and cars, accessible routes, wayfinding tools, furniture, lighting, trash collecting areas as well as Kengo Kuma's indoor and outdoor swimming pool building are all an integral part of this intricate commission. To be completed in 2024.

Papirøen was one of the last remaining city islands that still had a rustic harbour feel to it. We used Andersen's fairy-tale papercutting to define the island's visual complexion. Patterns will be projected onto the in-situ concrete floor and span the entire island, spreading out underneath the buildings, from the central square onto the quays, and creating continuity between indoors and outdoors. The four sturdy quays, popular place for festivities, pop-up restaurants and sunbathing, will remain free of built structures or trees to preserve the island's flexibility and ensure unobstructed views stretching out across the sea – the source of human destinies in Andersen's fairy tales. But, as soon as you walk from the quay through one of the alleys towards the central plaza, nature begins to assert itself: the alleys protected from wind by trees and decorated with climbing plants that cover them like a pergola; the plaza adorned with circular carpets of flowers that echo the trees' crowns – a sheltered warm hub in the colder seasons and a cool hideaway during the hot summer months; the roof gardens filled with blossoming fruit trees, spices and edibles.

"Early on, somewhere in early autumn, visiting the site that overlooks the sea from a certain height and feeling the salted breeze in our faces, we heard a distinct sigh. And again, a sigh, rising from the sea. And there they were: a large group of dolphins swimming in gentle cadence, repeatedly surfacing for a moment, their gleaming round backs in the evening sun... then diving under again. Magnificent." PB

LOCATION	Sardinia, Italy
CLIENT	Private owner
STATUS	Ongoing
SCOPE	Landscape restoration, maintenance of protected estate
MATERIALS	Local plantings and rock formations
SCALE	10 ha
COLLABORATORS	Marina Perot, Sergio Rolland, Carlo del Bene, Aura Luz Melis, Gianluca Tramutola
DESCRIPTION	This protected nature reserve, with its native, mixed vegetation of shrubs and herbs and its monumental rock formations, was severely damaged by motor sports and rubbish dumps. The denuded areas caused erosion on the steep flanks of the reserve and damage to the indigenous vegetation because they were now exposed to heavy winds from the sea due to the absence of sturdy shrubbery all around. We restored the damaged areas by strengthening the steepest slopes with dug-in wooden planks and replanting hundreds of shrubs of local mix, approved and delivered by the local forest ranger. We also cleaned the entire 10 ha of rocky land of deposits such as old refrigerators, cookers, mattresses, boat pulls, construction debris, etc. All with the consent and advice of the forest ranger and the municipality.

"The patchwork pattern of our garden design refers to the agricultural fields that covered this site at the start of Rishon's existence; we chose the terracotta brickwork – unusual in this area – not only for its warm colour but also in response to the brick building of the Carmel-Mizrahi Winery, situated nearby. (NB: This winery was established under the patronage of Baron Edmund James de Rothschild in 1886. David Ben-Gurion was one of three prime ministers who worked at this winery before entering into politics.)"

"Tel Aviv is a beautiful and lively city; the food is great and the colleagues and friends we made there over time are the best. As always, we learnt a lot from them – about language and its connection to agriculture; names of trees, crops and tools; about climate and the landscape; about historic sites, facts and myths; about social structures and (im)possibilities, religion, mutual tolerance and daily life in the private sphere. We were introduced to the most amazing kibbutz architecture, to fantastic Art Nouveau buildings and hidden gardens, to the spacious Rabbin Square and to hilly estates with beautiful stands of trees glowing in the pink of the setting sun with the sound of gunshots in the background from the nearby military training grounds." PB

"We presented the developing project a couple of times to the mayor and the local city architects and councillors. Along with the architects' team of Efrat and Kowalsky, we made sure to be thoroughly prepared, as our audience was well informed about local regulations, funding and priorities and therefore very critical. However, when we explained our idea for the continuous 'pergola security fence,' in which the standard security fence becomes an integral part of a romantically overgrown pergola space, there was not the immediate rejection that we feared. First a doubtful silence, then an appreciative murmur and then collective agreement that the possibility should be seriously investigated! And yes: we did get official permission from the security department – and thus, our newest invention saw the light – a bright yellow, overgrown and inhabitable (security) pergola in the heart of Israel." JC

LOCATION	Rishon LeZion, Israel
CLIENT	Municipality of Rishon LeZion
STATUS	First phase completed in 2019, second phase ongoing
SCOPE	Connective landscape for the International Center for the Hebrew Language, Haviv elementary School, Museum of Hebrew and Medalya Coffee House; a continuous greened pergola as security fence and inhabitable shaded space
SCALE	1.3 ha
COLLABORATORS	Efrat-Kowalsky Architects, Moria Architects/Studio MA
DESCRIPTION	A long, narrow, sloping site on the high point of the town, completely encircled by a sombre collection of different security fences that are essential to the safety of the primary school pupils, is earmarked to house three buildings: the future Haviv Primary School, the Museum of the Hebrew Language, together with the Bait La Ivrit (House of Hebrew) that will inhabit the charming old building at the current entrance gate. Our two main design proposals suggested reshaping the narrow rectangular site into a continuous, gentle slope (keeping all trees) and to replace the cacophony of fences by one continuous, well-designed, friendly fence that would be welcoming instead of frightening – without losing its function as a security tool.

Overgrown with blooming and fruit-bearing climbers, this green frame would unify the campus and create an abundance of cool, sheltered outdoor places to be used by school children and visitors for play, outdoor classes, gatherings, private reading and as a restaurant and terrace. Three types of pergolas form the green frame: a one-sided open shading device, a two-sided pergola that shelters people both inside and outside the fence; and a so-called "berceau," a closed green tunnel for total privacy and shade.

The gently sloping garden itself is covered with a colourful patchwork of rectangular flower beds and brick pavement – each brick "carpet" laid out in a different pattern and each plant bed filled with scented, ornamental and edible plants of different kinds and heights. Ball fields and a running track are cut out of the garden surface. Different species of old and young trees are spread throughout the entire site, most of which play a specific role in the Hebrew language. The brick 'carpets' flow into the open interiors of the school and the museum, where they create a sturdy base for large gatherings and where yellow curtains form flexible rooms for performances large and small.

The colourful top layer of the running track is still missing and the pergola is not yet complete, but the school opened, the garden is planted, the kids are playing. What a joy!!!

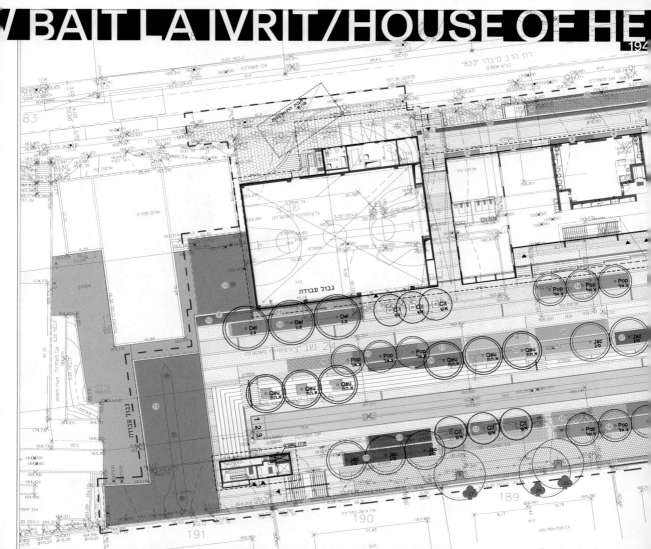

Only half of the project was realised at this point, thus this 50% construction plan drawing showing the floor plan of the school's entrance level, sports fields and garden

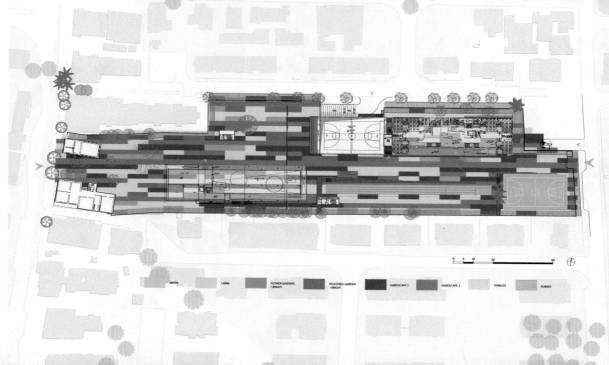

The definitive design drawing of the entire site, including school, museum, language centre and cafe

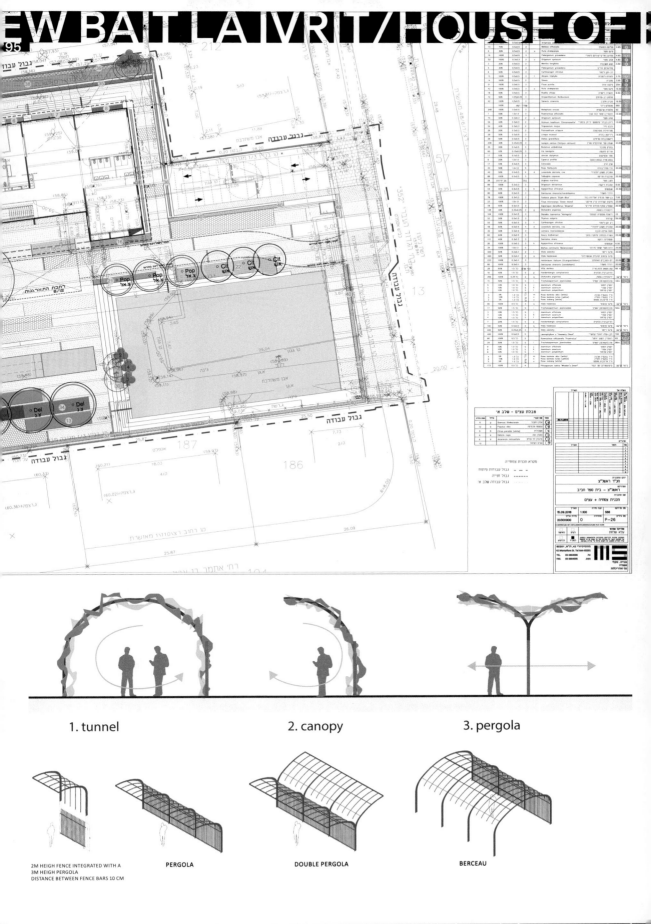

1. tunnel

2. canopy

3. pergola

2M HEIGH FENCE INTEGRATED WITH A
3M HEIGH PERGOLA
DISTANCE BETWEEN FENCE BARS 10 CM

PERGOLA

DOUBLE PERGOLA

BERCEAU

We invented a new form of security fence for this project because the gloomy jumble of aggressive fences we encountered on site got to us. Protection yes, of course, but in another form. So now the entire site is embraced by a continuous, bright yellow, greened, flowering, shading pergola with integrated, inoffensive security fences. We were proud that the municipality and the security department granted us an official permit for this fence design.

CONCEPT / 10 GARDENS FOR EUROFLORA

ORNAMENTAL GRASSES ③

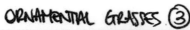

SUCCULENT ON PUBBLES ⑤

LAWN ①

STONE X PATHS

LOCATION	Parchi di Nervi, Genoa, Italy
CLIENT	Municipality of Genoa
STATUS	Completed
SCOPE	Garden installation at Euroflora Genova 2022 based on our linear Parco del Polcevera design
MATERIALS	Plants and various finishes for upstanding edges, paths and areas
SCALE	940 m²
COLLABORATORS	Studio Laura Gatti
DESCRIPTION	The municipality of Genoa asked Inside Outside and Studio Laura Gatti to participate in the 2022 Euroflora, held in the Parchi di Nervi. We were to represent the city by giving a glimpse of the future Parco del Ponte that we will design and realise in the coming years. Of course, we complied, and started to study the plots into which the park is divided to choose an appropriate one for our installation.

Where a Floriade usually exhibits special plants, we showed a scale model of our design: a miniature representation. We created a series of stripes, each different in width and each representing a different garden typology – both in section (topography) and in planting composition. Existing trees needed to be integrated – no problem of course – and our choice of plants would be re-used for the park's forthcoming restoration.

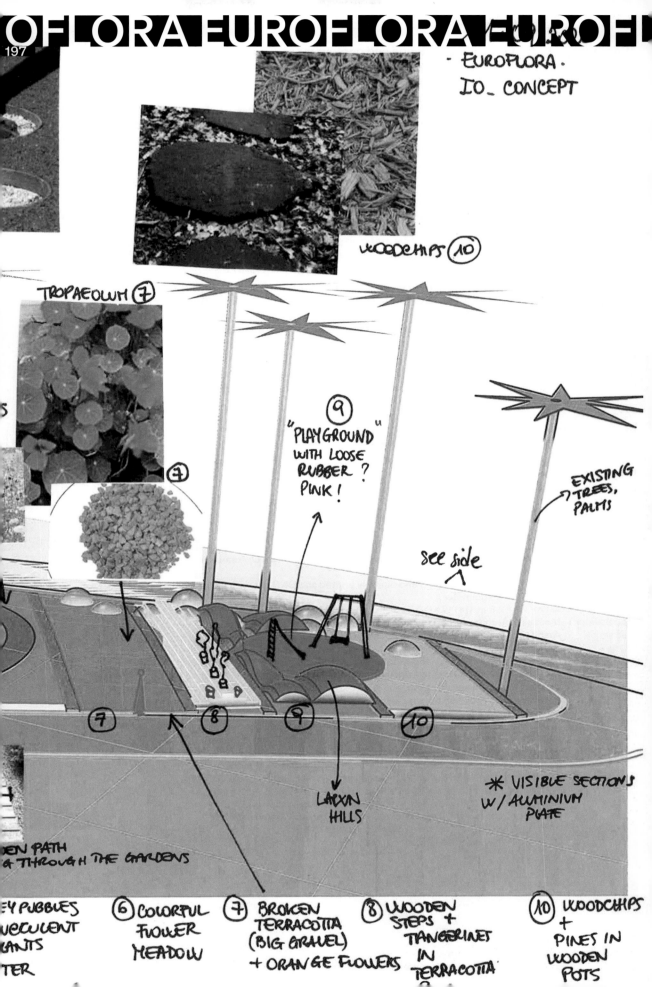

- EUROFLORA.
IO_ CONCEPT

WOODCHIPS (10)

TROPAEOLUM (7)

(7)

(9)

"PLAYGROUND"
WITH LOOSE
RUBBER?
PINK!

EXISTING
TREES,
PALMS

see side
︿

(7)   (8)   (9)   (10)

LAWN
HILLS

✳ VISIBLE SECTIONS
W/ ALUMINIUM
PLATE

EN PATH
G THROUGH THE GARDENS

EY PUBBLES
UCCULENT
ANTS
TER

(6) COLORFUL
FLOWER
MEADOW

(7) BROKEN
TERRACOTTA
(BIG GRAVEL)
+ ORANGE FLOWERS

(8) WOODEN
STEPS +
TANGERINES
IN
TERRACOTTA

(10) WOODCHIPS
+
PINES IN
WOODEN
POTS

"Some projects demand a lot of patience and perseverance. The idea seemed so simple, just a few curtains outside instead of inside to shade the interiors. But the relatively simple technique of a motorised track system for indoor use becomes rather complex when it has to perform in its entirety (including the motors) in all kinds of outdoor weather conditions, rain and shine, pulling out and folding back a soft, perforated surface. Thanks to our client, himself an architect, we got in touch with a creative steel and engineering company in Portugal that was interested to make a customised system. But after the first promising mock-up in 2019 that only needed a few adjustments, the firm stopped working on the commission and could not be persuaded to continue. After almost two years of calling, mailing and almost begging them to finish the job, we simply had to accept that their decision was final."

"It was already mid-2021 when we found a party from Germany that was confident they could make an appropriate system. They just needed to do a few calculations. With new-found energy we restarted working on the technical aspect of the project. Then, a few weeks later, our client gave us a call: "Hello, I'm on the verge of signing a contract with a Chinese fashion house that wants to rent the lower two floors of my building. The good news is that they like the outdoor curtains, but… they want to participate in the further development of your design. Are you willing to adjust it?" Of course. Our 'extra client' told us to integrate the following words into our tree: Desire/Dream/Hope/Fear – words that would communicate the fashion house's mentality. Okay, we thought, no problem… but doesn't this recall well-known 'wordworks' of certain established artists? Anyway, they changed their minds after receiving our modest quote and were happy to accept our wordless tree design. On to finalising the curtain."

"Alas the German firm's test proved negative. Their product tracks, carriers, cable and motor systems were not strong enough to guarantee good performance in extreme weather. Finally we found a capable company in the Netherlands. They addressed the situation with optimistic fervour and figured out a system that would work. After carefully adapting the details of our design to the requirements of their system – it FINALLY happened. Date of installation: October 2022."   PN

LOCATION	Le Marais, Paris, France
CLIENT	Moussafir Architectes
STATUS	Completed
SCOPE	Facade curtain (shading/glare control) for fashion/office/residential building
MATERIALS	Gauze curtain dipped in PVC and digitally printed and CNC cut with perforations of 16 mm diameter
SCALE	131 m²; 12 × 2.8 m, (1×) 12 × 2.5 m
COLLABORATORS	Moussafir Architects, Lenco Zonwering
DESCRIPTION	Architect Jacques Moussafir had been working on the renovation of a modest building in Paris to convert into an office and private residence. He asked us to design an outdoor solution for the intense sunlight and the lack of privacy. We presented several concepts from shifting, inflatable screens to translucent parasols that were placed perpendicular to the facade in a clever configuration, but eventually we picked the simplest idea: outdoor curtains, opening and closing along a motorised track. For the material we chose white translucent PVC mesh, with perforations for the wind to pass through, making sure that the curtains could withstand the forces of nature. The curtains were digitally printed in a solid grey-blue that forms the background of an image transcending the limitations of the floors of the five-storey building. Together they create the silhouette of a tree, the *Prunus lusitanica* that grows in the same street. Circular perforations in a firm grid shape the tree and make the mesh even more permeable for wind in these areas while casting patches of daylight inside and illuminating the facade in the evening by the light shining from inside out.

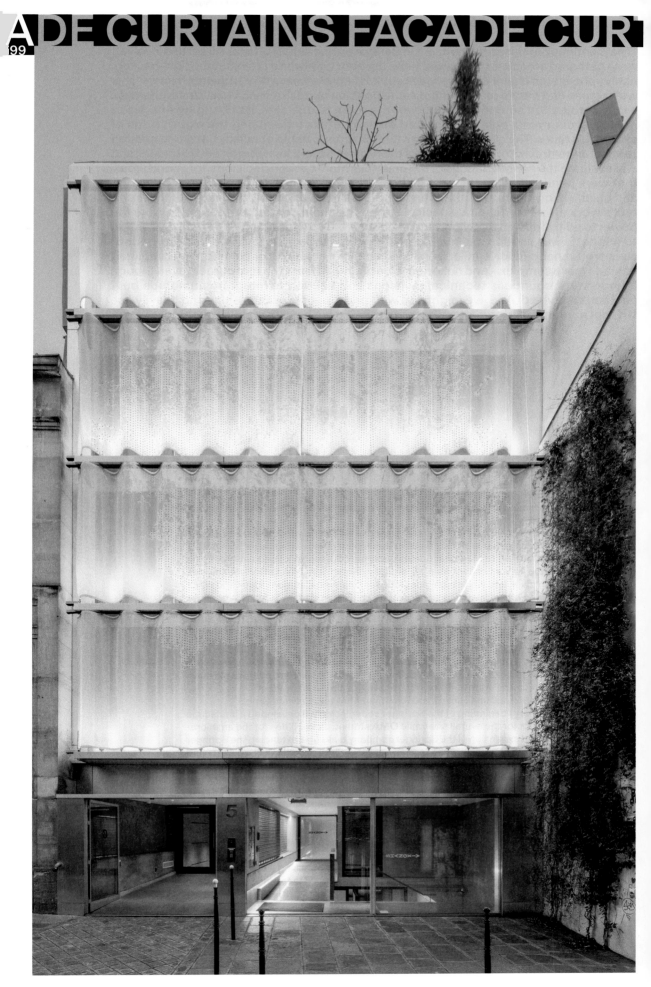

"The meetings organised by the client in Berlin were incredibly official. All parties involved were gathered around an O-shaped table covered with white tablecloths. High-backed, richly upholstered chairs were placed at equidistant intervals with pen, paper, microphone, water glass and carafe placed in the same position opposite each chair. Unsurprisingly, a large projection screen towered over the room to one side, its changing images of numbers, diagrams, photographs and design details influencing the expressions of everyone's faces. The atmosphere was far from comfortable or relaxed, and one needed to stay concentrated for every minute of every meeting and for hours on end to understand and evaluate the consequences of the many German-spoken decisions, large and small, that were being taken on the spot. The project was developed on the basis of 'design and build,' which means that the client appoints a main contractor to take over the architect's work after the 'definitive design' stage. This main contractor seemed to have the power to adjust design decisions and to economise on everything – so special attention to this party was needed. We too, experienced what this meant: prices went up, materials were exchanged for 'similar' versions, technical solutions or connections simplified or made more complex – and not often to our liking. At least the roof garden, even though it underwent countless technical revisions and needed to integrate numerous built additions, survived! And, we might add with pride, people greatly enjoy and heavily use the roof garden, even long after closing hours – so we have been told repeatedly."   PB

LOCATION	Berlin, Germany
CLIENT	Axel Springer SE
STATUS	Competition, 1st prize / completed
SCOPE	Landscape masterplan, landscape around building, roof garden, floors, curtains
MATERIALS	Grey stage net with rectangular transparent plastic window (offices/west), white stage net with rectangular transparent plastic window (offices/east), grey and white stage net (Idealo), soft pink dupioni silk lined with soft pink cotton velour (visitors' lounge), digitally printed light pink cotton velour, lined with black and white high gloss lacquer (Learning Campus), black and white lacquer strips following the floor pattern (Forum curtain 1), white high gloss lacquer with vertical transparent plastic windows (Forum curtain 2), CNC cut silver/white mesh (furniture pods), plantings, black and white ceramic tiles (entrance hall), black and white tiles and white concrete tiles
SCALE	Masterplan, 1.9 ha; realised landscape design of ground floor, 5,000 m²; roof garden, 7,000 m²; 102 curtains, 1,955 m²; 76 office curtains, 1,279 m²; 17 furniture pods: 190 m²; one visitors' lounge curtain, 53 m²; two campus curtains, 157 m²; four Forum curtains, 180 m²; two Idealo curtains, 96 m²
COLLABORATORS	OMA, Simons und Hinze Landschaftsarchitekten, Gerriets GmbH
DESCRIPTION	In the very beginning of the Springer commission we developed a landscape concept for the overall site while OMA studied possibilities for the amelioration and expansion of the Springer company buildings, extending the Springer site to the other side of the former, now demolished, Berlin Wall. This resulted in a very explicit organisation of the exterior spaces, a bold black-and-white composition that we thought necessary to connect the different buildings and areas (not all visually connected when standing on the ground) as a single entity. This organisation would later flow inside and up the new Springer building, which OMA was commissioned to build after winning the international competition.

Once architectural planning was activated, we stayed involved in the process as part of the OMA team and pursued the idea of the landscape as an integral part of the new building. Focusing on the public spaces inside, directly around it and on the roof, we drew up several designs for an elevated public park. This roof garden was an important political element, because the building occupied an open green public space, so our plan projected this green onto the roof as a publicly accessible garden.

In the meantime, it became clear that the interiors would need a great many curtains to fulfil multiple functions: glare control, darkening, space defining and space creating. We ended up producing 102 curtains, each series its own character, function and materialisation.

L SPRINGER MEDIA CAMPUS

.09 . Springer curtains overview . Inside Outside

tain type	curtain code	quantity	track length (m)	track length (m) check on-site	total tracks (m)	width pleated (m)	width pleated (m) check on-site	width flat (m)		curtain height (m)	curtain height (m) check on-site	total (m2)	Curtain Weight (g)	Track Weight (g)	material	tracks notes
ND FLOOR	EAST															
1 curtain	00-01	1	16,17		16,17	12,50		15%	15,43	4,05		62,5	28121,2	8505,4		
1 curtain	00-02	1		13,26	13,26	13,26		15%	15,30	4,05		62,0	27884,3	0,0		
3 curtain	00-03	1	6,70		6,70	6,70		15%	7,70	3,63		28,0	12577,95	3524,2		
4 curtain	00-04	1	6,70		6,70	6,70		15%	7,70	3,63		28,0	12577,95	3524,2		
OOR	EAST															
curtains	01-01 top			6,63	6,63		6,63	50%	9,95					3487,4	WHITE NET	
	01-01 bottom	1					7,09		10,64	3,04	3,04	32,3	4528,4			
curtains	01-02	1		3,91	3,91		3,91	50%	5,87	3,04		17,8	2496,1	2056,7	WHITE NET	
curtains	01-03	1		6,60	6,60		6,60	20%	7,92	3,04		24,1	3370,8	3471,6	LINEN GREY	
curtains	01-04	1		1,17	1,17		1,17	50%	1,76	3,04		5,3	746,9	615,4	WHITE NET	
curtains	01-05	1		6,60	6,60		6,60	20%	7,92	3,04		24,1	3370,8	3471,6	LINEN GREY	
curtains	01-06	1		6,61	6,61		6,61	50%	9,92	3,05	3,05	30,2	4233,7	3476,9	WHITE NET	
curtains	01-07	1		3,92	3,92		3,92	50%	5,88	3,04		17,9	2502,5	2061,9	WHITE NET	
curtains	01-08	1		3,91	3,91		3,91	50%	5,87	3,04		17,8	2496,1	2056,7	WHITE NET	
curtains	01-09	1		10,69	10,69		10,69	20%	12,83	3,04		39,0	5459,6	5622,9	LINEN GREY	
curtains	01-10	1		9,31	9,31		9,31	20%	11,17	3,04		34,0	4754,8	4897,1	LINEN GREY	
curtains	01-11	1		3,91	3,91		3,91	50%	5,87	3,04		17,8	2496,1	2056,7	WHITE NET	
curtains	01-12	1		3,91	3,91		3,91	50%	5,87	3,04	3,04	17,8	2496,1	2056,7	WHITE NET	
curtains	01-13	1		3,91	3,91		3,91	50%	5,87	3,04		17,8	2496,1	2056,7	WHITE NET	
curtains	01-14	1		5,01	5,01		5,01	50%	7,52	3,04		22,8	3198,4	2635,3	WHITE NET	
	WEST															
curtains	01-15	1		1,23	1,23		1,22	50%	1,83	3,04		5,6	778,8	647,0	GREY NET	
curtains	01-16	1		1,21	1,21		1,20	50%	1,80	3,04		5,5	766,1	636,5	GREY NET	
curtains	01-17	1		3,91	3,91		3,90	50%	5,85	3,04		17,8	2489,8	2056,7	GREY NET	
curtains	01-18	1		5,31	5,31		5,30	50%	7,95	3,04		24,2	3383,5	2793,1	GREY NET	
curtains	01-19	1		6,71	6,71		6,69	50%	10,04	3,04		30,5	4270,9	3529,5	GREY NET	
curtains	01-20	1		3,90	3,90		3,89	50%	5,84	3,04		17,7	2483,4	2051,4	GREY NET	
curtains	01-21	1		1,21	1,21		1,20	50%	1,80	3,04		5,5	766,1	636,5	GREY NET	
curtains	01-22/A	1		2,61	2,61		2,60	50%	3,90	3,04		11,9	1659,8	1372,9	GREY NET	Track already installed
curtains	01-22/B	1		2,61	2,61		2,59	50%	3,89	3,04		11,8	1653,5	1372,9	GREY NET	Track already installed
curtains	01-22/C	1		5,32	5,32		5,30	50%	7,95	3,04		24,2	3383,5	2798,3	GREY NET	Track already installed
curtains	01-22/D	1		5,32	5,32		5,30	50%	7,95	3,04		24,2	3383,5	2798,3	GREY NET	Track already installed
curtains	01-22/E	1		5,29	5,29		5,27	50%	7,91	3,04		24,0	3364,4	2782,5	GREY NET	Track already installed
curtains	01-22/F	1		5,29	5,29		5,27	50%	7,91	3,04		24,0	3364,4	2782,5	GREY NET	Track already installed
curtains	01-22/G	1		5,32	5,32		5,30	50%	7,95	3,04		24,2	3383,5	2798,3	GREY NET	Track already installed
curtains	01-22/H	1		5,32	5,32		5,30	50%	7,95	3,04		24,2	3383,5	2798,3	GREY NET	Track already installed
curtains	01-22/I	1		2,62	2,62		2,60	50%	3,90	3,04		11,9	1659,8	1378,1	GREY NET	Track already installed
curtains	01-22/J	1		2,62	2,62		2,60	50%	3,90	3,04		11,9	1659,8	1378,1	GREY NET	Track already installed
curtains	01-23	1		1,22	1,22		1,21	50%	1,82	3,04		5,5	772,5	641,7	GREY NET	
curtains	01-24	1		5,31	5,31		5,30	50%	7,95	3,04		24,2	3383,5	2793,1	GREY NET	
curtains	01-25	1		6,71	6,71		6,69	50%	10,04	3,05	3,05	30,6	4284,9	3529,5	GREY NET	
OOR	EAST															
curtains	02-01	1		1,21	1,21		1,20	50%	1,80	3,04		5,5	766,1	636,5	WHITE NET	
curtains	02-02	1		3,90	3,90		3,89	50%	5,84	3,04		17,7	2483,4	2051,4	WHITE NET	
curtains	02-03	1		1,22	1,22		1,21	50%	1,82	3,04		5,5	772,5	641,7	WHITE NET	
curtains	02-04	1		3,91	3,91		3,90	50%	5,85	3,04		17,8	2489,8	2056,7	WHITE NET	
curtains	02-13	1		6,62	6,62		6,61	50%	9,92	3,04		30,1	4219,8	3482,1	WHITE NET	
curtains	02-14	1		3,91	3,91		3,90	50%	5,85	3,04		17,8	2489,8	2056,7	WHITE NET	
	WEST															
curtains	02-05	1		1,19	1,19		1,18	50%	1,77	3,04	3,04	5,4	753,3	625,9	GREY NET	Track already installed
curtains	02-06	1		2,51	2,51		2,50	50%	3,75	3,04		11,4	1596,0	1320,3	GREY NET	Track already installed
curtains	02-07	1		1,63	1,63		1,62	50%	2,43	3,04		7,4	1034,2	857,4	GREY NET	Track already installed
curtains	02-08	1		2,17	2,17		2,16	50%	3,24	3,03	3,03	9,8	1374,4	1141,4	GREY NET	Track already installed
curtains	02-09	1		5,32	5,32		5,31	50%	7,97	3,04		24,2	3389,9	2798,3	GREY NET	Track already installed
curtains	02-10	1		2,52	2,52		2,52	50%	3,78	3,04		11,5	1608,8	1325,5	GREY NET	presence of a column
curtains	02-11/A	1		3,42	3,42		3,42	50%	5,13	3,04		15,6	2183,3	1798,9	GREY NET	presence of a corner
curtains	02-11/B	1		4,97	4,97		4,96	50%	7,44	3,04		22,6	3166,5	2614,2	GREY NET	presence of a corner
curtains	02-12/A	1		1,23	1,23		1,22	50%	1,83	3,04		5,6	778,8	647,0	GREY NET	
curtains	02-12/B	1		3,92	3,92		3,91	50%	5,87	3,04		17,8	2496,1	2061,9	GREY NET	
curtains	02-15/A	1		3,56	3,56		3,55	50%	5,33	3,04		16,2	2266,3	1872,6	GREY NET	
curtains	02-15/B	1		3,04	3,04		3,03	50%	4,55	3,04		13,8	1934,4	1599,0	GREY NET	
curtains	02-16	1		2,59	2,59		2,58	50%	3,87	3,03	3,03	11,7	1641,7	1362,3	GREY NET	
OOR	EAST															
ure pods	03-PR01HC	3	2,825		8,46	2,82		50%	4,23	2,135		27,09315	10295,4	1486,0		
ure pods	03-PR03C	1	15,08		15,08	15,08		50%	22,62	2,135		48,2937	18351,6	7932,1		
OOR	WEST															
rs' Lounge	04-01A+	1		15,30	15,30		13,60	50%	20,40	2,58		52,6	34210,8	8047,8		
	EAST															
curtains	04-02	1		1,22	1,22					3,03	3,03			641,7		Only track
curtains	04-03	1		1,21	1,21					3,03				636,5		Only track
OOR	EAST															
ampus	05-PD7A	1	24,86		24,86	24,86		20%	29,83	2,635		78,60	77030,01	26724,50		
ampus	05-PD7B	1	24,86		24,86	24,86		20%	29,83	2,635		78,60	77030,01	26724,50		
	WEST															
ture pods	05-PR04HC	3	1,52		4,56	1,52		50%	2,28	2,14		14,61	5552,9	800,0		
OOR	EAST															
ture pods	06-PR01HC	2	2,83		5,65	2,83		50%	4,24	2,14		18,1	6875,8	1486,0		
ture pods	06-PR03C	1	15,08		15,08	15,08		50%	22,62	2,14		48,3	18351,6	7932,1		
curtains	06-09	1		1,21	1,21		1,20	20%	1,44	3,00		4,3	604,8	636,5	LINEN GREY	
curtains	06-10	1		1,16	1,16		1,15	20%	1,38	3,00	3,00	4,1	579,6	610,2	LINEN GREY	
curtains	06-11/A	1		2,88	2,88		2,87	50%	4,31	3,01	3,01	13,0	1814,1	1514,9	WHITE NET	
curtains	06-11/B	1		1,31	1,31		1,31	50%	1,97	3,01		5,9	828,1	689,1	WHITE NET	
	WEST															
ture pods	06-PR04HC	4	1,52		6,08	1,52		50%	2,28	2,14		19,5	7403,9	800,0		
OOR	EAST															
curtains	07-07	1		2,50	2,50		2,50	50%	3,75	3,01	3,01	11,3	1580,3	1315,0	WHITE NET	
OOR	EAST															
ture pods	08-PR04HC	3	1,52		4,56	1,52		50%	2,28	2,14		14,6	5552,9	800,0		
curtains	08-06	1		3,91	3,91		3,91	50%	5,87	3,02	3,02	17,7	2479,7	2056,7	WHITE NET	
curtains	08-08	1		5,30	5,30		5,30	50%	7,95	3,01		22,9	3203,5	2787,8	WHITE NET	
OOR	EAST															
curtains	09-01	1		4,79	4,79		4,79	50%	7,19	3,01	3,01	21,6	3027,8	2519,5	WHITE NET	
curtains	09-02	1		2,62	2,62		2,62	50%	3,93	3,01		11,8	1656,1	1378,1	WHITE NET	
curtains	09-03	1		5,40	5,40		5,40	50%	8,10	3,01		24,4	3413,3	2840,4	WHITE NET	
curtains	09-04	1		4,80	4,80		4,80	50%	7,20	3,01		21,7	3034,1	2524,8	WHITE NET	
curtains	09-05	1		2,48	2,48		2,48	50%	3,72	3,01		11,2	1567,6	1304,5	WHITE NET	
curtains	09-06/A	1		2,57	2,57		2,57	50%	3,86	3,01	3,01	11,6	1624,5	1351,8	WHITE NET	
curtains	09-06/B	1		1,61	1,61		1,61	50%	2,42	3,01		7,3	1017,7	846,9	WHITE NET	
curtains	09-07/A	1		2,60	2,60		2,60	50%	3,90	3,01		11,7	1643,5	1367,6	WHITE NET	
curtains	09-07/B	1		8,01	8,01		8,01	50%	12,02	3,01		36,2	5063,1	4213,3	WHITE NET	
curtains	09-07/C	1		8,01	8,01		8,01	50%	12,02	3,00	3,00	36,0	5046,3	4213,3	WHITE NET	
curtains	09-08	1		3,90	3,90		3,90	50%	5,85	3,01		17,6	2465,2	2051,4	WHITE NET	
curtains	09-09	1		1,20	1,20		1,20	50%	1,80	3,01		5,4	758,5	631,2	WHITE NET	
curtains	09-11	1		5,32	5,32		5,32	50%	7,98	3,01		24,0	3362,8	2798,3	WHITE NET	
curtains	09-12	1		2,60	2,60		2,60	50%	3,90	3,01		11,7	1643,5	1367,6	WHITE NET	
	WEST															
o curtains	09-13	1		10,60	10,60		10,60	50%	15,90	3,01		47,86	21536,6	0,0		
o curtains	09-14	1		10,60	10,60		10,60	50%	15,90	3,01		47,86	21536,6	0,0		
	Total	102 items	119,66 m		479,1 m	129 m						1953,4 m2	563670,2 g	251131,9 g		

l m2 Office curtains	1279,1	m2
unt of Office curtains	75	

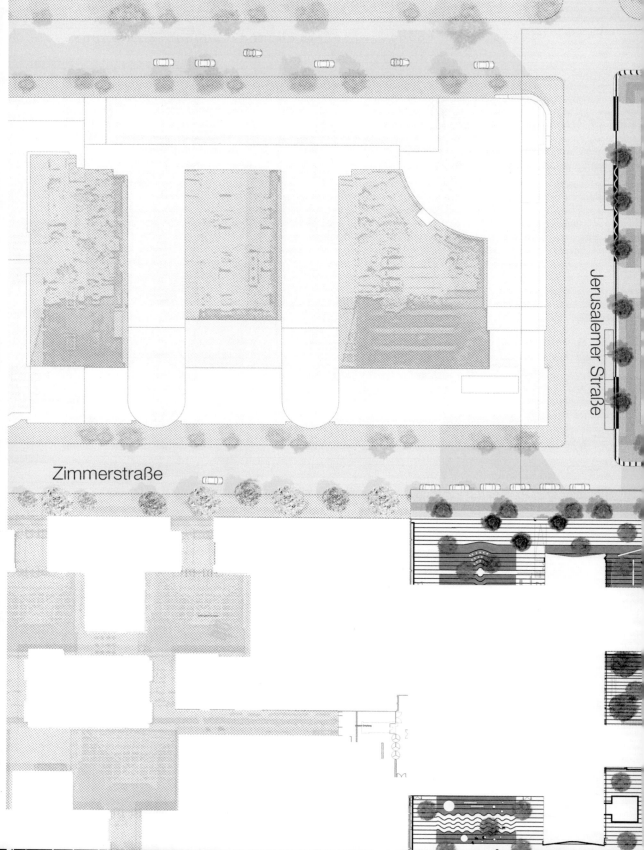

Jerusalemer Straße

Zimmerstraße

First we developed this landscape masterplan to tie the eastern and western halves of the Axel Springer campus together. We used natural black and white stone pavement of 5 × 5 cm that is typical of Berlin to create this very graphic pattern, which continues from the outside into the entrance halls of each building – both old and new. The pattern, by the way, is three-dimensional, so the landscape has a distinct topography and creates enclosed rooms, auditoriums, water features, sports fields and the like.

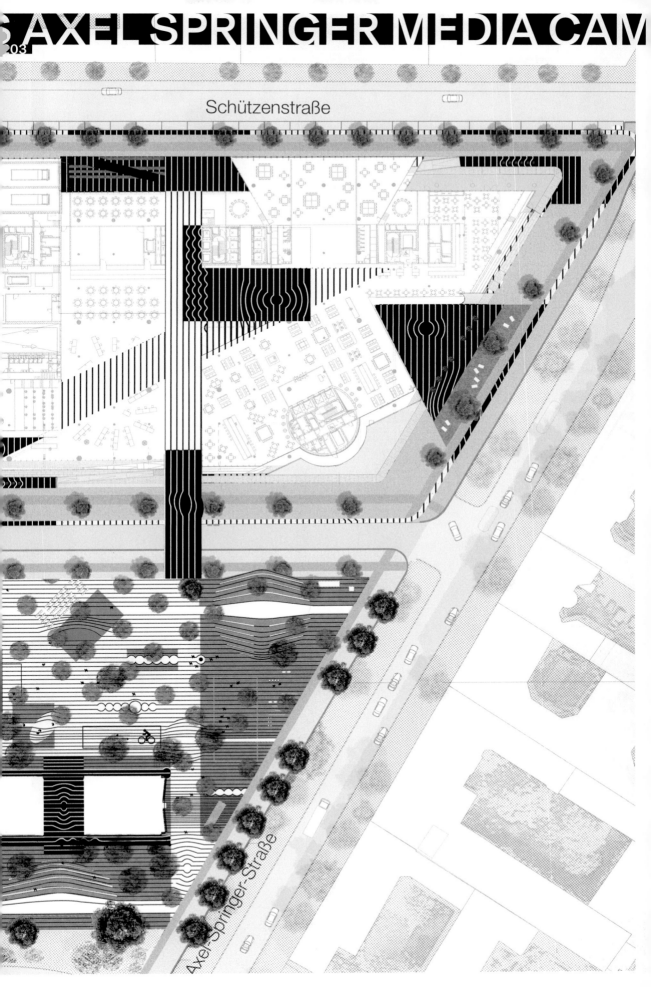

Schützenstraße

Axel-Springer-Straße

The curtains pick up on the striped patterns of the black-and-white floors that we designed, and become pleated, vertical planes that darken the glazed workspaces around

stairwell
restroom

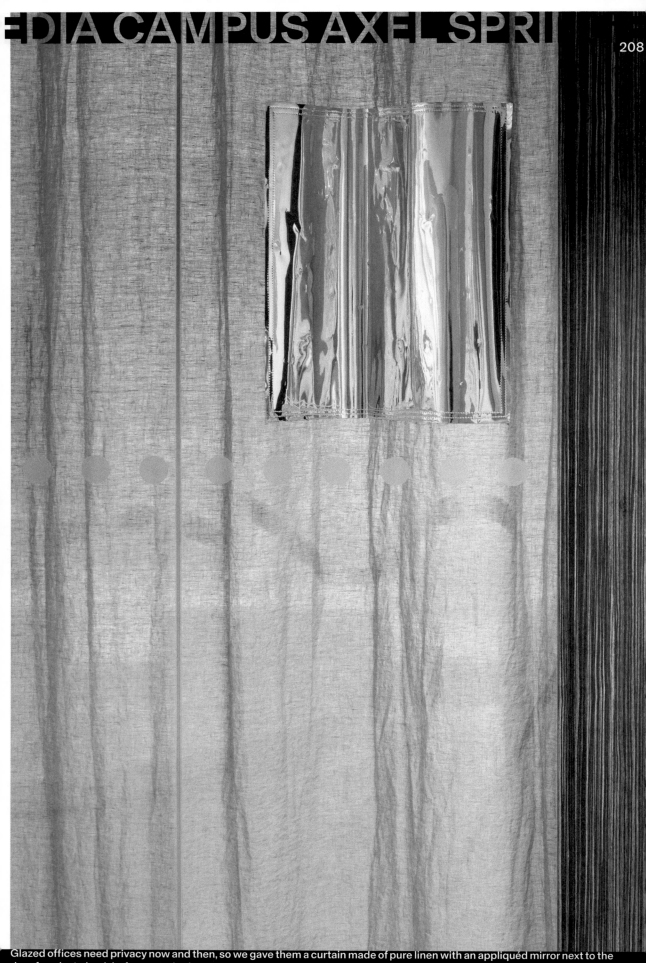

Glazed offices need privacy now and then, so we gave them a curtain made of pure linen with an appliquéd mirror next to the door for a last check before entering!

Here you are looking into one half of the Lern Campus, a space in the shape of the numeral eight that can be configured into two separate rooms or one large one. Inside, one half is white, the other black. The double layer of velvet and lacquer mutes the sounds from the surroundings, creating intimate rooms for study.

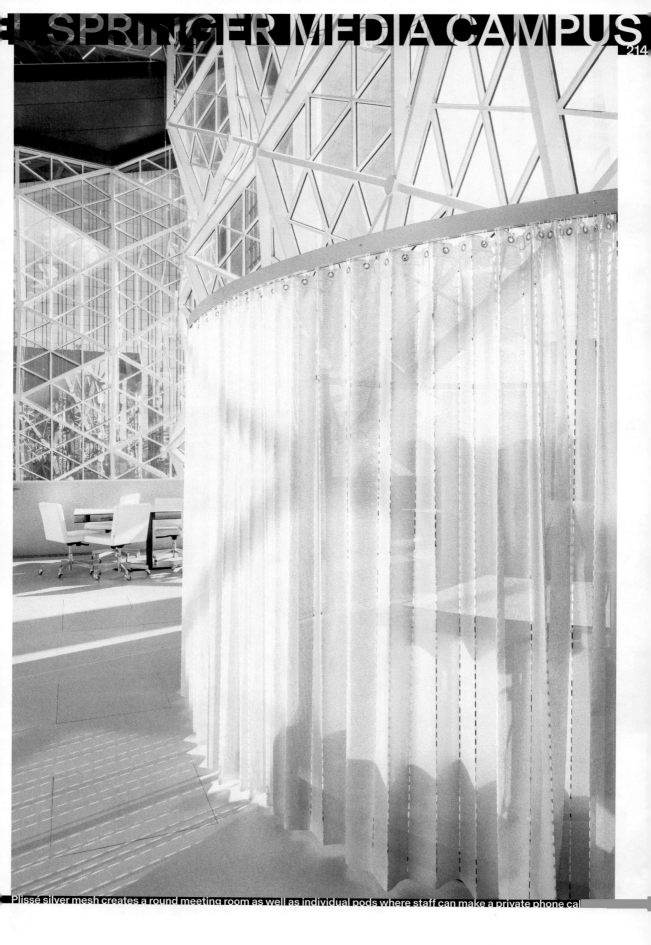

Plissé silver mesh creates a round meeting room as well as individual pods where staff can make a private phone call

the black-and-white floor pattern has integrated textures for the visually impaired

The black-and-white natural stone floor moves in and out of the building like a rectangular carpet, inviting people in, showing people out

The formerly spacious roof garden slowly filled up with a huge amount of emergency exits and enormous aluminium-clad technical equipment. We suggested turning our generous, mostly edible greenery into an aluminium forest with steel flowers, but the city and staff preferred "real nature."

"Visiting the site, we were struck by its energy even in its then current state. It was embedded in the vibrant, charismatic city, surrounded by an elevated train track, a hectic shopping and business area, college buildings with sports fields and busy roads. The previous building, lying at the foot of a large, green hill, was actively used day and night as a food market and a parking lot. We ate amazing food late at night at the bustling food market and realised that indeed, as the architects had already pointed out, this market had to stay. To keep it alive, OMA planned to lift the building and create a large square underneath. We envisioned the building with its three floating auditoriums as a lively, energy-transmitting machine that would radiate its energy to the square and the city around. The square, therefore, needed to become a muscular, multifunctional and inviting public space that would generate a counter flow of energy streaming back into the building, sucking the public in and up to its roof to enjoy the sky and the amazing views."

"To be able to work closely on the interiors of the building with the OMA TPAC team, based in Hong Kong, Taipei and Rotterdam, we 'detached' two of Inside Outside's treasured colleagues at the time, designer Marieke van den Heuvel (now writing a book on circular economy) and architect Aura Melis (now IO partner), to the OMA office in Hong Kong in 2010. They stayed for more than a year (during which both met their future spouses). Needless to say, I visited the TPAC team regularly for workshops and meetings, and we visited Taipei on several occasions to understand the context of the project in depth. Our work consisted of formulating strong concepts for the building's interiors and landscape, finding the right finishing and cladding materials, patterns for carpets and floors, upholstery for theatre seating, configurations and materials for the stage curtains in the three theatres, curtains and acoustic screens for the rehearsal studios and the GT foyer, lighting atmospheres, logistics and trajectories from surrounding streets through gardens and plaza into and through the building, demarcations for wheelchair accessible roads, etc. – AND a striking colour palette for the building as a whole (we suggested: all public spaces blue, all studios pink, technical rooms green and all backstage spaces dark brown!). In other words: easy task."   PB

LOCATION	Shilin District, Taipei City, Taiwan
CLIENT	Department of Cultural Affairs, Taipei City Government
STATUS	Competition, 1st prize / completed
SCOPE	Landscape design, including a public square for food markets and fairs, public garden areas, streetscape as well as roof, terrace and interior gardens; colour and material concept for entire building; upholstery for seating in three auditoriums; consultant for all wall, floor and ceiling finishes; stage curtains for two main auditoriums
MATERIALS	Light-blue glass fibre fabric with vertical slits of light-blue voile (Grand Theatre); 3 overlapping white, PVC, translucent front-and-rear projection screens (Proscenium Play); pink and white Trevira CS fabric, natural wool felt panels (rehearsal rooms); green cotton velvet (green room); double-layered light-blue glassfibre fabric (foyer GT); plantings, earth, black-and-white pigmented concrete, black pebbles, lighting, red and blue paint
SCALE	Landscape, 4.6 ha; Grand Theatre curtain, 20.3 × 14.45 m; Proscenium Play stage membrane, 20 × 12.15 m
COLLABORATORS	OMA, Artech, dUCKS scéno, Gerriets GmbH
DESCRIPTION	To preserve the existing food market, the architects elevated the TPAC building and left generous space for a large square to run through underneath. We designed an "indestructible" square that can withstand extremely heavy use. Its play of black and white lines invites people coming from the city or metro to enter the building at its centre. All technical necessities for flexible, intense use are integrated in the square, such as water, electricity and internet points, elements to attach tent-like structures, drainage lines, lighting, seating, rubbish bins, planters on rollers for occasional subdivisions, etc. Two sides of the square are flanked by elevated gardens conceived as podiums for actors, namely, a composition of single, extremely distinctive trees that seem to be performing in a stage play. Paths and small circular squares are cut out of these podiums. This pattern of circles connected by lines is repeated on the building's roofs, where they form roof gardens and viewing decks on different levels.

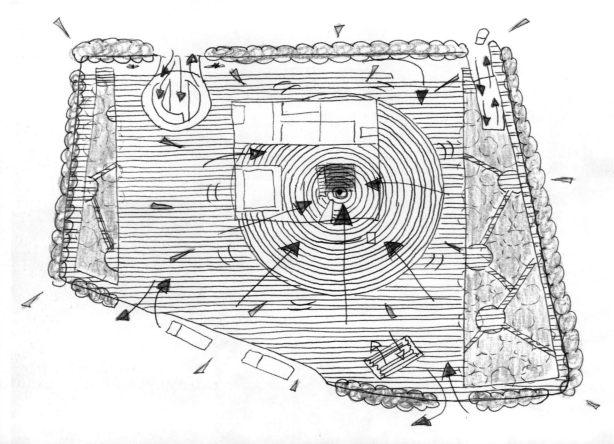

Sketches communicate precisely what one has in mind

And when the architects construct a 3-D collage, we fill in the gaps

Reference image symbolising our intention to use "character" trees

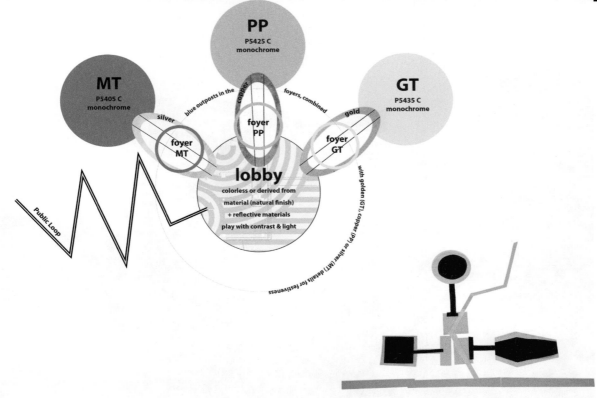

Handmade drawings, collages and studies of movement, material and colour form the base for architectural directions and decisions

CONCEPT FOR INTERIOR OF AUDITORIUMS:
EVERYTHING DIPPED IN PAINT!

FLOORS, WALLS &
CEILINGS ARE ONE
CONTINUOUS, SEAMLESS
WHOLE. THE USE OF
CAREFULLY CHOSEN
MATERIALS IS ESSENTIAL

THE BLUE COLORS ARE HIDDEN INSIDE THE AUDITORIUMS, ONLY THE GLOW IS
SOMETIMES VISIBLE...

ALL COVERED IN UNIFYING COLOR!

FLOOR, WALLS, CEILING AND CHAIRS BECOME ONE CONTINUOUS PLANE. (CONCEPT IMAGE)

THE ADDITION OF "SCRATCHY" PRINT ADDS DEPTH & NARRATIVE TO THE BALCONY WALL & DOORS

(1) paint applied as photocopy technique → silkscreen

WOOL VELVET COVERS THE AUDITORIUM CHAIRS.

SMOOTH SHOTCRETE COVERS ENTIRE VOLUME OF THE SPACE

INTERIOR OF FACADE WALL

(2) canvas, dipped or roller painted surface → atmosphere

CEILING & UNDERSIDE OF "OPEN" METAL

MULTIFORM THEATER

THIS THEATER IS THE "TOUGHEST" AND IS COLORED WITH THE DARKEST HUE OF THE GREY-BLUE FAMILY THAT WAS CHOSEN.

TECHNICAL CEILING

(1) rubber parquet floor (recycled rubber)

(5) Blue denim- with roller painted surface

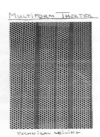

THE INTERIOR WALL OF THE EXTERIOR FACADE IS COVERED WITH ISOLATION BLANKET, LEFT U.S.A. BLUE (PROTECTED IN HEAT HERE)

PERFORATED WOODEN WALL FOR ACOUSTIC ABSORBANCE

THE ENCIRCLING WALL : POLYCARBONATE

IN THE FOYER : A SILVER CARPET

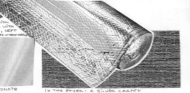

IN THE FOYER : A CUSHIONED CEILING

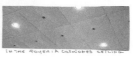

GRAND THEATER :

ONE SINGLE COLOR. MATERIALS CHOSEN FOR STRUCTURE & LIGHT REFLECTION / ABSORPTION

SPRAY-ON CONCRETE FOR A "MINIMUM" EFFECT

" SPONGE " FOR ACOUSTIC ABSORBANCE

STAGE CURTAIN COMING HANG INSIDE THE AUDITORIUM SO THAT ENTIRE "FACADE" IS A PLEATED, SOFT SURFACE

→ CEILING STRUCTURE

(1) Poured polyurethane (seamless) floor

(1) Faux leather smooth

METALIC BLUE "FAUX" LEATHER FOR THEATER CHAIRS

GOLDEN-BLACK 2ND CURTAIN AT BACK OF AUDITORIUM

→ CEILING STRUCTURE

GOLD FOIL OF BACK WALL OF V.I.P BALCONY

→ STAGE CURTAIN OUTSIDE THE SHADE (INSIDE AUDITORIUM), FIRE RETARDANCY A 2/B

Reality takes shape

Different positions for the "membrane" stage curtain illustrated

For the Proscenium Play stage we used a smooth, translucent projection membrane that absorbs and diffuses light. Lit from the back, it can show silhouettes and shadow plays. Different sections slide open in all directions like the shutter of a lens. It is located after the elliptical opening, on the stage side. There are two lateral curtains (one on each side) and one upper curtain. They can all travel along the entire proscenium opening to create countless different stage openings.

The rehearsal rooms HAD to be pink. Not only to complement and soften the naked skin of dancers and performers, but also to communicate pink externally, softening the building itself. So, pink plasterboard on almost all planes, and white curtains with a pink lining looking out: white at night becomes pink glow by day.

When I visited the building site many years ago, the temporary security fence looked like this – amazing!

Roof gardens in the making: circular terraces and viewpoints to be embedded in a carpet of evergreen shrubbery

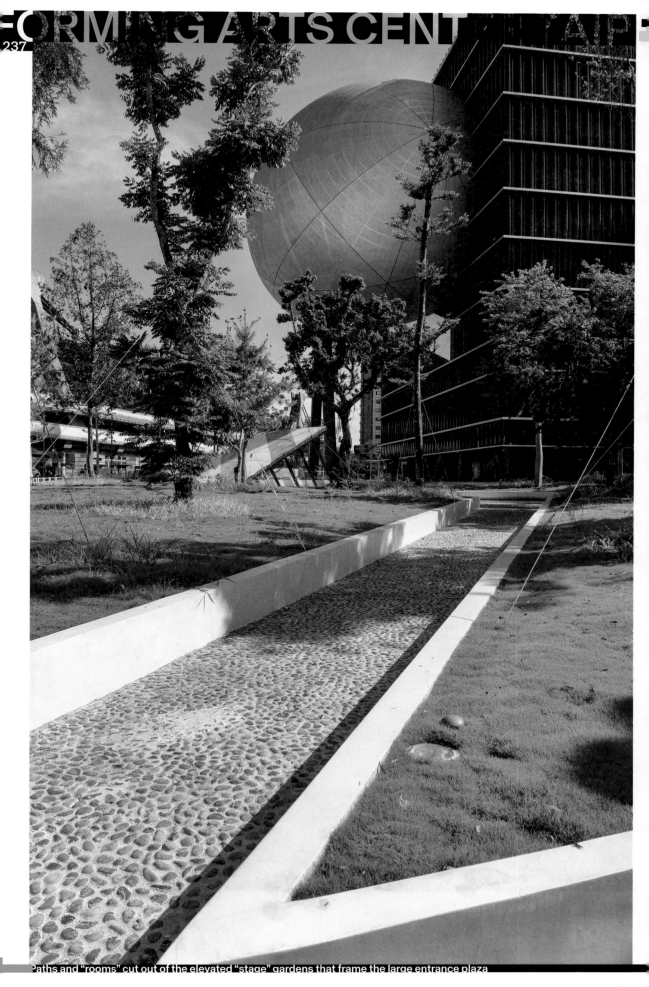

Paths and "rooms" cut out of the elevated "stage" gardens that frame the large entrance plaza

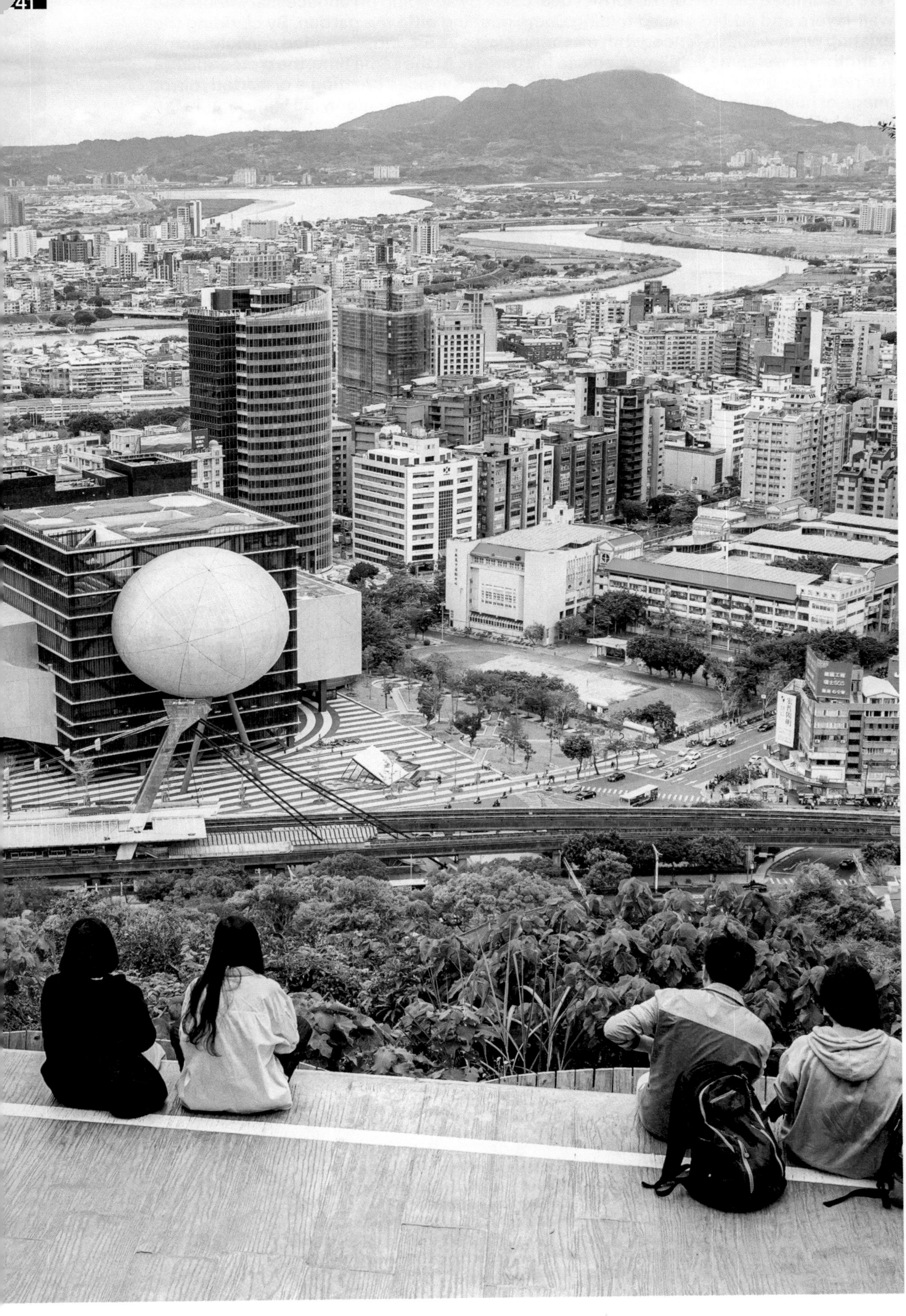

"We maximised the size of the former coal cellar by scraping off unnecessary floor- and wall-layers and added glazed folding doors opening onto the garden. By cladding the existing worn wooden fences with mirroring plates all around, we added sunlight, some warmth and welcome lighting effects to the garden. At the same time, the plates enlarge the relatively small garden visually, their irregular surfaces creating a distorted mirror image of house and garden, like an impressionist painting. At night, the lights inside the house reflect back, lighting up plantings nearby."   PB

LOCATION	Amsterdam, the Netherlands
CLIENT	Private owner
STATUS	Ongoing
SCOPE	Private garden installation and maintenance
MATERIALS	Plantings, water, water-life and PVC mirror plates
SCALE	18 × 11 m
DESCRIPTION	Inside the early-1900s building block, the gardens have two levels as each building was originally a one-family house with lots of open fireplaces and was later divided into separate apartments in the 1960s. The sunken ground floor was used to store coal and as living quarters for the staff, while the family lived upstairs with balconies overlooking the north-facing garden. A small area of the garden, 70 cm lower than the rest, was reserved for the rubbish to be put out by the staff. The family used the stairs connected to the first-floor balcony to reach the higher-level garden.

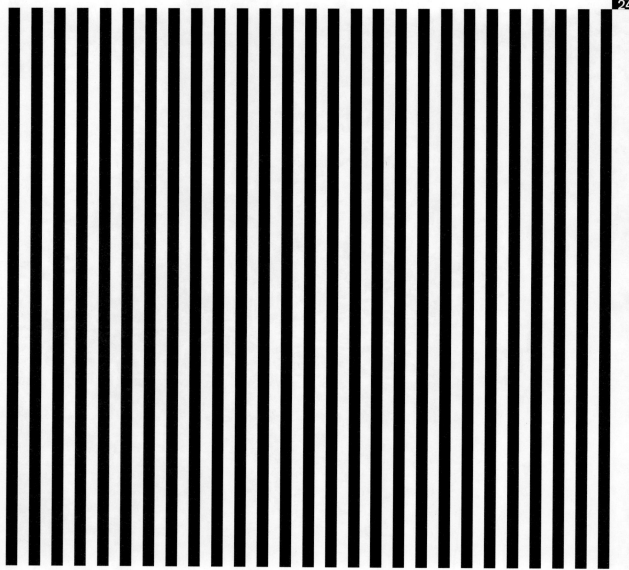

LOCATION	Ghent, Belgium
CLIENT	Grand Café Vooruit
STATUS	Completed
SCOPE	Acoustic and darkening curtains for music performances and events, integration of the curtains to the historic facade; interior and planting advisory
SCALE	Four curtains, 3.95 × 5.88 m, 7.87 × 5.87 m, 3.42 × 5.89 m, 9.94 × 5.92 m
COLLABORATORS	B-ILD, Chris Pype lighting, Kahle Acoustics
DESCRIPTION	In the Grand Café Vooruit we advised on the interior finishes in order to make this crowded hot-spot seem larger and more contemporary. We worked in close collaboration with B-ILD architects. Large, festive curtains of alternating black and white stripes of heavy velour cover the two main facades from floor to ceiling, providing the acoustic and darkening conditions required for the music performances and events that are regularly organised in this space. Importantly, the curtains relate to the historic facade and enhance the allure of the building.

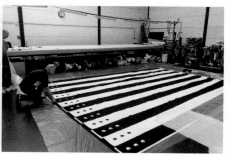

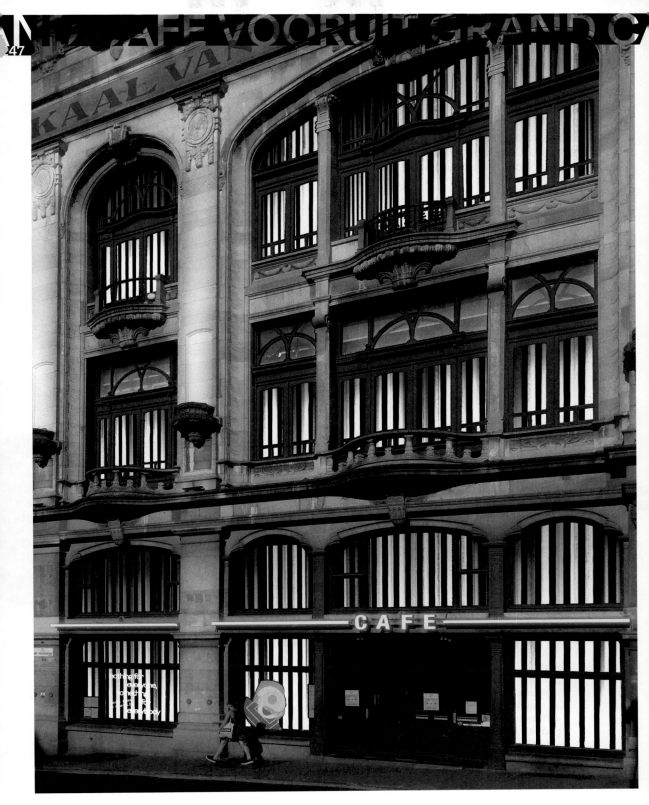

"This piece of land, for many years seemingly empty and forgotten but for the train tracks and the occasional train, was my favourite view from the terraces of Fondazione Prada. Wilderness! Turning red and orange in autumn, transparent in winter, it also inspired the OMA team (with office on site), because they 'transplanted' Porta Romana's plant composition onto the roof of one of the Fondazione buildings. The contrast between the high-end design of Fondazione Prada, with its golden tower, white high-rise, tasteful interiors and art exhibits, strengthens both worlds. Now that Porta Romana will be developed into a dense urban area, the rooftop garden will be the only remaining reference to the original wilderness that once thrived right next door. We shall miss it."   PB

GROUND LEVEL FOREST WITH ELEVATED SPIRAL RAMP

LOCATION	Milan, Italy
CLIENT	Coima, Covivio, Prada
STATUS	Competition
SCOPE	Landscape masterplan around Olympic city; commercial and residential towers, including large, circular wildernesses
SCALE	16 ha
COLLABORATORS	Studio Paola Vigano, Office KGDVS, Piovenefabi, TPS pro Srl, Ambiante Italia, F&M Ingeneria Spa
DESCRIPTION	Porta Romana is being reimagined as an "open urban parkscape" that will contain housing, offices, art galleries, a new train station and – importantly – the temporary Olympic Village, which in the future would be transformed into student housing. Essential to making this new development a "parkscape," 40% of the surface is expected to become park. In our proposal, we drew a grid of man-made "natures" – orchards, nurseries, gardens and sports fields – that bind the entire site together. Spread throughout the site and bridging the central train track, we proposed a series of circular "green sanctuaries" – different landscape typologies that are left to develop naturally after installation as a memory of the overgrown "wilderness" that once dominated the abandoned railyards of Porta Romana.

GROUND LEVEL
FOREST

MONUMENTAL
WILDERNESS MOUND

1:3000

Open com

ban farming

TA ROMANA PORTA ROMANA

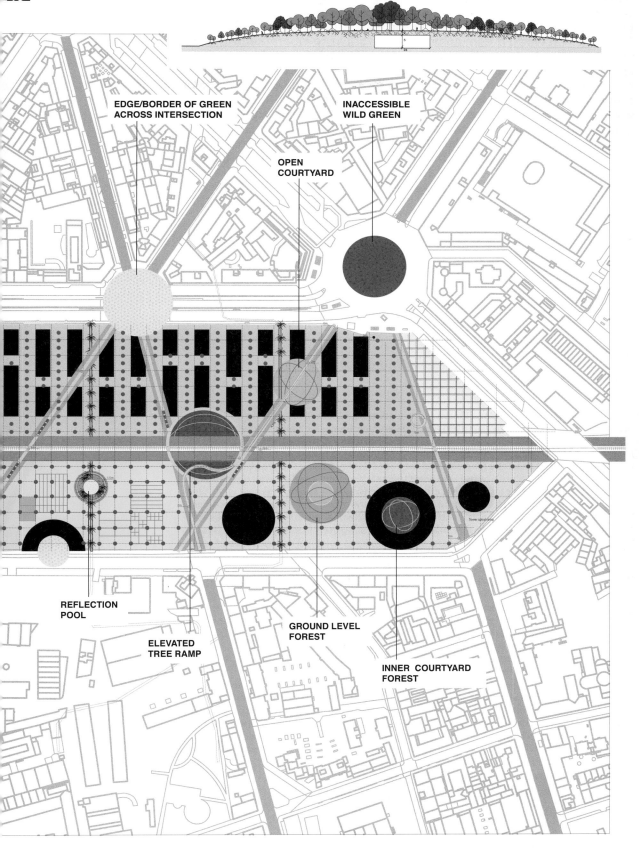

EDGE/BORDER OF GREEN
ACROSS INTERSECTION

INACCESSIBLE
WILD GREEN

OPEN
COURTYARD

REFLECTION
POOL

ELEVATED
TREE RAMP

GROUND LEVEL
FOREST

INNER COURTYARD
FOREST

ard   Urban green plaza

What FUN we had designing this fantastic Olympic Village with Office KGDVS and the rest of the competition team. We could so clearly envision the circular wildernesses spread over the site, bridging train tracks, connecting buildings and plazas, forming walled gardens; the elegant pedestrian bridges overcoming heights and distances; the vast sports fields, sculpture parks and orchards flowing underneath everything… Too bad!!!

"On the occasion of the tenth anniversary of Rome's first museum of contemporary arts, we were invited to design the exhibition *A Story for the Future – MAXXI's First Decade*, highlighting the museum's engaging and diverse program and revisiting its rich archive.

It was a dream come true to work in collaboration with a client as open-minded as Hou Hanru and his museum team. Experienced in teamwork, appreciative of experimental ideas, and trained to meticulously realise them to everyone's liking (within budget!) they gave us the freedom to express our ideas spontaneously, to present truly rough sketches and playful cardboard study models (now in the museum's collection) as well as numerous collages and samples. It all made the design process an energetic 'ping-pong match,' our collaboration with the museum smooth and fun. Besides the fact that the MAXXI is filled with inspiring, forward-looking art and architecture exhibitions, the elegant and well-organised hospitality (during this Covid pandemic!) of our hosts was unbeatable. Delicious lunches and even more fantastic dinners with local cuisine accompanied by evening-long conversations after work… what more could one wish for?" AM

LOCATION	Rome, Italy
CLIENT	MAXXI – Museo Nazionale delle Arti del XXI Secolo
STATUS	Completed
SCOPE	Exhibition design
SCALE	586 m^2
COLLABORATORS	Hou Hanru, Elena Motes, Silvia Lapergola, Etaoin Shrdlu Studio
DESCRIPTION	In Zaha Hadid's curved and fluid architecture, which also defines Galleria 4, we uncovered all roof windows to invite daylight in and transformed the curved space into a linear one by introducing two straight, paper-thin walls that lined the long sides of the room. To emphasise the urban concept, the entire length of the slim, longitudinal floor, thus created, was divided into a white and a black half, creating a highway-like space. The new walls were connected to the floor: one side white, the other matt black. The backbone of the exhibition consisted of black and white banners hung centrally in a repetitive rhythm from the ceiling, communicating the museum's initiatives through the years in chronological order. Numerous colourful collages spread out on the walls showed Hou Hanru's narrative on the museum's ongoing activities, the themes announced in large fluorescent lettering above each collage: 1. "MAXXI and the City," 2. "The Multitude," 3. "Worlds," 4. "The Challenges of Reality," 5. Do You Believe in Innovation? We cut two narrow, ceiling-high slits out of the black and white lateral walls, through which people could squeeze into leftover spaces. Each of these organically shaped rooms was dipped into one single energetic colour that leaked through the narrow slits into the main, black and white exhibition space – inviting people in from afar for a more focused introduction to monitored interviews with artists and staff and a collection of books. The collage-like layout and colour-coding referred to the curator's detective-like mapping of his "cold case" research on ten years' work. The tube-lettering of title and themes was inspired by the Hong Kong student demonstrations of 2019–2020. These ideas for the graphic representation of the exhibition's titles and collages, presented in our design concept, were further developed into a strong, well-balanced and colourful composition of texts and images by graphic designers Etaoin Shrdlu Studio.

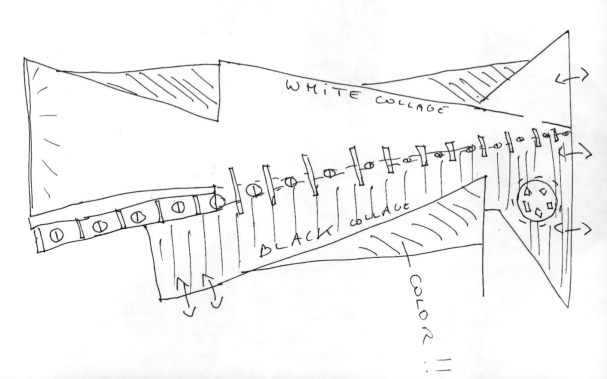

I made these sketches while talking with Hou Hanru on the phone as he told us what he had in mind for the exhibition and what it should communicate about MAXXI's ten-year existence

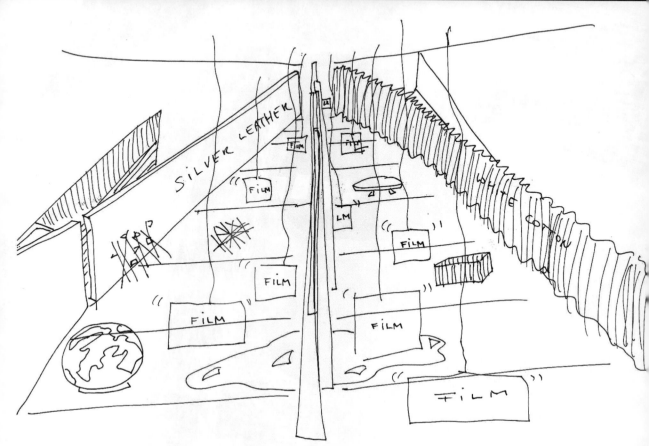

Needless to say, we made working models to experiment with colour and to study the potentials of the given space and the placement of possible objects. We also started to fantasise about different ways to compose the collages that Hanru had talked about, each representing a specific theme. How to form subgroups of subjects, how to connect subjects within the themes, etc. From detective boards (who's the murderer?) to street signage (where do I go?) and so on, we composed miniature collages on our studio walls with the imagery we received from the MAXXI team, presenting our ideas in this physical manner when they visited us during the design process. Energising!!

ATLAS B

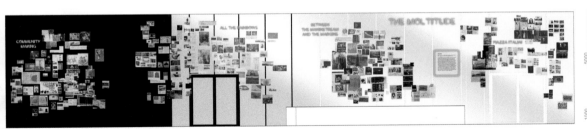

8609

8609

29456

5912

9258

20848

5678

5000

6000

1000

Each year was represented by a banner, so ten banners hung from the ceiling (where the skylights were uncovered to let daylight in) in the middle of the "street." One side of each banner was black with white text; the other side covered with coloured images of the various installations and/or performances of that specific year. The row of banners accentuated the division between the white and the black side of the long, narrow room.

Straightening Zaha's curved walls with paper-thin walls of equal height and length created "secret" niches behind. We cut out sliver-thin openings so that the intense colours of these niches would spread an inviting glow into the black-and-white main room. Lettering was composed with tube-lights, inspired by the Hong Kong protest marches the year before.

Nach der Natur
Humboldt Labor Exhibition at Humboldt Forum

"There are so many anecdotes which could describe the complexity and impossibilities of the design process of this ambitious exhibition at this particular new site. But maybe one of the most striking developments was that requirements changed 180 degrees in the process. During our first site visit, Petra and I were informed by the main curators that most of the exhibited objects that would be borrowed from Humboldt University's age-old archives could be touched by the public, as they were not particularly precious. There were no real restrictions on how to display them. This appealed to us and led to the idea of the Wunderkammer, where hundreds of objects would cover the ceiling and walls, only to be studied closely if pulled down with a cord (or similar device) or taken off the wall with a hook. The idea of creating a hanging storage system was born, and we worked with studio Cookies from Rotterdam to develop this idea further. In the process of finding the right mechanical system to enable the up and downward movement we envisioned, the requirements for the selected objects became stricter and stricter, resulting in the complete opposite of the envisioned nonchalant flexibility: in the end each object had to be installed in a closed, climatised, acrylic showcase, each made to size, sensitively lit and accommodating the objects according to museum standards. This obviously increased the weight of the system, the size of the steel structure and the required strength of the aluminium tracks. It also doubled our work on the detailed construction drawings and the complexity of installations. When you add the fact that we already had to detail the entire electricity and alarm systems as well as draw each and every screw and centimetre in detail – our workload multiplied fivefold along the way." AM

"One of the things of interest to us was that the scientists were adding four texts to each showcased object, describing each from four different perspectives – for example from biological, political, artistic and anthropological points of view. All this text takes a lot of space in a made-to-size showcase in which the object should get the most attention, so it was a challenge to solve this riddle without affecting the legibility of the texts, especially in the sparsely lit context." PB

LOCATION	Berlin, Germany
CLIENT	Humboldt University
STATUS	Competition, 1st prize / completed
SCOPE	Exhibition design, technical detailing and tender documents for the three-year+ installation *Nach der Natur*
SCALE	735 m²
COLLABORATORS	Cookies, Arup, Jens Casper, Julia Neller, Schnellebuntebilder
DESCRIPTION	Inside Outside won the competition for the design, detailing and construction of the prestigious natural science exhibition for the Humboldt University of Berlin. This three-year exhibition highlights their current cutting-edge research, scientific objects inherited from the original Wunderkammer – objects that were crucial to the development of the University – and an extensive sound collection (*Lautarchiv*) of the German language. The exhibition took place in two spaces inside the controversial, newly built Humboldt Forum (a copy of the former Berlin Palace). This architecture, together with the anticipated content, inspired our team to turn the appointed, generic gallery spaces into a theatre-based combination of foyer and backstage.

The foyer attracts attention through the gallery's glazed doors with a rounded curtain onto which swarms of fish and birds are projected – very visible from the large staircase that leads to the first floor. In the same room, aligning the walls, research projects by "excellent" students are shown. In the second, larger room, a steel theatre grid is installed, onto which a motorised system of 38 scissor arms is attached, each arm holding a different made-to-size Perspex vitrine. Each vitrine contains an object, chosen by a curator – a scientist – of Humboldt University. The 38 floating, climatised vitrines are movable in X – Y and Z direction depending on how the curators wish to group the objects by theme or event. Each object is visible from all sides, and each has four descriptions to cover an equal amount of historic / scientific / political / creative perspectives on the object in question. The system of vitrines is interactive with the Digital Wall, lining them to one side, when activated through a mobile phone. Along the opposite facade wall, with its grand windows, the sound archive is exhibited in a sequence of folded spaces, alternating dark and light (painted blue or white): small rooms, each meticulously detailed to allow as much concentration as possible to listen and read through the extensive and rich archive of the German language.

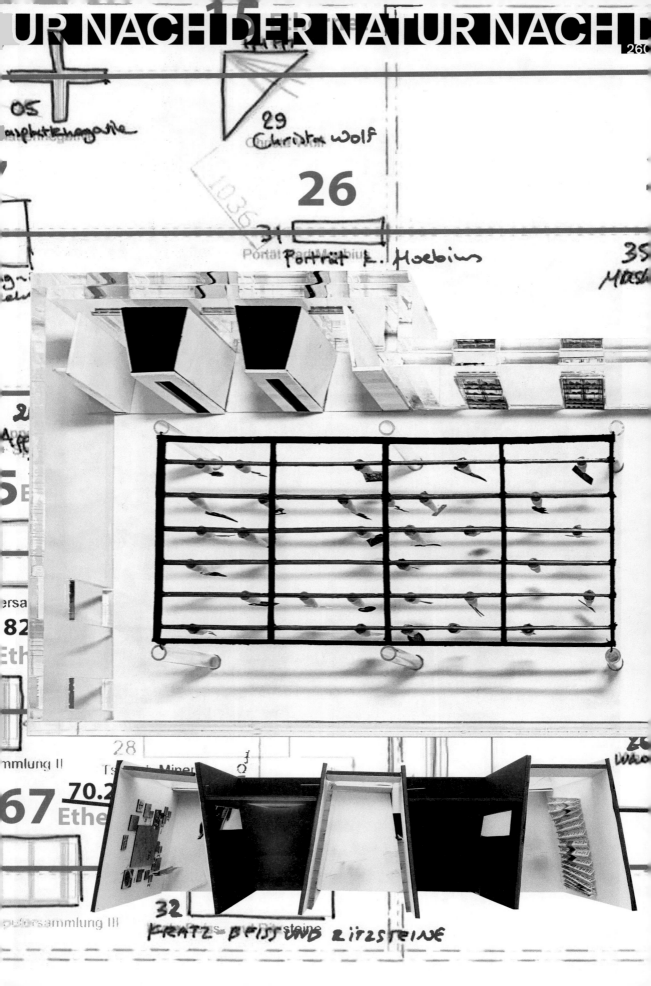

261

Models, models, models: where would we be without them?

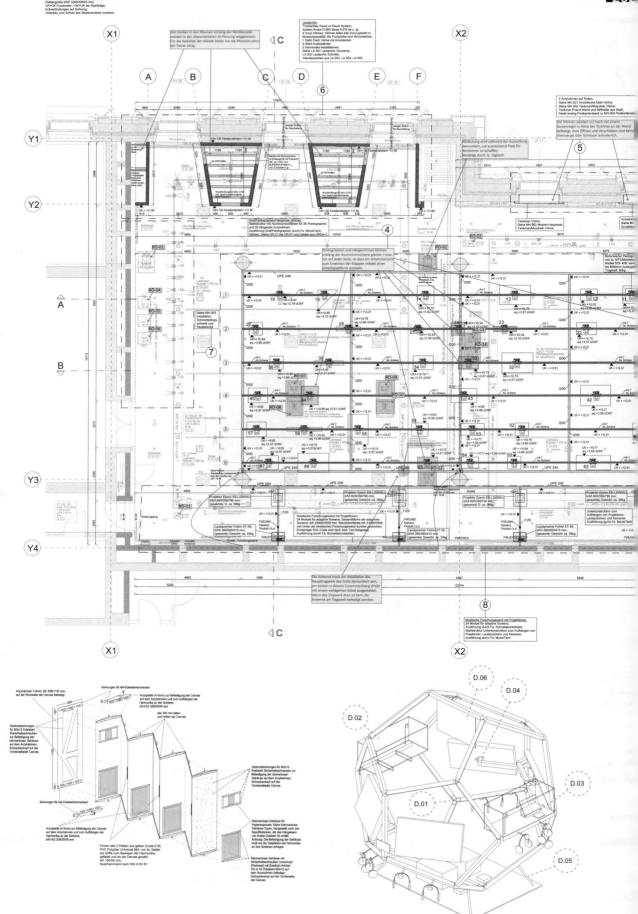

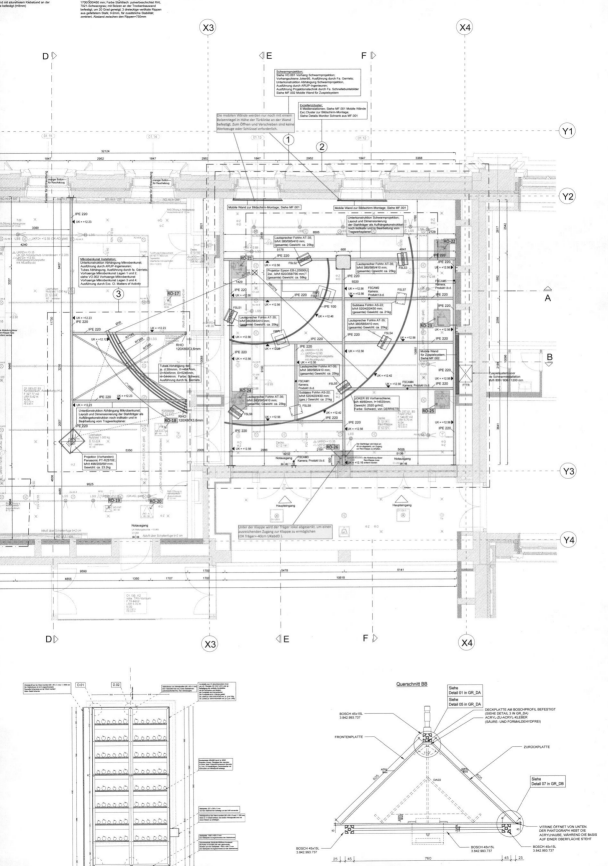

If not for our collaboration with the studio Cookies from Rotterdam, we never would have come this far. Incredible how they managed to design each and every Perspex showcase in detail, including light, climate control, graphics and enough space for the objects themselves – each one more weird, smelly or fragile than the next! And look at this moment where everything comes together: our work, their work, Arup's meticulous structural calculations, all enriching the characterless Humboldt room... vitrines wrapped in light-catching plastic – so beautiful!

The circular projection curtain that defines the entrance or "reception room," onto which interactive projections of fish shoals are projected

The cabinets we created for Humboldt University's *Lautarchiv*, which contains their collection of 710 recordings of German dialects, created in the 1920s, '30s and '40s, then expanded onto contemporary language forms, such as sign language and contemporary jargon (*Kiezdeutsch*); the ethnographic photo collection of the Hahne Niehoff archive; the Prisoners of War collection; and the Jahn archive, that includes correspondence between Western and African intellectuals and writers and conference recordings around African identity from a non-Western perspective.

The Prisoners of War collection display

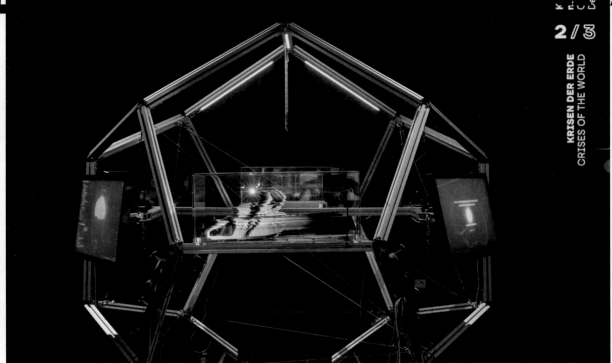

SO proud of our team at Inside Outside, Aura and Nafsika who never lost their cool, drew every %^&* detail and learnt the German language along the way; of Jens, our local saviour-in-need when it comes to German regulations and daily presence on site; of Julia, that patient and precise graphic designer who printed, glued and rubbed text after text on planes both soft and hard. Unbeatable professionals – no, fantastic human beings.

This ever-changing, interactive digital wall works in conjunction with the exhibited works when activated by the public. Each vitrine moves up or down individually, so that the scientists who curate the show can reorganise its content at will, even clearing the entire floor. When all the objects are pulled up towards the ceiling, a real Wunderkammer is born.

Sessions Auditorium Curtain
     Mingei International Museum

"Landscape architect and horticulturist Kate Sessions (1857–1940) had an enormous influence on the beautification of some 570 ha of parkland, previously called City Park, which was opened to the public in 1868. From 1892 onwards, Sessions had 100 trees planted each year, including the purple-flowering jacaranda tree. This tree was a real inspiration when I first worked in Los Angeles for a while (on Universal Headquarters) and saw the tree's elegant mimosifolia leaves through which the sunrays sparkled, its luscious, fragrant purple blossoms and – very important – the purple carpet of flowers that circle around the bottom of its trunk when the blooming season reaches its end.

The leaf became the inspiration for the curtain design. Though heavily abstracted, the leaf pattern offers the opportunity for rounded shapes and irregular openings, referring to the layers of jacaranda leaves fluttering in the wind when looking up into its crown – forming abstract, colourless light-and-dark patches against the sun."   PB

CLIENT	Mingei International Museum
STATUS	Completed
SCOPE	Textile art object (darkening, cooling, filtering)
MATERIALS	Wool felt, 6 mm thick, in two layers, each 3 mm thick, royal blue on the outside, light grey on the inside; digitally printed Trevira CS
SCALE	15.5 × 3.85 m
COLLABORATORS	LUCE et studio
DESCRIPTION	Architects LUCE et studio from San Diego renovated the Mingei International Museum and transformed a former loading dock into a 120-seat theatre; a concrete box with a terrace on its roof. They invited four artists to create special works for the building, and Inside Outside was one of them. We created a thick curtain of layered sheets of grey and blue felt, laser-cut with a pattern of abstract jacaranda leaves. An L-shaped rail allows the fabric to be hung either in front of the room's side wall – as a decorative sound improving element – or slid in front of the glass facade, where it filters daylight and forms the backdrop of performances.

To work with thick felt is great because it's a non-woven fabric and as such, you can cut it any way you want: you can sit on it, glue it, stack it, wallpaper it, lay it out or hang it, fold it, stitch it, pierce it, hammer it or scratch it – it will absorb sound and keep cool. One of our proposals for the curtain included a transparent plastic cover over the "leaves" (see previous page) because we thought we needed to spice the object up a bit, make it a bit kinky! But a shiny surface didn't fit the room nor the museum, and since we didn't like the intense blue as a permanent presence anyway, we turned the outside in so that the grey connects to the concrete walls. Shiny snaps were added for subtle light effects.

DAWN
Wall Piece for Private Apartment

"The first (online) meeting with the client started like this: 'Listen, I'm open to anything but you have to know that I really don't like curtains!' Okay... Our client's apartment is in a very high building in the middle of Manhattan overlooking the city and an enormous and very busy traffic intersection. She has two other houses, one in Montana and one in California. One house has a view over the beach and out to the sea, and the other has a view of a mountain landscape. When our client asked us to make an 'art piece' to act as a flexible wall in her Manhattan apartment, we were thinking of an abstract composition. But it soon became clear that what she really wanted was the representation of a landscape. To inspire us, she sent us numerous images of both the seascape and the mountain views from her houses under different lighting conditions and times of day. Beautiful!"

"The idea for the sunrise/sunset wallpaper and screen was born, and also the idea of a transparent curtain with a mountain landscape drawn onto it. We tested a couple of our client's photos by enlarging and drawing over them. Aura started making a rough sketch on top of a mountain image and Petra then made an almost Keith Haring-like drawing of that same view, more like a line drawing. Both had their own qualities, so we merged the two, sketch and drawing, as an experiment. The two proved to blend perfectly and this collaged image, much enlarged, became the print on the silk curtain. The result: sunrise behind mountain landscape. Our client proved to be very open indeed; she loves it!"   PN

LOCATION	Manhattan, New York, USA
CLIENT	Private owner
STATUS	Completed
SCOPE	Design of a flexible, space defining wall
MATERIALS	Digitally printed seamless Airtex wallpaper, digitally printed silk voile, digitally printed PVDF screen
SCALE	Wallpaper, 2.96 × 3.28 m; screen, 2.96 × 3.25 m; curtain, 6.69 × 3.24 m
COLLABORATORS	LUCE et studio
DESCRIPTION	The client had bought an apartment in New York City as a pied-a-terre and architect Jennifer Luce was about to renovate and decorate the place. Jennifer suggested removing a significant part of the wall between the living room and the guestroom for a more spacious effect, knowing that Inside Outside could provide a flexible solution for the issue of privacy in the guest and living room. So, we were introduced. We integrated the leftover piece of wall – with the front door in it – into our wall piece by covering it with a vinyl wallpaper that has the same print as the translucent screen that connects to it: a gradient from deep maroon to the lightest sky blue. For the screen we cut the print in very thin stripes that alternate with a diluted pale blue to maintain the translucency of the material. To finish it off we put the thinnest silk curtain in front of it, digitally printed with a black-and-white scenic image of a mountain landscape.

A translucent screen defines and divides living and guest room in a loft-like flat on an upper floor of a high-rise in mid-Manhattan. This screen is one of three components that collectively form one work: wallpaper (opaque, static), screen (translucent, sliding back and forth) and curtain (transparent, gently pleated, billowing).

LOCATION	Zurich, Switzerland
CLIENT	gta Exhibitions, ETH Zurich
STATUS	Completed
SCOPE	Drawing(s) for digital and physical exhibition on the subject of confinement (Covid)
MATERIALS	3 *cadavres exquis* drawings on paper of various colours
SCALE	3 sheets of A4 paper
COLLABORATORS	The three IO partners

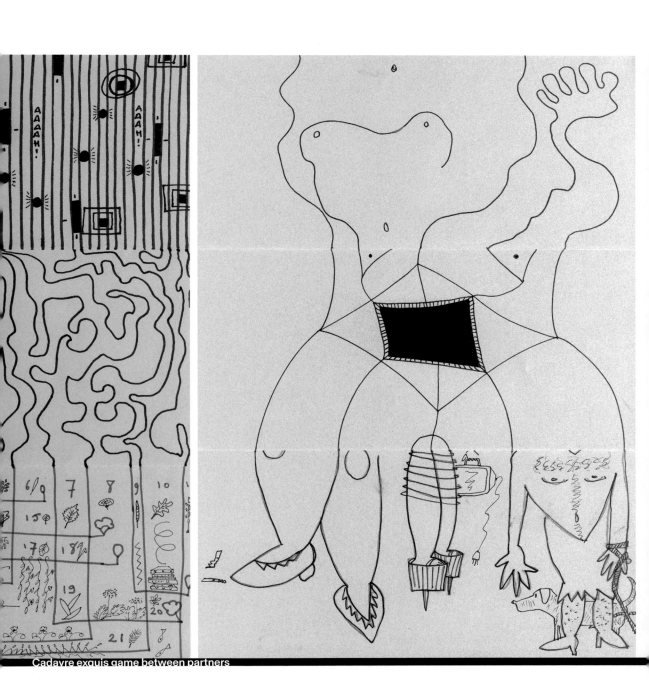

Cadavre exquis game between partners

"A developer sails the Mediterranean seas, discovers a Greek island with an available, steep plot along the sea and asks us to do a study on the plot's potential as future 'sustainable tourism' destination. This we do, in our turn discovering the beauty and potential of the place through paging through its history, biology, ecology, economy, commodities, climate; getting to know its residents, visitors, users and traders. But no – he sails on, the businessman."   PB

"In this context of mass tourism developments, the only way we could conceive a project on this site was by setting a completely new standard for the way site and landscape are treated, fostering thriving local biodiversity, involvement of the local community and respect for local resources and waste management."   NE

LOCATION	Santorini, Greece
CLIENT	Home Center Management GmbH
STATUS	Commissioned study
SCOPE	Site study and landscape concept for an agro-tourism development
SCALE	6.38 ha
DESCRIPTION	Our brief was to evaluate the suitability of a given plot for the development of a small-scale tourist accommodation facility. Santorini receives around two million tourists per year, inundating existing infrastructures. The sensitive eroding topography of the site, together with its volcanic geology and the arid and windy Mediterranean climate led us to take a regenerative landscape approach, where both terraces and architecture would be carefully embedded in the landscape, not least in order to stabilise it. We organised the landscape as a terraced agro-ecosystem, focusing on water retention and native, drought-resistant planting. Looking at the rich culture, local architecture and materials, we also proposed a series of cabins that could be literally shaped by the volcanic earth on site, using a minimum of imported materials and limiting the footprint.

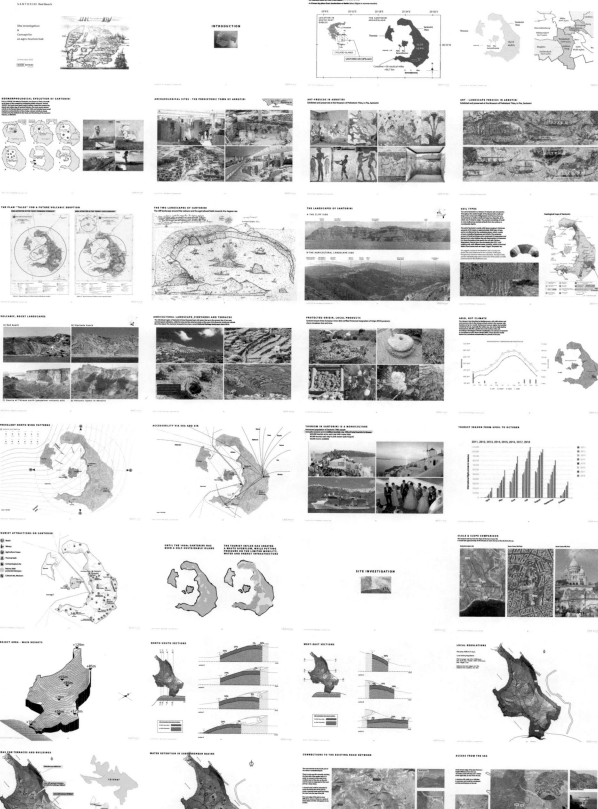

A developer sails the Mediterranean Sea, discovers a Greek island with a steep plot available on the water and asks us to do a study on the plot's potential as a future sustainable tourism destination. This we do, and in turn discover the beauty and challenges of the place through examining its history, biology, ecology, economy, commodities, climate; by getting to know its residents, visitors, users and traders. But no – he sails on, the quintessential businessman.

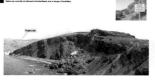
SOIL EROSION AT THE RED BEACH

Project site

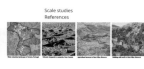
Scale studies
References

STEEP SLOPE FARMING IN THE ATLAS MOUNTAINS IN MAROCCO

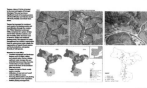
REGENERATIVE AGRICULTURE THROUGH WATER RETENTION IN TAMERA, PORTUGAL

WATER RETENTION IN SUBTERRANEAN BASINS

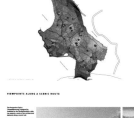

AGRICULTURE IN VOLCANIC LANDSCAPES IN LANZAROTE, GRAN CANARIA

THRESHING CIRCLES - AGRICULTURAL RUINS AT THE NORTH PART OF THE SITE

REFERENCE INSIDE OUTSIDE - QATAR NATIONAL LIBRARY

VIEWPOINTS ALONG A SCENIC ROUTE

TOURISM STRATEGIES - DISPERSED HOTEL IN MATERA, PUGLIA (IT)

PROGRAM + PHASING
LANDSCAPE REGENERATION + ARCHITECTURE STRATEGIES

OPPORTUNITIES AND LIMITATIONS

YEAR-ROUND PROGRAM

REGENERATIVE FARMING AS A BUSINESS MODEL

LANDSCAPE STRATEGIES

PATHWAYS

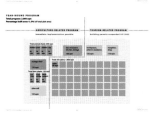
SCHEMATIC MASTERPLAN - SCENARIO 1

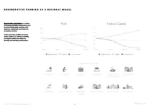
SCHEMATIC MASTERPLAN - SCENARIO 2

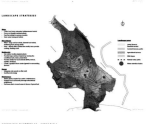
SCHEMATIC MASTERPLAN - SCENARIO 3

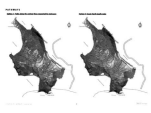
STUDY FOR HOLIDAY CABINS

CABIN TYPES AND SIZES

LOCAL MATERIALS FROM LAVA, PUMICE

REPURPOSED BUILDING MATERIALS

BUILDING TECHNIQUES

WIND-FORMED ARCHITECTURE

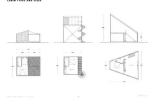

PRINCIPLES OF VERNACULAR ARCHITECTURE IN THE CYCLADES

INTEGRATING TO THE LANDSCAPE

VERNACULAR COOLING TECHNIQUES

CONCLUSIONS AND NEXT STEPS

WATER STORAGE CISTERNS IN SANTORINI

CURRENT WASTE 'MANAGEMENT' IN SANTORINI

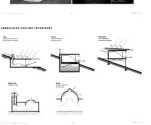
TOURISM STRATEGIES - ECOSYSTEM RESTORATION CAMPS AND COMMUNITY-BASED TOURISM

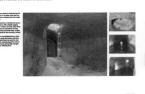

"Seeing the sobriety of the bedroom made us want to add something contradictory and lively to the space: reflective darkening; sensual functionality. We kept the foil widths half a millimetre apart to fold the silk lining forward through the slits. In this way, the silk forms thin, green 'fins' at the front. Daylight peeps through the tiny slits and stitching holes, adding a romantic detail at the start of day."

"The three images below show the damaged areas of the previous version of the Bedroom Curtain, where we used silver leatherette for the mirroring effect. This material has a foam-like filling that mimics the feel of real leather. It turned out that it reacts to intense manipulation and the human touch. The filling pulverised – over a period of seven years in this case. At our request, another firm developed (what seems to be) a sturdier version of silver and gold leatherette. But in the meantime, we had introduced a very shiny and reflective mirroring PVC for the new version – not only more daring and fun, but also stronger we think. Time will tell!"   PB

LOCATION	Amsterdam, the Netherlands
CLIENT	Private owners
STATUS	Completed
SCOPE	Darkening curtain for master bedroom
MATERIALS	Polyester silver foil and silk in 2 shades of green (mustard and military)
SCALE	3.5 × 3.87 m

"A restoration project makes designing additional objects to a building a very delicate process. The '70s architecture has so much character: a sculpture in itself! So, we first studied the restoration plans thoroughly with the architects and realised that they were very respectful of the original design, going back to its original colours for carpets, columns, window frames, etc. and adding only the most necessary modifications to comply to current safety and climate regulations. They had hired a colour specialist, Professor Schmuck, to advise on all colour interventions. The most sensitive issue of our work was the fact that we brought in new colours, which became one of the main topics." NE

"The acidic, lime-green colour of the foyer curtains was a bold choice, but we liked it in combination with the typical '70s salmon-coloured marble floor with orange Perspex poofs (lighting up from within!) scattered around. Professor Schmuck grew appreciative of the colour effect on the foyer's interior, but was worried about the impact of it towards the outside, as it lines an enormous glazed facade overlooking the neighbouring park. We didn't quite understand why at first, but soon did when he showed that the curtain shouldn't distract the attention from the building's white, sculptural volume when coming closer from a distance. He was right! He proposed the perfect shade of moss green which, in combination with the glass facade's greyish sheen, became olive green – exactly as he had envisioned!"

"To cover the walls along the circular balconies overlooking the foyer, we developed the thick, densely woven bronze/golden curtains to improve the acoustics of the entire foyer. The size and hew of the bronze background and golden blocks refer to Gunter Grote's mosaic artwork placed in the centre of the curved wall of the balcony. The colour accents of this curtain piece were discussed thoroughly. The architects strongly preferred the subdued bronze version of our tests in the given context, even leaving out the decorative golden elements in the first few meters touching the centre art piece. This we did, introducing a gradually increasing configuration for the golden blocks, so that the curtain's full glamour comes into its own at a polite distance from Grote's mosaic in both directions."

"Before the actual cloth was woven, we hung the various samples on site, for the theatre staff and architects to comment on. The moment we opened the folded samples we discovered that, with the soft lighting, the back of the weave looked much more attractive than the actual front: the soft pink yarns, only sparsely visible in front, formed the overall base at the back, and with the pattern of gold blocks twinkling away, the cloth looked subtle and elegant, lighter and more festive than the official, brownish front. Backsides often turn out more exciting – but here the more conservative front was preferred." PB

LOCATION	Düsseldorf, Germany
CLIENT	Düsseldorfer Schauspielhaus
STATUS	Completed
SCOPE	Curtain design, advisory on interior of foyers and restaurant for the restoration of the Düsseldorfer Schauspielhaus
MATERIALS	Restaurant (Schillings im Schauspielhaus), digitally printed mesh with sewn fins; foyer (Grosses Haus), two lime-green curtains of heavy cotton velour with a window of transparent plastic and organza; balcony, custom woven fabric of floating gold blocks on a grey and brown background, black Caban lining for acoustics; foyer Kleines Haus, blackout fabric with a digital print
SCALE	Restaurant, 36.9 × 3.6 m; foyer: curtain 1, 20.5 × 3.6 m, curtain 2, 32.8 × 3.6 m; gallery: curtain 1, 50.9 × 2.45–2.93 m (sloping ceiling), curtain 2, 85.9 × 2.46–2.96 m (sloping ceiling); foyer Kleines Haus, two curtains, 21 × 2.32 m each
COLLABORATORS	Ingenhoven Architects, Professor Schmuck, EE Exclusives
DESCRIPTION	The Schauspielhaus is a quintessential architectural masterpiece from the '70s designed by the architect Bernhard Pfau and enriched with artworks by Günter Grote. Collaborating on the renovation conducted by Ingenhoven Architects, we carried out an on-site, archaeologist-like exploration to extract the most idiosyncratic details of the existing building, which we re-purposed in our intervention: a series of four site-specific curtains, of which the two main ones for the Grosses Haus were requested by the theatre's director, Wilfried Schultz, to improve the overall acoustics of the main foyer. Here, public gatherings and festivities were to take place. We designed two flamboyant darkening acoustic curtains of lime-yellow/green in the foyer, a boundless curtain of elegant luxury for the balcony, a mesh curtain with a colour gradient like a dewy sunset for the restaurant and two wall covering curtains reminiscent of liquid concrete in the Kleines Haus.

For this curtain, we copied the typical '70s shape of the control window in the main theatre to scale, improving the acoustics of the central foyer without taking away the beautiful view of the adjacent park

Although the lime green in the interior is intense, the lining is executed in a more neutral shade of green so as not to detract attention from the sculptural architecture and to blend in with the park's planting

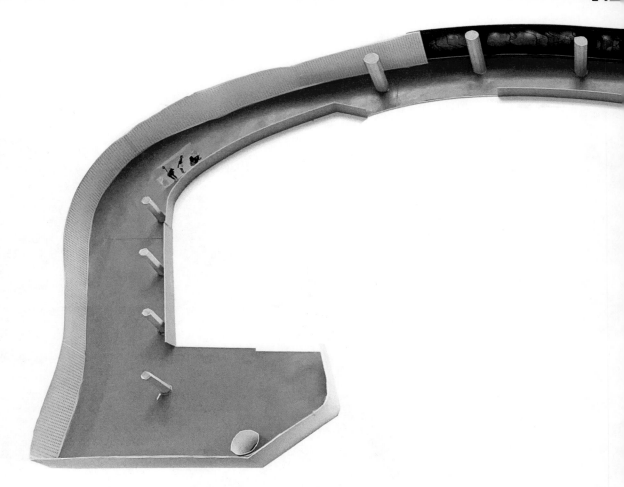

This is the model we made of the balcony to study which colour and pattern would best fit the place while also complementing the important mosaic artwork by Günter Grote at its centre and the colourful surrounding surfaces

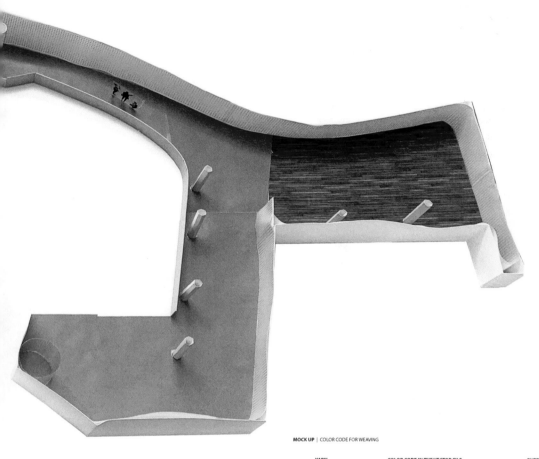

MOCK UP | COLOR CODE FOR WEAVING

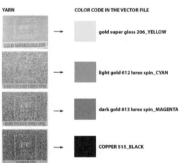

YARN	COLOR CODE IN THE VECTOR FILE	OVERVIEW OF THE VECTOR FILE
GOLD SUPERGLOSS 206	→ gold super gloss 206_YELLOW	
LIGHT GOLD 612 LUREX SPIN	→ light gold 612 lurex spin_CYAN	
DARK GOLD 613 LUREX SPIN	→ dark gold 613 lurex spin_MAGENTA	
COPPER 515	→ COPPER 515_BLACK	

EE-EXCLUSIVE MOCK UP | 20 February 2019

INSIDE OUTSIDE

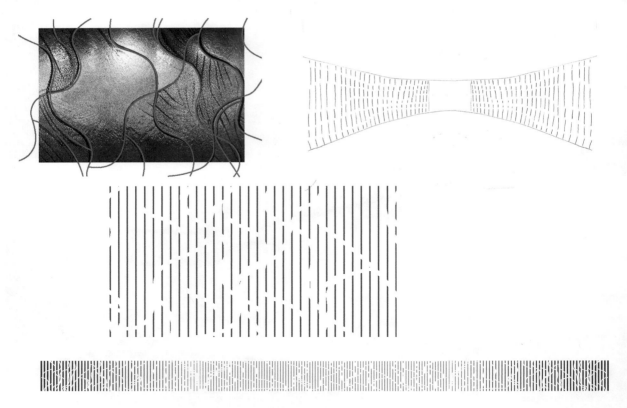

Taking the central mosaic artwork by Günter Grote as inspiration for the theatre's restaurant curtain, we cut through the vertical fins that were folded into the curtain's surface to create a wavy pattern. We then cut out vertical windows for a more direct view out during the day.

After photographing the existing bare-concrete foyer walls of the Kleines Haus, we superimposed the image onto the soft cloth, which we used to cover tubings, cables and storage niches that inhabit the opposite wall

"The Klepperstee Holiday Park is a family business. This always adds a personal dimension to a project in which you become acquainted with each family member, their relationships and sensitivities. In this case, the middle-aged son, Jeroen den Hollander, was our direct client and contact person, a positive man with the bold vision of transforming the park he had inherited from his father into an ecological resort based on 'efficiency' and a circular economy. His tranquil, Scandinavian mother went into more detail, envisioning a natural type of architecture that blends in with nature and a minimal, subtly coloured overall design for the future reception building as well as tiny holiday houses with lots of wood and wool rugs. She was also emphatic about the wellness atmosphere, which resulted, among other things, in a natural swimming pond. The daughter was in charge of the financial side of the business and was the one behind budget cuts, keeping an eye on the level of our involvement and insisting on the number of parking lots. Their different roles and focusses resulted in a balanced family team!"   AM

"The realisation of the continuous and spacious wooden terrace – pierced by trees at strategic points – was a first step. The terrace envelops and enters the new (wooden) reception building to form an interior 'play' garden, softening the boundaries between inside and outside. Also, and to our great pleasure, our (self-cleaning) natural swimming pool was realised – which has proven to be a great success in the past Corona years – so our child-rich neighbours and friends who love camping tell us! Now let's anticipate the next steps, when the owner implements some of our ideas for the landscape; hopefully also involving the foldable 'tiny houses' that Aura and architect Barend Koolhaas had so much fun sketching."   PB

LOCATION	Ouddorp, the Netherlands
CLIENT	Vakantiepark de Klepperstee
STATUS	Ongoing
SCOPE	New, sustainable landscape concept for holiday park; design and realisation of natural swimming pond and clubhouse terraces
SCALE	2 ha; masterplan, 28 ha
COLLABORATORS	Suzanne Loen, Vakwerk Architecten, De Bomenconsulent
DESCRIPTION	The Klepperstee Holiday Park, created in the 1970s, lies within a historically and ecologically complex region of the Kop van Goeree, South Holland. The land is formed by wind, sea and human engineering. The site is surrounded by low dunes and a dune forest. The new owner, in fact the son of the founder of the park, asked the Inside Outside team and their consultants to make a study on how to transform the strict, almost suburban organisation of the land into a much more natural, sustainable and biodiverse landscape with a more fluid layout. In other words, to turn it into a nature-based holiday park that reflects the times: the sensitivity and awareness of a better environment that connects us humans to nature, and vice versa.

One step was to "massage" the clearly defined '70s design language into a more organic organisation and definition of the different plots. The other was to break open the strict ecological partitioning of the site to let the local surrounding landscape flow freely into the park. As the landscape typologies differ along each side of the terrain, we allowed these different natural environments to enter the park – from sandy dunes to dune forest to a more traditional organisation of agricultural land, in which cultivated fields were divided by linear mounds of sand, created by farmers when cleaning the top layer of windblown sand off their fields.

Another step was to address the existing organisation of the entrance area and shared spaces (parking, reception, restaurant, in- and outdoor playgrounds), and the existing plantings. We wanted to loosen up, improve, embellish and naturalise these areas, adding a mix of native trees to each zone and replacing the strict hedge formations with more natural green patches. We softened the boundaries between inside and outside the reception building and between the individual holiday spaces (tent, caravan, villa), and introduced a natural swimming pond, numerous routes for nature exploration and conceptual ideas for tiny holiday houses.

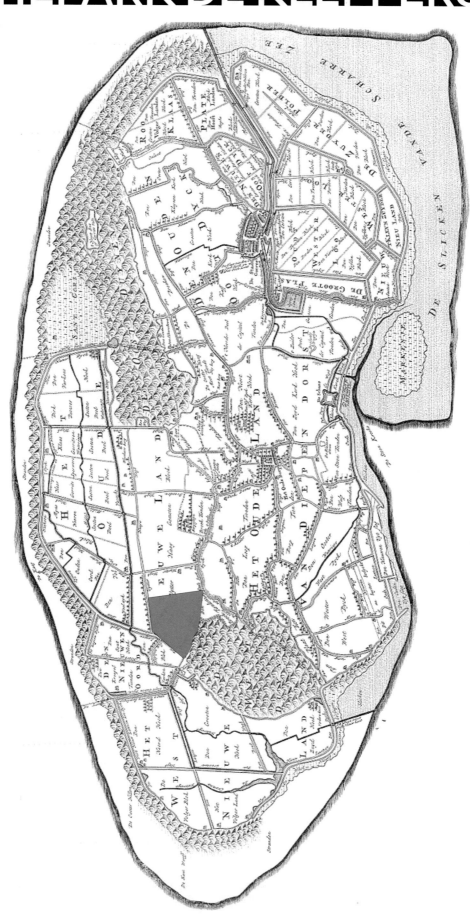

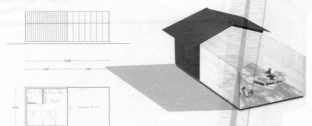

PROTOTYPE 1: WINTERTUIN

Deze cabin is opgebouwd uit een 'dichte' helft en een open helft die als een transparante kasconstructie is vormgegeven. Het is een aangename binnentuin/wintertuin conditie waar in geleefd kan worden.

De kas is ook een bron van energie: In zonnige wintermaanden warmt het op en verwarmt het de rest van het huis. Planten kunnen hier beschut overwinteren.
In de zomermaanden kunnen het dak en de gevel open wat het huis tot een ideale binnen-buiten ruimte maakt. Verder kunnen textiele doeken een aangename schaduw in de kas creëren tijdens hete zomerdagen.

De kasconstructie kan bestaan uit zilver gegalvaniseerd staal met polyester golfplaten, polycarbonaat of glas.

dichte deel afgewerkt met eterniet (vezelcementplaten)

1:200

PROTOTYPE 2: VERANDA

De minimale binnenoppervlakte van 25 m² wordt uitgebreid door het leven op de veranda. Een flexibel kookstel kan naar buiten worden verreden en er is ruimte voor een lange eettafel of lounge stoelen.

Het verandadak kan van 'outdoor textiles' gemaakt worden wat veel flexibiliteit biedt. Het kan ook uit polyester golfplaten bestaan dat uit te klikken is of simpelweg uit bamboo-matten over een elegant staketsel. De keuze bestaat in het wel of niet creëren van een overkapping.
Het dak van het gesloten gedeelte is volledig geïsoleerd.

een textiele verandadak dat flexibel hoog of laag te reguleren is en bij vertrek opgerold kan worden

1:200

PROTOTYPE 3: 'HOOG EN LAAG'

Interessant aan dit ontwerp is dat er 2 condities worden geschept vanwege het toelopen van zowel de plattegrond als het dak. Het lage brede raam kijkt uit op de tuin en de tegenoverliggende slanke hoge ramen bieden ver uitzicht over het landschap. De begane grond en eerste verdieping zijn samen 69 m² en de totale hoogte is 9.36 meter.
De plattegrond biedt de flexibiliteit om boven te slapen en beneden te wonen of juist andersom; boven te wonen genietend van het verre uitzicht en beneden te slapen.

De gevels kunnen met het duurzame western red cedar bedekt worden of met een andere houtsoort die met de Japanse techniek: 'Shou Sugi Ban' verduurzaamd wordt door het hout te verbranden. Een andere mogelijkheid is zwart verven, zoals in traditionele huizen van Oudorp wordt gedaan.

niveau 0

ELZENMETEN

Western red cederhout wordt silvergrijs in de loop van tijd wat goed bij de kleuren van een duinlandschap past

vakantiehuis in Almen, Melis /Koolhaas

niveau +3

1:200

To transform a '70s holiday resort into a contemporary, sustainable holiday landscape was an interesting challenge! Our team developed a masterplan including tiny collapsible (tree) houses, the introduction of indigenous plants and a sustainable sewage and composting system with step-by-step instructions for adaptations for the coming five to ten years. The first thing that was realised was the new reception building and our natural swimming pool, in which aquatic and moisture-tolerant plants as well as a natural filtering system keep the water clean and free of mosquitos.

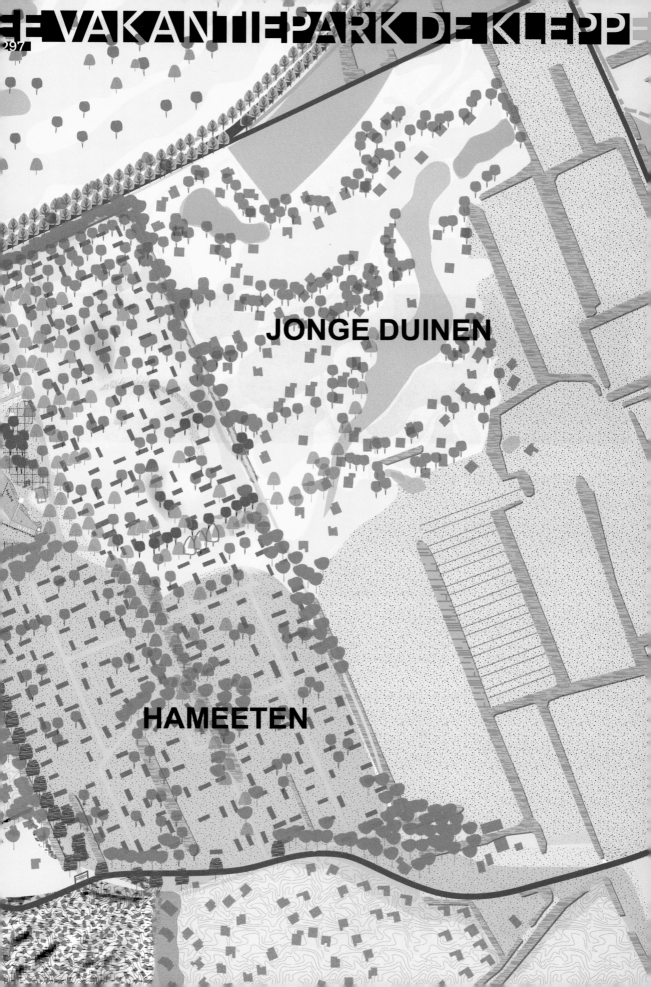

JONGE DUINEN

HAMEETEN

"Here Dieter Roth, Pierre Cardin, Emma Peel, Petra Blaisse and Irma Boom come together." PB

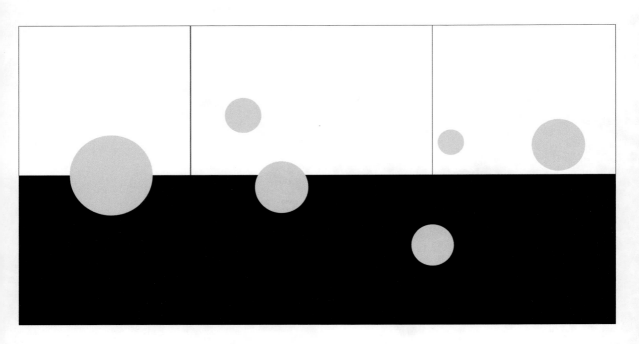

curtain-interior view

LOCATION	**Amsterdam, the Netherlands**
CLIENT	**Private owner**
STATUS	**Completed**
SCOPE	**Darkening curtain for the library's meeting and (re-)presentation room facing south**
LOCATION	**Amsterdam, the Netherlands**
SCALE	**8.5 × 4 m – in three parts**
MATERIALS	**White and black high-gloss PVC film (frontside facing the interior); white and black polyester blackout fabric (backside, facing the street); transparent PVC film (round windows)**
COLLABORATORS	**Owners**
DESCRIPTION	**A darkening curtain was needed for this semi-public library / exhibition space facing south**

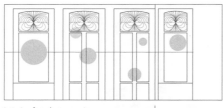

interior facade + openings

curtain-exterior view

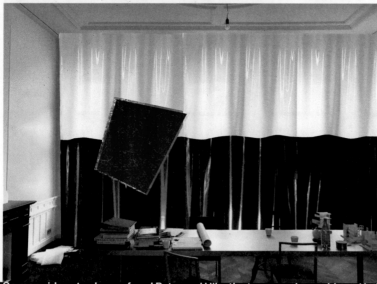

So many ideas to choose from! Peter and I like the top one where a hinged half-moon mirror covers the half-moon window of the curtain. But the owner, who knows our work well, preferred the version with many round openings, which allows for welcome viewpoints to the outside.

"It's always the hardest thing not to fall in love with the existing situation. In the middle of construction, we often think: don't do anything, it's good as it is; stop right there, it's perfect. A walk through the estate revealed a variety of conditions: a driveway that meanders left and right through the forest, passing a sloping meadow and ending up at a typical American country house with a porch and a rocking chair. An undulating lawn encircling the house; a barn where monkeys used to be kept; and, to the east, a filtered view over the Hudson River. The lawn then continues up to a worn sun terrace and swimming pool, shaded by a stately blue cedar (*Cedrus atlantica* "Glauca") on one side and a dark red, multi-stemmed Japanese maple on the other. North of the house a wide lawn slopes up, punctuated by various single trees, each one an object of beauty and a great spot for hiding and climbing. Walking farther up you reach an abandoned, dilapidated teahouse, overgrown with wild roses and honeysuckle. Along the left flank of the lawn a forest is taken over by vines and climbers, with strangely distorted trees piercing through a thick blanket of suffocating green. Walking into the forest along a narrow path, past rows of blue irises, you enter a dream world filled with pleasant surprises: a hidden pond under low-hanging branches, wild roses swaying down and catching the lace-like leaves of ferns, the play of light and shadow between the trees, the smell of moist soil and honeysuckle, the rustle of squirrels and birds. Looking out from the kitchen window at dusk you see deer and turkeys crossing the lawn, their shadows prolonging their silhouettes."

"The owners acquired the house to escape city life, a hideout for the entire family. We fantasised about the garden, worked on it together and stayed over for a few days on several occasions in different seasons. We discussed our plans with the local gardener and learnt about deer- and rabbit-proof plants from his years of experience, dreamt of a gated 'secret garden' filled with herbs and vegetables, discovered qualities and special places in the far corners of the estate, decided to re-work the pool and sun-terrace and the topography around, studied possibilities for turning the existing barn into a painter's studio, for shading the south-facing balcony with a pergola, went through plant books and lists of favourite flowers and colours, and learnt more about each other's lives, passions, routines, preferences and sensitivities along the way – all of this together only deepened our friendship." PB

LOCATION	Piermont, Hudson Valley, New York, USA
CLIENT	Private owners
STATUS	Completed
SCOPE	Landscape strategy, garden design, restoration of pool, planting plan
MATERIALS	Plantings, natural stone, pool, steel structures, wood
SCALE	2 ha
COLLABORATORS	James Sullivan

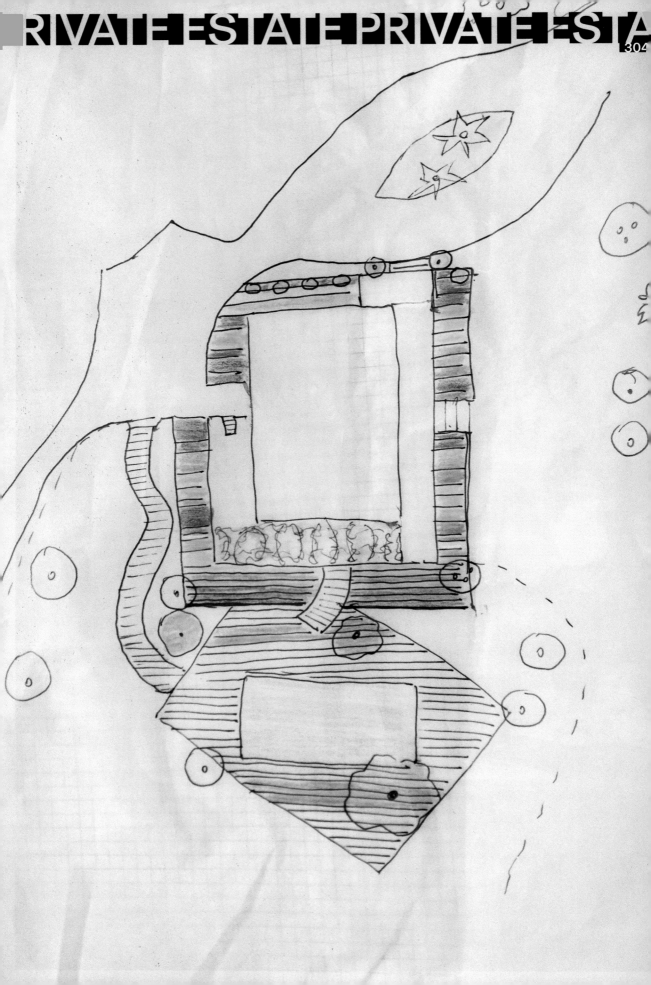

M

5 M

30

0

70

0

32 1

.20

.70

—0.

50-D

75

75

.70

12

40

50

.20

60

60

10

10

...BUCUS NIGRA „BLAC...

...A ----- OR: PAEONIA R...
„...

...US SEMPERVIRENS

...EMATIS RECTA / C. HER...
„EDWAR...

...ZA MEDIA

...ICUM VIRGATUM „HEA...

...EMISIA ALBA „CAN...

...OUSKIA ATRIPLICIFOLIA
„BLUE S...

...NOPS BANNATICUS
„TAPLOW B...

...NIA „SANCTUS"

...IA NEMOROSA „LUBE...

...IA × SUPERBA

...HORBIA CORNIGERA

BLUE OR WHITE (+) IRIS SIBIRICA

...IS - BEARDED HYBRIDS

...IOPOGON PLANISCAPUS „...
...ANDULA × INTERMEDI...

...ETA FAASSENII „WAL...

...BENA BONARIENSIS

...ACHYS OFFICINALIS

...TIBIDA COLUMNIFER...

...OMIS TUBEROSA / P. SAM...
...BASCUM CHAIXII...

BLUE ...| IRIS RETICULATE ...

SILVER Euphorbia myrsinite...
(DONKEY TAIL ...

PINK/MAUVE 18) ORIGANUM VULGARE

SILVER +Daylily) Rudbeckia ... (HRID, CULT...
+ Coreopsis ⊙ BEAUTY „lanc...

"The Arup Berlin team made careful calculations so that steel structures could replace the eliminated, load-bearing wooden beams resulting in a climatised house with triple (towards the outside) and double-layered almost colourless (important!) glass facades; and to ensure the right weight balance down through the 'mother building,' as this structure had to carry all additional weight.

     As the client wanted gardens around the glass house, we strategically cut openings in the attic roof, which we then covered with a glasshouse system of operable panels. These incisions opened unexpected views on the surrounding roofscape and on the treetops of Charlottenburg. A planting plan was developed for the now daylit attic." PB

"Although we were building in Germany, where regulations are strict and generally inflexible, the site was owned by an adventurous Israeli developer who provided us with an experimental playground where everything seemed possible. He accepted our idea almost without hesitation – except, of course, for the first price estimate. The project needed to be realised under the management of the client's Israeli staff, with a Romanian contractor. This eventually resulted in crisis management as many mistakes were made by the builders on site and we had to do lots of 'fixing' and re-detailing. Pouring the concrete floor 10 cm thicker than intended is but one catastrophic example that made us almost need to start from scratch. Yet with the courage and support of our diverse team, we managed to convince the Heritage Committee of Berlin to grant permission for the insertion of the long glass facade, 15.2 m in length, into the protected building's northern facade and to perforate the roofscape with gigantic sky lights, measuring a total of 138 m^2. To reach for the stars you have to think big!" AM

"This project, drawn up to the smallest detail, each material sampled and tested, halfway under construction and suspended in total silence for two years, was verbally put on permanent hold by our client in 2020: the developer had started a new life at sea and was no longer interested. He sold the attic with our unfinished project, and the new, unknown owner hired architect Henning Larsen from Denmark. Needless to say, we contacted Mr Larsen to discuss the situation. Naively, we hoped that we could stay involved in our treasured architectural intervention, officially approved by the Berlin authorities and partly realised. Mr Larsen found our call 'very sweet' but was as unmistakably firm as he was friendly in dismissing us, assuring us that he could understand our frustration, but that the new owner wanted something different – a completely climatised space, among other things. For sustainability reasons they would re-use the steel beams and the northern glass facade and, of course, the 138 m^2 of electrically operated skylights. Very nice to finally meet us, and who knows – maybe we could collaborate on another project someday. And that was that." PB

LOCATION	Berlin-Charlottenburg, Germany
CLIENT	Home Center Management GmbH
STATUS	Unrealised
SCOPE	Private house in the attic of the former hospital Joli Cœur
SCALE	Attic, 374 m^2; glass house, 15 × 7 × 4 m in height; landscape masterplan, ca. 6 ha
MATERIALS	Steel beams, aluminium profiles, glass plates, concrete floor.
COLLABORATORS	Paul Friedrich Bratring, 1900; Arup; Reinier Suurenbroek
DESCRIPTION	Inside Outside first designed the landscape masterplan for this former hospital-turned-residential area and developed interior concepts for all public spaces. Then our client asked us to create a "unique" apartment in the building's spacious, pitch-dark wooden attic. I accepted his invitation out of enthusiasm although I don't have an architecture degree. So, I invited architect Aura Luz Melis, with whom I had collaborated in the past, to join me in implementing this project.

     A one-storey glass bungalow, the same size as Philip Johnson's Glass House, has been "slid" through the northern flank of the gigantic sloping roof on top of the former hospital, and lands inside the attic. The cut in the roof creates a large opening that becomes the northern facade of the glass house with a long, adjoining terrace. To fit the glass box into the attic, numerous wooden structural beams had to be cut off and the weight shifted to the load-bearing steel structure (thank you, Arup Berlin!). We now have a transparent, climatised home in a rough unfinished and non-climatised attic. A separate bedroom is placed in the attic's south tower – under the cupola, with three round windows looking out over the entrance garden.

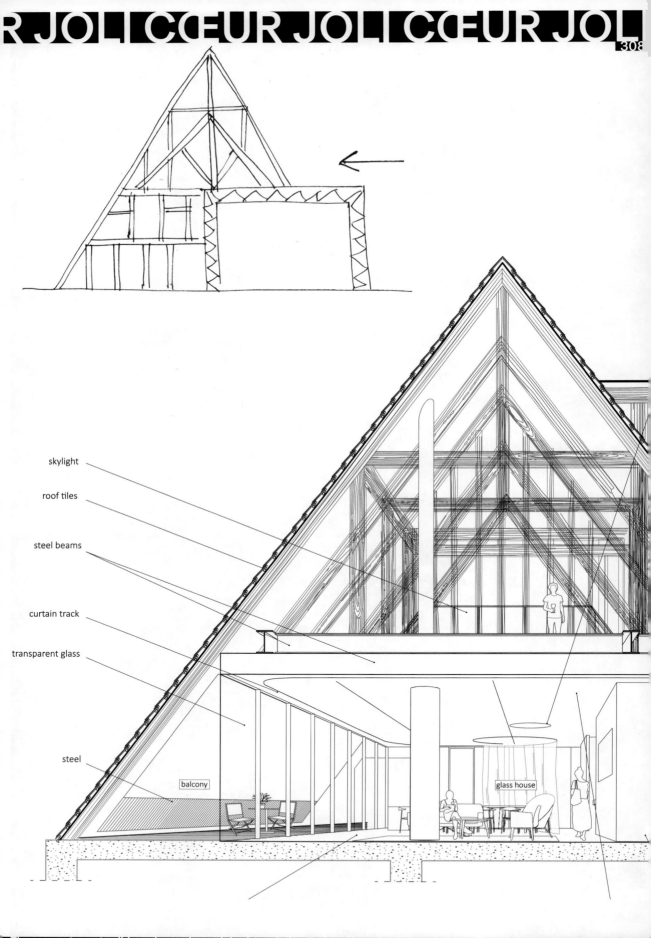

skylight

roof tiles

steel beams

curtain track

transparent glass

steel

balcony

glass house

The concept was to slide a glass volume right through the tiled roof into the dark wood attic. The Landmark Preservation Commission didn't allow it to stick out of the roof's surface, but we were allowed to cut out a piece of the north-facing roof so that the glass house, behind the newly created terrace, remains a visible object.

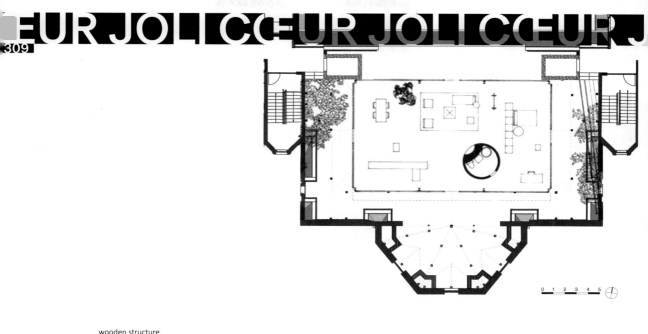

0 1 2 3 4 5

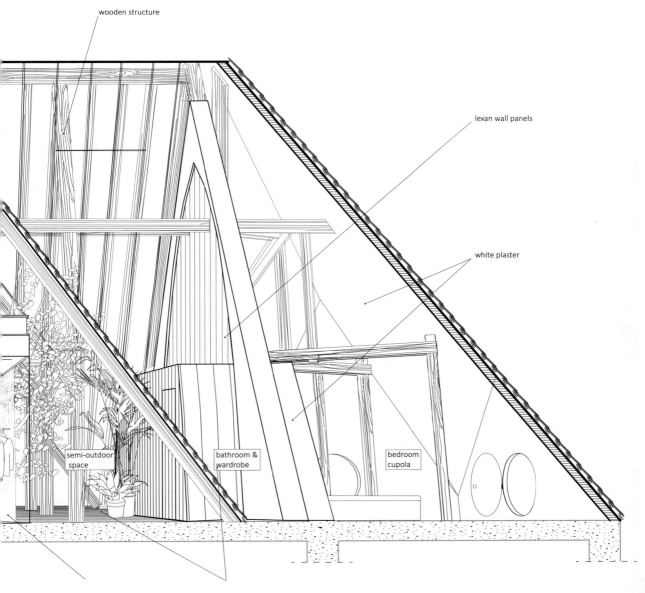

wooden structure

lexan wall panels

white plaster

semi-outdoor space

bathroom & wardrobe

bedroom cupola

The climatised glass house inhabits the non-climatised attic. Gardens, a long terrace, an outdoor bathtub and a spiral stair-case, which accesses the roof of the glass house for an amazing view over the city, will animate the space. The master bedroom and bathroom are separate, placed on the southern side, under the roof of one of the building's towers.

roof scape with skylights
on the south, west and east

skylights in eastern roof area

View of the outdoor terrace

READYMADES BELONG TO EVERYONE
Swiss Institute

"The curtain 'Don't pinch!' was a compact and fun project that gave us a chance to play around! We made it in our studio with the help of two interns. They were architecture students and neither had any experience in sewing. So, we made a curtain without yarn, needles or sewing. With the given theme in mind, we used bubble-wrap, transparent PVC, tape and bolts – leftover materials that everyone knows and has used for all kinds of things except curtains. The top triangle was made of four panels of transparent PVC welded together. The bubble-wrap panels of the bottom triangle were connected with bolts through eyelets that the interns hammered in. Then they cut the materials in two equal triangles and taped them together with yellow/black striped tape. Done! A hands-on project, quick and easy – just the way we like it!"   PN

LOCATION	New York, USA
CLIENT	Swiss Institute, New York
STATUS	Completed
SCOPE	Production of a ready-made curtain for the exhibition *READYMADES BELONG TO EVERYONE*
MATERIALS	Curtain of transparent PVC, big-size bubble wrap, black-and-yellow striped tape, bolts and eyelets
SCALE	6.48 × 4.79 m
COLLABORATORS	Niels Olsen and Fredi Fischli (curators)
DESCRIPTION	The curators of the show invited us to participate in the exhibition *READYMADES BELONG TO EVERYONE* with a typically Inside Outside curtain composed of "as found" material

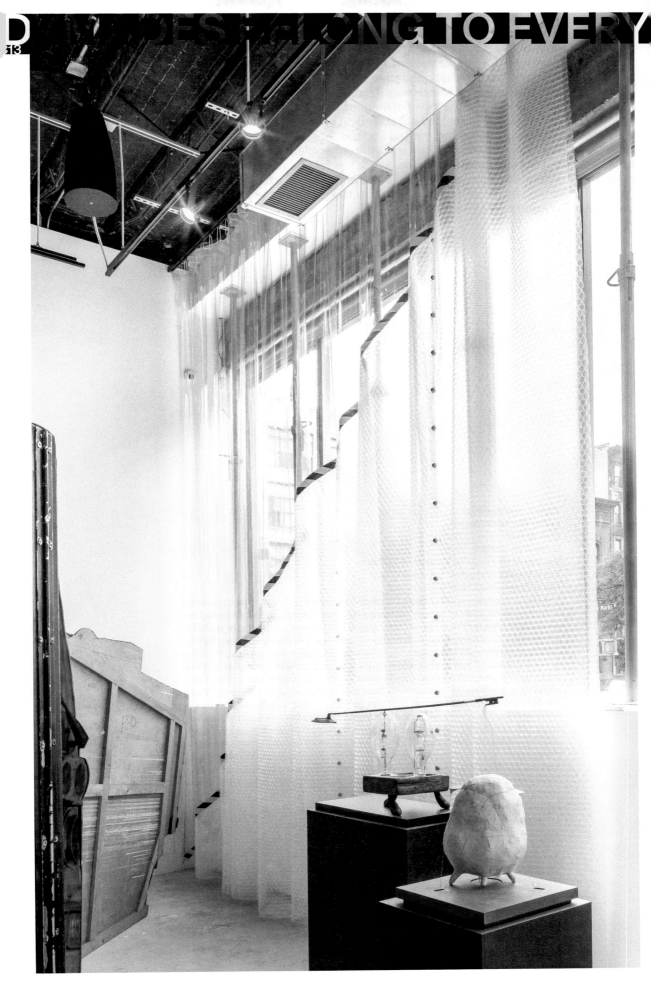

Theft is Vision
Luma Westbau

"We had the museum's thin steel structures repainted, doubled them and added necessary interconnections for reinforcement. As the level of reinforcement depended on the weight and number of works that needed to be attached, each screen became different: less structure with fewer works and more if more. The wrapping of the thin tubular structure with cling film resulted in a series of elegant, transparent screens with the intensely wrinkled but taut plastic animating the surface. The paintings, collages and prints were exhibited on this shiny, quivering, ruffled surface. The back of each art piece was visible (think Lina Bo Bardi) and through the transparent enfilade one could experience all the other works throughout the entire space. Almost weightless and non-existent, the screens nevertheless defined rooms of different sizes and created a trajectory from one themed gallery to the next. With all windows open to the city and the sky, the views outward became an integral part of the exhibit." PB

LOCATION	Zurich, Switzerland
CLIENT	Luma Westbau, Zurich
STATUS	Completed
SCOPE	Exhibition design
SCALE	4 screens of 218 m² in a space of 267 m²
MATERIALS	Steel frames and plastic wrapping film
COLLABORATORS	Niels Olsen, Fredi Fischli (curators)
DESCRIPTION	The Luma Westbau space needed to be divided into a series of rooms to house a themed exhibition of recent works by different artists. We were asked to develop an idea for the division of the space with screens, curtains or walls to achieve the necessary spatial definitions. Looking at the works chosen by the curators, we thought the walls should express the same character as the title of the exhibition *Theft is Vision*. Why not make transparent walls that display every work from front and back and provide an overview of all the works at the same time, but through increasingly thick layers of transparent material? First we thought of scaffolding, but that has become a cliché in the art world, so Niels and Fredi immediately killed that trajectory. We then looked for another structure combined with kitchen wrap, a transparent stretching and self-adherent material that we had in mind for a slightly obscene effect. We were offered the use of Luma's elegant metal "wall" structures, beautiful but so thin that we doubled them for stability and three-dimensionality. We had those tightly wrapped with transparent foil over and over again until it formed a strong but transparent surface.

The Vertical every 1250 mm

The Horizontal every 625 mm

Paintings floating on quivering cling film

"For extra acoustic absorbance we lent them two Garden Carpets from our collection, but we also asked Claudy for some of her felt scraps and raw materials to use for the curtains. She generously gave us a big collection of colourful felt fabrics, handspun yarns in different hues and a beautiful collection of the ingredients she uses for dying her wool, such as flower seeds, nuts, leaves and other materials."

"As a contrast to the abundance of expressive, organic elements that define Claudy Jongstra's art pieces, we meticulously separated and organised the ingredients according to colour, size and shape, and then selected one for each curtain. With almost mathematical precision we sandwiched the woollen balls, nuts, dried flowers and felt colour samples (all cut in equally sized squares) between two layers of transparent plastic – like samples in a laboratory."

"The systematically exhibited ingredients that form the base of Jongstra's work thus floated in space as visible thought-bubbles. Integrated in transparent fleeces, these materials were acting as separation between the different 'work rooms' that Claudy and her team created in the large, open space, where they taught printing, felting, colouring, cooking and bread-baking."   PB

LOCATION	Groningen, the Netherlands
CLIENT	Municipality of Groningen, Claudy Jongstra
STATUS	Completed
SCOPE	Space-defining, acoustic curtains and textile walls for a temporary educational building
MATERIALS	100% polyamide, digitally printed with pictures of grasses; transparent plastic, felt samples, woollen balls, pigments, seeds and nut shells
SCALE	Carpet, 2.7 × 2 m; curtains, 4.6 × 2.87 m, 2.3 × 2.5 m
COLLABORATORS	Claudy Jongstra team, Jeroen Kooistra
DESCRIPTION	In 2018 Claudy Jongstra started the Waste no Waste project as part of the Leeuwarden Cultural Capital of Europe with the aim of teaching people about inclusive, sustainable and vital communities. For this program of workshops and exhibitions she designed a temporary wooden building to be erected in the city centre of Groningen and Claudy asked Inside Outside to design curtains that could act as flexible (acoustic) walls to divide the large space of the temporary building into smaller, more practical ones for the different workshops and exhibitions that she was planning to organise there.

Intercity Next Generation
Dutch Railways

"What could be better than to be involved in the interiors of fast trains with shifting views of passing landscapes on all sides? One can see it as the epitome of everything Inside Outside stands for. And what could be more rewarding than to be invited by one of the Netherlands' largest national institutions: the Nederlandse Spoorwegen (Netherlands Railways)? Together with firms such as the former PTT (national post) and KLM (national airlines), the NS is one of the institutions that Petra and I – two different generations – were proud of as kids living in foreign countries." AM

"And what could be more interesting than to witness, step by step, the development of a new design for a train by an established French company, with the most modern digital means, in close communication with the NS staff and, in the process, to be invited to advise the client on the train's interior? Astonished to see absolutely everything presented digitally – even materials and colours – we persuaded our client to request physical samples. They did so from then on, and it turned out to be indispensable. After all, you need to feel materials and test colours, if possible, in full 1:1 scale. Tiny colour samples on paper don't show what they do in large scale and with a specific material. Smooth, irregular, soft, hard, shiny, matte… it all influences the colour. Additionally, all ingredients that add up to an interior need to connect, to complement or enrich each other, so you have to see them all together to be able to decide on the right combination and quality of things. Three-dimensional digital representation just doesn't do it." PB

LOCATION	The Netherlands, Belgium
CLIENT	Dutch Railways
STATUS	Competition, 2016, 1st prize; completed, train in use 2023
SCOPE	Artistic application on all interior glass and wall partitions and toilet units
MATERIALS	Ceramic print on glass, prints on anti-graffiti foil
SCALE	30 glass partitions per train, 222 m²; foil prints, 21 m² per train; total trains, trains, 99 for the Netherlands, 22 for Belgium
COLLABORATORS	Alstom Paris, Frans Parthesius, Jesse Koolhaas
DESCRIPTION	Sound waves became the theme for IO's designs for the requested "artistic decoration" of the glass partitions in the trains. We developed three patterns that were each printed in white on one side and in black on the other side of the thick glass plates and shifted them slightly to create a shadow effect. We used a ceramic print technique. When asked to also design the new toilet units in the train, we introduced two softly pleating Inside Outside curtains as wall-papered imagery on the exterior of the toilet booths, with "typical" Dutch landscapes occupying their interior. Everything, needless to say, vandal-proof and maintenance-free.

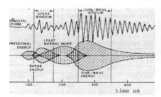
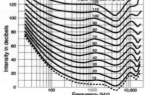
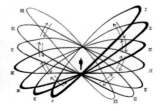

Official presentation of true-to-scale mock-up of the front section of the Intercity New Generation designed by Alstom (with "art" contribution by Inside Outside) to selected press, Dutch Railway staff and collaborators in a train-yard in Utrecht, 2019. Bottom: one of the Dutch Railway directors being interviewed in one of the accessible toilets decorated by IO.

PARTITION G6_SILENCE   SCALE 1:1   PARTITION F4_MEET AND GREET   SCALE 1:1   PARTITION I1_WORK AND QUIET   SCALE 1:1

We chose sound symbols or waves for each compartment type: left, Silence; middle, Meet & Greet; right, Work & Quiet

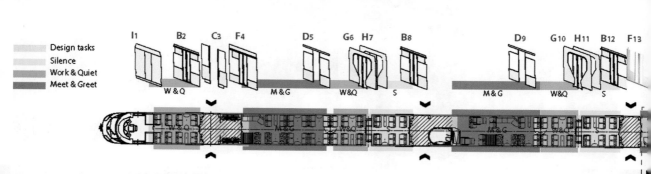

Design tasks
Silence
Work & Quiet
Meet & Greet

I1   B2   C3   F4   D5   G6   H7   B8   D9   G10   H11   B12   F13

W & Q   M & G   W & Q   S   M & G   W & Q   S

Design tasks

Where what would go in a typical high-speed train wagon configuration

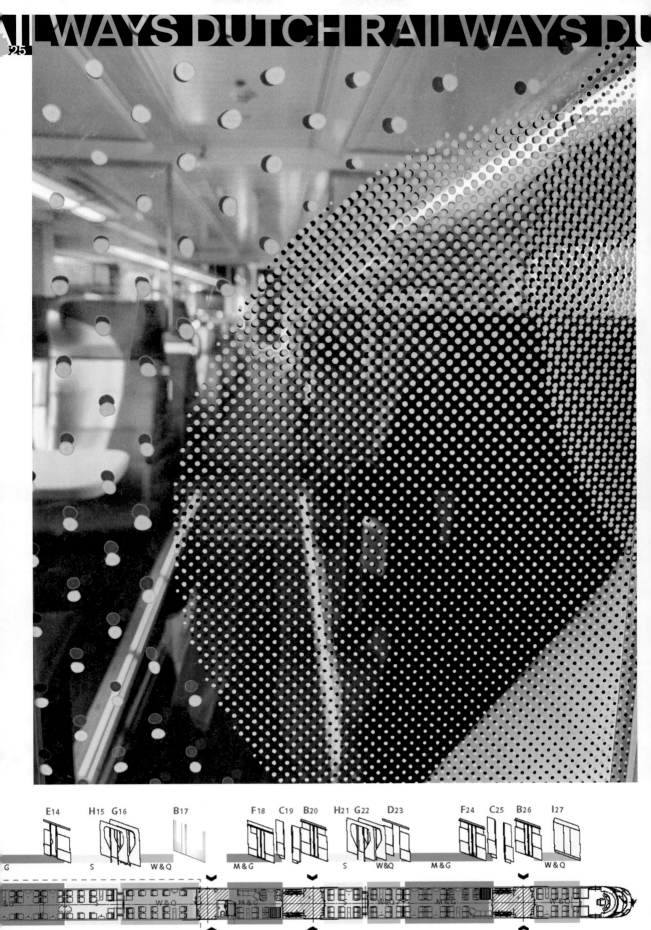

These were our original proposals for the toilet interiors. We truly wished the NS would accept these; they're so much fun! But – much like Schiphol Airport – the railway preferred to have Dutch landscapes, plus a "wiggly" wallcovering to prevent graffiti.

WC

We chose two of Inside Outside's famous curtains to cover the two toilet typologies: the Rothschild Bank curtain for second class compartments (lending an impression of transparency) and the Nederlands Dans Theater curtain for first class (we got permission to use them from both institutions)

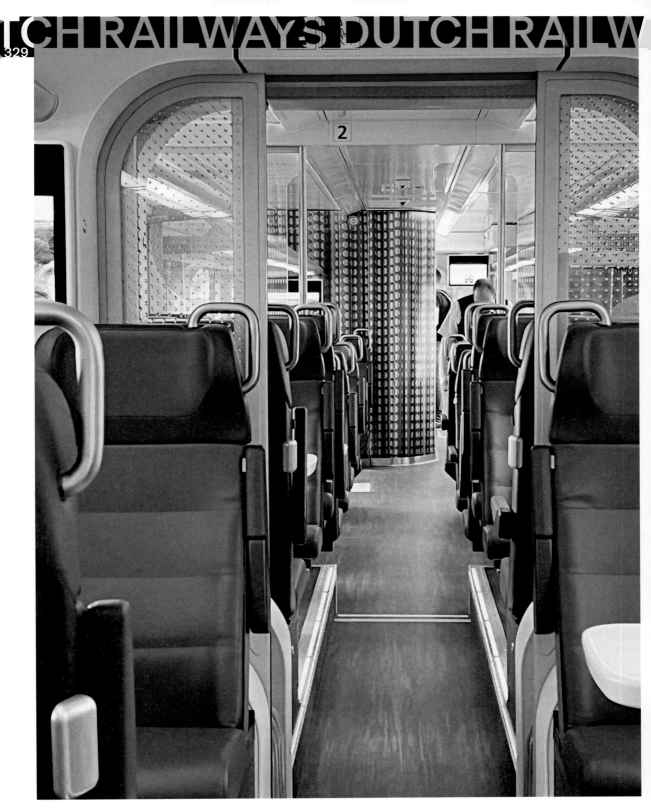

"We were asked to weave all textiles at the Textile Lab in town, although our plan was to make them from re-used industrial materials to seamlessly match the muscular, industrial look of the building. But the mayor insisted, as the Textile Museum and its Lab are the pride of the town. We had already developed different, fantastic textiles with the Lab, first for the Dutch Embassy in Berlin and later for the National Library in Doha, so we had no qualms about working with them again, except that weaving requires a lot more time and money than working with existing materials!"

"The Lab wanted to develop something 'unique' for this honourable project in their own city, but for this context we needed to disappoint them: we wanted to develop what we had in mind, namely a thick, canvas-like cloth – a tight, classic weave that mimics the industrial look of a sail. And to ensure the necessary transparency of the curtains – to provide views of the entire interior of the building and to complement the heavy drapes – we needed to develop an extremely transparent weave. After installation we realised that the delicate-looking, slightly uneven weave that came out echoes the sensitivity of the building's ancient and breakable 'curtain wall.' It catches every ray of light, making their gigantic surfaces look like waterfalls." PB

"We decided to experiment with a transparent monofilament yarn, very thin and extremely strong, commonly used for fishing, because we wanted to weave a sturdy yet 'completely' transparent fabric. What a challenge it would prove to be! Test upon test, from plissé structures to four-layer samples, we explored the boundaries of available weaving techniques for more than a year. In the end, we discovered that the best aesthetic effect was achieved by producing a double-layer weave, connected only by the thinnest single yarn (so-called floating threads), and to then separate the two layers by cutting them loose. Due to the enormous scale of our curtains and the need to weave continuous rolls of cloth, these floating threads needed to be introduced not only to hold the two layers loosely together, but to prevent the machine from blocking. When the floating threads were removed, we saw that small unsightly spots remained so we designed little angular and X-shaped forms of a different binding around these points – different in every curtain and visible only on closer study. The bindings we applied here are copies of ones used in Tilburg's traditional cloth." NE

LOCATION	Spoorzone Tilburg, the Netherlands
CLIENT	Municipality of Tilburg, Library Midden-Brabant, Seats2Meet, BKKC
STATUS	Competition, 1st prize / completed
SCOPE	Flexible textile architecture, interior landscape, "style rooms," moving furniture, interior moving gardens
MATERIALS	Trevira CS, monofilament, transparent plastic, Kevlar cords
SCALE	Interior, 4,125 m²; curtains A1, A2, each 47.3 × 14.85 m; curtains B1, B2, each 32 × 10.8 m; curtains C1, C2, each 57.8 × 11.16 m
COLLABORATORS	Civic Architects, Braaksma & Roos Architecten, Arup, TextielLab Tilburg, LevTec, Seilemaaker, Theatex
DESCRIPTION	The municipality of Tilburg rescued this large locomotive repair shop of elegant proportions by giving it landmark status. A good decision, as this steel-and-glass twin-structure, aligned with the train tracks that fed its purpose, is still in its original state: a hugely attractive industrial building inside a new urban development area. Owned by the municipality, this building will accommodate the city's public library, a commercial firm called Seats2 meet, an art foundation and other cultural foundations.

Together with architects and engineers we developed a plan that respects and protects the building's raw beauty. We focused on the contrast between its weightless skin and the enormous, heavy steel beams from which train wagons were suspended and shifted around for repairs. We kept everything intact, including the worn patches of colour on beams, tubes and concrete floor, the aged glass facade, the tracks and the smell of oil. Although the city's competition brief specified two separate volumes inside the existing building, each with its own function, our team treated the twin building, seemingly divided by a central steel structure, as one continuous open space. In its entire width, we implemented a folded landscape of stairs to connect three floors. Into this stepped landscape we cut openings to bring light into the space underneath. Three pairs of monumental curtains, hanging from ceiling to floor on each floor, create flexible rooms. Along the remaining tracks on the south-facing, concrete ground floor – now the main entrance hall – "garden wagons" slide into different positions, from inside to outside.

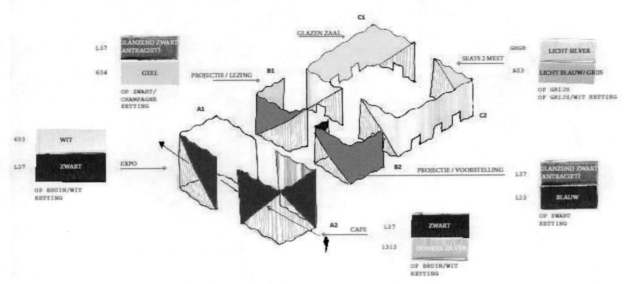

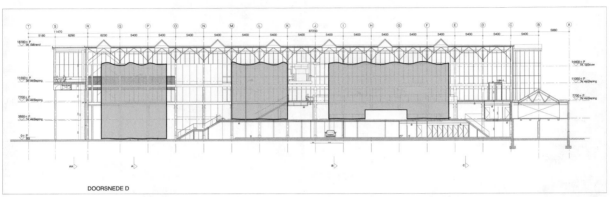

DOORSNEDE D

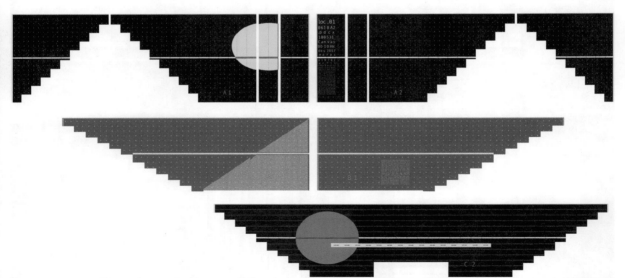

These drawings represent the basic principles of the three curtain pairs: their basic division between opaque and transparent, their colours, their placement and sizes, and, at the bottom, an impression of the way the thick, jacquard woven cloth-widths are horizontally assembled, including the literal; division of each curtain in two horizontal halves, to later be connected on site (thin yellow line at the centre)

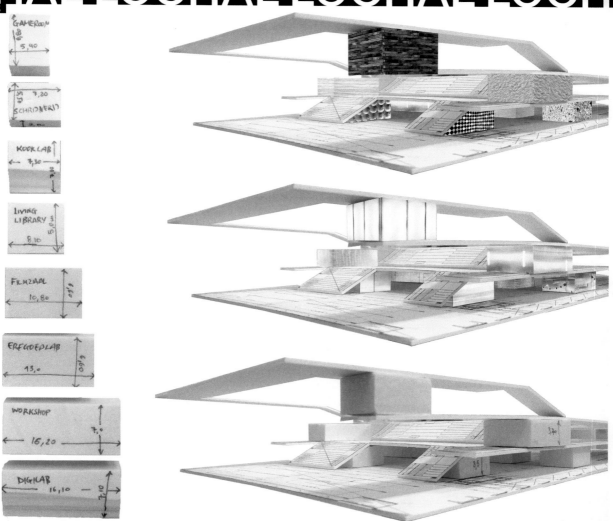

GAMEROOM
5,40

SCHRIJVERIJ
7,20

KOOKLAB
7,30

LIVING LIBRARY
8,10

FILMZAAL
10,80

ERFGOEDLAB
13,0

WORKSHOP
16,20   7,0

DIGILAB
16,10   7,10

Together with the competition team, we developed the organisation of the interior and the general finishes for the building. This included the stepped landscape and eight period rooms – small, eye-catching identifiable boxes, which were spread throughout the space and in which specific educational programs would take place, from cooking to writing, from film studio to digital lab. Their interiors were later developed by Mecanoo, who won a separate competition for the interior furnishing of the library.

The fishing line (monofilament) being woven to create the transparent sections of the curtains

Here half of a curtain is hanging; the transparent half made of fishing line will come underneath

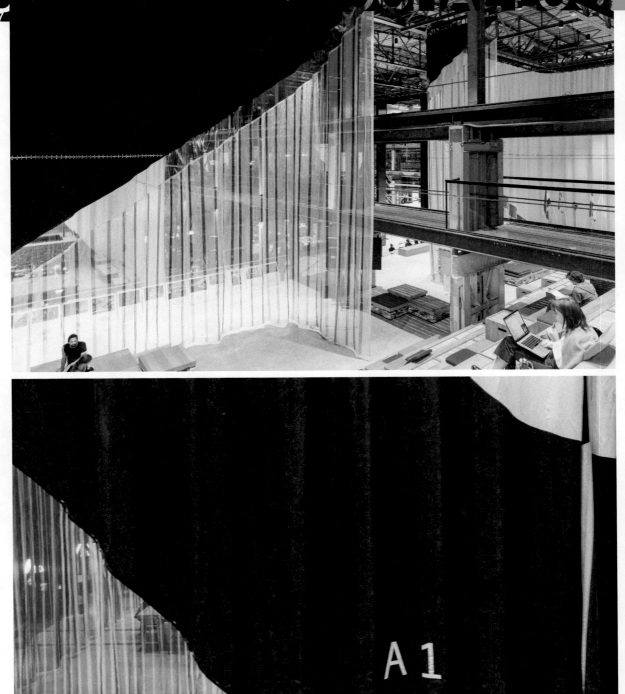

These photographs by Ivan Baan give a good impression of the curtains' scale and degree of transparency

For Seats2Meet we made two curtains; one enveloped the workplace and meeting space, the other the glass concert room next to it. Students from a local art academy furnished each of the workrooms.

King Abdulaziz Center for World Culture

"This art commission was managed by an Australian company on behalf of the client Saudi Aramco Oil Company in Dhahran. They had recommended us as one of seven artists to make a site-specific installation. We were to create a stage curtain for the main auditorium of the new King Abdulaziz Center for World Culture, built by the competition winners Snøhetta from Norway. Here, we were looking at Snøhetta's 'landmark' building in the making, with its organic phallic shapes that apparently represent desert rocks and crystals. I went to Oslo to visit him and his team to check on the interior of the building and in particular to see the finishes and colour scope of the auditorium in question. There was no huge interest in close collaboration, but they gave us useful information. We decided to develop a three-dimensional guillotine curtain that would integrate the irregular, angular shapes of the crystal-shaped balconies of the main theatre."

"For the longest time we had to communicate through the Australian firm, without ever talking directly to our actual clients. Very frustrating indeed. Suddenly, they announced that they were going to visit us in our studio in Amsterdam. Two women appeared on our doorstep, both fashionably dressed from top to toe. They told us that they headed up the building project from within Aramco and that it was about time to meet. They came with beautiful presents – dates and perfume – were charmingly funny and sharp as a razor. Meeting each other, creating a connection and speaking with one-another directly for a better understanding of each other's perspectives makes all the difference – it improves the work and accelerates the process."

"After working on tests and samples in Sharjah, my colleague Peter and I travelled on to Dhahran. On site, all the ins-and-outs of the architecture and surrounding landscape (designed by Snøhetta) as well as the ambitions for the building were carefully explained. Business-like and knowledgeable, playful yet efficient, feminine and bossy at the same time, the two women coordinated everything and oversaw our work with open minds and smart comments all the way. When we had installed the curtain after a weeks' work with the Showtex team, they reserved three whole days with us and the lighting technicians to create the right lighting for the work. Here our intention was to let the light – an essential part of every design – slide in an east-west direction along the golden crystal, as if a day passes and the position of the sun shifts – accentuating the glow and shape of the suspended sculpture that graced our curtain with an ever-changing play of shadows. What a luxury to be given time and technical support." PB

LOCATION	Dhahran, Saudi Arabia
CLIENT	Saudi Aramco
STATUS	Completed
SCOPE	Art commission for guillotine stage curtain
MATERIALS	Gold faux leather, digitally printed polyester velvet, blackout cloth, Polaris voile, steel rings
SCALE	210 m², 20 × 10.5 m
COLLABORATORS	Arup, Octatube, ShowTex Middle East
DESCRIPTION	Grasping the opportunity to NOT make a fluid, soft curtain but to integrate a stiff structure into a textile surface, we teamed up with Arup engineers in Amsterdam who jumped at the chance to work on something different, small and "simple." We wanted to follow the crystal shapes that dominate the main auditorium's interior: ceiling, balconies, surfaces. Dark reds and browns all around. So, we folded pieces of paper to explore scale and fold directions, studied weight and volume restrictions and came up with a tensegrity system of thin steel rods and cables. This structure was later covered with gold faux leather. The "crystal" is positioned centrally in relation to the curtain (at the height of the balconies), protruding forward and backward. The velvet curtain, attached to the crystal structure above and below, is printed with a colour gradation from white to dark blue/from dark blue to white. The lower part is pleated, the top part stretched. The diagonal folds of the crystal are continued as holed lines in the curtain through which back-light is projected when lights are dimmed in the room. The golden crystal is softly lit from different directions by spaciously placed, masked lamps that light up from left to right and back again, so that the crystal glows in different places at different moments. It is a gold rock with a soul, alive and glowing.

Backstage view

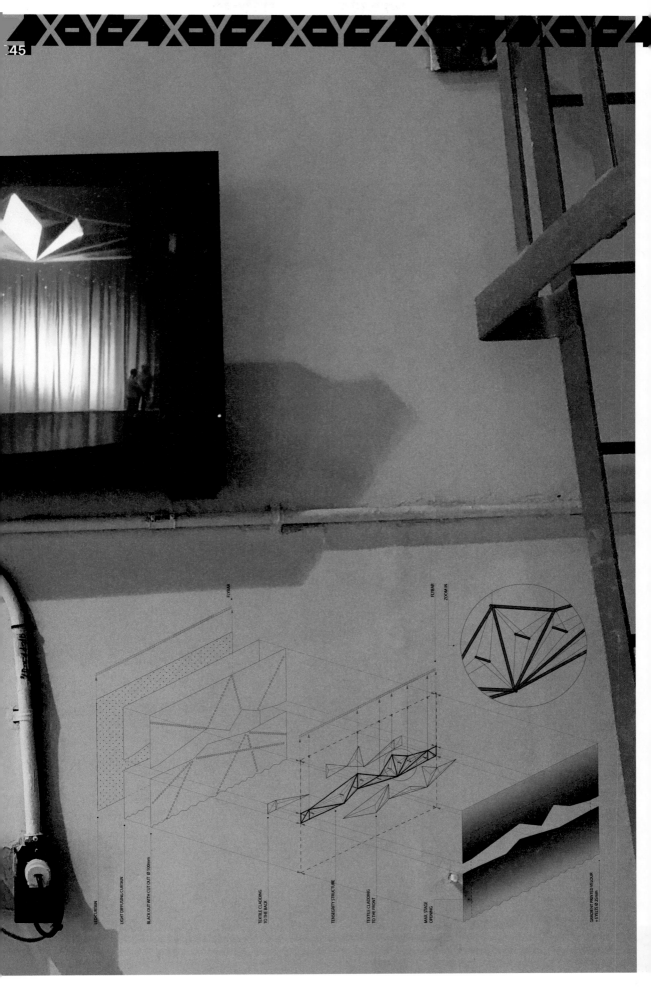

FLYBAR

FLYBAR

ZOOM IN

LED V CURTAIN

LIGHT DIFFUSING CURTAIN

BLACK OUT WITH CUT OUT Ø 100mm

TEXTILE CLADDING TO THE BACK

TENSEGRITY STRUCTURE

TEXTILE CLADDING TO THE FRONT

MAX. STAGE OPENING

GRADIENT PRINTED VELOUR + EYELETS Ø 25mm

Here, the last task to be completed during installation: the finishing of the hem. The client was always present and reserved a number of days to compose the lighting for the stage curtain after installation. Six projectors were placed at different points throughout the theatre so that light would move from one lamp to the next, creating the impression of the sunlight's changing position throughout the day.

"We were invited by the municipality of Milan to join this closed landscape competition, and Inside Outside was to be the leading party. We invited others to join our team. Mirko Zardini, urban theorist from Milan, was introduced to us, and he proved to be essential in understanding the ins and outs of the local urban logistics and of the local political and social structures. I then invited the other members, with whom I had repeatedly collaborated, like Michael Maltzan as architect for the Fashion Museum and School and specific pavilions that were part of the brief and would inhabit the park. As I envisioned the park as a botanic collection of gardens very early in the process, we invited Irma Boom to join us for the botanic and wayfinding texts, Piet Oudolf for one of the garden typologies and Rod'or for the landscape engineering."

"Our energetic team felt we had nothing to lose, and we were all really interested and passionate about the challenge of the project description (a connective public park with 'fashion' as main theme and a request for sports facilities) and the site itself: in the middle of Milan, a rough, empty plot with a few ancient buildings, embedded in a web of fierce traffic arteries and large-scale train and metro stations, underbuilt by tunnels and infrastructural networks and encircled by a palisade of future real estate developments. In the years after winning the project, we didn't hear from the municipality, but we wanted to realise the park one day, whatever it took. So when we – Inside Outside – finally signed an agreement with the city of Milan, we developed our park design with the support of local partner Franco Giorgetta and his daughter Simona (whom we had chosen as partners from six other possible parties earlier). Step by step it became a real, built project. Whatever happened during the process, the essence of our design survived. That resilience was surprising and comforting because, needless to say, a lot of shaping, scraping and economising went on between 2009 and 2018, when the park finally opened its gates on a rainy day in October. We might be 'nice girls' at Inside Outside, but we are bull terriers: we fight for what we believe in, however long it takes."   PB

LOCATION	Porta Nuova, Milan, Italy
CLIENT	Municipality of Milan/INGRE
STATUS	Competition, 2003–2004, 1st prize/completed 2018
SCOPE	Urban park design, planting plans, infrastructure, furnishings, lighting plan; fences around site of Fondazione Riccardo Catella
SCALE	10 ha
COLLABORATORS	Mirko Zardini, Michael Maltzan Architecture, Piet Oudolf, Irma Boom, Ro d'Or/Rob Kuster (competition team); Franco e Simona Giorgetta (local landscape architects); Piet Oudolf (plant recipe for Piet Garden); Irma Boom (graphic interventions); Carve (advisory on fence detailing)
DESCRIPTION	Here the competition plan that we developed with the Inside Outside Team proved resilient, which meant that the basis of the park design remained the same: a web of efficient paths connecting important points and shaping irregular fields with varied garden typologies and a confetti of 22 Circular Forests, each representing one species of tree and together forming the Biblioteca degli Alberi. The park covers a network of train and metro tunnels and infrastructure, as well as a very busy street. It integrates air intake and exhaust chimneys, emergency exits and maintenance spaces for the underground metro and train tunnels. It connects the various levels (difference of six to ten metres) of the surrounding city with its folded topography (slopes, stairs), which also creates interesting viewpoints and niches, while muting the sound of the surrounding traffic. Needless to say, the many trees, shrubs and plantings filter and improve the air, attract insects and birds and form welcome microclimates.

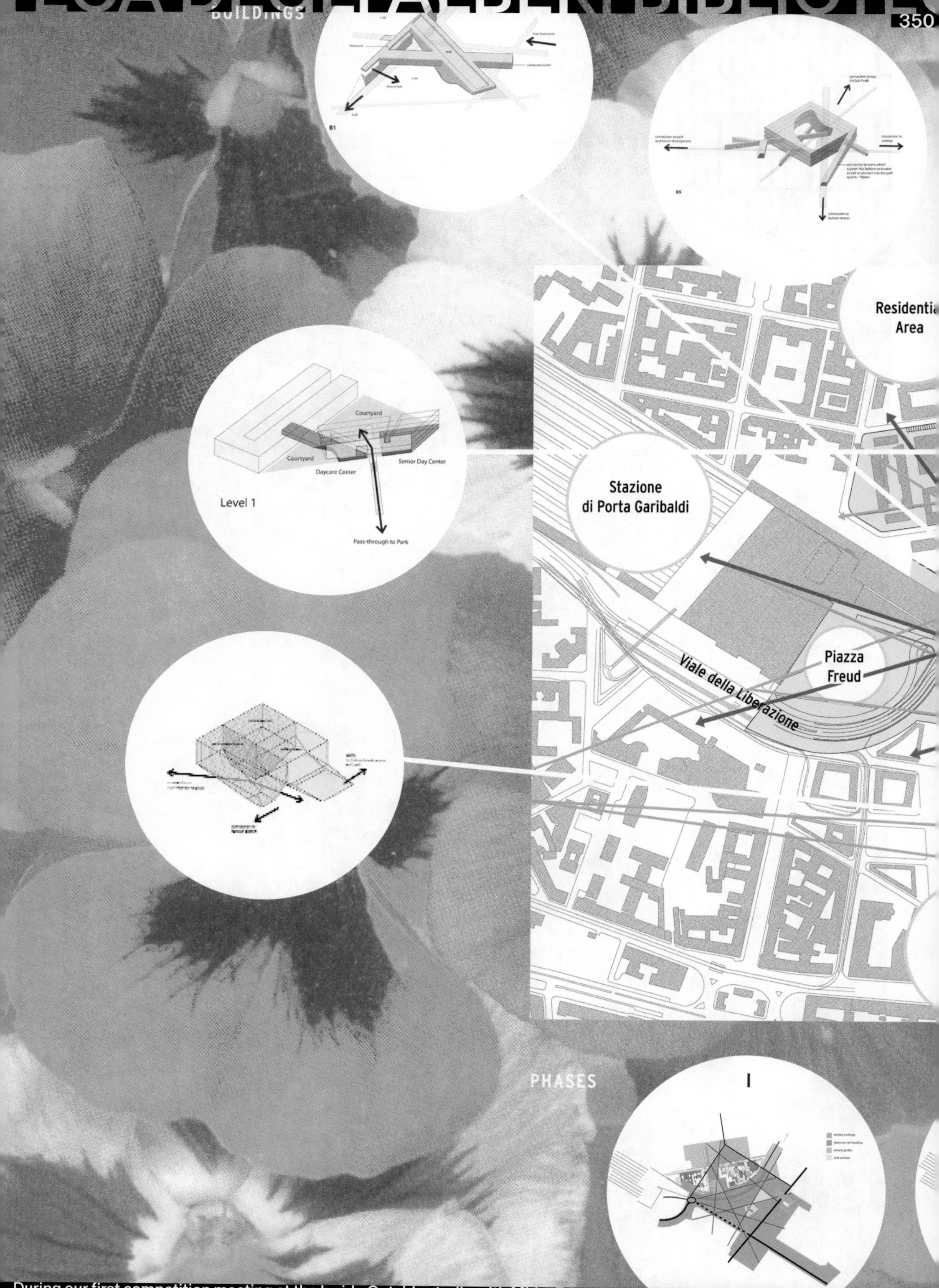
B1
B5
Courtyard
Courtyard
Daycare Center
Senior Day Center
Level 1
Pass-through to Park
Residentia
Area
Stazione
di Porta Garibaldi
Piazza
Freud
Viale della Liberazione
PHASES
I

During our first competition meeting at the Inside Outside studio with Mirko Zardini and Michael Maltzan, we drew straight lines through the given site to create direct connections between points of interest. This criss-cross of lines formed the web of paths that shapes the fields within, while also opening up all edges of the plot, as lines can continue endlessly, both literally and figuratively.

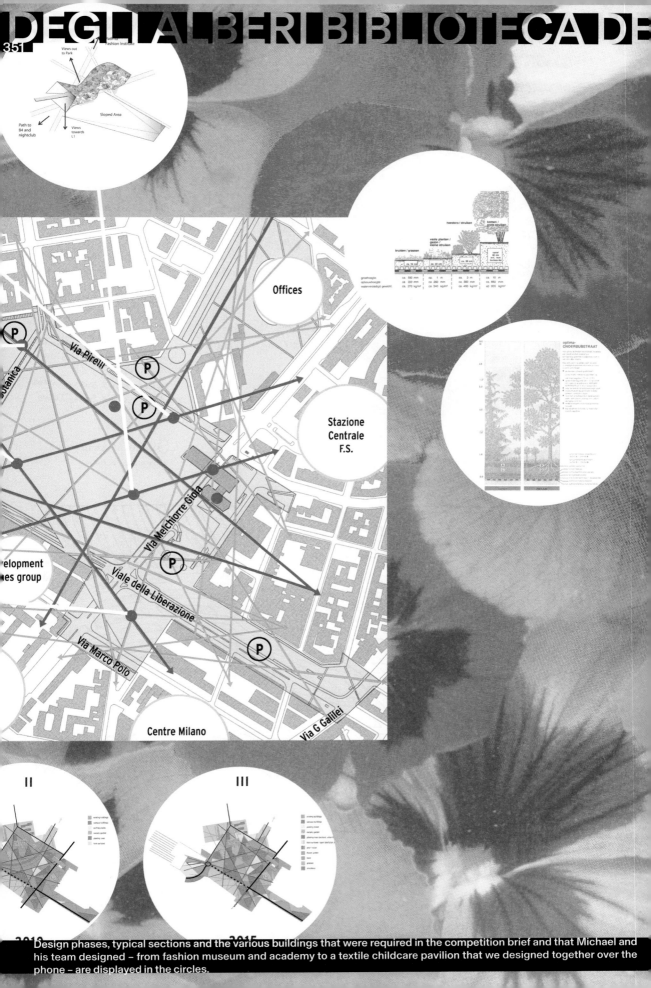

Offices

Stazione
Centrale
F.S.

Via Pirelli

Via Melchiorre Gioia

Viale della Liberazione

Via Marco Polo

Via G Galilei

Centre Milano

...elopment
...es group

II

III

Design phases, typical sections and the various buildings that were required in the competition brief and that Michael and his team designed – from fashion museum and academy to a textile childcare pavilion that we designed together over the phone – are displayed in the circles.

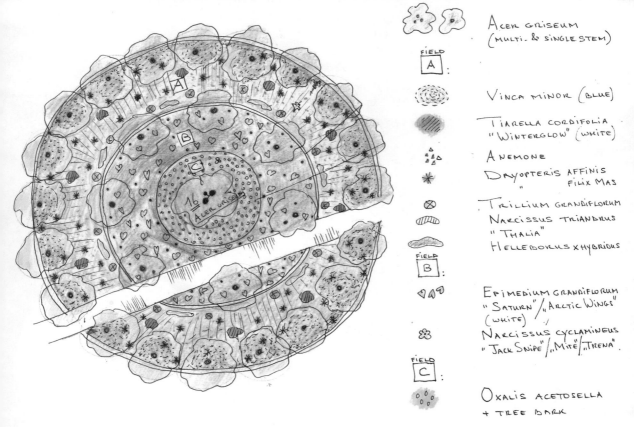

Acer griseum
(multi- & single stem)

FIELD A:

Vinca minor (blue)

Tiarella cordifolia
"Winterglow" (white)

Anemone

Dryopteris affinis
filix mas "

Trillium grandiflorum
Narcissus triandrus
"Thalia"
Helleborus x hybridus

FIELD B:

Epimedium grandiflorum
"Saturn"/"Arctic Wings"
(white)
Narcissus cyclamineus
"Jack Snipe"/"Mite"/"Trena".

FIELD C:

Oxalis acetosella
+ tree bark

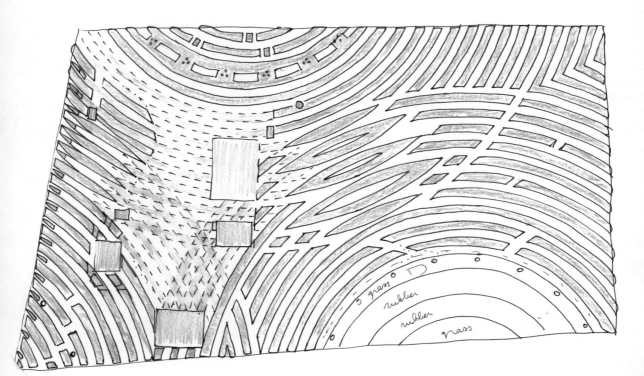

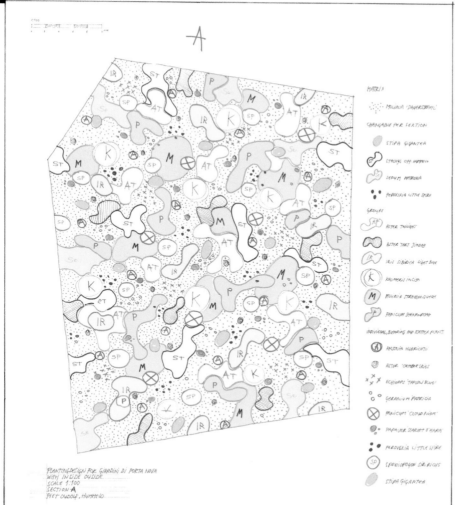

Both Piet Oudolf and I draw by hand. Top left: Acer Griseum circle; bottom left, the maze; top right, Piet's "Oudolf garden" typology; bottom right, my conceptual sketch, showing the complexity of the park's section (interplay between above and underground worlds) and the fact that the park will be viewed from different perspectives and at different speeds.

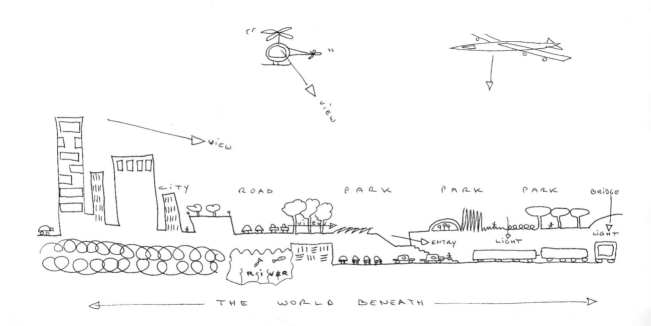

BIBLIOTECA DEGLI ALBERI
Progetto

INSIDE OUTSIDE

PETRA BLAISSE

INTERIORS · EXHIBITIONS · GARDENS

EERSTE NASSAUSTRAAT 5 · 1052 8D AMSTERDAM
PHONE: 00 31 (0) 20 6810 801 · FAX: 00 31 (0) 20 6810 466
WWW.INSIDEOUTSIDE.NL E-MAIL: OFFICE@INSIDEOUTSIDE.NL

Local Architect
Franco Giorgetta
Architetto Paesaggista
Via Fiori chiari 8
20121 Milano
tel. 02 863288

FASE 1 — GENERAL PLAN technical

Data	Scala
06—09—2010	1:1000

In the analysis phase, our team spent the first six months collecting necessary information from all of the parties involved with the underground infrastructure

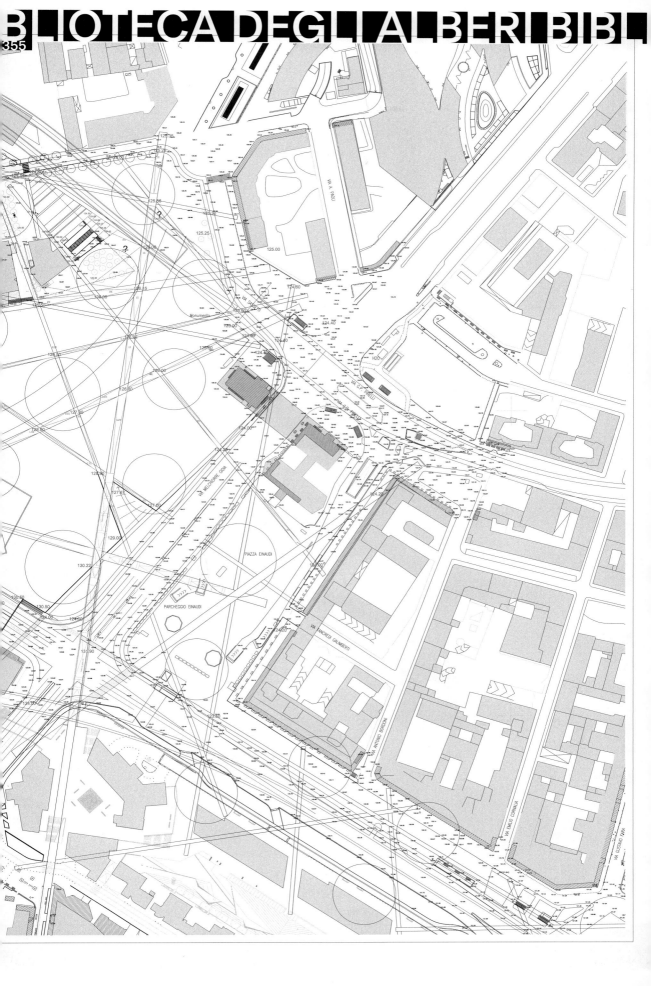

Our competition model. The base is made of different kinds of wood, revealing the various garden typologies of the park and of continuous, paths with Latin names of plants and trees, poems and wayfinding information (Irma Boom Office) written on them; Circular Forests float above the park, and buildings – models made by the Michael Maltzan team – are spread throughout. All together, they form the "cultural campus" inside the public park that we named Biblioteca degli Alberi.

Here you see the site after the ground has been cleared, freshly covered in a layer of sub-soil and later to be covered by the actual topsoil. I took the picture from one of Bosco Verticale's balconies when Stefano Boeri showed us around ca. 2016. Right before I took this picture, the American artist Agnes Denes had turned the site into a temporary wheat field as part of the Milan Expo.

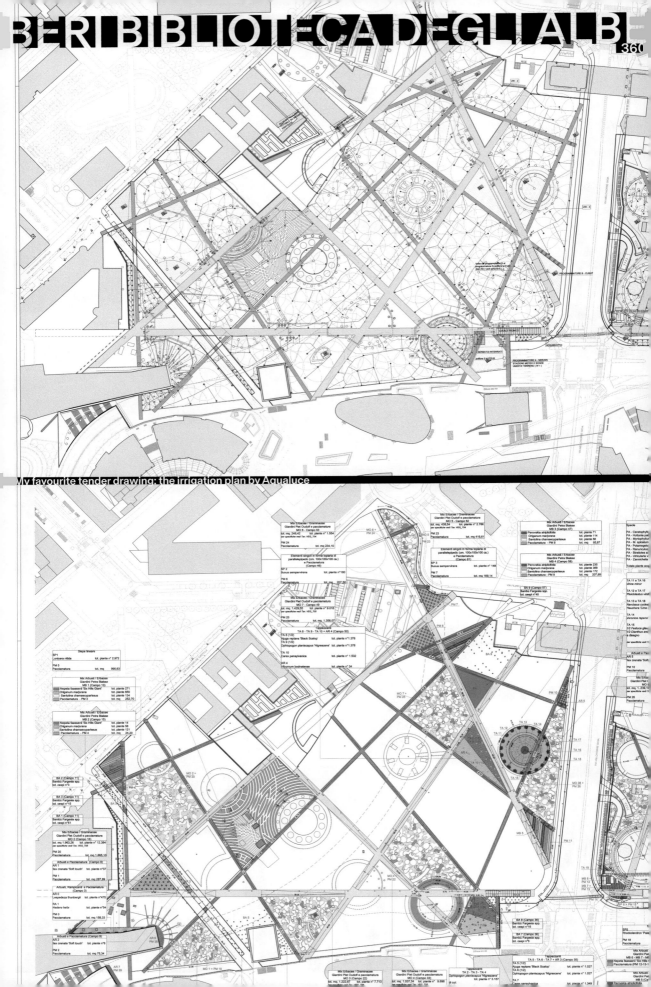

My favourite tender drawing: the irrigation plan by Aqualuce

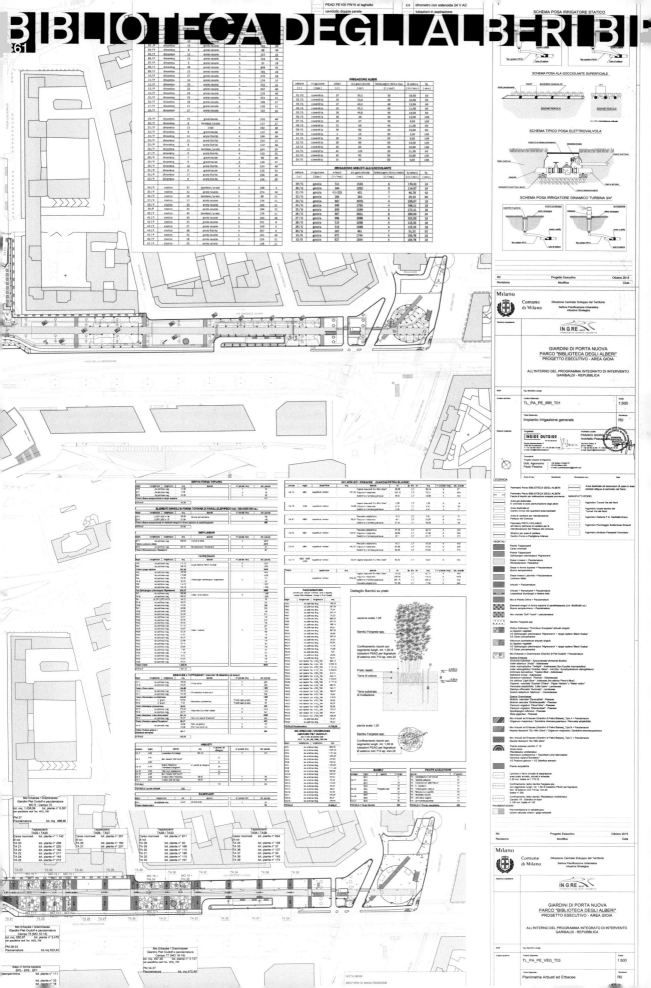

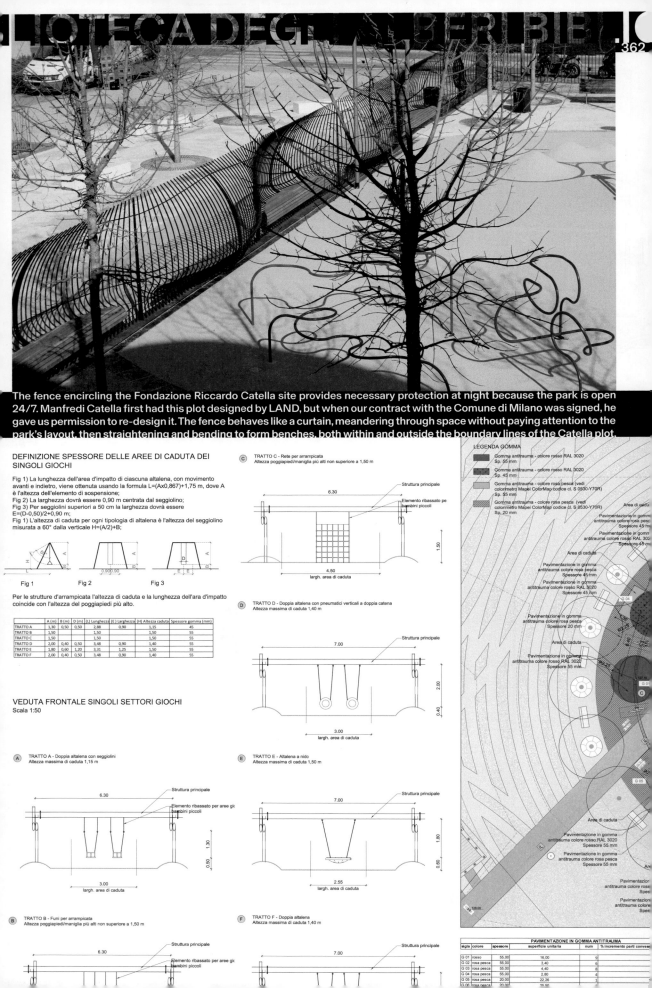

The fence encircling the Fondazione Riccardo Catella site provides necessary protection at night because the park is open 24/7. Manfredi Catella first had this plot designed by LAND, but when our contract with the Comune di Milano was signed, he gave us permission to re-design it. The fence behaves like a curtain, meandering through space without paying attention to the park's layout, then straightening and bending to form benches, both within and outside the boundary lines of the Catella plot.

DEFINIZIONE SPESSORE DELLE AREE DI CADUTA DEI SINGOLI GIOCHI

Fig 1) La lunghezza dell'area d'impatto di ciascuna altalena, con movimento avanti e indietro, viene ottenuta usando la formula L=(Ax0,867)+1,75 m, dove A è l'altezza dell'elemento di sospensione;
Fig 2) La larghezza dovrà essere 0,90 m centrata dal seggiolino;
Fig 3) Per seggiolini superiori a 50 cm la larghezza dovrà essere E=(D-0,50)/2+0,90 m;
Fig 1) L'altezza di caduta per ogni tipologia di altalena è l'altezza del seggiolino misurata a 60° dalla verticale H=(A/2)+B;

Fig 1   Fig 2   Fig 3

Per le strutture d'arrampicata l'altezza di caduta e la lunghezza dell'ara d'impatto coincide con l'altezza del poggiapiedi più alto.

	A (m)	B (m)	D (m)	(L) Lunghezza	(E) Larghezza	(H) Altezza caduta	Spessore gomma (mm)
TRATTO A	1,30	0,50	0,50	2,88	0,90	1,15	45
TRATTO B				1,50		1,50	55
TRATTO C				1,50		1,50	55
TRATTO D	2,00	0,40	0,50	3,48	0,90	1,40	55
TRATTO E	1,80	0,60	1,20	3,31	1,25	1,50	55
TRATTO F	2,00	0,40	0,50	3,48	0,90	1,40	55

VEDUTA FRONTALE SINGOLI SETTORI GIOCHI
Scala 1:50

(A) TRATTO A - Doppia altalena con seggiolini
Altezza massima di caduta 1,15 m

6.30
Struttura principale
Elemento ribassato per aree gi bambini piccoli
1.30
0.50
3.00
largh. area di caduta

(B) TRATTO B - Funi per arrampicata
Altezza poggiapiedi/maniglia più alti non superiore a 1,50 m

6.30
Struttura principale
Elemento ribassato per aree gi bambini piccoli

(C) TRATTO C - Rete per arrampicata
Altezza poggiapiedi/maniglia più alti non superiore a 1,50 m

6.30
Struttura principale
Elemento ribassato pe bambini piccoli
1.50
4.50
largh. area di caduta

(D) TRATTO D - Doppia altalena con pneumatici verticali a doppia catena
Altezza massima di caduta 1,40 m

7.00
Struttura principale
2.00
0.40
3.00
largh. area di caduta

(E) TRATTO E - Altalena a nido
Altezza massima di caduta 1,50 m

7.00
Struttura principale
1.80
0.60
2.55
largh. area di caduta

(F) TRATTO F - Doppia altalena
Altezza massima di caduta 1,40 m

7.00
Struttura principale

LEGENDA GOMMA

Gomma antitrauma - colore rosso RAL 3020 Sp. 55 mm

Gomma antitrauma - colore rosso RAL 3020 Sp. 45 mm

Gomma antitrauma - colore rosa pesca (vedi colorimetro Mapei ColorMap codice cl. S 0530-Y70R) Sp. 55 mm

Gomma antitrauma - colore rosa pesca (vedi colorimetro Mapei ColorMap codice cl. S 0530-Y70R) Sp. 20 mm

Area di cadu

Pavimentazione in gomm antitrauma colore rosa pesc Spessore 45 m
Pavimentazione in gomm antitrauma colore rosso RAL 302 Sp. 45 mm

Area di caduta

Pavimentazione in gomma antitrauma colore rosa pesca Spessore 45 mm
Pavimentazione in gomma antitrauma colore rosso RAL 3020 Spessore 45 mm

Pavimentazione in gomma antitrauma colore/rosa pesca Spessore 20 mm

Area di caduta

Pavimentazione in gomma antitrauma colore rosso RAL 3020 Spessore 55 mm

Area di caduta

Pavimentazione in gomma antitrauma colore rosso RAL 3020 Spessore 55 mm
Pavimentazione in gomma antitrauma colore rosa pesca Spessore 55 mm

Pavimentazione antitrauma colore ross
Pavimentazione antitrauma colore

		PAVIMENTAZIONE IN GOMMA ANTITRAUMA			
sigla	colore	spessore	superficie unitaria	num	% incremento parti conves
G 01	rosso	55,00	16,00	6	
G 02	rosa pesca	55,00	3,40	9	
G 03	rosa pesca	55,00	4,40	8	
G 04	rosa pesca	55,00	2,80	4	
G 05	rosa pesca	20,00	22,26	4	
G 06	rosa pesca	20,00	25,50		

Seventies colours for the children's playground, where all conditions were meticulously monitored to meet prescribed security regulations

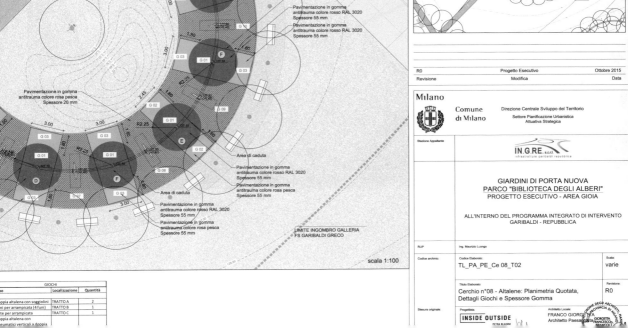

Scarico meteorico allacciamento a caditoia esistente

Fontanella tipo "Milano" (vedi TL_PA_PE_MAN_T02)

Pozzetto d'ispezione

Area di caduta

Pavimentazione in gomma antitrauma colore rosa pesca Spessore 55 mm

Pavimentazione in gomma antitrauma colore rosso RAL 3020 Spessore 55 mm

Area di caduta

Pavimentazione in gomma antitrauma colore rosa pesca Spessore 55 mm

Pavimentazione in gomma antitrauma colore rosso RAL 3020 Spessore 55 mm

Area di caduta

Pavimentazione in gomma antitrauma colore rosso RAL 3020 Spessore 55 mm

Pavimentazione in gomma antitrauma colore rosso RAL 3020 Spessore 55 mm

Pavimentazione in gomma antitrauma colore rosa pesca Spessore 20 mm

Pavimentazione in gomma antitrauma colore rosso RAL 3020 Spessore 55 mm

Pavimentazione in gomma antitrauma colore rosa pesca Spessore 55 mm

Area di caduta

Pavimentazione in gomma antitrauma colore rosso RAL 3020 Spessore 55 mm

Pavimentazione in gomma antitrauma colore rosa pesca Spessore 55 mm

LIMITE INGOMBRO GALLERIA FS GARIBALDI GRECO

scala 1:100

NOTA BENE 2 - Per strutture altalene vedi tavole TL_PA_PE_ST 06_T01-T02-T03-T04

CAROSELLO

R0	Progetto Esecutivo	Ottobre 2015
Revisione	Modifica	Data

Milano

Comune di Milano

Direzione Centrale Sviluppo del Territorio
Settore Pianificazione Urbanistica
Attuativa Strategica

Stazione Appaltante

IN.GRE s.c.r.l.
infrastrutture garibaldi repubblica

GIARDINI DI PORTA NUOVA
PARCO "BIBLIOTECA DEGLI ALBERI"
PROGETTO ESECUTIVO - AREA GIOIA

ALL'INTERNO DEL PROGRAMMA INTEGRATO DI INTERVENTO
GARIBALDI - REPUBBLICA

RUP: Ing. Maurizio Luongo

Codice archivio:	Scala:
	varie

Codice Elaborato:
TL_PA_PE_Ce 08_T02

Titolo Elaborato:
Cerchio n°08 - Altalene: Planimetria Quotata, Dettagli Giochi e Spessore Gomma

Revisione:
R0

Stesura originale

Progettista:
INSIDE OUTSIDE
PETRA BLAISSE

Architetto Locale:
FRANCO GIORGETTA
Architetto Paesaggista

GIOCHI		
Tipo	Localizzazione	Quantità
Doppia altalena con soggiolini	TRATTO A	2
Funi per arrampicata (4 funi)	TRATTO B	1
Rete per arrampicata	TRATTO C	1
Doppia altalena con pneumatici verticali a doppia		

The park in a number of conditions, seen from tower or drone: in the beginning, after the first year, covered in snow and during a public concert organised by Francesca Colombo, general and cultural director of the park

Betula urtilis 'Doorenbos

Jubilee in Gold
50 years gta Institute

"We discovered that the back side of the imitation leather looked like pale skin, more the skin colour of a very clean pig, so we liked being able to see that through the long slits that made the double-layered entrance curtain look like a sloppy, oversized dance dress. The second gold curtain was more restrained, more aesthetic and simpler – typically more to my liking, less ugly, therefore not so exciting, haha! The effect of both is beautiful when looking in from outside through the reflecting windows: they transmit a warm golden glow that melts into the autumn leaves of the trees. And the installation, consisting of organised rows of glass-covered table vitrines, reflected the gold curtains from unexpected angles. A daring engagement with the works on display!" PB

LOCATION   Zurich, Switzerland
CLIENT   Institute for the History and Theory of Architecture (gta), ETH Zurich
STATUS   Completed
SCOPE   Jubilee curtains for the exhibition
MATERIALS   Gold faux leather, steel rings, digital print
SCALE   2 curtains: 3.12 × 10.4 m
COLLABORATORS   gta Exhibitions
DESCRIPTION   For a festive exhibition celebrating the gta Institute's 50th anniversary, we designed two gold imitation leather curtains. The one at the entrance, functioning as division screen between entrance and exhibition, is printed with the words "50 years gta" and cut open vertically for a view into the exhibition. The other, covering the large window at the end of the show, is perforated and printed in a pattern that represents festive champagne bubbles.

One Line Workshop
Domaine de Boisbuchet

"Contrary to the expectations of the multinational group of interior architects and designers who attended our Boisbuchet summer workshop, we didn't introduce them to the art of curtain-making but went into the landscape to discover the estate's illogical path structure and decided to create a new, efficient path – ONE straight LINE that would connect everything despite all obstacles. They were delighted and felt better by the hour, the daily rains notwithstanding."

"Although it was summer when we gave the workshop at Domaine de Boisbuchet, the weather was mostly foul: it rained and rained. Of course, it smelled delicious, and the landscape with its castle, monumental trees, blooming meadows, mirroring lakes, horses and sheep in the mist looked cinematic – Hitchcock would have loved it. Due to the damp weather, salamanders found their way in the wet grass along the sandy paths in the early morning, their black and yellow colours standing out brightly. Our 'students,' inventive enthusiasts, made improvised raingear, covering themselves head to toe in black rubbish bags, changing into elegant-looking farm girls with hats, dresses and boots working the land, the whole picture brightened up by our colourful umbrellas. Fashion and countryside melted into one."   PB

"Designing a landscape on paper feels so easy when compared to physically creating one! This workshop turned out to be a test of the physical limitations of the body, about strength and energy, working long days during a wet French summer. All this to accomplish the goal which we all were passionate about: creating a perfectly straight path with an endless view to connect and open up the entire landscape. It was so liberating to step out of one's mind and focus on measuring, marking, rolling, mowing and clearing to create an outdoor line 830 metres in length!"   AM

LOCATION	Lessac, France
CLIENT	Alexander von Vegesack and Mathias Schwartz-Clauss,
STATUS	Completed
SCOPE	Week-long workshop on the French estate with 12 international interior architecture students of varied ages and levels of experience
MATERIALS	People, rope, rocks, meadow, forest, pigment powder and mowing machine
SCALE	Line: 830 m long × 2.8 m wide in an area of 150 ha
DESCRIPTION	After a guided tour of the property, we realised that it focused on small architectural jewels made by different famous architects but did not address the landscape itself. So, we undertook our own tour through the vast estate and walked through thick forests, swamps, prairies, meadows with horses, climbed over fences and … totally lost our way. Clearly, the estate needed a bit of "opening up" and an efficient, straight path to "unlock" the whole and interconnect the various landscape conditions! After studying satellite images and a physical model of the Boisbuchet estate, we discovered that a line running southeast – northwest, with the castle as central point, would do the trick. So we measured and marked out the line with body and rope – using the strength of 15 student and IO bodies and the help of the local farmhand to define and mow a straight path, in the end 2.3 metres wide and 830 metres long, enabling a new perception of the Domaine de Boisbuchet estate.

Substantial obstacles on the way were the forested blocks in between the hilly meadows, rivers and lakes. The forest's edges, straight and massive, were so densely filled with shrubbery and climbers that there was no way that you could pass through or even look in! We decided to cut a few openings into these vegetal walls. With the help of Paul, the neighbouring farmer, we created spacious windows, opening the view into the forest's endless rows of trees, their barren trunks rising like columns out of fresh green carpets of ferns and the whole area lit up by splashes of sunlight – a fairy tale uncovered.

Europa
Banco Popular Headquarters

"The strong black, white and gold graphics of this double-layered curtain design pleased the Ayala architects, not least because the abstract lines dictated by the Euro's diverse linear patterns proved to echo the abstract op art of the '70s. This struck a chord in the heart of architect Ayala Snr, a passionate lover of '70s abstract and kinetic art – like myself. It was also much appreciated by the client, the Banco Popular directors, as their former main office, housed in a beautiful '70s building and still functioning at the time, was decorated with an amazing collection of abstract, linear compositions, kinetic pieces and sculptures throughout. What a beautiful coincidence!"

"The buildings designed by the Ayala office are abstract compositions in themselves, with an endlessly layered, linear play of thin white steel structures inside and out. Our curtains blend in, merging and extending through the reflections in the glazed facades." PB

LOCATION	Madrid, Spain
CLIENT	Banco Popular, Inc.
STATUS	Completed
SCOPE	View-filtering and acoustic curtains with patterns based on € paper money and vertical, black-and-white, darkening screens for the main glazed auditorium
MATERIALS	Front screen mesh, Trevira CS voile, gold and silver faux leather, transparent plastic, lacquer foil; blackout cloth, white and black
SCALE	645 m², 68.42 × 9.42 m (double-layered)
COLLABORATORS	Arquitectos Ayala
DESCRIPTION	"Europa" became the theme for the enormous curtains that cover three of the four glazed facades of the bank's main auditorium. Black, white, silver, golden and yellow prints and appliquéd shapes, with cut-outs and slits together form the two-layered curtain of mesh and voile. The composition of abstract patterns and forms are graphic representations of patterns taken from euro bank notes. The two layers play with light and shadow and the gold additions reflect each ray of light. The separate blackout screens can be lowered from the ceiling on all four sides of the room. By having these vertical screens alternate between white and black, we completely changed the spatial experience of the auditorium.

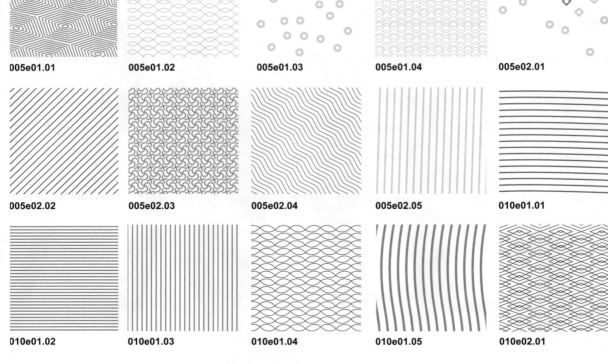

005e01.01   005e01.02   005e01.03   005e01.04   005e02.01

005e02.02   005e02.03   005e02.04   005e02.05   010e01.01

010e01.02   010e01.03   010e01.04   010e01.05   010e02.01

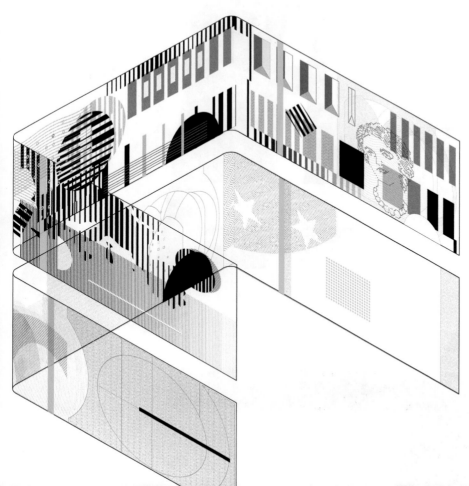

For the transparent auditorium of the Banco Popular building designed by Arquitectos Ayala of Madrid, we chose to analyse all euro bank notes to identify each pattern integrated into their design. Then we used these single patterns to create an abstract composition in which two layers interact with each other's shapes and openings, with the changing daylight and with the architectural structures visible through the glazed facades. To darken the space, alternating black and white screens roll down from the ceiling, creating a vertically striped room.

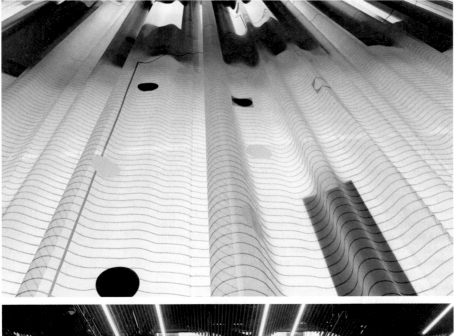

"The then director Olga Viso and curator/graphic designer Andrew Blauvelt started by introducing us to David Adjaye and Ai Wei Wei so that we could form a team to analyse and suggest improvements on the situation of the interior and exterior public routings (which, with the addition of the new building, were not considered convenient) and to think about the form and content of an additional entrance on the garden side. We met in our studio in Amsterdam, at Ai Wei-Wei's heavily guarded workshop in Beijing and at the Walker in Minneapolis a couple of times, and each of our threesome came up with suggestions that we discussed in depth with the museum. While these sessions were very inspiring, in the end Inside Outside was appointed to design the landscape in collaboration with local architects HGA and develop an integrated whole in which entry, parking and outdoor areas come together to form a coherent whole."

"Enthusiastically integrating the landscape and the architectural design for the new entrance, the HGA team helped us by calculating and solving all structural complexities below and above ground. First of all, Herzog & de Meuron's underground parking structure was not strong enough to support the large hill that we envisioned, which meant doing research to find alternative techniques. An exciting process followed, in which the mound was built up of 80% foam and 20% soil, with lightweight granulates mixed in. Secondly, they managed to relocate below-ground rooms along the edges of the building, so that we could recreate the soft green landscape around Barnes's brutalist brick volume that he himself had designed. And thirdly, the existing technical spaces underground were relocated to create accessible routes and easy pedestrian access over the hill – a difficult job. This is what you call constructive collaboration!" PB

LOCATION	Minneapolis, Minnesota, USA
CLIENT	Walker Art Center
STATUS	Completed
SCOPE	Landscape design, enhancing visibility of existing entrance on Hennepin Avenue and integrating new entrance wing on Vineland (HGA); Advisory on interior and exterior circulation
MATERIALS	Plantings, earth, black brushed concrete; foam (lightweight filling for hill)
SCALE	2.1 ha
COLLABORATORS	HGA/J. Sorrano, J. Cook, Olga Viso, Andrew Blauveld; Research phase: David Adjaye, Ai Wei Wei
DESCRIPTION	Michel Desvigne's proposal for the landscape of the Walker was made parallel to the development of the Herzog & de Meuron extension, but only part of it was realised: the treatment of the surrounding hardscape and one or two tree groupings along the top edge of the site. The rest of the ground sluggishly sloped down to one side, covering the newly built parking lot below. The residential buildings that surround the Walker site are not particularly attractive, and the adjacent sculpture park didn't feel connected to the Walker garden because an extremely wide road cuts through the site. Around the Barnes building, wide tiled steps form a hard edge that covers the below-ground rooms, which Barnes himself designed in a later stage to accommodate the need for additional space.

The most urgent issues, according to us, were softening up the edges around the Barnes building and reshaping the sloping field into an attractive mound. The latter would improve the perspective in all directions, while also screening off the surrounding buildings. In addition, we proposed opening up the museum towards the garden by adding a door for direct public access to the garden. Spread strategically over the hill, a series of rectangular tree "rooms" and green or flowering "carpets" mimic the galleries of the Barnes building. An irregular, zigzagging path connects street to hill and the "vegetal rooms" to each other. Each room has its own purpose: restaurant terrace, performance space, classroom, garden, entrance to James Turrell's installation. The essential role that the Walker prescribed for the hill is that of outdoor auditorium for the annual concerts attended by thousands of enthusiasts! So, the placement of the tree groupings had to be carefully considered.

TOPOGRAPHY   PATHS   TREES

TOOLS

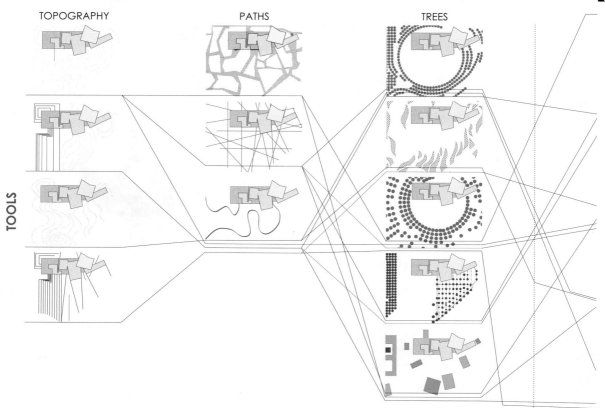

For the Walker garden we developed a multiple-choice system; the client could choose the tools they found most appropriate for their programed garden, in which educational art sessions and public concerts were to take place on a regular basis

COMBINATIONS

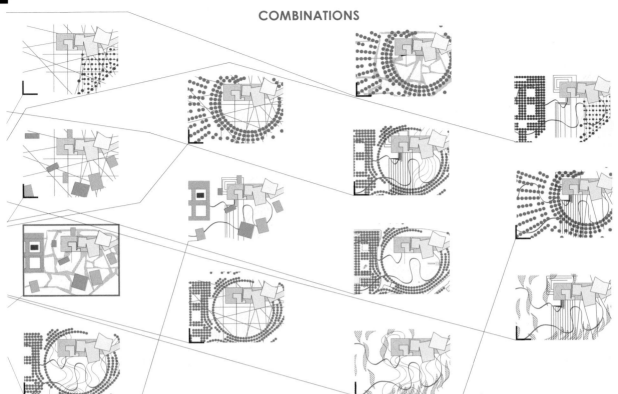

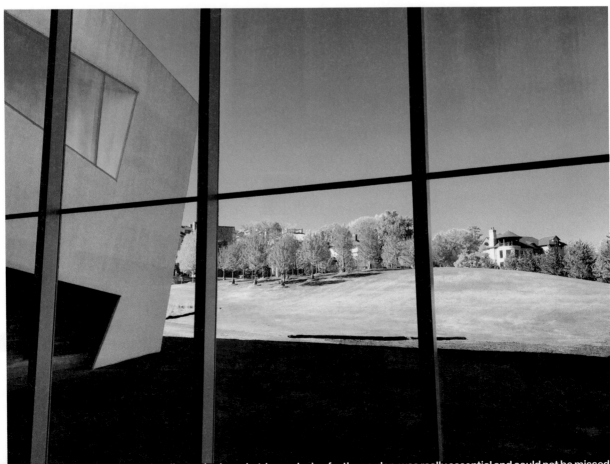

In an urgent budget meeting, the client asked us what, in our design for the garden, was really essential and could not be missed. Our response: the hill. The hill is the main intervention, the tool that creates perspective, that causes a garden to climb and descend, that offers different views, that functions as an auditorium during concerts and as wind protection for the terrace.

Multi-stem birch trees encircle and announce the parking entrance

James Turrell's installation lies embedded in a rectangular carpet of high grasses through which a path zigzags up and down. In the foreground: one of the garden's sunken air exhausts is hidden in the centre of a biodiverse (indeed!) flowering carpet.

The new entrance and restaurant addition by HGA, with terrace, path, stairs and *Gleditsia triacanthos* "Sunburst" trees in winter. On top of the roof, a viewing terrace with a floor by Sol LeWitt; the museum owns an impressive collection of his work.

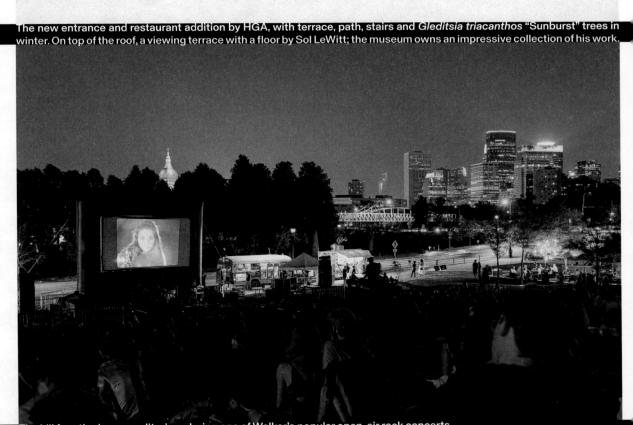

The hill functioning as auditorium during one of Walker's popular open-air rock concerts

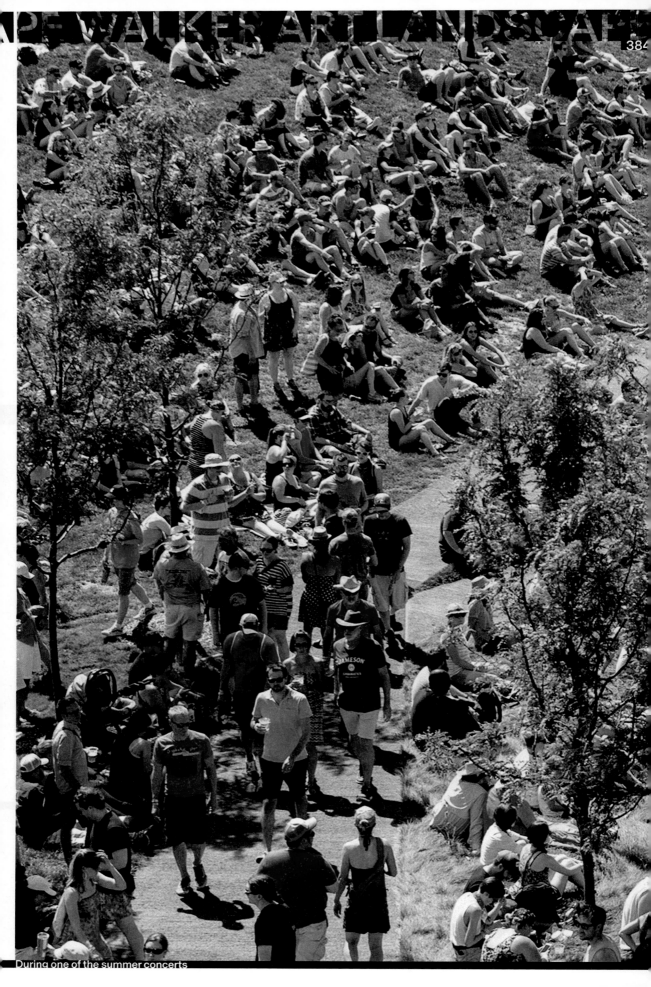

During one of the summer concerts

Roeterseiland Campus
University of Amsterdam

"Connecting and opening up every area on site, the white 'ribbon' doesn't need to be used as a path but can be followed as a seductive wayfinder: along its curves and loops, one finds the entrances and exits of the various faculties while experiencing the landscape as a trajectory of changing spatial sensations. From the main entrance square along historic facades and stepped water edges, over blooming meadows and through crowded terraces, into the most silent and hidden, scented courtyards." PB

"As is almost customary at Inside Outside, the hand of the person that draws the concept and actual plan of landscape designs – in this case our colleague Céline, who drew the ribbon of Roeterseiland – is translated into reality almost literally. In some places one can even identify the 'imperfections' of the sketched curves, which were kept deliberately – aiming for artistic 'coincidence' and avoiding perfection at all costs." JC

"We make hundreds of concept sketches for a project, searching for the right language, the essence of the given site and its future forms of use. Here, we wanted to unify the typical campus situation, where many buildings of different generations and architects are placed quite chaotically on a piece of land, closed off from the outer world, with very diverse and not particularly inviting outdoor spaces. As in our prison garden's path of the late 1990s, we found that an intuitively meandering line dancing through the whole site and, in this project, not ignoring logic and boundaries but rather emphasising them, would not only give the university a distinctive 'handwriting,' but would also energise the campus by playfully guiding people through every aspect of the site – and all in one movement." PB

"The winding ribbon can be seen as a metaphor for the phases students go through during their studies: rather than being a direct line from A to B, the path of their formation will take them along detours and loops through various gardens, fostering their objectives, influencing the course of their studies and lives and opening up new opportunities." JC

"Do you know the 'flirting bridge'? It is the bridge that crosses the main canal and connects the two peninsulas of the campus, forming the most direct internal connection between faculties. In our attempt to create a maximum amount of outdoor seating for the students to meet – and flirt – we equipped both sides of this bridge with linear benches, which you can not only sit on, but that also serve to prevent casual bike parking against the bridge's balustrades. The result is a prime place to relax and enjoy the beautiful folks passing by in the summer sun." JC

LOCATION	Amsterdam, the Netherlands
CLIENT	UvA Universiteit van Amsterdam
STATUS	Completed
SCOPE	Design of all public spaces and inner courtyards
SCALE	Landscape, 2.2 ha; total surface, 4.5 ha
COLLABORATORS	Arcadis, AHMM Architects
DESCRIPTION	The UVA campus site lies along our city's canals. For our project, we removed the grey 30 × 30 concrete tiled surface and instead worked with the principal ingredients that have been used for centuries for the streets that line Amsterdam's canals. The new finishes include the famous rows of elm trees lining the water's edge, the warm red-brick paving and the natural, blue-grey stone street margins. The exceptions in our design lie in the modern streetlamps and in the way the typical white zebra brick is used as a device to draw a romantically meandering ribbon that guides students, teachers and visitors through the campus and from one exit or entrance to the next, creating playful garden areas and intimate patio gardens on the way. At key moments, the path seems to rise to become a wooden bench or table that hovers above the white ribbon or that is aligned with a pedestrian bridge. These seating elements are spread over the campus inviting students to be outside, to study and meet in the fresh air. Where the ribbon crosses green fields, we replaced the white brick with white flowering perennials and bulbs. Seen from above, the white ribbon creates coherence with its intriguing, connective pattern. Today, the campus is open to the general public and functions as a park to be enjoyed by residents from the neighbourhood.

With our design, we remodelled the topography and logistics of the entire site to reduce traffic, to improve pedestrian flow and general connections, to insert water storage systems, to open up and soften the edges along the various canals and to create inviting garden and seating areas for outdoor study and meetings. We re-organised car and bicycle parking, trash storage and garbage collection systems.

Here we used normal materials in an abnormal way. While white brick usually represents crossings or parking areas, here we use it to form a decorative element: a continuous, meandering ribbon that ties the university campus together, that leads the way to entrances and exits of the various buildings, forming flowerbeds and seating areas along the way.

"When starting on this project we had no idea that this picturesque Tuscan town had one of the biggest Chinese communities in Europe. Textile workers from Wenzhou had immigrated to this centre of the Italian textile industry in large numbers to work in and later take over the small companies of the city, leading it to be called Italy's 'Little China'. Wenzhou, the origin of most of the Chinese immigrants, is famous for its plant-based indigo textile dye." JC

"The strength of Prato's textile industry comes from the collective collaboration of many small enterprises that produce the textiles together. Like the artisans from Prato and other parts of Italy, immigrants have the potential to contribute to – and to guarantee the continuation of – ancient local traditions; in this case the production of textiles. Yet in practice, the different populations work and live in their own cultural bubble. Imagine if these different cultures within Prato could inspire each other and learn from each other's heritage! This is what we set out to achieve with our design: a park that could produce ingredients for the creation of textiles and therefore become a platform for cultural exchange. Alas, we were not selected for the job and made way for our respected colleague Michel Desvigne." PB

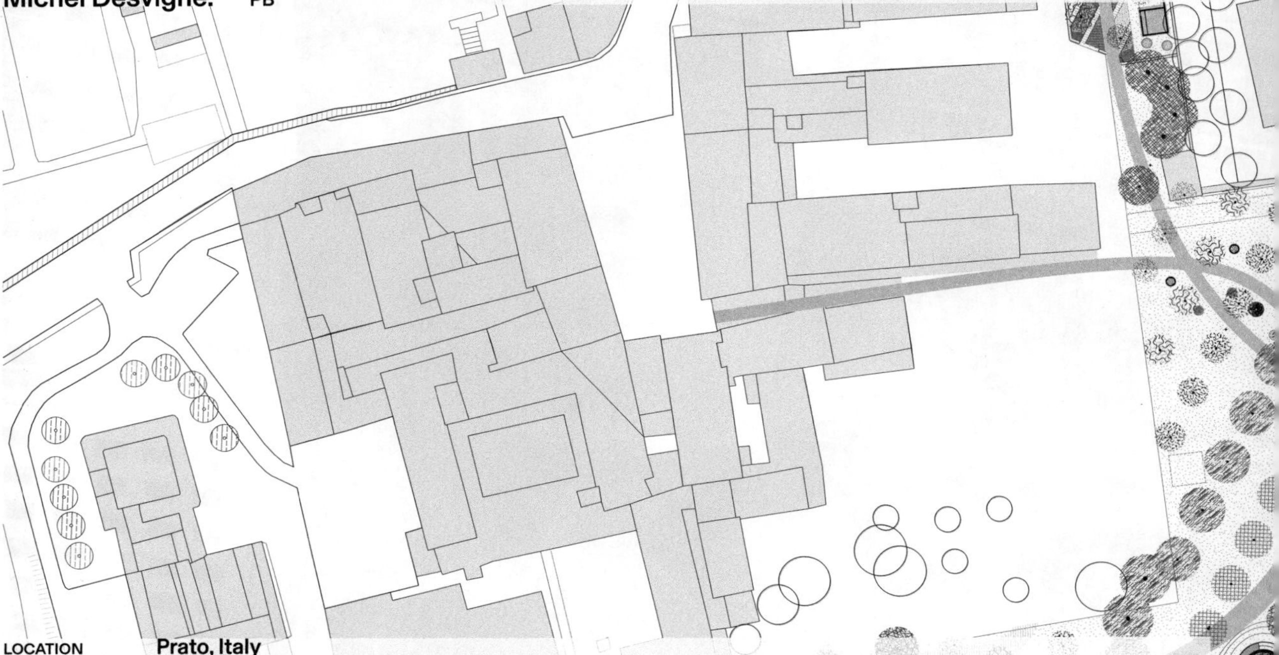

LOCATION	Prato, Italy
CLIENT	Municipality of Prato
SCOPE	Landscape design for a new park in the heart of the old city
SCALE	3.3 ha
COLLABORATORS	Alvisi Kirimoto Architects
DESCRIPTION	The team created a productive landscape, inviting the mixed community (mainly Italian and Chinese) of this textile-producing town to meet and collaborate, and stimulating visitors to learn about the basic ingredients for the production of yarn and pigments. Each new tree or plant and every animal introduced to the new park is related to textile-making in some way. These ingredients can be explained and studied but also used and exchanged during workshops, at markets and in classes that will take place in the park, inside the new pavilions and in spaces around town.

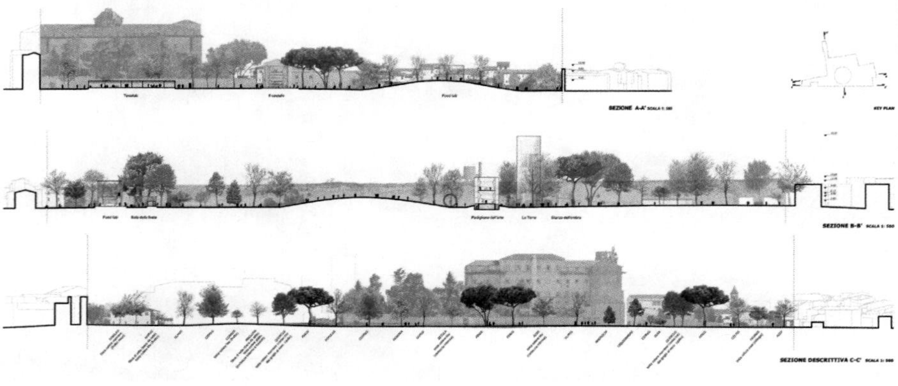

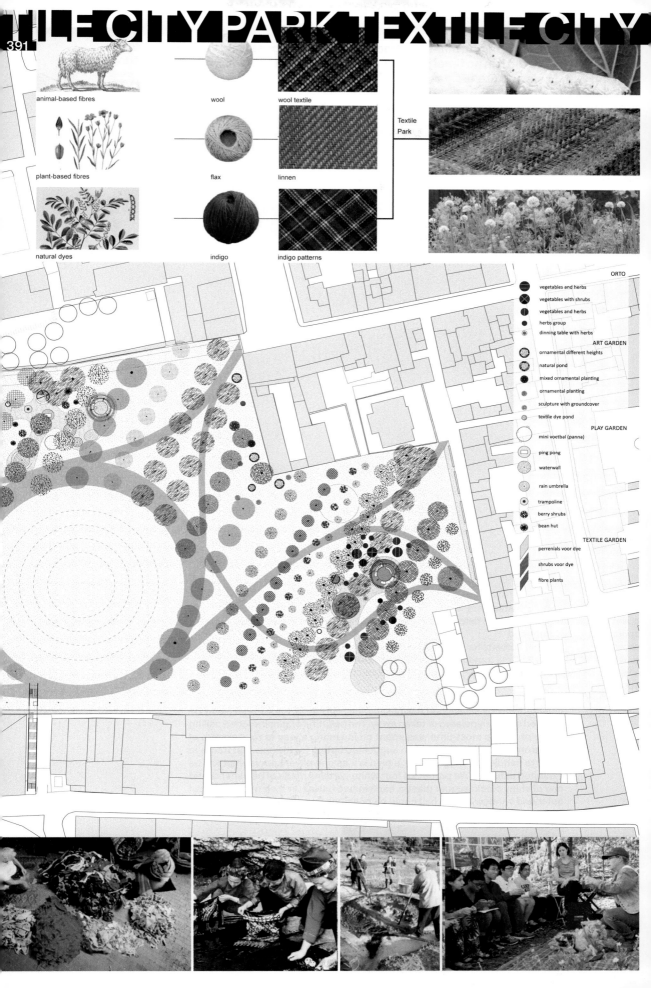

animal-based fibres

wool

wool textile

plant-based fibres

flax

linnen

natural dyes

indigo

indigo patterns

Textile
Park

ORTO
- vegetables and herbs
- vegetables with shrubs
- vegetables and herbs
- herbs group
- dinning table with herbs

ART GARDEN
- ornamental different heights
- natural pond
- mixed ornamental planting
- ornamental planting
- sculpture with groundcover
- textile dye pond

PLAY GARDEN
- mini voetbal (panna)
- ping pong
- waterwall
- rain umbrella
- trampoline
- berry shrubs
- bean hut

TEXTILE GARDEN
- perrenials voor dye
- shrubs voor dye
- fibre plants

"With just a couple of straight, muscular tracks, a few white sheets and some kinky black lacquer plastic, we did it in no time! Hahaha, everything needs to be quick and clear when working with Niels and Fredi!"   PB

LOCATION	Zurich, Switzerland
CLIENT	Institute for the History and Theory of Architecture (gta), ETH Zurich
STATUS	Completed
SCOPE	Flexible screens for gta Exhibitions gallery space
MATERIALS	White cotton, transparent plastic, black lacquer foil
SCALE	3.13 × 18.86 m; 3.13 × 21.72 m; 3.13 × 21.98 m; 3.13 × 26.14 m; 3.13 × 11.77 m
COLLABORATORS	gta Exhibitions
DESCRIPTION	To organise the large exhibition space into smaller galleries, curators Niels Olsen and Fredi Fischli envisioned flexible screens – curtains – that could easily be handled and manipulated or taken away. The beautiful original wooden ceiling is sculptural, so most time was spent on inventing a way to fix a system of tracks onto it. We succeeded and suggested opting for the heaviest tracks in order to handle the weight of large pieces – as one never knows what will be exhibited in future. We produced four white curtains made of bed sheets and one of shiny black lacquer plastic, each in two halves. In their middle, we cut out round windows. Each half could be positioned at will since they matched in size (more or less). With their free pleating, widths could be easily adjusted.

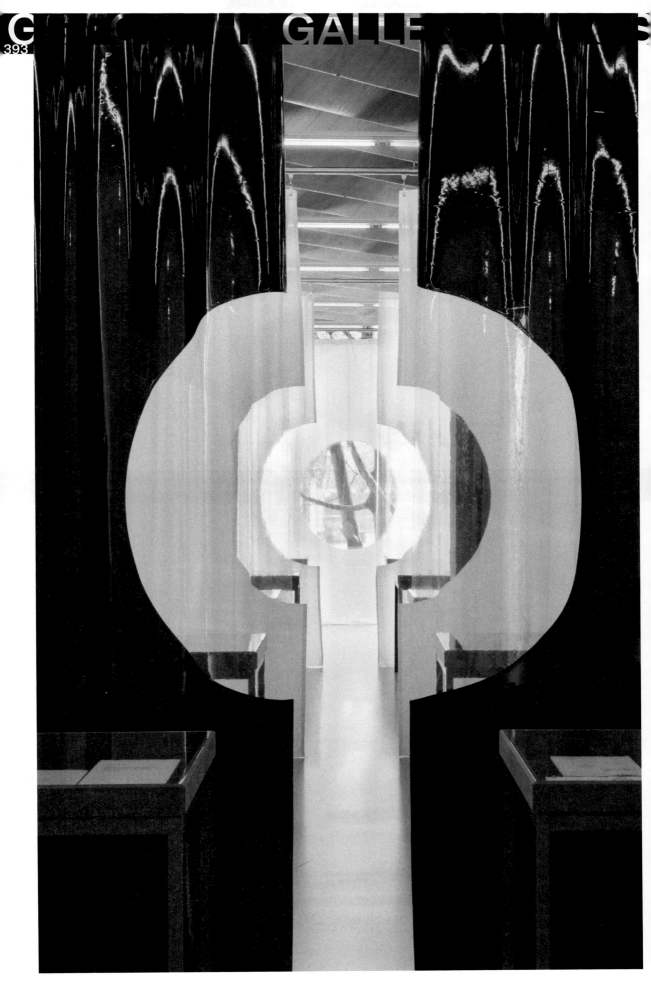

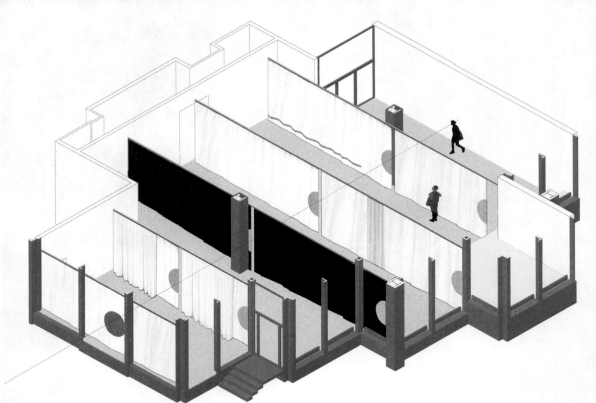

The gta/ETH called us out of the blue and asked if we could create flexible divisions for their (beautiful, '70s) gallery space (with an amazing, sculptural wooden ceiling) so that they could create smaller rooms if needed. Low budget, little time. Interested? Of course!

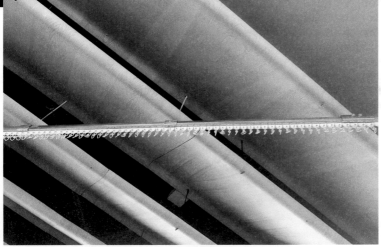

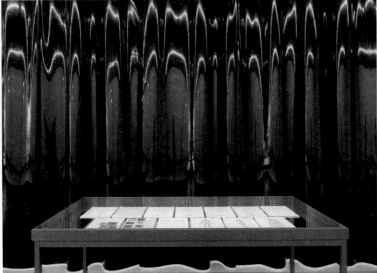

At first we thought: simple white cotton sheets, that'll do the trick. You can draw on them, wash them, tear them to pieces – doesn't matter. Then the unavoidable happened; the designer in us started to draw details – ugh! – like round windows and plissé areas. And THEN we thought: let's add some kinky stuff too, after all, we're in Switzerland. So, along came a shiny black lacquer version – looking like a waterfall of crude oil.

"We joined OMA on this competition too, because one cannot turn down the chance to work on such a challenge – an area that one has visited on so many occasions through the years, to enjoy the fantastic architecture of Sharun and Mies and other buildings in the area. Each one is a work of art, not only as an architectural object but as a visual, auditive, spatial and physical experience both inside and out. Created at different times, they transmit an incredible aura, so an architect who has been offered a building site right in their midst has a task that carries a lot of weight. OMA developed a sculptural, 'collage' building in four parts, with each of the sections reacting to the architecture facing it. The result was an intricate pyramid of art that has never been seen before (not an entirely objective comment). We participated, anticipated, integrated and connected – museum to gallery to church to historic buildings to concert hall to library to existing public spaces and streets, as well as implementing entrance and patio gardens within the OMA structure." PB

LOCATION	Berlin, Germany
CLIENT	Stiftung Preussischer Kulturbesitz
STATUS	Competition, 2nd prize; honorable mention
SCOPE	Landscape design for the new museum's surrounding, streetscape and plazas, its roof and inner gardens
SCALE	ca. 1 ha
COLLABORATORS	OMA
DESCRIPTION	The placement of the new museum building along Potsdamer Strasse, between Mies van der Rohe's impressive Nationalgalerie on one side and Sharun's amazing Berlin Philharmonie on the other, creates a long, enclosed, rectangular plaza onto which the main entrance of the museum opens up. St Matthäus Kirche at the south-western end of the square faces the Grosse Tiergarten park straight ahead. Along the west side, the square is flanked by the Kunstbibliothek and the Kunstgewerbe Museum between which a generous slope leads from the square to the Gemaldegalerie on top of the hill. Square and slope are considered as one in our landscape design, and the treatment of paving and green are continuous. Plantings enter the museum, shading a terrace, animating a patio, forming an exaggeratedly "formal" garden on one of the roof terraces.

Pierre Paulin
Centre Pompidou

"The invitation for us to install a curtain in the already designed retrospective exhibition of Pierre Paulin's furniture and designs came from the Centre Pompidou itself. Pleased, we jumped in, worked frantically on scale models, technical systems and material samples, and then presented our ideas. They were appreciated at first sight and approved. We were about to get the official OK when the museum discovered that their budget was insufficient for our intervention. Luckily, we were 'rescued' by a private friend of the museum willing to sponsor our work. The curtain, 77 m in length, is now in the museum's collection, and sections of it are used for other Pompidou exhibitions when suitable. After the festive opening, where our entire team was present, the widow of Paulin, Maia, thanked us wholeheartedly for our addition to the exhibition. She felt that the curtain complemented her husband's work and enhanced the exhibit's time-line concept. A great compliment." PB

LOCATION	Paris, France
CLIENT	Centre Pompidou
STATUS	Completed
SCOPE	A timeline and backdrop curtain for the retrospective exhibition *Pierre Paulin*
MATERIALS	Front screen mesh, silver faux leather, lacquer foil, transparent plastic
SCALE	77 × 3.6 m
DESCRIPTION	The exhibition covered Paulin's work from the '50s to the '90s, presenting about 70 pieces of furniture and 50 drawings in chronological order in the museum's Gallery 3. We were asked to add curtains to the linearly arranged installation drawn by the museum's exhibition designer. We produced one continuous curtain that meanders through the room as a backdrop for the exhibited works, cutting through the podiums onto which the objects were placed. By treating one translucent material in different ways, continuously changing its profile, the curtain communicated the era of the object's realisation and logically led the visitor through the exhibition space. Its translucency added depth to the installation, as light and street life shimmered through in one direction, and objects from another era were vaguely visible on the other – predicting the future. Cut-outs and windows created unexpected views onto adjacent objects and spaces and out into the city. Where documentary films on the designer's life and oeuvre were shown, the curtains became massive and opaque, darkening the space in question on one side, reflecting daylight on the other.

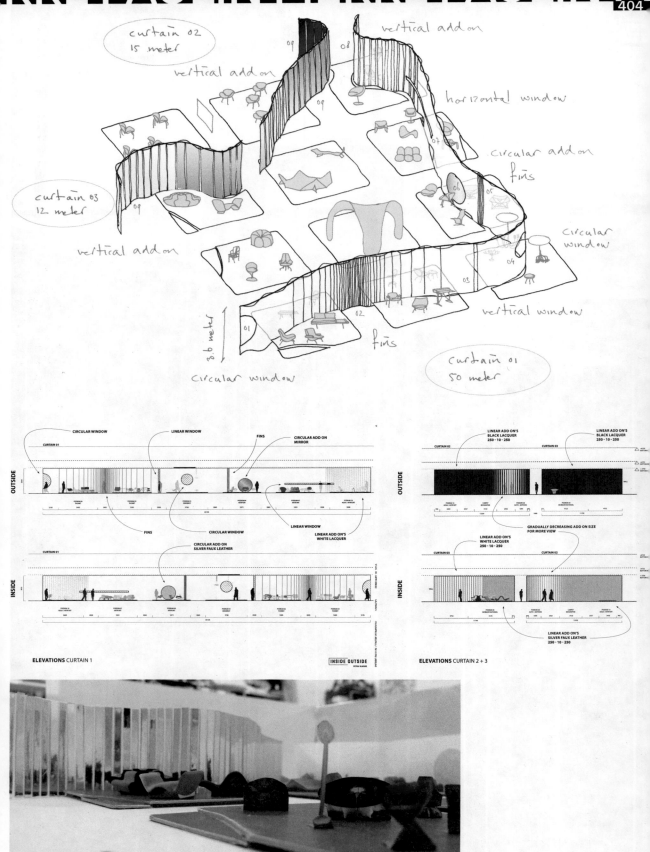

curtain 02
15 meter

vertical addon

vertical addon

horizontal window

circular addon
fins

curtain 03
12 meter

vertical addon

circular window

vertical window

0.6 meter

circular window

fins

curtain 01
50 meter

ELEVATIONS CURTAIN 1

INSIDE OUTSIDE

ELEVATIONS CURTAIN 2 + 3

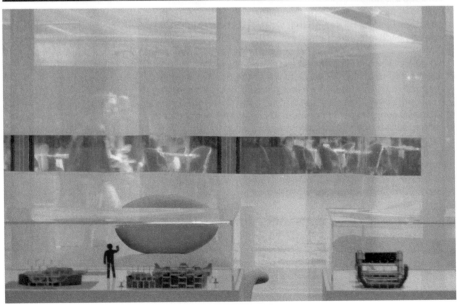

Two Family Tales and Heritage Gardens
Qatar National Library

"We made at least six designs for the shaded Heritage Garden that had no plants – models with torn paper, lumps of cane sugar, sand, transparent foils or wood scraps, depending on the typology (water film, sand dunes, travertine boulders, travertine screens) – fewer for the stone-covered main garden itself – and at least six designs for the curtains, represented as scale drawings and prints on paper, cotton and woven tests to scale, each with a different theme and materiality. Choices were finally made after very critical and well-informed meetings with the representatives of the client in the air-conditioned building shacks on site."

"To work in that climate is a challenge for a Northern European person. It can be 45–50 degrees Celsius outside and on the building site it often seems even hotter. Regulations require sturdy boots, helmets and orange or yellow dayglo vests. You also need to take socks with you if you borrow boots from others, and you tend to wear slippers or sandals on your way to the site. Of course, legs and arms need to be covered, as well as your hair. Scaffolding that you need to climb is boiling hot, so gloves are no luxury. Builders' heads are wrapped in cloth, eyes covered with sunglasses. So, you are surrounded by beautifully dressed, colourful, friendly zombies who carry heavy building materials over narrow platforms, construct intricate structures or manage the temporary elevators – sitting on the most amazing self-made chair – and show you the way through a pile of structures that will, eventually, form the building. Signs inform you about regulations and risks; graffiti and stickers tell you about the builders' emotions and jokes. Views out over the sand-coloured city are tremendous. Pieces of coloured plastic flutter in the hot wind, inspiring future curtains." PB

LOCATION	Education City, Doha, Qatar
CLIENT	Qatar Foundation
STATUS	Completed
SCOPE	Landscape design for the surrounding garden, patios and heritage garden
MATERIALS	Agaves and acacias, limestone, travertine slabs and leftover pieces, gold mosaic, white concrete furniture, lighting
SCALE	Total area 4.3 ha, gardens 2.3 ha
COLLABORATORS	OMA, Sergio Roland, Solid Nature
DESCRIPTION	The surrounding limestone landscape design that we developed exhibits two xerophytic plant families, each species planted inside its own circular cavity: acacia and agave. The concave plant areas protect the plants against the predominant winds and collect the night's dew and the sparse rainwater. We had difficulty convincing the maintenance crew not to water the plants, as especially the agave family suffers a great deal from too much moisture. One of the roof's overhanging corners covers a pedestrian bridge to the Heritage Library entrance. Under that roof, a sunken space for a shaded landscape was created where we composed a meditative stone garden with rows of upstanding travertine slabs, their top edges broken off to form mountain-like profiles. This "mountain landscape" looks like a stage-set, the cut-out mountain shapes rising from a carpet of broken travertine particles. This "puzzle" of broken pieces is made of recycled travertine leftovers from the interior of the Heritage Library. No irrigation required in both gardens.

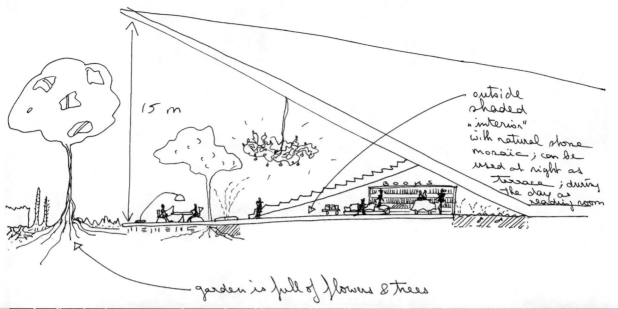

outside shaded "interior" with natural stone mosaic; can be used at night as terrace; during the day as reading room

15 m

BOOKS

garden is full of flowers & trees

One of my first sketches to communicate to the architects our blurred landscape/interior boundary intention

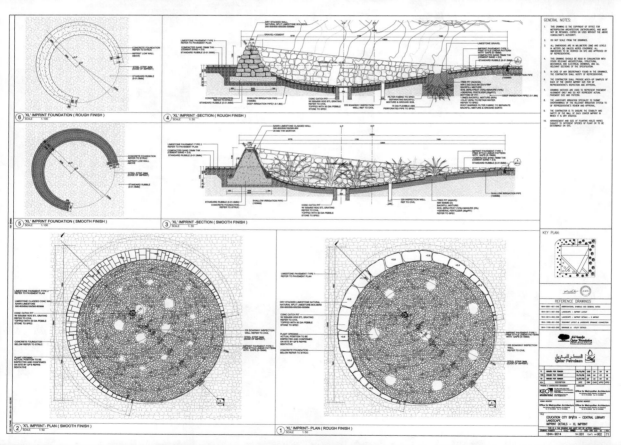

Construction drawing of the limestone "craters" that form the garden structure around the Qatar National Library

the selection of agave plants and acacia trees – the two families that will inhabit the "craters" of the library's garden

The 1:1 (full scale) off-site test made of the typical planting situation, with integrated lamps, plant holes and plants

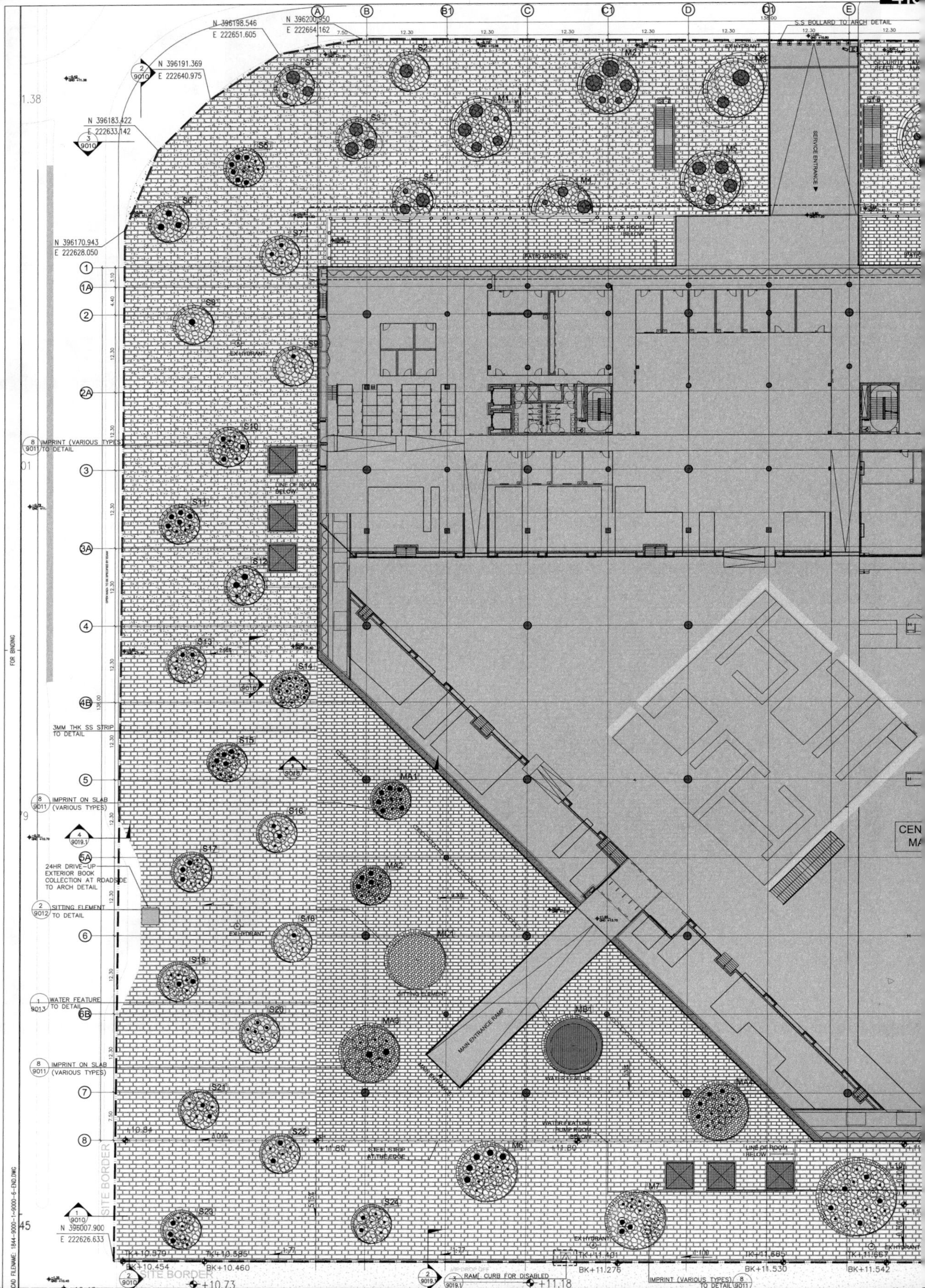

Technical drawing of garden, including lines for the visually impaired, security fences, water drains, etc. The drawing also shows the trucking bay (at the top), two entrance bridges (bottom left and right) both shaded by the lifted corners of the building, the Heritage Garden (bottom right corner) and the two sunken patio gardens (top edge along building).

OPEN WADI- TO BE SPECIFIED BY EDAW

N 396199.616
E 222827.000

SITE BORDER

IMPRINT (VARIOUS TYPES) 8
TO DETAIL 9011

PATIO GARDEN TO DETAIL 1 9015

DRAIN PIT TO DETAIL 4 9000

IMPRINT (VARIOUS TYPES) 8
TO DETAIL 9011

PAVEMENT TO SPEC 1 9000.3

MESH OPENING TO DETAIL

FINISHES AS PER NEIGHBORING LOT

3MM THK SS STRIP AT THE
EDGE OF PAVEMENT TO DTL

IMPRINT PLANTING TO SPEC 1 9000.4

HERITAGE ENTRANCE GARDEN 1
TO DETAIL 9016

DRAIN PIT TO DETAIL 4 9000

IMPRINT VARIOUS SIZES 8
TO DETAIL 9011

IMPRINT (VARIOUS TYPES) 8
TO DETAIL 9011

PAVEMENT 1
TO SPECIFICATION 9000.3

HERITAGE ENTRANCE GARDEN

HERITAGE COLLECTION ENTRANCE RAMP

SITE BORDER

ONE OF ROOM BELOW

GENERAL NOTES:

1. THIS DRAWING IS THE COPYRIGHT OF OFFICE FOR METROPOLITAN ARCHITECTURE (NETHERLANDS), AND MUST NOT BE RETAINED, COPIED OR USED WITHOUT THE ABOVE CONSULTANT'S AUTHORITY.

2. DO NOT SCALE FROM THE DRAWINGS.

3. ALL DIMENSIONS ARE IN MILLIMETERS (MM) AND LEVELS IN METERS (M) UNLESS NOTED OTHERWISE. ALL DIMENSIONS TO BE VERIFIED ON SITE AND APPROVED BY QF REPRESENTATIVE.

4. THIS DRAWING SHOULD BE READ IN CONJUNCTION WITH OTHER RELEVANT ARCHITECTURAL, STRUCTURAL, MECHANICAL AND ELECTRICAL DRAWINGS, AND ALL RELEVANT SECTIONS OF THE SPECIFICATION.

5. IN CASE OF ANY DISCREPANCY FOUND IN THE DRAWINGS, THE CONTRACTOR SHALL NOTIFY QF REPRESENTATIVE.

6. THE CONTRACTOR SHALL PROVIDE MOCK-UP SAMPLES OF EACH OF THE CRATER IMPRINT SIZE FOR QF REPRESENTATIVE'S INSPECTION AND APPROVAL.

7. DRAWING HATCHES ARE USED TO REPRESENT PAVEMENT ALIGNMENT ONLY AND DO NOT REPRESENT ACTUAL PAVEMENT SIZE AND PATTERN.

8. THE LANDSCAPE IRRIGATION SPECIALIST TO SUBMIT SHOPDRAWINGS OF THE RELEVANT IRRIGATION SYSTEM TO QF REPRESENTATIVE'S REVIEW AND APPROVAL.

9. THE CONTRACTOR IS TO ENSURE THE STABILITY AND SAFETY OF THE WALL OF EACH CRATER IMPRINT IN WHICH IT IS DRY STACKED.

10. ARRANGEMENT AND SIZE OF PLANTING HOLES VARIES SUBJECT TO DIFFERENT SPECIES OF PLANT OR TO BE DETERMINED ON SITE.

LEGEND:

IMPRINT LOW WALL TO DTL
IMPRINT LABEL
IMPRINT (VARIOUS TYPES)

EXTERNAL HYDRANT

ACACIA

AGAVE

FLOOR LAYING SETTING OUT POINT

SITE BOUNDARY

KEY PLAN:

HATCHED AREA:
LANDSCAPE'S SCOPE OF WORK

(MAIN BUILDING WORK)
(BY OTHERS)

OMA

REFERENCE DRAWINGS

| 1844–0001–001–END | ABBREVIATIONS, SYMBOLS AND GENERAL NOTES |
| 1844–0051–001–002 | GROUND LEVEL SITE PLAN |

Qatar Foundation

Qatar Petroleum

T1	ISSUED FOR TENDER	06/12/08	CAD	LH	CY	V
T00	ISSUED FOR TENDER	15/10/08	CAD	LH	CY	V
T0	ISSUED FOR TENDER	12/07/08	HP	LH	CY	V
REV.	DESCRIPTION	DATE	DWN	CHKD	APPD	AP

PROGRAM & CONSTRUCTION MANAGEMENT
KEO

CONSULTANT
Office for Metropolitan Architectu

DESIGN ARCHITECT
Office for Metropolitan Architecture

EXECUTIVE ARCHITECT
Office for Metropolitan Architectu

TITLE
EDUCATION CITY BP#7A – CENTRAL LIBRARY
LANDSCAPE
KEY PLAN

THIS IS A CAD DRAWING AND MUST NOT BE ALTERED MANUALLY

| DRAWING NUMBER: | SCALE 1:250 | ORIG. DWG SIZE: A0 | R |

1844–9000

N

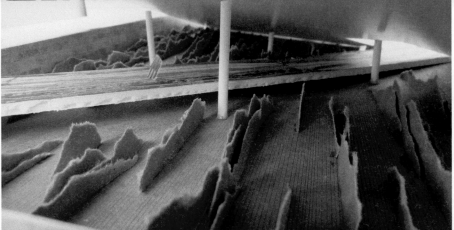

We made a couple of versions for the Heritage Garden, a sunken, shaded area underneath a sloping pedestrian bridge that leads to the underground level entrance of the Heritage Library, where historical manuscripts and documents are preserved and exhibited. No water allowed, of course! So, we proposed travertine landscapes, first a scale model composition of square boulders that we visualised with lumps of cane sugar; and the second of a "mountain range" of travertine plates, as shown here, first visualised with torn brown paper.

Lines of LED light align one side of the travertine slabs for a night-time effect

We used small left-over particles of travertine to cover the floor. It looks like a dried-out clay landscape with mountains rising from it. In its entirety, I think it looks like a Japanese stage set, but here it changes all the time, depending on natural conditions.

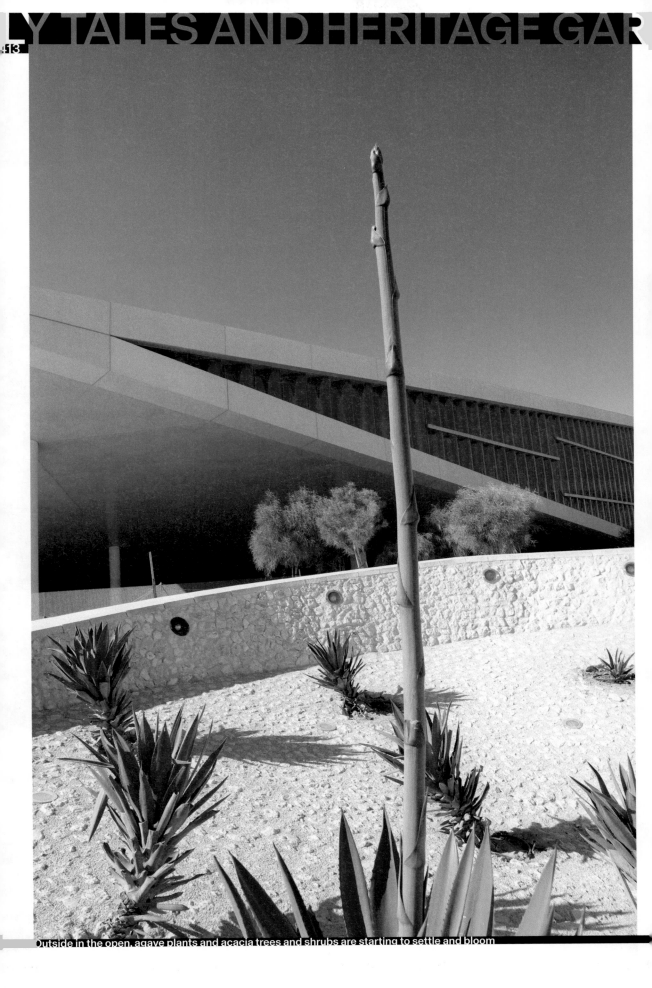

Outside in the open, agave plants and acacia trees and shrubs are starting to settle and bloom

Cosmic Curtain
Qatar National Library

"When you work in different cultures, you meet women. Women on the building site, women as colleagues, women as clients, local women at the market or on the street. There is always a particular click, brief eye contact, an eyebrow raised, a smile, a gesture. In Doha, I got a lift from a beautifully manicured woman wearing a djellaba, who had just returned from a medical conference, where she had been one of the speakers. She was driving a large four-wheel drive, and she was about to drop off an American colleague – also a woman – at her hotel. She happened to see me looking for a taxi, late one night. She stopped to say that such a phenomenon doesn't exist in Qatar, and if she could give me a ride? I first sat in the back listening to the two women commenting on their conference. Once she dropped off her colleague, she invited me to join her in the front. We chatted a bit about where I come from, what brought me to Doha, etc, and then she said: "We feel very sorry for you western women: you have to work SO hard. You take care of your children, your house, your husband plus a job, and you hardly ever have help! No wonder only a few women reach the top… it seems impossible! We, here, are lucky: we have assistance in abundance and live with the family. We can study here or abroad, go places, build a career and a family at the same time. But poor you." PB

LOCATION	Education City, Doha, Qatar
CLIENT	Qatar Foundation
STATUS	Completed
SCOPE	Art commission for a monumental curtain that creates a deployable auditorium in the main hall
MATERIALS	Viscose raffia (tree bark), silk, flame proof impregnated
SCALE	700 m², 100 × 4.9–6.4 m
COLLABORATORS	OMA, J&C Joel, TextielLab Tilburg, Arup
DESCRIPTION	For this art commission, we made a large curtain that creates an auditorium in the huge, open volume of the white and reflective interior of the library building. It is woven with a triple Jacquard technique (creating different inside and outside colour surfaces thanks to hidden yarns) with – in vertical direction – a slippery viscose yarn that allows the cloth to adjust to its diagonal versus horizontal positions. With a gradient from black to blue on the inside and a constant silver-white surface on the outside, the curtain forms an intimate room and is a perfect match for the sparkling white library space outside. The design refers to the starry desert skies (here in linear formation), enlivened by enlarged drawings of different astrolabes from the collection of the Museum of Islamic Art in Doha. (Astrolabe means "the one that catches the heavenly bodies" – an elaborate inclinometer, historically used by astronomers and navigators to measure the inclined position in the sky of a celestial body, day or night. Invented by the Greek astronomer Hipparchus, 190–125 BC.)

ACCE ←

This collage is appealing – a stark juxtaposition of sturdy construction site versus elegant outcome. This difference between rough and elegant would disappear eventually, as the interior of the library became extremely refined, and the curtain became an integral part of its aesthetic. But this moment is so nice.

CESS →

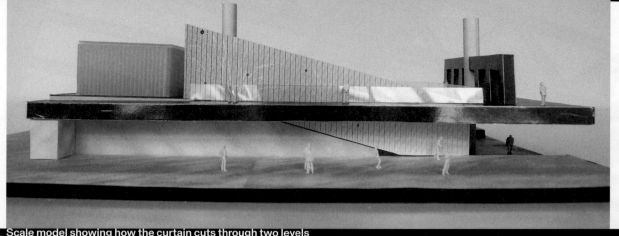

Scale model showing how the curtain cuts through two levels

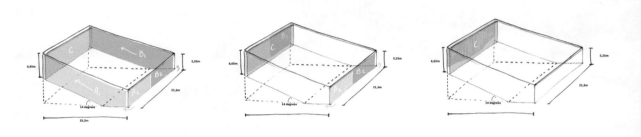

Drawing showing the different positions of the curtain

Because of the vertical weave of smooth raffia – made of tree bark – the cloth can adjust to its straight or sloping position

Because both the track and the floor are sloping, the curtain is definitely NOT a straight piece of cloth

Because of the three-layered jacquard weaving technique, the curtain has a very different colour on each side. Outside, it is silver and white with black decorations. Inside, it is blue-turning-to-black with silver and white decorations.

Water Recipe Garden
Qatar Foundation Headquarters

"It was so interesting for us to be introduced to the local desert planting communities of the Qatari desert, to drive into the sandy, hilly and sometimes rocky landscape and discover the influence of the fluid topography that changes with the wind, the different ways plants catch and store moisture in the overbearing heat, the effect of salination of the groundwater (due to desalination of seawater for human use), the positive effect of animal manure, the damage caused by animal fouling and the many different plant combinations fostered these physical conditions. It was equally interesting to meet Qatari agronomists, botanists and ecologists, to read their publications, to visit the university's botanic collection, to meet with local gardeners and to collaborate with representatives of the large American landscape firm AECON (whom we previously knew as EDAW), which designed the overall landscape masterplan for Education City and the separate entity within it, Oxygen Park. It is good that we all try to work in a sustainable manner by using a minimum of water and introducing indigenous plants (what that means is still debated: "those native to the specified locale; growing in that region for a considerable amount of time (longer than the plants that have merely naturalised in the region)." Yet we dare to state that we did this differently from the general concept for the area. For our QFHQ roof garden, we implemented a systematic exhibit of plant communities with an experimental 'combing out' rhythm to study the effect of collaboration between their root and soil life systems, and an equally experimental watering system – a gradation from ample to none. A garden that is meant to be an active laboratory for local universities, botanists, ecologists and pedologists, to measure the response of the plant communities, singular plants and the composed soil on the given, man-made, contained circumstances." PB

LOCATION	Education City, Doha, Qatar
CLIENT	Qatar Foundation
STATUS	Completed
SCOPE	Experimental, ecological, semi-public garden on concrete plate above parking lot; street furniture and lighting plan; design of darkening curtains for the building's two auditoriums
MATERIALS	Perforated projection screen with mother-of-pearl coating, custom-dyed orange netting, light-blue Trevira CS voile, indigenous plantings, rocks, travertine, lighting, furniture
SCALE	3.8 ha
COLLABORATORS	OMA, Dr. Ekhlas M. M. Abdel Bari, Prof. Dr. Kamal Batanouny
DESCRIPTION	We referenced the Qatar Foundation Headquarters' square volume with its irregular rhythm of openings by introducing a grid of planters that fold out of a travertine surface. Its intense, warm colour covers the concrete roof-plate of the open parking garage underneath. The two buildings sink through this plate into the parking space below, where their shaded and protected main entrances are placed next to the drop-off area.

The grid of planters is organised from large to small and from high to low, each one exhibiting a specific plant community of the Qatari desert. Starting as complete communities in the largest planters, they are thinned out as planters get smaller – experimenting with the effects of progressively less "collaboration" between the different root systems. Using a gradual irrigation system, planters "evolve" from lush green to dry and rocky. Spread throughout this system of desert planting compositions, we inserted planters filled with foreign trees, perennials and succulents that can tolerate the heat but that have a more sculptural or colourful appearance throughout the year.

A planter is taken out at regular intervals to create an opening of the same size, allowing trees to grow through the surface from the garage below and reveal their crowns with their fragrant white blossoms to the public in the gardens above. Some planters fold down to become staircases, creating direct access to and from the garage. Both types of openings create a welcome air flow to cool the parking lot and entrance areas. In between the planters and scattered throughout, "street trees" grow directly out of the travertine floor, providing more shade for visitors. Air exhaust and intake for the parking garage below, trash cans, lighting, irrigation and drainage systems are all integrated in the planters. Two planters are transformed into security booths, welcoming guests at the two entrances. Along the outward-looking edges, the travertine-plated flooring slopes upward to a height of 120 cm, forming a dike-like protection edge around the lifted garden and eliminating the need for guardrails.

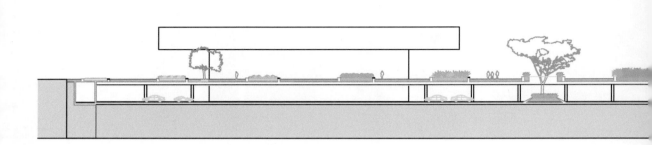

Section drawing of roof garden on top of parking garage showing the gradation of irrigation from more (right) to none (left) and the tree planted underneath at parking level, its crown sticking through an opening at the garden level

ENDEMIC PLANTS, SHRUBS, TREES, GRASS, BULBS & SUCCULENTS IN COMPOSED GROUPINGS ARE WATERED TO DIFFERENT DEGREE IN RICH TO ARID SOIL TO STUDY PLANT BEHAVIOUR

My first sketch showing the essence of the design intent

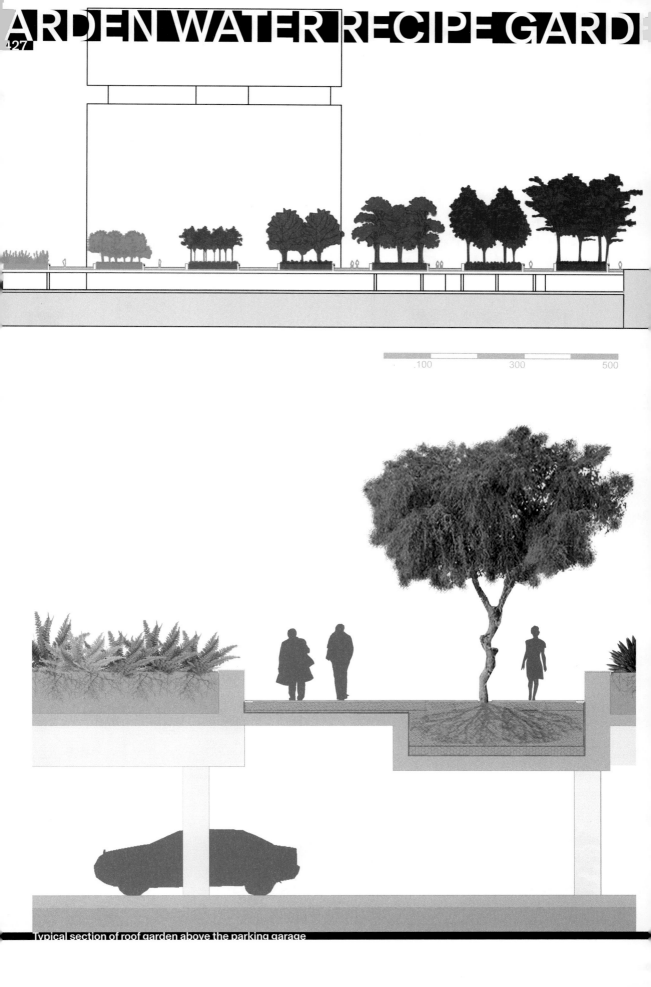

.100   300   500

Typical section of roof garden above the parking garage

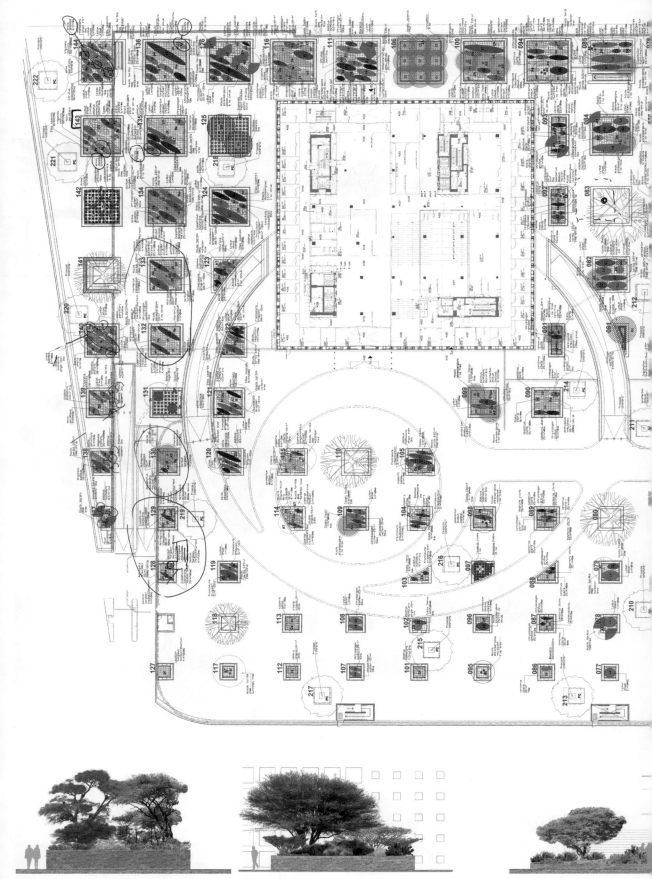

LEVEL-1. OVERALL PLANTING PLAN
(SCALE 1:400)

1

As always, our work refers and reacts to the architectural context, to the users' demands, to the local climate, to regional tastes and to the ambitions of the community. The foundation disseminates information about Qatar's (natural) history, its talents and its (hidden) treasures, and thus the garden is a showcase of the Qatari desert's various plant communities – albeit in an urban setting and in the form of research. Our aim is to have the botany and ecology departments of local universities adopt and tend our garden while also using it as a base for soil, plant, insect and bird research.

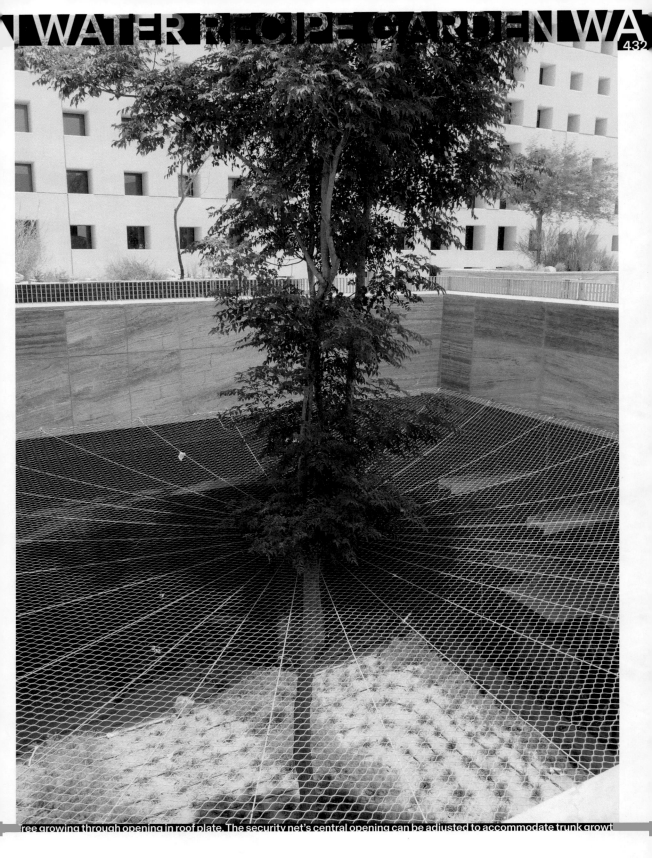

ree growing through opening in roof plate. The security net's central opening can be adjusted to accommodate trunk growt

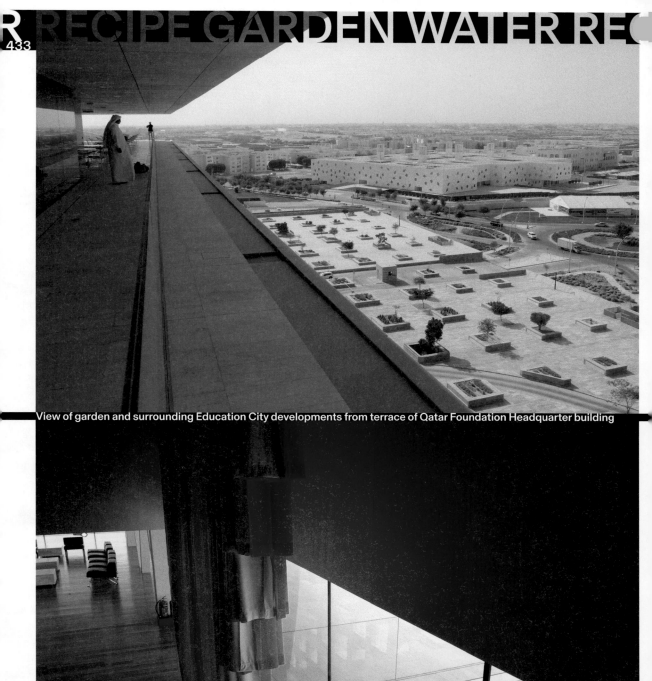

View of garden and surrounding Education City developments from terrace of Qatar Foundation Headquarter building

Inside the Qatar Foundation Headquarter building, our curtains for one of the auditoriums with a white interior and dayglow orange exterior

Night view of Qatar Foundation Strategic Studies Center's roof garden. This is the hour that temperatures drop, and visitors and families with children start to go outside to walk the city streets and visit gardens, playgrounds and beaches.

This is the office of Sheikha Moza, director of the foundation, which contains several reception areas and meeting rooms as well as a private bathroom. We were asked to select all finishing materials for the interior facade, walls, ceilings and floors. OMA chose the furniture. To the left, you see the special box we made with all the finishing samples. We put a beautifully designed lid on it, then wrapped it and shipped it to Sheikha Moza's personal staff.

2013–2015   **Solar Curtain Research**

"One of the main challenges of the research was how to integrate the available (affordable) monocrystalline silicon plates and conductive copper wire into a translucent, knitted fabric. We found a composite copper yarn that ensured flexibility. Before being slid in staggered position into the incorporated sachets of the fabric, the solar cells are placed on lightweight pyramids to maintain their optimal angle to the sun. The positive and negative conductive yarns, not interfering with one another, come together at specific points where they transmit the energy to a battery. We calculated that the curtain, covering the textile museum's facade, would generate enough energy for a knitting or weaving machine to run for a whole year. In 2016 a new prototype, based on the previous research, was developed."   PB

2002   **Mobile HIV Clinic**

"I formed a team with a medical doctor and two architects, and we formulated and illustrated our concept and created a prototype. Triangular loose parts of a sturdy, UV tolerant, water- and windproof material, with zippers along the sides, would be covered with regularly spaced round solar cells, connected by energy-transporting copper yarns – positive and negative. These met at the extreme tip of the triangle to transfer the absorbed energy to the devices to be charged: a small fridge to store medicines, a kettle to sterilise instruments. The other side of the cloth was to be printed with information on hygiene to prevent contamination, under which numerous small bags of packaged condoms were lined up. This mobile HIV clinic could be easily dismantled and divided into small units to be transported elsewhere on foot, horseback or camel, by bicycle, motorcycle or car. The essence was that these units could spread over large distances like the HIV virus itself. No trucks or elaborate transport required. The units could then be reactivated and reconnected to form sheets as large as necessary and in any shape. We sent our invention to the organisation in a modest cardboard tube – and never heard back."   PB

LOCATION	Case study sites: Textile Museum, Tilburg (northern European climate) and Qatar National Library, Doha (desert climate)
CLIENT	TextielMuseum, Tilburg
STATUS	Commissioned research
SCOPE	"Develop a test of something you have wanted to test for a long time…"
SCALE	Varied
COLLABORATORS	TextielLab Tilburg, Solar Fiber, Eindhoven University of Technology
DESCRIPTION	Our team, with Carmen Buitenhuis and Peter Niessen, collaborated with the Textile Lab in Tilburg, the Eindhoven University of Technology and Solar Fibre, to do research on an outdoor, solar-energy-absorbing shading curtain. We chose two theoretical locations: a glass facade in a northern European climate and one in the Middle East for a desert climate.
LOCATION	Sub-Saharan countries
CLIENT	Architecture for Humanity, San Francisco
STATUS	International competition
SCOPE	Design for a Mobile HIV clinic for the Sub-Saharan countries
SCALE	Multiple units of each 1.2 × 2.4 m
COLLABORATORS	Irene Curulli, Rebecca Gomperts
DESCRIPTION	We entered an open competition, organised in the United States, for a "Mobile HIV Clinic for the Sub-Saharan countries." It seemed urgent to do something in support of the AIDS pandemic that affected us all so much, and logical for us at IO to develop an idea that involves fabric as an exceptionally flexible, foldable, rollable and lightweight material. Textiles can be shaped into numerous forms fulfilling multiple functions; they can easily be transported anywhere and attached to any given structure at any time in any climate; they can be deployed as a shading device, wind screen and protective, enveloping layer; they can transmit information through "decoration" (logos, illustrations, narratives). Variations on curtains in the form of tents, sheets, carpets and clothes are and always have been indispensable for us humans through the ages.

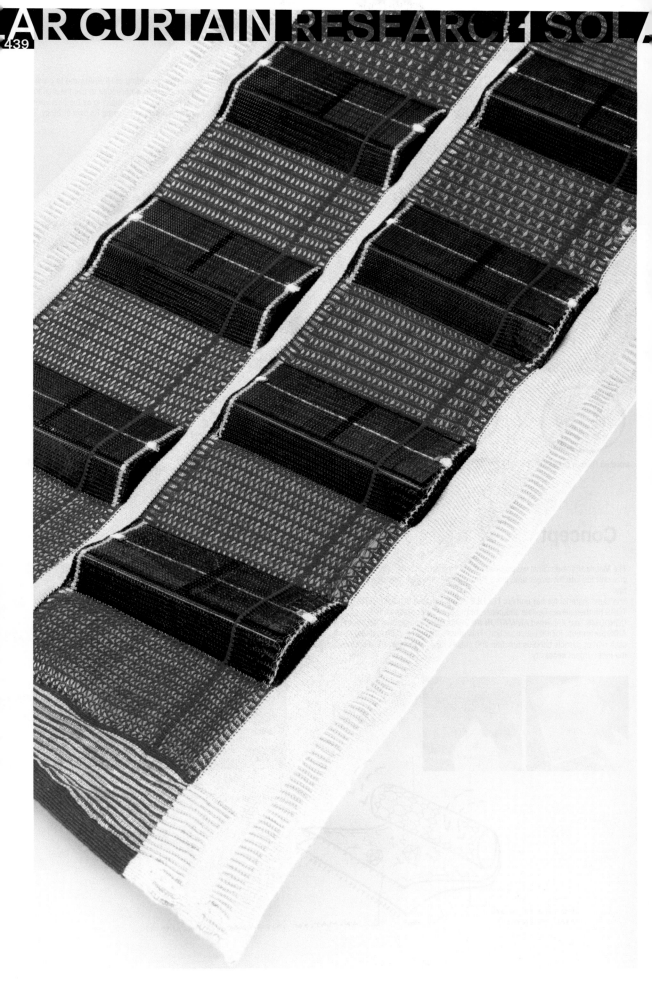

HIV - MA mature form

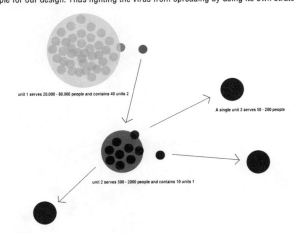

The mobile HIV clinic is a tool to prevent the spreading of HIV/Aids and to provide treatment to those already infected. For our mobile unit we propose to use the characteristics of the virus: its system of dismantling, copying and multiplying as the basic principle for our design. Thus fighting the virus from spreading by using its own strategy.

unit 1 serves 20,000 - 80,000 people and contains 40 units 2

A single unit 3 serves 50 - 200 people

unit 2 serves 500 - 2000 people and contains 10 units 1

The HIV virus is the leading cause of death in sub-saharan Africa. It spreads through blood, sperm, vaginal discharge and breast milk

Once the virus enters the human body it invades CD 4 cells. In the CD 4 cell the Viral RNA (genetic material) is transformed into DNA (genetic material is nucleus of cell) and then built into the DNA of the human cell's nucleus. Here the viral RNA is multiplied and copied and released again.

Infected Human CD 4 Cell

Multiplying of HIV viral RNA in CD 4 cell nucleus

Releasing daughter HIV virus

Daughter HIV virus in: Sperm, Blood, Mother-milk

Infecting new human CD 4 Cell

Concept

The Mobile HIV/Aids clinic we propose here consists of 3 units, whereby each smaller size unit fits into the larger unit, like a Russian doll; although here in multiple quantity.

The basic material for our units is TEXTILE with integrated SOLAR ENERGY COLLECTORS (in themselves flexible and paper thin); sown-on pockets for male- and female CONDOMS, and imprinted ANIMATION INFORMATION, images that tell about HIV and AIDS prevention, identification, action. This means that even in dismantled form, each unit or particle beholds function and attains its aim: the spread of information as the most urgent necessity.

SUN COLLECTOR

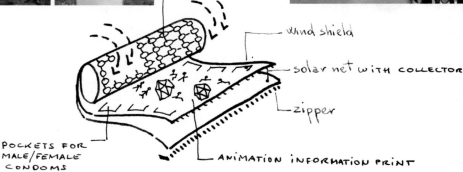

wind shield

solar net with collector

zipper

POCKETS FOR MALE/FEMALE CONDOMS

ANIMATION INFORMATION PRINT

Unit Network

Unit 1 :

Concept: Through distributing the smaller units 2 (the daughter units)Unit 1 functions as the [infe]cted human CD 4 cells (the mother unit) that produce daughter HIV particles .

[T]he main unit that holds and transports all other units is the container. It travels from a given [p]oint in Europe or the United States to a sub-saharan country, where it is placed in a context [th]at has a basic form of infrastructure. The unit in itself, once emptied of it's 40 smaller units [th]at each contain 10 even smaller units) can, by unfolding it, be transformed into an open [w]orkspace, information and training centre and laboratory. Unit 1 will organise the transport of [un]it 2's to their own destinations support the work done in the 40 units 2. In its basic form the [co]ntainer measures 12 x 2.5 x 2.50 meter. It can extend its volume with the 'survival blankets' [th]at can act as roofs or walls. Because these blankets are imprinted with the HIV 'logo' and [st]ory-telling animation figures, they communicate the function and purpose of the initiative to [th]e passer-by in a very direct manner. The unit generates its own energy with a second textile [sh]eet: the solar cell blanket. Armed with materials, tools and only a few staff members, Unit 1 [ca]n serve a population of 20.000 to 80.000 people.

[F]unctions of the mother unit :

- [In]formation, education, training (health workers for unit 2 and local shamans for unit 3), [di]agnostics, treatment, storage (medicines, tools etc.), research.

[E]quipment connected to this unit:
- Small laboratory to do the Western Blott test (final HIV test) and CD 4 count (to establish the [ef]fect of the treatment provided in unit 2)
- Space for training, educating the health workers of unit 3 and 2
- Storage space for packages of unit 2, HIV medicines, condoms, other
- Computer for research purposes
- Solar electricity blankets that can be zippered onto or used separately from:
- Information blankets with printed-on education about HIV/Aids and condoms in sewn-on [po]ckets.
- Watercooker and water storage cans, light, refrigerator etc.

[H]uman resources:
[1] or 2 laboratory specialists, 1 midlevel health provider, 1 special trainer to educate the health [w]orkers that will work with unit 2, and 1 researcher to analyze the data. Back up support from [a] local medical doctor.

Distances + Transp. means

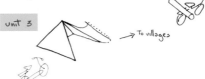

Unit 3

To villages

25 Km

Unit 2

50 Km

Unit 1

Unit 2:

Concept: Unit 2 functions like the daughter HIV particles after being released by the CD 4 cells.

This is a box-like unit that fits onto or into a jeep or medium sized car. This aluminum and textile subunit contains information- and medical tools, solar electricity blankets, a fold-up bicycle & 10 smaller units for distribution. In this unit, people can get a HIV fast test with a blood drop from finger tip or sputum. When the HIV fast test is positive, extra blood will be sent to the laboratory at Unit 1 for the final HIV test, the Western Blott. If this test is positive, medication will be transported back to unit 2 where the patient will receive the treatment. To follow the effect of the treatment, blood is drawn in unit 2 and then transported to Unit 1 for a CD4 count. To prevent transmission of the HIV virus, condoms and milkpowder with boiled water (mother-child transmission) are distributed.

Each unit 2 will serve 500 to 2000 people. Unit 2 will distribute 10 packages of unit 3 (that is slightly smaller than unit 2) to local medicine man or heads of the villages.

Function: Provision of information, diagnostics, treatment, distribution and coordination of 10 unit 3's.

Equipment:
- HIV fast tests
- Bloodtubes, needles, needle-containers
- Small fridge, water cooker, light, etc.
- Bicycle (foldable). To transport blood samples to and medicines from unit 1. To transport Units 3 to destination
- Solar electricity blankets for the unit itself, with zippered-on or separately used.
- Survival blankets with information animation about HIV/Aids and sewn-on pockets that contain condoms and milkpowder
- 10 packages of unit 3 that will be distributed to the local population

Human resources:
1 trained health workers, with local assistance.

Multiplying 1x40 x10= 400 units 3

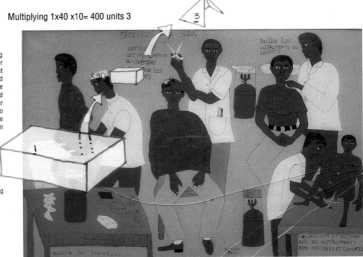

Unit 3 :

Concept: Unit 3 functions like the primary HIV virus that infects a human for the first time.

It is a rolled-up package of 4 double-layered triangular sun-collecting and information-spreading textile sheets (each double layer connected onto each other by zippers) that can be seperately or together used as tent, roof, blanket, dress, hat, belt, bed, base, shelter (sticks added). To prevent HIV transmission, the most basic tools are information, education and condoms. Cartoons and texts about HIV/Aids transmission and prevention are printed on the survival blanket. With the water cooker and light attached to the solar energy blanket, the generated electricity can be used for basic hygiene such as clean water that is needed to diminish the chance of other (opportunistic) infections. Condoms (for men and women alike) and milkpowder can be used to prevent the further spreading of the HIV virus and new infections. The condoms function like the viral envelope. The solar electricity and survival blanket function like the viral RNA. Each unit can serve 50 to 200 people

Function:
- Information, shelter, assistance, prevention.

Equipment:
- Solar electricity blankets, zipped onto - or separate from:
- Survival blankets with animation information about HIV/Aids and sewn-on pockets containing condoms and milkpowder.
- Water cooker, light, -etc

Human resources:
- local village heads, medicine man/women or inhabitants.

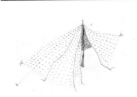

Even in dismantled form, each unit or particle beholds function and attains it's aim: the spread of information as the most urgent necessity.

"When we didn't win first prize – much to our surprise ;-) – my colleague (now partner) Jana Crepon and I went to see the jury members in Antwerp to understand what made them choose another, definitely more conservative, design. The answer was clear enough: our project was too radical."   PB

LOCATION	Zuiderdokken, Antwerp, Belgium
CLIENT	Municipality of Antwerp
STATUS	Competition, 2nd prize
SCOPE	Design flexible, multipurpose public park in the historical heart of Antwerp
SCALE	3.4 ha
COLLABORATORS	BEL Architecten, Landschaap, Witteveen & Bos, Roel Huisman
DESCRIPTION	Our team focused on retaining the impressive scale of the former Zuiderdokken (Southern Docks), ignoring its current division in three zones defined by intersecting streets, each zone with its own purpose: sports, parking, garden.

We envisioned one continuous rectangular lawn with extra enforcement to allow for any form or scale of use. This spacious lawn is inlaid with a series of circular gardens, terraces, pavilions, playgrounds and sports fields – flat, concave or convex, these inlays sometimes contain a structure for shading or a small pavilion. Flanking the fields, we projected lively pedestrian avenues paved with black-and-white natural stone slabs and lined with monumental trees and occasional newspaper and coffee stands.

The old below-ground retaining walls of the former water basins would be repurposed to accommodate parking for cars and bicycles. We carved a trench down from the walls' entire height to make their monumental, ancient presence visible and also to provide daylight and fresh air for the underground spaces. On both outer ends of the park, we designed wide entrances for bicycles and pedestrians, elegant spirals flowing down into the underground parking spaces.

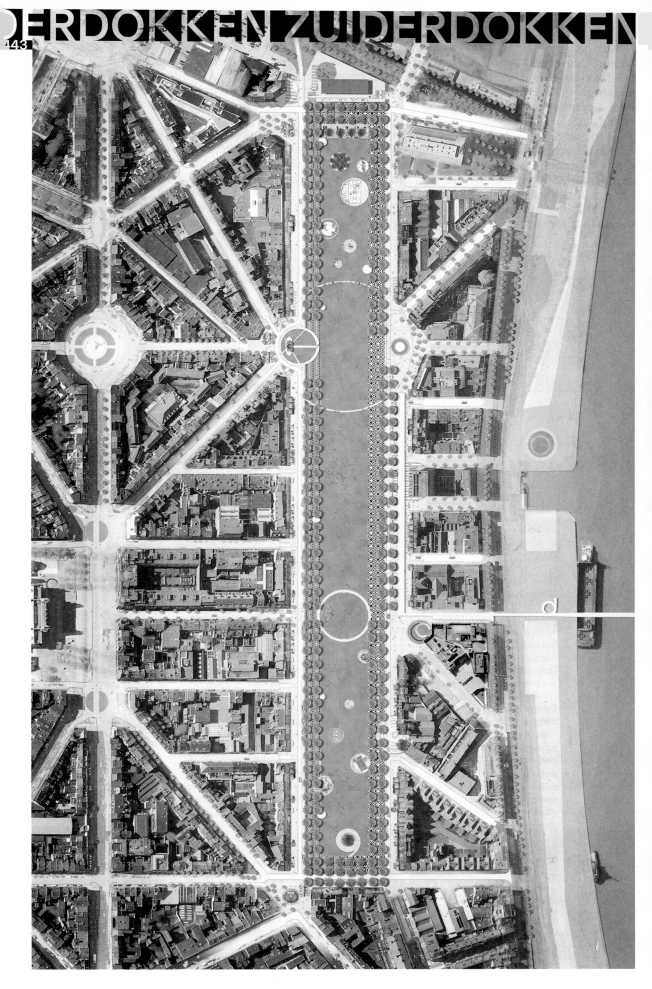

d

"It was not easy to convince Anne and Jean-Philippe to join us in this Art Mill competition, as they didn't feel particularly comfortable with the political mentality of the country. But we convinced them that ART and SCIENCE should transcend politics and be used as an important, influential tool to connect people and to break down political barriers of any kind. So, they agreed to join us."

"Not to our surprise Jean-Philippe turned out to be totally absorbed in growing parasitic plants such as orchids in a self-made glasshouse inside their office, and Anne and the entire team there seemed to follow a very eco-conscious lifestyle: the fact that the entire studio was lined with plant cuttings and rooting seeds told us that they must definitely share our belief in leaving as little a carbon footprint on this earth as possible, reusing the existing whenever possible and respecting all living things. So we were pleased to discover this overlap of interests during – and in favour of – this Art Mill project."   PB

LOCATION	Doha, Qatar
CLIENT	Qatar Museums
STATUS	Competition
SCOPE	Convert the flour mill into an Art Mill, with gallery and studio spaces, screening rooms, classrooms, gardens, restaurants, terraces, parking lots
SCALE	9.4 ha with 3.2 ha of gardens
COLLABORATORS	Lacaton & Vassal Architects
DESCRIPTION	One large, continuous, horizontal shading "fleece" of aluminium shingles covers the entire Art Mill area at considerable height, thus creating a new climatic zone: a whole city section with a cooler climate, where one can move freely from one building or garden to the next on foot, uncovered. Plantings of varied height and mass, both on land and in the sea, help achieve the right level of shading and cooling. Air turbulence is caused through natural air movement, caused by the strategic placement of open and closed volumes, of openings and closures. Diving into the history of Middle Eastern architecture, where natural cooling has been applied in cities and homes for centuries, together with our passionate, shared interest in natural processes between natural space and living environments made our collaboration with Lacaton & Vassal vibrant and inspirational.

In order to lower the temperature under the open frame aluminium roof and facades covered with solar cells, we planned for soil mass, plants and trees in the site's interior as well as the implementation of mangrove forests along the edges of the site, which would cool down the air as it blows onto the site with the predominant winds

USE SITE WATER SOURCE FOR EVAPORATIVE COOLING

Shaft connected to an underground tunnel

Room with shafts connected to underground tunnel

Low tide: temperature of the air is cooled in tunnel

Low tide: cooled circulation will cool outdoor space

High tide: blasts of water from below - a fountain

High tide: blasts and mist of water cooling the space

USE LOCAL COASTAL ECOLOGY: MANGROVE GARDENS

Shelter from sand storms and heavy wind

Nursery grounds/shelter for marine organisms

Filtering and purifying the sea water

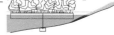

Sand accumulation on edges creating a beach

THE 'SKY' LEVEL
+35m

Embedded inside the structure of the roof, terraces, cafés, restaurants and lounges have the best view around, and access to the top of the silos.

MUSEUM'S LAYER
+27m

All the exhibition rooms of the museum are located at this level, in a quiet situation.

GARDEN LAYER
+15m > +30m

A ground of gardens and terraces, with a theatre, library and education program.

PUBLIC LAYER
+0m > +15m

The natural ground, a large public space widely open, in free access for permanent activities.

The visitors arrive at the centre by car or coach to be at an equal distance to all the site's spaces .
The car parking is created in the existing building

SITE

The main existing buildings are preserved and new volumes are built to supplement the program

DESIGN OF THE SHADING - Opacity

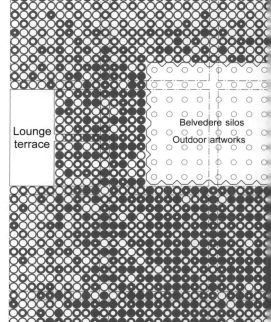

Lounge terrace

Belvedere silos
Outdoor artworks

In addition to the roof cover, as many trees as possible were projected on the site to achieve a temperature ten degrees lower than the outdoors. The shade generated by the leaf cover, protecting the parking lot and the entrance zone, would further contribute to a cooler climate.

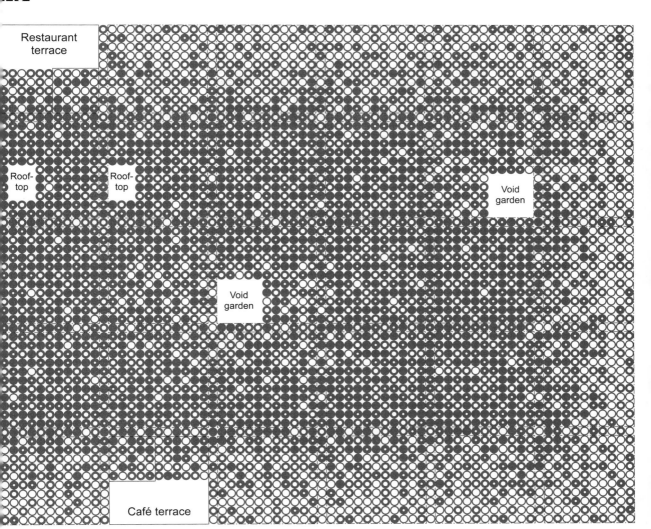

Restaurant terrace

Roof-top

Roof-top

Void garden

Void garden

Café terrace

"The then director of Het Nieuwe Instituut (which includes the Netherlands' Architecture Institute) Guus Beumer had decided to liven up Huis Sonneveld, a monument from the '30s owned by the institute and open to the public. On an annual basis, he invited designers and artists for an intervention of a half year. After Richard Hutten, who decorated the house with furniture pieces and objects of his own design, I was the second artist to be invited. It's a modernist, white villa with beautiful proportions, a wonderful garden, lots of light, balanced colour scope, crafted details. Although Guus gave us the opportunity to add our own designs – such as replacing the original curtains – my first thought was to react to the architecture, as we always do, in this case by inviting nature in with the help of mirrors, to accentuate the building's essence and let it shine. And that's what we did."   PB

LOCATION	Rotterdam, the Netherlands
CLIENT	Het Nieuwe Instituut
STATUS	Completed
SCOPE	Temporary art installation in the museum Huis Sonneveld
MATERIALS	Wooden underlay and PVC mirroring plates
SCALE	Ground floor, 33 m²; first floor, 167 m²; second floor, 61 m²; roof, 22 m²
COLLABORATORS	Brinkman en Van der Vlugt (1933), Herman Pols/Castano Xylos, HNI team
DESCRIPTION	Amplifying the theme of Het Nieuwe Bouwen's early modern architecture, Licht Lucht en Ruimte (light, air and space), we covered indoor floors, terraces and roof landing with mirroring PVC plates, meticulously fitted under each heater, wash basin, edge and closet, and removed the translucent curtains from the windows and carpets from the floors. Daylight flows in, sun hits the floor and bounces back to the ceilings, secrets are unveiled and falling curtains become sturdy structures.

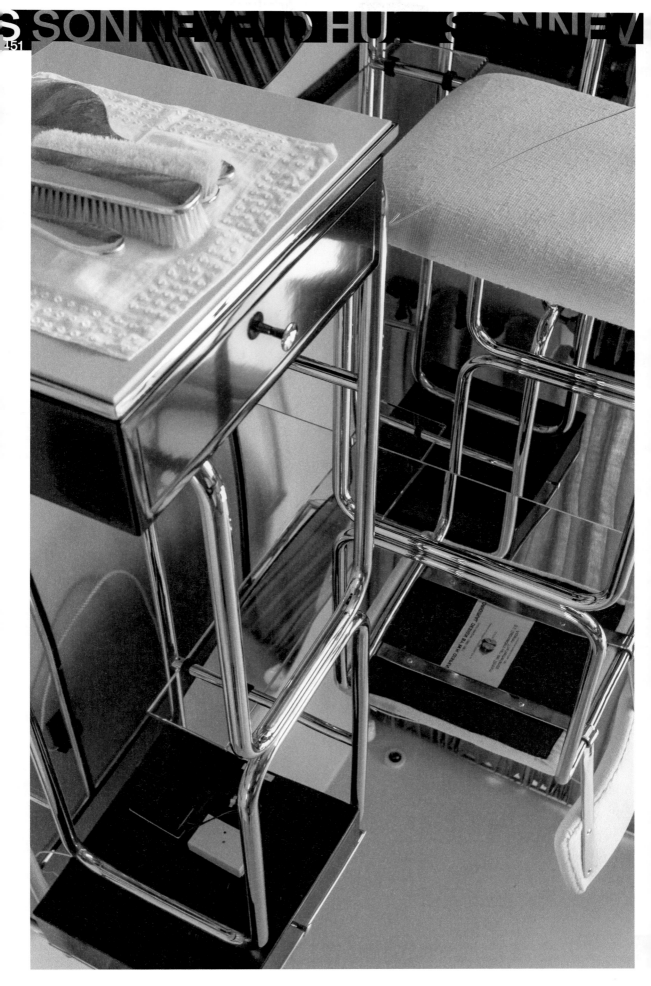

We got permission from the curators of the New Institute (former Netherlands Architecture Institute) to remove the sheer curtains and loose carpets during our six-month installation period in order to open up all windows and install our mirroring floor. First a subfloor was installed, and then large plates with aluminium mirror foil were glued onto it.

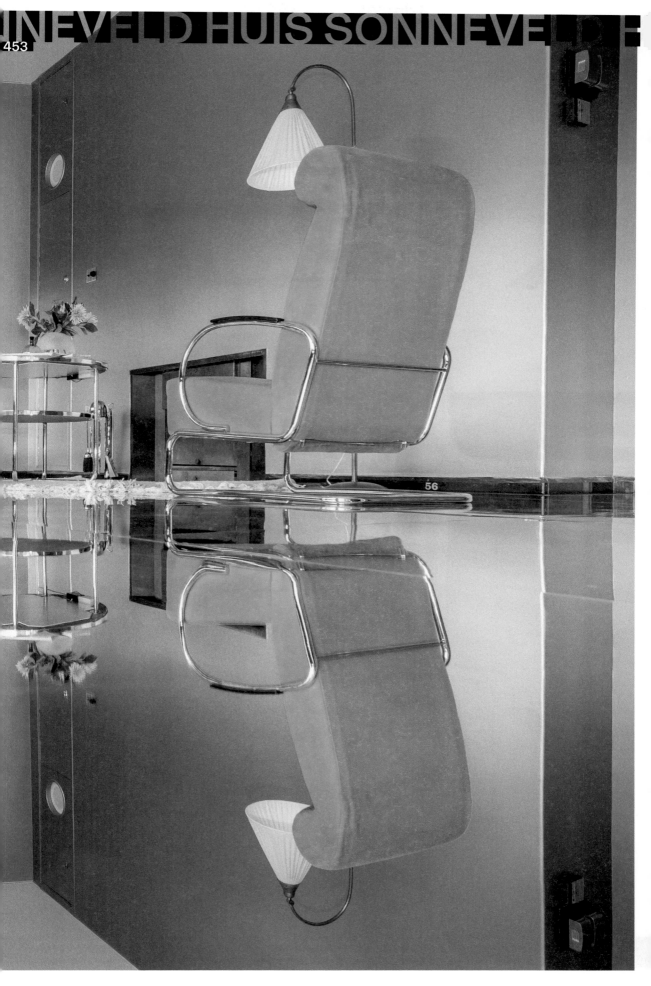

Each custom-made plate was meticulously placed to fit seamlessly under each object and edge condition, including heating, cupboards, toilet and sinks. This made all hidden surfaces visible, exposing the architecture's detailing as well as the alarm systems and labels underneath the pieces of furniture, making it clear that they are objects in a museum.

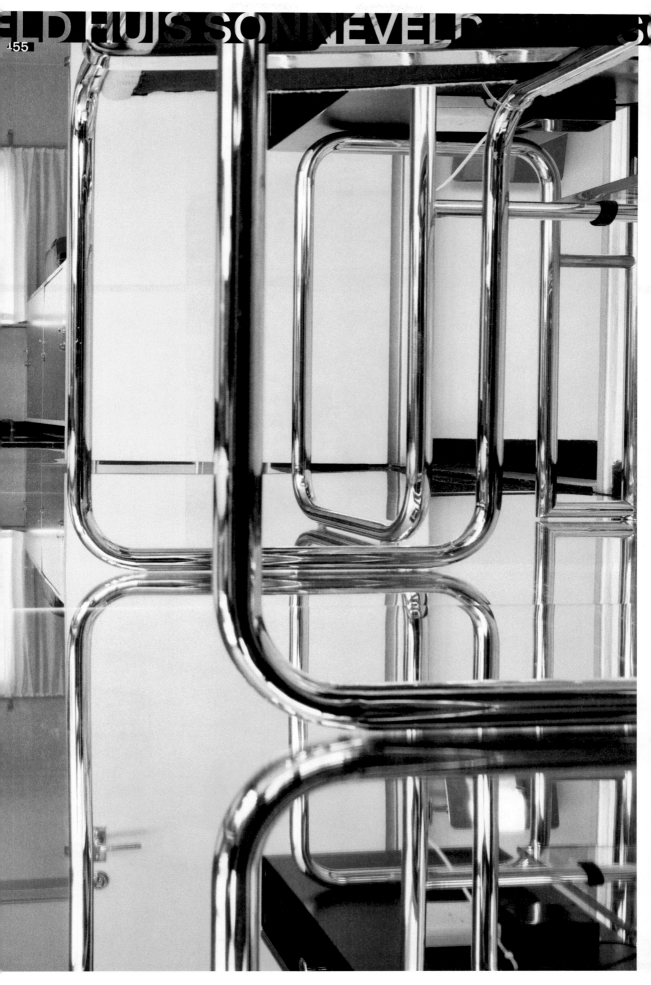

The way we presented our idea to the clients was the existing interior versus the proposed intervention

Living room view in the fifth month

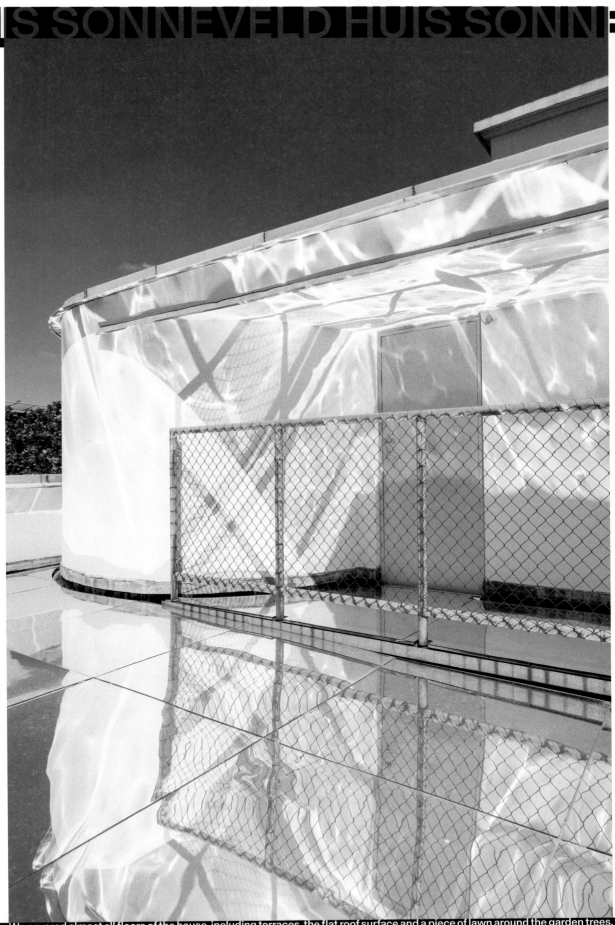

We covered almost all floors of the house, including terraces, the flat roof surface and a piece of lawn around the garden trees. The garden reflected inward, the house reflected outward, daylight flowed in and out in all directions. The given six-month period covered a few seasons; the daylight had amazingly strong effects in some months, whereas colours and reflections got more subtle in others.

Knoll Showcase
Salone del Mobile

"Three years in a row our massive curtains defined the Knoll furniture pavilion in one of the huge halls of Milan's Salone del Mobile. For two years they shaped various rooms and embraced their furniture pieces a bit sensually with falling layers of whites and soft greys. The third year, we exchanged the installation for a kinky black lacquer and silver faux leather composition. So exciting to see the dramatic effect of relatively simple interventions on the atmosphere of a place, a room, and on the character and aesthetic of an object. To have short, hands-on projects such as these now and then is very welcome!" PB

LOCATION	Milan, Italy
CLIENT	Knoll International
STATUS	Completed
SCOPE	Space defining curtains
MATERIALS	Cotton velvet, Trevira CS voile, faux leather, plastic lacquer, blackout cloth; stainless-steel rings, steel snaps, etc.
SCALE	2013–2014, 153 × 4.75 m; 2015, 2 curtains (exterior, 180 × 4.75 m; interior, 195 × 4.75 m)
COLLABORATORS	OMA

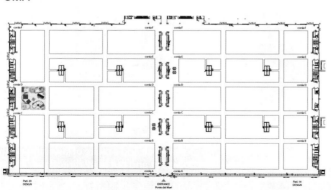

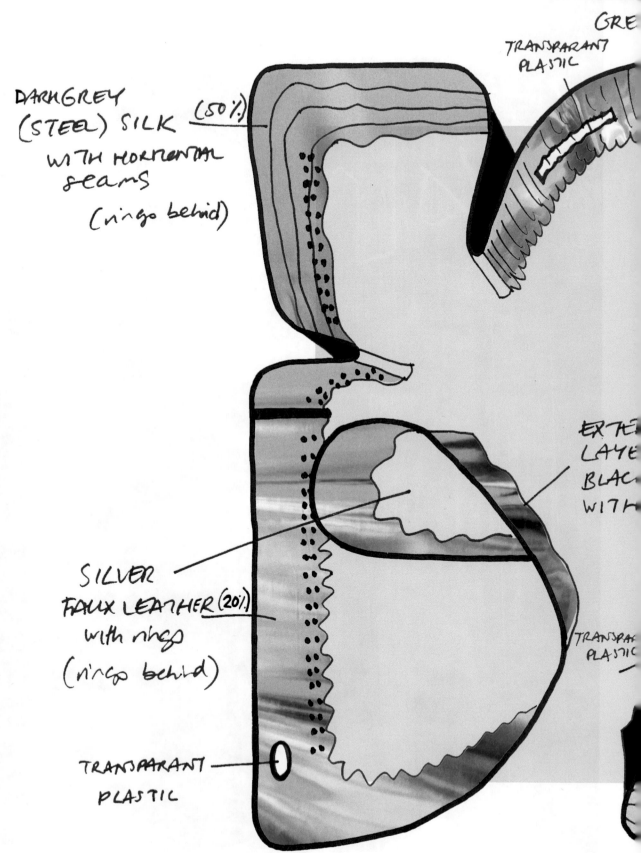

GRE

TRANSPARANT PLASTIC

DARK GREY (STEEL) SILK (50%) WITH HORIZONTAL SEAMS (rings behind)

EXTE LAYE BLAC WITH

SILVER FAUX LEATHER (20%) with rings (rings behind)

TRANSPA PLASTIC

TRANSPARANT PLASTIC

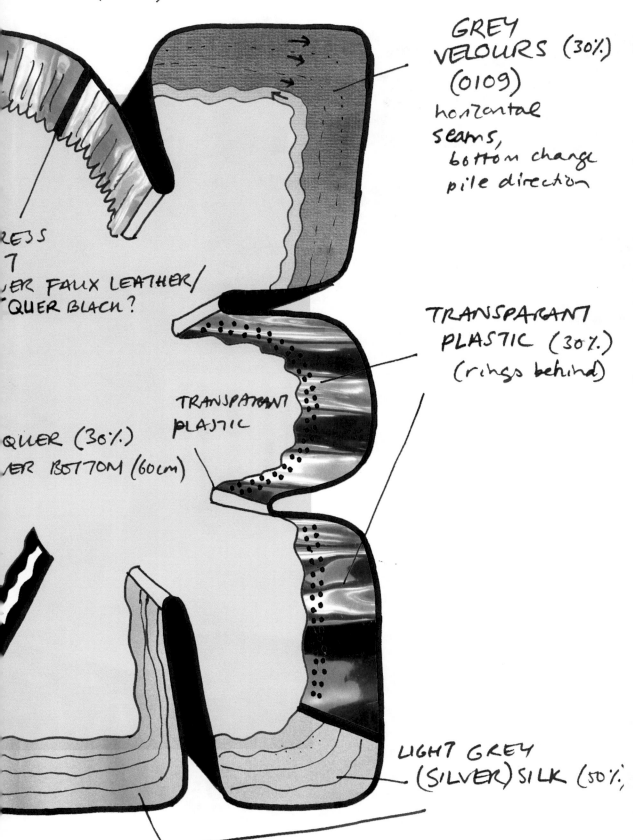

CQUER (100%.)

GREY
VELOURS (30%)
(0109)
horizontal
seams,
bottom change
pile direction

RESS
7
ER FAUX LEATHER/
QUER BLACK?

TRANSPARANT
PLASTIC (30%.)
(rings behind)

TRANSPARANT
PLASTIC

QUER (30%.)
ER BOTTOM (60cm)

LIGHT GREY
(SILVER) SILK (50%.

Peepholes and slits allow for anonymous views in

The white version of our intervention at the Knoll pavilion for the first two years of the Milan Furniture Fair

Espace public (Limites)
AGORA 2014 Biennale de Bordeaux

"Violent, political, restricting, liberated, menacing, shared, respectable… The public space remains complex. Nothing should have the power to deprive people of it. Especially not formal regulations. What if we decided to assume power over them? The public space is mouldable, even if – and perhaps because – it is complex to define. Public space isn't common space, shared as its name implies by a community. Public space isn't even a private space, even if its separation – certainly in France – is less visible than in other countries or other civilisations. Public space is not – or not only – republican because public space can seem strangely colonialist: its beaches, the slopes of Mont Blanc, leisure complexes and commercial centres: are they public spaces? Public space is violent. And in general, whatever isn't considered necessary there is easily destroyed. The public space is the political place par excellence. It is a place for demonstrations, for the liberation of Paris, the fall of the Berlin Wall, the revolutions of the Arab Spring. Public space is that of transport links, but also of the removal of past conquests, the mastery of culture over nature: it's the Roman road, the super-highways, the streets of our villages. But public space is also the Greek agora, the Forum, a meeting place, of beginnings, of sharing, where the question of limits remains important; the limits of the public space can be physical, functional or symbolic. It changes according to its use. The risk of fixing them too rigidly can restrict their diverse and lively uses. Is the public space endangered? At a time when cities are trying to create inclusive, sympathetic public spaces, free of cars, can it really be possible for the public space to be a place of possibilities, a place of experimentation for all of life?" STATEMENT BY YOUSSEF TOHMÉ, AGORA PRESS TEXT, SEPTEMBER 2014

"In uneasy, even anguished times, searching for 'absolute zero risk,' the norm quickly colonises all sectors of the public sphere. For each question, for each eventuality, for each doubt, the answer is the same: to legislate or regulate. Obligation or prohibition, whichever the case, produces a conditioned reflex; it imposes itself in its uniformity, its rigidity, and often its absurdity on a place or on its local circumstances, whatever they might be. The norm also imposes itself in its excesses on the citizen whom it is meant to serve and protect… The vital organs of democracy are affected by the roughly 400,000 technical prescriptions that today are applicable to territorial collectives: the law, robbed of its credibility and authority, of judicial security, becomes a direct victim of a textural frenzy that is now chronic; local elected officials in particular, are bureaucratised, even infantilised… Conventional centralism transforms these elected officials into mere administrators, substituting technical expertise for the legitimacy of the ballot box, and changing governance by action into action by maintenance." INFORMATION REPORT BY CLAUDE BELOT, SÉNAT, 16 FEBRUARY 2011, AGORA PRESS TEXT SEPTEMBER 2014

LOCATION   Hangar 14, Bordeaux, France
CLIENT   Municipality of Bordeaux
STATUS   Completed
SCOPE   Exhibition design for the 6th edition of the AGORA Biennale
SCALE   Scenography, 5,400 m², including 212 gabion exhibition panels on the ground
               floor and a large curtain (195 × 3.62 m) on the first floor
COLLABORATORS Youssef Tohmé and team, Studio DB

467

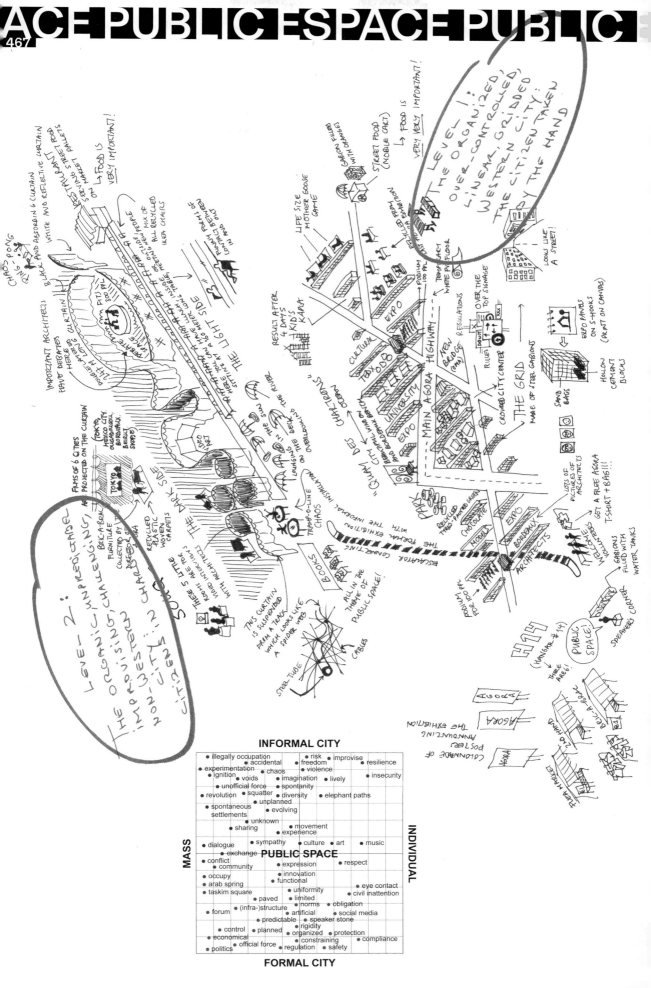

LEVEL 1 : THE ORGANIZED, OVER-CONTROLLED, LINEAR, GRIDDED WESTERN CITY : THE CITIZEN CITY, TAKEN BY THE HAND

LEVEL 2 : THE ORGANIC, UNPREDICTABLE, CHALLENGING, IMPROVISING NON-WESTERN CITY : THE CITIZENS IN CHARGE

CHAOS PONG PING PONG

IMPORTANT ARCHITECTS PLAYED DEBATES HERE

BLACK AND ABSORBING CURTAIN, WHITE AND REFLECTIVE CURTAIN

SERVING STREET FOOD ON MARKET PALLETS → RESTAURANT!

↳ FOOD IS VERY IMPORTANT!

FILMS OF 6 CITIES PROJECTED ON THE CURTAIN (TOKYO, MEXICO CITY, GUADALAJARA, BORDEAUX, BEIRUT, SKOPJE)

DOUBLE HEIGHT! LIGHT HANGING CURTAIN OF A PIT, 200 M2

BRIC-A-BRAC FURNITURE COLLECTED BY THE DIRECTORS OF TOKYO

RECYCLED PLASTIC WOVEN CARPETS

THESE LITTLE SPOTS WITH ARCHITECTS, 100 INTERVIEWS

THE DARK SIDE / SETTING AT THE LIGHT SIDE

IN THE SUN

THE RIVER

VIDEO ART

LOUNGING ON THE DECK OVERLOOKING THE RIVER

"QUAI DES CHAOS" / TRAM-P-LINE

RUNNING POINTS OF FITNESS DINING INSIDE? ALSO CHAIRS? → WHERE PEOPLE ARE CHILLING IN A RANDOM MIX OF ALL RECYCLED IKEA CHAIRS

STEEL TUBE / CABLES

THIS CURTAIN IS SUSPENDED FROM A TRACK WHICH LOOKS LIKE A SPIDER WEB

ALL IN THE THEME OF PUBLIC SPACE!

BOOKS

LIFE SIZE MOTHER GOOSE GAME

RECYCLED PAPER EXHIBITION

TRANSPARENT WHITE PE FLOOR

MID/OLD PPL 100 PPL

GABION FILLED WITH ORANGES

STREET FOOD (MOBILE CART) ↳ FOOD IS VERY VERY IMPORTANT!

LOOKS LIKE A STREET!

EXPO PANELS ON S-HOOKS (PRINT ON CANVAS)

OVER THE TOP SIGNAGE

REGULATIONS RULES

CROWDED CITY CENTER

THE GRID MADE OF STEEL GABIONS

SAND BAGS

HOLLOW CEMENT BLOCKS

EXPO

CULTURE TEXDDB

UNIVERSITY

EXPO

NEW BRIDGE (OMA)

MAIN AGORA HIGHWAY

BEAUTIFUL VIEW ON THE CITY?

THE FORUM EXHIBITION WITH THE INFORMAL INSTALLATIONS

ESCALATOR BROCHURE

PODIUM PPL

PLAN

RECYCLED TYRES-PLANTED GARDEN

CHOCOLATE

MODELS

EXPO

BORDEAUX

LOTS OF PICTURES OF ARCHITECTS

ARCHITECTS

WELCOME VOLUNTEERS GET A FREE AGORA T-SHIRT + BAG!!!

GABIONS FILLED WITH WATER TANKS

SPEAKERS CORNER

RESULT AFTER 4 DAYS KIDS KAPLA

H14 (HANGAR #14) THERE ARE 6!

PUBLIC SPACE!

AGORA

AGORA

COLONNADE OF POSTERS ANNOUNCING THE EXHIBITION

BRIC-A-BRAC

PRINT ON 2D

FLEA MARKET

AGORA

Diagram grid

INFORMAL CITY

MASS ← → INDIVIDUAL

- illegally occupation
- accidental
- experimentation
- ignition
- voids
- chaos
- unofficial force
- spontanity
- revolution
- squatter
- diversity
- unplanned
- spontaneous settlements
- evolving
- unknown
- sharing
- risk
- freedom
- improvise
- violence
- imagination
- lively
- resilience
- insecurity
- elephant paths
- movement
- experience

PUBLIC SPACE

- dialogue
- sympathy
- culture
- art
- music
- exchange
- conflict
- community
- expression
- respect
- occupy
- innovation
- arab spring
- functional
- taskim square
- uniformity
- eye contact
- paved
- limited
- civil inattention
- forum
- (infra-)structure
- norms
- obligation
- artificial
- social media
- predictable
- speaker stone
- control
- planned
- rigidity
- organized
- protection
- economical
- constraining
- compliance
- politics
- official force
- regulation
- safety

FORMAL CITY

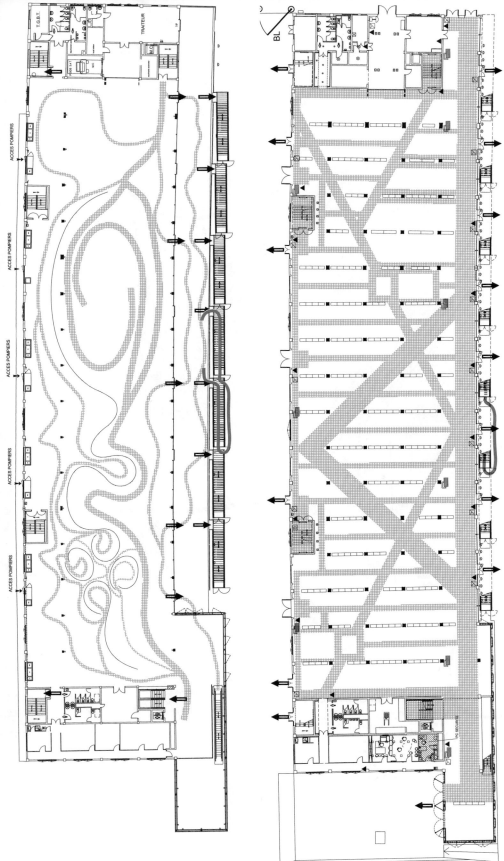

The two floorplans above show the different way we designed the two floors, one representing the fixed, well-organised, censored and secured "public space" in the Western world (right side, ground floor) and the other showing the fluid, mouldable and ad-hoc public spaces with improvised programming in the rest of the world (left side, 1st floor). Right page: 1st floor (2×) and ground floor just before the press opening.

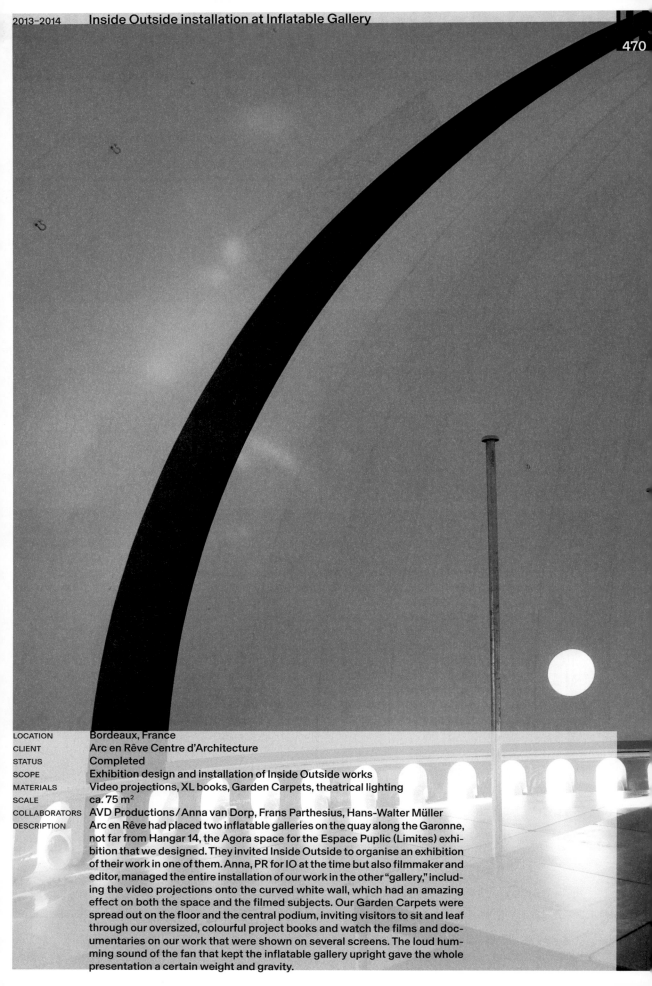

LOCATION	Bordeaux, France
CLIENT	Arc en Rêve Centre d'Architecture
STATUS	Completed
SCOPE	Exhibition design and installation of Inside Outside works
MATERIALS	Video projections, XL books, Garden Carpets, theatrical lighting
SCALE	ca. 75 m²
COLLABORATORS	AVD Productions / Anna van Dorp, Frans Parthesius, Hans-Walter Müller
DESCRIPTION	Arc en Rêve had placed two inflatable galleries on the quay along the Garonne, not far from Hangar 14, the Agora space for the Espace Puplic (Limites) exhibition that we designed. They invited Inside Outside to organise an exhibition of their work in one of them. Anna, PR for IO at the time but also filmmaker and editor, managed the entire installation of our work in the other "gallery," including the video projections onto the curved white wall, which had an amazing effect on both the space and the filmed subjects. Our Garden Carpets were spread out on the floor and the central podium, inviting visitors to sit and leaf through our oversized, colourful project books and watch the films and documentaries on our work that were shown on several screens. The loud humming sound of the fan that kept the inflatable gallery upright gave the whole presentation a certain weight and gravity.

Narcissus Flying Curtain

"The musicians seemed to float on water, and the veil falling from the ceiling looked like a frozen waterfall. For each performance we had to re-install the balloons and fill each one with equal amounts of helium, then attach them at regular intervals to the extremely thin glass fibre stick inserted in the top hem of the curtain. Depending on the respective temperature and air movement, we attached the floating curtain with thin fishing rods to a stable object in the space or on stage, predicting – so to speak – possible movements of this independent, slightly fluctuating object. One evening, with the installation completed, lighting balanced and musicians ready to go, the public streamed in through the two entrance doors opposite the stage. It was winter, and cold air flowed in. When the orchestra started, the curtain – independent indeed – started to react to the cold air by suddenly and passionately moving forward, completely enveloping the musicians from behind! As if caught in a web, they couldn't move. Oh... the shame! The music stopped, we ran forward to restore the damage – and on the performance went." PB

LOCATION	Travelling concert scenography, several theatres in the Netherlands: Hervormde Kerk, Den Bosch, Muziekgebouw aan het Ij, Amsterdam, Korzo Theater, The Hague, De Vereeniging, Nijmegen
CLIENT	Nieuw Amsterdams Peil, Calliope Tsoupaki
STATUS	Completed
SCOPE	Scenography for a chamber music performance
MATERIALS	Silver voile, helium balloons, black high gloss dance floor
SCALE	Floor, 7 × 6.4 m; curtain, 36 × 7 m; approx. 40 helium balloons
COLLABORATORS	Tanja Durloo (scent expert), Calliope Tsoupaki (composer)

Sino-European Gardens
Shenzhen Stock Exchange Headquarters

"One of the things one learns is that each culture needs a different manner of representation. I feel very European in the sense that I care for a level of naivety and spontaneity in the conceptual phases of a project. We envision landscape as a rich and living world in which anything can happen over time. Provided, of course, that we create a liveable base from which 'nature' can grow, expand and thrive – even on a roof. Representing and designing the first steps therefore tends to be graphic, simple and fun, sort of animation movie imagery, children's book typology with lots of idealism about biodiversity and beauty. The graphic element is important to create a resilient base from which a landscape can develop further (with or without human intervention) without undermining its essence, the 'big gesture' of a design. But the SZSE client requested true-to-life renderings from the very beginning. As it happens I can't stand digital renderings because they are ugly and pretend to be something they are not: the reality they communicate will not come about. But – and this was inspiring – the clients also took every choice of planting and shape very seriously, as the Chinese culture believes in the explicit meaning of each living thing and of each shape and colour. Meaning in all senses of the word: mythological, historical, medical, biological, philosophical. This impelled us to dig up totally different information about our plant choices and design directions." PB

LOCATION	Futian District, Shenzhen Shi, China
CLIENT	Shenzhen Stock Exchange
STATUS	Completed
SCOPE	Landscape design: public park, entrance areas and plazas; vertical, interior and patio gardens; floor patterns for entrance halls and restaurant; roof garden
SCALE	ca. 6 ha
COLLABORATORS	OMA, SADI Engineers, SED, Verte Asia
DESCRIPTION	The brief for this project was to create a composition of gardens on all levels – from street to roof. Thus, we designed all of the green spaces for this building, including plazas, sidewalks, public park, interior gardens and both indoor and outdoor vertical gardens. We decided to re-introduce the Sino-European garden, an almost forgotten tradition. This concept is made visible in the park area on street level, with its stepped "rice fields" filled with grasses and perennials; but more so in the roof garden (approximately 11,000 m², at an altitude of 60 metres), where we used mediaeval floral patterns – quite similar to Chinese paper cuttings – as the basis for our design. Translating these floral shapes into cut shrubs and grasses with small groups of red-flowering perennials created an elegant, ever-changing pattern of rooms, spaces and trajectories. As the shrubs grow taller, protection from sun and wind improves. Water features mute the city sounds and floral smells fill the air. Sports fields, running tracks, yoga and tai chi spaces, terraces, tea gardens, roofed television and film rooms and meeting spaces can be shared here by the SZSE staff of 10,000 employees.

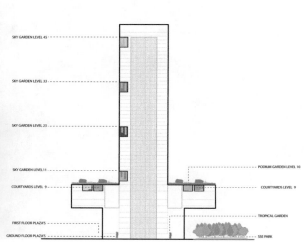

Photoshop image of the suspended columns we developed for all interior terraces that welcome the ten thousand-strong staf

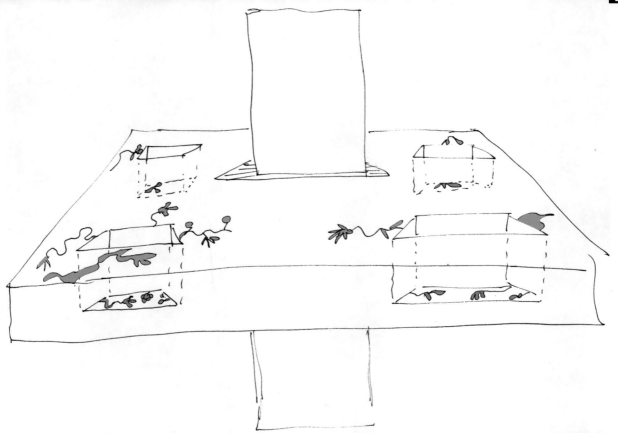

Sketch to clarify our interventions on the roof and inside the (sunken) patios of the horizontal slab of the SZSE Tower illustrating the fact that the roof garden "sinks down" into the four patio gardens below

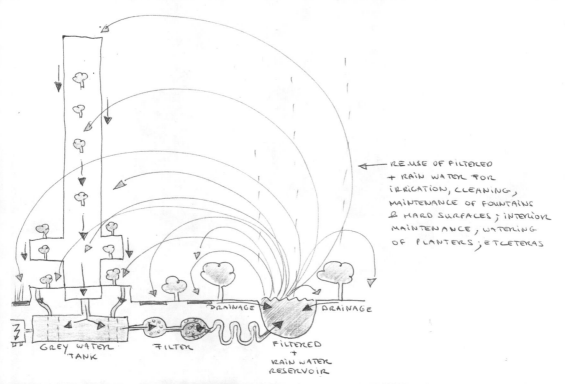

REUSE OF FILTERED + RAIN WATER FOR IRRIGATION, CLEANING, MAINTENANCE OF FOUNTAINS & HARD SURFACES ; INTERIOR MAINTENANCE , WATERING OF PLANTERS ; ETCETERAS

DRAINAGE

DRAINAGE

GREY WATER TANK

FILTER

FILTERED + RAIN WATER RESERVOIR

Sketch to clarify our intention to work with a circular (rain and grey) water system which uses the garden soil as a filtering layer and the natural pond as a water buffer

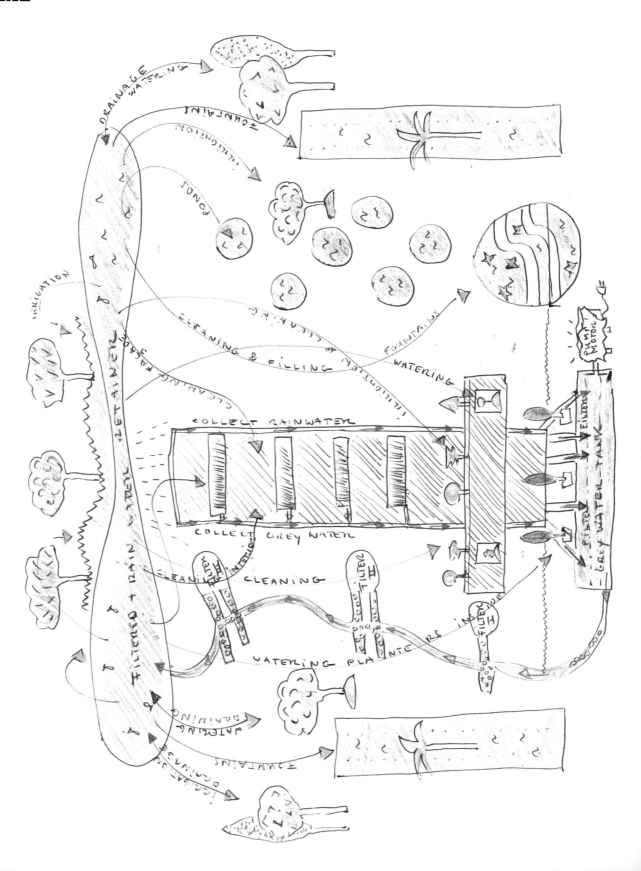

Labels within sketch: DRAINAGE WATERING, FOUNTAIN, IRRIGATION, PONDS, IRRIGATION, CLEANING & FILLING, CLEANING FACADE, FOUNTAIN, WATERING, COLLECT RAINWATER, COLLECT GREY WATER, CLEANING, FILTER I, FILTER II, FILTER III, WATERING PLANTS INSIDE, WATERING DRAINING, FOUNTAIN, IRRIGATION DRAINAGE, FILTERED + RAIN WATER RETAINED, IRRIGATION, PUMP MOTOR, FILTER, GREY WATER TANK

The Middle Ages prescribed certain floral patterns to be used in architectural decorations. We thought that these Western patterns related to Chinese paper-cuttings, and could therefore reinforce our Sino-European art concept for the landscape that we were to develop in, on and above ground level here in Shenzhen.

At the clients' request, awful true-to-life illustrations of the future

五节芒 Miscanthus floridulu

纤细狼尾草 Pennisetum setaceum

鹅掌柴 Schefflera arboricola

小驳骨 Gendarussa vulgaris

锦熟黄杨 Buxus sempervirens

福建茶 Carmona microphylla

大叶红草 Alternanthera ficoidea

龙船花 Ixora chinensis

萱草 Hemerocallis fulva

红花鼠尾草 Salvia coccinea

石蒜 Lycoris radiata

LEGEND
图例

RED PERENNIALS/BULBS	红色宿根/球
GRASSES+BULBS	观赏草+球根花卉
LOW SHRUB	矮灌木
HIGH SHRUB	高灌木
LAWN	草

深圳证券交易所广场
SHENZHEN STOCK EXCHANGE SQUARE

工程名称	PROJECT
深圳证券交易所广场	
SHENZHEN STOCK EXCHANGE SQUARE	
建设单位	CLIENT
深圳证券交易所	
SHENZHEN STOCK EXCHANGE	
建设地点	SITE
深圳市福田区	
FUTIAN DISTRICT, SHENZHEN	
建筑设计	ARCHITECT
大都会建筑事务所	
OFFICE FOR METROPOLITAN ARCHITECTURE	
国内建筑设计单位	LOCAL ARCHITECT & ENGINEER
深圳市建筑设计研究总院	
SHENZHEN GENERAL INSTITUTE OF ARCHITECTURAL DESIGN AND RESEARCH	
景观设计	LANDSCAPE ARCHITECTURE
INSIDE OUTSIDE	
国内景观设计单位	LOCAL LANDSCAPE DD SUB-CONSULTANT
深圳市新西林园林景观有限公司	
SHENZHEN SED SITELINE ENVIRONMENT DESIGN CO.,LTD	

修改记录
REVISION REMARK

版次 EDITION No.	修改日期 REVISION DATE	说明 DESCRIPTION

加盖图章处
STAMP AREA

合签
COORDINATION

建筑 ARCHI.		结构 STRUCT.	
给排水 PLUMBING		电气 ELEC.	
暖通 HVAC		燃气 GAS	

	印刷体 PRINT	签署 SIGNATURE
审定人 APPROVED BY		
审核人 EXAMINED BY		
项目负责人 CAPTAIN		
项目经理 PROJECT MANAGER		
专业负责人 DISCIPLINE RESPONSIBLE		
校对人 CHECKED BY		
设计人 AUTHORIZED BY	KUNLE ADEYEMI	
制图人 DRAWN BY	KUNLE ADEYEMI	

绝对标高: ± 0.00 = 8.00 m
ABSOLUTE ELEVATION: ± 0.00 = 8.00 m

图名

植物种植平面
VEGETATION PLAN

合同号	4000617	100% DD 景观扩初	阶别
比例	1:200	A0	图纸尺寸
日期	2009-08-27	V1.2	版次

图号

AL- 1-06

DRAWING NOT TO SCALE @ A3

Roof garden in the making, hurrah!

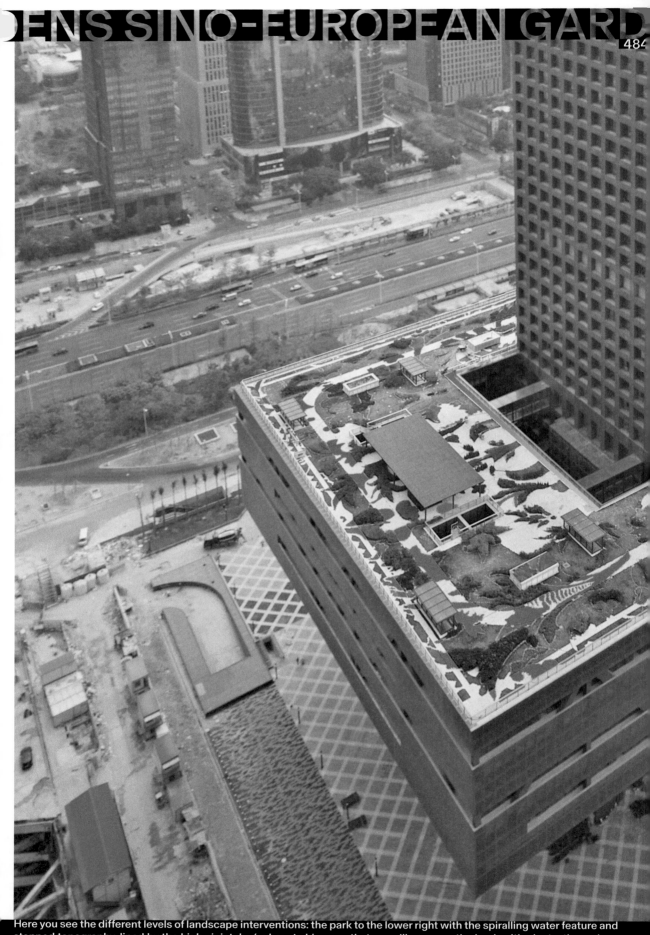

Here you see the different levels of landscape interventions: the park to the lower right with the spiralling water feature and stepped topography, lined by the high air intake/exhaust chimneys that we will cover on the back with plants; the various plazas on different levels and the sidewalks that we designed with enough porous surfaces and integrated green to comply with Chinese norms for water storage; and the Sino-European roof garden, not quite finished but getting there.

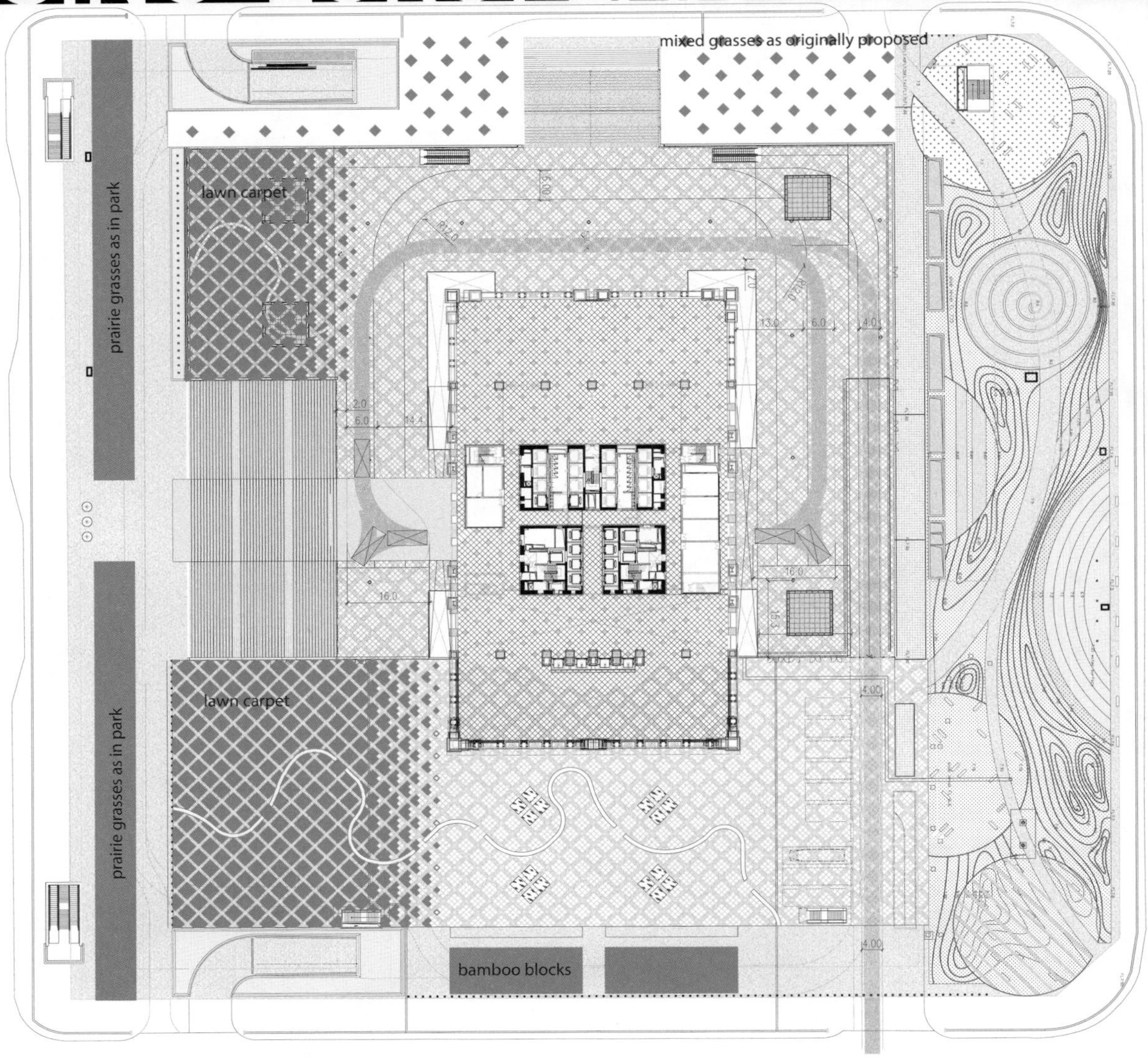

mixed grasses as originally proposed

prairie grasses as in park

lawn carpet

lawn carpet

prairie grasses as in park

bamboo blocks

深南大道

福中三路

Plazas, sidewalks, parking entrances, stairs, water features

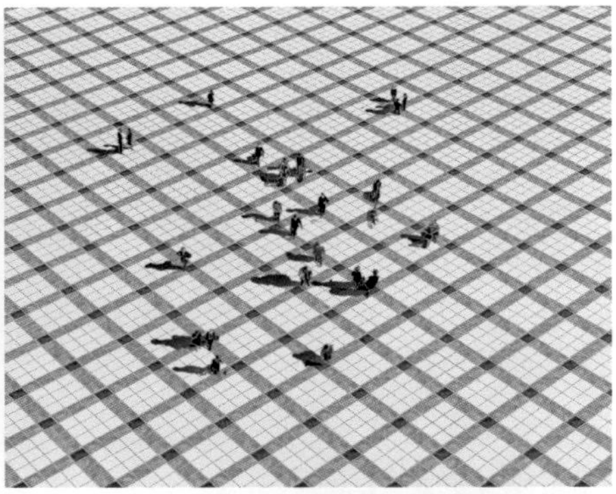

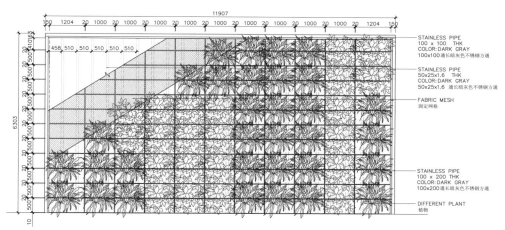

11907

STAINLESS PIPE
100 x 100 THK
COLOR: DARK GRAY
100x100通长暗灰色不锈钢方通

STAINLESS PIPE
50x25x1.6 THK
COLOR: DARK GRAY
50x25x1.6 通长暗灰色不锈钢方通

FABRIC MESH
固定网格

STAINLESS PIPE
100 x 200 THK
COLOR: DARK GRAY
100x200通长暗灰色不锈钢方通

DIFFERENT PLANT
植物

(5) SOUTH ELEVATION,4,5,6,7#COOLING TOWER 4,5,6,7#冷却塔南立面图
SCALE   1:50

Plantings for immense exhaust chimney surfaces outside, and to animate walls and improve the air quality and atmosphere indoors

Pink!
Private Apartment
"No, no, no, no, please no visible detailing or artistic additions – just PINK!"

"The apartment was meticulously furnished in a minimalist composition of pure forms in whites, greys and cream. A window the size of the entire southern facade overlooked Vondelpark and formed the fourth wall of the living room, which had a very low ceiling. When I visited the place to discuss the client's expectations for a shading curtain, the idea of PINK immediately came to mind. There was an instant thrill at the thought that a 'presence' – not a backdrop – would soon inhabit their home. And man, did it change the place when bright sunny daylight shone through, smouldering pink through the cracks of the front door, pink on your skin, in your body, heart and soul!"   PB

LOCATION	Byzantium building, Amsterdam, the Netherlands
CLIENT	Private owner
STATUS	Completed
SCOPE	Create darkening and cooling curtain along glazed south facade
MATERIALS	Pink cotton velvet; a lining of blackout cloth with golden faux-leather bottom edge (invisible from the inside, visible from the terrace)
SCALE	9.8 × 2.4 m

"During our four years in Amsterdam, we lived with only one artwork in our apartment: a large pink velvet curtain that we commissioned from Petra to span the long, wall-to-wall, floor-to-ceiling sliding glass balcony door in our living room. Our apartment was a long rectangular box that culminated in an extraordinary aperture to the Vondelpark. In spanning the entire south wall, the window occupied the width of the apartment. The interior plan for the apartments, known as the Byzantium (1985–1991) – one of the earliest projects of OMA – was altered by the developer to add an additional floor, which reduced the heights of the units. That compromise to the design compressed the space, emphasising the horizontality and length of the apartment. The low ceiling blocked the view of the sky, which had the effect of turning the window into a framing device – the band of trees outside became pictorial content.

We initially wanted something that would significantly reduce the south-facing light so that we could safely hang light-sensitive works in the room. We also wanted to introduce colour into the space – the walls were heavily textured and bright white, the floor was warmer white marble tile, and our furniture was neutral grey. Together with Petra, we chose a cool pink cotton velvet. We imagined a solid block of colour and opted for unadorned velvet – without the combination of materials or the perforations that are more typical of Petra's remarkable use of curtains to blend inside and outside. We envisioned that the thickness of the velvet (also backed with an additional layer of a white, light blocking drape) would completely block the light from entering, and also any visibility of the pink from the outside. Unexpectedly, the light still penetrated, and the curtain became a stunning filter for the intense south-facing sunlight. When closed, the light passed through and infused the entire space in a deep pink glow, and the limbs and leaves of the trees were still visible as wavering patterns of silhouetted light. When the curtain was pulled to one side, it condensed into a stunning block of pink against the leaves and the hundreds of bright green parrots that alighted in them every evening at dusk. At night, the drawn curtain glowed in the interior light.

Ultimately, we never ended up hanging any other artworks in the apartment – nothing else seemed necessary – the curtain alone was perfect. The pink curtain was not only beautiful, but also comforting and enlivening; we wanted our home to feel like a refuge, and fortunately it did. Only some years later did we learn that a certain shade of pink (just a little warmer than ours) is known as "drunk tank pink" because it is proven to have a calming effect on agitated people. Considering the stress of the Stedelijk directorship on both of us, we certainly made an uncanny and fortuitous selection! When we departed Amsterdam, we unfortunately had no choice but to leave the custom-made curtain in its place, anxiously hoping that the owners would choose to retain it. It gave us such pleasure to learn that they, too, embraced it."

ANN GOLDSTEIN AND CHRISTOPHER WILLIAMS
25 MAY 2020

"It is not really fair to include this garden as part of the Inside Outside collection of private garden designs as the owner originally designed it around 1985 with landscape architect Liesbeth Sillem. But I helped with the installation and for many years since then, I have helped to take care of its maintenance and planting choices in close collaboration with the owners, bringing it to maturity and photographing its plant combinations, colour and light effects through the years, until 2010 when the house was sold. Many of the photographs I took of the plants became the basis of our Garden Carpets, first introduced during our solo exhibition at Storefront for Art and Architecture New York in 2000."   PB

LOCATION	Wassenaar, the Netherlands
CLIENT	Private owner
STATUS	Completed
SCOPE	Private garden, installation and maintenance
MATERIALS	Plantings, brick, water, awnings
SCALE	4,000 m²
COLLABORATORS	Owner

Re-Set, new wings for architecture
Dutch Pavilion – Venice Architecture Biennale

"For us, this installation brought together everything our work with curtains stood for during all the previous years of training and experimenting. A large-scale piece of falling cloth, slightly pleated, that moves through space. A composition of different 'textiles' – woven and non-woven – that work together to create various effects. One curtain that changes the architectural context by taking on different shapes in space. A flexible wall that contains most architectural qualities: opaque versus transparent, open versus obstructed view, vertical versus horizontal, massive versus lightweight, colourless versus colourful, reflective versus absorbent, porous versus airtight, heavy versus weightless."

"A curtain is not about the cloth, its qualities, colour, sheen, feel, pattern, structure, behaviour, wear-and-tear; it is also about the way it is put together and detailed, draped, doubled and pleated. And it all starts with the shape and potential of the technical installation from which it hangs, to which it's attached, along which it slides, moves, shifts, where it is stored, how it curves. Here, the motorised bicycle-chain technique allowed the curtain to take extremely sharp turns: the cloth literally folded onto and into itself, doubled up, stretched out and around like a living creature."

"I look back on this exceptionally rewarding collaboration with gratitude. It was an honour for Inside Outside to represent the Netherlands at the Venice Architecture Biennale; really something to get excited about. And the way everything came together was truly miraculous: apart from our own top team and the NAi director's and staff's help, we managed to get the best engineers, craftsmen, technicians, inventors, graphic designers, composer and sponsors on board. Everyone gave their best for many months and, at the end, during the weeks on site." PB

LOCATION	Venice, Italy
CLIENT	NAi (Netherlands Architecture Institute)
STATUS	Completed
SCOPE	Installation representing flexible use of vacant buildings
MATERIALS	Bicycle chain, aluminium rods, motors, found materials; Trevira CS voile, leatherette, tape, cotton velvet, plastic
SCALE	Curtains, 21 × 5.4 m (2×); track length, 148 m; loop of 12 configurations, 90 seconds per stop; speed, 4 sec/m; total duration, ca. 22 minutes
COLLABORATORS	Gerrit Rietveld (1950s), Gerriets GmbH, Rob Nijsse, Hans Jansen, Landstra & De Vries
DESCRIPTION	This installation communicated different messages: the materials we used could be found and put together anywhere in the world; the installation demonstrated an economic and flexible means of reviving a vacant building, and the curtain's 12 positions referred to the 12 hours of the day and of the night. This was our response to the theme of common ground that David Chipperfield, director of the Biennale, had introduced that year.

Another message we communicated was about light. In contrast to many museums today, where daylight is forbidden and we are doomed to look at art in dim, dead light, we took every filtering layer off to let in natural daylight and sunlight – and the weather in general. Out went the white foil that covered the roof windows and thousands of milk-white lamellae that spread the daylight evenly.

The mirrors on the roof reversed the typical trajectory of the sun inside. So, the installation was also about time. By re-setting the position of the curtains 12 times a day in reference to the 12 hours of day and night, we reconfigured the experience of space and light. The entire cycle of the curtain's movements took about 24 minutes, requiring commitment and patience of the viewer. A series of steel "fingers" attached to the top hem of the curtain that would scrape past found objects was attached here and there to the track: pieces of metal tube, stretched metal, metal mesh and such. These sounds would suddenly give the space a different atmosphere to which everyone responded differently. Except for diagrams of the 12 curtain positions on the entrance facade, we did not provide any printed or other explanation to the public. This was an installation to experience individually, instinctively. Nothing to take home, nothing to guide you.

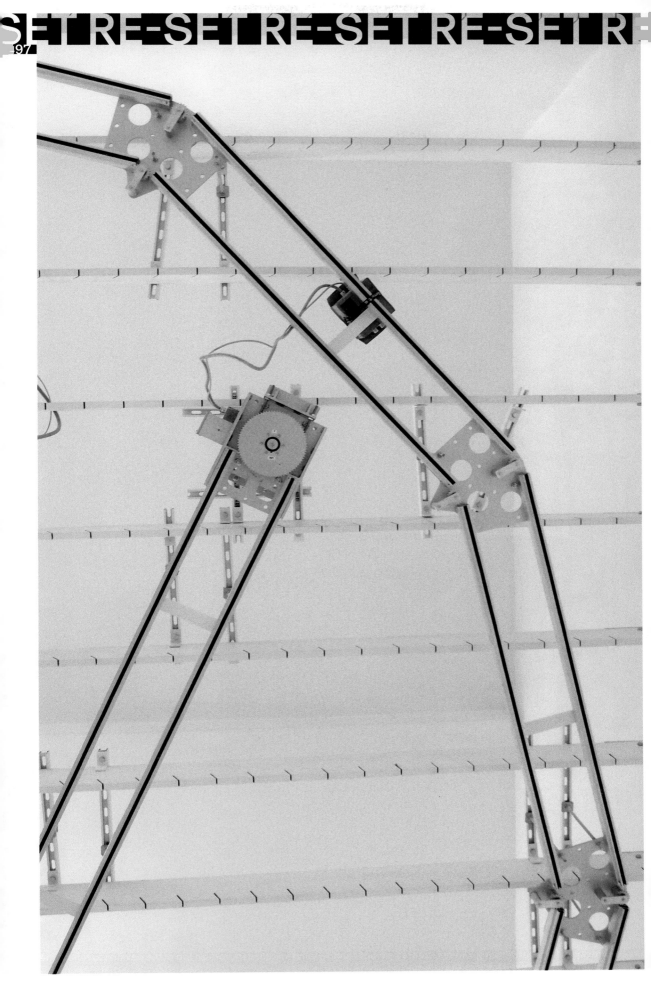

We took away all the light-filtering louvres, cleared all roof windows and installed mirrors on top of the pavilion to reflect the sunlight from all directions back into the interior

We were not allowed to touch the ceiling of the Rietveld Pavilion, a protected monument, so we attached the tracks and motors to the wooden louvre beams. You see the layered shadow effects of direct sunlight via the mirrors here

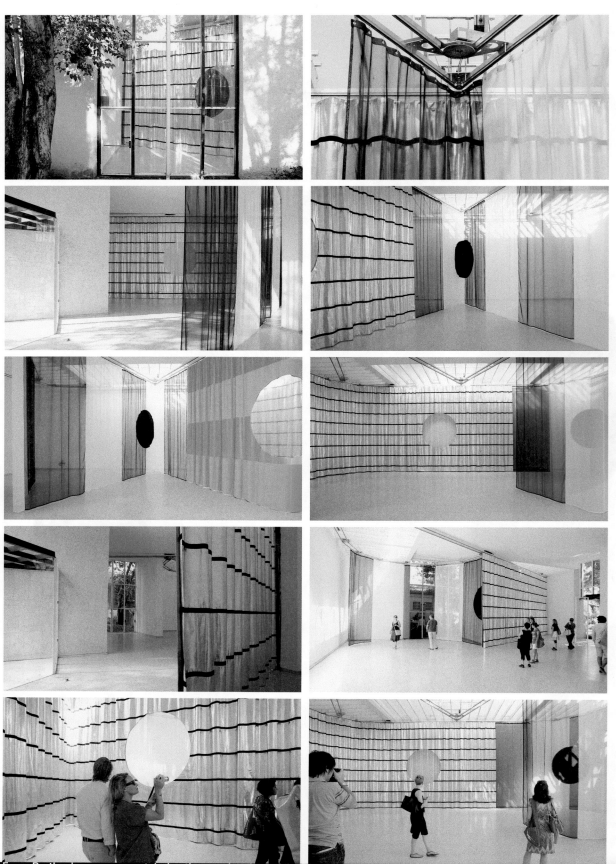

Frans Parthesius was present during the opening days of the Biennale in the summer of 2012, filming the space with visitors and their reactions and behaviour in relation to the moving curtain. He and I went back to film the empty space in late autumn to properly document all the movements of the curtain from different angles as well as the shifting play of shadow and light in the space. He merged these two moments with his edit and we chose a series of stills from it.

"This photo is not about the content. It's about the composition of transparent acrylic shelves attached directly to the wall with thick screws that, by sheer luck, didn't hit any interior wiring; it's about how they reflect and spread light into the space and onto the objects in mysterious ways.

　　　It was my birthday present from Rem. He and carpenter/designer Johan invented it. We first made a scale model at the Inside Outside studio, with each future object represented by beads, screws and other little things we found around. So, each object fits perfectly and the installation lights up the room every day of the year."　PB

Damask Tapestry
Stedelijk Museum

"For this commission, we are indebted to Ann Goldstein, then director of the Stedelijk Museum in Amsterdam, who entrusted us with the creation of a wall carpet to improve the acoustic quality of both restaurant and entrance lobby, and to visually connect both the restaurant to the museum and the new, slick addition to the old brick building. We were given very little time, and we were to work with the Dutch carpet company Desso, who sponsored the work and would produce it. Although Desso counted on a 'tufted' wall carpet, we insisted on it being woven into a tapestry – like the ancient ones that depicted landscapes, heroic figures and historic moments, adding to the spatial and acoustic experience of a room, while covering thin walls and door openings to keep out the cold."

"Working closely with the production company and with the machines available, my then colleague Marieke van den Heuvel and I developed this layered composition, a diverse three-dimensional weave. I was really nervous about creating a work that didn't move, pleat or billow! Flat and motionless scares me. We did all we could to add three-dimensional effects to the composition, the illusion of depth and movement. Strategic lighting helps enhance the shadow effects of the work as well. Ann, Patrick van Mil, the museum's financial director, Mels Crouwel, architect of the new wing, and Gilian Schrofer, designer of the restaurant, regularly reviewed the process. We did a great collaborative job with all parties involved, and I think we quite fulfilled our ambitions."   PB

LOCATION	Amsterdam, the Netherlands
CLIENT	Stedelijk Museum Amsterdam – director Ann Goldstein
STATUS	Completed
SCOPE	Tapestry in restaurant and on walls of the entrance hall to improve acoustics
SCALE	Tapestry restaurant, 14 × 10.4 m; tapestry foyer, 20.5 × 3.15 m; total, 210 m²
COLLABORATORS	Desso Tarkett, Aura Luz Melis
DESCRIPTION	We developed a woven woollen tapestry in black, greys and whites for the new entrance hall and restaurant of the museum. The grey was introduced for optical effect but also to express our concern about the black-and-white thinking that seemed to prevail in political and social discussions at the time (and actually still does).

The tapestry, up to 12 metres high in places, illustrates the layering of old (1895) and new architecture (2012), with integrated hand-drawn floorplans by architect Adriaan Willem Weissman, an AutoCAD section drawing of the actual wall and spaces behind the work and with hand-drawn sketches by Mels Crouwel. The flower-repeat is the ancient *Angelica archangelica* (named in the fourteenth century) and refers to the former museum garden that disappeared under the new museum extension. This herb once grew freely in the humid soil when the site was still farmland. We developed 15 different weave bindings – one binding type for each ingredient – to create different rhythms and thicknesses for depth and play of shadows. A regular rhythm of small rectangles stabilises the entire surface, at the same time connecting the new and old Stedelijk: the aligned rectangles shift into a brick pattern when the work moves closer to the old brick building. The gradation of vertical lines, from thin to thick in repetitive waves, make this flat and static tapestry pleat and billow when seen from afar. The work is integrated into the Stedelijk's textile collection. It can be reproduced by Desso Tarkett if the museum considers it necessary due to irreparable damage.

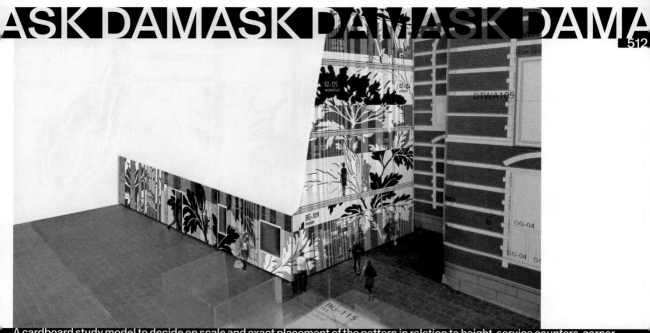

A cardboard study model to decide on scale and exact placement of the pattern in relation to height, service counters, corner, actual floors and rooms behind the tall wall

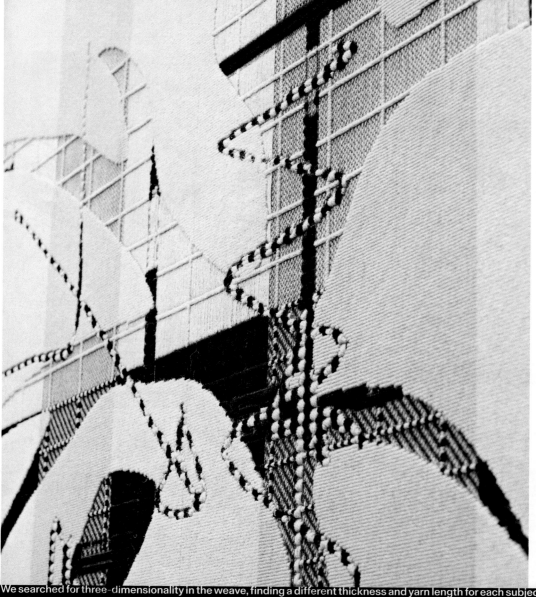

We searched for three-dimensionality in the weave, finding a different thickness and yarn length for each subject. The entirety is held together by a backdrop pattern that, when shifted, mimics the brick pattern of the old Stedelijk building.

03-106
patchkast

02-125
verdeelkast

01-122
gang

BG-109
publieksrestaurant keuken

We used the architect's CAD section drawings to represent the actual spaces and floors behind the wall that is covered by the tapestry, including the figures typically used to help visualise scale

Piranesi Pixel
Landscape CCTV Headquarters and TVCC Conference Centre

"I think this was the most challenging commission we had accepted so far. Designing the CCTV landscape – with all its security regulations, climate conditions and urban logistics – was difficult enough to develop into an accepted, definitive design, but drawing up architectural details without professional landscape experience within our team proved an almost impossible task. I certainly couldn't do it and neither could Yukiko Nesu, my much-appreciated colleague at IO, although we really did our utmost best. Not to the amusement of the (German) architects who led the project at OMA. Normally we are able to overcome the harshest challenges with our creative energy, but this time that didn't work. When architects Rosetta Elkin and Mathias Lehner joined us in the definitive design phase, we were able to catch up and restore our position within the CCTV team. Our design proved to be robust and, in essence, it survived." PB

LOCATION	CCTV Headquarters and TVCC Conference Centre, Beijing, China
CLIENT	Chinese Central Television (CCTV)
STATUS	Completed
SCOPE	Landscape design of streetscape, security zones, roof gardens, public garden and entrance areas; design of street, path and interior finishes of entrance halls
SCALE	10 ha + interior spaces
COLLABORATORS	OMA, ECADI
DESCRIPTION	To introduce the small scale of the old city of Beijing in this project, OMA and Inside Outside decided to use etchings by Piranesi, depicting floorplans of streets, courtyards and houses. We collaged sections of several etches together into a convincing composition. Then we translated Piranesi's black outlines into trimmed shrubbery of various heights. These green screens form a system of outside rooms and paths, offering the CCTV staff space on the flat roof for work, relaxation, filming and recording. Around the entire site at the street level, a negative version of the Piranesi pattern forms a security belt of dense, evergreen, trimmed shrubbery, out of which circular "rooms" are cut. An invisible security fence is placed inside this green, continuous plane with its round cut-outs. Around the TVCC hotel and congress building a more playful public park was projected, with entrance areas, parking areas and driveways as an integral part of the landscape.

As we needed to communicate our design long distance to unknown sub-contractors, we made a pixelated version of the intricate Piranesi design. Everything was integrated within the pixels of this design shift, which we named "Piranesi Pixel," including plantings, furniture, emergency and maintenance stairs and air exhausts and intakes. The pixel pattern spread out into the lawn and travertine pavement areas – paths, "rooms" and squares – as well as into the interiors of the CCTV building, where they form trajectories and sometimes climb walls. Much later Inside Outside won first prize for the landscape design of the Media Park, an area adjacent to CCTV. The client introduced us to a local landscape firm, which eventually took over our design and made it theirs. Copyright and personal merit is not recognised in China.

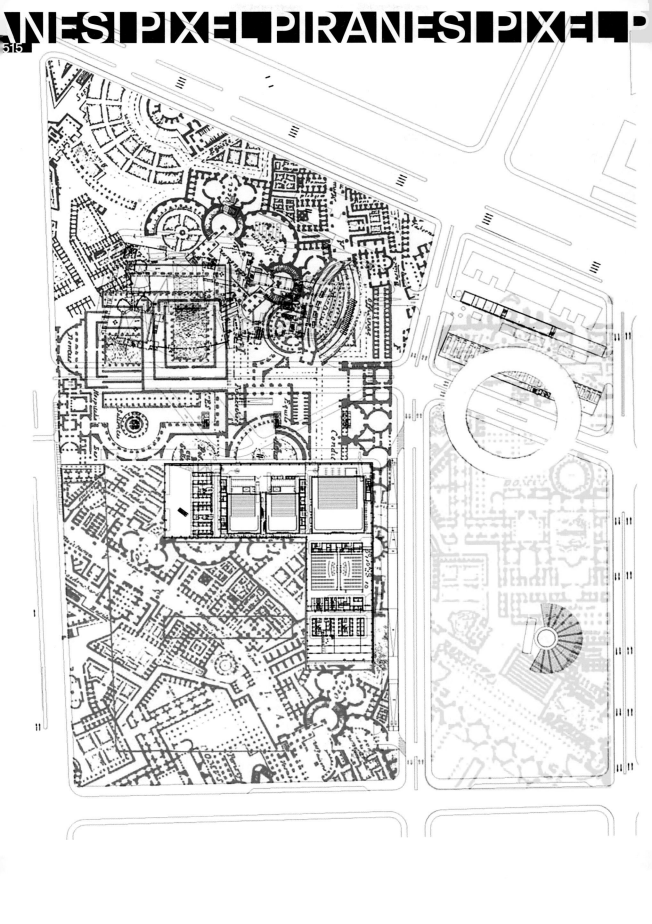

4.3. 像素单元

像素点是位于一个三角形的网格中，由直径为1。2米，间距为40厘米的圆形成。每个像素点根据分配于其上的区域，位置和功能而转译为不同的像素。

1。2米的直径对于像素来说是一个相宜的尺度，这些像素可转化成为建筑元素，可成为花盆或圆形表面处理。

这些圆形令其间的空间成为流动空间，尽管圆形之间最小的距离仅有40cm，这些路径却不断扩宽并分裂成为3条新路径。

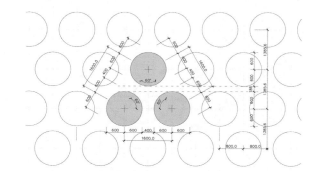

4.3 Pixel Unit

A Pixel is a 1.2 meter diameter circle positioned in a triangular grid. The distance between the circles is 40 cm.

Every pixel can be translated differently depending on the zone, location and programm that apply to the pixel.

The 1.2 meter diameter is an easy dimension for a pixel. A pixel can be transformed into an architectural element, become a planter or just be a circular surface treatment.

The circular shape makes the space in between very dynamic. Although the distance between the pixels at its smallest point is only 40 cm, the 'paths' are widening up and split in 3 paths.

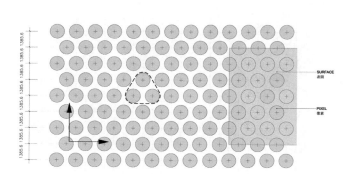

SURFACE
表面

PIXEL
像素

The Piranesi landscape pattern was transformed into a dot pattern to make the complex plan easier for the builders to comprehend and execute

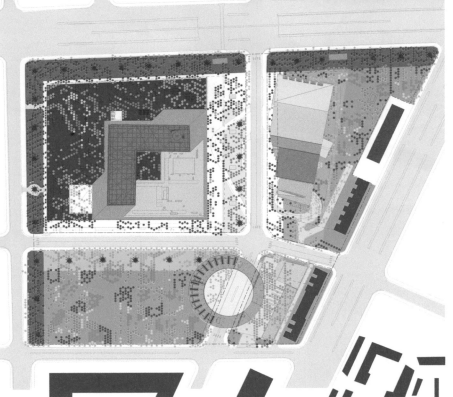

This drawing illustrates the different zones of the CCTV and TVCC landscape: security zones, elevated garden for staff, entrance gardens, public garden, media park, technical zone, green roofs.

OMA model of buildings and gardens

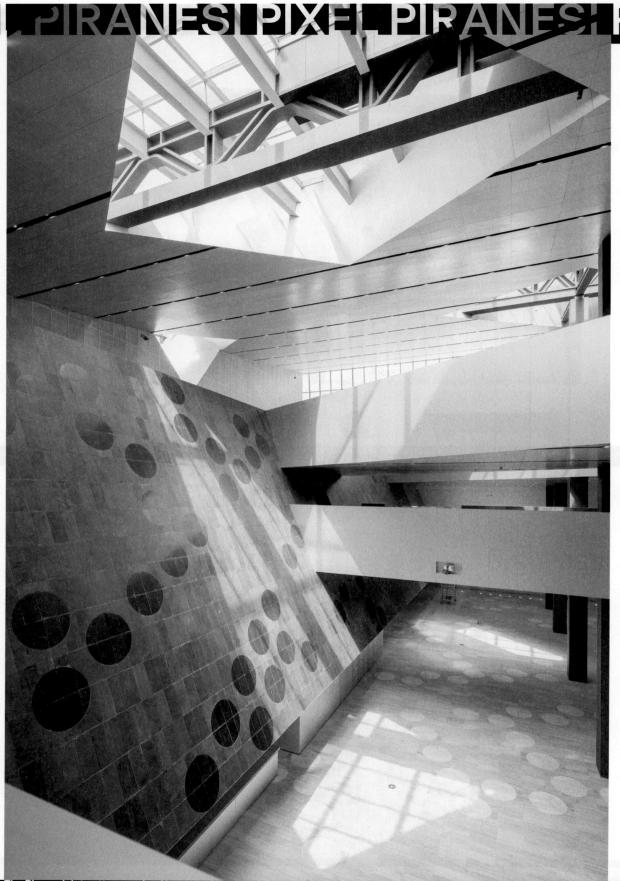

The Piranesi dot pattern evolved into a series of round planters scattered across the lawns, each containing shrubs, trees or flowering plants, exhaust and air-intake chimneys, emergency stairs, furniture, etc. – not quite what we envisioned. What remains from our first drawing are the dot patterns in the natural stone surfaces of paths, plazas and entrance lobbies, some-times escaping their horizontal confinement by climbing onto the interior's monumental sloping walls.

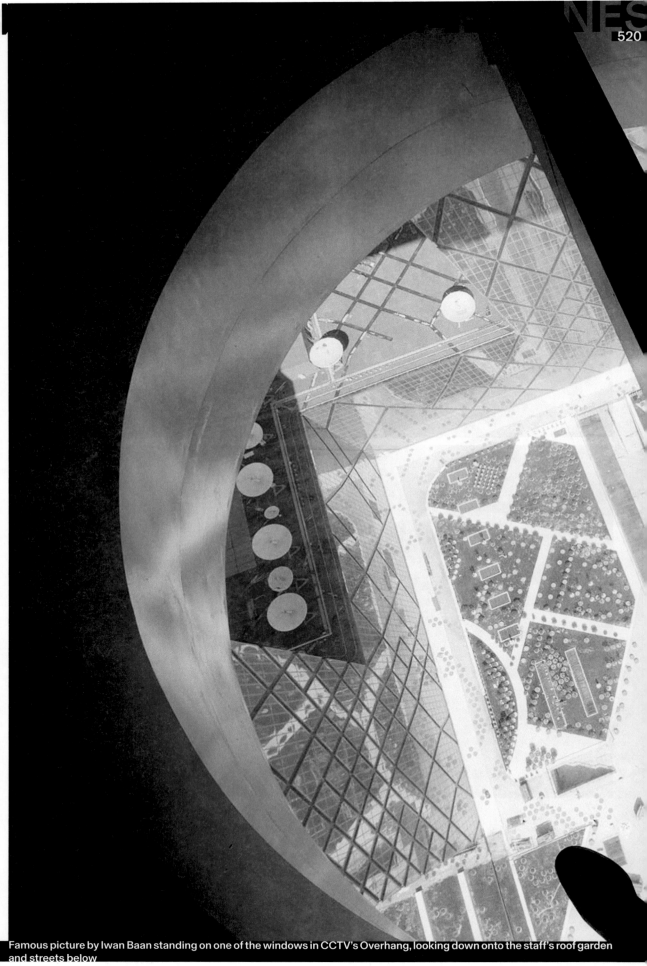

Famous picture by Iwan Baan standing on one of the windows in CCTV's Overhang, looking down onto the staff's roof garden and streets below

Our CCTV and TVCC gardens, heavily simplified through years of traditional Chinese maintenance methods, photographed with iPhone on a grey day through the security fences in March 2023

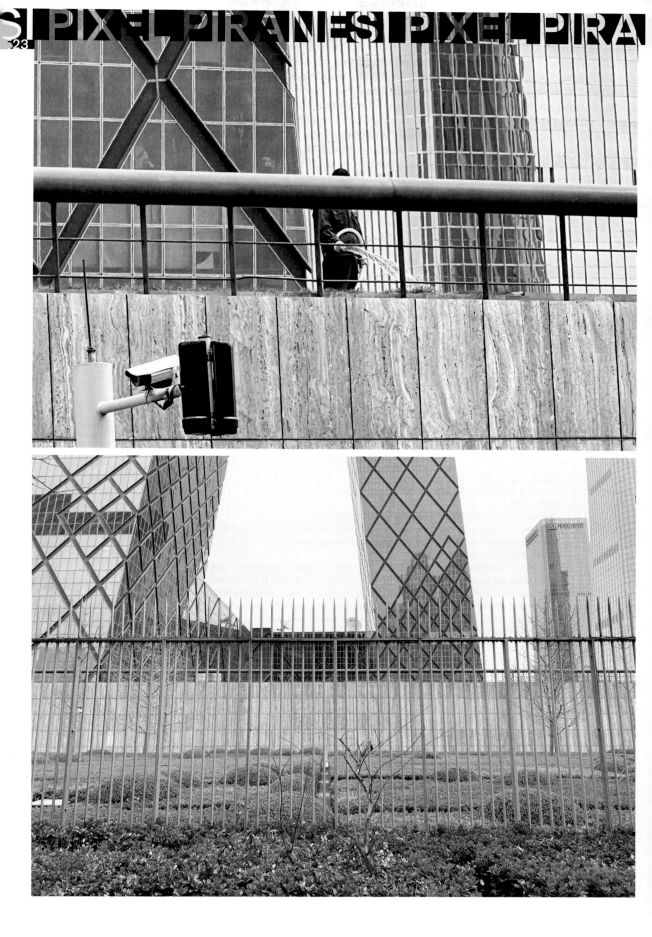

Piper Auditorium
Harvard GSD

"When Mohsen Mostafavi invited us to think of a textile division for the large Piper Auditorium, I was intrigued. I had visited the building years before, and only remembered the exciting, spacious, stepped floor with architecture students working away on drawing boards with study models all around and daylight flowing in generously from one side, and a visiting professor jumping from one level to the next to review the students' completed work. When I visited again, works by Olafur were being exhibited in the hall. The auditorium in question was a mess: filled with drawings boards crisscross over the floor on one side, leaving little space for an auditorium on the other. I thought: one thin layer of cloth won't do – we need mass here for the sound; and serious presence for visual effect! The curtain became a room in itself – sturdy and technical outside, gentle and lovely inside. A nightgown inside a man's raincoat." PB

LOCATION	Cambridge, USA
CLIENT	Harvard University Graduate School of Design
STATUS	Completed
SCOPE	Space-dividing curtain for the Piper Auditorium
MATERIALS	Grey PVC truck cloth, transparent plastic, gold, brocade-like fabric, black fishnet, transparent reinforcement tape, lead fishing weights
SCALE	33.5 × 5.8 m (double-layered)
DESCRIPTION	The Piper Auditorium is a beautiful '70s building, a bold concrete volume on stilts with an irregular window pattern cutting across the front facade and framing the cascade of stepped workspaces inside. We copied the composition of the windows for our curtain as it needed an opening for views and projections. In the process, the dividing curtain became a narrow oval-shaped room with the track designed as a continuous narrow oval, so that the curtain, when pulled out completely, forms a small, oval room. Here one can hide things, install a long table with models or use the space for a meeting. The outside of the curtain is made of grey truck plastic, the interior of a heavily pleated, glimmering gold theatre cloth. As always, the manner in which widths are stitched together and the top, bottom and side seams are treated is important. Here the weights along the lower hem of the gold layer are pearl-shaped lead fishing weights, hanging inside loose translucent covers. They look like elegant earrings.

The curtain's name, Bon-Bon Box, echoes the contradiction between exterior and interior, functional versus theatrical. One can choose which background to use behind a speaker or for a presentation. Its (storage) position is free, the curtain can be shifted in all directions by hand. A cord to minimise the storage volume was added later.

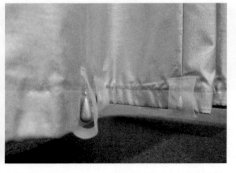

"We made an irregular composition of gold and silver faux leather and gauze, cut in rectangles and all vertically positioned on a transparent organza. The silver and gold rectangles are double-sided, each side its own colour, with the organza in between. The track has an unequal U-shape and the curtain is hand pulled."

"To study the Rothschild collections, we went through many a book and, together with the OMA architects working on the project, visited one of the family's country houses in England where a great many portraits, landscape paintings and furniture pieces are stored. Needless to say, there were many remarkable art works and objects including chinaware, richly embroidered and printed drapes in front of windows and a series of wooden panels that were obviously taken from other buildings as part of a special collection. We studied the detailing of the floors, doors, windows and ceilings and also the views out onto the estate. Finally, we took a walk through the gardens, enjoying the well-maintained lawns and forest-like areas with ancient trees and rhododendrons, generous paths defined by upstanding steel edges, on-and-on meandering, suddenly standing face-to-face with a very large, old aviary – beautiful. Empty of course, but with signs of former residents. We took lots of pictures as a source of inspiration for the bank's future interiors and roof gardens."

"We organised workshops at our studio in Amsterdam. The project leader of OMA Ellen van Loon and her colleagues Isabella and Carol would come for a day – sometimes two – to go through the building floor by floor, room by room, looking for inspiration from our collected samples and tests as well as our library of books and projects. We created all kinds of new material samples, selected the best, made combinations, photocopied them and made numerous to-scale paper collages onto each floor plan: parquet flooring with different patterns for each room and floor, different carpet series in various colour tones – modern and classic – looking for the right way to complement antiques from the Rothschild collection as a welcome contrast to the clear lines and 'pure' materials of the architecture. This included some of the wall panelling and doors, tables, chairs, paintings and more. We thought about ways to embellish the necessary acoustic wall coverings and window shadings – especially for the bank's library of old books – with images of the family's portrait paintings, trying to make them abstract by enlarging them ten-fold or by making paper weaves of copied portraits mixed with abstract patterns of super-enlarged paint structures... etc: fun! Of course, many ideas were taken to a higher level by the OMA team, for which we can only compliment them."   PB

LOCATION	New Court, London, United Kingdom
CLIENT	NM Rothschild & Sons
STATUS	Completed
SCOPE	Acoustic, space-defining and view-filtering curtain for the entrance lobby; outside entrance areas; roof gardens on three levels; advisory on interior finishes; colour and furnishing concepts
MATERIALS	Curtain of colourless polyester organza, golden and silver faux leather, silver grey polyester gauze; plantings; natural stone; travertine; study models for interiors and curtain
SCALE	Lobby curtain, 54.4 × 5.2 m; interiors, 13,000 m²; entrance plaza, roof gardens, 15,000 m²
COLLABORATORS	OMA, Ken Creasey Ltd
DESCRIPTION	The curtain needed to soften the space and filter the urban environment outside without obstructing the daylight. It also needed to create an extra room, when necessary, to act as security sluice or cloakroom. In addition to this specific commission, we studied all interiors and rooms of the building and advised on floor and wall patterns, images and finishes. For the exterior entrance area, we echoed the tombstone pattern of the beautiful old neighbouring church's cemetery by inlaying roughened slabs of travertine in between the smooth ones. On the lower roofs of the building, we envisioned patterns of different colours and structured greens, which could be seen from the office tower. The roof garden on the highest level became a classic design of trimmed shrubbery and carpets of lawn, together forming a series of "meeting rooms" varying in size and shape, embedded in a light-coloured travertine floor.

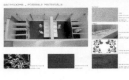

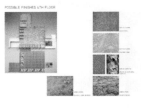

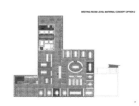

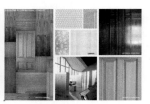

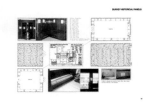

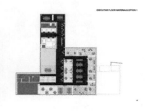

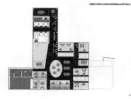

We held regular workshops about the interior with the OMA staff at our Inside Outside studio to develop ideas for floor and wall finishes and concepts for the furnishings. Inspired by the Rothschild family's art and furniture collections and OMA's building materials (steel and glass), we tried to exaggerate the contrast between classical and modern.

Along the way, we developed ideas for the entrance square and roof gardens

the roof garden on top of the bank has a 360-degree of the city as well as "vegetal rooms" for meetings, lunches and tea breaks

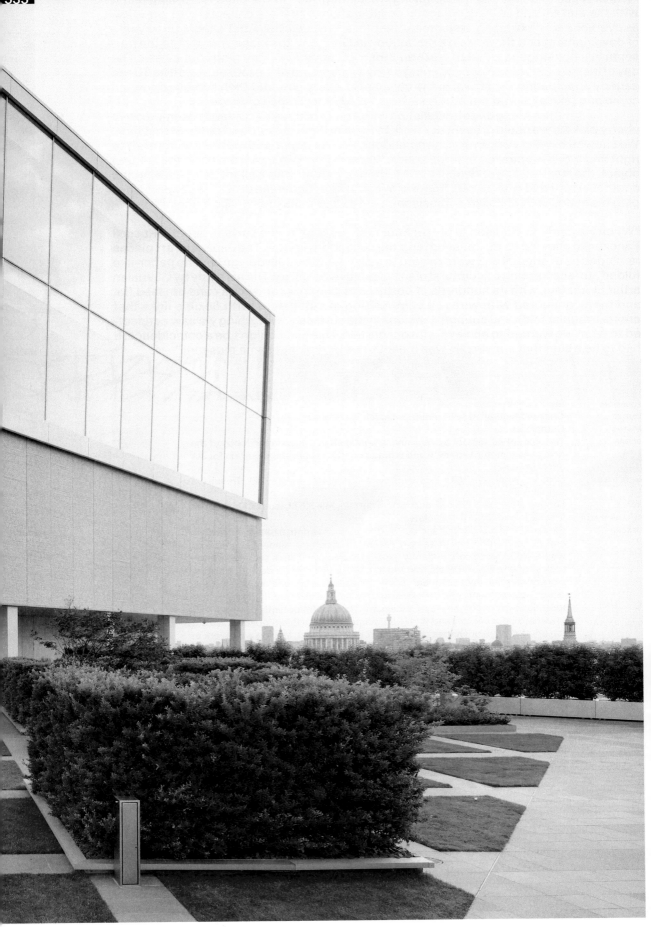

"The process of designing the spiralling track integrated in the panelled ceiling along with the curtain and lighting object (in collaboration with the architects) was a real joy, as everyone was extremely welcoming, helpful and respectful. After almost three years of development and the curtain's production in Germany, the piece was sent to the museum in a humongous wooden crate and then left standing in the lobby for a week. The day of installation was a real happening as many members of the museum staff had been eagerly anticipating the arrival of the curtain. So, every now and then somebody would come and take a peek at our progress, hoping to get a glimpse of the result.

   After a long day of installation with a team of three people and two impressive cherry pickers we could present our work to Russell Panczenko, the director at that time. We showed him the curtain in all its splendour, with its motorised movement from left to right and into the spiralled storage space. There the curtain swirled around the lighting object, the loose silk layer dancing and fluttering behind with a slight delay, leaving the director in awe and with a smile from ear to ear. 'Like a Cinderella dress,' he gasped, clapping his hands with childlike enthusiasm, 'Like a Cinderella dress… Do it again!'"   PN

"When we came to Madison to present our first concept for the curtain, director Russell Panczenko showed us the museum and the collection on view. The Japanese art pieces reminded us of origami and were related to our 'defiant' curtain design with its paper-like folded surface forming a sculptural plane of relative flexibility. The art piece by Ghanaian artist El Anatsui, with its hundreds of bottle caps from beer and soda cans pressed flat and then connected with wire is a composition of stiff pieces with flexible links that create irregular folds and counter-tensions in the surface… everything we saw connected to what we wanted to achieve with our curtain. This just couldn't be a coincidence; it had to be a sign that our curtain was meant to be part of that same museum."   PB

LOCATION	Madison, Wisconsin, USA
CLIENT	Chazen Museum of Art – director Russell Panczenko
STATUS	Completed
SCOPE	Translucent curtain for privacy and acoustic absorbance in the lobby of the new annex; motorised track and storage configuration; stage curtain for auditorium; lamp
MATERIALS	CNC cut wool felt, digital print on Trevira CS voile, silver-grey silk; Trevira CS taft, fibrefill; tube light
SCALE	Lobby curtain, 20 × 6.94 m; auditorium curtain, 14 × 5.5 m; lamp, 6.94 × 0.15 m
COLLABORATORS	Machado and Silvetti Associates
DESCRIPTION	We wanted to make a "defiant" curtain this time, not a soft, pleated and flexible one, but one with a will of its own. Fantasies of stiff translucent shapes that would "kink" along soft, radiantly glowing, transparent lines seduced us and took shape in several tests that led to our original curtain design. At some point during the process though, the fire department pointed out that the curtain covers the main emergency exit and would, due to its relative rigidity, take too long to get out of the way if necessary. Thus we (reluctantly) reversed our idea: hard became soft and thin/transparent became thick/opaque. We cut the original angular shapes out of a thick grey wool felt, leaving a network of opaque lines. To create stability, we attached the felt where the lines intersected to a transparent voile that we bloused a bit, to create more depth. This white voile is printed with a slightly shifted echo of the felt network. In parallel, we designed a track configuration that spirals around a vertical lighting object of our own design, making the stored curtain a lighting sculpture and a landmark of the museum.
	In a next phase, we were invited to design the stage curtain alias backdrop for the museum's auditorium. Here, we created the opposite of the entrance lobby curtain: a thick, duvet-like object that can take different positions while improving the room's acoustic quality.

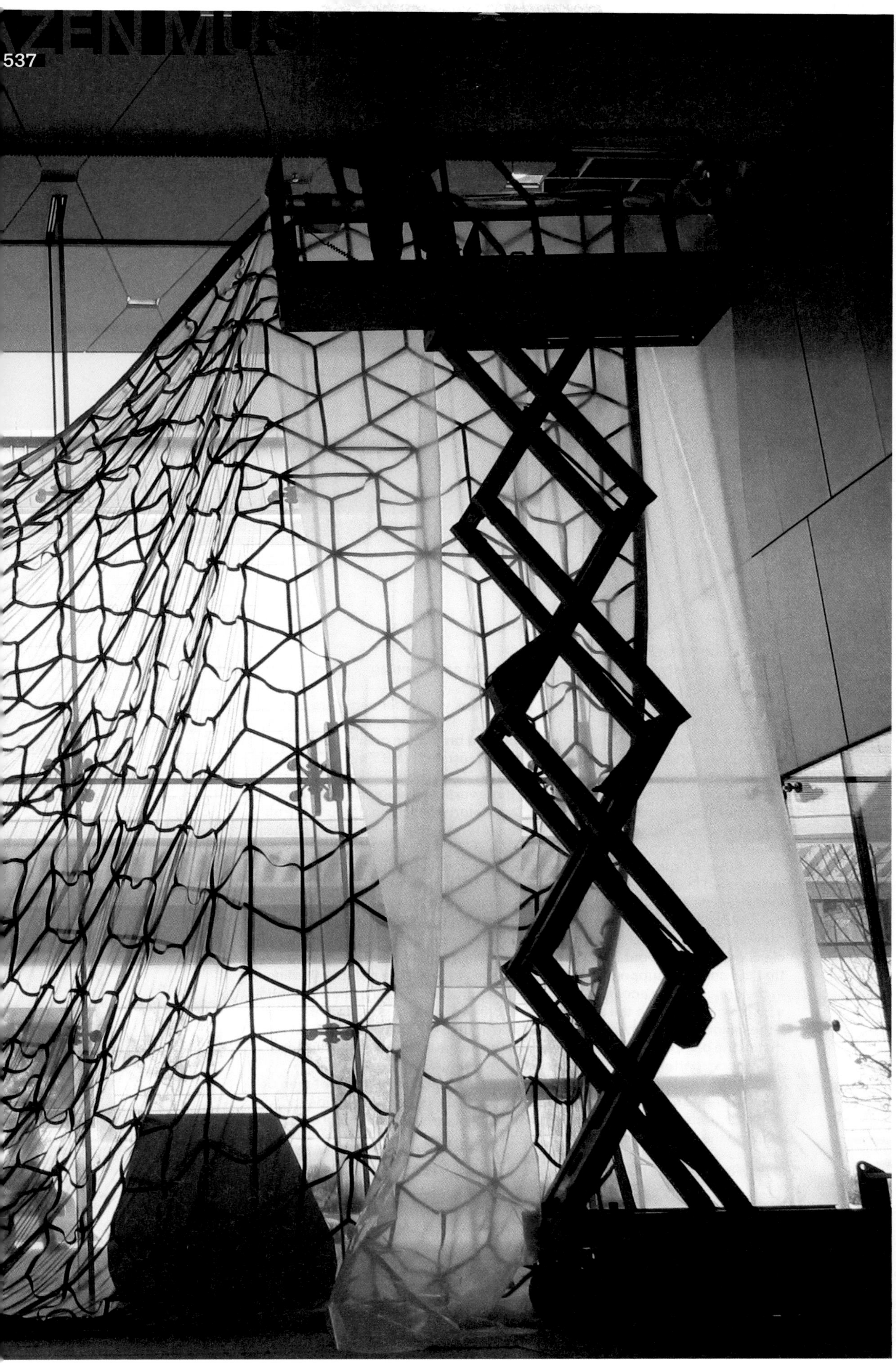

Hans Vredeman de Vries Curtains
Cornell University College of Architecture

"We wanted to tease the architects with this design, challenging their very modern building by adding classic columns and structures – providing the missing columns for OMA's almost floating architecture. In the study rooms upstairs, the mesh curtains with Vredeman's drawings printed in dark brown ink filter daylight while affording a 'veiled' view of the campus landscape and the other buildings. Here, the architectural perspective drawings add an extra layer to the architectural structures nearby, while the small perforation lines project playful patches of light onto the floor and the students at work." PB

"At the official opening party a few students invited us to join them later for a drink at another party close by. After a short walk across Cornell's beautiful campus, we arrived at the place, welcomed by the usual towers of beer crates, loud music and (mainly male) architecture students having agitated discussions. They invited us in and proudly showed us their place where – among the collection of road signs, posters and other treasures – we saw one of Millstein Hall's delicately embossed aluminium ceiling panels hanging on the wall like a hunter's trophy: a clear token of their appreciation of OMA's architecture." PN

LOCATION	Ithaca, New York, USA
CLIENT	Cornell University, College of Architecture, Art and Planning
STATUS	Completed
SCOPE	Darkening curtains for Milstein Hall auditorium; view filter and glare control curtains for AAP forum
MATERIALS	Printed and perforated blackout cloth; printed projection mesh, steel rings
SCALE	Auditorium curtain, 47.4 × 3.7 m; AAP Forum curtain, 31 × 3.7 m
COLLABORATORS	OMA
DESCRIPTION	The auditorium of the Millstein Hall has three vertical glass surfaces that give it an open and transparent character. The motorised curtain darkens the auditorium when necessary and maintains the transparency of the facades when it's stored around the auditorium's stairs.

Since Cornell University is renowned for its architecture department, we zoomed in on the architectural drawings of Dutch artist/architect Hans Vredeman de Vries (1527–1607). He was one of the first to discover and master the rules of perspective. For the auditorium we chose a drawing of columns that we printed on both sides of the curtain. From the inside it suggests a classical landscape outside the auditorium while from the outside it suggests that the columns support OMA's modern architecture. The perspective lines in the drawings are accentuated by perforations with metal eyelets and add a bit of light(ness). As the same image is printed on both sides of the curtain – the inside drawing mirroring the outside image – the perforations will only match the perspective lines of the drawings on the inside, creating an apparent random pattern of perforations on the outside image.

In the AAP forum we combined other drawings of Hans Vredeman de Vries to create a false perspective of mysterious spaces in or outside the forum and printed them on the outside of the chosen mesh in a sepia colour to relate to the old brick wall of the adjacent Sibley Hall.

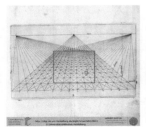

No.2

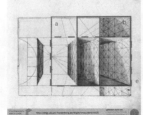

No.4

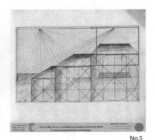

No.5

No.13

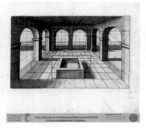

No.14

We visited the print collection of the Rijksmuseum, found the perspective etchings by Hans Vredeman de Vries we were looking for and got permission to borrow them for digital reproduction. The red frames show the parts we selected for the two curtain collages.

Auditorium Darkening Curtain 1A

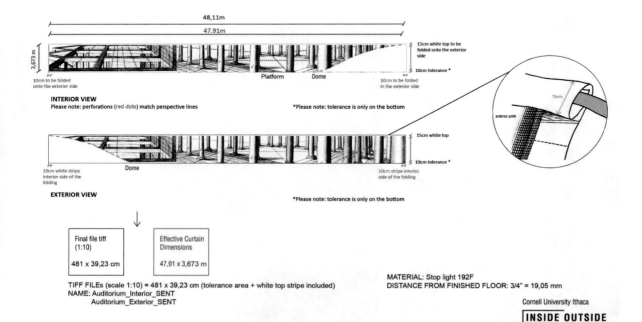

48,11m

47.91m

3,673 m

15cm white top to be folded onto the exterior side

10cm tolerance *

10cm to be folded onto the exterior side

Platform   Dome

10cm to be folded in the exterior side

70mm

exterior print

INTERIOR VIEW
Please note: perforations (red dots) match perspective lines

*Please note: tolerance is only on the bottom

15cm white top

10cm tolerance *

10cm white stripe interior side of the folding

Dome

10cm stripe interior side of the folding

EXTERIOR VIEW

*Please note: tolerance is only on the bottom

Final file tiff (1:10)	Effective Curtain Dimensions
481 x 39,23 cm	47,91 x 3,673 m

TIFF FILEs (scale 1:10) = 481 x 39,23 cm (tolerance area + white top stripe included)
NAME: Auditorium_Interior_SENT
          Auditorium_Exterior_SENT

MATERIAL: Stop light 192F
DISTANCE FROM FINISHED FLOOR: 3/4" = 19,05 mm

Cornell University Ithaca

INSIDE OUTSIDE
PETRA BLAISSE

page **1**

Typical example of the way in which a curtain is represented in a tender document: one page includes information about material, cuts and finishing for the top edge

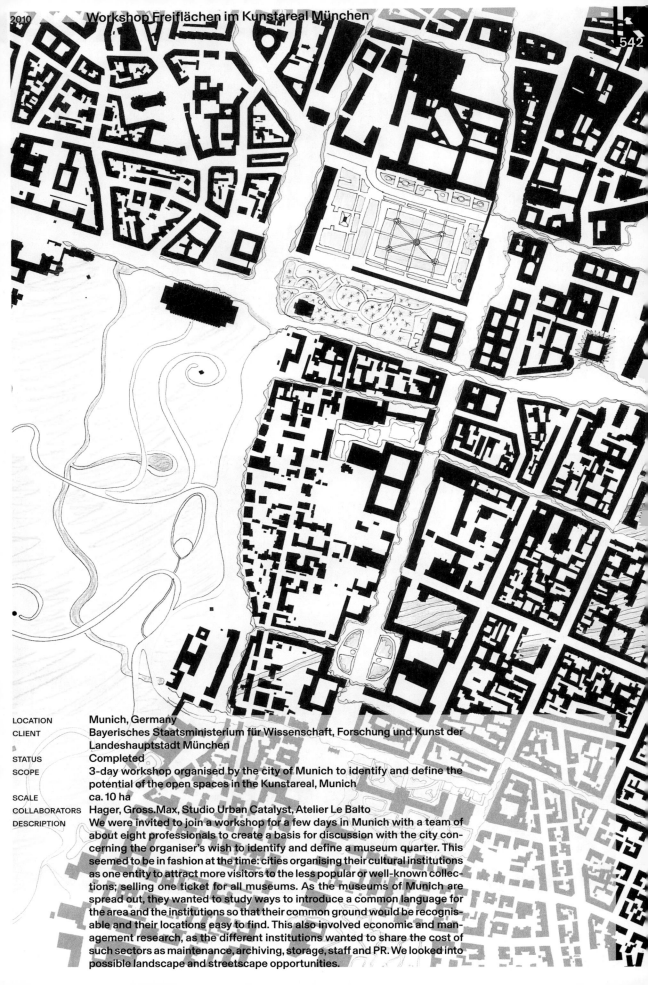

LOCATION	Munich, Germany
CLIENT	Bayerisches Staatsministerium für Wissenschaft, Forschung und Kunst der Landeshauptstadt München
STATUS	Completed
SCOPE	3-day workshop organised by the city of Munich to identify and define the potential of the open spaces in the Kunstareal, Munich
SCALE	ca. 10 ha
COLLABORATORS	Hager, Gross.Max, Studio Urban Catalyst, Atelier Le Balto
DESCRIPTION	We were invited to join a workshop for a few days in Munich with a team of about eight professionals to create a basis for discussion with the city concerning the organiser's wish to identify and define a museum quarter. This seemed to be in fashion at the time: cities organising their cultural institutions as one entity to attract more visitors to the less popular or well-known collections; selling one ticket for all museums. As the museums of Munich are spread out, they wanted to study ways to introduce a common language for the area and the institutions so that their common ground would be recognisable and their locations easy to find. This also involved economic and management research, as the different institutions wanted to share the cost of such sectors as maintenance, archiving, storage, staff and PR. We looked into possible landscape and streetscape opportunities.

Park of the New Horizon
West Kowloon Cultural City

"Once again, we discovered how important landscape is as a tool for new urban developments. In developing the urban plan, it is the first layer to be incorporated into the organisation of the infrastructure. Not only is the health of the soil and the life underground essential – even underneath future buildings – but nature and infrastructure go hand-in-hand and can work in parallel to cool, protect and anchor structures. A landscape can also buffer water and organise air flow because it is a porous layer that can be opened for maintenance of underground systems at any time. Landscape plays a role in the early stages, but also in the final ones by soothing tensions, giving (temporary) free green space to inhabitants for numerous activities, upgrading the value of an area, and preparing ground levels and systems for future buildings. Landscape can open up unexpected qualities and possibilities: viewpoints, natural shading, spatial organisation, wayfinding, wellbeing, health, beauty, open space – happiness!" PB

LOCATION	West Kowloon, Hong Kong
CLIENT	WKCD Authorities
STATUS	Competition, 2nd prize
SCOPE	Landscape masterplan, including all infrastructure above and below ground
SCALE	42 ha
COLLABORATORS	OMA, Atelier Urbanus Shenzhen, Mc Kinsey & Company, Michael Schindhelm, Hou Hanru et al.
DESCRIPTION	This long and narrow site that follows the shoreline opposite Hong Kong City is new land regained from the sea when the tunnel was built to connect Kowloon to the city; a landfill, in other words, mainly used for the storage of building materials and otherwise left alone, used only by locals to grow vegetables, to fish, picnic and play. Views from here are staggeringly beautiful in all directions: the sunset, the high-rise profile of Hong Kong seen through a glittering haze, large ships passing by…

Inspired by the local fish-farming ponds with their irregular, angular shapes and in view of OMA's plan to build three small villages spread over the site, each with their own art program (rather than a series of buildings for culture), we composed a continuous, flowing carpet of fields, the pattern drawn by an intricate system of paths. The program and character of each field changes between one village and the next. Topography is an important tool here to connect the park with the underground world, buildings with landscape and shore, bridgeheads with the surrounding city and also to cover the underground road system and technical infrastructure. Moving from east to west, the park includes a host of uses: open-air auditoriums, sunken terraces and orchards, sculpture gardens, running tracks, fishponds and water containment pools, playgrounds, areas for sports, picnicking, tai chi and skateboarding, vegetable and flower gardens, plazas, viewing decks and hills. A continuous feng shui forest (mixed trees, shrubbery and undergrowth bearing fruit and nuts) snakes over the fields, providing the necessary shading for pedestrians and connecting the entire park.

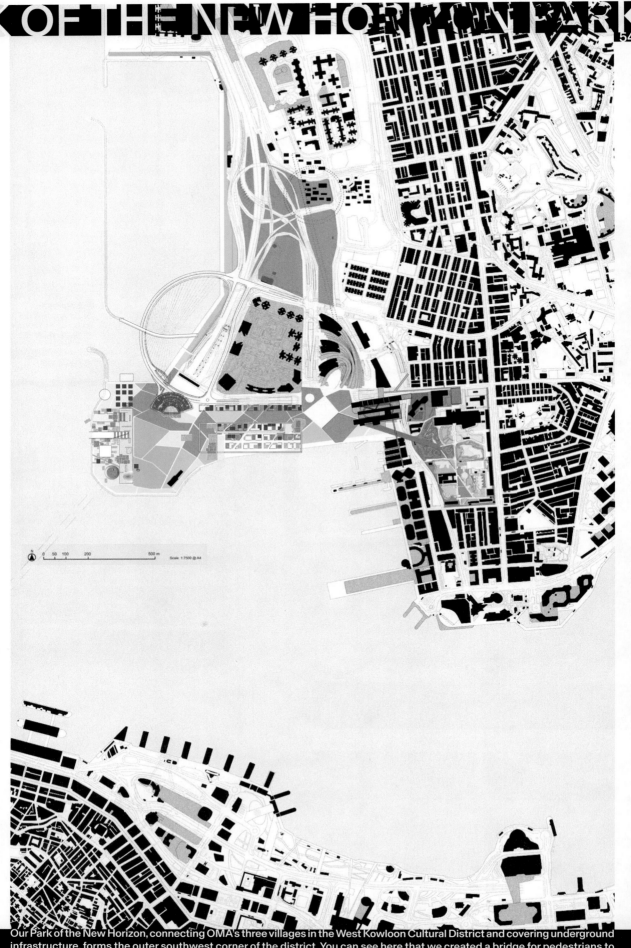

Our Park of the New Horizon, connecting OMA's three villages in the West Kowloon Cultural District and covering underground infrastructure, forms the outer southwest corner of the district. You can see here that we created a bridge for pedestrians to reach the existing Kowloon Park.

Fishing

Climbing

Kiting

Sun bathing

Surfing

Graffiti

Dogs allowed

Feel the plants

Hawking

Bird feeding

Skateboarding

Keep clean

Cycling

Lying on benches

Lying on lawn

We always want to liberate public parks from the usual restrictions!

(CHINESE) THEATRE GARDEN

CHILDREN'S PLAYGROUND

LAKE AND TEAHOUSE

HARBORS & QUAYS

AGRICULTURE FIELD
(VEGETABLES, HERBS, FRUIT)

BIKE & SKATE FIELDS

CHILDREN'S FARM

MAIN PLAZA

ORCHARD + ART

My sketches, representing the different forms of use that the Park of the New Horizon offers, surround a few of the collages we made to illustrate some of the park's different attractions, areas and viewpoints

PERGOLA ROUTE   MARKET PLACE

SPORTSFIELDS

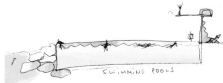

SWIMMING POOLS

REED FIELD

ROCK FORMATIONS

FLOATING DECK
FOR MUSIC ETC.

CONTINUOUS
COAST LINE

OPEN LAWNS

OPEN FIELDS

MIXED FOREST

Flora and fauna
Vegetation fields: Forest Garden, Meadows and Water Bodies

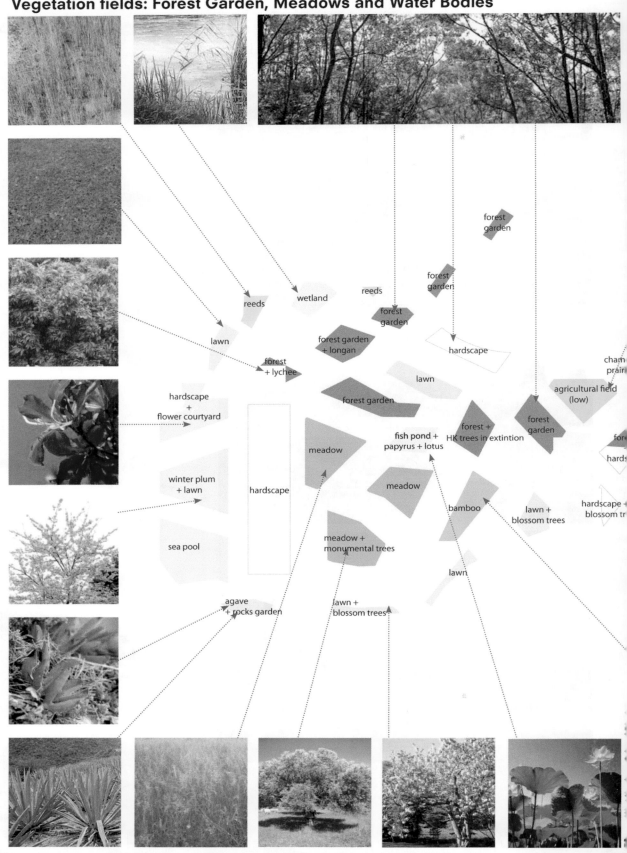

forest garden

forest garden

reeds

wetland

forest garden

forest garden + longan

hardscape

cham prairi

lawn

forest + lychee

reeds

agricultural field (low)

hardscape + flower courtyard

forest garden

forest garden

lawn

fore hards

fish pond + papyrus + lotus

forest + HK trees in extinction

winter plum + lawn

hardscape

meadow

meadow

bamboo

lawn + blossom trees

hardscape + blossom tr

sea pool

meadow + monumental trees

lawn

agave + rocks garden

lawn + blossom trees

Each field has its own character and function, with matching blue, green and/or water-retaining surface (meadow, wetland, lawn, porous surface, water reservoir) and plant/tree selection. Here an expanded view of the fields with their typologies symbolised by one typical plant or tree. Together with the shaded food forest that connects all conditions from east to west, the park becomes an extremely biodiverse environment.

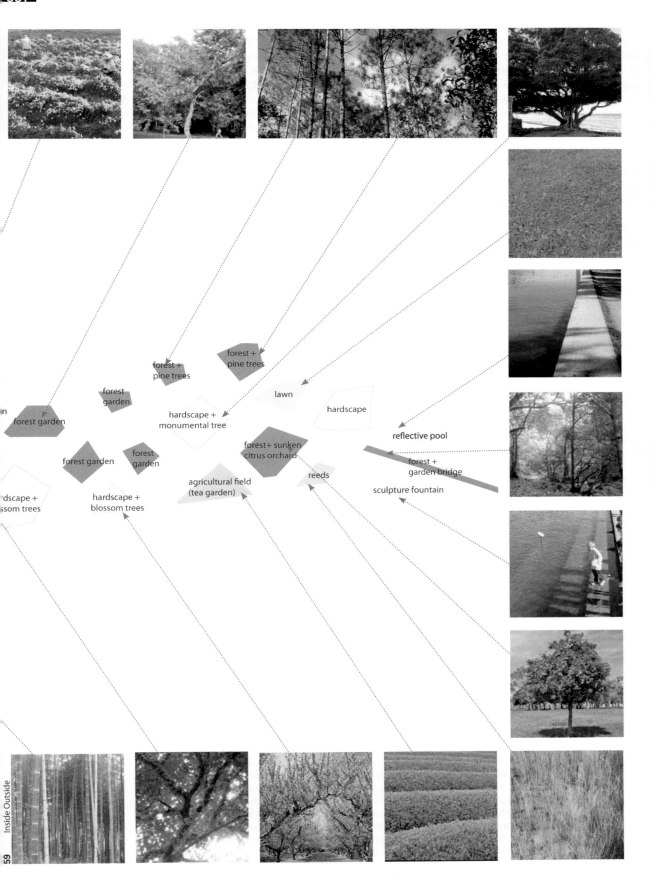

forest + pine trees

forest + pine trees

forest garden

lawn

hardscape

forest garden

hardscape + monumental tree

reflective pool

forest garden

forest garden

forest+ sunken citrus orchard

agricultural field (tea garden)

reeds

forest + garden bridge

sculpture fountain

dscape + ssom trees

hardscape + blossom trees

Desert City
Masterplan for Ghadames

"Visiting the Libyan city of Tripoli with its Italian influence, its unprotected and unkempt Roman ruins along the sea (not a single fence or other barrier, a seamless continuation of the city!), experiencing the endless drive through a monotonous desert landscape (asphalt road lined with electricity poles, cutting straight through a stony beige flatness with sparse tufts of growth and sudden odd rock formations) towards the desert town of Ghadames was, again, a unique experience. Old Ghadames, an intricate weave of narrow, walled alleys with openings slanting to the left and right, leading to yet another web of shaded alleys, which led to wooden doors that in turn led into living quarters with uneven whitewashed walls, softly shining lanterns and sumptuous cushions in reds on the floor. Houses that families now living in Tripoli kept to preserve memories of the past or as a holiday home. Walled gardens where once vegetables and fruit trees thrived, now abandoned and dried out. A walled town that was once fertile inside and barren outside is now barren both inside and out. A road cuts through the old and the new town of Ghadames. On one side the centuries-old Ghadames, on the other its 'Rorschach image' of the '70s: same size and shape but filled with low, concrete housing blocks and linear streets."

"Whether we should accept work in places or with clients that one might not consider 'politically correct' is always an issue for us and others around us. I find it hard to answer to criticism of that order. Of course, it is an important point, but wherever we go to work, we communicate with local colleagues, builders and inhabitants. Everyone stresses the necessity for us all to stay connected and to keep exchanging knowledge and creativity with others. Many people don't agree with their own government or can explain very well why our Western European perspective is limited or outright wrong. It is so easy for us Westerners to point a finger at differences that we don't understand. We are often wrong or just naïve in our judgement – and our fears." PB

LOCATION	Ghadames (World Heritage Site), Nalut district, Libya
CLIENT	Wahat, developers and architects
STATUS	Schematic design
SCOPE	Landscape masterplan and phasing plan for the abandoned, ancient desert town; landscape design for a new film festival and tourist spa on a former military site nearby; gardens for a planned hotel on the former airplane landing strip
SCALE	268 ha
COLLABORATORS	OMA
DESCRIPTION	The Libyan government wanted to re-vitalise their desert towns by fostering culture and tourism. Naturally, restoration of the original structures – including gardens and street systems – was an integral element of these projects. OMA and Inside Outside needed to address three sites: the ancient Ghadames village itself, a former runway to the east and a former military site to the west. Ancient Ghadames is still owned by families living elsewhere, for example, in the capital Tripoli or the city of Benghazi. They would occasionally come back to their houses for holidays. As is customary in the desert, the town is walled in for protection against wind, sand and unwelcome visitors; each garden plot within the walls is also walled in. The first thing we envisioned was to restore the water systems and gardens, so that vegetables, fruit, herbs and other goods could be produced. Outside Ghadames, a bit farther up the asphalt desert road, an old military base was chosen to accommodate the future film festival where the VIPs of cinema were to gather. A whole village was proposed, with villas and theatres, pools and spas, restaurants and sports facilities, golf courses and shaded gardens – above and below ground.

Right next to the old Ghadames village, on the former runway that left a long linear scar in the landscape, OMA envisioned a linear, beam-shaped hotel punctuated with a series of patios, connected by narrow corridors, actually a chain of independent white bungalows, framed by a continuous wall. The hotel had only one storey and measured a few hundred metres in length. Open patio gardens each with its own characteristic features function as cooling elements. The composition of built and unbuilt – closely positioned volumes versus gardens and narrow alleys – was organised in the traditional way, where shade, air flow and water evaporation provide for natural cooling. Rainwater and dew were to be collected and used for irrigation and cleaning. We developed all the designs in collaboration with the climate engineers of the team, as water management, natural cooling and sustainability in general were high on the agenda. The project was aborted when the political situation of the country escalated in 2011.

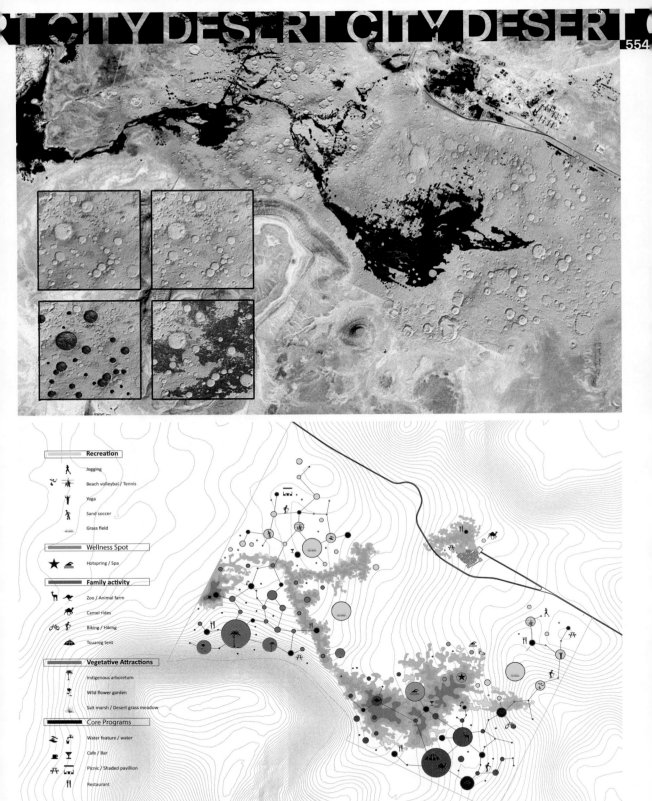

Recreation
- Jogging
- Beach volleybal / Tennis
- Yoga
- Sand soccer
- Grass field

Wellness Spot
- Hotspring / Spa

Family activity
- Zoo / Animal farm
- Camel rides
- Biking / Hiking
- Touareg tent

Vegetative Attractions
- Indigenous arboretum
- Wild flower garden
- Salt marsh / Desert grass meadow

Core Programs
- Water feature / water
- Cafe / Bar
- Picnic / Shaded pavillion
- Restaurant

N   0   100   250m

For the landscape of this film festival site we chose to introduce clearly defined, circular areas that could be concave or convex, above or below ground, uncovered or covered by a shading device, each circular intervention with its own program

Old city
Phase 1
Phase 2
Phase 3

N 0 100 250m

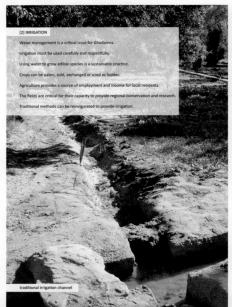

[2] IRRIGATION

Water management is a critical issue for Ghadames.

Irrigation must be used carefully and respectfully.

Using water to grow edible species is a sustainable practice.

Crops can be eaten, sold, exchanged or used as fodder.

Agriculture provides a source of employment and income for local residents.

The fields are critical for their capacity to provide regional conservation and research.

Traditional methods can be reinvigorated to provide irrigation.

traditional irrigation channel

restored irrigation channel

Restoration works in the ancient desert town on the one hand (above); the scientific organisation of cooling gardens in a totally new architectural structure on the other (right page)

Ventilation by Arabic principle of "hot" and "cold" courtyards

- Courtyards have to be integrated in the site
- Courtyards with different sizes to provide different qualities
  sun exposed hot courtyard → higher pressure (used in winter)
  shaded small courtyards → lower pressure (used in summer)
- Cold courtyards shaded and vegetated, hot cold yards paved and less shaded
- Open for the main wind direction
- Sloping heights of buildings (within the stripe the wind speed will be reduced by buildings and other obstructions). By sloping heights wind can be cached also in the southwestern end of the stripe

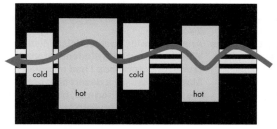

Concept hot and cold courtyard

Plan

Main wind direction

A ── A'

Schematic section AA'

Sloping heights

Wind caught by higher buildings

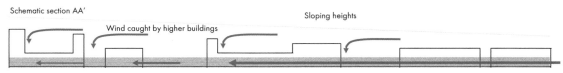

Wind slowing down

Con los Ojos Abiertos
La Casa Encendida

"As usual, we did some research and discovered that Madrid lies on a plateau 635 metres above sea level and is surrounded by very different natural environments including the Sierra de Guadarrama of the Sistema Central to the West (with Peñalara, the highest mountain in Madrid, at an altitude of 2428 metres), savannas, wetland marshes in the low-lying plains and along rivers in various directions. Because of this, it is one of the most important resting places for migrating birds. We decided to concentrate on both the migrant and the local bird populations, and to make birds the symbol of the awareness of nature in the city. After reading numerous articles on the subject, IO's Karin and Carmen went to Madrid to meet with Mr Fernando Barrio and colleagues of the Sociedad Española de Ornitología to get more detailed information. We collected images of all the birds and habitats in question and composed a continuous runner for the stairs as well as a series of 'positive' and 'negative' sunscreens and awnings – sunscreens with bird cut-outs in the opaque surface and with birds 'appliquéd' onto the translucent mesh base. As a result, patches of sunlight or shadows in the form of flying birds moved through the interior spaces throughout the day. The 'bird-carpet' ran from the entrance up to the roof terrace, where a bird's nest-like curtain waved in the wind. On the third floor, a large print covered a wall, including a map of Madrid surrounded by its natural environments as well as our findings and ideas about greening the city. We also added very direct questions to the visitors to stimulate their awareness, inviting them to write their reactions onto the poster itself with supplied felt pens. The mayor of Madrid was impressed and asked us to reproduce the 'bird runners' as a carpet for his office in the city hall, but, alas! To produce such a unique piece in the right quality proved too costly."   PB

LOCATION	Madrid, Spain
CLIENT	Fundación Montemadrid
SCOPE	Site-specific installation
MATERIALS	Printed project carpets and CNC-cut sunshades; roof curtains of silk, choucroute (all materials recycled after closure)
SCALE	Facade, 34 "bird" sunshades, 2.38 × 1.8 m; one continuous ribbon carpet over five flights of stairs, 102 × 0.6 m; roof curtain, 51.5 × 4.5 m; interactive poster, 2 × 2 m
COLLABORATORS	Ariadna Cantis, Sociedad Española de Ornitología, La Casa Encendida team
DESCRIPTION	When I worked with students at the architecture faculty in Madrid – an invitation for a workshop I had received from Juan Herreros – they told me that Madrid is actually a desert city: only greened in the touristic centre of town, the remainder a dried-out, barren environment where nothing grew or lived – except people. We visited some neighbourhoods and discussed what could be done to improve the environment without using water or investing money, and by involving the different communities. In the meantime, Ariadna Cantis invited Inside Outside to do a site-specific, temporary installation somewhere in Madrid. She proposed La Casa Encendida, a cultural centre with a rich, varied program of exhibitions, concerts and performances as well as creative, social and educational spaces, services for free and a world crafts shop – all accommodated in one large nineteenth-century building.

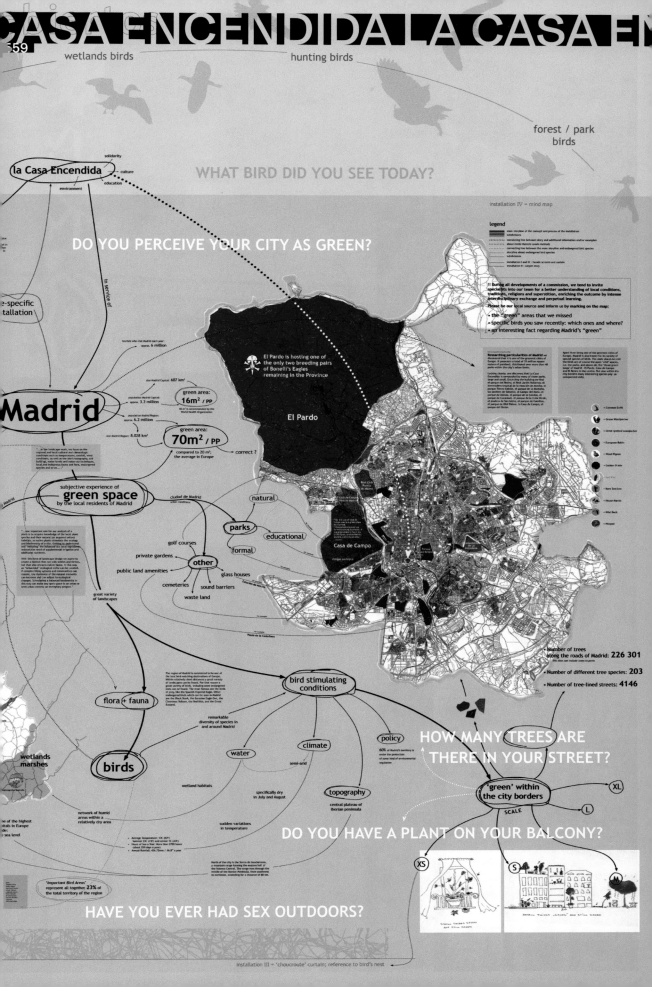

1 2 3 4 5 6 7a 7b 8 9

LOCATION	Amsterdam, the Netherlands
CLIENT	Private owner
STATUS	Completed
SCOPE	Design of private garden, installation and maintenance
MATERIALS	Plantings, concrete tiles, wood, water
SCALE	8 × 10 m
DESCRIPTION	The garden, situated inside a closed building block and facing southwest, developed like small lacework over a period of 24 years. It became an enclosed gazebo and had special effects every season. It attracted insect and bird life as well as amphibians with the help of the neighbouring gardens, which had little water features here and there and were filled with fruit trees (and chickens). A monumental chestnut tree bloomed profusely and shaded our gardens. Unfortunately, it got infected by leaf miners and its dry leaves covered our gardens from early summer on.

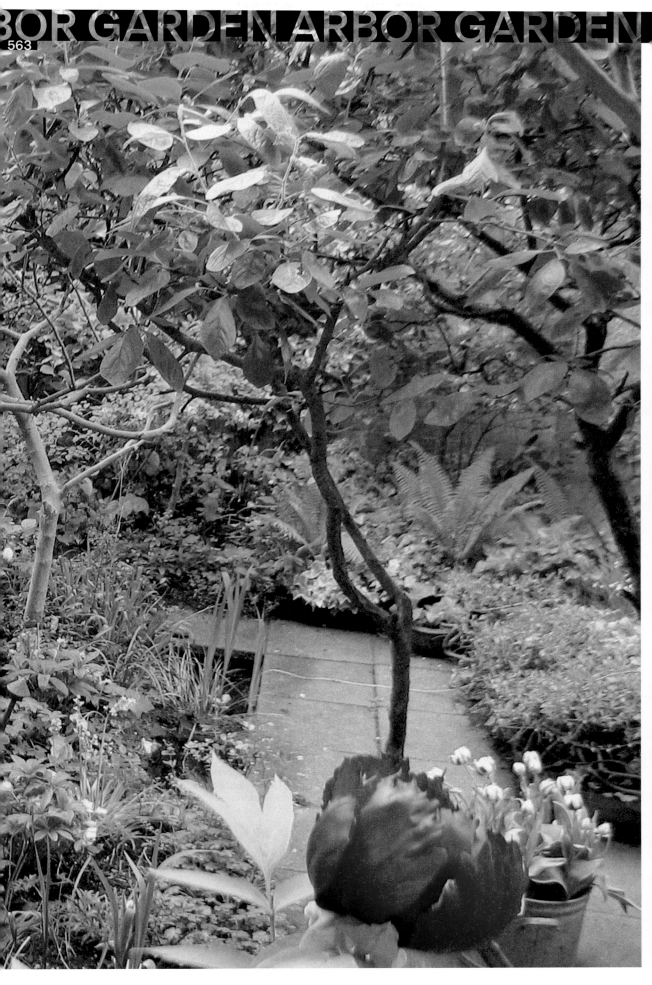

"Inspired by the collages made for our first prison garden commission in the late '90s, we made lots of collage-like illustrations for these two very different design proposals. However, unlike the Nieuwegein prison, prisoners in these two institutions mostly stay there for a considerable time, which gave us the possibility to offer gardens in which one can really live and work, gardens where food is produced and health is improved, and where initiatives can be taken by the prisoners themselves – hopefully helping them to cope with their fate and to work towards a better future."   PB

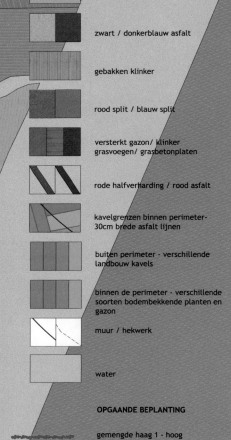

gazon

zwart / donkerblauw asfalt

gebakken klinker

rood split / blauw split

versterkt gazon/ klinker
grasvoegen/ grasbetonplaten

rode halfverharding / rood asfalt

kavelgrenzen binnen perimeter-
30cm brede asfalt lijnen

buiten perimeter - verschillende
landbouw kavels

binnen de perimeter - verschillende
soorten bodembekkende planten en
gazon

muur / hekwerk

water

OPGAANDE BEPLANTING

gemengde haag 1 - hoog

LOCATION   Beveren and Dendermonde, Belgium
CLIENT   Regie der Gebouwen / Jan de Nul Group
STATUS   Competition
SCOPE   Landscape masterplans and design of all prison gardens, walls, exterior en-
                trance and parking areas
SCALE   Dendermonde, 13 ha; Beveren, 12 ha
COLLABORATORS   51N4E, Hootsmans Architectuurbureau
DESCRIPTION   Two new prisons were the substance of this competition. The architects and
                contractor invited us to design and organise the outside spaces, including
                walls and parking lots. Although the architects designed identical prison
                buildings for both sites, the surrounding contexts were totally different as
                reflected in IO's landscape designs. One design reacts to the hectic stress of
                the urban context (zigzag pattern, square prison wall), the other echoes the
                relaxed pattern of the countryside (agricultural fields, circular prison wall). The
                gardens also had different purposes: the first concentrated on sports and
                workouts, the second on gardening and food production. Our projects came
                in second – the winner was the team of Stéphane Beel Architecten.

State Detention Centre Beveren: landscape designed for inmates with long prison sentences. The gardens are set up for them to create and maintain vegetable and herb gardens. The design takes the surrounding agricultural fields as inspiration. In this "softer" mentality with a lower security level, the prison wall is round.

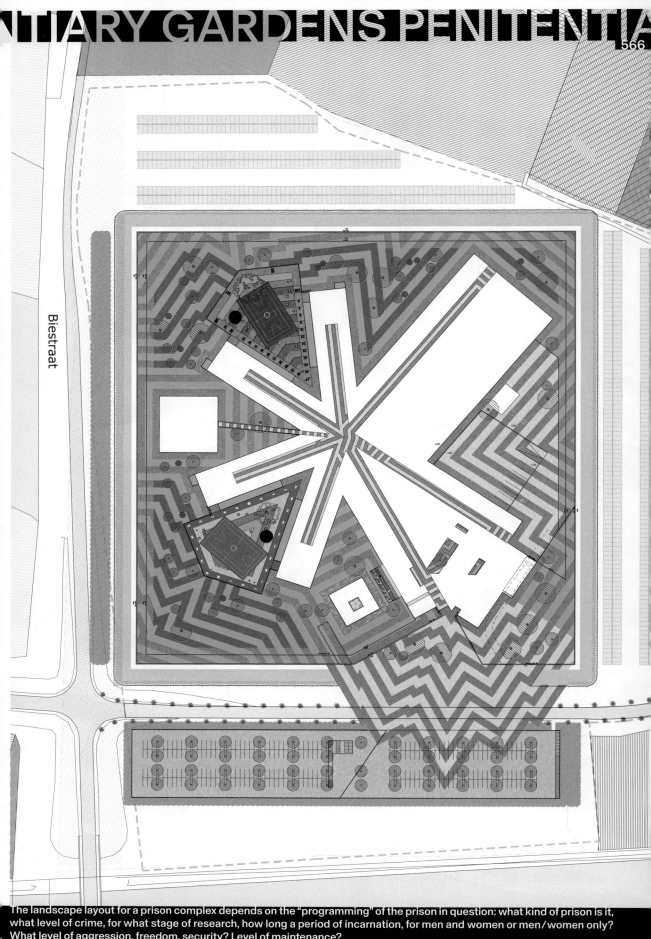

Biestraat

The landscape layout for a prison complex depends on the "programming" of the prison in question: what kind of prison is it, what level of crime, for what stage of research, how long a period of incarnation, for men and women or men/women only? What level of aggression, freedom, security? Level of maintenance?

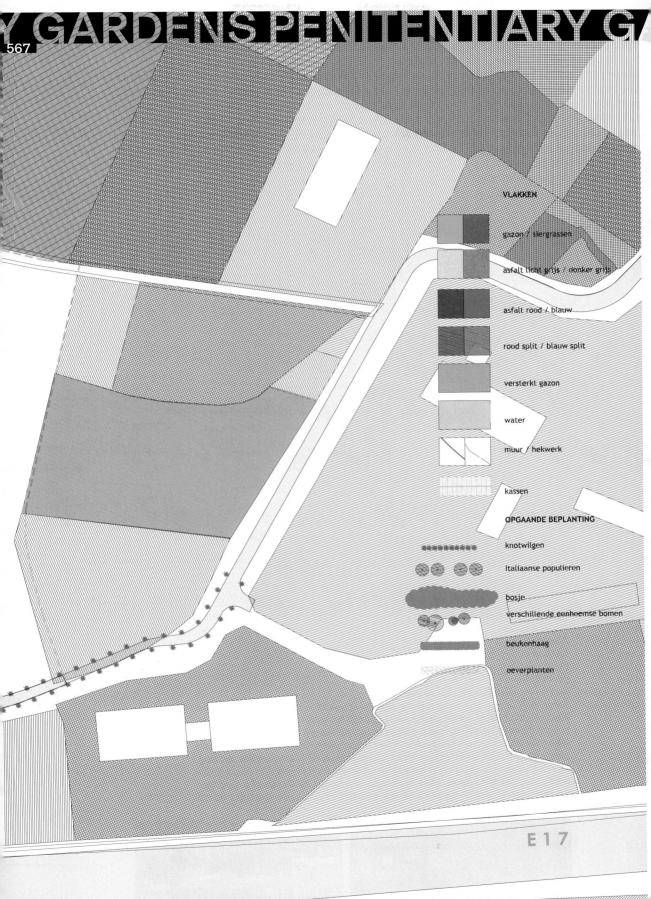

VLAKKEN

gazon / siergrassen

asfalt licht grijs / donker grijs

asfalt rood / blauw

rood split / blauw split

versterkt gazon

water

muur / hekwerk

kassen

OPGAANDE BEPLANTING

knotwilgen

Italiaanse populieren

bosje

verschillende eenheemse bomen

beukenhaag

oeverplanten

E 17

State Detention Centre Dendermonde: Energetic landscape design related to urban context and short-term detainees, the outside spaces aimed at sports and work-outs. Inmates are stressed as they await their sentence, so security here is high.

"Our clients believed in our design but were terrified of what had to be done first to make their dream happen. They let us go ahead but kept a sharp eye on the gardener and us during the entire process. Every move was discussed and many agreed to but without joy. No helping hand, no collegiality, no cup of tea: we were suspect employees – and nothing more. The day Jana and I finished the job, we said goodbye to a happy garden full of life, light and flowering plants, a sunken trampoline for the daughter, a cabinet for garden furniture integrated into a sun-bathed, floating deck overlooking the creek and the new jetty for the rowing boat and then waved farewell to the welcoming front garden. Never to be visited again, we quickly and secretly took some photos – a strictly forbidden act – with our sandy hands."   PB

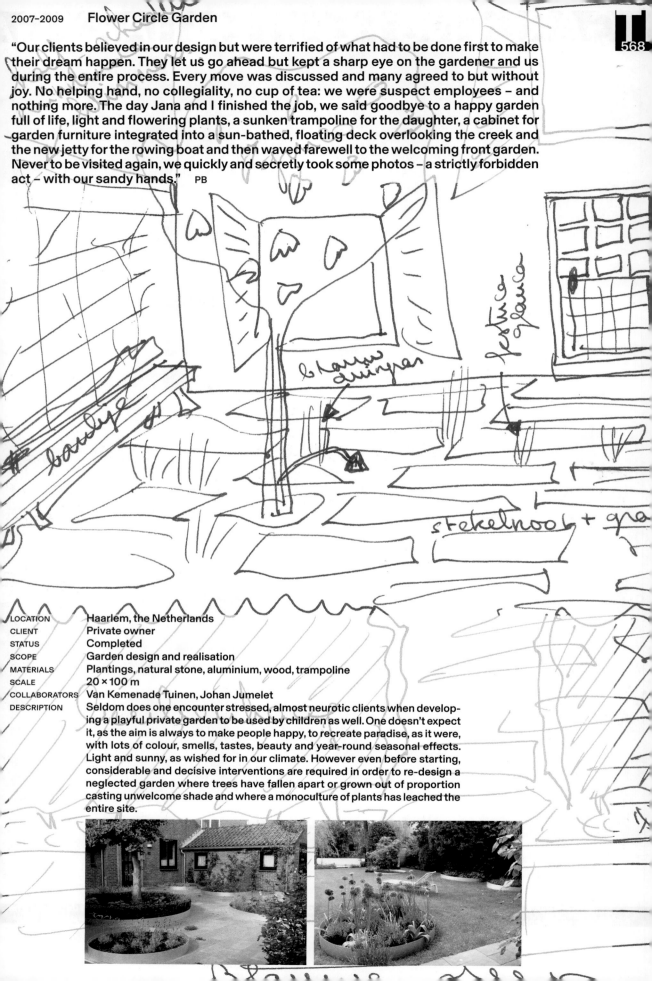

LOCATION	Haarlem, the Netherlands
CLIENT	Private owner
STATUS	Completed
SCOPE	Garden design and realisation
MATERIALS	Plantings, natural stone, aluminium, wood, trampoline
SCALE	20 × 100 m
COLLABORATORS	Van Kemenade Tuinen, Johan Jumelet
DESCRIPTION	Seldom does one encounter stressed, almost neurotic clients when developing a playful private garden to be used by children as well. One doesn't expect it, as the aim is always to make people happy, to recreate paradise, as it were, with lots of colour, smells, tastes, beauty and year-round seasonal effects. Light and sunny, as wished for in our climate. However even before starting, considerable and decisive interventions are required in order to re-design a neglected garden where trees have fallen apart or grown out of proportion casting unwelcome shade and where a monoculture of plants has leached the entire site.

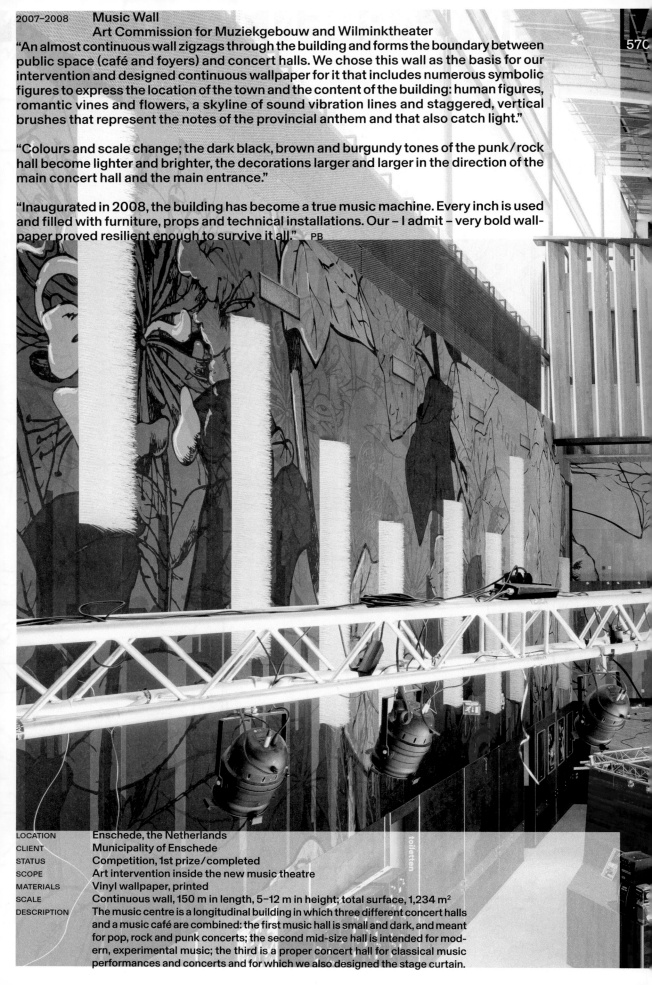

2007–2008
Music Wall
Art Commission for Muziekgebouw and Wilminktheater

"An almost continuous wall zigzags through the building and forms the boundary between public space (café and foyers) and concert halls. We chose this wall as the basis for our intervention and designed continuous wallpaper for it that includes numerous symbolic figures to express the location of the town and the content of the building: human figures, romantic vines and flowers, a skyline of sound vibration lines and staggered, vertical brushes that represent the notes of the provincial anthem and that also catch light."

"Colours and scale change; the dark black, brown and burgundy tones of the punk/rock hall become lighter and brighter, the decorations larger and larger in the direction of the main concert hall and the main entrance."

"Inaugurated in 2008, the building has become a true music machine. Every inch is used and filled with furniture, props and technical installations. Our – I admit – very bold wallpaper proved resilient enough to survive it all." PB

LOCATION	Enschede, the Netherlands
CLIENT	Municipality of Enschede
STATUS	Competition, 1st prize/completed
SCOPE	Art intervention inside the new music theatre
MATERIALS	Vinyl wallpaper, printed
SCALE	Continuous wall, 150 m in length, 5–12 m in height; total surface, 1,234 m²
DESCRIPTION	The music centre is a longitudinal building in which three different concert halls and a music café are combined: the first music hall is small and dark, and meant for pop, rock and punk concerts; the second mid-size hall is intended for modern, experimental music; the third is a proper concert hall for classical music performances and concerts and for which we also designed the stage curtain.

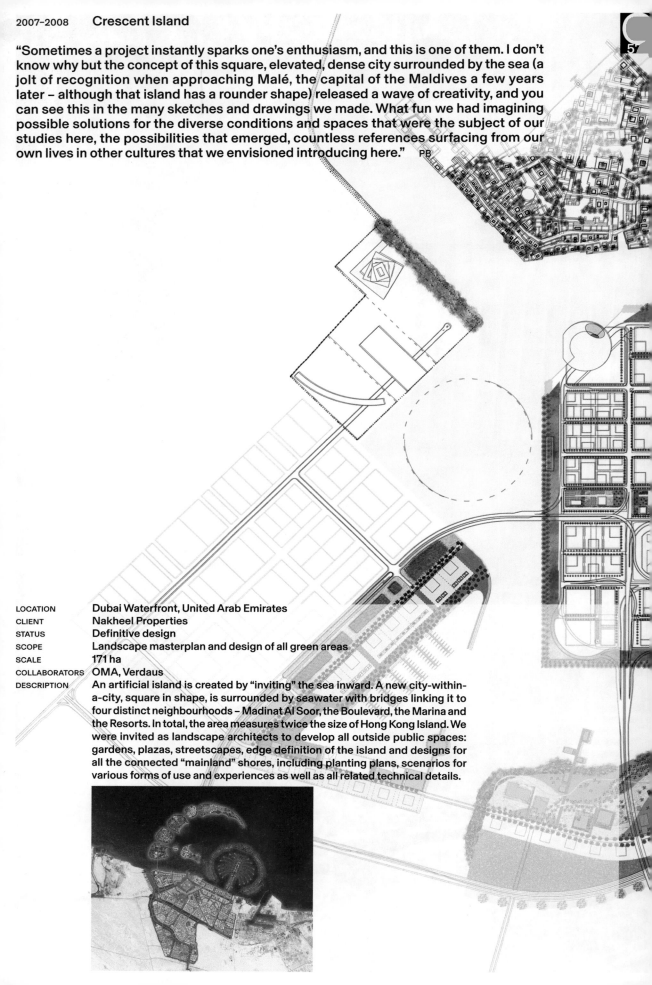

"Sometimes a project instantly sparks one's enthusiasm, and this is one of them. I don't know why but the concept of this square, elevated, dense city surrounded by the sea (a jolt of recognition when approaching Malé, the capital of the Maldives a few years later – although that island has a rounder shape) released a wave of creativity, and you can see this in the many sketches and drawings we made. What fun we had imagining possible solutions for the diverse conditions and spaces that were the subject of our studies here, the possibilities that emerged, countless references surfacing from our own lives in other cultures that we envisioned introducing here."   PB

LOCATION	Dubai Waterfront, United Arab Emirates
CLIENT	Nakheel Properties
STATUS	Definitive design
SCOPE	Landscape masterplan and design of all green areas
SCALE	171 ha
COLLABORATORS	OMA, Verdaus
DESCRIPTION	An artificial island is created by "inviting" the sea inward. A new city-within-a-city, square in shape, is surrounded by seawater with bridges linking it to four distinct neighbourhoods – Madinat Al Soor, the Boulevard, the Marina and the Resorts. In total, the area measures twice the size of Hong Kong Island. We were invited as landscape architects to develop all outside public spaces: gardens, plazas, streetscapes, edge definition of the island and designs for all the connected "mainland" shores, including planting plans, scenarios for various forms of use and experiences as well as all related technical details.

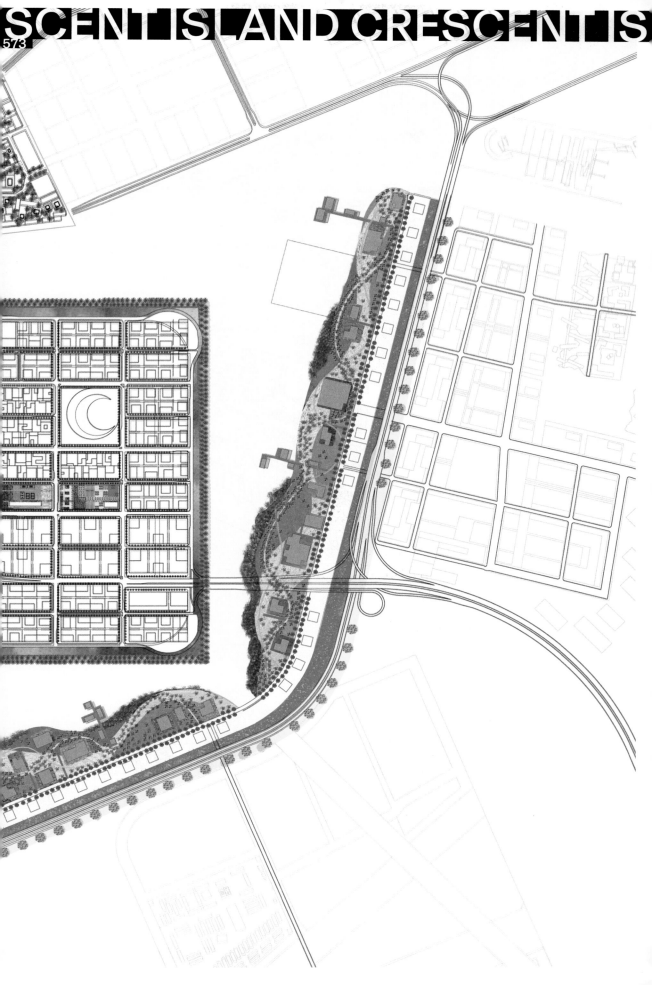

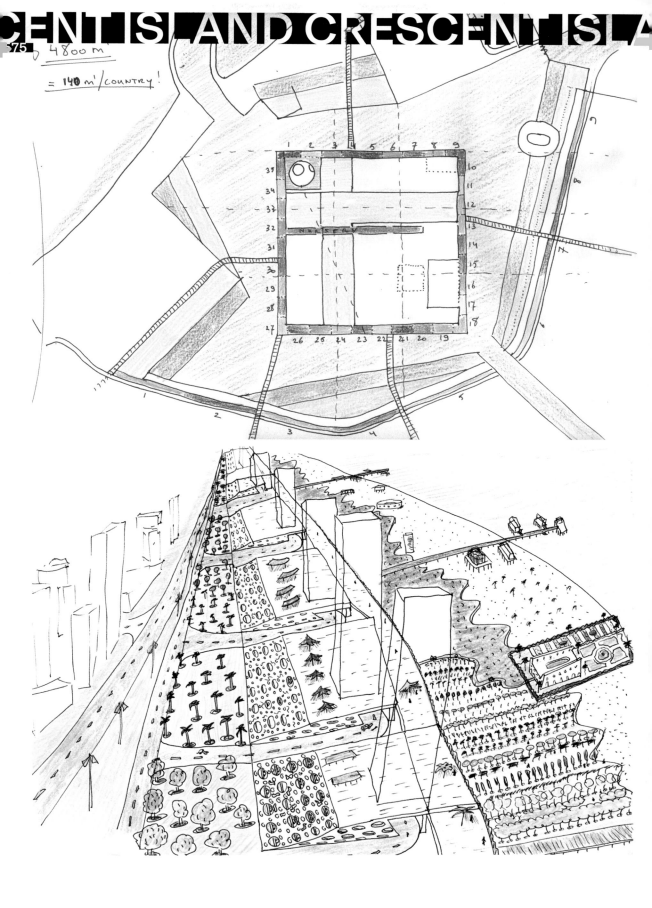

4800 M

= 140 m¹/COUNTRY!

"We visited the different sites and Mr Slim's former museum and his art collection as a basis for further thought. As Fernando was married to Mr Slim's daughter Soumaya at the time – we were witnesses at their wedding at the Catedral Metropolitana de la Ciudad de México – we were introduced to the family and taken on various outings in the city. When you are in Mexico City you are inevitably introduced to its beauty, its layers and layers of architecture through time, its intricate urban tissue, its beautiful parks, trees, avenues and alleys, colours and street life. In our day-to-day life in the city, we passed and visited unbelievable buildings and public places of all ages, from ancient cathedrals, museums and parks to 1970s beauties to recent inventions. No face-lifting here, everything is original. What a relief, what sheer beauty to witness the lives these buildings have lived!!"

"After a local breakfast (spicy scrambled eggs, papaya with lime and hot chocolate), walk past the fences of Chapultepec Park in the morning, through Parque Alameda in the early evening. Visit Ciudad Universitaria on a Saturday, Jose Vasconcelos Library on a Sunday (reinforcing our ideas about LocHal's furniture concept), Casa Barragan during lunch break, dinner at Casa Gilardi, meet someone at the Palacio de Bellas Artes or the Museo Nacional de Antropologia, have a hot chocolate afterwards at a place nearby. After lunch near Diego Rivera and Frida Kahlo's studios, pass the fantastic high-rise cacti hedge, meander through rooms bathed in daylight streaming in through enormous steel-framed windows, past outside steps and bridges to the house next door, get inspired to go visit Casa Azul as well, discover the beauty of its inner garden, its worn windows and gates … it is all too much to even start describing how lucky I've been to be in Mexico City through the years."

"On two of these visits and, later, for various conferences in the city, I invited colleagues Marieke, Rosetta and, later, Aura to join me, not only to participate in the work but so that they could also be inspired by Mexico City, by its social, architectural and artistic culture, and be introduced to local and other visiting professionals. To become part of a day-to-day working culture is the best way to get to know a place and its people: transport systems, finding your way, communicating, eating, meeting others, helping with chores, organising your laundry, your digital world: daily routines that make you part of a community. Such collegial changes of scene work well for bonding; they foster mutual respect and appreciation and are essential to the health of our studio and the quality of our work."   PB

LOCATION	Private house (Villa S) and Museo Soumaya, Mexico City, Mexico
CLIENT	LAR, Fernando Romero
STATUS	Completed
SCOPE	Workshops on ideas for interiors and landscaping; logistics of movement around and through the buildings; facade and interior surface treatment; colour scope for each floor; site visits and studies
MATERIALS	Drawings and models, pen, (coloured) paper, cardboard, sponge, paint, found objects, vegetal materials, glue, photographs and photocopies
COLLABORATORS	LAR, Fernando Romero
DESCRIPTION	I was asked to join Fernando Romero's team to inspire the projects and his team of young architects on a few occasions, once for a private house and its gardens and once for the new Museo Soumaya building. Fernando and I had collaborated at OMA when he worked there for a couple of years (on a private house and Casa da Musica, among others), and we liked working together. My task was to think with him and his team about the basic concept of a project, inspire modelmaking, drawing and collage, diving into detail and material research. This would traditionally mean interior finishes, lighting and colour scheme, inside-outside connections, green additions and the landscape in general. A public building like the Museo Soumaya involves landscaping of the immediate surroundings, logistics of movement around and through the building, facade and interior materials, colour scope for each floor and room, etc.

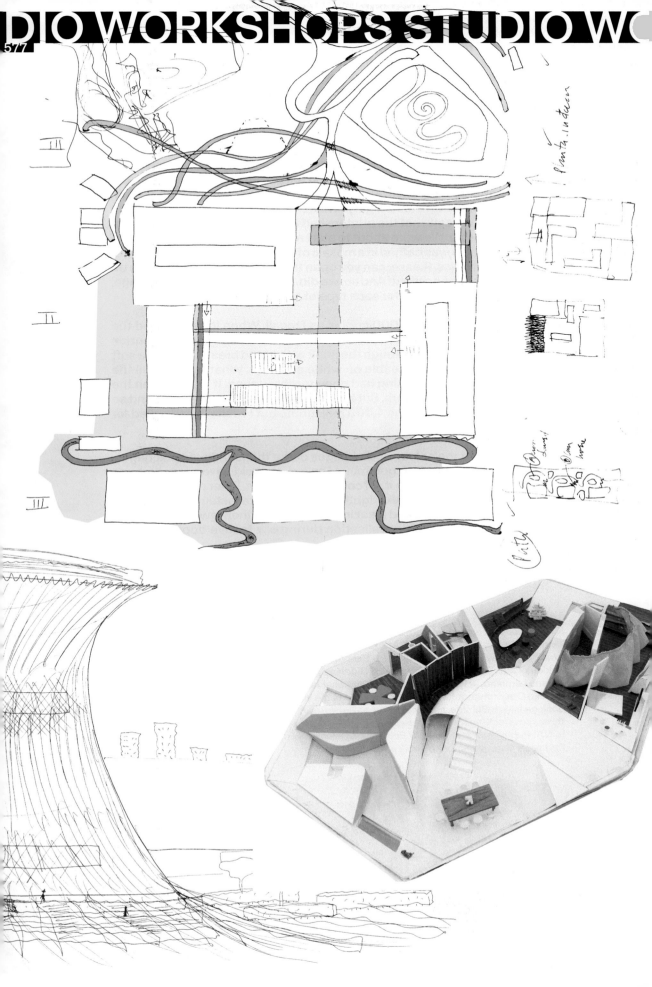

2002–2007   Inside Outside Petra Blaisse
Monograph

"Kayoko and Irma decided to show seven 'typical' projects, representing a selection of our multidisciplinary work with other works in between to present specific themes, and articles by 'critical authors' interwoven throughout. In the last section, a sketchbook would illustrate the work process of various projects in the form of spreadsheets of stamp-sized images. To my surprise NAi asked me to write the introductory text. I wrote one very long sentence that starts on the cover and meanders into the book like a river."

"I remember driving with Irma to Belgium, to the printers, in her old dark-blue BMW. She is a slow driver, it was a sunny day, we enjoyed the views and were in good spirits: we were to do a final check of the print quality – colour and focus – so, the end was near and we were excited! The printing company was housed in a very old building with a large, wood-panelled meeting room with stained glass windows above heavy wooden doors that opened onto a garden. We saw that the printers had laid out all of the book pages on the dark wooden meeting table. We were about to start and then looked at each other in despair: everything on the table was bathed in a mosaic of colours because of the daylight shining through the stained glass. Please, can you open the garden doors, we have to do this work in the open air, in bright daylight! And so, we did. Page by page, image by image. We left sticky notes – a different colour for each type of comment."

"Then the books were printed, about 4,000 copies as I recall. When Irma received the first copy I biked to her studio as fast as I could! Rushing in, I didn't pay much attention to Irma's expression, but as we leafed through the book with bated breath, we saw a soft pink haze all over the book, most noticeable on white surfaces. What to do?! Call the publisher of course and tell him something had gone terribly wrong. It was hard on the publisher, and even harder on the printers. But there you go: it had to be redone, and so it was. I don't know what happened to the 4,000 pink prints but I wish we had asked for a few copies for our archives. Forgot."

"The bookbinders had cut off the colour-coded edges of the thousands of book pages, resulting in heaps of colourful shreds. A goldmine! I asked if I could have a few garbage bags full, so we could do something with it. Of course, no problem. Peter made a number of transparent plastic cushion covers with brightly coloured Velcro fastenings, which we stuffed with the book scraps. They looked amazing, and we gave them away as presents to all the people involved in the book's realisation during our festive book launch at Architectura & Natura."   PB

PUBLISHER   NAi Publishers, Rotterdam, with Birkhauser, 2007. ISBN 9789056624538
REPRINT   Monacelli Press, New York, with NAi Publishers, 2009. ISBN 9781580932585
COLLABORATORS   Irma Boom, Kayoko Ota; authors, Cecil Balmond, Bernd Baumeister, Gaston Bekkers, Chris Dercon, Tijs Goldschmidt, Dirk van den Heuvel, Sanford Kwinter, Helene Lemoine, Renz van Luxemburg, Tim Ronalds, Michael Shermer
DESCRIPTION   Kayoko Ota, architecture critic from Tokyo, was the initiator and editor of this book on Inside Outside, and Irma Boom was the designer. We were quite the threesome looking for a suitable publisher. We found a courageous partner in NAi Publishers with director Eelco van Welie, who appointed Veronique Patteeuw as coordinator and editor.

Swamp Garden
                   Public/Private Parking

"The location in the polder meant that water levels could rise up to 50 cm above the parking level, depending on weather conditions. As I dislike the obvious solutions of a closed planter with upstanding walls, I thought of the natural upward pressure of the groundwater and came up with the idea of a 'crack' in the floor: the concrete slab of the parking garage breaks open violently, creating oblique fissures, irregular wedges of concrete. Large, moisture-loving trees would grow from the long crevice. The trees would grow right through the parking garage roof and spread their branches over the public plaza above. People would experience the crowns of the trees from their vantage point, witnessing unusual sights."

"The mathematics to calculate the exact slant of the upward sloping concrete fins in all their variations and the effect of the horizontal fold at the point where the large concrete slab changed from flat to sloping were complex. As we definitely wanted to show this moment of folding, we didn't want a cut at this point – something the builders preferred. The cut, or dilatation joint, needed to shift away from the fins and folds to line up with the security fences that run along the parking lots on both sides."

"As far as I was concerned, the fin structure had to look natural and elegant, so we saw to it that from the required critical watertight point – up to which point they are quite thick to be able to hold soil and water – they would taper up – so that their visible, free-floating edges were as thin as possible."

"Apart from the complexity of the shapes (each fin was different, upfolding, irregular, tapering, poured on site), the fins also had to be watertight up to the specific height of 50 cm above ground level, not only by securing the connections between them, but also by applying a different concrete substance up to that point. I am still thankful that I had just hired Simao Ferreira, who set up my first computer system and has a knack for maths, and that we worked with great engineers and contractors, everyone intrigued by the design and passionate about getting the intended results. They did a perfect job. Now, 30 years later, the Almere municipality still considers the installation 'very successful' with its full soil condition and thriving plants, its open roof and trees for fresh air, the flyover parking entrance street and spacious sidewalk with the pi number 3.14159 26535 89793 23846 26433 83279 50288 41971 69399 37510 5 printed on it."   PB

LOCATION	Almere Stad, the Netherlands
CLIENT	Municipality of Almere
STATUS	Completed
SCOPE	Underground linear garden to separate public from private parking
MATERIALS	Plantings, reinforced concrete, earth, lighting
SCALE	2,000 m²
COLLABORATORS	Pieters Projectbureau, Bureau Bouwkunde, Kleinjan Advies – en ingenieurs-bureau/Team Groen, Water en Natuur
DESCRIPTION	We had been invited to create an underground linear garden strip to liven up and separate the planned parking garage that was to be placed in two sections underneath the large public plaza above. The client expected us to design an elevated planter of some kind to limit costs and simplify works. This we did not do.

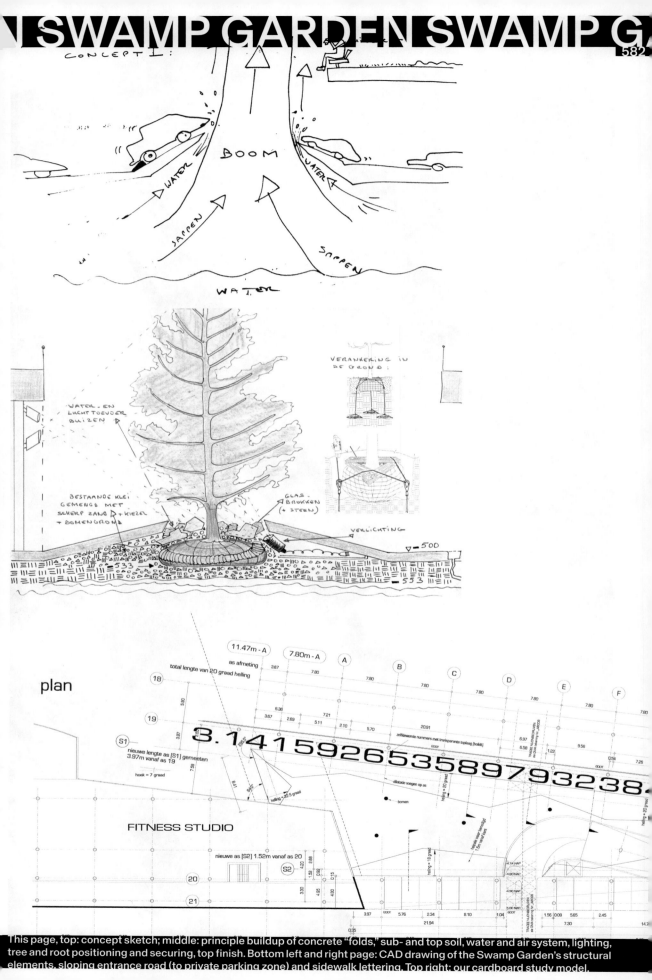

CONCEPT I:

BOOM

WATER

SAPPEN

WATER

SAPPEN

WATER

VERANKERING IN
DE GROND:

WATER- EN
LUCHT TOEVOER
BUIZEN

BESTAANDE KLEI
GEMENGD MET
SCHERP ZAND + KIEZEL
+ BOMENGROND

GLAS-
BROKKEN
(+ STEEN)

VERLICHTING

▽ -500

-533

-553

plan

11.47m - A   7.80m - A   A   B   C   D   E   F

as afmeting

total lengte van 20 graad helling

18

19

S1

nieuwe lengte as [S1] gemeeten
3.97m vanaf as 19

hoek = 7 graad

3.14159265358979323 8...

FITNESS STUDIO

nieuwe as [S2] 1.52m vanaf as 20

S2

20

21

This page, top: concept sketch; middle: principle buildup of concrete "folds," sub- and top soil, water and air system, lighting, tree and root positioning and securing, top finish. Bottom left and right page: CAD drawing of the Swamp Garden's structural elements, sloping entrance road (to private parking zone) and sidewalk lettering. Top right: our cardboard study model.

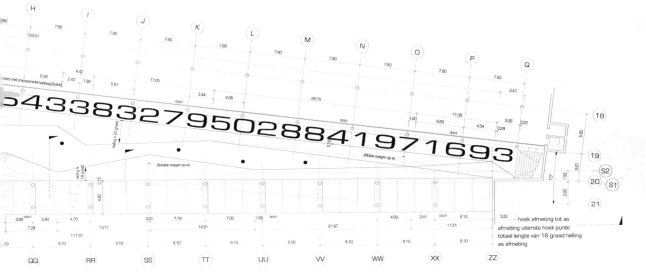

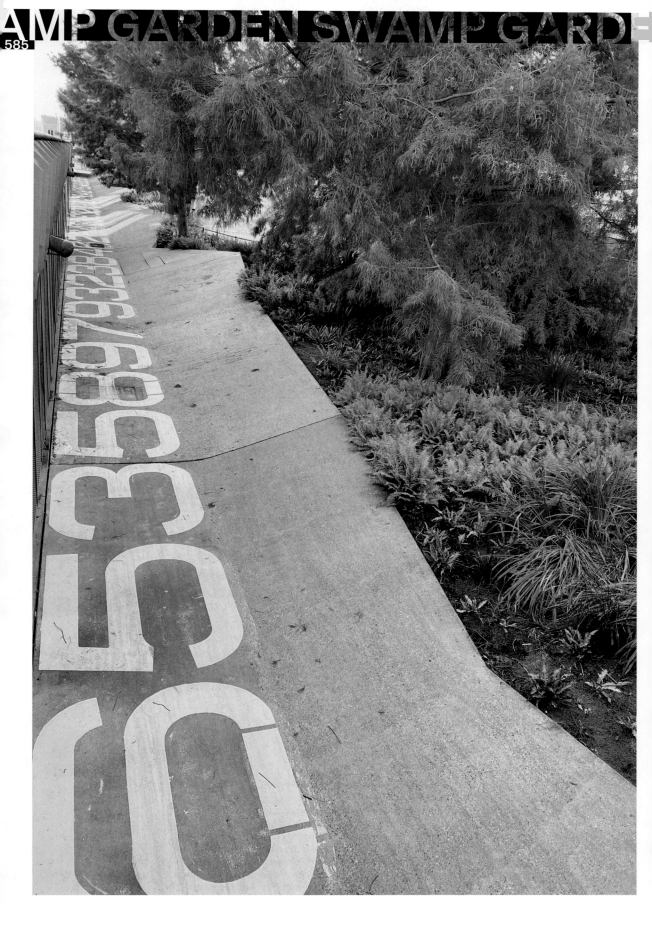

Genesis. Life at the End of the Information Age
Centraal Museum Utrecht

"One of the greatest things about being involved in designing exhibitions is that one can really dive deep into the subject matter, in this case DNA manipulations, a complex scientific issue now presented in the domain of art. We were asked to illustrate and exhibit the material and make it accessible to the public. Everything from early pioneers to the latest Artificial Intelligence robots had a platform in this exhibition. Together with the curatorial team we were able to figure out the essence of each artist's contribution and tried to make a design that would convey this essence in a playful manner: rational versus irrational, know-how versus instinct and experimental versus artistic. We produced floor-to-ceiling wallpapers with codes and recipes, filled rooms with rows of aquariums containing swarms of tiny, mutated fish and had smelly chicken runs inhabited by the most amazing chickens and cocks. We created warm, humid rooms with exotic plant mutations, surreal under blue and purple light – all very colourful, inventive and sometimes hilarious!" PB

LOCATION	Utrecht, the Netherlands
CLIENT	Centraal Museum Utrecht – director Pauline Terreehorst
STATUS	Completed
SCOPE	Exhibition design
MATERIALS	Various
SCALE	1,011 m²
COLLABORATORS	Dr. Emilie Gomart
DESCRIPTION	This themed exhibition explored the intersection of art and science. We created a different room for each theme, starting with the long entrance corridor lined on one side with integrated vitrines and continuing up the stairs into a series of exhibition spaces. We regarded the corridor as an overture to the exhibition and treated the row of vitrines as enlarged, vertical slide tables covered with large "slides" of scientific formulae and microscopic photographs with cut-outs through which objects in formaldehyde could be seen.

The first room represented the brain and tools of the scientist, with wallpapered notes, sketches and formulas taken from actual scientific documents. It was filled with objects and tools used for study and calculations. The following rooms each showed the work of artists that illustrate or use scientific discoveries or research as integral part of their creations. Sometimes this results in machines or robots that produce and manipulate processes; sometimes it results in an exhibit of animals (chickens, fish), plants or humans that underwent or are the result of experiments.

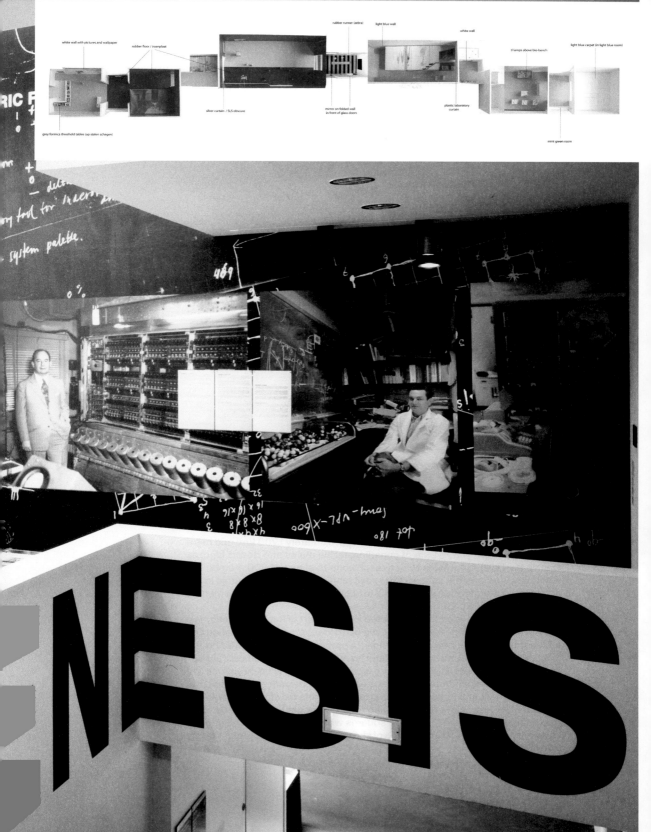

white wall with pictures and wallpaper

rubber floor / rraanplaat

rubber runner (zebra)

light blue wall

white wall

tl lamps above bio-bench

light blue carpet (in light blue room)

silver curtain / SLS obscure

mirror on folded wall
in front of glass doors

plastic laboratory
curtain

mint green room

grey formica threshold tables (op stalen schagen)

Urban Oasis
City in the Desert

"We divided the site into sections to illustrate the area's natural soil formation and topography with its dramatic height differences that would form canyons, valleys and hills. We also indicated the shady, more moist conditions versus the dry and sun-drenched ones, creating a series of very different biotopes. Our aim was to make a stark contrast between the 'wild' landscape and the organised, modern city – an exciting contradiction that we thought would enrich life inside the city and the experience of the park, while also stimulating biodiversity. Meandering through the park – in the shape of a snake biting its tail – one would encounter many different natural conditions (lush, semi-lush, semi-arid, arid and canyon) and plantings, at times walking through a fresh fruit orchard, at times down into a hot and arid canyon, with the city towering high above."   PB

LOCATION	Ras al Khaimah, United Arab Emirates
CLIENT	RAK Gateway Authority
STATUS	Competition 2nd prize
SCOPE	Landscape masterplan for a new city in the desert, with biodiverse, shaded green zones and cooling airflows as major focus. Includes sports and play areas, intimate patio gardens. Outside the city's defined boundaries, tree and shrub formations protect against wind and sand storms.
SCALE	Total city of ca. 120 ha
COLLABORATORS	OMA
DESCRIPTION	The emirate of Ras al Khaimah measures approximately 1,700 km² and has a varied landscape with 64 km of coastline, fertile plains and desert land, as well as the Hajar Mountains, which reach heights of up to 1,900 metres. The weather varies over the course of the year, ranging from hot and humid in the summer (with highs often above 40°C) to cooler and drier in the winter months (with highs of 25–30°C).

A new city needed to be projected in the desert of Ras al Khaimah, as a gateway to the country. While OMA developed ideas for a square-shaped city with some landmark buildings outside its protective walls, we studied the existing topography and soil conditions (sand, large rock formations, subsoil of clay and limestone) as well as future urban climate and wind directions. We came up with a meandering landscape – a continuous park – that would run through the new, mainly dense, urban structure. Inside the closed built blocks, defined by narrow alleys for pedestrian flow, we suggested regular cut-outs to create outside "rooms," intimate squares with shading trees. Outside the city walls, we projected large groups of shrubbery and trees to protect the city from sandstorms.

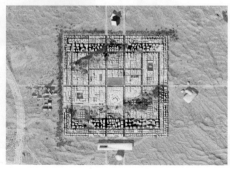

VEGETATIVE BARRIER

1:15000

CANYON:
ROCK SUBSTRATE
NO VEGETATION

ARID:
SAND SUBSTRATE
DESERT VEGETATION
NO ADDITIONAL
IRRIGATION

SEMI-ARID
SAND SUBSTRATE
DESERT VEGETATION
ADDITIONAL IRRIGATION

SEMI-LUSH
GRASS AND SOIL SUBSTRATE
INTRODUCED VEGETATION
ADDITIONAL IRRIGATION

LUSH
SOIL AND GROUNDCOVER SUBSTRATE
INTRODUCED VEGETATION
ADDITIONAL IRRIGATION

While making sketches, you first fantasise about all possible conditions in a designated development area, then you dive into the actual ground and climate conditions of the given site as well as the indigenous trees and plant communities. Then the ping-pong with the architects / city planners starts in order to find the right way to make their urban plan liveable, enjoyable and sustainable.

LUSH	SEMI-LUSH	SEMI-ARID	ARID	CANYON
15-25 m	25-35 m	35-45 m	45-55 m	55-65 m

"We proposed to use only black and white for all street materials and plantings. Streets, sidewalks and squares with black and white paving in various patterns; trees with very light and dark trunks; white flowers, black seed pods, black succulents and perennials, dark-coloured ornamental grasses, etc. Our team was familiar with the local ceramic and cement industries, which was useful and inspired our choices of street materials. It wasn't easy to find trees and plantings that were only black and white, but it was a stimulating challenge to limit our scope to the absence of colour in living things."   PB

LOCATION   Dubai, United Arab Emirates
CLIENT   Dubai City
STATUS   Schematic design
SCOPE   Landscape masterplan for a large new urban area, including a new saltwater
                waterline
SCALE   5.7 ha
COLLABORATORS   OMA
DESCRIPTION   The landscape masterplan for this large new urban area, included not only a
                new saltwater line but also streetscapes and greening. We decided on a very
                graphic treatment of the area that would clearly set it apart from the other
                developments in Dubai.

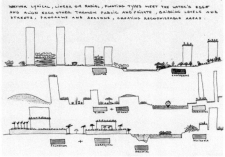

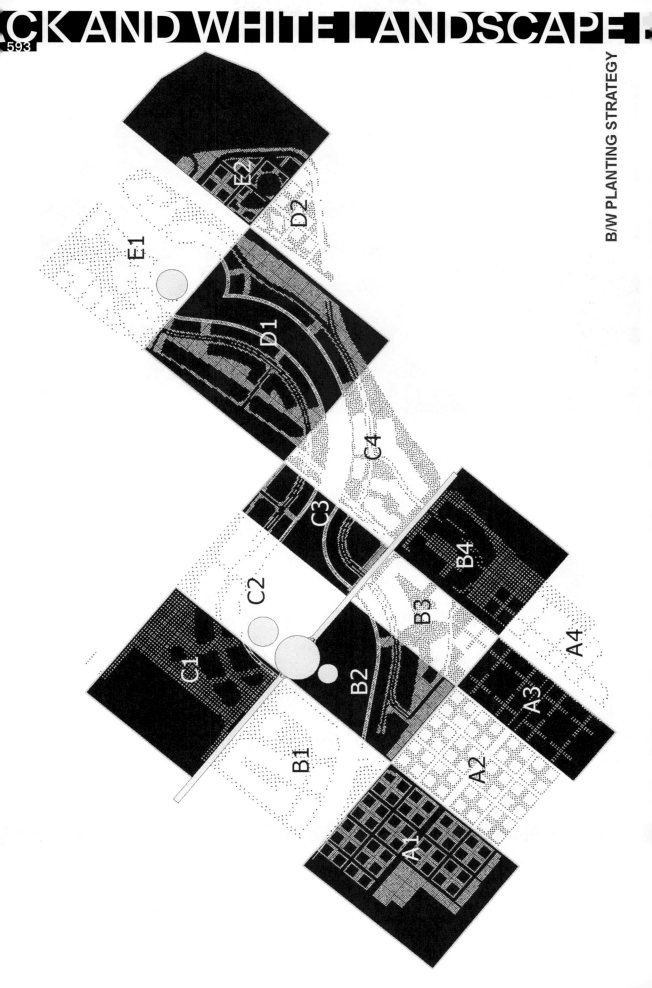

BLACK

WHITE

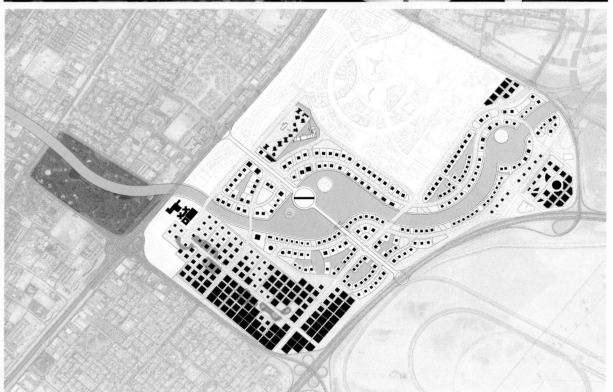

The idea to make both the pavement and the plantings black and white was so exciting! We looked for trunks, leaves, flowers, seeds and fruit with the least amount of colour – not an easy task but inspiring.

PARK GARDENS	GENERAL SPECIES	PLANT/PATH FORM	COOLING	IMPRESSION	TEXTURE	WILDLIFE VALUE

P. PALMETUM
a showcase of palms
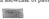

Aiphanes erosa
Cocos nucifera
Phoenix dactylifera
Rhapis excelsa
Washingtonia filifera

P. SCENTED
a seasonal mix of scented
and flowering trees

Bauhinia purpurea
Cassia hybrid
Delonix regia
Pulmeria rubra
Gardenia

P. AQUATICS
outdoor pools filled floating
and submerged plants

Aponogeton
Echinodorus
Nymphaea
Salvinia cucullata
Trapa bicornis

P. STREET
formal trees that form a
wide crown

Bursera simaruba
Capparis odoratissima
Elateriospermum tapos
Ficus retusa
Hymenaea courbaril

P. FIELD
layers of desert grasses

Nopalea coccinellifera
Opuntia depauperata
Panicum
Penisetum
Wedelia trlobata

P. XERPHYTIC
requires little water, planted in native sands

Agave americanan
Aloe arborescens
Fourcroya geminispina
Kalanchoe
Yucca aloifolia

P. CONIFEROUS
rolling hills and
tropical forests

Araucaria excelsa
Pinus ponderosa
Pseudotsuga menziesii
Samanea saman

P. HERBACEOUS
plants that hold water
in their leaves

Alpinia purpurata
Crinum amabile
Dieffenbachia
Pandanus veitchii
Sanseviera

P. HELICONIA
bright foliage in waves of
wide planting

Alpiniia purpurata
Heliconia Stricta
Strelitzia reginae
Tapeinochilus ananassae

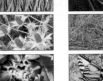

Shifted Room
Haus der Kunst

"Chris Dercon, the director of the museum at the time, brought the Haus der Kunst back to its (almost) original state by peeling off the layers of paint that hid the building's true history. The beautiful marble of the columns was revealed, narrative mosaics reappeared on the walls, and floors were stripped naked for everyone to see. One thing couldn't be restored however: the stained-glass ceiling of the Mittelhalle, which diffused the daylight so beautifully. The ceiling used to have a continuous decoration of swastikas around its edge. One side of each swastika drawing had been removed at some point, leaving an innocent, swirly pattern in its place. It was not the first time that I realised how complex restoration can be – but this case was further complicated because of its compromised past. Here in the Netherlands, street names in cities that refer to our colonial past are changed into new, 'innocent' ones; and sculptures of former 'heroes,' who are now considered controversial, are taken down. Is that a good thing...? Is it better to eliminate the past or preserve it and be confronted with what we now consider 'wrong'? Maybe we could take the sculptures off their pedestals and place them on the ground, at our own level, so that we can look them – and our past – straight in the eye."

"The ceiling of the Mittelhalle was still in its original state, which meant that it was filled with straw. Therefore it could never hold the weight of the curtains, and the tracks had to be fastened to walls and columns instead. Track lengths and curves were attached to steel profiles, mounted at regular intervals on the surrounding walls. It became a costly but technically exciting undertaking. Muscular yet elegant, and pulled by hand, the curtain's weight and size required two people – one in the front pulling, one in the back pushing, guiding the curtain along the turns, including the intricate C-shaped storage configurations that we designed in two corners of the hall. Once stored, the curtains became solitary figures on the side, giving way to the Mittelhalle's original 1930s design."

"Years later Moritz Küng told me that he had visited Haus der Kunst to see our curtains but couldn't find them. They had apparently been removed. Indeed, the system had been dismantled and the curtains had been stowed away in plastic bags in the storage cellars of the institution without our knowledge. We were flabbergasted, but what to do? Time had passed when the chairwoman of the Friends of Haus der Kunst contacted me to ask for my permission to repurpose the curtains for a good cause. I responded positively, saying it would be wonderful if they could be put to use in another cultural building in Munich. But no, they had another plan altogether: they wanted to produce handbags from the fabric – with our label on them to increase their saleability, and they would then invest the proceeds in cultural activities for the city..." PB

LOCATION	Munich, Germany
CLIENT	Haus der Kunst – director Chris Dercon
STATUS	Completed
SCOPE	Sound regulating and film projection curtains, encircling the main hall
MATERIALS	Dove-blue cotton velvet, projection screen, front screen mesh; printed Trevira CS voile; emergency exit signs and slit-definitions; pulling cord; weight, 500 kg, hand pulled/pushed by two
SCALE	38.2 × 9.1 m; 39 × 9.1 m; 20.7 × 9.1 m
COLLABORATORS	Boesel Stahlbau, Hespe & Woelm GmbH, Theatex
DESCRIPTION	This central hall, or *Mittelhalle*, where Hitler often gave his speeches under numerous national flags hanging from the balconies, is used for exhibits and openings, but is also a space that can be rented out for dinners, fashion shows and festivities. The acoustics were bad and the room lacked privacy, so a curtain seemed to be the solution. But instead of installing two curtains behind the row of columns along each length, we created a shifted snail loop, with one length of the curtain hanging in front of the columns and the other behind. Encircling the entire space, the curtain can also take an earlier turn to form an entrance or cloak room. By applying two layers in varied combinations, a large projection surface was created on the curtain's inner side while a thin, elegant layer covered the outer side, facing the adjacent exhibition rooms. The Haus der Kunst floorplan guides visitors through these rooms.

ERD-GESCHOSS

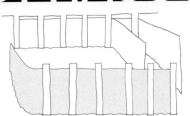 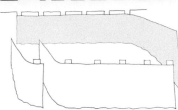 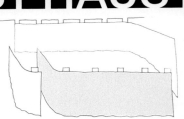

Change the architecture in one single move

Studying the history of the room, we found photographs of official dinners given in the '30s and '40s. Textile drapes hovered in the space and pleated cloth covered the walls

Track configuration (red) with two storage places (green)

HdK floorplans, printed on the outer, white voile layer

Curtain seam with holes for airflow

"Our team of three, Rosetta, Aura and I, really enjoyed getting to know the harbour site and the city of Riga. We didn't have much free time there, but when we could make some, I remember walking in the old city over cobblestones and – like a real tourist – going to the market, buying fresh fish eggs, wooden kitchen tools, bread and some fruit from the farm women who were warmly clothed in layers of woollen coats, skirts, stockings, gloves, scarves. They stood behind little tables, selling small bunches of violets, forget-me-nots and meadow flowers, fresh from their land. I also remember Aura and Rosetta jumping like mad on a large trampoline in a small park – a welcome way to release stress after our long meetings with the OMA team and the very young developers who were our optimistic commissioners at the time ;-)! as Latvia had recently joined the European Union in 2004. When Russia took over again a few years later, the project was abandoned until further notice." PB

LOCATION	Riga, Latvia
CLIENT	New Riga Development Company
STATUS	Commissioned study
SCOPE	Landscape development strategy (re-use of materials, introduction of temporary nurseries, playgrounds and recreation areas and phasing plan); landscape masterplan for the transformation of former harbour and waterfront of Riga into a commercial, cultural and residential area
SCALE	100 ha
COLLABORATORS	OMA
DESCRIPTION	We were looking at a large, old harbour site that the young local developers aimed to transform into a new district where cultural, commercial and residential areas were to be combined. OMA divided the longitudinal, rough harbour site along the river into three linear areas, with the cultural district aligning the Daugava River, the high-rise commercial district in the middle and the residential district land inwards. Here we used landscape as a tool to bridge the sequence of phases from demolition to cleaning, developing and building: by integrating and reusing building materials, all leftover spaces could be shaped, greened and transformed into temporary vegetable and fruit gardens, play and sports areas and thus be made accessible to the inhabitants for their personal use and enjoyment. By using the old infrastructure as well as the existing tracks and railway carriages, electricity could be generated and rolling nurseries installed to implement plantings close by, wherever and whenever needed. Organised in organic tree "blobs," a reference to Latvia's spread-out forest patches, the landscape would eventually define traffic flows, parking lots, infrastructure and security zones. Strategically placed, these groupings of trees, shrubs and undergrowth would provide protection against the icy winds and ward off the heavy snow. Covered gardens and greenhouses would lead pedestrians from place to place in the harsh winters.

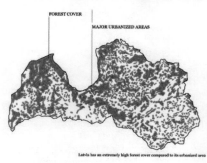

FOREST COVER

MAJOR URBANIZED AREAS

Latvia has an extremely high forest cover compared to its urbanized area

0m 100m 200m   500m   1000m

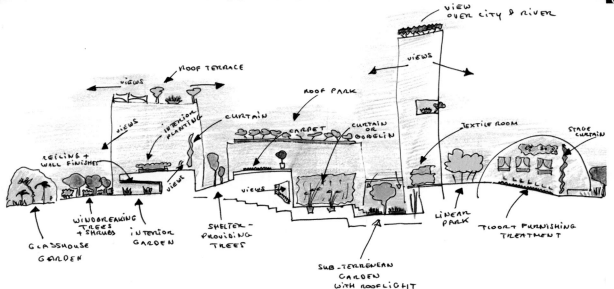

The harsh climate of Riga gave plants and trees an important role as windbreaking tools and made seamless connections between inside and outside a necessity

Riga Port City will be a continually changing site under observation and assessment by the community of Riga. The landscape offers an opportunity for the public to take part in registering the growth of this new part of their city. Inside Outside proposes to achieve this by planting two large nurseries to supply the new neighborhoods with street trees, and the residents with the advantages of mature plantings: increased shading, wind and snow breaks and cleaner air. Aged trees also add character and contribute to the perception of the new forms. Just as streets, sidewalks, public buildings and recreational facilities are part of a community's infrastructure, so are publicly owned trees. The street trees in Riga Port City are important assets, which require care and maintenance the same as other public property. The first phase of work is located in the area closest to the existing city, which

is the most direct connection to the activity to the old city. Therefore, the first phase will offer an opportunity to connect the existing open space system with the proposed plan. As residents begin to use this new trajectory they will begin to access the waterfront for the first time in an unobstructed way. This connection to the Daugava will eventually lead to more commercial viability for the adjacent land. As people start to populate the site, more and more amenities will be required. Public parks, while admittedly serving public purposes, often exhibit a structural separation, one that lacks a connection to the land around it, and to other parks within a green space system. Such distinctions are not present in the open space system designed for Riga Port City, rather the landscape forms a contribution to the flexible program, through the patch concept, the patches will serve to connect the entire site, regardless of a potentially fragmented time frame of development. The role of the landscape masterplan is a one that will shape the most immediate public acknowledgment for Riga Port City.

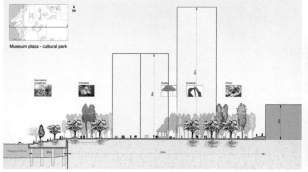

Museum plaza - cultural park

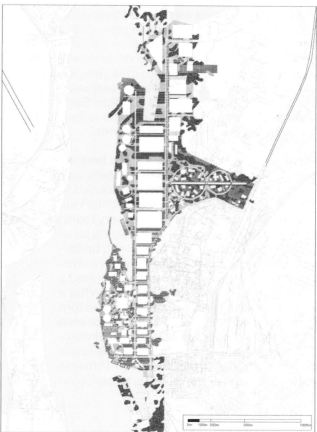

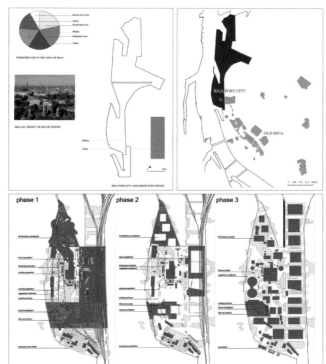

The landscape masterplan for Riga Port City is an ongoing and multi-staged design process, which benefits from a close cooperation between the various design disciplines and the collaboration of the future inhabitants themselves. The world is changing fast. Most design fields are disposing of their autonomy, due to a rapid multiplication of digital techniques and the incredible production of "designed" artifacts. Architecture and urban design are slower to adopt this change. The scale and complexity of Riga Port City emphasises the need for strong between collaboration between disciplines. The ongoing stimulation between architects, landscape architects, designers, engineers and clients encourages our professions to think more deeply about the significance of each other's decisions and their eventual impact on the overall plan.

A masterplan aims to give comprehensive instructions for the development of a site. As such it usually concerns itself with built form and infrastructure. Where will the structures be built, and how will they be served? The landscape masterplan operates at the same scale and in conjunction with the masterplan itself, but it poses a different set of questions. What is the street quality, how do pedestrians move, what is the vegetative character of the neighborhood, what features can help make the climate more comfortable? These are some of the immediate issues that can encourage familiarity and help to support users as they find their way in a new environment.

Looking at the map of Latvia you discover that the country is covered with forested areas that have undulating shapes. We scaled down these shapes and projected them onto the designated cultural and residential areas. In the central business area we moulded the forest areas into a linear formation (think Richter) to fit the Manhattan-like grid of city blocks.

"Naturally, the line drawings Mies made of the crowns of trees, which we copied and enlarged, were the inspiration for the curtain prints. The trick here was to print the black-out cloth on both sides, positive/negative, and in such a way that, when sewing the widths together, the shapes, which outsized the width of the cloth, would fit together on both sides. This was a challenge for us (working drawings), the printers (soft material tends to stretch) and the seamstresses (the cloth is opaque, only one side visible while sewing). Behind the continuous glazed facade lie three different rooms. Although seemingly identical, each curtain has its own detailed finish, depending on the room's function. Seen from outside, however, the glass facade looks like one continuous entity, and the reflection of the street trees on the tree pattern of the curtains dissolves all boundaries."

"I was standing with architect Mathias Lehner, who was working with me at the time, on the scaffolding to hang one of the curtains. The scaffolding was wrapped in plastic and the heavy bulk of folded cloth bundles had been carried up little by little). We started to pull out and lift the top edge of the curtain to attach it to the runners with the zip ties we carried in our pockets. To begin hanging a large and heavy curtain, you attach every fourth ring to the runners to first spread the weight and organise the cloth, as it takes a lot of muscle to pull, hold and attach such a soft, falling object of considerable weight. Underneath, two men were rolling our scaffolding from left to right to accommodate our movement. We were about halfway and just getting the hang of it when we suddenly heard a frightful sound to our left: a tearing sound – *krrrrrrraaaah!* – and down it fell... What a SHOCK! Our hearts stopped as we realised that the curtain, with all its weight, had torn loose from its reinforced top edge. But why?! We analysed the situation and discovered that a terrible mistake had been made: the top hem, thrice folded and filled with reinforcing tape (then holed and ringed), was not correctly sewn to the cloth along the lower edge. It was stitched under the layered hem instead of through it. Luckily, a local firm was found to do the repair work – but not before we took detailed pictures of the situation for further discussion."   PB

LOCATION	Chicago, Illinois, USA
CLIENT	IIT Illinois Institute of Technology
STATUS	Competition 1st prize/completed
SCOPE	Darkening and blackout curtains for entire west facade, interior finishes, patio and "flying" gardens, surrounding landscape
MATERIALS	Blackout fabric, digitally printed in black and white on both sides
SCALE	Curtains, 17.2 × 8.4 m, 19.4 × 8.4 m, 18.9 × 6.4 m; carpets, various sizes; landscape, 1.6 ha
COLLABORATORS	OMA, 2 × 4; Peter Lindsay Schaudt, Kate Orff
DESCRIPTION	For the integrated gardens – a triangular garden, a flying garden and two patios – we chose local plantings to suit the conditions (dry, wet, windy, sunny or shaded). I found it essential to plant a large, mature pine tree inside one of the patios to provide shade. Growing taller than the roof, it becomes visible from afar and also influences the interior light and atmosphere. The flying garden sprouted from an abandoned idea: original plans for a bowling alley gave way to an open-roofed, linear garden filled with local grasses and herbs. The triangular patio facing the professors' glazed dining room became a reflective water garden: an irregular surface of natural black stones is covered with a film of water and enlivened by large, transparent chunks of ice-blue glass that reflect and transmit light in all directions. A necessary addition given the dark wall of engraved donors' names as a backdrop! A grid of planted and furnished circles around the outside of the building was projected in response to the facade's speckled graphics designed by 2 × 4 – combined with systems of inlaid paths, sport fields and entrance zones.

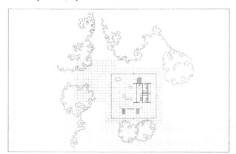

Because of the large black-and-white pattern, the curtain looks continuous along the entire, west-oriented glass facade; it is, however, treated differently in each room. Above you see the ballroom curtain that we stitched through vertically without yarn to let light in during the day and out at night.

IIT Mies Trees Darkening Curtains
Overview

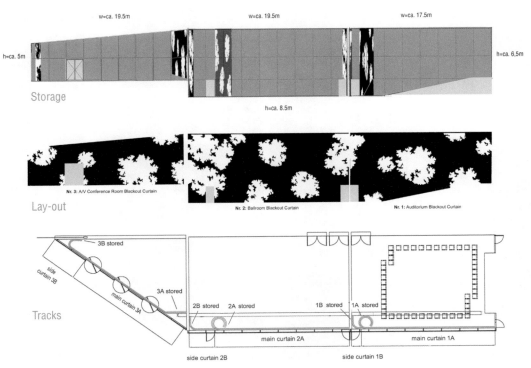

w=ca. 19.5m   w=ca. 19.5m   w=ca. 17.5m

h=ca. 5m   h=ca. 6,5m

h=ca. 8.5m

Storage

Lay-out

Nr. 3: A/V Conference Room Blackout Curtain

Nr. 2: Ballroom Blackout Curtain

Nr. 1: Auditorium Blackout Curtain

Tracks

3B stored

side curtain 3B

main curtain 3A

3A stored

2B stored   2A stored

1B stored   1A stored

main curtain 2A

main curtain 1A

side curtain 2B

side curtain 1B

INSIDE OUTSIDE

PETRA BLAISSE ©2003

Left page: landscape sketches. Right page top: OMA drawing with my notes on interior finishes; bottom: OMA drawing representing both the "mineral" and vegetal landscape elements.

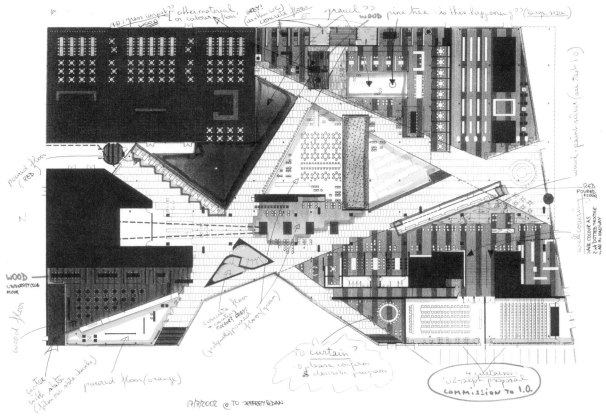

Handwritten annotations around plan:

no gum carpet?? other material or colour?? floor wood

GREY! (as thin WC) concrete floor

gravel??

WOOD pine tree - is this happening?? (large size)

wall colour as fade colour as 2 w/ dotted texture as used in hallway

poured floor (red)

N

RED POURED FLOOR

WOOD UNIVERSITY CLUB FLOOR

wood floor

concrete floor + colour?? colour grey (industrial) poured floor (green)

water with stout (from our site chunks)

poured floor (orange)

to curtain? - pl lease confirm & describe program

17/7/2002 @ TO JEFFREY & DAN

4 curtains '02-Sept proposal COMMISSION to I.O.

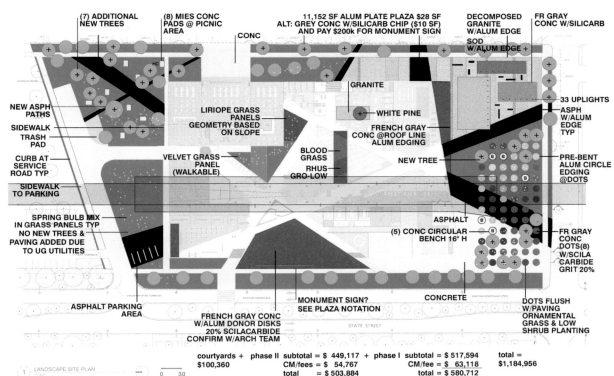

(7) ADDITIONAL NEW TREES

(8) MIES CONC PADS @ PICNIC AREA

CONC

11,152 SF ALUM PLATE PLAZA $28 SF ALT: GREY CONC W/SILICARB CHIP ($10 SF) AND PAY $200k FOR MONUMENT SIGN

DECOMPOSED GRANITE W/ALUM EDGE

SOD W/ALUM EDGE

FR GRAY CONC W/SILICARB

NEW ASPH PATHS

GRANITE

WHITE PINE

33 UPLIGHTS

ASPH W/ALUM EDGE TYP

SIDEWALK

TRASH PAD

LIRIOPE GRASS PANELS GEOMETRY BASED ON SLOPE

FRENCH GRAY CONC @ROOF LINE ALUM EDGING

NEW TREE

PRE-BENT ALUM CIRCLE EDGING @DOTS

CURB AT SERVICE ROAD TYP

VELVET GRASS PANEL (WALKABLE)

BLOOD GRASS

RHUS GRO-LOW

SIDEWALK TO PARKING

SPRING BULB MIX IN GRASS PANELS TYP NO NEW TREES & PAVING ADDED DUE TO UG UTILITIES

ASPHALT

(5) CONC CIRCULAR BENCH 16" H

FR GRAY CONC DOTS(8) W/SCILA CARBIDE GRIT 20%

ASPHALT PARKING AREA

MONUMENT SIGN? SEE PLAZA NOTATION

CONCRETE

DOTS FLUSH W/PAVING ORNAMENTAL GRASS & LOW SHRUB PLANTING

FRENCH GRAY CONC W/ALUM DONOR DISKS 20% SCILACARBIDE CONFIRM W/ARCH TEAM

STATE STREET

1 LANDSCAPE SITE PLAN   0   30

courtyards + $100,360

phase II subtotal = $ 449,117
CM/fees = $ 54,767
total = $ 503,884

+ phase I subtotal = $ 517,594
CM/fee = $ 63,118
total = $ 580,712

total = $1,184,956

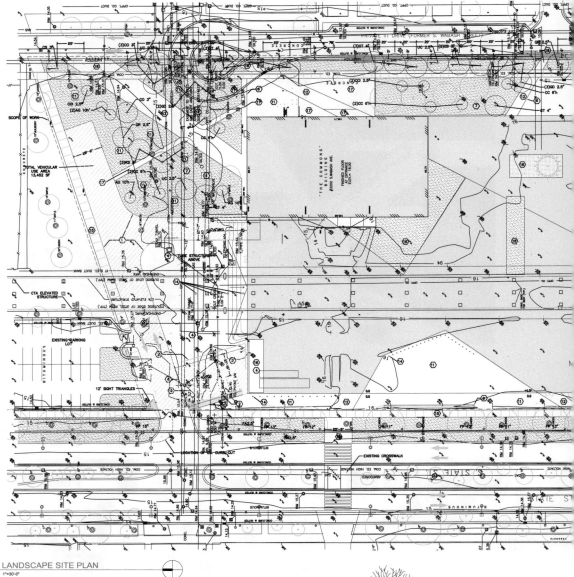

1 LANDSCAPE SITE PLAN
1"=30'-0"

PRE-PURCHASED TREE

SYMBOL	QUANTITY	BOTANICAL NAME	COMMON NAME	SIZE	SPACING	REMARKS
PSP	1	Pinus strobus	Eastern White Pine	25' B+B	See plan	Pre purchased pine from ......

CANOPY TREES

SYMBOL	QUANTITY	BOTANICAL NAME	COMMON NAME	SIZE	SPACING	REMARKS
AF	3	Acer x freemanii	Freeman Maple	4" cal. B+B	See plan	Clear wood height 6' - 7' min. single trunk
CO	3	Celtis occidentalis	Common Hackberry	3-4" cal. B+B	See plan	Clear wood height 6' - 7' min. single trunk
CS	1	Catalpa speciosa	Northern Catalpa	3" cal. B+B	See plan	Clear wood height 6'-7' min. single trunk
FA	15	Fraxinus americana 'Autumn Purple'	Autumn Purple White Ash	3-4" cal. B+B	See plan	Clear wood height 6' - 7' min. single trunk
GD	3	Gymnocladus dioicus	Kentucky Coffeetree	3" cal. B+B	See plan	Single trunk
GT	9	Gleditsia triacanthos var. inermis	Thornless Honeylocust	3-4" cal. B+B	See plan	Clear wood height 6' - 7' min. single trunk
PS	3	Pinus strobus	Eastern White Pine	3-4" cal. B+B	See plan	Limb up to 6' on site per L.Arch. instruction
QB	4	Quercus bicolor	Swamp White Oak	2.5" cal. B+B	See plan	Clear wood height 6'-7' min. single trunk
QR	6	Quercus rubra	Red Oak	2.5" cal. B+B	See plan	Clear wood height 6' - 7' min. single trunk

ORNAMENTAL TREES

SYMBOL	QUANTITY	BOTANICAL NAME	COMMON NAME	SIZE	SPACING	REMARKS
AC	9	Amelanchier canadensis	Shadblow Serviceberry	6'h B+B	See plan	
CC	8	Cercis canadensis	Redbud	6'h B+B	See plan	

BULBS

SYMBOL	QUANTITY	BOTANICAL NAME	COMMON NAME	SIZE	SPACING	REMARKS
CB	235	Crocus tommasinianus 'Barr's Purple'	Barr's Purple Crocus	BULB	See plan	Sited by landscape architect in field
SS	220	Scilla siberica	Siberian Squill	BULB	See plan	Sited by landscape architect in field
DA	340	Daffodil 'February Gold'	February Gold Daffodil	BULB	See plan	Sited by landscape architect in field

VINES

SYMBOL	QUANTITY	BOTANICAL NAME	COMMON NAME	SIZE	SPACING	REMARKS
PQ	9	Parthenocissus quinquefolia	Virginia Creeper	36" O.C.		At trash compactor screen wall

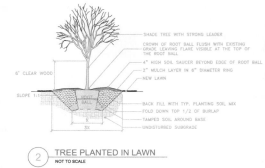

SHADE TREE WITH STRONG LEADER
CROWN OF ROOT BALL FLUSH WITH EXISTING GRADE LEAVING FLARE VISIBLE AT THE TOP OF THE ROOT BALL
4" HIGH SOIL SAUCER BEYOND EDGE OF ROOT BALL
2" MULCH LAYER IN 6" DIAMETER RING
6" CLEAR WOOD
NEW LAWN
SLOPE 1:1
BACK FILL WITH TYP. PLANTING SOIL MIX
FOLD DOWN TOP 1/2 OF BURLAP
TAMPED SOIL AROUND BASE
UNDISTURBED SUBGRADE

2 TREE PLANTED IN LAWN
NOT TO SCALE

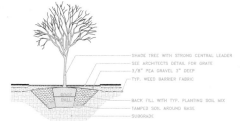

SHADE TREE WITH STRONG CENTRAL LEADER
SEE ARCHITECTS DETAIL FOR GRATE
3/8" PEA GRAVEL 3" DEEP
TYP. WEED BARRIER FABRIC
BACK FILL WITH TYP. PLANTING SOIL MIX
TAMPED SOIL AROUND BASE
SUBGRADE

3 TREE PLANTING DETAIL WITH GRATE
NOT TO SCALE

LEGEND

1. 6" STEEL CURB
2. STEEL TUBE CURB-STOP 6" HIGH
3. CRUSHED STONE WITH STABILIZER
4. SMOOTH BLACK RIVER STONE, OVAL SHAPE (3-4" LONG)
5. REFLECTIVE DOTS
6. FLUSH STEEL EDGE BETWEEN MATERIALS
7. SOD LAWN OVER 6" TOPSOIL TYPICAL
8. 9'-6" STEEL FRAME WALL WITH POLYCARBONATE PANELS (SEE ARCHITECTS DRAWINGS)
9. OUTDOOR SPORT SURFACE
10. 18" HIGH SEATWALL. CONCRETE VENEER TO MATCH PRECAST CONCRETE PAVERS.
11. PRECAST CONCRETE PAVERS
12. EXTRUDED ALUMINUM
13. SAND
14. UPLIGHTS
15. CONCRETE
16. COURTYARDS
17. EXPOSED AGGREGATE CONCRETE SIDEWALK
18. STEEL GRATE (SEE ARCHITECTS DRWGS.)

KEY

— · — · — · — PROPERTY LINE

— — — — — SCOPE OF WORK

SOD LAWN

VEHICULAR USE AREA

EXISTING TREE TO BE PRESERVED AND PROTECTED (TYP.)

PROPOSED TREE

EXISTING TREE IN GRATE

PROPOSED TREE IN GRATE

LARGE GRANITE BOULDERS (2" HIGH X 3' WIDE MIN.)

LAWN MOUND (SEE DETAIL 7)

18' HIGH SEAT. CONCRETE VENEER TO MATCH PRE-CAST CONCRETE PAVERS.

PROPOSED SHRUB AND PERENNIAL PLANTING, SEE PLANT SCHEDULE

ILLINOIS INSTITUTE of TECHNOLOGY

Heer Bokelweg 149, 3032 AD Rotterdam, The Netherlands Tel +31 (10) 243 8200 Fax +31 (10) 243 8202

ARCHITECTURE

300 West Adams Street, Chicago, IL 60606-5174, USA Tel +1 (312) 726 5960 Fax +1 (312) 726 1118

ARCHITECT

OFFICE FOR METROPOLITAN

WITH HOLABIRD & ROOT

INSIDE OUTSIDE
PETRA BLAISSE

EERSTE NASSAUSTRAAT 1, 1052 BD AMSTERDAM
PHONE +31 20 20 6810 841 FAX +31 20 20 6810 446
WWW.INSIDEOUTSIDE.NL E-MAIL OFFICE@INSIDEOUTSIDE.NL

NO.	DATE	REMARKS
	11-01-03	RECORD DRAWINGS
	07-11-03	REISSUED FOR BID
34	04-04-03	ISSUED FOR BULLETIN #34

PROJECT:

McCormick-Tribune
Campus Center

TITLE

SHEET NO. :

DRAWN

PROJECT NO.

SCALE:

N KEY PLAN

SHRUB DETAIL

3 INCHES MULCH, CREATE SAUCER
PLANT TOP OF BALL 3" ABOVE FINISH GRADE
EXISTING GRADE
TYP. PLANTING SOIL MIX
LOOSENED SOIL
UNDISTURBED SUBGRADE

DIAMETER

WITH SPADE ... 8" DEPTH

PLAN

SECTION

STAGGER PLANT ROWS
1" MULCH
3" PLUG
TYP. PLANTING SOIL MIX
SUBGRADE

(5) TYPICAL PERENNIAL AND GROUND COVER DETAIL
NOT TO SCALE

SCHEMATIC SECTION OF PLANTER

PLANTING (SEE PLANT SCHEDULE)
1" MULCH
TYPICAL PLANTING SOIL MIX
STEEL EDGE (SEE ARCHITECTS DRAWINGS)
PRECAST CONCRETE PAVERS, EXTRUDED ALUMINUM OR LAWN (SEE PLAN)
SUBGRADE

10'-0"

...ATIC SECTION OF LAWN MOUND

SOD LAWN
TYPICAL PLANTING SOIL MIX
STEEL EDGE (SEE ARCHITECTS DRAWINGS)
PRECAST CONCRETE PAVERS, EXTRUDED ALUMINUM OR LAWN (SEE PLAN)
SUBGRADE

10'-0"

PERMIT NOTES

1. SEE CIVIL AND ARCHITECTURAL PLANS FOR ALL OTHER SITE INFORMATION REFERRED TO ON THIS PLAN.

2. TREE PLANTING IS TO BE COMPLETED IN TWO PHASES 1ST - FALL 2002, 2ND - SPRING 2003.

3. OWNER STATEMENTS
A. "The undersigned acknowledges that the landscape planting shown on the landscape plan(s) for the Illinois Institute of Technology (IIT) property at the Northeastern corner of State and 33rd Street, bounded to the East by former Wabash St. (Private IIT drive) and to the North approximately to the former 32nd St. location (where there is a curb cut on State St.), Chicago, Illinois 60616, to the best of the undersigned applicant's knowledge has been designed and will be installed, maintained, and replaced, as required, by the current and subsequent owners in accordance with the requirements of Title 10, Chapter 32 of the Chicago Municipal Code, the landscaping standards of the Guide to the Chicago Zoning Ordinance."

B. "Existing parkway and on-site interior trees are to be protected while project is under construction and will be replaced by current and subsequent owner if damaged."

"Owner"   Date
Terence Frigo
Illinois Institute of Technology

4. SWORN STATEMENT BY REGISTERED LANDSCAPE ARCHITECT
"The undersigned landscape architect, registered in the State of Illinois, acknowledges that the landscape plan(s) for the property at the Northeastern corner of State and 33rd Street bounded to the East by former Wabash St. (Private IIT Drive) and to the North approximately to the former 32nd St. location (where there is a curb cut on State St.), Chicago Illinois 60616 to the best of the undersigned applicant's knowledge has been designed and will be installed, maintained, and replaced, as required, by current and subsequent owners in accordance with the requirements of Title 10, Chapter 32 of the Chicago Municipal Code, the landscaping standards of the Chicago Zoning Ordinance, and the Guide to the Chicago Landscape Ordinance."

Landscape Architect   Date
Peter Lindsay Schaudt, ASLA
Illinois Registration #157-000214, Expires 08/31/2001

5. ANY QUESTIONS REGARDING THIS PROJECT CAN BE DIRECTED TO:

Mr. Terence Frigo "Owner"
Director Design and Construction Illinois Institute of Technology
Machinery Hall, RM. 203
100 W. 33rd St.
Chicago, IL 60616
312.567.8973

Interiors as landscapes and landscapes as rooms connect the new building to Mies's building, and different levels to each other, allowing daylight to flow inward and animating the interiors with plants and reflections

The Professor Club dining room with our log motif carpets and "liquid" courtyard

Looking up from the students' canteen before the furnishings arrived

The "flying" garden, in autumn gold, lighting up the students' canteen in autumn gold

Textile Works
Vlaams Nederlands Huis De Buren

"The presentation of each curtain without colour and in the right proportions resulted in abstract compositions built up of rectangles and squares of different materiality and levels of transparency – really beautiful objects in themselves, mathematically compiled and all the same size." PB

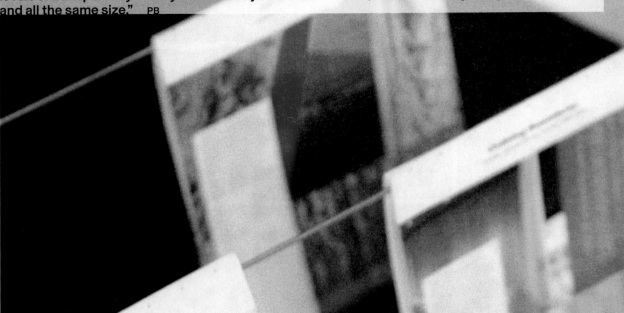

LOCATION	Brussels, Belgium
CLIENT	Vlaams-Nederlands Huis de Buren
STATUS	Completed
SCOPE	Solo exhibition on Insight Outside's textile works
MATERIALS	Curtain samples, photo prints on PVC, Garden Carpets, IO holed flags, video films of IO curtains and gardens
SCALE	2 carpets; 6 curtains; 13 digitally printed panels; 2 banners; video loop and sound installation
COLLABORATORS	Stephan Willenborg, Frans Parthesius
DESCRIPTION	The exhibition showed the materials of our curtains in a dry, analytical manner: we had a series of banners made, all the same size of the textiles/nonwovens/plastics in question and according to the percentage of each material used in the real object. We showed the materials without colour so that the banners were all white/beige/light-grey cloth, each cut in rectangular pieces and then sewn together. This resulted in abstract compositions. The banners were hung flat on steel cables, facing the entrance/exit door.

Against their backdrop we added a second layer, which showed photographic reproductions of the real curtain to scale and in its modified context: colour, print, manipulation of the fabric. This side was seen when leaving the space, when turning back towards the exit/entrance door. A number of our Garden Carpets were laid on the floor, and we had the film screened in a little black niche with one stool and a darkening cloth.

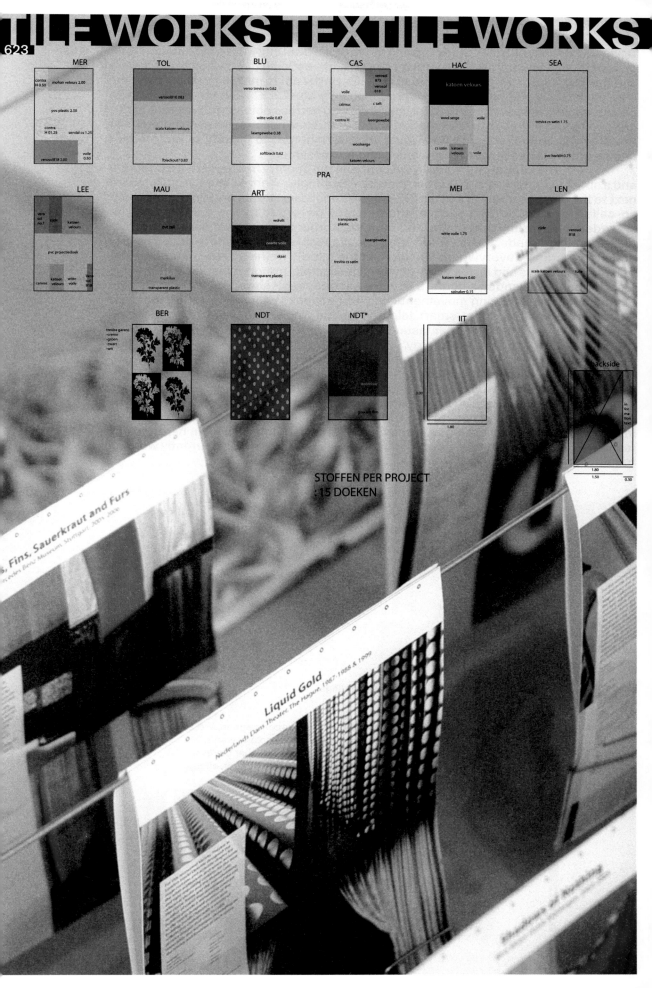

MER
contra H 0.50 / mohair velours 2.00
pvc plastic 2.50
contra H 01.25 / sendal cs 1.25
verosol818 2.00 / voile 0.50

TOL
verosol816 083
scala katoen velours
?blackout? 0.83

BLU
verso trevira cs 0.62
witte voile 0.87
lasergewebe 0.38
softblack 0.62

CAS
verosol 875 / verosol 818
voile
calmuc / c taft
contra H / lasergewebe
woolserge
katoen velours

HAC
katoen velours
wool serge / voile
cs satin / katoen velours / voile

SEA
trevira cs satin 1.75
pvc backlit 0.75

PRA

LEE
vero tol no.7 / zijde / katoen velours
pvc projectiedoek
canvas / katoen velours / witte voile / vero sol 818

MAU
pvc zeil
markilux
transparant plastic

ART
wolvilt
zwarte voile
skaai
transparant plastic

PRA
transparant plastic
lasergewebe
trevira cs satin

MEI
witte voile 1.75
katoen velours 0.60
spinaker 0.15

LEN
rijde / verosol 818
scala katoen velours / tulle

BER
trevira garens
-creme
-groen
-zwart
-wit

NDT

NDT*
wolvelour
gouden film

IIT
3.00
1.80

backside
in for ma tion text
1.80
1.50   0.30

STOFFEN PER PROJECT
: 15 DOEKEN

Fins, Sauerkraut and Furs
Mercedes Benz Museum, Stuttgart, 2001-2006

Liquid Gold
Nederlands Dans Theater, The Hague, 1987-1988 & 1999

"It was essentially an urban study trip and as we drove from city to city, the outside world passed by, mysterious, humid, soothingly warm and – noticing the tension of our drivers and the weapons in the car – dangerous at times. Better not to make any stops along the way. Each city was totally different – predominantly Muslim Kano in the north, with its palace, ancient mosques and mud houses in varying earthen colours, its weavers, leatherworkers and indigo dyers, its markets, yellow three-wheelers, horses and emirs in amazingly beautiful robes, staffs in hand. All this right next to the city's ultra-modern centre, and bossy Lebanese hotel owners and businessmen.

The capital city Abuja in the centre of the country has modern architecture and a spacious, linear, late '70s urban plan by – excitingly – Kenzo Tange. A city created next to the gigantic, round rock Aso (936 metres above sea level). And finally, the then-so-called 'dysfunctional' Lagos, at the time still governed by the military, with its crowded, energisingly rhythmic, and for a Westerner seemingly chaotic but in fact well-organised roads, traffic, trade, garbage disposal and social networks. There is activity practically everywhere you look: in the middle of the street, under bridges, between highways and inside every cavity – for example, a shop, a market, a gathering, a performance, a vendor, a home, a laundromat or a repair shop. You feel the tension of unheeded laws, fleeting movements and hurried looks while discovering the most humorous, interested, street-smart, talented people who shape their lives with strong conviction while undertaking fantastic initiatives worldwide and with immense creativity, know-how and bursting energy.

When we visited Lagos's architecture faculty to meet and talk with students, I not only received a portrait photograph of a young man who wanted to meet my daughter, whom he assumed would be beautiful, he also asked me to hand her the photograph with his name and address on it. We also met architecture student Kunle Adeyemi, who later came to the Netherlands to join OMA. He eventually led the competition project in Abuja for which we developed ideas for the landscaping – as shown here. He has managed his own architecture studio for many years now, and we are currently working together on a project in Kigali, Rwanda." PB

LOCATION	Abuja, Nigeria
CLIENT	Nelson Mandela Institution
STATUS	Competition: 2nd prize
SCOPE	Landscape design for campus and surroundings
SCALE	112 ha
COLLABORATORS	OMA, Arup
DESCRIPTION	We joined the OMA team as landscape architects for this competition, and, of course, this new university campus for science and technology wanted to represent the newest and most advanced mentality, meaning that the "landscape" had to integrate the latest findings for climate improvement, energy saving and water management.

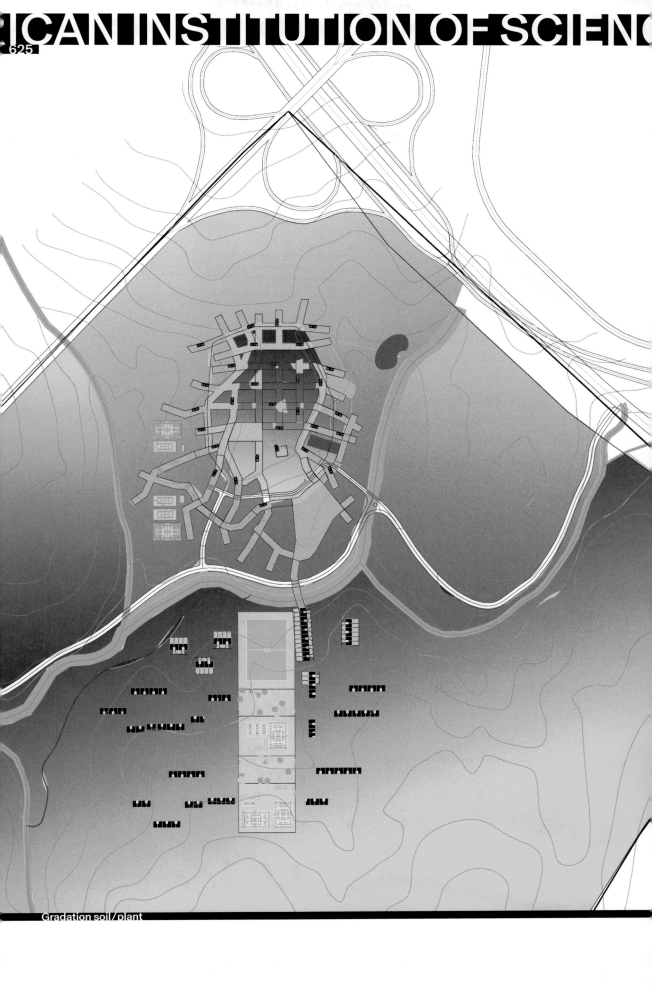

Gradation soil/plant

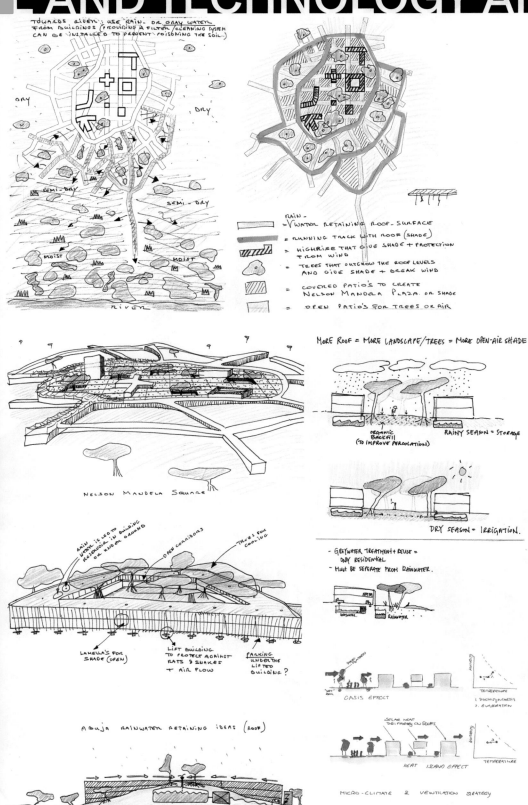

Studies to see how roofs, building and topography can interact to organise greenery as well as water- and airflows with the aim of improving soil and climate

Visualising patios, open facade structures and balconies

Adding more trees to OMA's presentation material

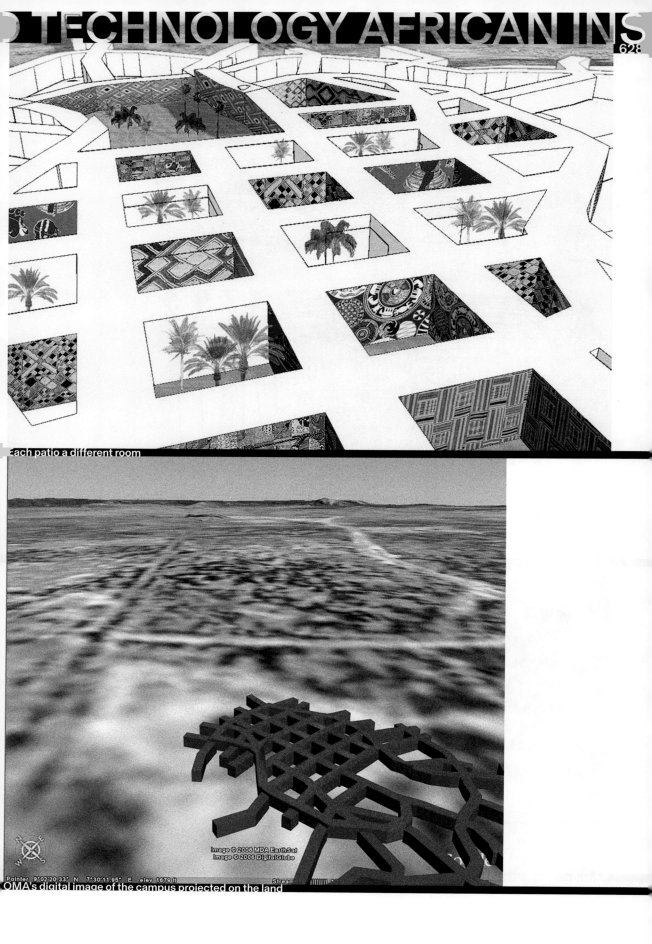

Each patio a different room

OMA's digital image of the campus projected on the land

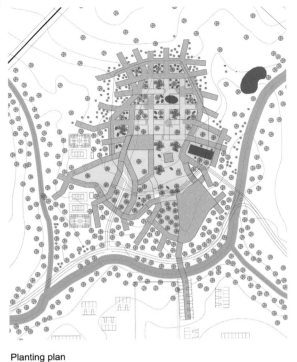

Planting plan

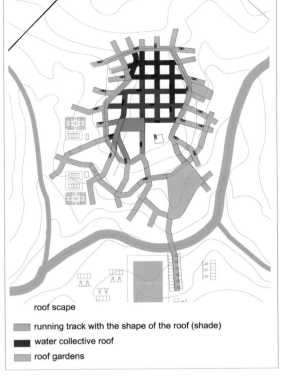

roof scape

▨ running track with the shape of the roof (shade)
■ water collective roof
▨ roof gardens

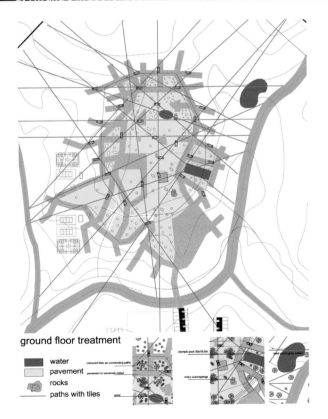

ground floor treatment

■ water
▨ pavement
▨ rocks
— paths with tiles

coloured tiles as connecting paths
pavement in savannah colour

olympic pool 50x18.5m

rocky outcroppings

pond

1m above ground   8m above ground

2002–2005 Invisible Presence
Glass Pavilion, Toledo Museum of Art

"Only one curtain was to be typically 'Petra' (very present and expressive, that is, according to Sejima!), namely in the multipurpose room, where we designed an ingenious shape for the tracks so that many different rooms and conditions inside that space could be formed by one and the same curtain. For the cafeteria we designed a sturdy, easy-to-clean, white gauze curtain with round holes and windows. We had to prove that it would be easy to clean in the 1:1 mock-up on site, so we threw ketchup and coffee onto it and then wiped the surface with a moist cloth. Ketchup got caught inside the tiny openings of the gauze but disappeared with a brush. As the roof of this elegant building was extremely thin, both the curtains that were provided, and the strategically placed plantings in the patio and adjacent park helped to cool the interior. In the end, only our track systems and configurations were installed. At the request of the then newly appointed museum director, the shading/UV filtering curtains were produced by a local firm on the basis of our research and design." PB

LOCATION	Toledo, Ohio, USA
CLIENT	Toledo Museum of Art
STATUS	Partially realised
SCOPE	Space-defining, acoustic and darkening curtains for multipurpose room; sun and UV screening voiles for exhibition spaces; washable view-filter curtain for canteen; shading plan for interior spaces through plantings in surrounding museum garden (not realised); rack and storage configurations and all test samples (realised)
MATERIALS	Yellow silk (multipurpose room), perforated white projection mesh (canteen), grey/silver Verosol with stainless-steel top and bottom seams (exhibition spaces and Hotshop)
SCALE	Space 1, 75.3 × 4 m; space 2, 34 × 4 m; space 3, 60.4 × 4 m; space 4, 95 × 4 m
COLLABORATORS	SANAA, TRANSSOLAR Energietechnik GmbH/Matthias Schuler
DESCRIPTION	It was an interesting 2.5 years of collaboration with SANAA (Kazuyo Sejima + Ryue Nishizawa) with Floris Idenburg as well as the light and climate engineers on developing functional yet invisible curtains for the Toledo Glass Museum. All curtains were to regulate the light and the UV levels in the rounded, glazed exhibition spaces. They were neutral and colourless, designed with open top edges for the fire sprinklers. We studied the surrounding park for its ability to provide natural shade for the building.

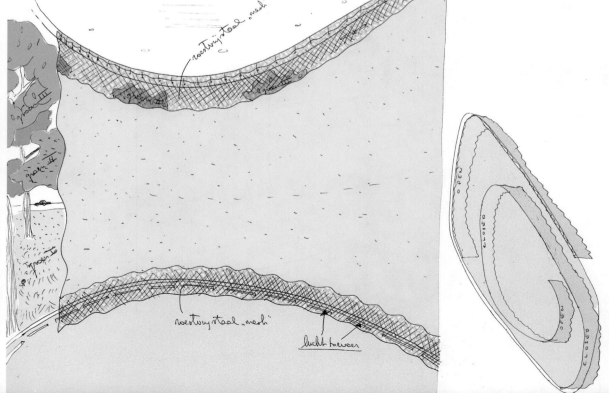

"DARKENING CURTAIN-CONFIGURATION"
= GRADUAL LIGHT CONTROL
= ATMOSPHERE TO EXHIBIT/OBJECTS
= TRANSLUSCENT FILTER

"DRAMATIC CURTAIN"
= DARKENING
= DIVIDING
= ACOUSTIC
= DECORATION

AUDITORIUM

REST

EXHIBITION

EXHIBITION

FOOD

HOT SHOP

S

"LINEAR CAMELEON"
= SHADING
= SCREENING
= ACOUSTIC ABSORBANT
= TRANSPARENT → OPAQUE

"TRANSPARENT MASS"
= SHADING/COOLING
= PROTECTING

"GARDEN STRATEGY"
= SEASONAL SHADE EFFECTS
= ADDITION TO PARK PLANTING
= SUBCONSCIOUS ROUTING TO BUILDING
= OPEN / CLOSED COMPOSITION AROUND BUILDING

Studies for the dramatic curtain for the multipurpose room: one curtain that can divide a large space into different rooms, simultaneously creating sound and light conditions

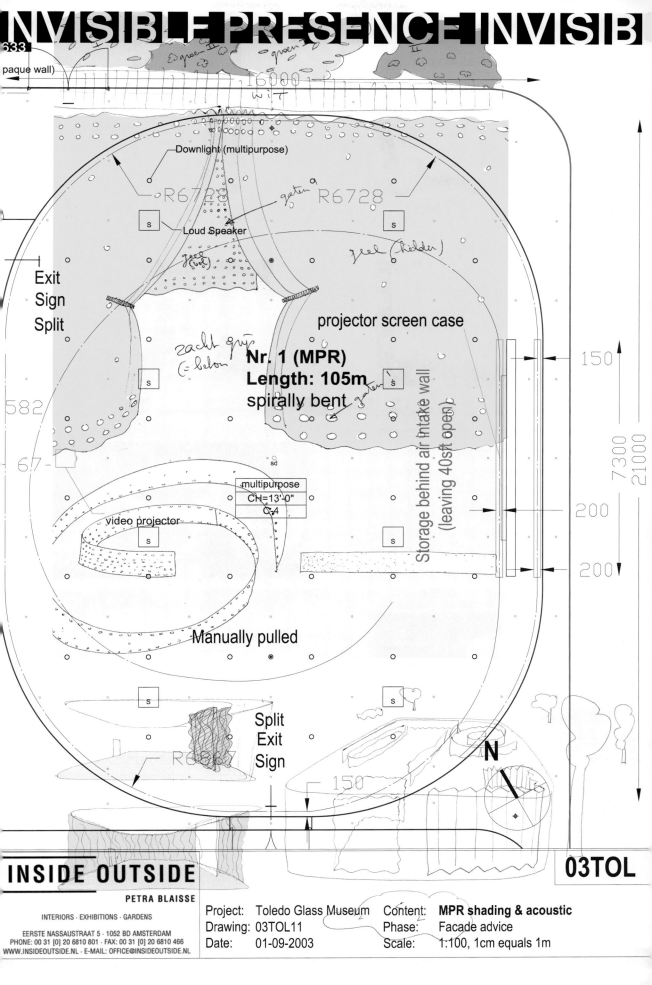

INSIDE OUTSIDE

PETRA BLAISSE

INTERIORS · EXHIBITIONS · GARDENS

EERSTE NASSAUSTRAAT 5 · 1052 BD AMSTERDAM
PHONE: 00 31 [0] 20 6810 801 · FAX: 00 31 [0] 20 6810 466
WWW.INSIDEOUTSIDE.NL · E-MAIL: OFFICE@INSIDEOUTSIDE.NL

Project:	Toledo Glass Museum	Content:	**MPR shading & acoustic**
Drawing:	03TOL11	Phase:	Facade advice
Date:	01-09-2003	Scale:	1:100, 1cm equals 1m

03TOL

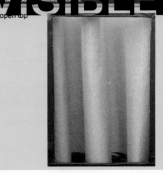

With open top

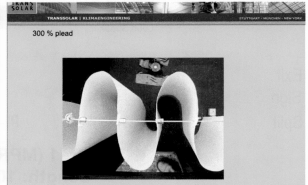

300 % plead

Top view of the test box with the window opening and the horizontal and vertical sensor

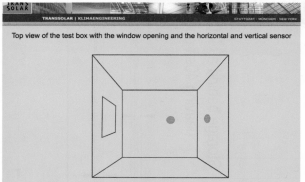

100 % plead

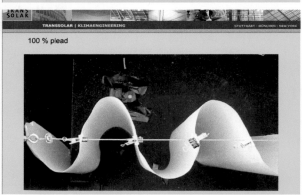

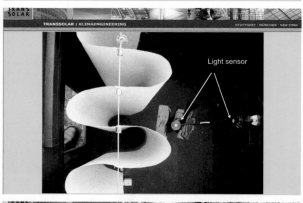

Light sensor

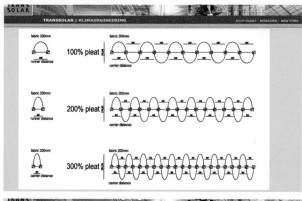

Front view to the window of the testbox with the pleated curtain

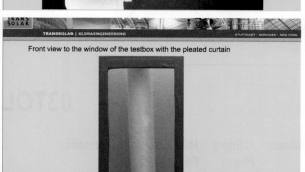

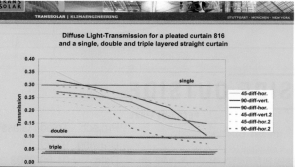

Diffuse Light-Transmission for a pleated curtain 816 and a single, double and triple layered straight curtain

Analysis of heat gain and light transmission due to different pleat percentages in relation to the curtain's position along the glass facade

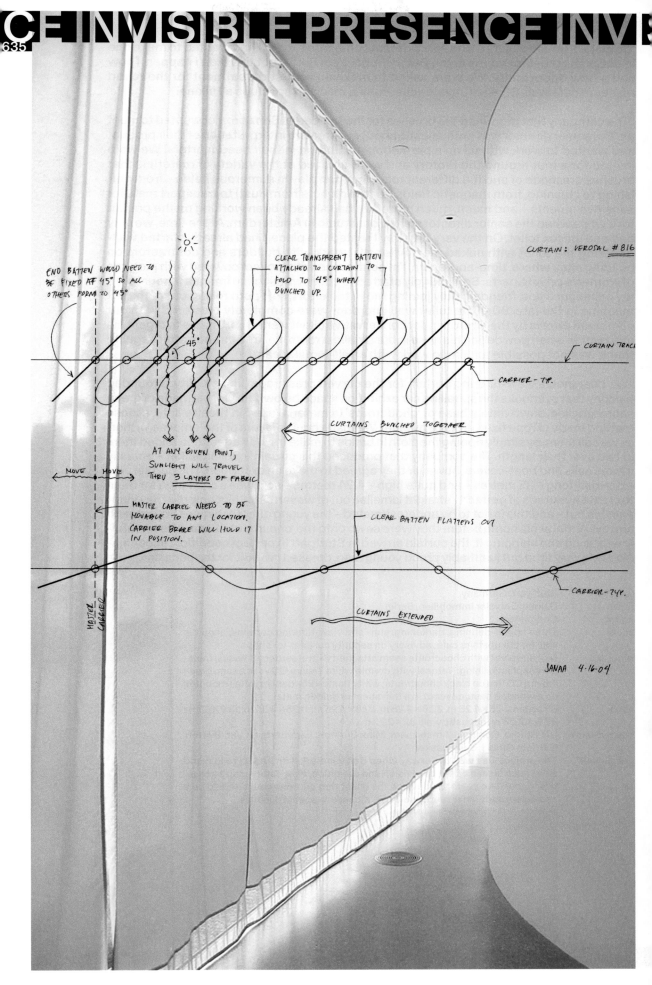

CURTAIN: VEROSAL #816

END BATTEN WOULD NEED TO
BE FIXED AT 45° SO ALL
OTHERS FORM TO 45°

CLEAR TRANSPARENT BATTEN
ATTACHED TO CURTAIN TO
FOLD TO 45° WHEN
BUNCHED UP.

45°

CURTAIN TRACK

CARRIER - TYP.

CURTAINS BUNCHED TOGETHER

MOVE   MOVE

AT ANY GIVEN POINT,
SUNLIGHT WILL TRAVEL
THRU 3 LAYERS OF FABRIC

MASTER CARRIER NEEDS TO BE
MOVABLE TO ANY LOCATION.
CARRIER BRAKE WILL HOLD IT
IN POSITION.

CLEAR BATTEN FLATTENS OUT

CARRIER - TYP.

MASTER CARRIER

CURTAINS EXTENDED

SANAA 4·16·04

Hairs, Fins, Sauerkraut and Furs
Mercedes-Benz Museum

"To make a brush-covered wall was a dream come true for me: I had wanted to make one in one of the meeting rooms at the Dutch Embassy in Berlin, but this didn't happen. I now had a new opportunity. We were asked to make an acoustic treatment for the round museum café wall. Sensual, mysterious, subtle, chic and spacious all in one!"

"The company that produced the brushes for the Mercedes Benz project wanted to meet us. The senior director was enthusiastic about our creative interpretation of their product and wanted to work with us on a permanent exhibition in their headquarters. We were invited for a tour around the factory and were amazed at the variety of materials that brushes are made of and the different roles they can play in numerous fields – from polishing to cleaning, from magnetic fields (to free objects from dust) to transport mats for sensitive objects – and much, much more. We had already been working on the project for a while when the senior director visited our studio in Amsterdam. At the time, we only had one unisex toilet. On the very first day I rented the place, I had already started wall-papering the toilet with naked men. After all, I work with builders and contractors on building sites where, time-and-again, I'm confronted with lockers covered with pictures of women's private parts. So, I jokingly started to collect masculine images for our toilet, my colleagues and friends gladly joining me in the effort, soft porn rolling out of the fax machine in the late '90s! The toilet wall and door were completely plastered with our combined efforts by the time our poor conservative client visited us. Unable to digest his misfortune when powdering his nose in our smallest room, he fired us soon after, arguing that it was not possible for him to work with an all-female team."

"We designed a view-filtering curtain for the curved press room, in actuality, a rounded balcony that overlooks the spiralling car exhibition space below. The work is made of green satin lamellae, sewn onto a base of 'choucroute' (a material used in theatre sets, a loose matting made of rope fixed in place by glue). We made double layers of the lamellae, or 'fins' as we call them, by simply ripping the cloth in bands to make frayed edges, then folded them in two over their length. The company that produced this curtain – Seilemaaker – actually makes sails and boat-covers, however they agreed to make an exception. The curtain was extremely long – 35 metres – and quite high – 4.24 metres – so it was a challenge for them to create hundreds of perfectly straight lamellae out of woven satin. Not only did they manage this but – and this is not to be underestimated – the young director himself ironed each and every 'fin' at his home before they were sewn onto the 'choucroute' base. After carefully wrapping and shipping it, the curtain arrived in Stuttgart in perfect condition, accompanied by a very tired but justifiably proud young man, dressed in a suit for the occasion."   PB

LOCATION	Stuttgart, Germany
CLIENT	DaimlerChrysler Immobilien, Berlin
STATUS	Completed
SCOPE	Three space-defining, darkening, sun- and view-filtering curtains; acoustic wall for the upstairs café; advisory on security curtains for shops
MATERIALS	Mohair velvet with choucroute seam attached with steel corset hooks, transparent plastic lining; Verosol with double white Trevira CS voile seam; green Trevira CS fins on black choucroute; white flame-retardant brushes mounted on a wooden base, covered in a thin sheet of golden metal
SCALE	6 curtains: 35 × 4.25 m, 32.6 × 4.25 m, 27.8 × 4.25 m; 11.25 × 4.25 m; 13.6 × 3.7 m; 33.3 × 2.03 m; acoustic wall: 32 × 2.72 m
COLLABORATORS	UN Studio, Concrete Amsterdam, Mink Bürsten, Lammerts en Van Bueren, Gerriets GmbH, Seilemaaker
DESCRIPTION	The project was well underway when Ben van Berkel invited us to join and solve such issues as space division and definition, view-filtering and acoustics. It took two years to convince the client that curtains could indeed be a necessary addition in response to the museum's spatial qualities.

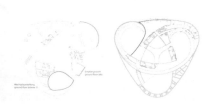

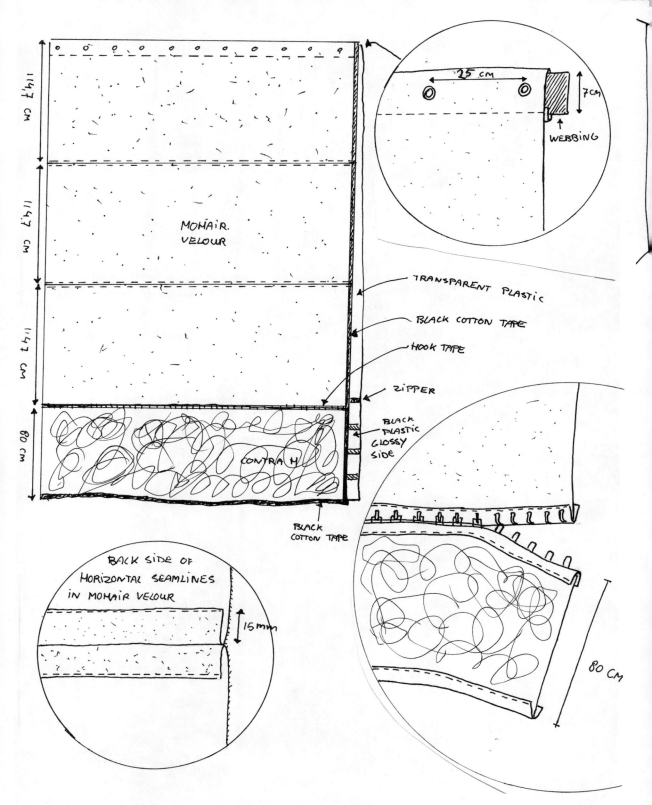

114,7 CM

114,7 CM

114,7 CM

80 CM

MOHAIR.
VELOUR

CONTRA H

25 CM

7CM

WEBBING

TRANSPARENT PLASTIC

BLACK COTTON TAPE

HOOK TAPE

ZIPPER

BLACK
PLASTIC
GLOSSY
SIDE

BLACK
COTTON TAPE

BACK SIDE OF
HORIZONTAL SEAMLINES
IN MOHAIR VELOUR

15mm

80 CM

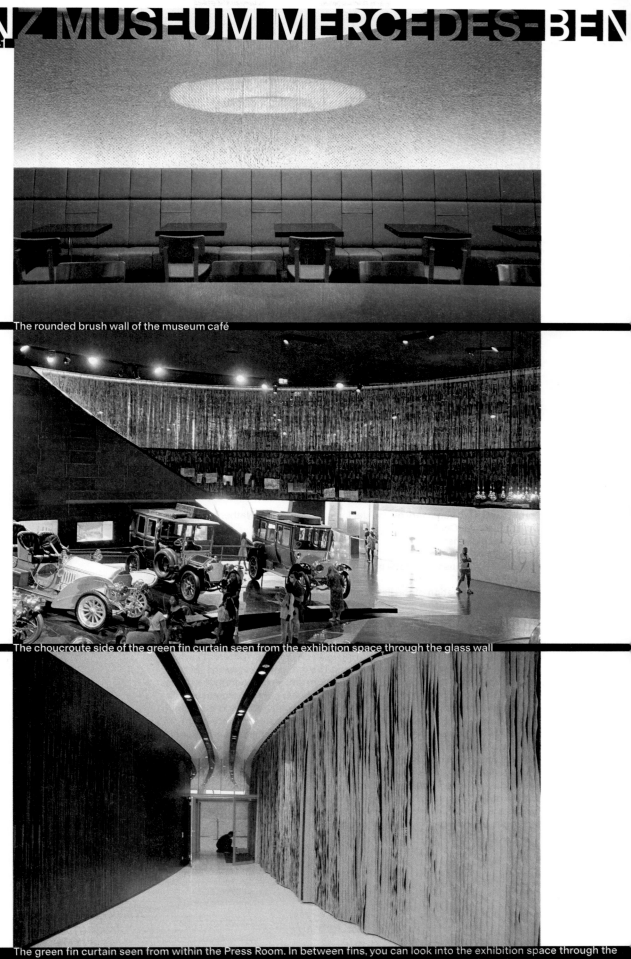

The rounded brush wall of the museum café

The choucroute side of the green fin curtain seen from the exhibition space through the glass wall

The green fin curtain seen from within the Press Room. In between fins, you can look into the exhibition space through the choucroute base layer.

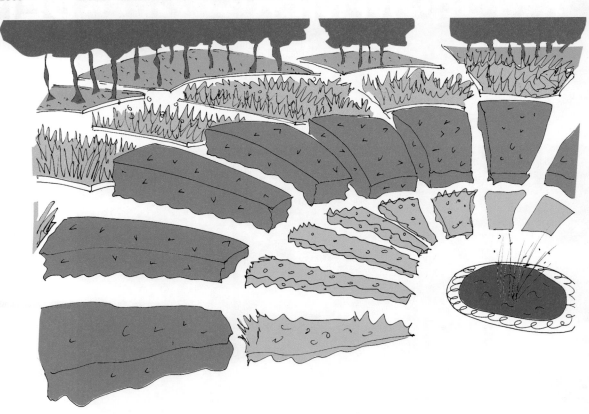

LOCATION	Former Catholic monastery by Van der Laan, Deventer, the Netherlands
CLIENT	Deventer Health Center
STATUS	2 Concept designs
SCOPE	Landscape design
SCALE	4 enclosed gardens with a total of 1,447 m^2
COLLABORATORS	One Architecture
DESCRIPTION	For the transformation of the listed monastery Sint Jozef – built by Van der Laan in the '50s – into a contemporary health centre, Matthijs Bouw/One Architecture invited us to re-design the four old dark, stark, evergreen and motionless gardens into lively ones with a more health-oriented and welcoming character. Each enclosed garden had its own ground condition (from concrete understructure to full soil), allowing us to design them differently while still treating them as a coordinated series. The two garden versions that we drew up refer both to the building's architecture and former cloister function. We designed one contemporary *Hortus conclusus* garden, organised in a radial layout of cultivated planting beds with special herbs and medicinal plants of different heights. The other version is an intricate linear composition that relates to the chapel's stained-glass windows. Water features are projected in the centre of both gardens, enhancing the microcosms and encouraging biodiversity, while a grid of small trees, scattered over paths and planting beds, adds verticality. We aimed to break open the architecture's introverted character by suggesting a floor finish with the same patterns and colours throughout the building's interior corridors and waiting rooms, thus connecting the different wings of the new health centre to each other.

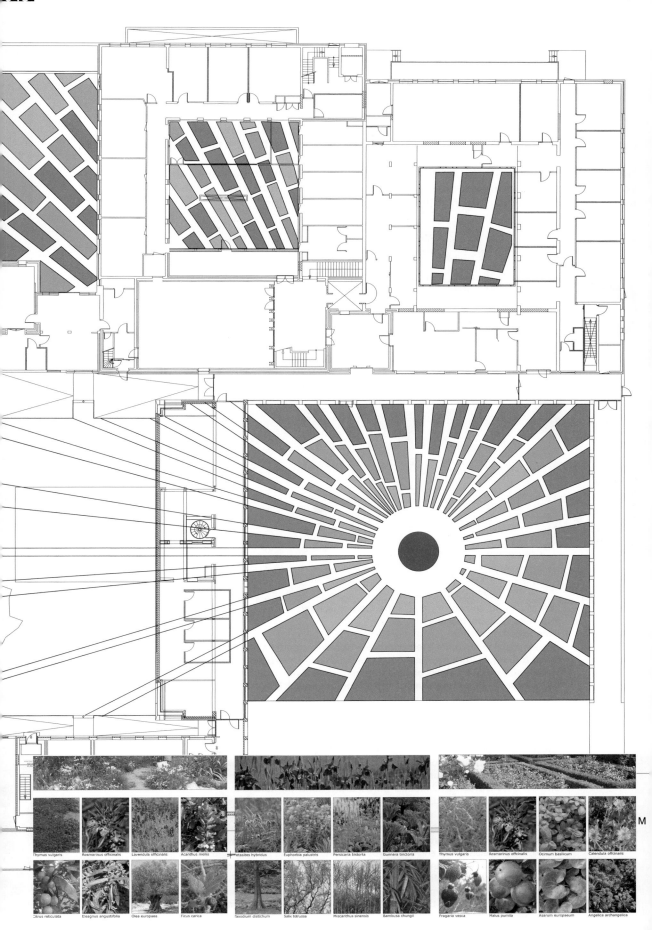

Thymus vulgaris Rosmarinus officinalis Lavendula officinalis Acanthus mollis Petasites hybridus Euphorbia palustris Persicaria bistorta Gunnera tinctoria Thymus vulgaris Rosmarinus officinalis Ocimum basilicum Calendula officinalis

Citrus reticulata Eleagnus angustifolia Olea europaea Ficus carica Taxodium distichum Salix totruosa Miscanthus sinensis Bambusa chungii Fragaria vesca Malus pumila Asarum europaeum Angelica archangelica

M

Rifletutti
Villa Manin

"We ordered 60 black umbrellas, ripped off the tops and replaced them with transparent silver foil. It was quite a hands-on job to figure out the right way to create an umbrella top, with folding seams, connection caps and a central cover. We also put our labels – numbered – on the handles. We made 57 of them in our studio, cutting, fitting, sewing (thank you Peter, Anky and Rosetta) and then wrapping and sending them to Francesco Bonami by registered post."

"When I escorted Rem, who was carrying two parasols out of sheer enthusiasm, and Kasper König over the spacious lawns, then through a wooded area, Kasper looked down into one of the mirroring drops and exclaimed: 'Trees are growing downward and the sky opens up beneath us. You have opened up the earth and created the sixth dimension!'"

"Rosetta and Peter nearly broke their arms and hands trying to hammer the long pins, soldered under the stainless-steel plates, into the dry and rocky soil of the Villa Manin forest grounds. A hellish job! Wet the ground, that really helps."   PB

LOCATION	Villa Manin Contemporary Art Centre, Codroipo, Italy
CLIENT	Francesco Bonami (curator)
STATUS	Completed
SCOPE	Art commission to create a temporary pavilion in the gardens of the estate
MATERIALS	Silver foil, steel structure, plastic handles; stainless-steel polished plates in various sizes with screwed-on pins to secure each plate in the forest soil
SCALE	50 'private pavilions' (translucent and mirroring parasols); 18 mirroring discs (polished stainless steel 5 mm thick) 10 pcs of 0.25 m; 5 pcs of 0.5 m; 3 pcs of 1 m in diameter
DESCRIPTION	The installation was planned as part of the Venice Art Biennale in the summer of 2005. Kasper König's collection was on view inside Villa Manin. Outside, follies and art pieces were to be spread over the estate, and Francesco asked us to develop a pavilion for the gardens. We thought we should make something that represents our mentality and approach to transformation and chance. So, we created 52 mobile "personal pavilions" for visitors to take into the gardens, plus 22 round, polished steel plates, forming "water drops" spread throughout a shaded forest area. The water drops guided visitors along an attractive trajectory through the woods, while reflecting light and mirroring the surroundings. The Rifletutti were umbrellas, clad in translucent silver foil to serve as parasols for sun and wind protection. At the same time, they formed a mobile, intimate space around each visitor. Their name refers to the reflection of the surroundings in both directions. We made small holes in each of them, so-called organised viewpoints. The holes projected playful patches of light on visitors' bodies and on the ground – like the butterflies in Garcia Marquez's fairy-tale world in *One Hundred Years of Solitude*.

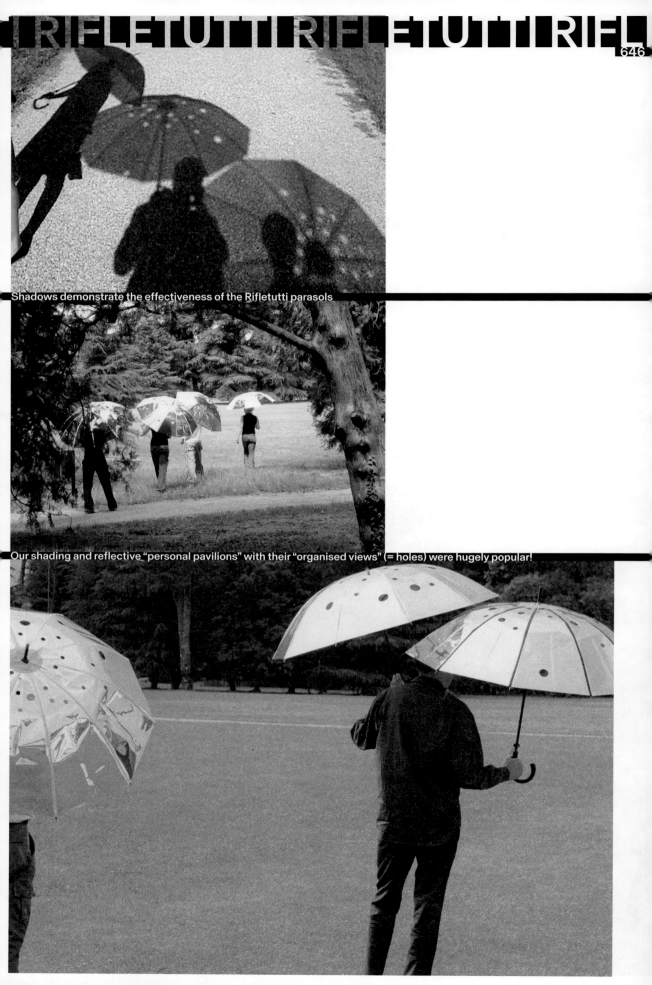

Shadows demonstrate the effectiveness of the Rifletutti parasols

Our shading and reflective "personal pavilions" with their "organised views" (= holes) were hugely popular!

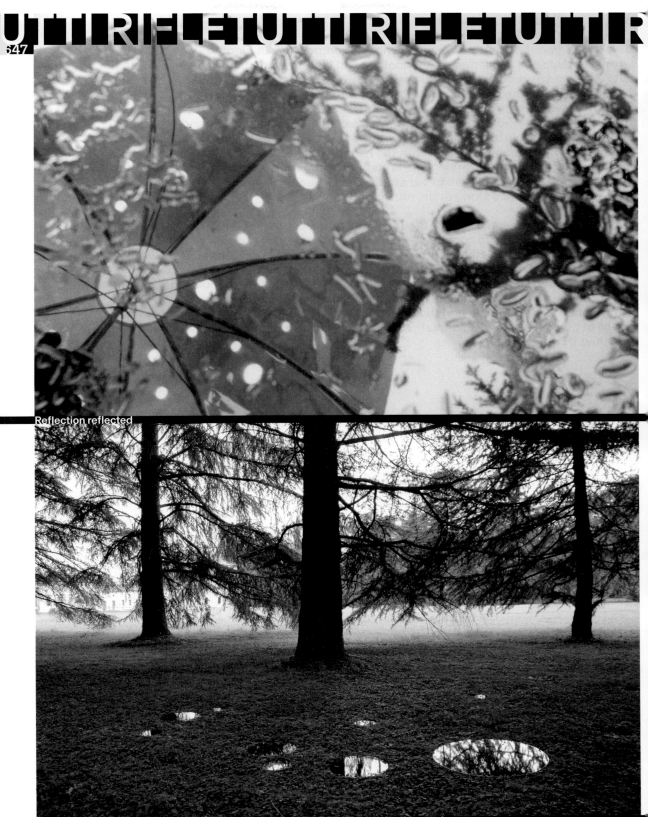

Reflection reflected

The embedded polished steel "water drops" are dispersed throughout the forested areas

Cool Inlays Landscape
Dubai Renaissance Tower

"This was a 'paper project' as we didn't win the competition. (It went to Zaha Hadid but was never realised.) In our design, technology and fantasy went hand in hand. Sustainability was key, so we communicated directly with the environmental engineers and Arup to make sure that the gardens and the architecture collaborated and reinforced each other. The revolving, circular base for the Renaissance Tower, placed in the saltwater of the sea inlet, triggered our imagination. We made numerous sketches and collages to explore garden opportunities and converted the strongest ideas into digital drawings – composed by colleague Rosetta with the help of architect Jason Lee, who lent us his time after working hours. Working late is standard procedure in our professions, and so we make it fun and cook dinner in our studio and, on lucky days, put a record on my old gramophone and dance along to the music!"

"Rosetta and Jason developed the digital drawings in beautiful detail. There was energy in the air and eagerness to come up with the best solutions for economic water use and re-use, and the most attractive, new typology for the sustainable garden and water islands. As usual, I made sketches in the course of our conversations and exchanges – sometimes absentmindedly on a newspaper or some other printed matter. The circular shape of the two garden/water islands took its cue from the pivoting circular disc onto which OMA's Renaissance slab is placed, and that makes the tower turn with the sun. That disc was meant to be covered with solar plates that would, at the same time, shade the parking lot below, if I remember well." PB

LOCATION	Dubai, United Arab Emirates
CLIENT	Dubai Properties
STATUS	Competition
SCOPE	Sustainable landscape design in connection to the high-rise building's energy- and water management ambitions
SCALE	3.8 ha
COLLABORATORS	OMA, Arup, Vincent de Rijk, Frans Parthesius, Hans Werlemann, Irma Boom
DESCRIPTION	The building is designed as a single monolithic volume that wastes no energy but rather collects what it needs: an almost flat, rectangular slab, 200 metres wide and 300 metres tall with a closed system of white solar cells as cladding for the facade. The building rises from a circular disc close to the Dubai city shore and rotates with one of its slim flanks following the movement of the sun, so that the rooms inside are always in the shade. Its grey water is taken down to the circular Garden Island, where a septic tank with cleansing bacteria stores it temporarily, after which it goes through filtration media (filled with nanofiber, rubble stone, grit or sand) and is further purified by root systems of strategically chosen aquatic and marsh plants, shrubs and trees (phytoremediation vegetation). Some of the purified fresh water is then transported back into the building for re-use, some to the Freshwater Island, where it fills a decorative fountain alias swimming pool. The Garden Island, in the meantime, welcomes the public into its cool microclimate, where floating terraces and bridges lead visitors through a shaded green world.

I had fun imagining ways to reach the Renaissance site over the water – a hovering bridge shaded by rows of trees at its centre

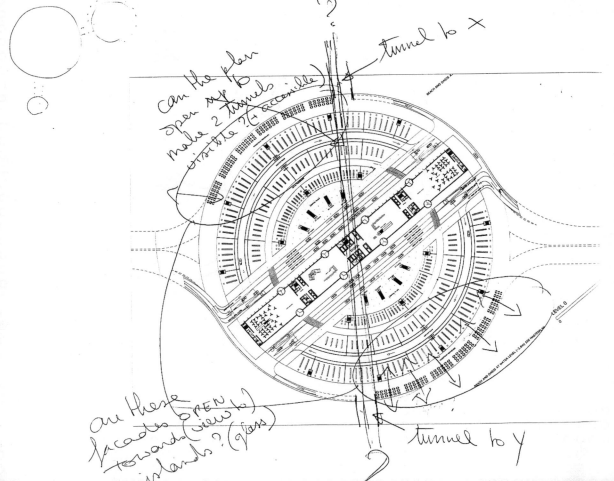

Questions to architects concerning the accessibility of the two garden islands

Sketch for Garden Island, showing the lifted path system that hovers above the vital, moist soil and meanders in between tree trunks and under the shading tree crowns

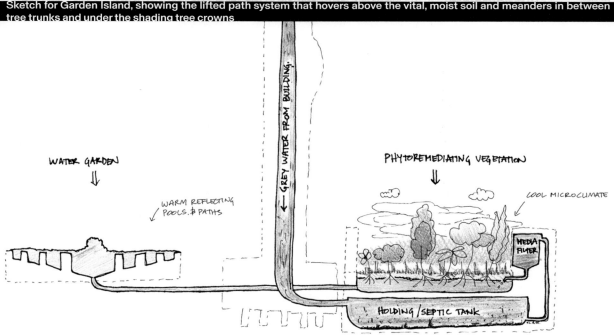

Sketch explaining circular, self-cleaning water system in which grey water is first filtered and then cleaned by root systems (soil particles and microorganisms) after which it is pumped onto the Water Garden, where the clean water can be used for fountains or for swimming

Window Windows
Architectura & Natura Bookstore

"This is certainly the smallest curtain we ever made for the smallest space we ever worked on. Not to say that it was easy, on the contrary: small is difficult. And, of course, we had grand ambitions: Apart from fulfilling the brief, we also wanted the curtain to become a backdrop for the books on display when not in use as a shading device, at the same time serving as a translucent screen between storefront and store to protect the cashier from the permanent gaze of passers-by; and it had to be stored away in such a way that the pleated volume would not obscure the view of the books. We found the right cloth, shaped the appropriate track, built the necessary structures and introduced a new lighting element. The silver side of the transparent cloth reflects the sun, and with its round windows, it looks like a facade when lit from the front. The print that covers the back shows an enlarged Santolina plant." PB

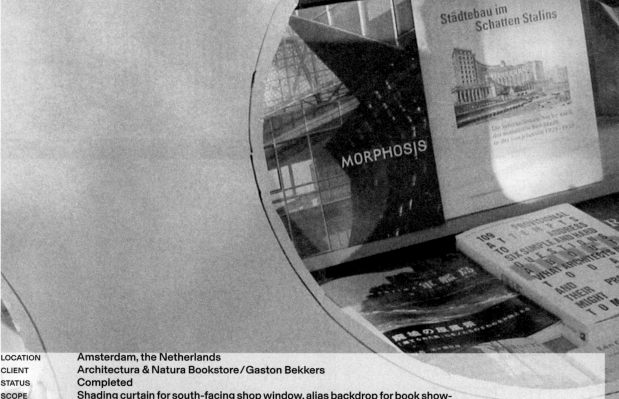

LOCATION	Amsterdam, the Netherlands
CLIENT	Architectura & Natura Bookstore / Gaston Bekkers
STATUS	Completed
SCOPE	Shading curtain for south-facing shop window, alias backdrop for book showcase; showcase lamp
MATERIALS	Printed and cut Verosol, transparent plastic
SCALE	4.75 × 3.55 m
COLLABORATORS	Johan Jumelet (lamp)
DESCRIPTION	We were asked to develop a shading/UV-filtering curtain for the south-facing storefront of the bookstore. In order to represent architecture AND nature and protect the array of books on architecture, design, landscape and natural science, the curtain needed to offer shade but not to close off the showcase.

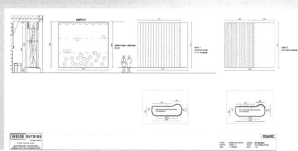

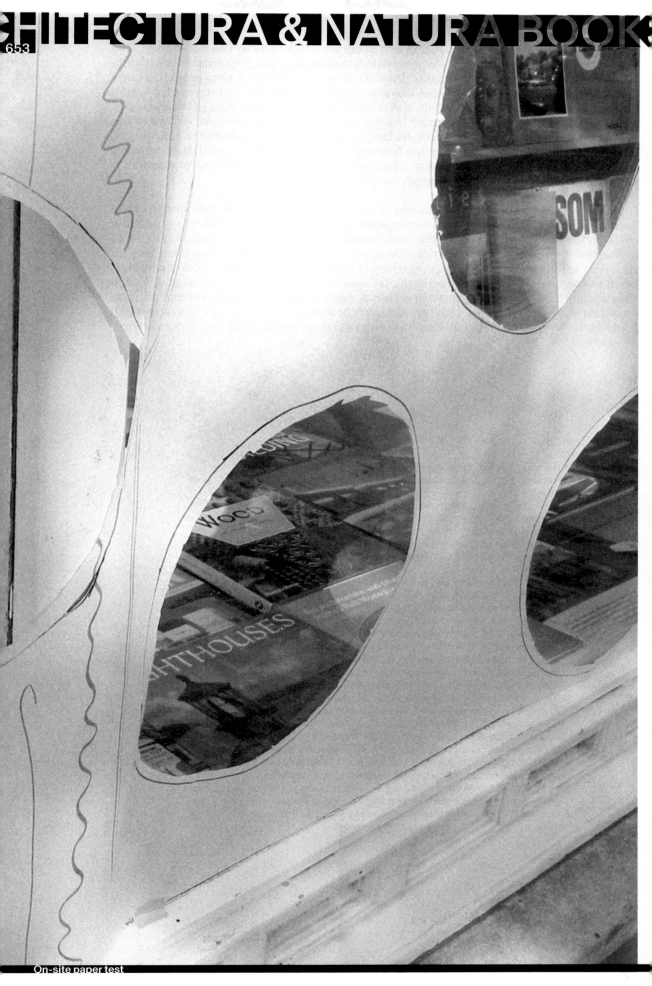

Restoration Revised
Curtains for Hackney Empire Theatre

"It was an amazing sight when, during one of our working visits to Tim Ronalds and his team, we went to the building site where restoration works were underway. In the middle of the theatre where there are usually rows of red-velvet chairs, we encountered a huge crane standing with its grasshopper-like legs on the bare ground, its long neck sticking through the open roof high above us. It was quite late, there were stars in the clear sky, and building lamps were illuminating the theatre's Victorian interior. We looked at the room rising up around the void with its balconies, colourful wall decorations, golden flower clusters and weird mix of lamps framing the bare ground, the earth that normally lies hidden under the carpeted floor and our feet in festive shoes. Earth and sky connected for just a few hours, overwhelmingly beautiful and symbolic."

"In the old days, the public was allowed to eat and smoke during performances at the Hackney Empire. The vaulted roof has a round window at its centre. This heavy window rests on two tracks on the top of the roof. At intervals, the window would slide open to air the theatre space: smoke and hot air would escape upward, refreshing the space for the next performance. Behind the upper ring of balconies, on both sides, round windows open to the city outside. They too could be opened for fresh air and views out. As the theatre functions day and night, with performances ranging from bingo to slapstick, from one-man shows to musicals and from concerts to theatre plays, daylight plays as much a role as darkness. The Hackney Empire is and will hopefully remain a place for everyone, all year round." PB

LOCATION	Hackney, London, United Kingdom
CLIENT	Hackney Empire Theatre, The Heritage Lottery Fund, The London Arts Council
STATUS	Completed
SCOPE	Guillotine house curtain and acoustic drapes for main auditorium; blackout and space-defining curtains for studios; darkening, acoustic and backdrop curtains for café; concept for wallpapers
MATERIALS	Velvet house curtains with gold cord; acoustic drapes, velvet and printed; studios, printed voile and wool serge; Pepys Pub, velvet and stainless-steel chain mill
SCALE	Main auditorium, 10.4 × 10.6 m, 9 × 5.6 m (2×); studios: 35.8 × 3.9 m, 15.3 × 4.75 m; Pepys Pub, 20 × 4.5 m, 11.3 × 4.5 m
COLLABORATORS	Tim Ronalds Architects, Ken Creasey Ltd
DESCRIPTION	A building by Matcham from the late nineteenth century initiated an interesting discussion about what restoration entails and to which exact state and date one should return. The decision was made to leave the colourful layers that were added through the years. These layers were cleaned and re-built and necessary structures – such as a stage tower – were added. Original elements of value were also restored while keeping the famous and much-loved décor. In response, we proposed textile and wallpaper interventions that would point to the future: a vibrant, black-and-white layer that would run behind and around the Victorian theatre box, a disconnecting factor that would accentuate the classical character of the theatre. After careful consideration of all those involved, it was decided not to implement this idea: the directors and boards found it important to give the public what they were used to before closure, namely a classical theatre with all the traditional and anticipated features. So, the house curtain had to be red velvet with gold cords and nothing else. So, yes, we switched direction and developed a classical red house curtain, using a conventional technique on a larger scale.

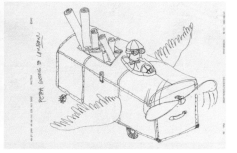

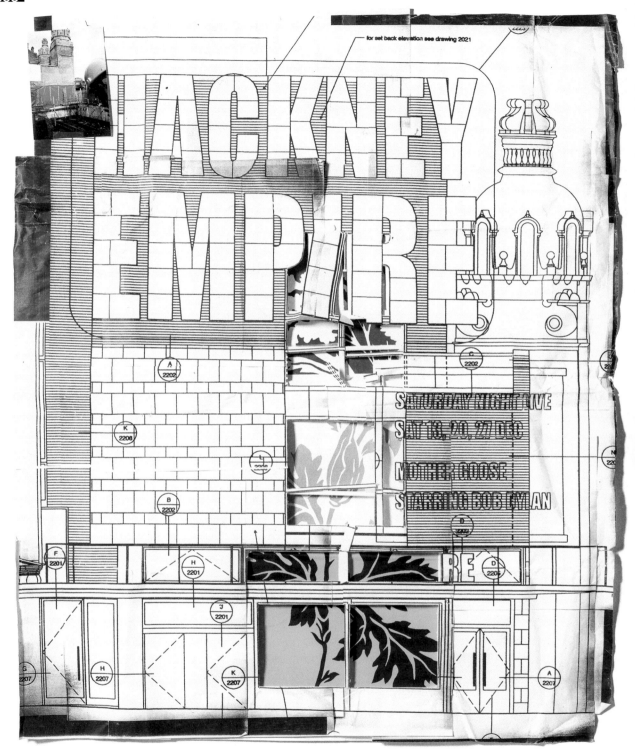

for set back elevation see drawing 2021

SATURDAY NIGHT LIVE
SAT 13, 20, 27 DEC
MOTHER GOOSE
STARRING BOB DYLAN

27/09/01 arrival London Luton

28/09/01: HACKNEY EMPIRE PRESENTATION

Sketches made after our important schematic presentation of our ideas for the front curtain to the clients. We took a lot of heavy 1:1 samples to London; I was accompanied by len Wiegers (financial adviser) and Lieuwe Conradi (creative architect/ strongman).

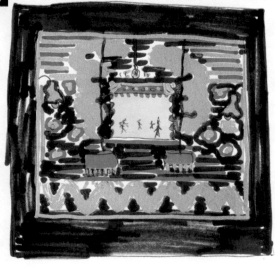

BEFORE   AFTER

Full-scale white-cotton model of future red-velvet stage curtain (by Ken Creasey Ltd London)

Preliminary studies

"I referred to the process of curtain-making in our 2007 Inside Outside book. That we developed 11 monumental curtains in parallel and as an integral part of the architectural birth of Casa da Música is still an exciting story for us. The building site was one of the most beautiful I have ever seen. I vividly remember that during one of my visits I literally held my breath at the beauty of the excavation works down below: from the wet, reflective, dark-grey concrete surface of the future basement floor, just being poured, to the sky-high fountains of thin, steel rods (the rebars for future concrete columns) jetting upwards, freely swaying in the wind – a bona fide ballet of rods dancing in front of a bright blue sky and mirrored in the shiny concrete below. Visual music."

"When you climb up the scaffolding to reach a high point of a building under construction, many sensations rush through your veins: danger, concentration, physical exertion, visual sensations, smells and sounds. One wrong step and you could fall, one split second of distraction and you could bump your head hard. You have taken on the challenge of climbing all the way up the teetering structure to hang or attach samples to dusty walls, unstable edges or thick round tubes. Your helmet is squeezing your forehead, the boots you borrowed are full of sand, the dayglo jacket is too big and weighed down by your tools (no phone yet), and you are surrounded by the people who will judge your ideas, which are about to be shown in the most unappealing circumstances for the object in question."   PB

LOCATION	Porto, Portugal
CLIENT	Porto 2001, Casa da Música
STATUS	Competition: 1st prize/completed
SCOPE	11 acoustic, blackout and view-filtering curtains and sunscreens; advisory on interior and exterior finishes; concept for public square
MATERIALS	Sala I, Trevira CS voile and fire-retardant fishnet (black and white), Verosol and Trevira CS voile (black and white with silver), wool serge (white and black) with printed blackout lining; Sala II, Choucroute and Trevira CS voile, velvet and stainless-steel rings; Rehearsal Rooms 1 and 2, wool serge (black and white) and plastic (for viewing slits and windows)
SCALE	Sala I: 3 curtains, 22 × 15 m, and 3 curtains, 22 × 13 m; Sala II: 2 curtains, 14 × 12 m, and 1, 14 × 7 m; Rehearsal Rooms, 65 × 8 m, 55 × 8 m
COLLABORATORS	OMA, Renz van Luxemburg, Gerriets GmbH
DESCRIPTION	Where the huge, corrugated glass facades looked like curtains, our curtains looked like walls: colourless flat surfaces of varied structure, material and performance that disappeared and appeared seamlessly and silently out of – and into – ceilings or hollow walls. Curtains and wall coverings refer to Porto's Catholic heritage (white and black lace, gold-leaf digital woodgrain, decoration of auditorium walls) and its craft traditions (white/blue ceramic tiles). The landscape refers to the nearby seashore with its rocks and rounded sand formations. The travertine topography has incisions with seats and a bus station hidden under its billowing surface. The lack of planting is intentional, as the site lies adjacent to the classic circular park Rotunda di Boavista with its tall, columnar sculpture showing a fierce lion overpowering an eagle on the top – the dramatic view from the Casa's glazed, eastern foyer. This *Monumento aos Heróis da Guerra Peninsular* commemorates the victory of the Portuguese and British over the French troops that invaded Portugal during the Peninsular War (1807–1814).

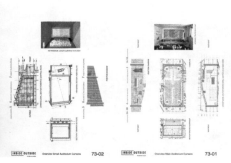

INSIDE OUTSIDE   Overview Small Auditorium Curtains   73-02   INSIDE OUTSIDE   Overview Main Auditorium Curtains   73-01

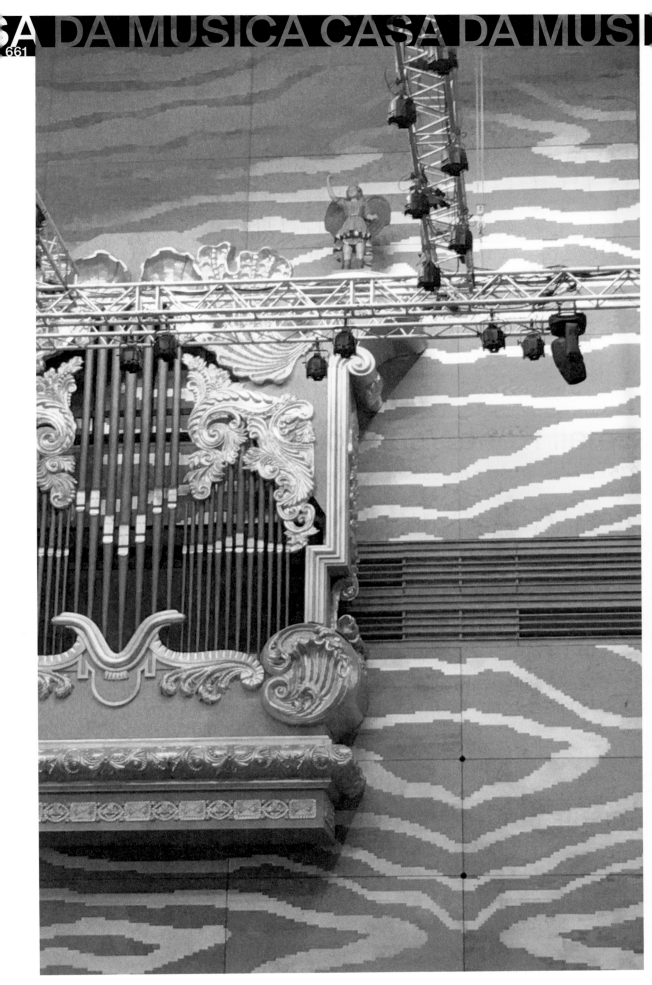

Large Rehearsal Room 1

325 carriers; *4 stops necessary for storage!*

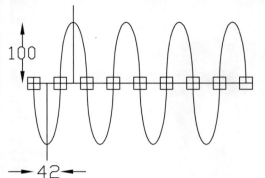

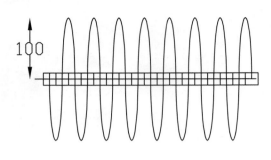

380% along mirror wall
length = 13.5m

900% around corners
325 carriers = 6.5m
storage length = 2 pieces of 3.25m
acousticly least effective

Small Rehearsal Room 4

275 carriers; *4 stops necessary for storage!*

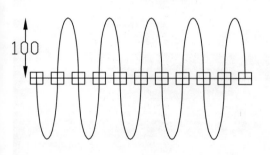

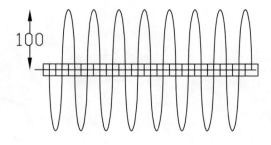

500% along mirror wall
length = 9.0m

900% around corners
275 runners = 5.5m
storage length = 2 pieces of 2.75m
acousticly least effective

INSIDE OUTSIDE

PETRA BLAISSE

INTERIORS · EXHIBITIONS · GARDENS

EERSTE NASSAUSTRAAT 5 · 1052 BD AMSTERDAM
PHONE: 00 31 [0] 20 6810 801 · FAX: 00 31 [0] 20 6810 466
WWW.INSIDEOUTSIDE.NL · E-MAIL: OFFICE@INSIDEOUTSIDE.NL

Project: Casa da Musica
Drawing: 03CAS20
Date: 01-10-2003

Content: **Runner Spacings & Pleat**
Phase: offer
Scale: 1:10, 1cm equals 10cm

03CAS

E OUTSIDE

PETRA BLAISSE

Curtain 1 and 2 sketches and details

73-28

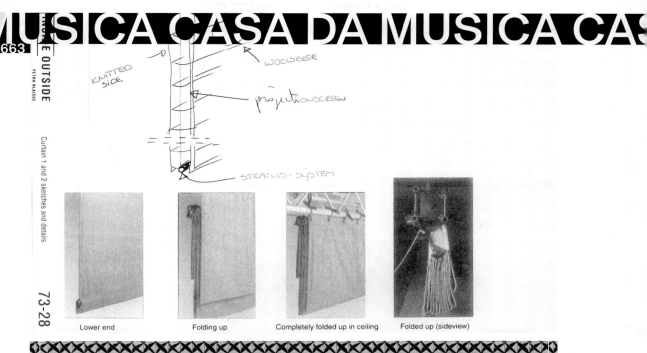

KNITTED SIDE

WOOLWEDGE

projectionscreen

STRATUS - SYSTEM

Lower end

Folding up

Completely folded up in ceiling

Folded up (sideview)

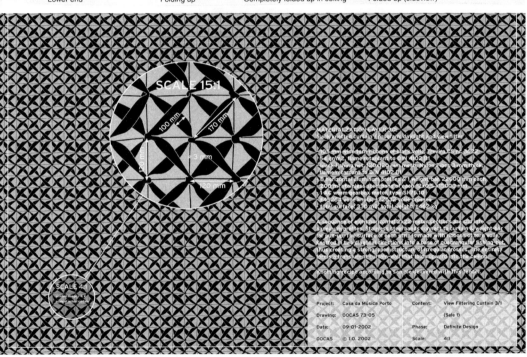

SCALE 15:1

100 mm

170 mm

120 mm

ø 3 mm

120 mm

SCALE 4:1
printed actual curtain

MATERIALZATION LAYER 3/1
black knotted curtain's program: daylight and view filter

- 105 mm wide torn ribbons of black voile, Trevira CS nr 3622, 54 gr/m2, flame retardant to DIN 4102 B1
- black fishing net, 130x130 mm mesh, Nylon Fiber 3 mm thick, flame retardant to DIN 4102 B1
- 8 horizontal aluminium profiles & 1 weight-bar 22000 mm each
- 200 st stainless steel bands of each ±0.5 x15000 mm
- 1 WC worm gearbox motor, type SK 15.10
- ±45264 voile knots, ±22632 voile crosses
- total surface: 330 m², total weight: ±462 kg

A sequence of eight horizontal 22-meter sections are cut into aluminium profiles. Stainless steel bands connect to curtain & weight-bar for roll-up. The surface of each strip is made with ribbons of torn voile, knotted in two diagonal directions into a base of quadrangular fishing-net, thus creating a strong open structure of irregular crosses. The entirety forms a translucent curtain-wall that folds upward into the ceiling.

Knotting recipe according to sample delivered with this tender.

Project:	Casa da Música Porto	Content:	View Filtering Curtain 3/1
Drawing:	00CAS 73-05		(Sale 1)
Date:	09-01-2002	Phase:	Definite Design
00CAS	© T.O. 2002	Scale:	4:1

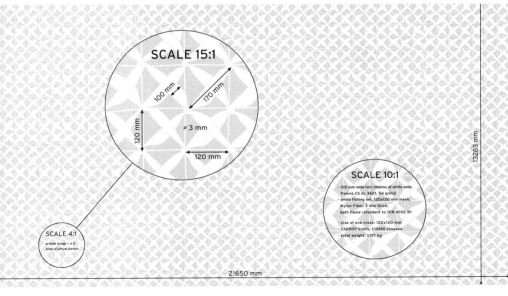

SCALE 15:1

100 mm

170 mm

120 mm

ø 3 mm

120 mm

SCALE 10:1

- 105 mm wide torn ribbons of white voile, Trevira CS nr, 3621, 54 gr/m2
- white fishing net, 120x120 mm mesh, Nylon Fiber, 3 mm thick; both flame retardant to DIN 4102 B1
- size of one cross: 120x120 mm
- ±36800 knots, ±18400 crosses
- total weight: ±391 kg

SCALE 4:1
printed image = 4 X
scale of actual curtain

13263 mm

21650 mm

Tests on building site

Knotted white curtain for the large concert hall (Sala 1) in the making

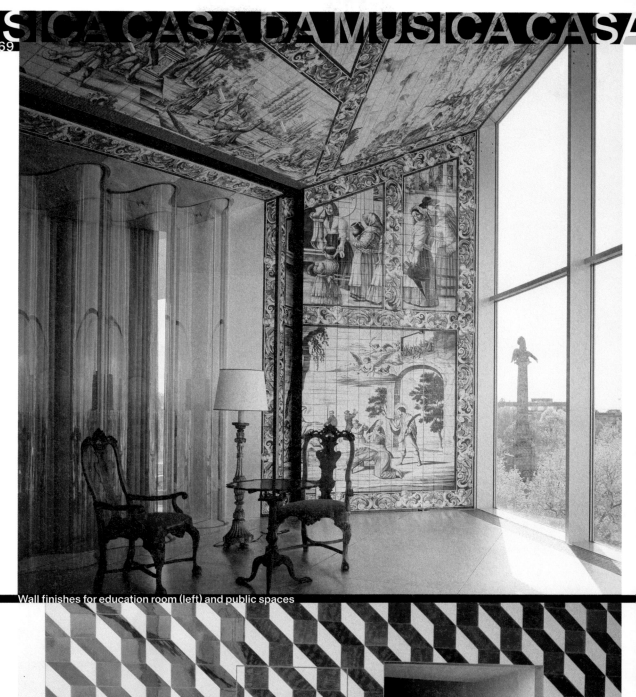

Wall finishes for education room (left) and public spaces

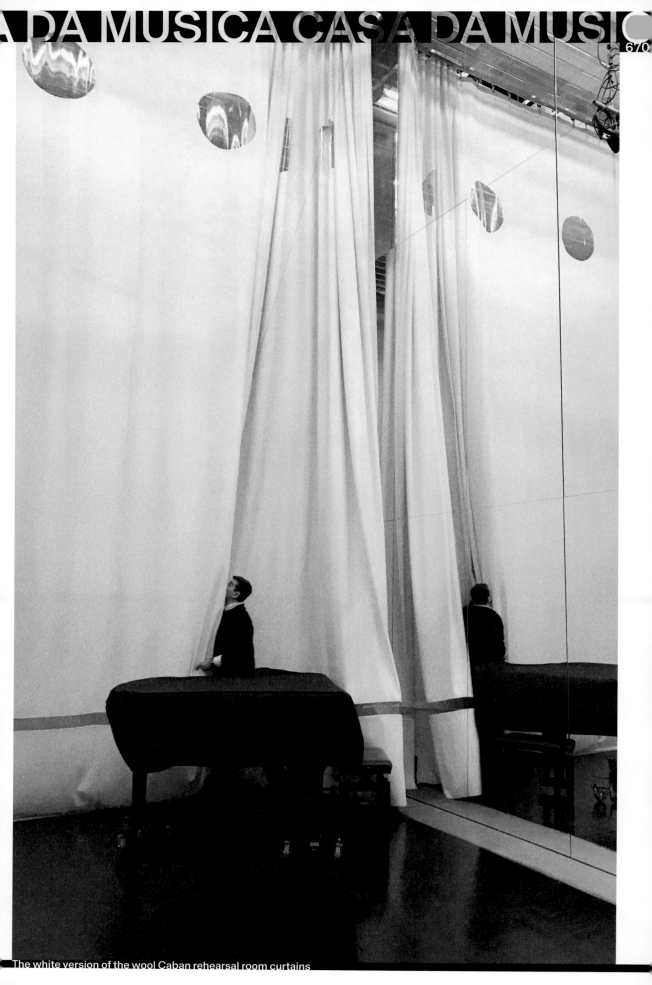

The white version of the wool Caban rehearsal room curtains

The exterior dune landscape made of travertine

Sun and Moon
Villa Leefdaal

"This small private villa is located in the midst of agricultural fields flowing into the wide-open horizon in all directions. The architects had already anticipated the implementation of our curtains on all three levels of the house: down in the study that cuts into the land, in the glazed space of the living and dining rooms, and in the two bedrooms upstairs that open up to a large roof terrace. Not afraid of colour, this television man applauded the introduction of bright pink into his minimalist house, which he would soon be sharing with his new spouse. We managed to darken the master and guest bedrooms with a layered composition of canvas and velvet that had strategic openings mimicking the sun and moon, inviting their light to shine in different, mysterious ways into each room."　PB

LOCATION	Leefdaal, Belgium
CLIENT	Private owner
STATUS	Completed
SCOPE	Design of multiple curtains to organise light, space and sound in bedrooms, living room, study
MATERIALS	Fuchsia-pink silk, grey velvet and Verosol (living room); bright-pink cotton velvet and dark-brown canvas lining (bedrooms); projection screen with *Helleborus niger* print (basement)
SCALE	20 × 2.75 m, 13 × 2.75 m, 8 × 3 m, 7 × 3 m, 7.65 × 2.2 m
COLLABORATORS	Macken & Macken, Theatex
DESCRIPTION	The question here was to design a space-enveloping curtain for the glazed living room, two darkening curtains for the bedrooms upstairs and – in a later stage – a glare-control curtain for the editor's digital work space on the lowest level of the house.

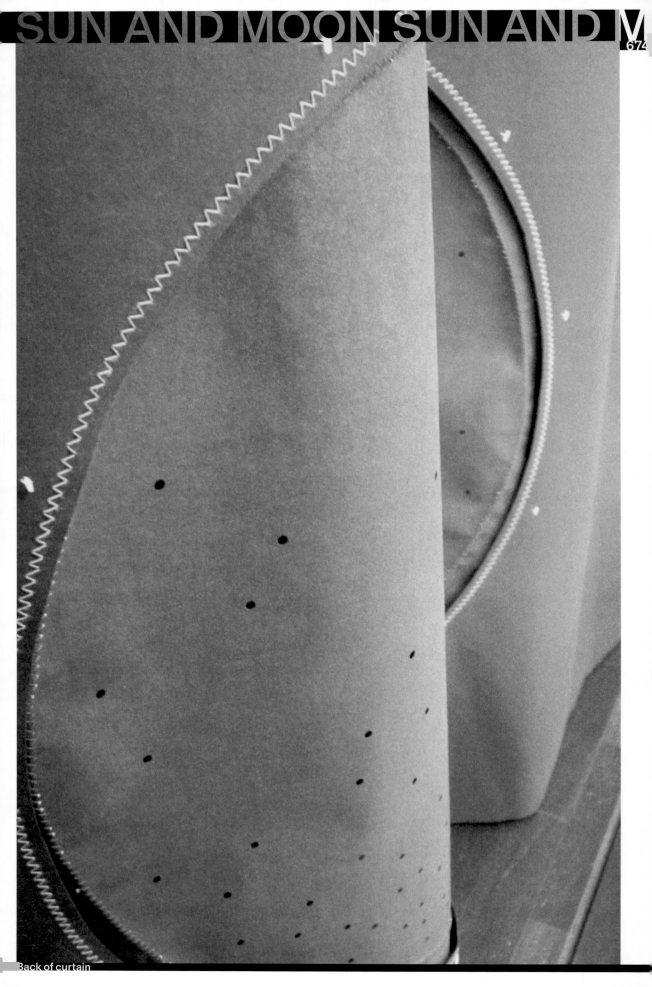

675

Front of curtain

2000–2003   **Angelica**
              The Embassy of the Netherlands

"This was the first time we had a curtain cloth woven. I happened to have met Frits Veenis during a trip in India years before, a wonderful guy who decided to adopt India as the base for his work after having been a travel guide in Asia for many years. He started a textile production line near New Delhi, travelling back and forth between his hometown in the south of Holland and Delhi. He connected to a whole 'family' of weavers and artisans who added prints, appliques and needlework to his designs, after which he exported the goods to the Netherlands and all over Europe. His experience in weaving helped us to understand the basic ins and outs of the craft. Naturally, the Textile Lab in Tilburg taught us a great deal too. Frits and Stef – together with my colleague Marieke – made it all happen. In the meantime, we were testing the colouring of the Trevira CS yarns at De Ploeg, as I wanted the green to be a lively lime green, the black to be deep and the white to be a tiny bit cream-coloured to make the cloth a bit classic – not contrasting too harshly."

"It feels like a miracle when one's design slowly slides out of a machine, a sensation of utter excitement after so many drawings, deliberations and tests that never quite reveal enough. Needless to say, such a gratifying "final result" only comes after a carefully considered, step-by-step process. For example, the thickness of the yarns and the intensity of the weave (amount of yarns per cm) had to be adjusted several times to meet the darkening and acoustic requirements for the room in question; the intensity of the green and white when seen on a large scale and backlit with daylight had to be rethought a few times; we had to refine our drawings in order to show weavers and seamstresses the exact points where the flowers overlap, each flower covering three widths up; and finally, the translation from our computer drawings to the lab's weaving computers produced errors that needed to be carefully monitored and corrected. But, finally, the two embassy curtains with their softly shining, heavy, tightly woven jacquard weave emerged and now darken, soften and colour the spacious reception room of the embassy, which overlooks the garden and the Spree River to one side and addresses the driveway entrance to the other."   PB

LOCATION	Berlin, Germany
CLIENT	Ministry of Foreign Affairs of the Netherlands
STATUS	Completed
SCOPE	Two darkening curtains for main reception room with track and storage configuration; glare control curtain concepts for all offices along the facade (tulip-printed Trevira CS voile – not realised); interior finishes advisory; concept for adjacent public parkland facing the Spree River
MATERIALS	Lime-green, cream and black/white Trevira CS yarns woven into thick jacquard weave
SCALE	2 darkening curtains, 17.4 × 5.1 m, 9.3 × 3.7 m
COLLABORATORS	OMA, TextielLab Tilburg, Frits Veenis, De Ploeg, Theatex
DESCRIPTION	The two curtains for the large reception room represent typical Dutch elements, such as the flat landscape with its broad horizon, the fresh green of spring, the black-and-white winter landscape and the wild *Angelica* plant that grows so well in our moist polder soils. The cloths were woven by the Textiel Museum in Tilburg; the Trevira CS yarns were produced and coloured by De Ploeg in Aarle-Rixtel and installed by Theatex from Vinkeveen – so an entirely Dutch crew created these very Dutch curtains, which was the point.

Zuidgordijn nr.1: afmetingen geplooid (met 38cm overlengte = 14.5m)
binnenste kader: wat van buiten te zien is (raamopening met dorpel)
stippellijn: wat van binnen te zien is

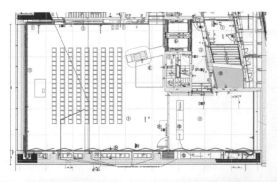

Noordgordijn nr.2: afmetingen geplooid
inclusief 1.10m extra lengte: 28,10m2
stippellijn: wat van binnen en buiten te zien is (raamopening)

Top image: north-facing Angelica curtain in black-and-white jacquard weave. Below: 2 working drawings of both curtains (the largest to be executed in lime green) with instructions; OMA plan drawing with, in red, hanging and storage positioning of curtains. Small image: photo sent to me by the embassy, showing a new Ikea cloth for sale, not long after installation of our curtains in Berlin.

Art intervention with Berend Strik
Embassy of the Netherlands

"We started a search for images that we could incorporate in these Persian carpets, symbols that both connect and distinguish German and Dutch culture. We found beautiful images of Persian carpets that we printed, then cutting specific details or patterns out of them that we replaced with tiny portraits of actors, politicians, public heroes and criminals, porn stars and artists; labels, products, ads; national flags and symbols of technical inventions over time. These details, carefully woven into the carpet patterns, were not readily visible to the casual observer, but could be discovered on closer inspection. A stair landing was transformed into an intimate niche, outfitted with lavish sofas and cushions: a place of rest for quiet conversations between diplomats."

"Because we did not have a computer at hand, we composed the 'unfolded floorplan' and the illustrative collages by hand and printed the booklet at the copy shop around the corner. Only minimal text was added. We sent our submission by registered mail with cautious optimism: who would dare choose our welcoming yet – admittedly – slightly confrontational proposal? Well – they didn't. The arts commission opted for an installation outside the main entrance, a cloud formed of steam onto which a waving Dutch flag is projected."   PB

LOCATION	Berlin, Germany
CLIENT	Ministry of Foreign Affairs of the Netherlands
STATUS	Art competition
SCOPE	Proposal for art intervention linking the Embassy's entrance plaza to its interior world
COLLABORATORS	Berend Strik
DESCRIPTION	Berend Strik invited me to enter a public arts competition with him, launched for the new Dutch embassy building in Berlin. This was a great idea because Berend, a respected Dutch artist, works with stitched yarns and fabric appliqué on his own photo prints and I often use textiles and graphic techniques in our applied work, and I also knew the embassy building inside out. We both wanted to make an "applied" work, something that could be experienced up close and on a day-to-day basis – not a typical art piece to be viewed from a distance. We came up with the idea for a runner, that is, a narrow, linear carpet that would run from the threshold of the embassy's main entrance over the central stairs and up to the top floor, linking the embassy's entrance plaza to its interior world, and accompanying staff and visitors up and down the building. It had to be a Persian carpet because of its historic value – a narrative object of sublime craftsmanship, filled with symbolic imagery and considered worthy enough to be used as a diplomatic gift. Such carpets are found in many historical paintings, royal and stately interiors and classical households. A symbol of globalisation and cultural exchange through time.

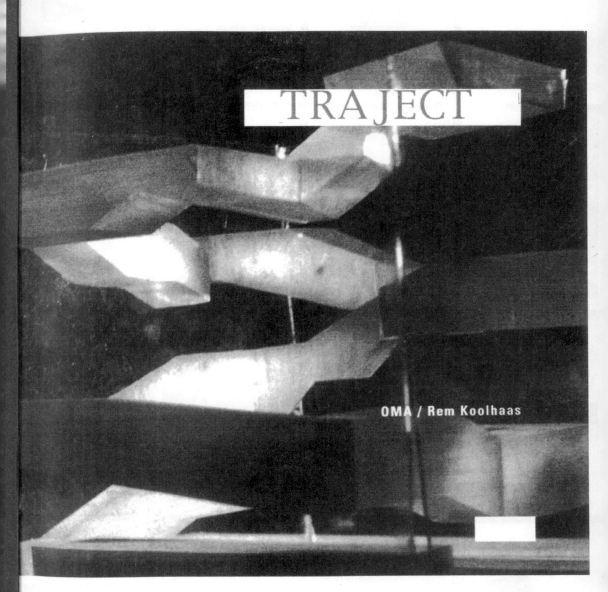

TRAJECT

OMA / Rem Koolhaas

Petra Blaisse   Berend Strik

Cover of our hand-made presentation booklet named *Trajectory*, handed to the art competition jury by post. The photocopied
pages are held together with a cheap plastic binding strip, and we politely put the credit to the architect of the appointed
building on the front image!

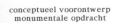

conceptueel voorontwerp
monumentale opdracht

Kanselarij Berlijn
architect: OMA

juni 1998

opdrachtgever:
ministerie van buitenlandse zaken

nederlands gebouw in berlijn

Glazen blok op metalen plein
transparant met een spiralend centrum
opgebouwd uit staal en hout:
HET TRAJECT

uitgevouwen Traject.

onderzoeksgebied voor
'monumentaal kunstwerk'

IDEE

Wij willen een monumentaal kunstwerk
aan deze dynamische ruimte verbinden.
Wij trekken als het ware de tuin/het
landschap door deze tunnel naarbinnen

Dit landschap wordt een
verhaal en krijgt een
identiteit en kan op
verschillende manieren
gezien worden:
als tegenstelling met
andere landen of
gedacht vanuit de
overeenkomsten.
Wij geven de voorkeur aan
het gezamelijke en overeenkomstige.

landschap is tapijt.

Het landschap wordt een
verhaal over
identiteit en deze kan op
verschillende manieren
verbeeld worden: als
tegenstellingen met
andere landen of juist
gedacht vanuit de
overeenkomsten. Wij
geven de voorkeur aan
het laatste.

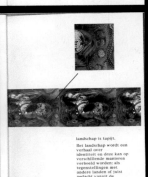

In de 16 de en 17 de eeuw
was nederland veel meer een
land wier identiteit bepaald
werd door de directe relatie
met de zee.

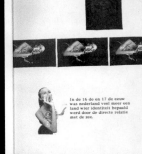

Wij moesten niet alleen de
zee bedwingen in directe zin-
het beschermen van ons eigen land-

maar ook de zee onderzoeken in
de meest ruime zin: landveroveren.

Vandaag is dit land
veroveren alleen nog
in de drooggelegde polders
te bespeuren.
Net als bij ieder europees
land is de nederlandse
identiteit in deze eeuw
veel multicultureler
geworden

schets voor
wand

Wij bezoeken niet meer
de culturen per schip maar
wij worden meer een inter-
nationaal hybride volk:
alle volkeren zijn overal

deze diffuse hybride identiteit
zouden wij willen vertalen in
iconografie die rijk zijn aan
interpretatie mogelijkheden zonder
daarbij de gebruiker direct te
confronteren.

vloer
wordt
wand
wordt
plafond

loper op nederlands grondgebied

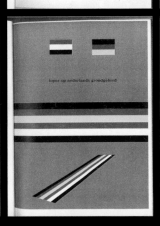

stalen vloer met ingelegde loper

Het geheel ademt een
klassieke bekende sfeer:
stijlvol, subtiel, geruststellend;
akoestiek en atmosfeer
worden verzacht en verwarmd.

Echter:
verweven in dit vertrouwd
uitnodigend object zitten
beelden en verhalen.

Een zachte loper ingelegd
in het metalen oppervlak.
meelopend met door de
architectuur gedicteerde
vormen.

uitgevouwen traject

alle verdiepingen

Op bepaalde plekken
klapt de loper omhoog
en wordt textiele wand
bespanning; comfortabele nis;
monumentaal gordijn,
plafond of hij verbreedt zich
tot een waarachtig tapijt.

Beate Uhse nis

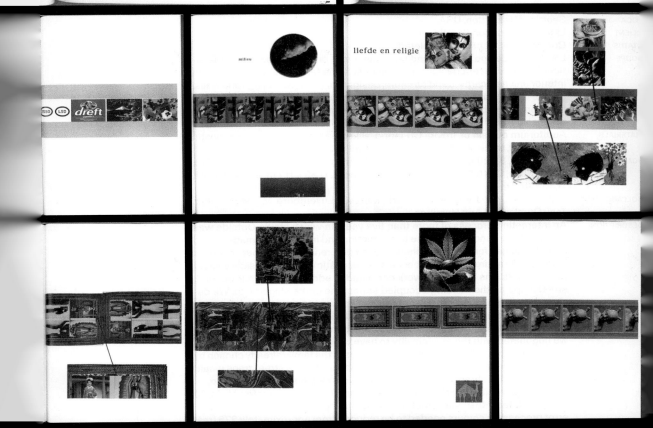

Undoing Boundaries
Seattle Central Library

"Seattle was and remains the city of Boeing, Microsoft and grunge. This metropolis is situated in an exceptionally beautiful environment, surrounded by volcanoes, sea inlets and wild forests. Mount St Helens, 2,550 m high, rises in the distance, the Canadian border is close by and the city's vibrant shore along the Puget Sound (a deep 160 km-long inlet of the northern Pacific Ocean) is dotted with bustling fish restaurants as well as lively markets and shops. A ferry takes you to nearby islands, where I once visited a wonderfully lush garden with the tallest growing, shade-tolerant Thalictrum I have ever seen."

"It was an intense task, one we shared with the interior team of LMN and the library staff, its board and the director, to create all of the interior atmospheres and materials, which were different for each space and each floor. The library board, mostly women, took our landscape and interior role extremely seriously as a way of introducing 'human scale' to the building. We did everything to achieve welcoming and comforting surroundings, both inside and out. As a social meeting place, cultural centre and learning campus, the library is open to everyone from early morning to late at night, seven days a week. Therefore, all furniture and finishes need to be 'vomit and flea proof,' as they humorously called it. While OMA and Maarten van Severen developed transparent bookcases, we recommended designers for 'safe' chairs and sofas: Quinze and Milan, two Belgian furniture designers who work with foam, like Maarten, but in bolder shapes and colours."

"Inside the auditorium on the ground floor, the 'garden soil' and streetscape is represented by the brown, polyurethane-poured floor with graphic inlays, the sloping 'nature' by Maarten van Severen's green chairs, and by the green plissé curtain that we installed. The plissé of the heavy cloth provides sound absorption while the curtain's backing, a thick plastic sheet printed with a brown bear-hair pattern, provides sound reflection when pulled behind the stage. The S-shaped track offers three main positions for the curtain: as cover for one side wall (acoustic function); as stage curtain (lightproof and sound absorbing); as backdrop (sound reflecting)." PB

LOCATION	Seattle, Washington, USA
CLIENT	Library Foundation Seattle
STATUS	Competition: 1st prize / completed
SCOPE	Landscape design for surrounding streetscape, entrance plazas and transitional areas; concept designs and colour scheme for all spaces; advisory on interior finishes, carpets and furniture; designs for acoustic ceilings and walls; double-faced curtain for auditorium, track configuration (S-shape to turn curtain from stage curtain to backdrop); project carpet design, ten patterns in three colours for the Garden Carpets
MATERIALS	Auditorium curtain of Trevira CS fabric, silkscreened and folded (= acoustic absorption), truck plastic with bear hair print (= acoustic reflection)
SCALE	Landscape, 3,320 m²; curtain, 24.75 × 8.75 m; green carpets, 19.75 × 10.7 m, 7.9 × 5.35 m, 1.7 × 6.9 m, 13.82 × 9.3 m; red carpet, 11.85 × 11.7 m; mauve carpet, 11.85 × 18.3 m
COLLABORATORS	OMA, LMN, Jones & Jones, Kate Orff, Renz van Luxemburg, Mathew Stadler, Tony Oursler and Ann Hamilton
DESCRIPTION	An interesting process of more than five years in which Inside Outside was involved from conceptual phase to production and installation. I made "mood board" collages for the atmosphere of each different space: colour schemes, materials, furniture typology, floor finishes, acoustic ceilings, possible wallpapers, carpets. The landscape work consisted of addressing the surrounding streetscape as the building occupied almost the entire sloped site. We designed a system of rectangular green carpets and terraces that follow the stepped and sloping topography of the site. Situated along each road, each carpet was a different composition of local plantings and families of trees. Then we negotiated with the municipality to have the single species of trees lining the streets replaced by a row of varied species of the family already chosen by the city. So, varieties of oaks, varieties of maples, etc. The street trees would thus represent a library of trees where they were aligned with the building. The Garden Carpet that we made for our exhibition at Storefront in 2000 was translated into (flame-proof and anti-static) "project carpets," a trial-and-error process, as colours needed to be reduced from approximately 275 (real photo) to 8–12 colours. In addition, we wanted to keep the three-dimensional effect and we had to find the right colours and scale of the images (larger and larger), which meant making many 1:1 tests (each 100 × 100 cm). This process alone took 2.5 years.

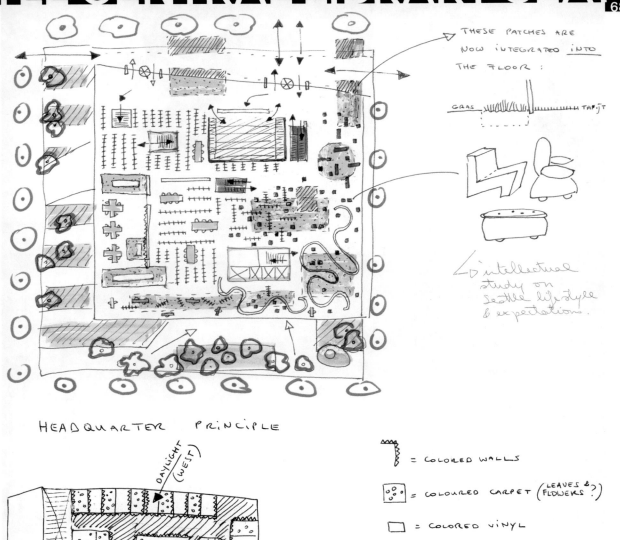

THESE PATCHES ARE
NOW INTEGRATED INTO
THE FLOOR :

GRAS   TAP. JT

↳ intellectual
study on
Seattle lifestyle
& expectations.

HEADQUARTER PRINCIPLE

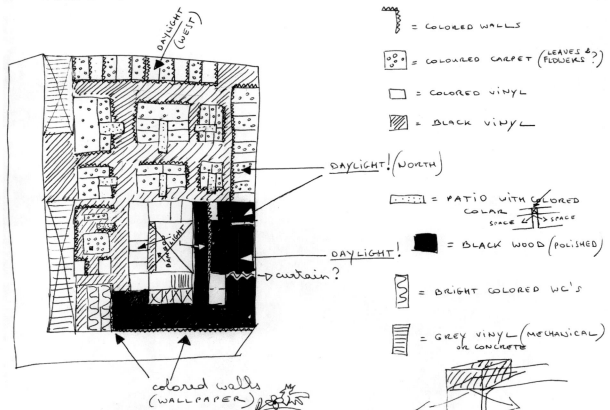

DAYLIGHT (WEST)

= COLORED WALLS

= COLOURED CARPET (LEAVES & FLOWERS?)

= COLORED VINYL

= BLACK VINYL

DAYLIGHT! (NORTH)

= PATIO WITH COLORED
COLAR
SPACE ←→ SPACE

DAYLIGHT!

curtain?

= BLACK WOOD (POLISHED)

= BRIGHT COLORED WC'S

= GREY VINYL (MECHANICAL)
or CONCRETE

colored walls
(WALLPAPER)

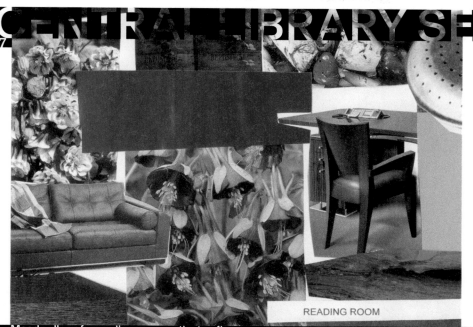

READING ROOM

Mood collage for reading room on the top floor

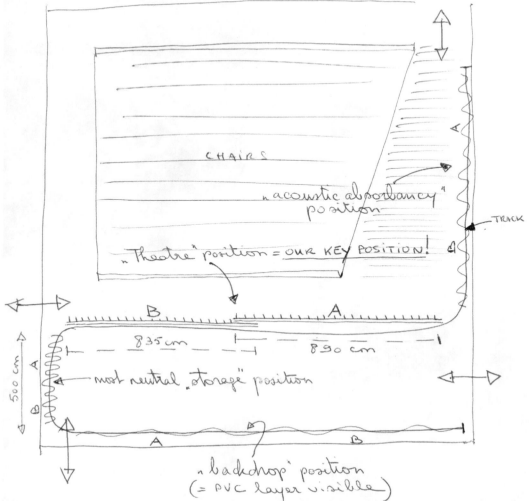

CHAIRS

„acoustic absorbancy"
position

„Theatre" position = OUR KEY POSITION!

TRACK

B   A

— 835 cm —   — 890 cm —

most neutral „storage" position

500 cm

„backdrop" position
(= PVC layer visible)

Above, top image: the curtain sliding into "theatre" position; below: sketch showing the curtain's different positions. Right image: at the instant of the shot the curtain is pulled past the "storage" bend into "backdrop" position, showing both the front (folded, silk-screened Trevira CS, sound absorbing) and the back (flat, digitally printed PVC lining, sound-reflective).

FAX

INSIDE OUTSIDE
PETRA BLAISSE

INTERIORS · EXHIBITIONS · GARDENS

EERSTE NASSAUSTRAAT 5
1052 BD AMSTERDAM

PHONE: 00 31 [0] 20 6810 801
FAX: 00 31 [0] 20 6810 466
E-MAIL: OFFICE@INSIDEOUTSIDE.NL
WWW.INSIDEOUTSIDE.NL

DATE: oct 31 - 2001

COMPANY: OMA - NY

FAX NR: oo.1.646 2306558

MR/MRS: Yoshua Ramus

NR OF PAGES
[INCL. THIS PAGE]: 1

CONCERNING: planters in Living Room / 5th Ave

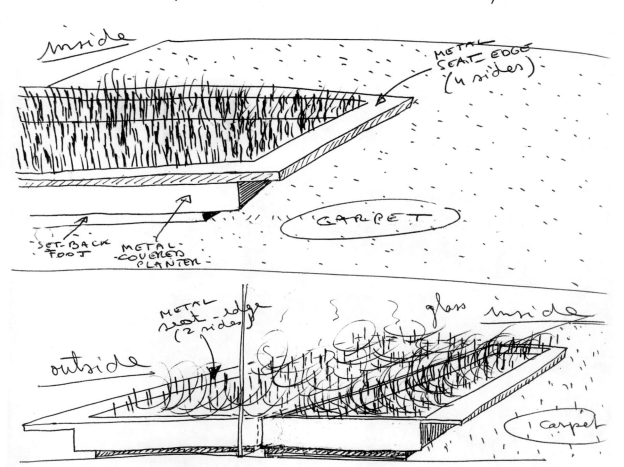

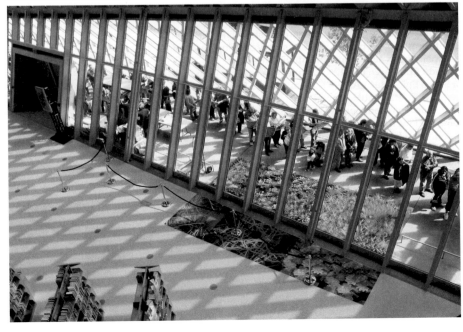

Whipped Cream and Knitted Sock
Prada Epicenters New York, Beverly Hills

"We had ordered the silver voile from Germany, for delivery to the Gramercy Park Hotel just before Christmas. Anky and I arrived at Kennedy Airport with our homemade XL knitting needles (thick wooden sticks, each pair connected with a piece of bright-green garden hose) in November 2011; we didn't get arrested. When we arrived at the hotel, we discovered that the rolls of cloth didn't fit in the elevator and asked the receptionist on duty if we could roll them out in the lobby next to the Christmas tree. 'Fine,' he said. We rolled out the endless lengths of cloth until a pile as high as the tree blinked faintly like a dirty snow heap beside it. We pushed the pile into the elevator and carried it into one of our rooms: the largest one, obviously.

There, we tore the silver transparent fleece, called Lasergewebe, into bands 10 cm wide and started knitting backwards in circles from each other's laps. We knitted for seven days, drank 100 litres of water, watched horrible American news programs and tree-sawing competitions on TV, scared the housekeeper with our climbing vine, exchanged thoughts about life in general and loves in particular and, in the end, created a sock of 10 × 4.75 metres, which we then threw out of the window in an XL garbage bag given to us by the hotel. We squeezed the bag into a taxi, arrived onsite – where people were working hectically on the final details and no ladder could be found – and installed it 30 minutes later, just in time for it to become the 'stretched metal' Sound Sock that covers the shop's audio installation, an integral part of OMA's hanging cupboard system." PB

LOCATION	Broadway, New York and Rodeo Drive, Los Angeles, USA
CLIENT	Prada
STATUS	Completed
SCOPE	Curtains for VIP dressing rooms; Knitted audio sock for NY shop, advisory on interior landscape and materials
MATERIALS	Knitted audio sock: Lasergewebe CS and transparent fishing line; VIP rooms: white Trevira CS cloth, transparent plastic, zippers, safety pins, Inside Outside labels; in LA: steel chain mesh along top edge of VIP curtains
SCALE	VIP curtains for Prada Epicenter, NY, 12 × 3.5 m (2×); sock, 5 × 4.75 m; VIP plissé curtain for Prada Epicenter, LA, 12.4 × 2.9 m, 14.7 × 2.9 m
COLLABORATORS	OMA, Helene Kierulf, Gerriets GmbH
DESCRIPTION	The Whipped Cream curtains produced by Helene Kierulf and her team for the VIP dressing rooms in New York were a heavy plissé structure with a transparent plastic lining. They function as flexible, sound-absorbing walls that create a spacious, private dressing room. Along their lower edge, vertical windows allow a limited view to check the availability of the room. In the Beverly Hills shop, a wide top-edge of stainless-steel chain mesh was inserted for the fire-sprinkler system. My assistant Anky and I knitted the sock by hand in Manhattan's Gramercy Park Hotel in November 2011. It took us a week, and we installed it on site just in time for the official opening festivities.

699

SOUND

EXPANDED
METAL CAGE

I x

KNITTED
VOILE SOCK (SILVER)
(DOUBLE LAYER)

PRADA NYC - 15/1/2

LIGHT IN "SOCK"
OR: SOFT CUPBOARD

Knitting the hanging sock at Grammercy Park Hotel, NYC and production of the VIP curtains at Helene Kierulf's studio (all video stills)

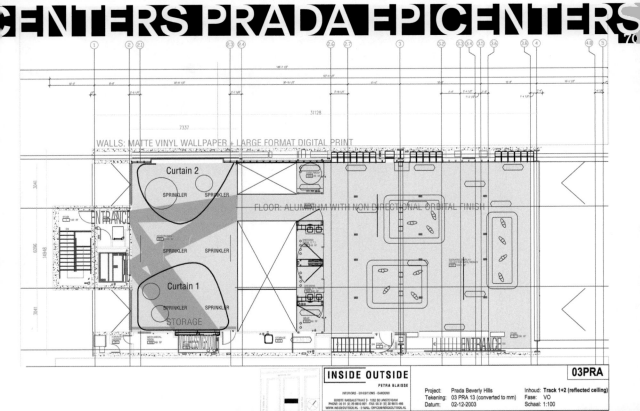

WALLS: MATTE VINYL WALLPAPER + LARGE FORMAT DIGITAL PRINT

Curtain 2

SPRINKLER   SPRINKLER

ENTRANCE

FLOOR: ALUMINIUM WITH NON DIRECTIONAL ORBITAL FINISH

SPRINKLER   SPRINKLER

Curtain 1

SPRINKLER   SPRINKLER

STORAGE

ENTRANCE

INSIDE OUTSIDE
PETRA BLAISSE

INTERIORS · EXHIBITIONS · GARDENS

EERSTE NASSAUSTRAAT 5 · 1052 BD AMSTERDAM
PHONE: 00 31 (0) 20 6810 001 · FAX: 00 31 (0) 20 6810 466
WWW.INSIDEOUTSIDE.NL · E-MAIL: OFFICE@INSIDEOUTSIDE.NL

Project: Prada Beverly Hills
Tekening: 03 PRA 13 (converted to mm)
Datum: 02-12-2003

Inhoud: **Track 1+2 (reflected ceiling)**
Fase: VO
Schaal: 1:100

03PRA

Recipe for VIP curtains Prada Epicenter. NYC

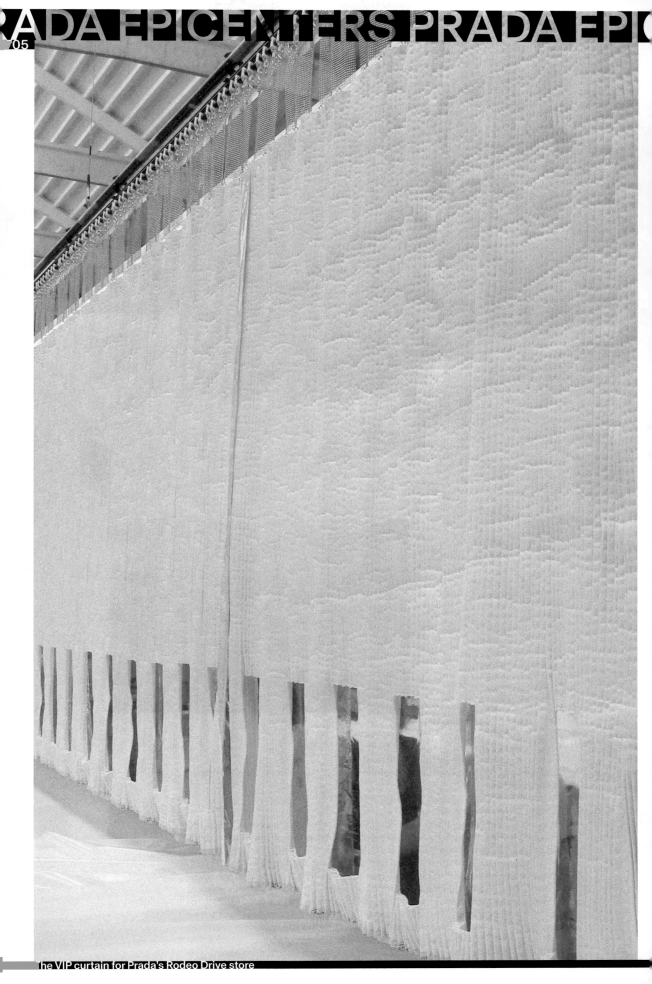

The VIP curtain for Prada's Rodeo Drive store

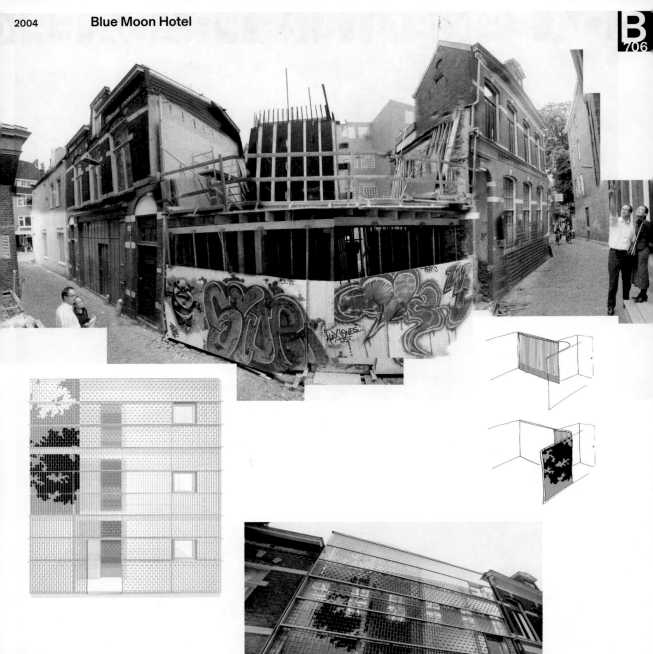

LOCATION	Groningen, the Netherlands
CLIENT	Toyo Ito & Associates
STATUS	Completed
SCOPE	Multipurpose curtains for two hotel rooms
MATERIALS	Orange verso quilted with large black tree-crown form, white voile with laser fabric bottom
SCALE	Floor 1, 63 × 2.7 m (2×); floor 2, 3.63 × 2.4 m (2×)
COLLABORATORS	Hosoya & Schäfer Architects
DESCRIPTION	In a tiny alley an equally tiny hotel for university professors stands squeezed between old brick buildings. Ito designed this hotel, a narrow infill with a transparent aluminium facade that mimics the rhythm and form of the surrounding brick facades but upended. Behind this aluminium cladding, a glazed facade. Two tiny "monk's cells," each on a separate floor, face the treeless alley. Our orange, two-sided, quilted curtains darken the bedroom, provide privacy, close off the entrance door, cover the wall facing the bed for comfort and improve the acoustic quality of the room – all in one. The dark profile of a tree crown is appliquéd on the two orange curtains, half of the crown on each curtain. As the tree drawing outgrows the two floors, the floors become one when seen from outside. The visitor, inside, has the impression that an actual tree casts its shadow on the building and into the room.

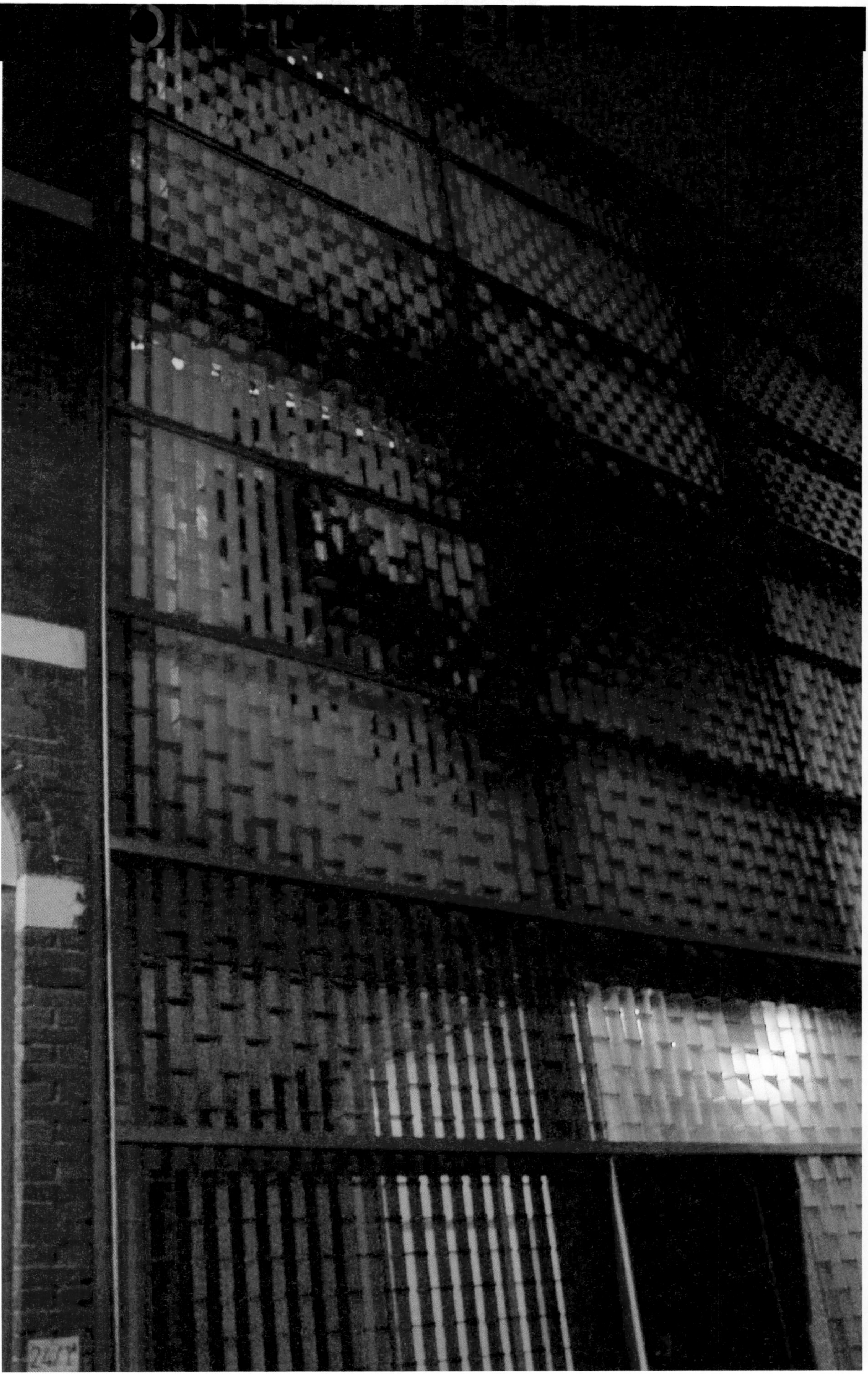

Garage Door Curtain
Lehmann Maupin Gallery

"Thanks to the fact that the gallery was able to register the curtain as an 'artwork,' we were able to use grey polyethylene, even though it didn't meet code for public buildings because it's not fire retardant. The curtain was logically stored within the hollow side-wall, so that it could be hidden away at any time. It functioned as a separation between the entrance and the exhibition gallery during installation, allowing people to peek inside through its large horizontal window. The window could be covered with a separate piece of the same material, attached with snaps. On the front we printed the large number of the gallery's address. At the entrance/exit slit of the curtain, we later added the words 'Entrance' and 'Exit' on each side. For total light blockage, we designed a second layer, which could be added when necessary. We also produced special bags to store the curtain." PB

LOCATION	Meatpacking District, New York, USA
CLIENT	Lehmann Maupin Gallery
STATUS	Completed
SCOPE	Space-defining and darkening curtain for art gallery, track and storage configuration, studies for other space-dividing interventions
MATERIALS	Grey truck plastic, transparent plastic for window slit, metal snaps for removable window cover, canvas as demountable 2nd layer for darkening
SCALE	12.5 × 4.35 m (2×)
COLLABORATORS	OMA, Irene Curulli
DESCRIPTION	The gallery had just moved to the Meatpacking District, where all spaces were former single or double floor storage and distribution buildings with large garage doors and deep, rectangular floors. OMA put in rooflights and developed an efficient floor plan with ample wall surface. After a few studies to see which curtains could suit both office and gallery space, we made the Garage Door curtain to define and close off the gallery. Hanging parallel to the real garage door and the facade facing the street, it creates a corridor between the entrance and gallery space when pulled out. A horizontal window allows views into the exhibition space. A separate cover made to close off this window also has a special bag for protection when stored. In a later phase, a blackout curtain was produced that could be attached to the runners along the top. The whole could be stored in its entirety in the specially made hollow of the side wall.

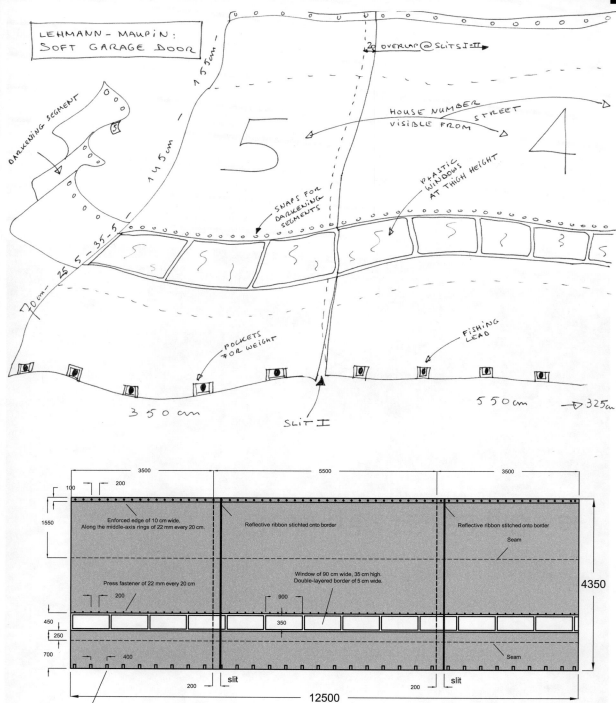

LEHMANN - MAUPIN:
SOFT GARAGE DOOR

DARKENING SEGMENT

145 cm

5 cm

2c OVERLAP @ SLITS I + II

HOUSE NUMBER
VISIBLE FROM STREET

5

4

PLASTIC
WINDOWS
AT THIGH HEIGHT

SNAPS FOR
DARKENING
SEGMENTS

70cm - 25.5 - 35.5

POCKETS
FOR WEIGHT

FISHING
LEAD

350 cm

SLIT I

550 cm

325 cm

Drawing Nr. 1 dimensions:

3500 — 5500 — 3500

100 — 200

1550

Enforced edge of 10 cm wide.
Along the middle-axis rings of 22 mm every 20 cm.

Reflective ribbon stitched onto border

Reflective ribbon stitched onto border

Seam

Press fastener of 22 mm every 20 cm

200

Window of 90 cm wide, 35 cm high.
Double-layered border of 5 cm wide.

4350

450

250

700

400

900

350

Seam

200   slit

200   slit

12500

Pocket with weight.
6 by 10 cm, every 40 cm.

20 cm overlap

Nr. 1: Darkening Curtain Galleryfront:
Total length of textile layed out flat incl. 15 % pleat: 12,50 m

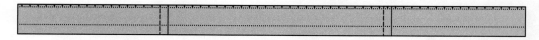

Nr. 2: Shutter
3 pieces of 350 cm, 570 cm and 370 cm long. All pieces 75 cm high.

Tracey Emin installing her show

installing gallery curtain

TOUCH
Wallpaper Series for Wolf Gordon

"We won first prize for our first-and-only mass product design in 2003, which was festively presented to us during a design fair in New York. Unfortunately, our product was only made for the American market. It would have been more successful in Europe, South America, Asia, where tastes for interiors are more daring, experimental – especially with the younger generation. Today, of course, vinyl is not considered sustainable, therefore it's improbable that we can still make it of use: 'a synthetic man-made material, it is a type of plastic that is made from ethylene (found in crude oil) and chlorine (found in regular salt). When processed, both the substances are combined to form Polyvinyl Chloride (PVC) resin, or – as it is commonly called – vinyl.'"   PB

LOCATION	New York/Long Island, USA
CLIENT	Wolf Gordon Inc.
STATUS	Completed
SCOPE	Designer wallpaper series for the US market (based on IO textile samples)
MATERIALS	Vinyl
SCALE	(8×) 54" wallpapers
COLLABORATORS	Four Color BV (technical photography)
DESCRIPTION	We were invited by Mary Beth Shaw, Wolf Gordon's creative director, to develop a special wallpaper series. On the basis of the samples that she showed, we decided not to focus on a creative pattern but rather on countering the harshness and functionality of the dead vinyl material, produced as hygienic, easy-to-clean wallpaper for public buildings, offices and hospitals. We took a series of our own textile samples – knits, knots, weaves, stitches – to a photographer specialised in documenting technical and medical objects in microscopic detail. The result was so sharp that we could enlarge the images ten-fold and still see the thinnest hair and smallest thread in detail. These images were sent to the Wolf Gordon lab and translated into copper print rolls. The vinyl was printed in several layers several times to achieve the intensity and three-dimensionality that we envisioned. Permitted to define some of the colours, we chose expressive ones for the selected patterns, as opposed to the greys and beiges that the company preferred with a view to sales in the US. The result was a series of six different wall covers: 1. felt sticks, thick; 2. felt sticks, thin; 3. zigzag stitch; 4. felt (chosen by the firm as a neutral, more saleable design); 5. knit (front, front lit)/knit (back, back lit); 6. bear hair.

LOCATION	Rotterdam, the Netherlands
CLIENT	Private
STATUS	Completed
SCOPE	Birthday present
MATERIALS	Silk, felt, plastic, snaps
SCALE	2.88 × 1.76 m
DESCRIPTION	Offered as a birthday present in the form of a small shoebox model with a representation of a sweet pink curtain. The final object looked quite different: apple-green felt, transparent plastic and silver silk with horizontal view-slit, held together with metal snaps. Not so sweet after all.

Radial Views
Penthouse

"We never met the golf-crazed owner, but it was great to drive through London on the back of the architect's motorbike, even though it was a challenge with my pencil skirt! I must have squeezed my gallant driver really hard with my thighs out of sheer fear as we zigzagged through busy traffic, but he politely refrained from commenting."

"The sunny and windy roof garden with its panoramic view asked for a design that accentuated the openness and energy of this close-to-the-sky place while also providing a feeling and situation of 'wellness'."

"This project was a pleasure in many aspects, but it was also an intriguing mathematic riddle. Not only was the ceiling of the beautifully redone penthouse interior round, but it also sloped, so the track needed to be bent in two directions and brakes needed to be invented to prevent the curtain from sliding down. The curtain itself had the weirdest shape in the end: we had to produce a complete 1:1 (true-to-scale) test curtain (in white cotton) to understand its exact configuration and used it as the model for the real curtains – including the steel chain-mesh curtain in the golf room. Outside on the roof, we built a spiralling wooden flooring that folded up into a bench. Plantings were naturally wind- and sun-resistant. We had the lighting and furniture stabilised and fastened. The curtains that encircled the round film room on that floor looked out onto the roof garden and echoed the plantings outside. It is important to work on private houses now and then because one can be more experimental. Both curtains and roof garden were made by wonderful craftspeople, who did all the detailed wood and textile work by hand." PB

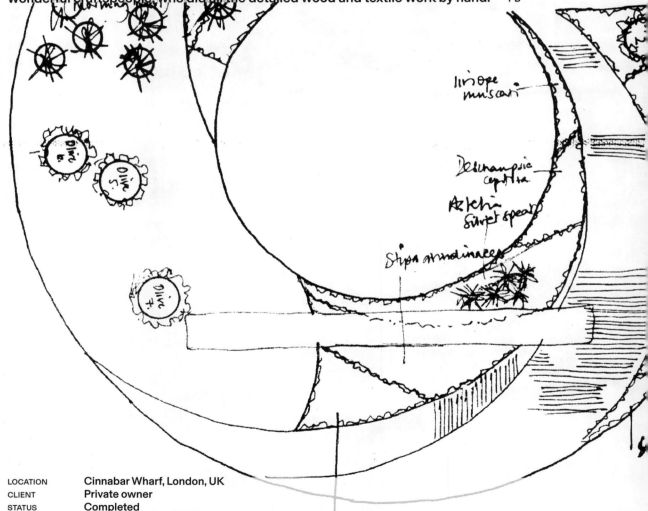

LOCATION	Cinnabar Wharf, London, UK
CLIENT	Private owner
STATUS	Completed
SCOPE	Roof garden and all curtains for this round, two-floor penthouse with sloping ceiling, including stainless-steel mesh curtain for golf room
MATERIALS	Digitally printed taffeta and orange velvet lined with blackout (film room); orange, cotton velour curtain lined with pink nylon (bedroom); Trevira CS voile combined with sun-reflective, aluminised Verosol, lined with silk and pink metal organza (living room); steel mesh (guest/golf room); plantings, wood
SCALE	Curtains, 19 × 3.1 m, 17.5 × 1.4 m, 82.8 × 3.3 m, 4 × 3.2 m; roof garden, ca. 80 m²
COLLABORATORS	Bushe Associates, Master Gardeners

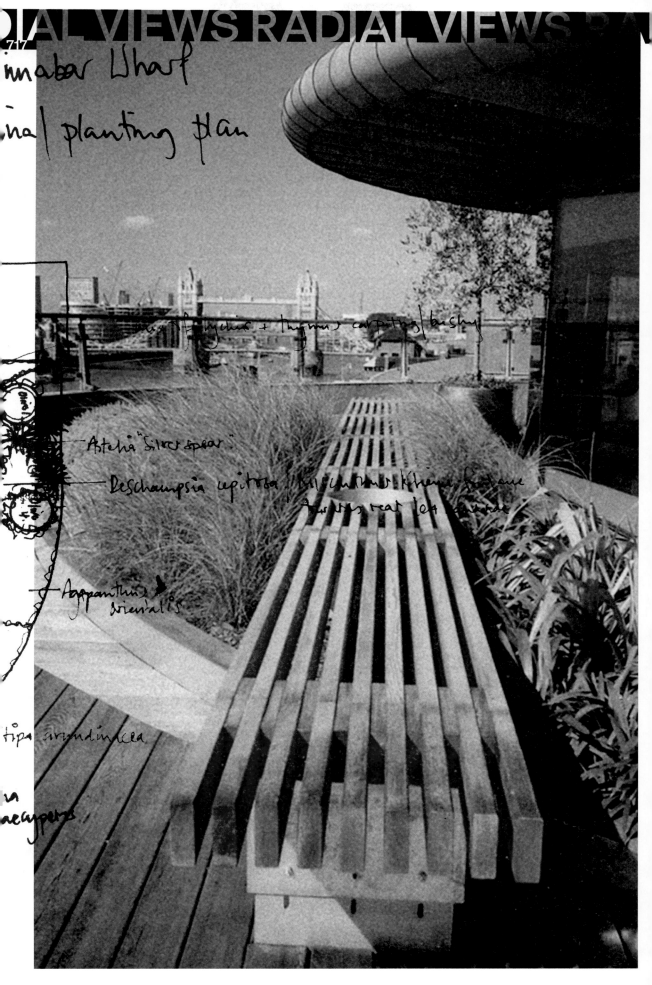

nnabar Wharf

inal planting plan

lycini + thymus carpeting/bushy

Astelia "Silver spear"

Deschampsia cepitosa / Miscanthus Kleinia fontaine
Purpurescat left avade

Agapanthus
orientalis

tipa arundinacea

a
aecypens

"The mound (childishly) refers to the upward pressure of crude oil and to the shape of rock strata from which natural gas is extracted, two raw materials used by Occidental Petroleum Corporation (owner of the museum) for hydrocarbon exploration and petro-chemical manufacturing. The founder and chairman of this firm, Armand Hammer, initi-ated and financed the building, designed by architect Edward Larrabee Barnes, whose doors opened for the public in the '90s. While we laughed about my evocative sketches, we were serious about the project, motivated and inspired, studying each situation and request, looking for the right solutions, making study models and collages and producing numerous material tests. In the end, though, director Ann Philbin was not convinced. She found the design too demanding and asked us to develop something simpler. We pre-sented the 'connecting lines' composition, installing our vision onsite with plants borrowed from a local nursery that we set up on the drawn lines. Samples of the blue 'water' surface were passed around, technical details explained and shown. But, in the end, our landscape was not realised. Maltzan built the Billy Wilder Theatre, the John V. Tunney Pedestrian Bridge, an updated restaurant/café, an education lab and, according to their website, they have completed outdoor courtyard improvements, so we guess that his office took over the landscape task in the end. But we liked the process of working on this project very much, enjoyed our LA workshops, meetings and presentations with the Maltzan and Lehrer teams, as well as getting to know the Hammer collection, the museum's spaces and Ann's strong viewpoints."　　PB

LOCATION	Los Angeles, California, USA
CLIENT	UCLA Hammer Museum
STATUS	Commissioned study
SCOPE	Landscape design for museum courtyard and streetscape
SCALE	Courtyard: 960 m^2; streetscape: 2500 m^2
COLLABORATORS	Michael Maltzan Architecture, Studio MLA
DESCRIPTION	Michael Maltzan was developing an extension to the Hammer Museum build-ing with a museum café elevated above the museum courtyard. Initially, we designed the courtyard as a spacious, sensuous wooden mound that would inhabit the entire courtyard. From this stepped mound plantings grew, stairs folded up and a water feature was cut out. The mound's stepped flank would flow down into the 300-seat Billy Wilder Theater to form the seating area. Al-though appreciated, this design was considered too costly and not practicable enough. We made a new design, in which straight, planted lines – each with a different colour scheme – connected all museum areas, entrances and exits. The courtyard itself was represented as water: a concrete floor covered with a transparent layer of blue epoxy, smooth in some places, wrinkled in others. The lines of plants had regular "bridges" directly connecting all important points of access and exit. Essential in both designs were large trees that would outgrow the courtyard's open roof. This meant that generous space for living soil and water storage would be organised under the porous top surfaces.

Mia & Sara

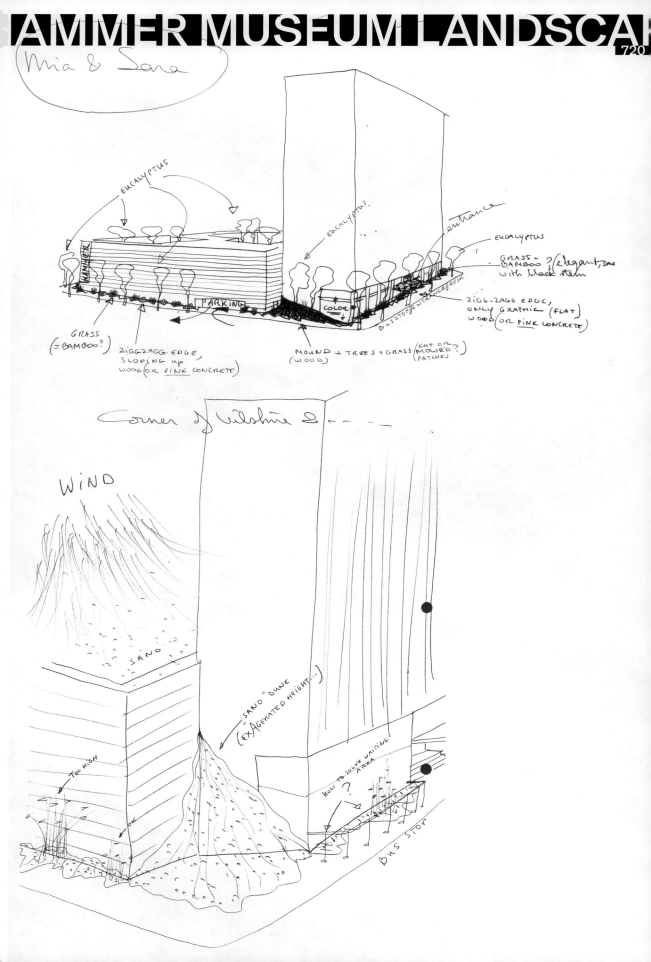

EUCALYPTUS

EUCALYPTUS

entrance

EUCALYPTUS

GRASS - ? (elegant, sma
BAMBOO ? with black stem

HAMMER

COLOR

PARKING

BUSSTOP/ENTRANCE/DESK

ZIGG-ZAGG EDGE,
ONLY GRAPHIC (FLAT)
WOOD (OR PINK CONCRETE)

GRASS
(= BAMBOO?)

ZIGGZAGG EDGE,
SLOPING UP
WOOD (OR PINK CONCRETE)

MOUND + TREES + GRASS (CUT OR
(WOOD)   MOWED?
                PATCHES

Corner of Wilshire &

WIND

SAND

SAND "DUNE
(EXAGGERATED HEIGHT...)

TOO HIGH

HOW TO SOLVE WAITING
AREA
?

BUS STOP

WATERFEATURE
UNDER STAIRS

FORM & BUILD-UP OF WATERFEATURE:

→ FORM OF STAIRS = FORM OF "POND" : SHADOW (+ LIGHT & INFORMATION & REFLECTION SOURCE)

MINIMAL
SAFETY RAILS

WATER IN MOVEMENT
LETTERS) BRUCE MAU DESIGN
LIGHT)
TECHNICAL
ISOLATION

STAIR = FOLDED-UP PLANE
OF COURTYARD MOUND

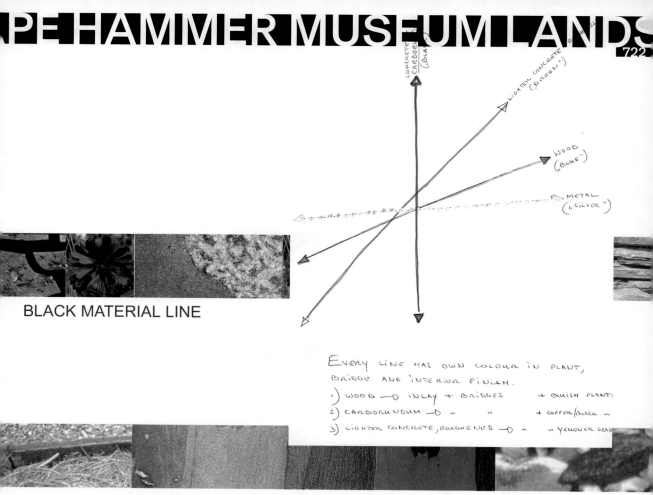

Handwritten labels on diagram:
- CONCRETE (CARBON...)
- LIGHTER CONCRETE ("GREEN")
- WOOD ("BLUE")
- METAL ("SILVER")

BLACK MATERIAL LINE

EVERY LINE HAS OWN COLOUR IN PLANT, BRIDGE AND INTERIOR FINISH.

1) WOOD —D INLAY + BRIDGES   + BLUISH PLANTS
2) CARBORUNDUM —D "   "   + COPPER/BLACK "
3) LIGHTER CONCRETE, ROUGHENED —D " " YELLOWER GRASS

COLOURED MATERIAL LINE

GREEN MATERIAL LINE

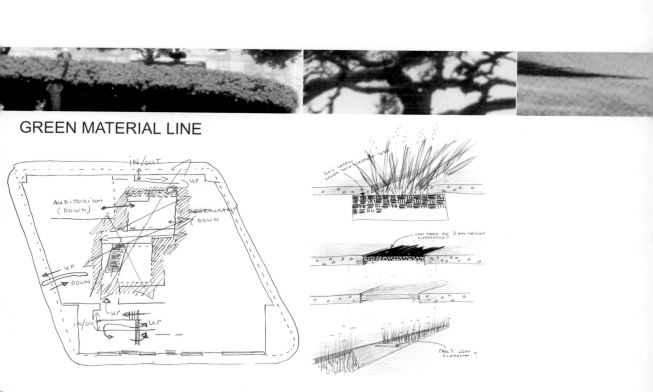

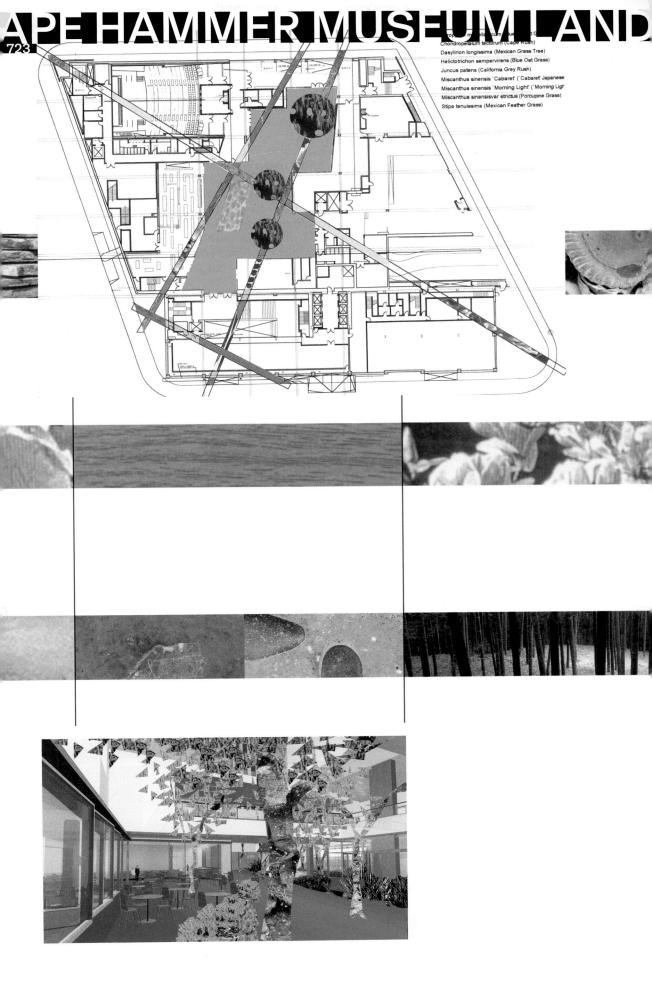

Tropae... myrtillum... Nasturtium C...
Chondropetalum tectorum (Cape Rush)
Dasylirion longissima (Mexican Grass Tree)
Helictotrichon sempervirens (Blue Oat Grass)
Juncus patens (California Grey Rush)
Miscanthus sinensis 'Cabaret' ('Cabaret' Japanese
Miscanthus sinensis 'Morning Light' ('Morning Ligh
Miscanthus sinensisvar strictus (Porcupine Grass)
Stipa tenuissima (Mexican Feather Grass)

"The outside curtain's large size, covering the entire front facade of the building, was to show the scale in which we usually work. It was also a good way to announce our show. First, we asked residents for permission because the translucent curtains would be covering the front windows on all floors, filtering their view and filling their interiors with bright colours for a couple of weeks. We appreciated their flexibility. The city did not raise any objections either, provided we complied to their strict rules."

"Anky and I sewed the facade curtain on the sidewalk in SoHo. The curtain was made of three layers of scaffolding netting in various colours, and it had a white, holed hem at the top that looked like stately mink fur from afar but was in fact a plastic anti-weed membrane used in agriculture. This was later sewed on by Helene Kierulf (via Mary Bright). Liz Diller helped us find mountaineers to install a series of parallel steel cables from the roof to the sidewalk to secure the curtain because the city did not permit them to billow out onto the street. For this reason loose belts connected the curtain to the cables, at the same time allowing for the curtain to be pulled up at night to prevent damage. Sarah Herda, the Storefront's director, and her team did this every single evening from the roof."

"Thanks to 2×4's Michael and Susan, very pregnant with their first child, the landscape collage on the exterior facade was immaculately printed and installed. Graffiti artists, who usually embellished the whole neighbourhood, left the surface alone during the show, much to everyone's surprise. The effect of the plants on the Garden Carpet inside was so three-dimensional that people hardly dared step on it. It became a big success with architects and we have been producing professionalised versions for public buildings ever since."   PB

LOCATION	Soho, New York, USA
CLIENT	Storefront for Art and Architecture – director Sarah Herda
STATUS	Completed
SCOPE	Design for retrospective exhibition *Inside Outside / Petra Blaisse*, including printed matter and site-specific installation
MATERIALS	Facade curtain of scaffolding nets (layered), strawberry plastic, steel cables and leather belts
SCALE	Curtain, 15 × 10 m; (3×) Grass Cushions, each 1 × 1.2 m, et al.
COLLABORATORS	Frans Parthesius, 2 × 4, Frits Veenis, Helena Kierulff
DESCRIPTION	Announcing the exhibit with a facade curtain that covered the entire height of the building, we installed the first version of the Garden Carpet (full-colour print on cheap project carpet) inside and made a few Grass Cushions for on the sidewalk. Four identical video films of our curtains and gardens by Frans Parthesius, projected on the diagonal backwall of the gallery, functioned as windows of varied size. Outside, a selection of our landscape projects was collaged on the concrete facade, while textile samples that lined the outer wall billowed out onto the sidewalk through Storefront's hinging facade openings.

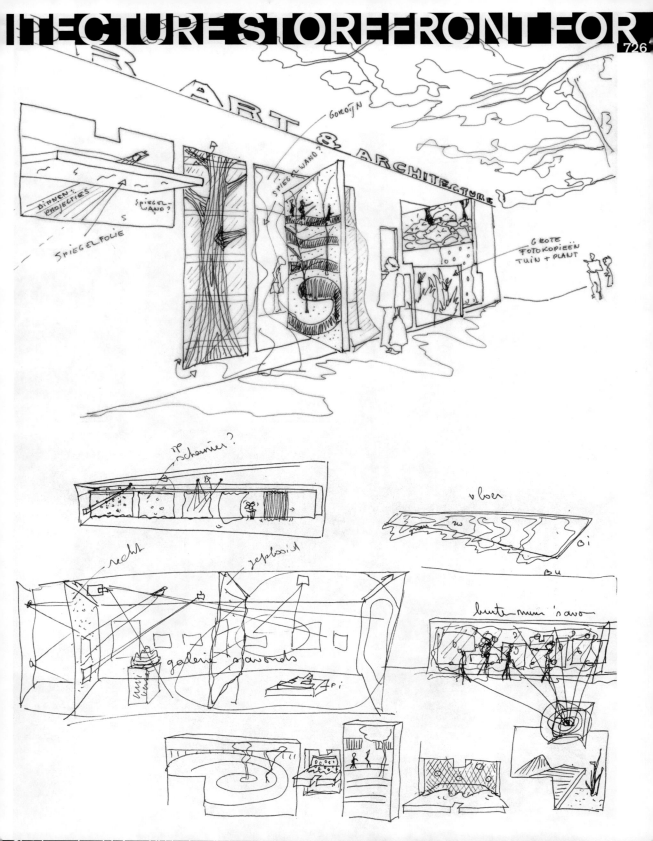

Director Sarah Herda's daily chore watering the Grass Cushions

Movements 25%
Introduction to a Working Process

"Irma Boom conceived the white booklet *Movements 25%: Introduction to a Working Process* in six weeks. It was great to share her small basement studio with her during that time, the roof light energising the already lively and inspiring working process. Although I had asked Irma to make a tiny booklet through which you could leaf backwards and forwards, seeing a plant grow and die in one direction and a curtain open and close in the other, she insisted the booklet should show my studio's work. Indeed, everything about the book illustrates the Inside Outside mindset: the embossed verbs on the white cover that you can feel but not see and that become more visible as they get dirty; the words 'inside' and 'outside' printed on the edge; the folded pages of the index front and back; the two-sided matte (landscape) versus shiny (interior) papers in different widths that creates this special effect when you flip through the book; the numerous holes that create connections between indoor and outdoor projects and beyond... It is a beautiful piece of work." PB

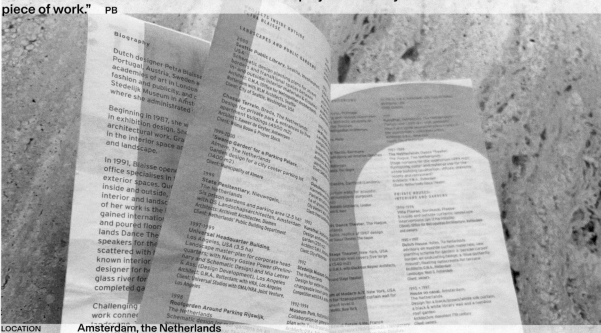

LOCATION	Amsterdam, the Netherlands
CLIENT	Storefront for Art and Architecture / Sarah Herda, Architectura & Natura (2012)
YEAR	2000 + 2012
STATUS	Completed
SCOPE	Exhibition catalogue *Movements 25%: Introduction to a Working Process*; Re-publication of exhibition catalogue *Movements 25%, Introduction to a Working Process*, including DVD of works filmed by Frans Parthesius and plastic cover by Irma Boom, on the occasion of the 13th Venice Architecture Biennial, 2012
SCALE	236 pages / 10 × 14.5 cm
COLLABORATORS	Irma Boom, Frans Parthesius

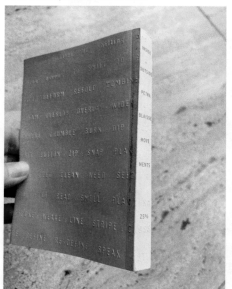

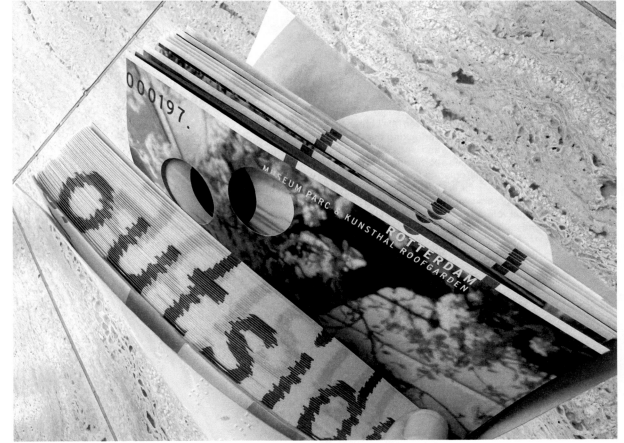

"I was fortunate to first meet Nancy Power, and then Mia Lehrer, both local landscape professionals who inspired, educated and supported me in the development of my ideas and my presentations to architects and clients. Mia and her colleague Esther showed me their urban landscape projects, and explained local regulations, safety codes for playgrounds and maintenance issues as well as the importance of involving residents. Nancy took me on fantastic drives through mountains that overlooked the ocean, where specialised nurseries exhibited 'Manhattans' of towering, tree-trunk-like cacti side by side, like a group of high-rise buildings: strangely-shaped euphorbias, fountains of grasses and rows of sculptural succulents that took my breath away. She showed me beautiful private gardens full of never-seen colours, leaf structures and flowers, with the sweet scents of the blossoms competing with the strong smell of coyote droppings. We experienced the cold mist of the sea in the mornings and enjoyed the midday heat as we visited the most amazing nurseries including that of John Greenlee with his vast collection of grasses, and other nurseries with exotic-looking plant species in hues of blue, black and purple, often with sculptural features and seed pods – very unusual for my Northern European eyes."   PB

LOCATION	Hollywood, Los Angeles, USA
CLIENT	Universal Studios
STATUS	Definitive design
SCOPE	Interior and terrace gardens, surrounding landscape and infrastructure
SCALE	3 ha
COLLABORATORS	OMA, Nancy Goslee Power, Mia Lehrer & Associates
DESCRIPTION	The steep hillside, overlooking the Universal film studios, is part of the Los Angeles earthquake and landslide area, characterised by hot winds coming in from the desert and a permanent shortage of water. The building cuts into a steep Hollywood hill, creating four conditions: a flat entrance area, a sloping street edge, a steep hill in the sun and a shaded garden under the elevated building.

We envisioned a garden of large white boulders under the hovering horizontal volume that rests on four large pillars, containing entrances, elevators and technical cores. Elevated paths zigzagging over its irregular surface connect the entrances. Groups of shade-tolerant plants form green fountains of life. The design for the sun-bathed, steep hill evolved into two alternative landscape schemes: a system of folded terraces in stepped formation, formed by white walls and filled with lawn and elegant bamboo, and a smooth slope, anchored underground and covered with overlapping grass carpets of various types and colours, in which concave steel/copper/stone circles lie embedded. Woven into the headquarters, shaded terraces and patio gardens enlarge and lighten the interior spaces, opening up each floor to different gardens (butterfly, bamboo, dragon, mound and roof) and to amazing views towards the mountains nearby.

SITE

AS UNIVERSAL CITY GROWS, THE EXISTING CHAPARRAL WILL BE REPLENISHED WITH IMPLANTS OF NEW INDIGENOUS DEPENDENCY ZONES. THESE NEW AREAS WILL CONTRAST AND AUGMENT THE NATIVE LANDSCAPE.

THE ENTRANCE TO UNIVERSAL PLANTED IN SEPTEMBER AND OCTOBER OF THIS YEAR - WAS THE FIRST AREA TO BE TREATED IN THIS WAY. THE NEXT AREA WILL BE THE LANDSCAPE SURROUNDING THE UNIVERSAL BUILDING.

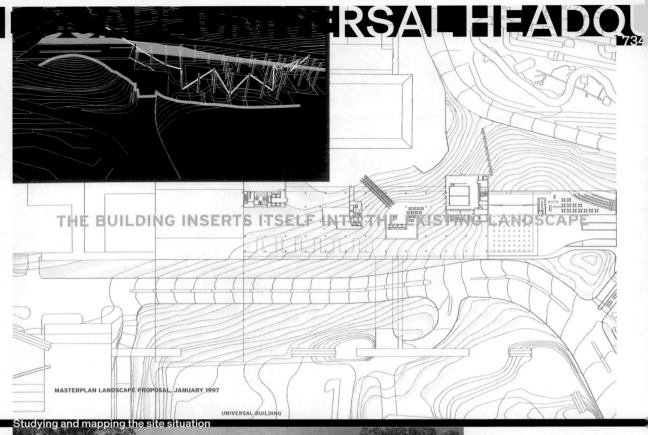

THE BUILDING INSERTS ITSELF INTO THE EXISTING LANDSCAPE

MASTERPLAN LANDSCAPE PROPOSAL, JANUARY 1997

UNIVERSAL BUILDING

Studying and mapping the site situation

FORECOURT • FOUNDATION PARK • SOUTH HILLSIDE • NORTH HILLSIDE • MALL • VERTICAL PLANES

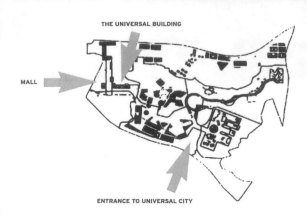

THE UNIVERSAL BUILDING

MALL

ENTRANCE TO UNIVERSAL CITY

Study models of steep hill with various landscape scenarios

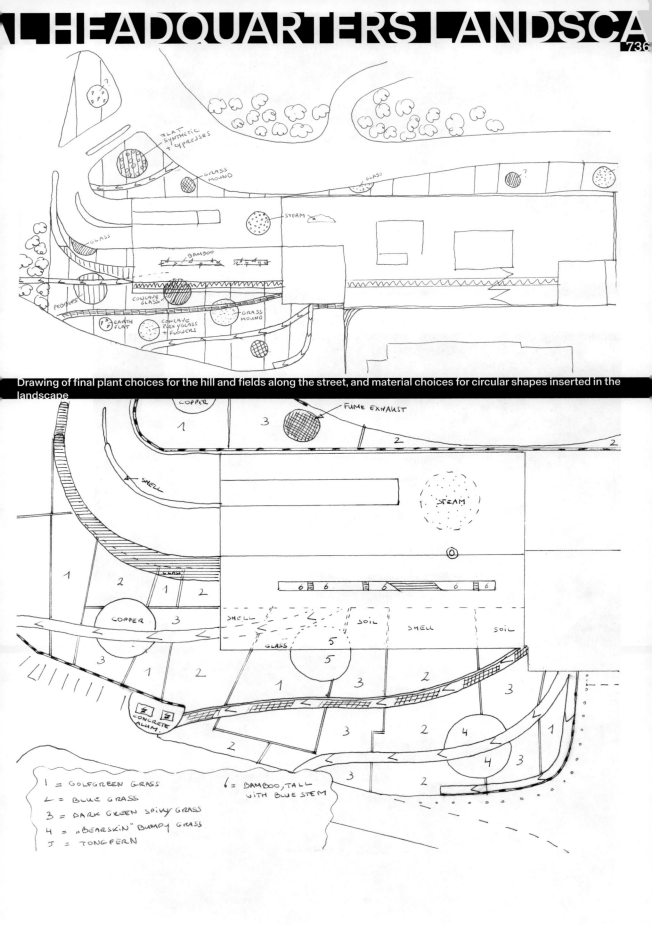

Drawing of final plant choices for the hill and fields along the street, and material choices for circular shapes inserted in the landscape

1 = GOLFGREEN GRASS
2 = BLUE GRASS
3 = DARK GREEN SPIKY GRASS
4 = "BEARSKIN" BUMPY GRASS
5 = TONGFERN

6 = BAMBOO, TALL WITH BLUE STEM

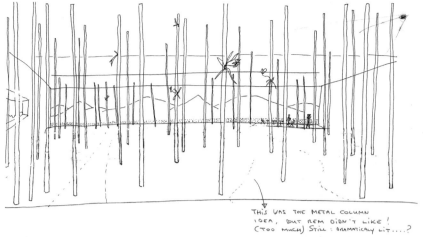

THIS WAS THE METAL COLUMN
IDEA, BUT REM DIDN'T LIKE!
(TOO MUCH) STILL: DRAMATICALLY LIT....?

13 / UNIVERSAL FLOOR, NORTH : ALUMINUM FLOOR - WAVING OUT; ALU/METAL SPIDERTHIN COLUMNS
88'.0" x 36'.0" = 3168 SF   + ORCHIDS. PATHS + ISLANDS : FLATTENED ALUMINUM PLANES
±26.5 x 11m = 291 m²   WITH OR WITHOUT CARPETS
height : 10'.5" = 3.20 m hoog

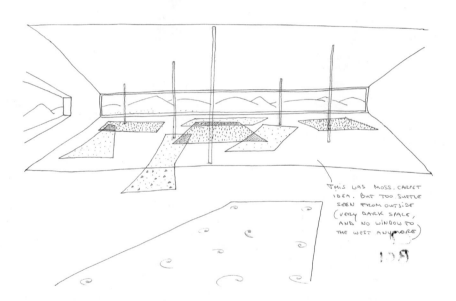

THIS WAS MOSS.CARPET
IDEA. BUT TOO SUBTLE
SEEN FROM OUTSIDE
(VERY DARK SPACE,
AND NO WINDOW TO
THE WEST ANYMORE)

Sketches for the patio and terrace gardens inside the towers

UNIVERSAL FLOOR - SOUTH WEST GARDEN - 64'.0" x 64'.0" + 24'.0" x 16'.0" = 4200 SF
(a)

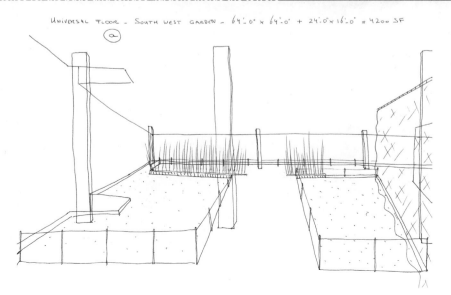

Conceptual collage and final plant choices

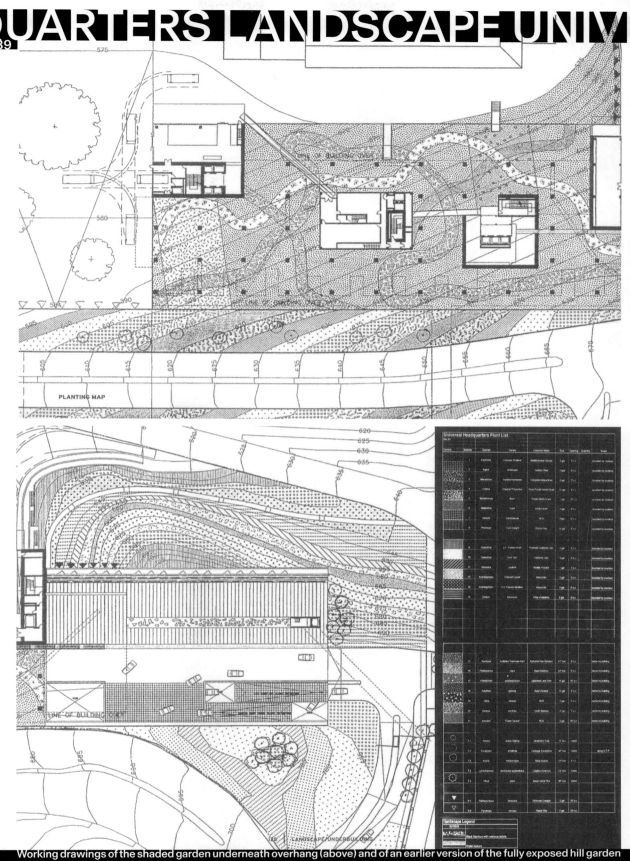

Working drawings of the shaded garden underneath overhang (above) and of an earlier version of the fully exposed hill garden (below)

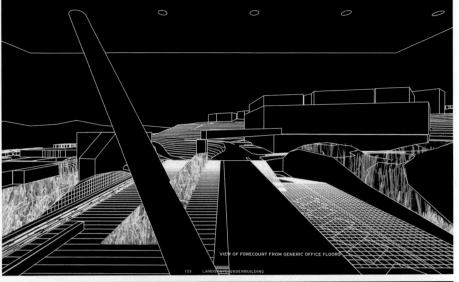

VIEW OF FORECOURT FROM GENERIC OFFICE FLOORS

133   LANDSCAPE UNDERBUILDING

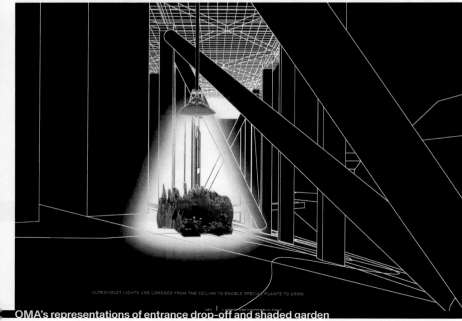

ULTRAVIOLET LIGHTS ARE LOWERED FROM THE CEILING TO ENABLE SPECIAL PLANTS TO GROW.

OMA's representations of entrance drop-off and shaded garden

PLANTS THRIVE WITHIN THE BUILDING'S COLUMNS AND DIAGONAL BRACES, WHICH CRISS-CROSS THROUGH THE FOUNDATION PARK LIKE BOLTS OF LIGHTNING. THIS EFFECT IS EXAGGERATED AT NIGHT, WHEN THE BRACES ARE ILLUMINATED. THE SOUTHERN EDGE'S RETAINING WALL IS BORED WITH LIGHT EMITTING HOLES THAT TRANSFORM THIS MASSIVE WALL INTO A THIN-SKINNED HOLLOW SPACE.

UNIVERSAL BUILDING

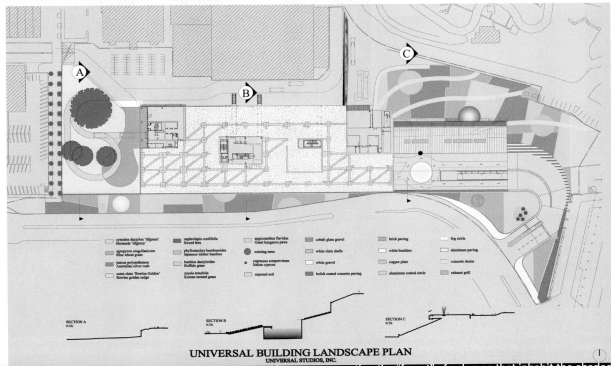

cynodon dactylon 'tifgreen' Bermuda 'tifgreen'	nephrolepis cordifolia Sword fern	anigozanthos flavidus Giant kangaroo paws	cobalt glass gravel	brick paving	fog circle
agropyron magellanicum Blue wheat grass	phyllostachys bambusoides Japanese timber bamboo	existing trees	white clam shells	white boulders	aluminum paving
juncus polyanthemos Australian silver rush	buchloe dactyloides Buffalo grass	cupressus sempervirens Italian cypress	white gravel	copper plate	concrete drains
carex elata 'Bowles Golden' Bowles golden sedge	zoysia tenuifolia Korean mound grass	exposed soil	bolodt coated concrete paving	aluminum coated circle	exhaust grill

SECTION A
N.T.S.

SECTION B
N.T.S.

SECTION C
N.T.S.

UNIVERSAL BUILDING LANDSCAPE PLAN
UNIVERSAL STUDIOS, INC.

Inside Outside text on OMA drawing (top); reference image representing the "forest" of columns that inhabit the shaded garden (middle); presentation drawing of the gardens (bottom)

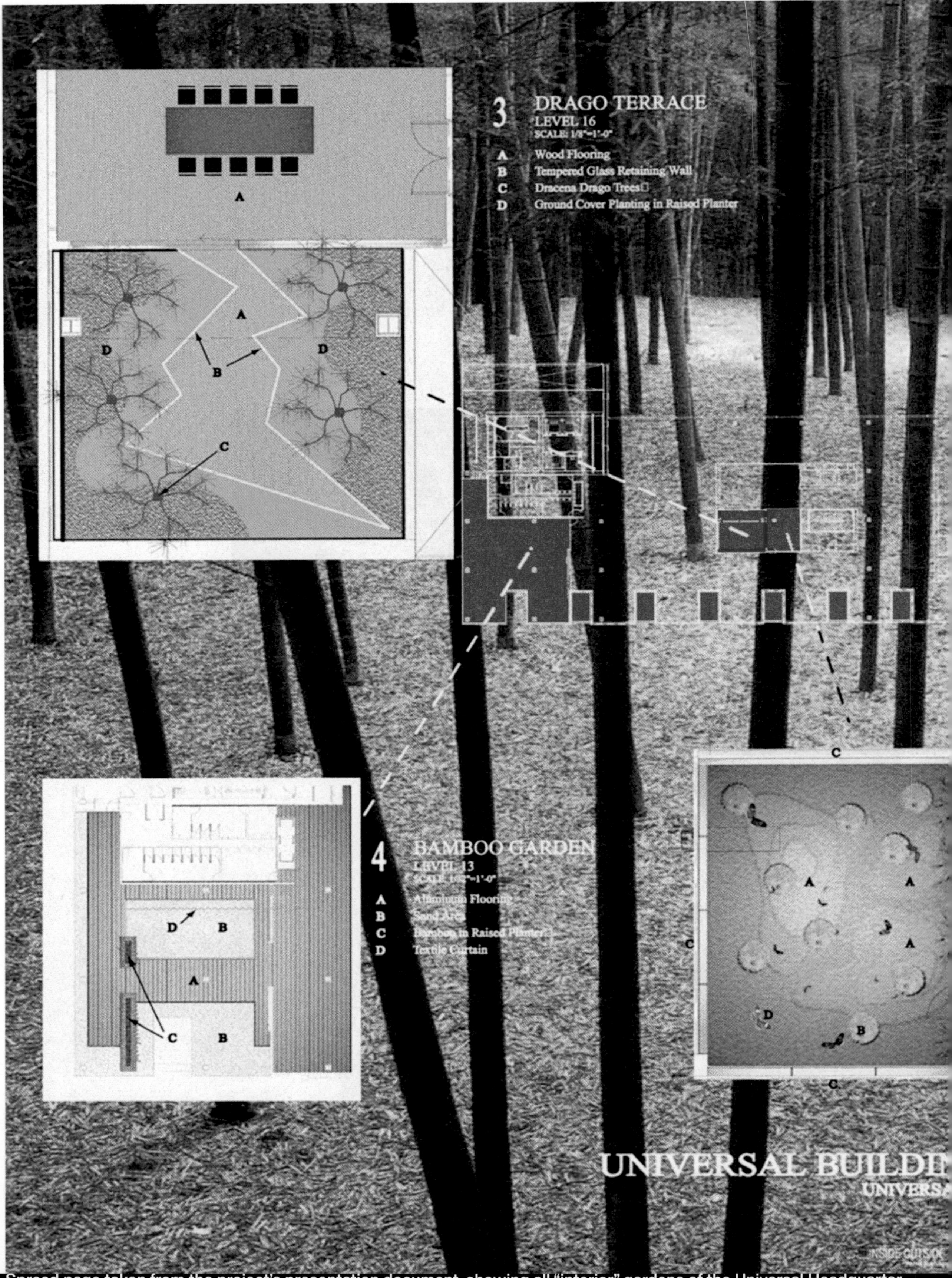

3 DRAGO TERRACE
LEVEL 16
SCALE 1/8"=1'-0"

A   Wood Flooring
B   Tempered Glass Retaining Wall
C   Dracena Drago Trees
D   Ground Cover Planting in Raised Planter

4 BAMBOO GARDEN
LEVEL 13
SCALE 1/32"=1'-0"

A   Aluminum Flooring
B   Sand Area
C   Bamboo in Raised Planter
D   Textile Curtain

UNIVERSAL BUILDI
UNIVERSA

Spread page taken from the project's presentation document, showing all "interior" gardens of the Universal Headquarter building. Only now, at this very moment, I see the misspelling of the word "Dragon" in the title of garden 3, top left... Strange that this slipped our attention at the time!

2 MOUND GARDEN
LEVEL 13
SCALE: 1/8"=1'-0"

A   Cast Aluminum Plate Mounds
B   Earth Mound With Moss
C   Copper Plate Surface
D   Solid Plexiglass Tubes
E   Glazed Glass Wall

5 BUTTERFLY GARDEN
LEVEL 13.5
SCALE: 1/8"=1'-0"

A   Earth Mounds with Ground Cover
B   Flowering Shrubs in Pots
C   Glazed Glass Wall
D   Butterflies

1 ROOF TERRACE
LEVEL 14
SCALE: 1/8"=1'-0"

A   White Roofing Gravel
B   Black Mexican Pebbles

TERIOR GARDENS
S, INC.

GRAPHIC SCALE

The Path as Spatial Tool
State Detention Centre

"The women's wing has only one fence, a single row inside the prison wall, while the men have two fences of different heights. Of course, numerous cameras are found everywhere. The prison director explained that historically the percentage of women trying to escape is much lower than that of the men. Women are reportedly aware of their responsibilities and are more able to accept the consequences of their own actions. Therefore, in this prison women are allowed to have their children and husbands visit. Two special apartments were made for this purpose and open up to the gardens, which contain a playground and a sandbox."

"As the building was totally new when I started this commission, the director asked me if I wanted to stay in one of the women's cells for a couple of days while the staff were familiarising themselves with the building and their routines – so that I could experience life in prison. I declined the offer, too scared I might be forgotten… maybe even more scared about the confrontation with myself, isolated in a bare cell for four days! My loss."   PB

LOCATION	Nieuwegein, the Netherlands
CLIENT	Rijksgebouwendienst (Dutch State Building Department)
STATUS	Completed
SCOPE	Landscape design of six gardens for female and male prisoners, entrance and parking areas; (separate) shelters for prisoners and guards; lighting and maintenance plan
SCALE	2.5 ha
COLLABORATORS	Archivolt Architecten, DS Landschapsarchitecten
DESCRIPTION	A meandering path ignores and escapes all boundaries. It enters the building and forces its way out into the free world beyond double fences and walls, creating different garden compositions on the way. Each garden is composed of different granulates and plantings, allowing the prisoners to find their bearings when looking through the cell windows behind the iron doors that line the endless corridors of the repetitive floorplan of the building's interior. Treetops change with the seasons. Round control rooms with mirroring windows are placed at the intersections on each floor. The main entrance is in the middle of the building, with the women's quarters to the left and the men's to the right. Separate parking for staff and visitors is placed in the lot outside the prison wall. We designed the parking lot as well as the entrance plaza with the word 'Love' in swirly letters, mimicking the language of the path. In our design of shelters for prisoners and guards in each of five gardens, the roofs had to be transparent for camera surveillance, and breakable to prevent prisoners from climbing onto them. Occasional trees were allowed, provided they were placed at a prescribed distance from each vertical surface, and with trunks trimmed to a height of three metres. The materials had to be small in scale and smooth to ensure they could not be used as weapons. I could not – as first intended – create rich gardens for the prisoners to work in as a form of therapy since this is an interim facility for detainees waiting to be sentenced and then relocated.

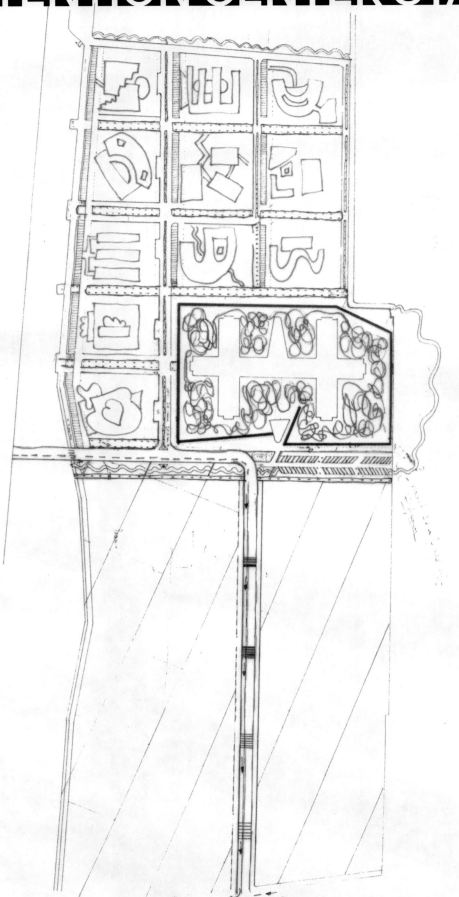

de gevangenis in relatie met de
omgeving

Presentation collage of gardens and entrance square minus prison building

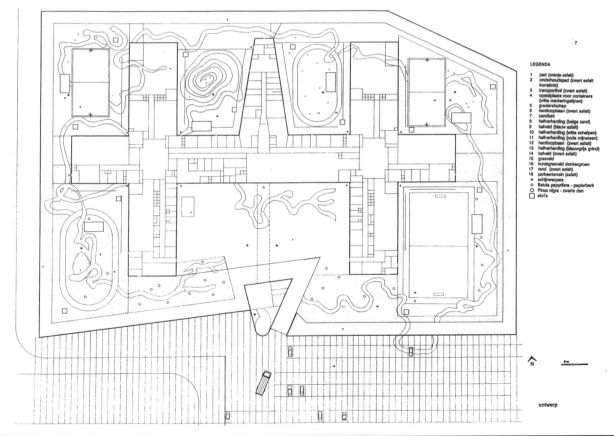

7

LEGENDA

1 pad (oranje asfalt)
2 onderhoudspad (zwart asfalt
   korrelmix)
3 transporthof (zwart asfalt)
4 opstelplaats voor containers
   (witte markeringslijnen)
5 graslandschap
6 hardloopbaan (zwart asfalt)
7 zandbak
8 halfverharding (beige zand)
9 balveld (blauw asfalt)
10 halfverharding (witte schelpen)
11 halfverharding (rode mijnsteen)
12 hardloopbaan (zwart asfalt)
13 halfverharding (blauwgrijs grind)
14 balveld (zwart asfalt)
15 grasveld
16 kunstgrasveld donkergroen
17 rand (zwart asfalt)
18 parkeerterrein (asfalt)
+ schijnwerpers
o Betula papyrifera - papierberk
O Pinus nigra - zwarte den
□ abri's

N   5m

ontwerp

Working drawing of landscape, parking lot and street plan

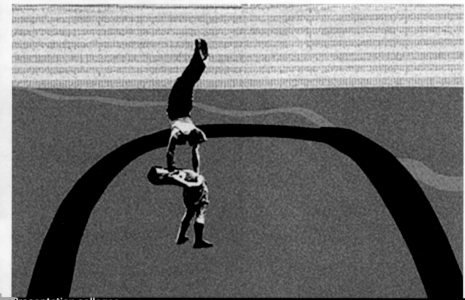

Presentation collages

Close-up of women's spiral garden

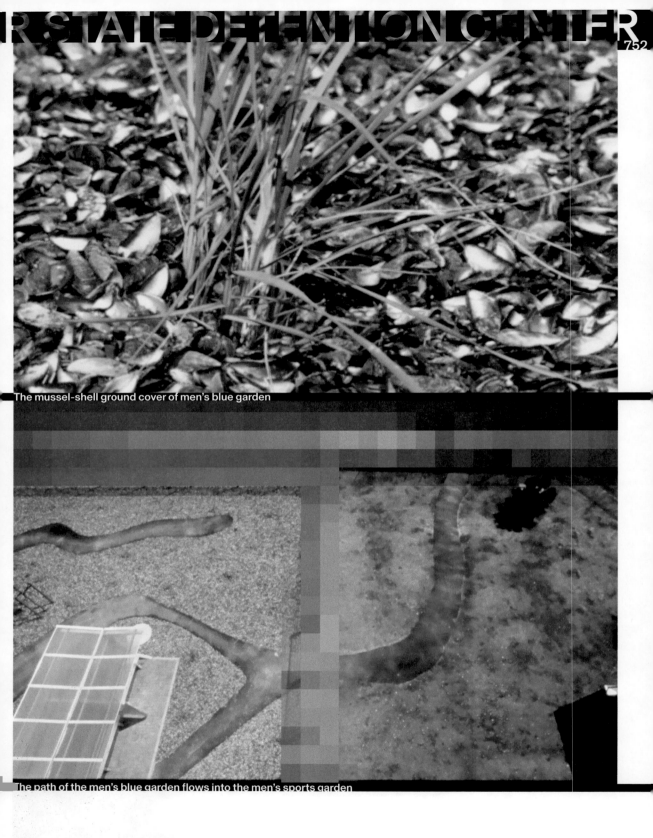

The mussel-shell ground cover of men's blue garden

The path of the men's blue garden flows into the men's sports garden

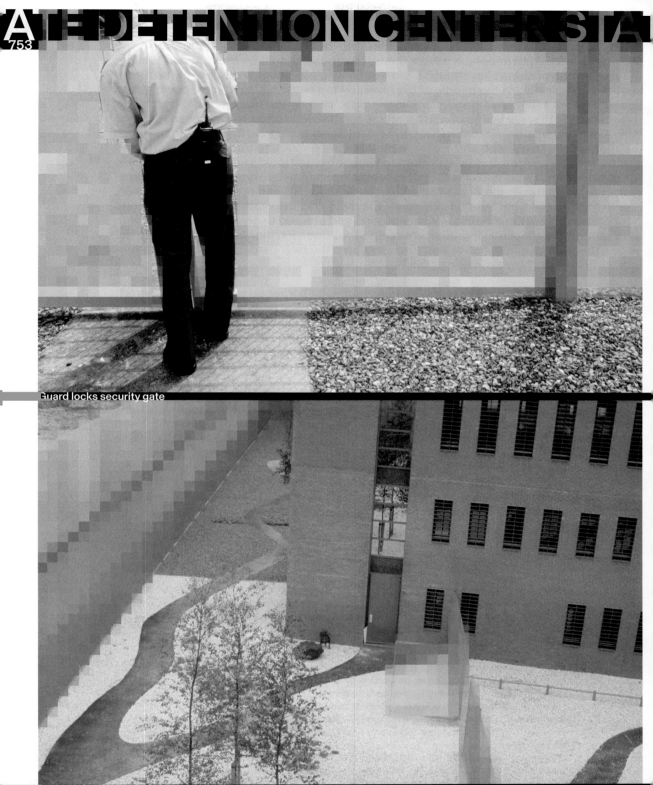

Guard locks security gate

Paths defy all boundaries

| 1994–1998 + | Water Fleece, Pink Bathrobe, Garden Mirror, etc |
| 2011–2012 | Maison Bordeaux |

"First the overgrown area was opened up here and there to allow entry to the site. As the architects wanted to ascertain where the future house should be located and this neglected forest-of-brambles situation did not allow us to get an overview of the site, a scaffolding was built in the middle of the forest on top of the hill, so that we could get an overview from a higher vantage point. Having decided on the placement of the house, the undergrowth was cleared of wild brambles and the dead branches removed to create view-lines towards the Garonne River and city of Bordeaux and to improve the development of existing trees and shrubs while maintaining enough natural mass to filter and scatter the city sounds. It was important to keep a 'natural look.' The heavy clay soil was full of stones and rocks and was therefore too hard to handle in dry summers, so rain was welcome when the shape of the terrain had to be modified and new additions planted. The extracted soil from the building site – the base was excavated to form the ground floor of the three-storey house – was moulded and shaped to create an intimate lawn area around the glazed living quarters on the first floor. Farther on, more towards the edge of the estate where it dropped down towards the river below, OMA created a biological, linear overflow swimming pool."

"The concrete driveway with drop-off had a (minimally!) greened turning-circle. We left the existing tree on the patio that divided the concierge and guest houses into two sections, which resulted in an open-roofed patio through which the tree grows over a carpet of bark chippings. We planted new trees close to the house to block the wind and provide shade. Paths were mowed in the wild meadows. The green of the driveway flows into the kitchen, laundry room and storage areas in the form of a polyurethane-poured floor in soft greens."

"In the meantime, we designed and produced all of the curtains for the house – curtains that complement the basic concepts of architecture: lightness versus weight; open versus closed; thick versus thin; colour versus colourlessness. The heart of the house was the disabled owner's study, a large platform that shifted vertically from floor to floor along a vertical cupboard that contained all that was necessary for his wellbeing. In the living room, two parallel tracks turn corners and run out over the open terrace. They carry art pieces and a curtain, one the backdrop for the other, both to be viewed in nature or somewhere along the glass facades that define the interior." PB

LOCATION	Floirac, Gironde, France
CLIENT	Private owner
STATUS	Completed
SCOPE	Garden interventions, interior finishes, kitchen flooring, design of all curtains; re-design of all existing curtains and two additional red carpets in 2012
MATERIALS	Blue tulle (living area/1998), white cotton with circular window and slit of transparent plastic (living area/2012); jute (terrace/1998); grey polyethylene stage mesh (terrace/2012); pale-pink, double-layered Honan silk (bathroom); pink Honan silk (master bedroom); double-layered mirror foil (balcony); white high gloss lacquer blocks sewn on white voile, backside of blocks in gold faux leather (bedroom 1); grey high-gloss lacquer with two horizontal slits of transparent plastic lined with blackout material and bottom of gold faux leather (bedroom 2); light-blue high-gloss lacquer with a bottom of white lacquer lined with light-grey blackout fabric and gold faux leather bottom (bedroom 2); two red wool carpets
SCALE	Seven curtains: 8.44 × 2.33 m, 12.96 × 2.28 m, 4.84 × 2.28 m, 5.76 × 2.38 m, 9.61 × 2.38 m, 20.74 × 2.4 m, 25 × 2.4 m; two carpets, 3.4 × 2.18 m, 5.97 × 2.5 m
COLLABORATORS	OMA; Maarten van Severen, Vincent de Rijk
DESCRIPTION	Eleven hectares of neglected forest on top of a hill overlooking the city of Bordeaux, the Garonne River and a network of highways. Determining the location of the house required extensive study of the landscape and views. We designed all track configurations and curtains for the house as a counterpoint to the architecture. The soft-green polyurethane floor of the kitchen and laundry room is conceived as a continuation of the driveway lawn outside. In 2012, two bright-red woollen carpets were added to the interior, warming up the living room on the first floor and the television room downstairs. A white curtain, made of cotton sheet with transparent plastic openings, encloses the living room and escapes outward when the weather allows. We produced a new exterior mosquito- and shading curtain that envelops the facade and terrace of the living room. In the master bedroom, the pink silk curtains and the mirroring terrace curtain were redone. We designed new curtains for all of the guest bedrooms.

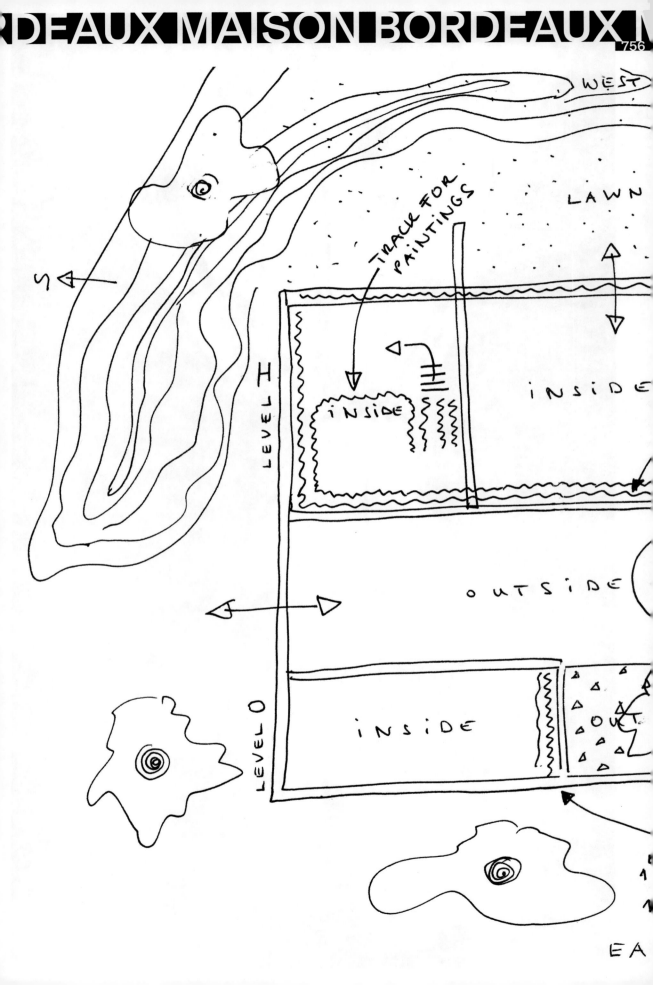

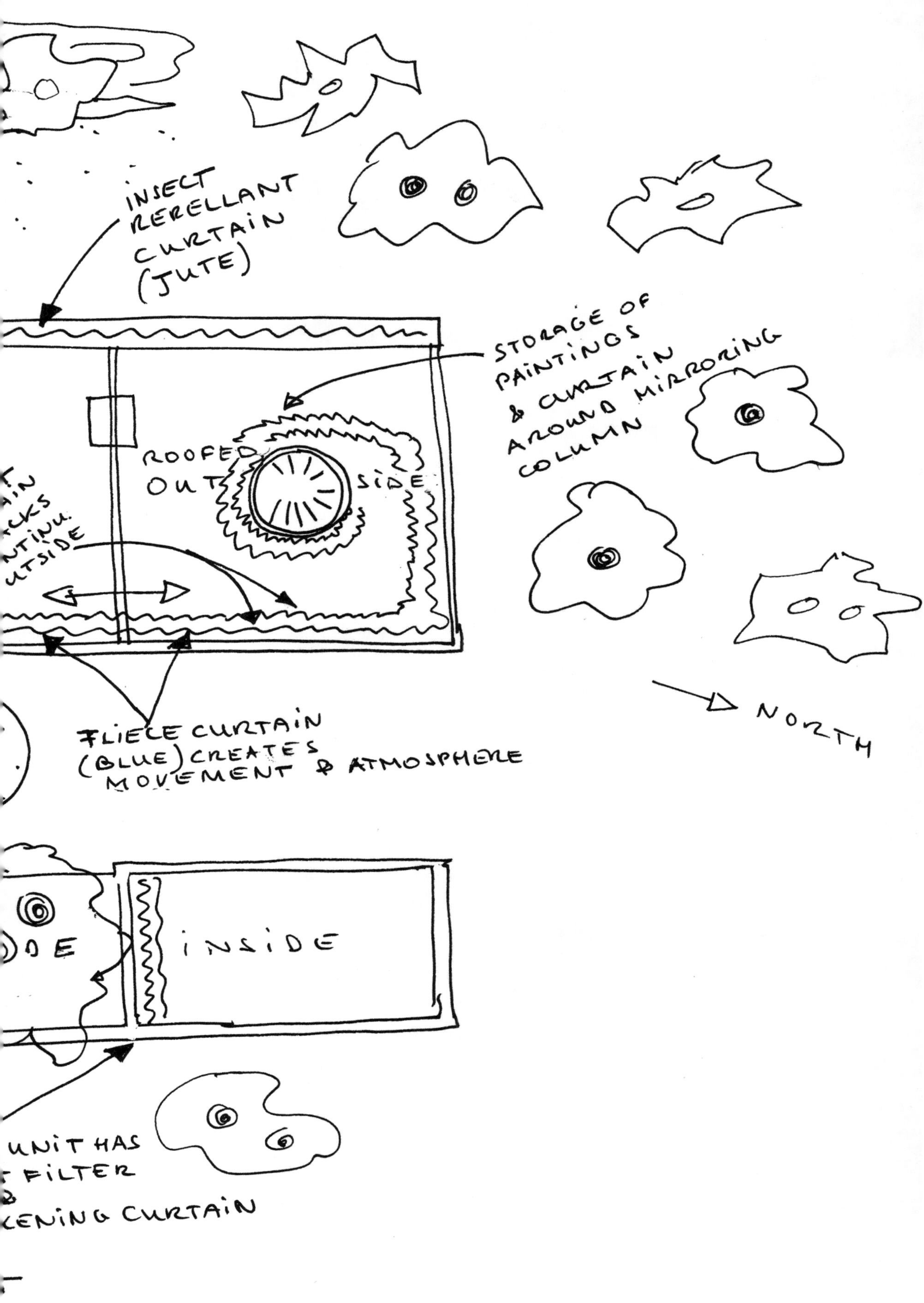

INSECT
RERELLANT
CURTAIN
(JUTE)

STORAGE OF
PAINTINGS
& CURTAIN
AROUND MIRRORING
COLUMN

ROOFED
OUT SIDE

IN
CKS
NTINU.
TSIDE

FLIECE CURTAIN
(BLUE) CREATES
MOVEMENT & ATMOSPHERE

NORTH

INSIDE

) E

UNIT HAS
FILTER
ENING CURTAIN

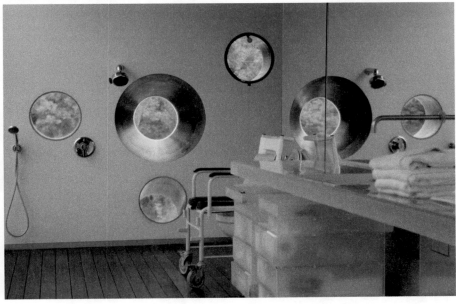

The silk soft-pink curtain creates privacy along the large facade window and envelopes the bath to form an intimate place, offering warmth and a beautiful skin complexion

761

Darkening curtains for guestrooms, formerly the children's bedrooms

Curtain for third guestroom, formerly daughter's bedroom

Mirroring curtain along outer edge of terrace enlarges bedroom and reflects both bedroom and garden

The carpet organises the wide-open living space and integrates the platform

Indoors and outdoors merge

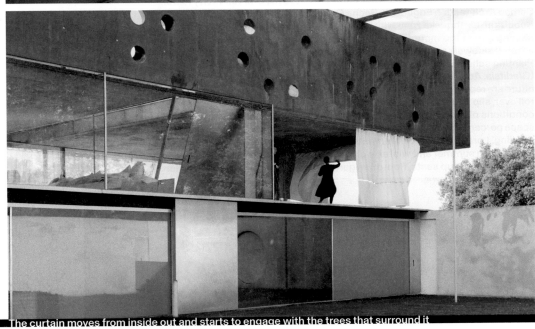

The curtain moves from inside out and starts to engage with the trees that surround it

Connective Green
H-Project

"A narrow street runs between the sunken OMA building and the steep rock-garden of Jean Nouvel's museum in the back. Beneath that street, a large support structure divides the underground parking garage of the OMA building from the canyon-like Nouvel garden. I wanted to replace this structural wall with a giant aquarium of the same volume and strength, a 'living window' between parking garage and canyon, an under-wonderworld in blues, with fish flying through nature."

"We ate the most amazing food on plastic stools along the streets in Seoul: fresh, crispy, spicy, full of raw garlic, sometimes overwhelmed by things that were served and that we couldn't quite recognise, pale strands that were cut into pieces with large scissors and thrown on the barbecue by a sturdy woman in a worker's outfit, with our faces green in the neon light shining out of the diner."

"I've never been so nervous presenting our work to a commissioner as in Seoul: standing in front of a large group of stern-looking men in black suits who seemed so clearly unintrigued by my story, which was translated from English to Korean sentence by sentence. It seemed as though there were no women in our professional field at that time in South Korea. The women I met served tea and welcomed guests. I was literally on my own in a man's world, addressing critical developers who placed a premium on efficiency, economy and clarity, while I was telling stories about nature and beauty with functionality hidden within. The second time I was to present the development of landscape to the client, I felt so nervous that I decided to ask a man to accompany me in the role of 'business partner'. I invited Michael van Gessel, an established Dutch landscape architect from Amsterdam and co-director of the studio B+B, to join me at my expense. He gladly accepted and helped me to prepare and keep my cool. A man at my side definitely helped give my input more 'weight' in the eyes of my audience. Heart-breaking in hindsight! Luckily, Michael was able to hand out his office's business card, which I hope helped generate work for him. In the end, everything worked out. The landscape was executed exactly as it was designed. On a trip to the site years later, Rem discovered, almost by accident, that the design was being realised. Nobody ever informed us."   PB

LOCATION	Seoul, South Korea
CLIENT	Samsung Cultural Foundation
STATUS	Completed
SCOPE	Landscape and infrastructure in the heart of the city, connecting three separate museum buildings by Botta, Nouvel and OMA and the clinic building by Terry Farrell
SCALE	4 ha
COLLABORATORS	Irene Curulli, Andrew McNair; Mario Botta, Jean Nouvel, OMA and Terry Farrell, Samoo Architects & Engineers, Sacha Curiel
DESCRIPTION	Seoul is an earthquake zone with very hot summers and very cold winters. The sloping site in the mountain foothills lies on rocky ground. In our design, a lettered sidewalk runs through the entire area, connecting all of the buildings. Planting schemes (shrub, rock, grass, perennial and bamboo gardens), trees (*Gleditsia, Acer, Pinus, Magnolia, Malus* and *Prunus*), materials and street furniture are repeated to reinforce unity. Gardens of varied typology run through, roll over, slip under or divide the buildings, enhancing the natural profile and conditions of the site, and fulfilling the strict Korean requirements for landscape percentage per built volume. For the public plaza on the roof of the OMA building, I proposed a few interventions to liven up the large aluminium surface in both summer and winter: a circle of trees, a liquid metal pond, turning sculptures, pop-up seats, flop-open gardens and a spiralling steam pavilion.

CRITICAL ISSUES AUGUST 1996

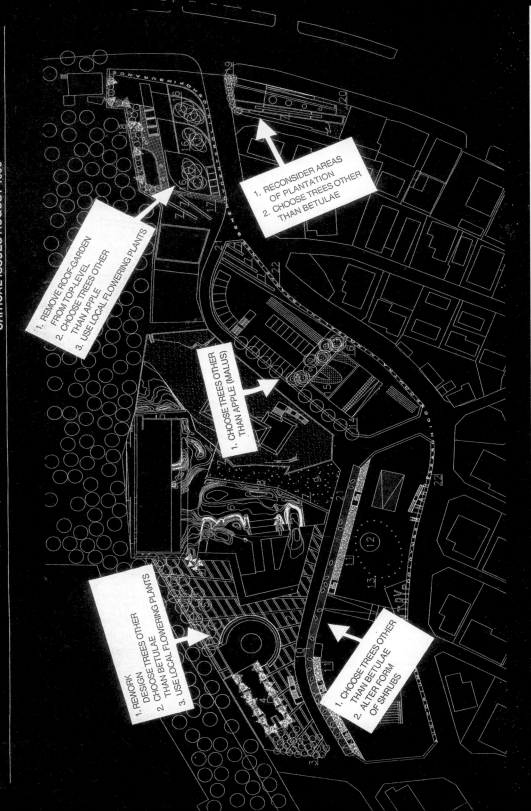

1. REMOVE ROOF-GARDEN
   FROM TOP-LEVEL
2. CHOOSE TREES OTHER
   THAN APPLE
3. USE LOCAL FLOWERING PLANTS

1. RECONSIDER AREAS
   OF PLANTATION
2. CHOOSE TREES OTHER
   THAN BETULAE

1. CHOOSE TREES OTHER
   THAN APPLE (MALUS)

REWORK
1. DESIGN
2. CHOOSE TREES OTHER
   THAN BETULAE
3. USE LOCAL FLOWERING PLANTS

1. CHOOSE TREES OTHER
   THAN BETULAE
2. ALTER FORM
   OF SHRUBS

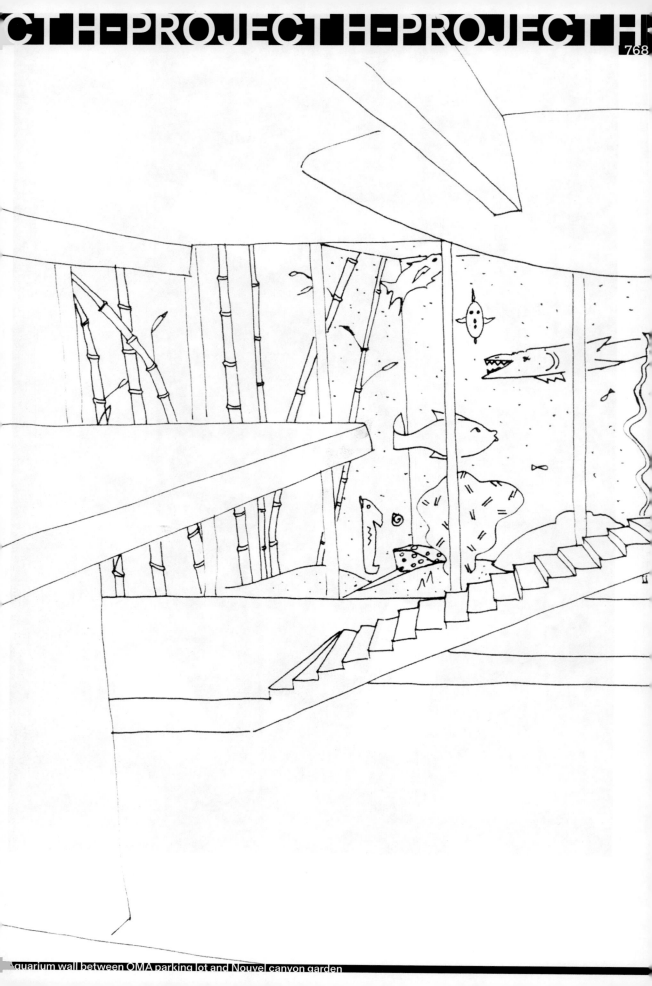

Aquarium wall between OMA parking lot and Nouvel canyon garden

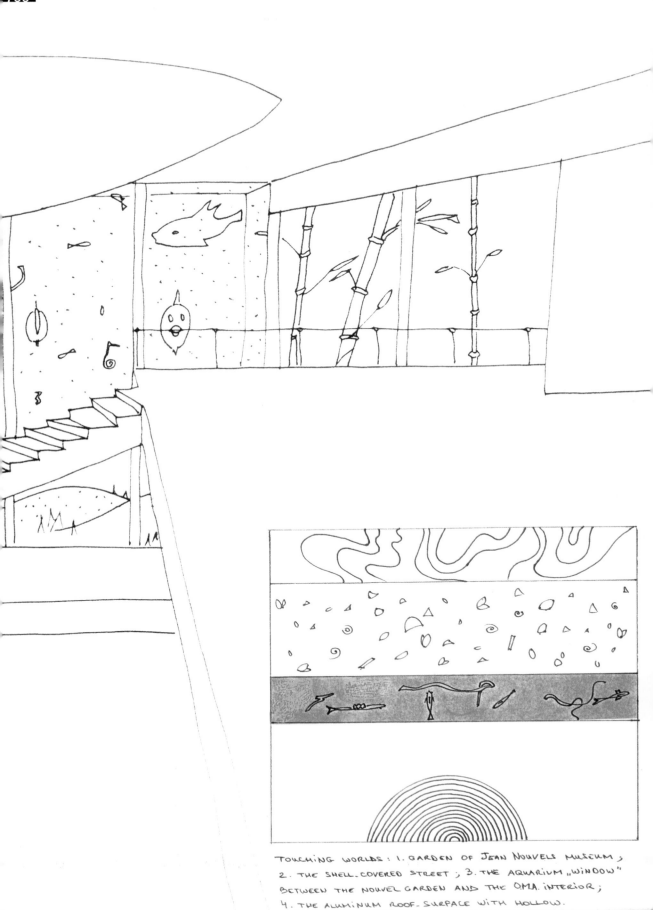

TOUCHING WORLDS: 1. GARDEN OF JEAN NOUVELS MUSEUM;
2. THE SHELL COVERED STREET; 3. THE AQUARIUM "WINDOW"
BETWEEN THE NOUVEL GARDEN AND THE OMA INTERIOR;
4. THE ALUMINUM ROOF SURFACE WITH HOLLOW.

FAX voor REM

Rem

je zou jullie project niet
alleen kunnen zien als „high
technology" met alle verbindingen
en bewegingen van dien maar
ons zou parametype werk ook als
„earthworks" : uitgravingen
inhepingen
vouwsels
stapeling
zonnestanden
schaduwen
windbeweging
etc etc

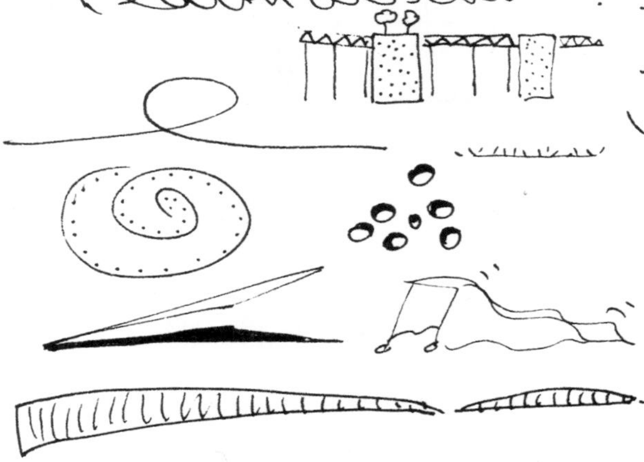

Dan kijk ik in elk geval heel
anders naar alles en dan krijgen
alle buiten gebieden meens die
verbinding :

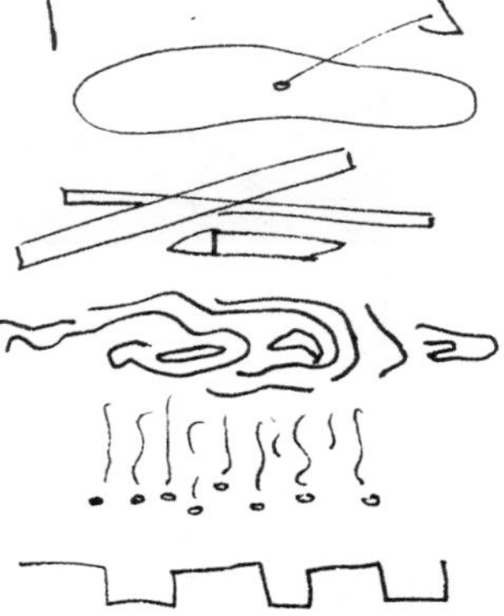

1	(CM)
2	(B)
3	(N)
4	(K)
5	(F)

interessant ?

getekend :
(de boenmonster)

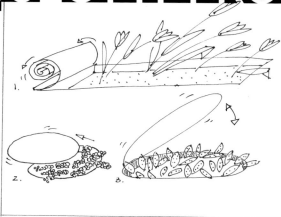

THREE PLANT AREAS "CUT" OUT OF THE ALUMINUM ROOF:
IN THEM ONE COULD PLANT 1. WHITE TULIPS, 2. STACHYS
BYZANTIA "SILVER CARPET" OR 3. SEDUM CYANEUM "ROSENTEPPICH"

A SPIRAL "BUILDING" IS CREATED BY THIN STEAM WALLS. PARALLEL
TO THE HOLES ARE WINDOWS FOR LIGHT TO THE OFFICES BELOW.

WHERE THE TWO ROOFS MEET, A CHILDRENS' PLAYGROUND.

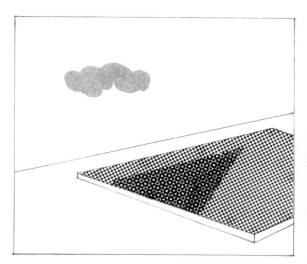

A TRANSPARENT SENSOR FIELD ON THE ROOF LOOKS
INTO THE RESEARCH CHAMBER BELOW.

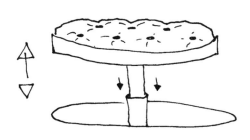

PUBLIC SEAT
(SILVER NYLON, UPHOLSTERED)

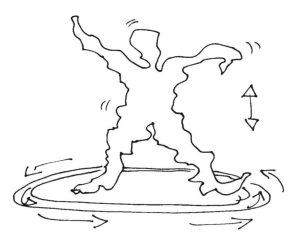

SOME SCULPTURES SLOWLY
ROTATE ON A DISC.
THE DISC ALSO LOWERS
INTO THE BUILDING TO
CHANGE THE WORK.

LANDSCAPE

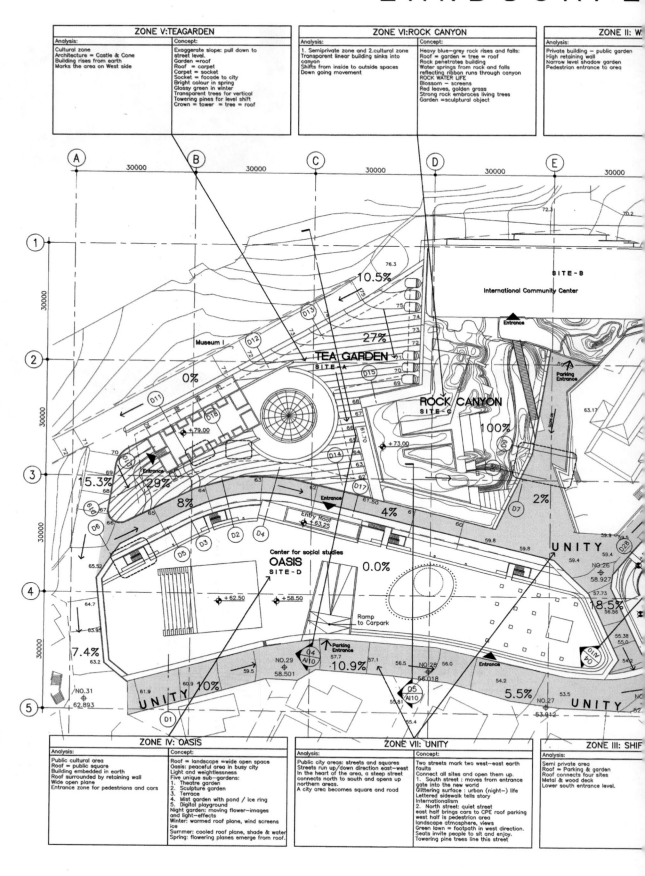

ZONE V:TEAGARDEN

Analysis:
Cultural zone
Architecture = Castle & Cone
Building rises from earth
Marks the area on West side

Concept:
Exaggerate slope: pull down to
street level.
Garden =roof
Roof = carpet
Carpet = socket
Socket = facade to city
Bright colour in spring
Glossy green in winter
Transparent trees for vertical
Towering pines for level shift
Crown = tower = tree = roof

ZONE VI:ROCK CANYON

Analysis:
1. Semiprivate zone and 2.cultural zone
Transparent linear building sinks into
canyon
Shifts from inside to outside spaces
Down going movement

Concept:
Heavy blue–grey rock rises and falls:
Roof = garden = tree = roof
Rock penetrates building
Water springs from rock and falls
reflecting ribbon runs through canyon
ROCK WATER LIFE
Blossom — screens
Red leaves, golden grass
Strong rock embraces living trees
Garden =sculptural object

ZONE II: W

Analysis:
Private building – public garden
High retaining wall
Narrow level shadow garden
Pedestrian entrance to area

ZONE IV: OASIS

Analysis:
Public cultural area
Roof = public square
Building embedded in earth
Roof surrounded by retaining wall
Wide open plane
Entrance zone for pedestrians and cars

Concept:
Roof = landscape =wide open space
Oasis: peaceful area in busy city
Light and weightlessness
Five unique sub–gardens:
1. Theatre garden
2. Sculpture garden
3. Terrace
4. Mist garden with pond / ice ring
5. Digital playground
Night garden: moving flower–images
and light–effects
Winter: warmed roof plane, wind screens
ice
Summer: cooled roof plane, shade & water
Spring: flowering planes emerge from roof.

ZONE VII: UNITY

Analysis:
Public city areas: streets and squares
Streets run up/down direction east–west
In the heart of the area, a steep street
connects north to south and opens up
northern areas.
A city area becomes square and road

Concept:
Two streets mark two west–east earth
faults
Connect all sites and open them up.
1. South street : moves from entrance
gate into the new world
Glittering surface : urban (night–) life
Lettered sidewalk tells story
Internationalism
2. North street: quiet street
east half brings cars to CPE roof parking
west half is pedestrian area
landscape atmosphere, views
Green lawn = footpath in west direction.
Seats invite people to sit and enjoy.
Towering pine trees line this street

ZONE III: SHIF

Analysis:
Semi private area
Roof = Parking & garden
Roof connects four sites
Metal & wood deck
Lower south entrance level.

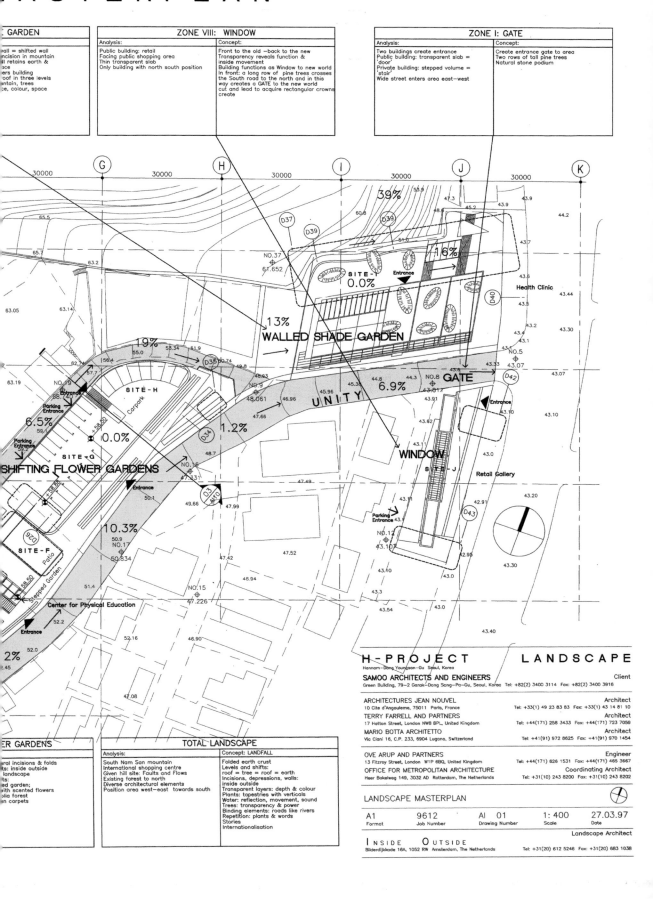

ZONE VIII: WINDOW

Analysis:	Concept:
Public building: retail	Front to the old —back to the new
Facing public shopping area	Transparency reveals function &
Thin transparent slab	inside movement
Only building with north south position	Building functions as Window to new world
	In front: a long row of pine trees crosses
	the South road to the north and in this
	way creates a GATE to the new world
	cut and lead to acquire rectangular crowns
	create

ZONE I: GATE

Analysis:	Concept:
Two buildings create entrance	Create entrance gate to area
Public building: transparent slab = 'door'	Two rows of tall pine trees
Private building: stepped volume = 'stair'	Natural stone podium
Wide street enters area east–west	

: GARDEN
- all = shifted wall
- ncision in mountain
- ll retains earth &
- ace
- ers building
- oof in three levels
- untain, trees
- e, colour, space

WALLED SHADE GARDEN
13%
39%
16%
SITE 0.0%
Entrance
Health Clinic

UNITY
6.9% GATE
WINDOW
SITE-J
Retail Gallery
Entrance
Parking Entrance

SHIFTING FLOWER GARDENS
19%
6.5%
0.0%
SITE-H Carpark
SITE-G
10.3%
SITE-F Patio
Stepped Garden
Center for Physical Education
Entrance
Parking Entrance
1.2%

H-PROJECT   LANDSCAPE

Hannam–Dong Youngsan–Gu Seoul, Korea

SAMOO ARCHITECTS AND ENGINEERS   Client
Green Building, 79–2 Garak–Dong Song–Pa–Gu, Seoul, Korea Tel: +82(2) 3400 3114 Fax: +82(2) 3400 3916

ARCHITECTURES JEAN NOUVEL   Architect
10 Cite d'Angouleme, 75011 Paris, France   Tel: +33(1) 49 23 83 83 Fax: +33(1) 43 14 81 10

TERRY FARRELL AND PARTNERS   Architect
17 Hatton Street, London NW8 8PL, United Kingdom   Tel: +44(171) 258 3433 Fax: +44(171) 723 7059

MARIO BOTTA ARCHITETTO   Architect
Via Ciani 16, C.P. 233, 6904 Lugano, Switzerland   Tel: +41(91) 972 8625 Fax: +41(91) 970 1454

OVE ARUP AND PARTNERS   Engineer
13 Fitzroy Street, London W1P 6BQ, United Kingdom   Tel: +44(171) 626 1531 Fax: +44(171) 465 3667

OFFICE FOR METROPOLITAN ARCHITECTURE   Coordinating Architect
Heer Bokelweg 149, 3032 AD Rotterdam, The Netherlands   Tel: +31(10) 243 8200 Fax: +31(10) 243 8202

LANDSCAPE MASTERPLAN

A1	9612	AI 01	1: 400	27.03.97
Format	Job Number	Drawing Number	Scale	Date

Landscape Architect

INSIDE   OUTSIDE
Bilderdijkkade 16A, 1052 RW Amsterdam, The Netherlands   Tel: +31(20) 612 5246 Fax: +31(20) 683 1038

TOTAL LANDSCAPE

Analysis:	Concept: LANDFALL
South Nam San mountain	Folded earth crust
International shopping centre	Levels and shifts:
Given hill site: Faults and Flows	roof = tree = roof = earth
Existing forest to north	Incisions, depressions, walls:
Diverse architectural elements	inside outside
Position area west–east towards south	Transparent layers: depth & colour
	Plants: tapestries with verticals
	Water: reflection, movement, sound
	Trees: transparency & power
	Binding elements: roads like rivers
	Repetition: plants & words
	Stories
	Internationalisation

R GARDENS
- ral incisions & folds
- ts: inside outside
- landscape
- ts:
- ed garden;
- ith scented flowers
- olia forest
- n carpets

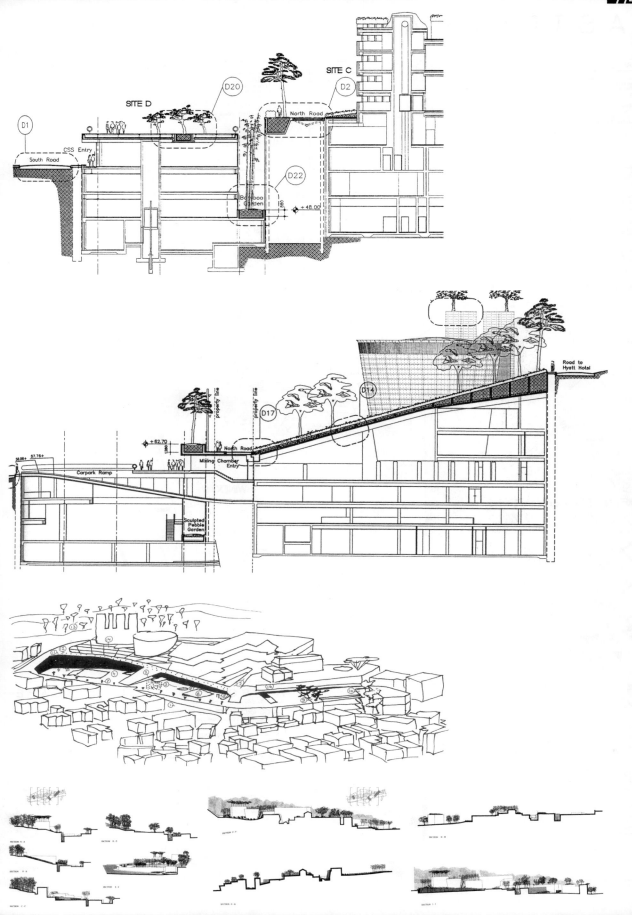

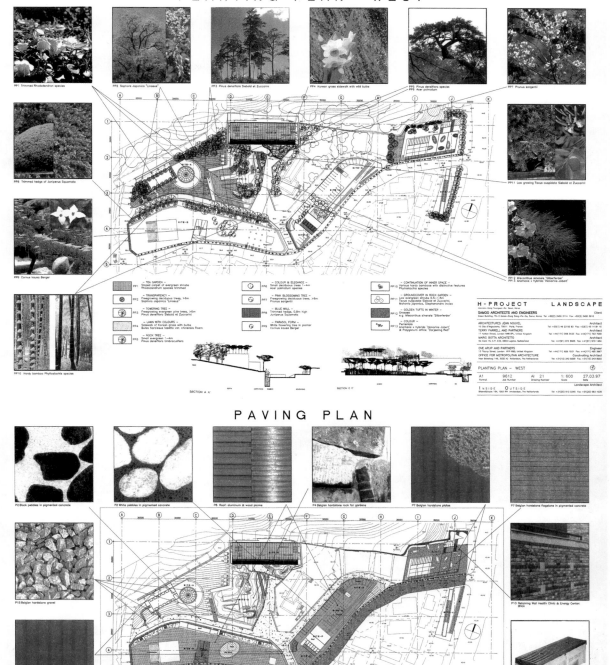

PLANTING PLAN - WEST

PAVING PLAN

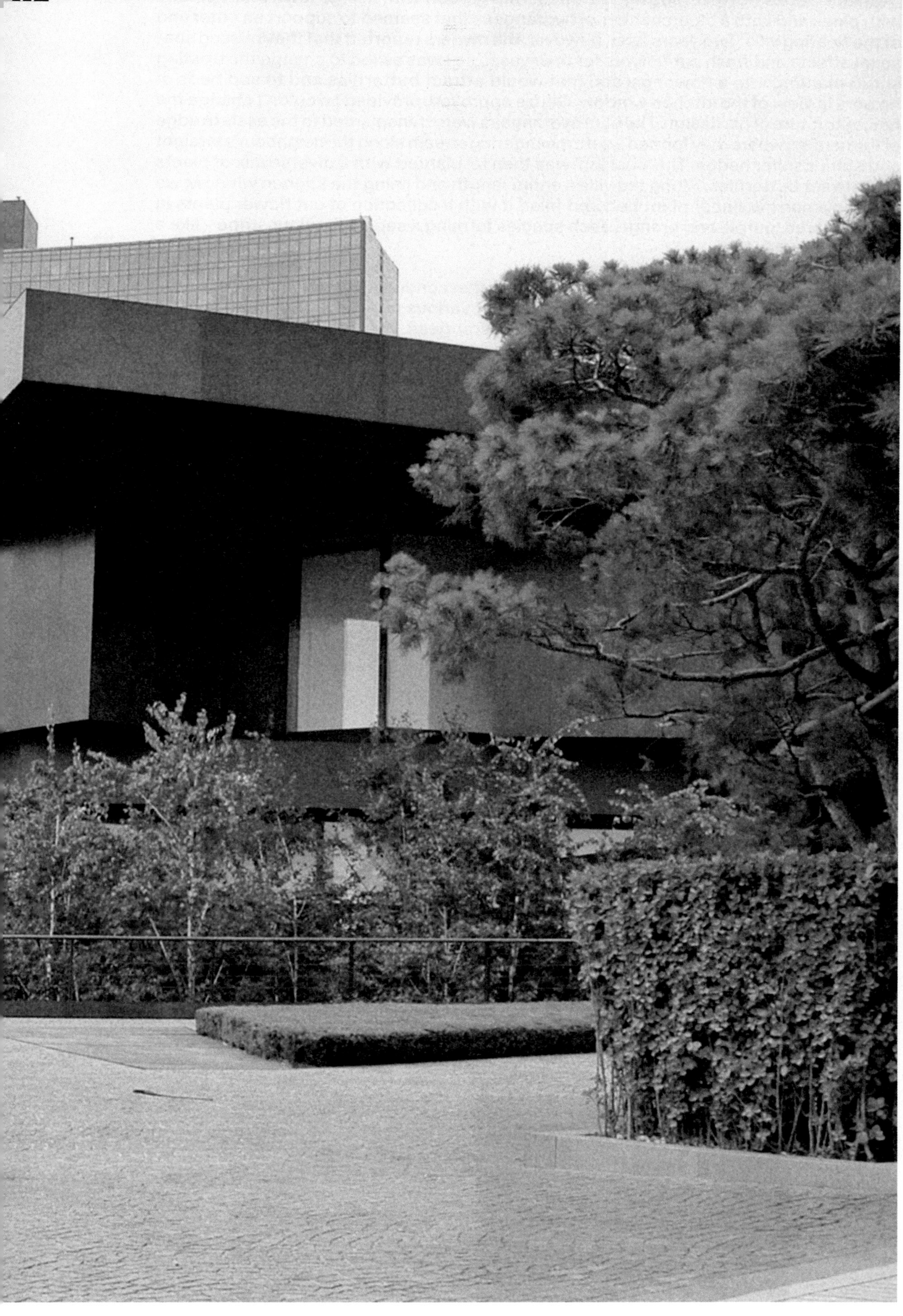

Shade Honey
Dutch House

"Adriaan Geuze of West 8 designed a beautiful garden with a large lawn interspersed with pines and with a blue 'cushion' of hydrangeas that seemed to support an outer end of the floating villa. Two years later, however, the owners reported that they missed seasonal effects and fresh cut flowers for their vases so I was asked to change the existing shrub planting into a flower garden that would attract butterflies and to add beds of flowers in view of the kitchen window. Geuze approved, provided I wouldn't change the basic structure of his design. The blue hydrangeas were transplanted to the eastern edge of the garden, where they formed a soft, meandering stream along the neighbour's straight and stark conifer hedge. The 'cushion' was then re-planted with a diverse mix of plants that attract butterflies. Along the villa's entire length and lining the kitchen window, we created a narrow, linear plant bed and filled it with a collection of cut flower plants in shades of red, purple and orange, each species forming a separate colour stripe – like a Persian carpet."

"In one week in the fall and under the worst of weather conditions, Liesbeth, her colleague and I chose and bought every plant and shrub at various nurseries, transported them to the site, then moved and re-planted the hydrangeas, prepared the ground of the 'cushion' and the 'Persian carpet' and planted hundreds of perennials, herbs, bulbs and shrubs. The rain never stopped. Covered in mud and dripping wet, we paused at intervals under the villa's 'belly,' gratefully accepting hot tea and eating our own whole-wheat peanut butter sandwiches and apples – Dutch gardener's tradition! Friday evening, after a week's hard work, we took a look at the (muddy) result and envisioned the garden's growth and effects in the near future, the pleasure it would bring its owners, the surprises it would unleash!"

"One full season after installation the client called me and said that all was beautiful and thriving, and that she and her husband were very happy with our interventions. With one exception: the plants we chose not only attracted butterflies but bees and hoverflies as well, which she was quite scared of… could we please DO something about this…?" PB

LOCATION	Holten, the Netherlands
CLIENT	Private owner
STATUS	Completed
SCOPE	Steel mesh and black voile exterior curtain, shading screens for terrace, design and installation of butterfly garden and "Persian carpet"
MATERIALS	Steel mesh, lined with black polyester voile; sunshades: perforated spinnaker, plantings
SCALE	Curtain, 35 m², garden works, ca. 400 m²
COLLABORATORS	OMA, West 8, Liesbeth Sillem and colleague
DESCRIPTION	We re-planted the "blue cushion" that appears to hold up the elevated villa and, along the west margin of the garden, we planted a "Persian carpet": a thin line of systematically organised beds of red-leaved and pink/red/orange blooming perennials and bulbs with a trimmed hedge of burgundy-red Berberis. A line of inserted ceramic pots, filled with seasonal bulbs, was added onto the linear flowerbed along the sunken driveway. We planted small groups of blue and white crocus bulbs throughout the lawn and within the forested buffer zone between the public road and garden, groupings of evergreen, flowering shrubs and shade tolerant perennials to ensure privacy.

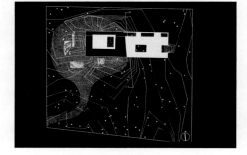

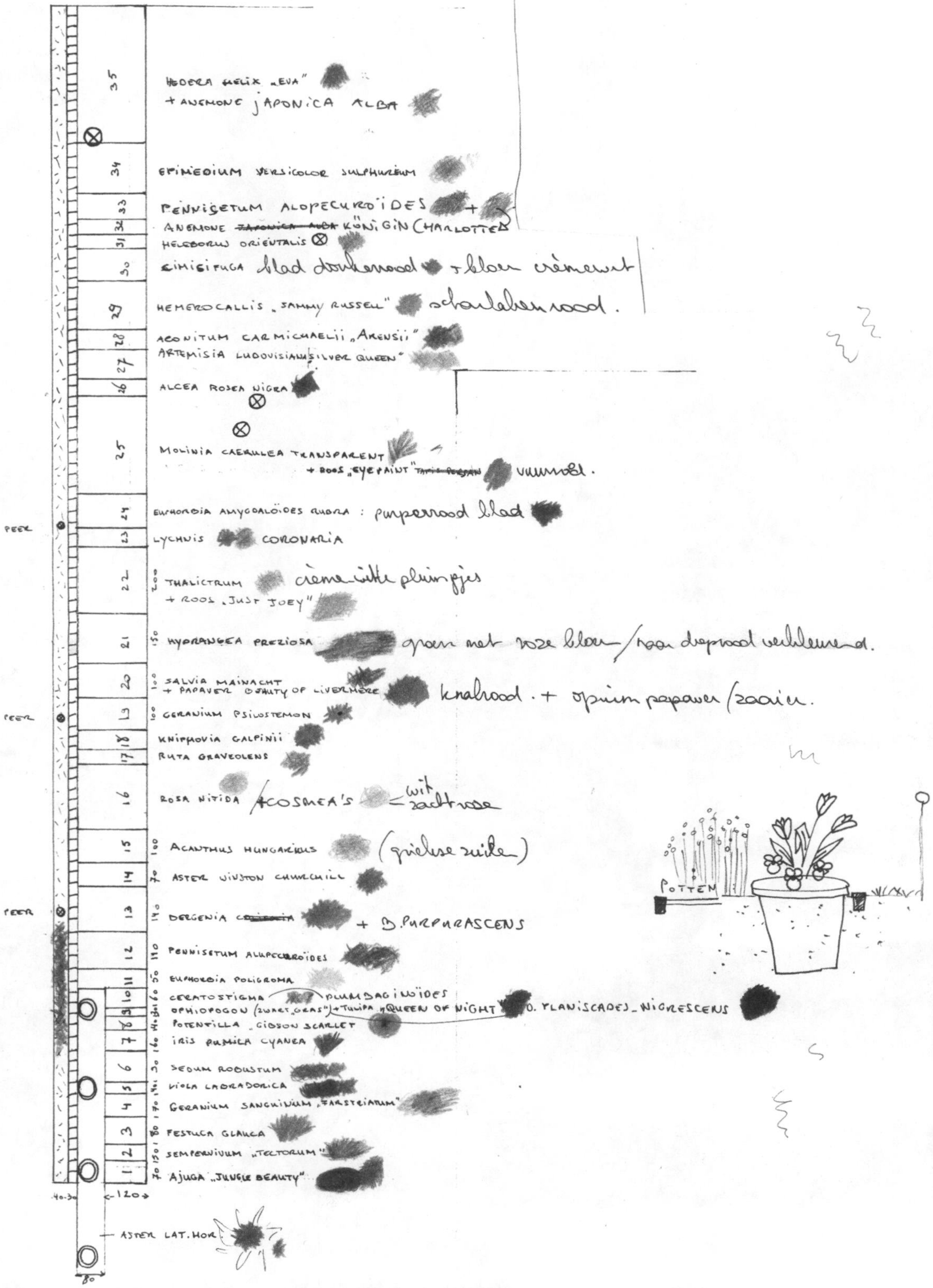

HEDERA HELIX "EVA"
+ ANEMONE JAPONICA ALBA

EPIMEDIUM VERSICOLOR SULPHUREUM

PENNISETUM ALOPECUROÏDES +
ANEMONE ~~JAPONICA ALBA~~ KÖNIGIN (CHARLOTTE)
HELLEBORUS ORIENTALIS ⊗
CIMICIFUGA blad donkerrood + bloem crèmewit

HEMEROCALLIS "SAMMY RUSSELL" scharlakenrood.

ACONITUM CARMICHAELII "ARENSII"
ARTEMISIA LUDOVISIANUM "SILVER QUEEN"

ALCEA ROSEA NIGRA ⊗

⊗
MOLINIA CAERULEA TRANSPARENT
+ ROOS "EYE PAINT" ~~THEE ROZEN~~ vuurrood.

EUPHORBIA AMYGDALOÏDES RUBRA : purperrood blad
LYCHNIS CORONARIA

THALICTRUM crème witte pluimpjes
+ ROOS "JUST JOEY"

HYDRANGEA PREZIOSA groen met roze blauw / naar dieprood verkleurend.

SALVIA MAINACHT
+ PAPAVER © FRUITY OF LIVERMERE knalrood. + opium papaver (zaaien.
GERANIUM PSILOSTEMON

KNIPHOVIA GALPINII
RUTA GRAVEOLENS

ROSA NITIDA / COSMEA's wit zachtrose

ACANTHUS HUNGARICUS (grielse weide)

ASTER WINSTON CHURCHILL

BERGENIA ~~CORDATA~~ + B. PURPURASCENS

PENNISETUM ALOPECUROÏDES

EUPHORBIA POLIGROMA
CERATOSTIGMA PLUMBAGINOÏDES
OPHIOPOGON (ZWART GRAS) + TULIPA "QUEEN OF NIGHT" O. PLANISCADES NIGRESCENS
POTENTILLA "GIBSON SCARLET"
IRIS PUMILA CYANEA

SEDUM ROBUSTUM
VIOLA LABRADORICA
GERANIUM SANGUINEUM "FARSTRIATUM"
FESTUCA GLAUCA
SEMPERVIVUM "TECTORUM"
AJUGA "JUNGLE BEAUTY"

40-30 ← 120 →

— ASTER LAT. HOR.

80

PEER
PEER
PEER

POTTEM

781

Collage representing colour scope of "Persian carpet"

Details of steel mesh curtain (with black voile lining) and folding system

Reflection of 'butterfly cushion' and steel curtain.

Butterfly "cushion" in bloom

Milky Way
         Lille Grand Palais

"The building was so huge that we walked for miles and miles every day. Eventually we started getting around on roller skates. All communications with the French teams were best completed before lunch, when wine and whisky were served. The focus altered considerably after 4 pm. Joep van Lieshout created all the public toilets and the main bar, living in a camper onsite during the week. Friday evenings we would sometimes drive back to Rotterdam together in his old Citroën – if I remember the car correctly! Mark Schendel and Jeanne Gang were both working for OMA at the time – Jeanne had recently joined – and this project is where we all got to know one another."

"OMA had designed a huge folding wall (about 40 × 12 metres) between the exhibition space and the adjacent rock concert hall so that the spaces could be connected. The new tenant of the building didn't like this form of flexibility at all and overnight secretly built a concrete stone wall, closing off the opening permanently – or so it seemed. Koolhaas discovered this first thing the next morning and was deeply shocked. The clock was ticking, the fight for the restoration of the door started and I raced to make a temporary drape of painter's linen to cover this ugly bricked-up wall. A long pipe was mounted from which the drape was to be hung. In the meantime I had (my own) enlarged hands painted on the linen – hands pushing the wall out with force! Because Nelson Mandela had just been inaugurated as president of South Africa, I took the opportunity to add the Mandela fist while I was at it. Then while standing on swaying cherry pickers, we threaded the leather belts through the steel eyelets, one by one by one, and affixed the gigantic linen to the tube. The wall remained and, sadly, within less than a year, the linen drape disappeared."   PB

LOCATION	Lille, France
CLIENT	City of Lille, SAEM Euralille, Association Lille Grand Palais
STATUS	Completed
SCOPE	Research and advisory on furniture, materials and colours, design of curtains, acoustic walls, restaurant, terrace floors
MATERIALS	Various fabrics, steel rings, polyurethane, plastic panels
SCALE	Main auditorium, 37 × 11 m; small auditorium, 16.8 × 12.3 m; entrance hall, 39 × 10 m
COLLABORATORS	OMA, François Delhay Architectes, Julie Sfez
DESCRIPTION	Curtains: dark-purple and light-grey cotton velvet, steel rings, aqua satin lining, salmon-pink cotton velvet, black Trevira CS voile, painter's linen, paint. Restaurant floor: poured polyurethane in three colours: pink (salmon), light-yellow (mayonnaise) and grey (concrete). Acoustic walls in the auditoriums: blue leatherette with foam filling and large buttons; soft-yellow glass wool, covered with transparent, corrugated plastic panels. Upholstery of seating in three auditoriums: a) woven wool cloth in five colours, b) dark-green perforated leatherette, c) salmon-coloured knitted stretch fabric.

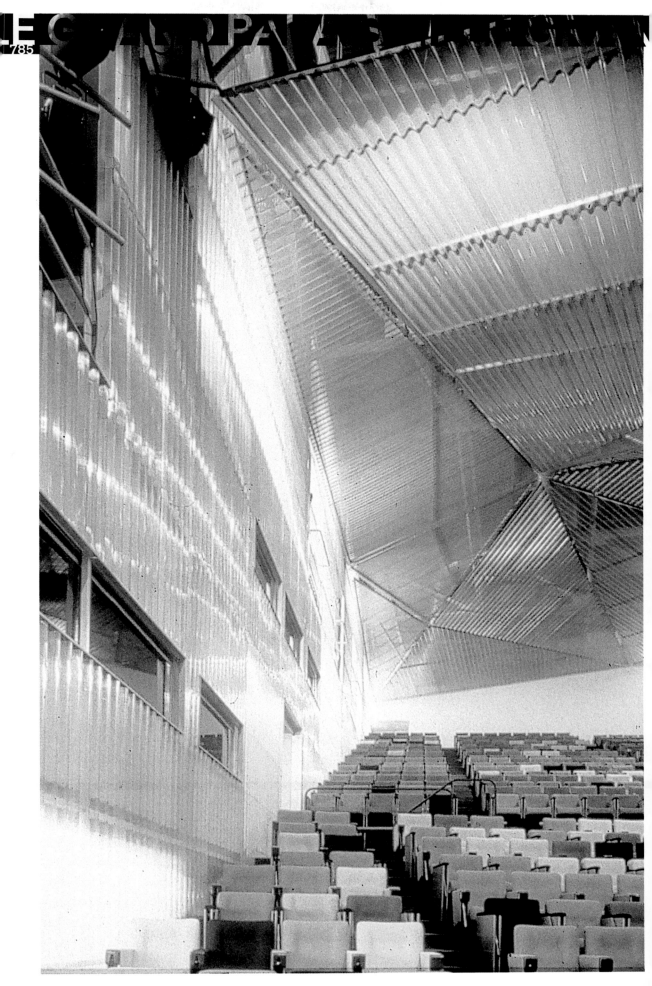

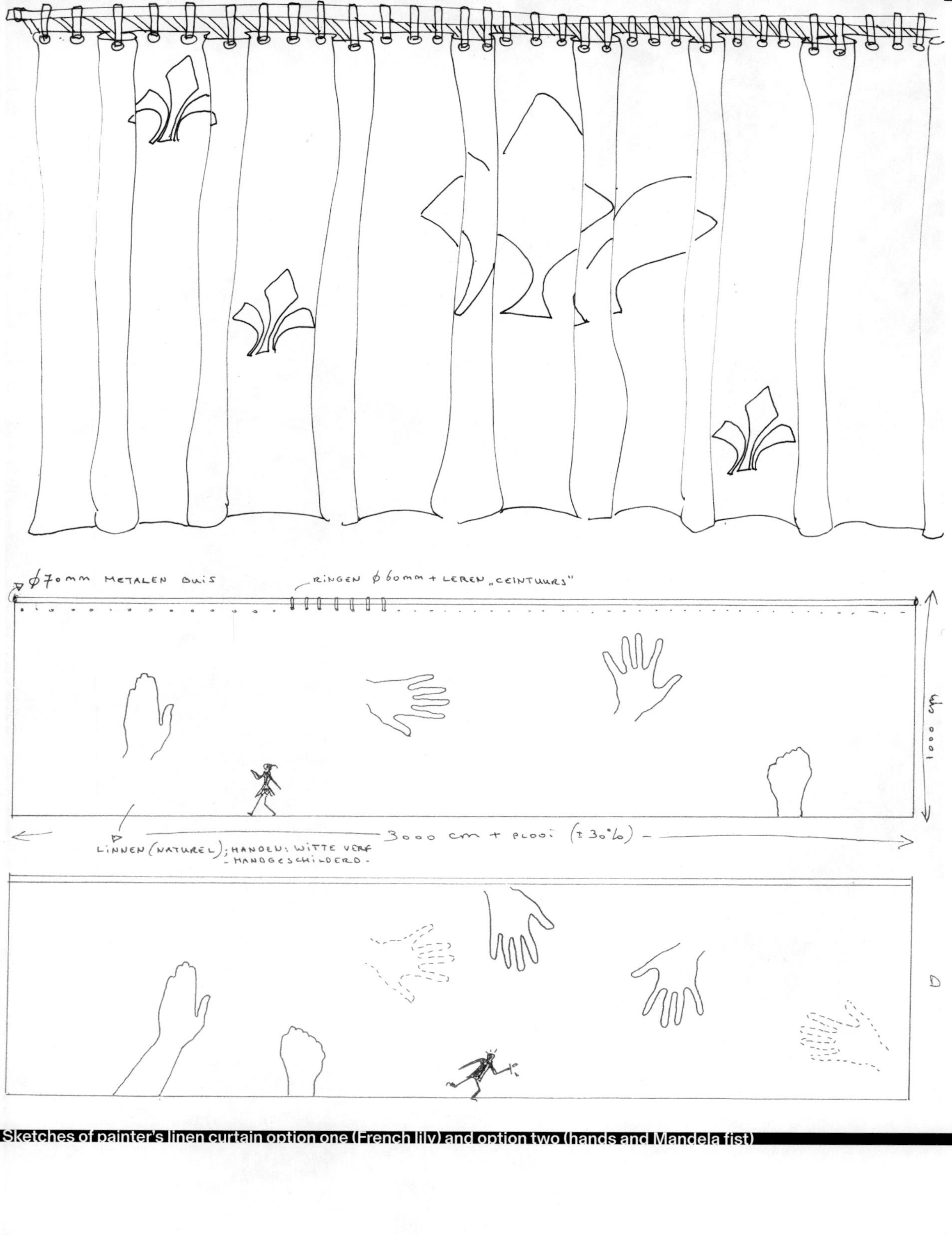
Ø70mm METALEN BUIS
RINGEN Ø60mm + LEREN „CEINTUURS"
1000 cm
3000 cm + PLOOI (± 30%)
LINNEN (NATUREL); HANDEN: WITTE VERF
- HANDGESCHILDERD -

Sketches of painter's linen curtain option one (French lily) and option two (hands and Mandela fist)

Installation of linen curtain, hiding the temporary wall

Linen curtain installed

Ah! This enormous drape, made of painter's linen and hand-painted with (my) pushing hands, covers the unauthorised wall placed overnight by the just-appointed tenant of the exhibition hall inside the Conference Centre. The drape was a last-minute move as well, meant to be a temporary coverage of a case pending.

BANDES TRANSPARENTES (VOILE NOIR)

RIDEAUX D'AVANT-SCÈNE

(VELOURS LILAS)

MUR BÉTON + CAPITONNAGE (BLEU)

200

136   136

200

BOUTON (BOIS + FAUX-CUIR, ⌀ 75 mm)
VISÉ

FAUX-CUIR (POREUX : SON)

LAINE DE VERRE (2 COUCHES)

ÉPAISSEUR ± 15 cm

BOIS

S ALLE C 2

— CAPITONNAGE → SUR MUR INCLINÉ.

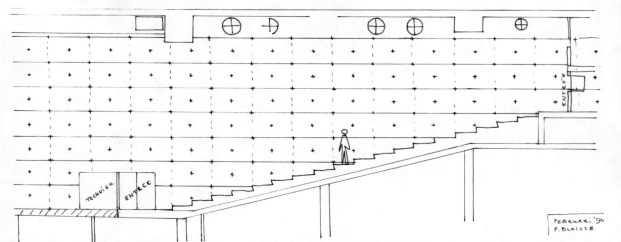

FEBRUARI '94
P. BLAISSE

Curtain (in movement) connects with wall

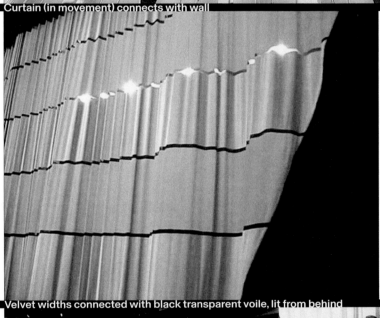

Velvet widths connected with black transparent voile, lit from behind

All ingredients together: blue cushioned wall, salmon-covered chairs, pale-pink back of curtain... so ugly :-)!!

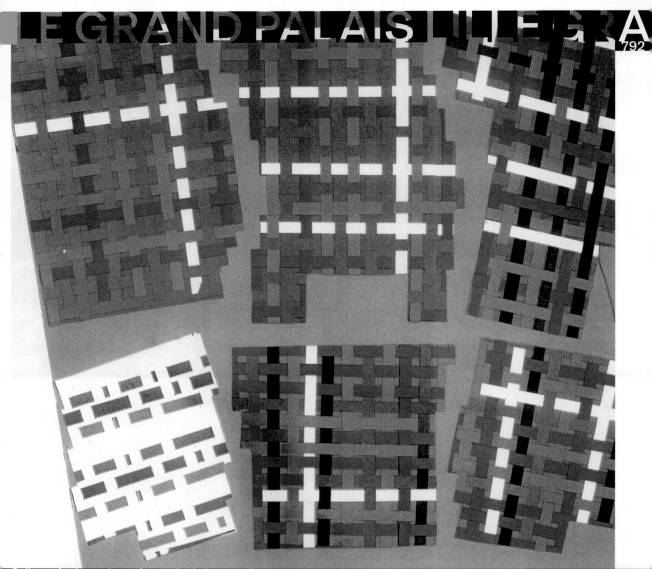

Collage of colour scheme for seating in large auditorium

Large auditorium seating viewed from stage

Detail of restaurant floor

Polyurethane restaurant floor connecting to wooden terrace floor

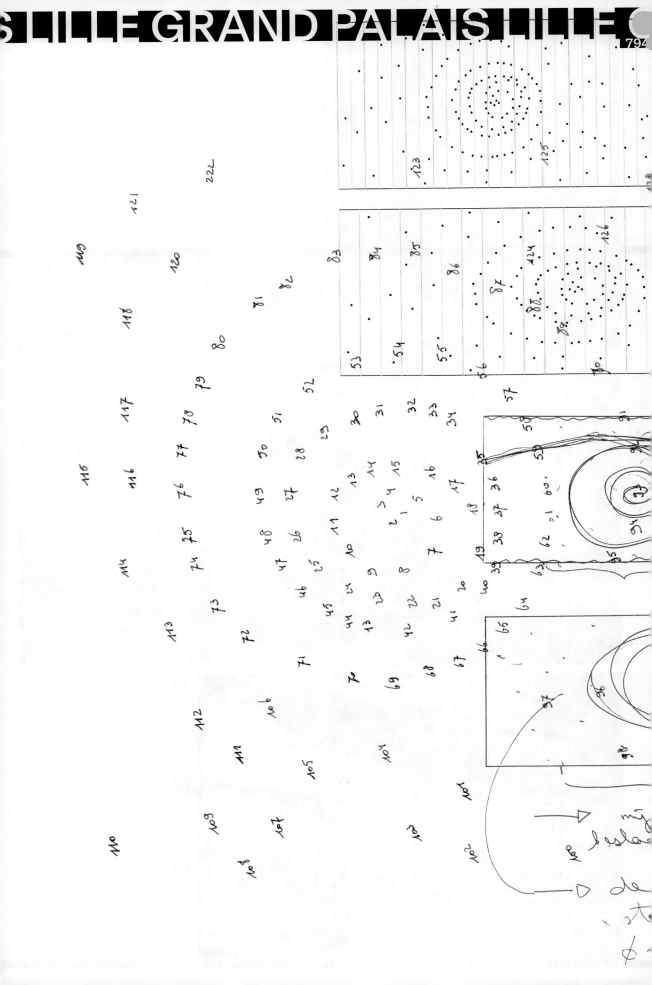

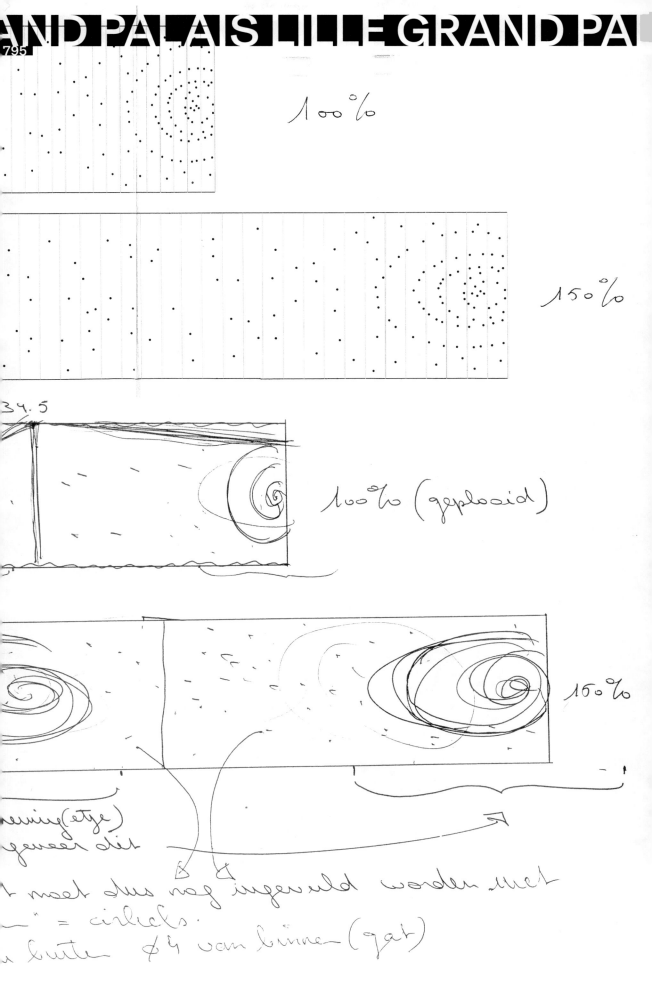

100%

150%

34.5

100% (geplooid)

150%

...ning(etje)
...ganeer dit

...t moet dus nog ingevuld worden met
...° = cirkels.
...buiten & van binnen (gat)

I invited a French photographer to take pictures of our curtains at the Grand Palais, soon after the opening. Here (and in the small auditorium), I asked him to leave the lens open so that the movement and speed of the stage curtain would be made visible – or tangible if you will. Two things differ from a classic stage curtain here: it moves sideways and disappears to one side (to the right), and it has separate colours on each side of the slit off the middle: the left plane is light grey, connecting to the light-yellow wall to its left; the right plane is dark purple and connects to the bluish wall to its right. The chairs of the theatre represent the world's continents, each continent its own earth-colour.

"Initially my job was to translate French into Dutch so that Yves could communicate with the environment department at the City of Rotterdam, but I ended up helping with the design, notably the stone river with glass chunks, the 'flying' bridge and the 'entrance room,' a white apple orchard with a mirroring wall. Later, I represented Yves during the realisation of the park when he fell ill."

"We started with rounded 'stones' of transparent glass made by glassblowers – gorgeous but too costly… and too perfect. Then I found out that glass ovens in various European countries are dismantled every ten years or so, leaving behind thick glass crusts and piles of irregular glass chunks. We were able to order a few tonnes of these rocks, transparent blue, beautiful, like glacial ice, frozen water. Perfect to represent the tribute to the former river that Yves had envisioned. The glass rocks caught every ray of light and turned the river of stones into a twinkling stream, like in a fairy tale."

"Together with the construction guys and wearing thick leather gloves, we glued each glass chunk to the layer of white boulders that formed the 'frozen' river's base. After a few months, all of the glass rocks had miraculously disappeared – later resurfacing in art pieces and on architects' desks."

"The blue-glazed bricks that form the main path and the square around the Kunsthal were acquired from a previous Dutch Floriade [an international horticultural exhibition, ed.]. They are made of mud from the river Thames and their multi-hued blue glaze gives them a lively, watery look. We later found out that mud from the river Thames is polluted, so the bricks were taken out of production. The Museumpark might be one of the last places where these beautiful, blue-glazed bricks can be enjoyed under foot."

"Eventually I was able to realise the seating islands that connect to the 'romantic path' of the Romantic Garden at regular intervals. They are made of two concrete plates, poured into a wooden mould into which colourful, glazed tiles – each with bevelled, serrated edges for grip – were glued in a playful pattern. When dry, the slabs were turned, the tiles cleaned, resulting in festive seating islands – each one with its own colour to make appointments more practical: "I'll see you at the yellow island." A small half-moon is cut out along the middle edge of both slabs, forming a hole for the centrally placed streetlamp (Friso Kramer). Two white concrete benches (Spanish-made) and a garbage bin (Bas Pruijser) were added later."   PB

LOCATION	Rotterdam, the Netherlands
CLIENT	Municipality of Rotterdam
STATUS	Completed
SCOPE	Assisting landscape architect Yves Brunier during the design of a public park as "living art piece"
SCALE	4 ha
COLLABORATORS	Yves Brunier, OMA/Rem Koolhaas, Fuminori Hoshino, Chris van Duijn; Ank van Peski
DESCRIPTION	This narrow, linear park (100 × 400 m), designed by Yves Brunier in the late '80s, was conceived as a sequence of "rooms," each with their own character. Yves worked from the OMA office, under the loving eyes of Rem Koolhaas, who had invited him. Rem and Yves called the park a "building on its side": four rooms in all, each one totally different from the next. First space, a white "entrance lobby" opposite the Dutch Architecture Institute (now The New Institute), is followed by an elevated "theatre plaza" of black asphalt with white graphics. This very urban podium is then followed by the romantic room, the "garden-by-numbers," with a flying bridge inlaid with glass "eyes," from which the garden can be viewed at a distance – like looking at a painting. The flying bridge lands on the blue-glazed "water square" that vanishes, to one side, under the Kunsthal building. The square serves as the terrace of the Kunsthal restaurant and connects the building to the adjacent Natural History Museum.

Sketches for romantic garden (top), art podium (middle) and apple orchard (bottom)

Footbridge in the making

Blue-glazed bricks for central path and plaza

Apple orchard with white shell ground cover and mirroring wall, just after installation

Noise Dress and Flower Field
Kunsthal Rotterdam

"To stand there on the steel roof structure in the blazing summer sun while the concrete for the Kunsthal roof was about to be poured; to help the builders bind the spiralling curtain track onto the rebar just in time for it to be poured over with fresh cement, disappearing completely inside the concrete ceiling... this was truly a historic moment."

"It was an adventure to find very old 'vintage' pear trees and to create the witch-like profiles that I envisioned for this place. The idea was that their naked winter profiles and their stark shapes would be visible through the translucent wall that aligns the garden along one side. The trees thrived and produced so many stewing pears that the whole Kunsthal staff could enjoy them through the winter. What a joy when a duck laid eggs and hatched seven ducklings in the thick ivy-bed. But tragically, the chicks had nowhere to go... We picked the whole family up and brought them down to the park below. Happy ending!"

"Discussing possibilities for the given site and circumstances with bulb growers and tree specialists, deciding about amounts and pricing: it's always a pleasure to learn from dedicated professionals, but it's also time-consuming because gardeners' stories flow like rivers!"   PB

LOCATION	Rotterdam, the Netherlands
CLIENT	Municipality of Rotterdam
STATUS	Completed
SCOPE	Advisory on interior finishes and furniture, auditorium curtain, restaurant sofa, design and implementation of sloping roof garden
MATERIALS	Glass-fibre and black-cotton velvet curtain, speakers, wood boards, electrical cords, plug; "flower field" of colourful stacking chairs for the auditorium; grey Bolidt polyurethane for the floor of the large exhibition space; ivy carpet on roof garden with seven pear trees and 6200 bulbs
SCALE	Curtain, ca. 240 m²; roof garden, 500 m²
COLLABORATORS	OMA, James Rubery, Mostert De Winter, Hans Werlemann/Hectic Pictures, Theatex
DESCRIPTION	Spiral track embedded in concrete roof/ceiling. Double-layered, sound-absorbing, darkening curtain to form a rounded auditorium when unfolded. Stored, it becomes an inclined column/an evening dress. The curtain has integrated speakers spread over its surface that transmit the high sounds, while the stepped seating area has integrated speakers for the lower tones (with James Rubery). The multicoloured auditorium chairs we chose represent a field of flowers; a continuation of Museumpark. On the sloping roof garden, concrete compartments prevent the soil from sliding down. Seven ancient pear trees, with their weird irregular shapes, stand on a carpet of ivy. 6200 bulbs of varied types introduce seasonal change and colour effects from spring through winter.

The snail-shaped track that organises the storage of the curtain with the fire alarm, installed at the last minute, in its centre; to the left you vaguely see the indentation where the switch is positioned to let the curtain go straight to the back wall

Emergency exit at top level of curtain

The "flower field" of chairs enveloped by the curtain. Here you can see little dots on the silver glass fibre surface: these are the speakers that transmit high tones. The lower-tone speakers are integrated in the risers of the stairs.

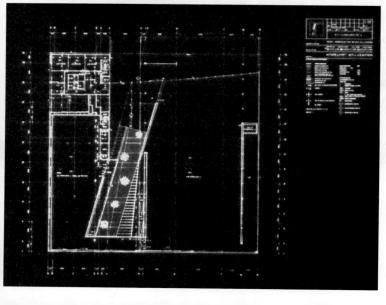

We designed this sofa in combination with Günther Förg's ceiling-light installation

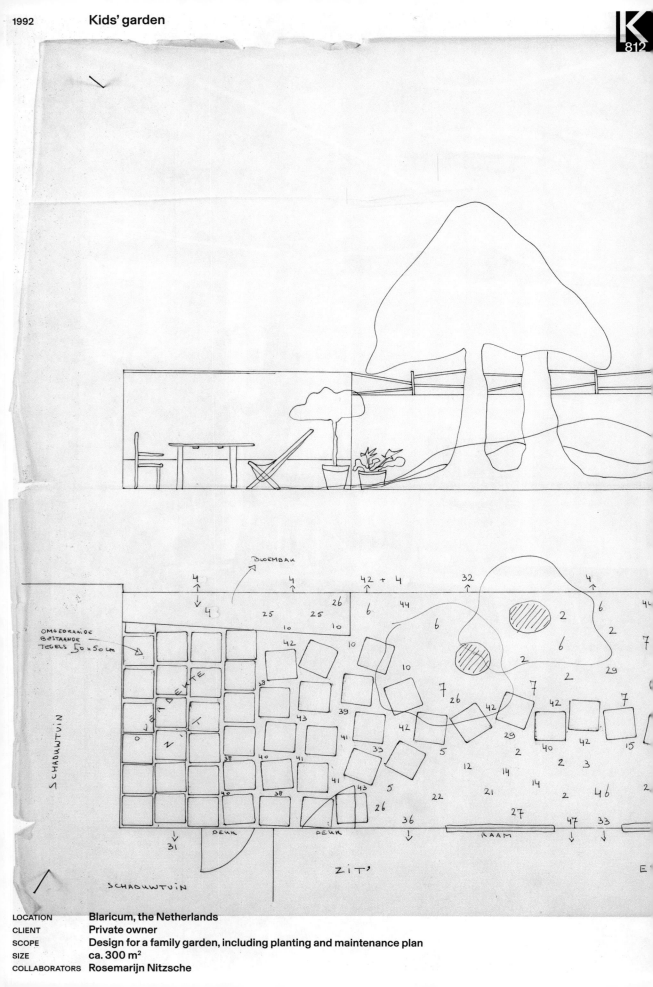

LOCATION   **Blaricum, the Netherlands**
CLIENT   **Private owner**
SCOPE   **Design for a family garden, including planting and maintenance plan**
SIZE   **ca. 300 m²**
COLLABORATORS   **Rosemarijn Nitzsche**

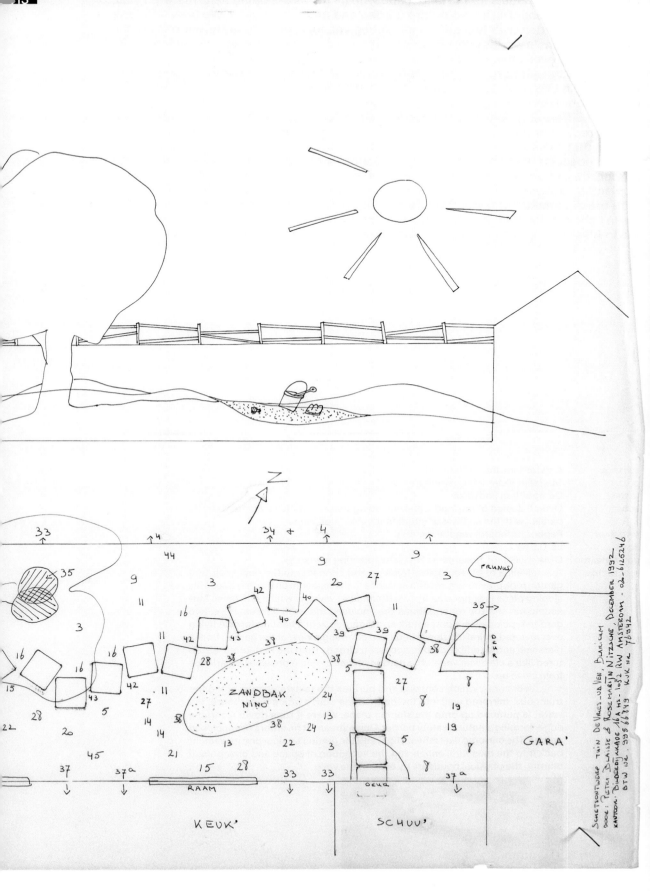

Multiple Choice
Two Gardens for the Stedelijk Extension

"We made study models for the landscape with its upward-sloping field, mirrored wall, circular flow channel, lifted sculpture garden and museum facade. We then filled the future inner garden with two different planting versions: one romantic and one edible. We collaged whole worlds with pieces of magazine clippings, fantasising about the most stunning and ever-changing plant compositions, considering edible versus aesthetic. Leafing through piles of plant encyclopaedias and drawing on our own experiences from the estate in Olst, the Museumpark and private gardens, we came up with numerous concepts: ornamental grass gardens, perennial gardens, trimmed shrub gardens, all in swirls of different greens and various leaf structures; and, for the second typology, a chequered vegetable garden with ancient apple-tree varieties in linear formation and colours that change with the seasons. For the competition presentation we made a separate landscape booklet with a lyrical, explanatory text about the two versions of the garden, their characteristics and potential, with colourful collages, pictures of the model, planting drawings and precise plant lists. It was to be presented to the jury in parallel with the documents of the architects, but unfortunately that didn't happen. Our team wasn't chosen. Too bad! We came in after Venturi, Rauch and Scott Brown, who lost the job to Álvaro Siza, who lost the job to Benthem en Crouwel. Hence, the bathtub." PB

LOCATION	Amsterdam, the Netherlands
CLIENT	Stedelijk Museum Amsterdam
STATUS	Competition 2nd prize
SCOPE	Overall design of the landscape, including two alternative inner gardens (in parallel with the architects' interchangeable floor plans)
MATERIALS	Paper, cardboard, vegetal material
SCALE	ca. 0.5 ha
COLLABORATORS	OMA (building), Rosemarijn Nitzsche (planting advisory)
DESCRIPTION	A small slice of Museumplein folds up and connects to the new sculpture garden roof, providing a second entrance to the museum on the 2nd floor. This sloping plane is supported by two (triangular) walls, of which one faces Museumplein and the other defines the enclosed museum garden. Here, two garden typologies are presented: an art garden with a floating terrace flying over lowered, spiralling flowerbeds and affording a view of the garden from a distance; and an edible garden accessed directly from the restaurant, structured like a classical vegetable garden and affording a physical experience from close up.

A channel, which contains and purifies the rainwater, runs along the triangular, mirrored wall into the patio of the staff's office wing. There, the water is pumped up onto the sloping plane, where it runs down along the edge, forming a natural safety barrier. Downstream, it re-enters the enclosed garden. The mirrored wall reflects light and the garden's colour and movement back into the museum, enhancing the sensation of space and change and blurring the physical boundary by erasing the wall.

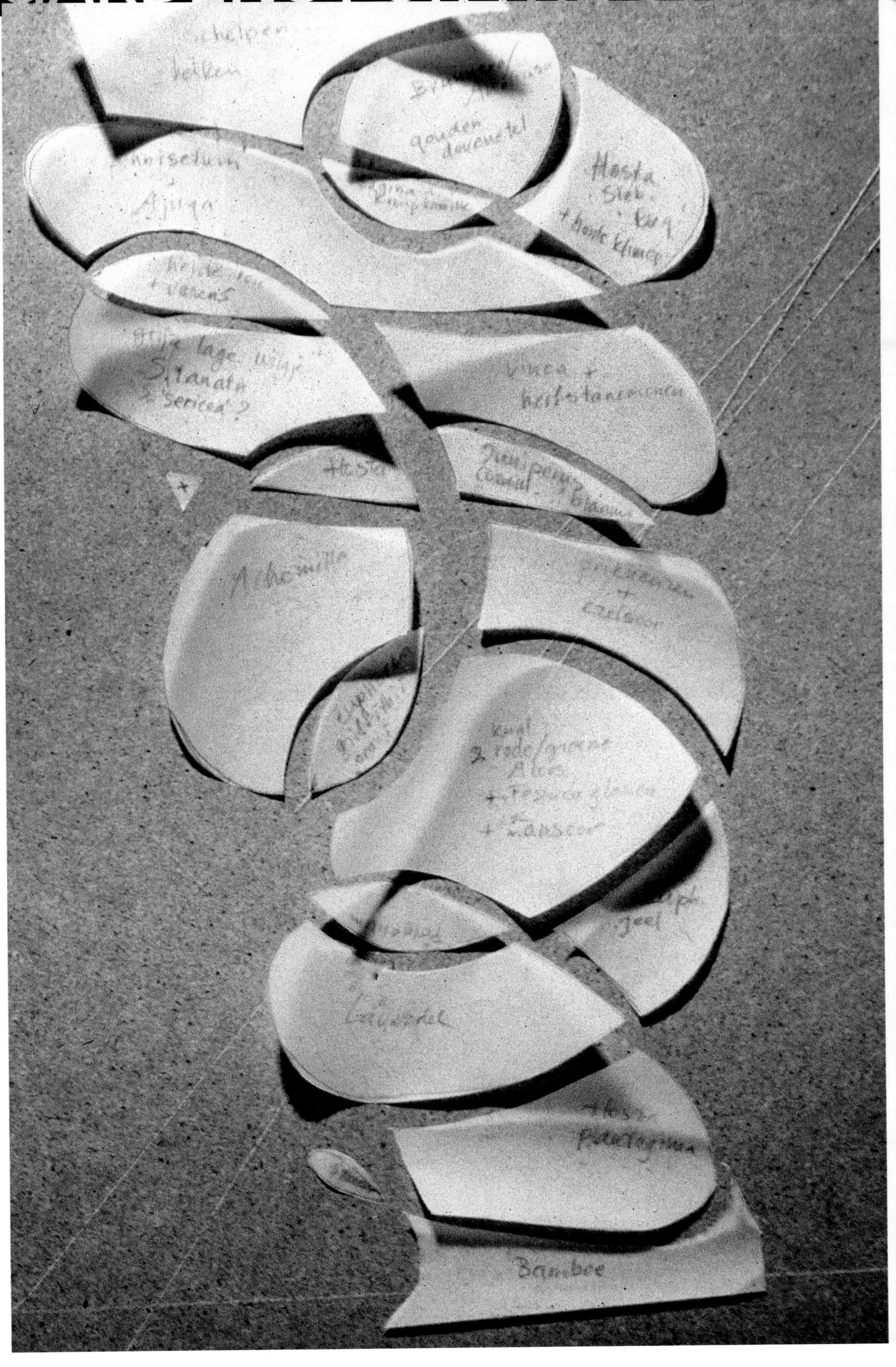
Ajuga
gouden dovenetel
Hosta
Alchemilla
Bamboe

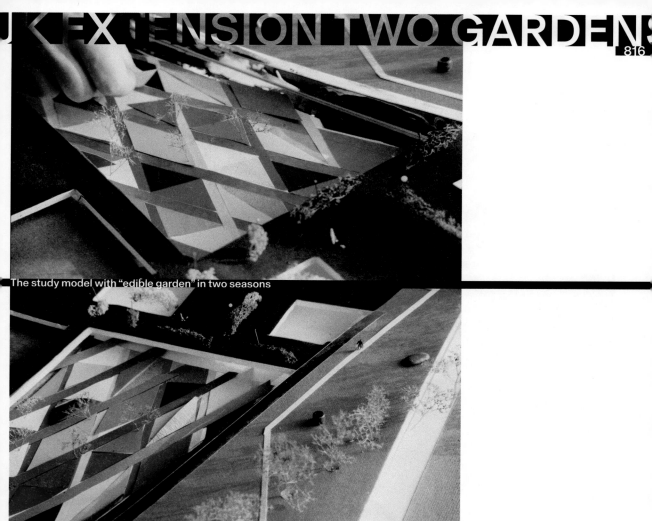

The study model with "edible garden" in two seasons

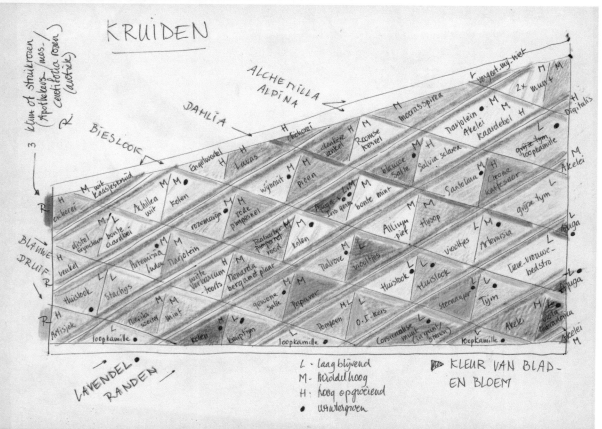

Rosemarijn Nitzsche's planting plans

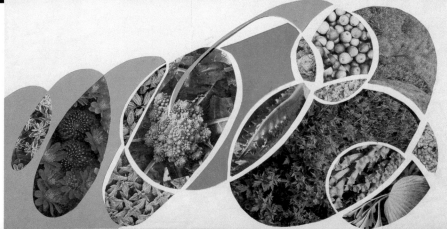

"Art garden" summer collage

"Art garden" autumn collage in the making

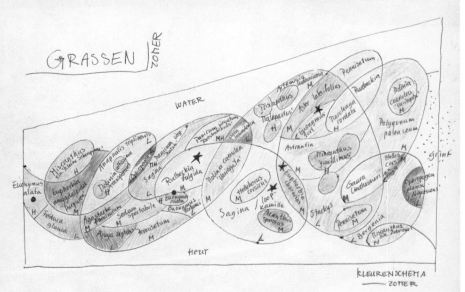

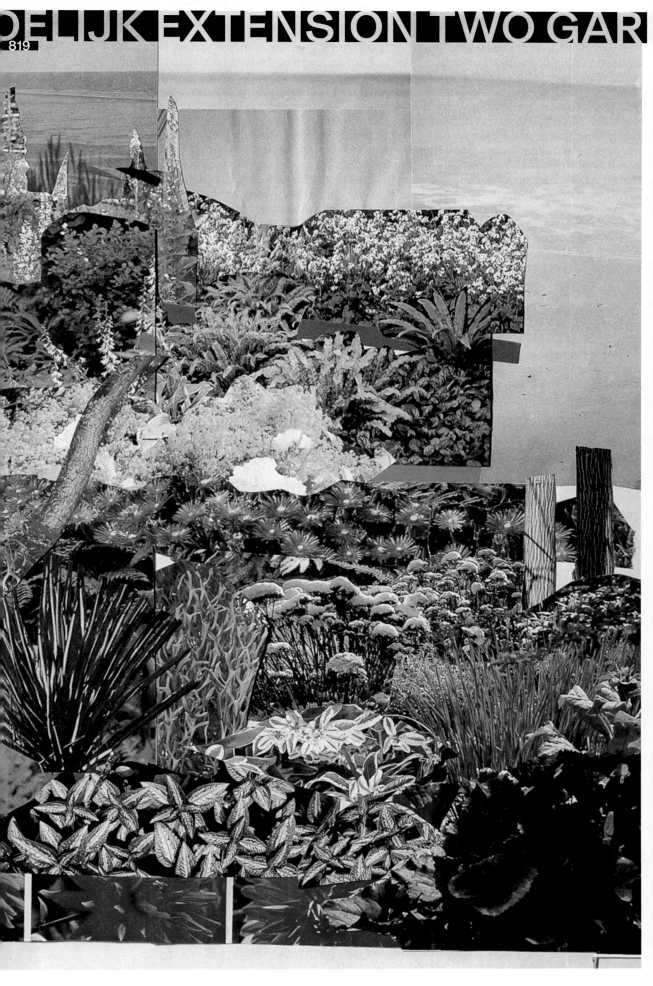

Private Estate De Putter

"It turned out that the lady who taught me 'everything' about gardening, Lily ter Kuile, believed in the philosophy of Rudolf Steiner. For two and a half years, I drove to her in my red VW Polo and stayed there for two to three days a week to work. We ate organic food, drank pure fruit juices and herbal teas and gardened according to the phases of the moon. We healed wounds and colds with chamomile tea, we checked our bodies for ticks every evening. The day started at half-past six and ended when darkness fell. I often slept in Lily's workspace, a wooden wagon on wheels with a biological toilet. I lay between her hand-dyed woollen yarns from which she knitted pastel cardigans, looking through the window at the forest outside, listening to the sound of wind, rain and birds and taking in the smell of moist ground. During the night, I heard each and every sound of the forest. I loved sleeping in that place. In the evenings, the gardening team (landscape architect Rosemarie Nitzsche and I) joined the owners inside the old pine grower's bungalow to eat and read garden books until we went to sleep, around 9.30 pm, dead tired and content. With the advent of the mobile phone, I have gotten used to working on exhibition and architectural projects under stress and often day and night. These garden days were the epitome of rest and contemplation."

"Lily was a master of painting Easter eggs in batik style with a modern version of the *canting* – a type of pen through which melted wax flows. You can make detailed drawings on the egg with this tool. First you have to make two holes in the egg: one at the top, one at the bottom. Then you blow out the raw egg (and use it to make scrambled eggs). You now have a hollow eggshell, light and beautiful, ready to paint. As you know, the batik method goes in layers and steps. After each drawing, you dip the egg in a dye bath, and after it dries, you dip it in hot water so that the wax melts off. Your first drawing appears. Then you draw again over this base. It's all about thinking backwards."

"The more I learnt, the more appreciation I received. In the end, I even got paid for my travel expenses and the work I did. I was proud. Sometimes we were treated to a study trip. We visited specialised nurseries all over the Netherlands, and once took a trip to England, by boat – Lily, Rosemarijn and I – driving around on the left side in a rented car, staying in typical English countryside bed and breakfasts with nylon duvets covered in flowery cloth, tea and toast in the morning, cottage pie in the evening. What amazing gardens and nurseries we saw! Lily was obsessed with ivy at the time, every section of her forest needed to be covered in a carpet of a different species: *Hedera nepalensis*, *Hedera hibernica*, *Hedera helix* 'Glacier,' *Hedera helix* 'Jake,' *Hedera helix* 'Ivalace' or 'Parsley Crested' (punctuated with *Hellebores*, *Digitalises* and groups of *Narcissi*). Along the edges of the forest, we had planted mixed shrubs, interlaced with ramparts made of sawed-off branches and twigs, upon which we wanted to plant climbing plants – a mixture of everything: roses, honeysuckle, clematis and so on. So, we looked for special varieties of those as well." PB

LOCATION	Olst, the Netherlands
CLIENT	Private owner
STATUS	Completed
SCOPE	Gardening education, including ground preparation; clearing and general layout of land; creation of nursery; soil, plant and root basics; botanical names; planting techniques; tool care; moon calendar
SCALE	ca. 2.5 ha
COLLABORATORS	Lily Terkuile; Rosemarijn Nitzsche, farmer De Jong and son
DESCRIPTION	A former pine tree nursery of approximately two hectares, neglected for many years by its ninety-year-old owner, was bought by an elderly couple from The Hague to be transformed into a private estate with a family home. The land lies low behind a dike that runs parallel to the large IJssel River. A creek defines the estate's eastern border. A tiny yellow-brick house stands by the creek, encircled by pine trees. The new owners lived there temporarily until the site of their "real" home was defined and could be designed and built by their son-in-law.

One part of the estate was devoted to edible plants: it had a vegetable and an herb garden, laid out in a classical manner. In the back you see our hand-made henhouse and ceramic chimes made by Lily, my gardening mentor.

OMA – Barcelona
Collegi d'Arquitectes de Catalunya

"We stayed in Barcelona for a few weeks to install the exhibit. The Collegi had a nice team assisting us with everything including finding tools and materials at the last minute to achieve the effects we wanted. I remember driving through Barcelona on the back of a scooter, the guy skilfully manoeuvring through tiny alleys and heavy traffic, efficiently zigzagging through town to find each address. A great way to experience a city!"

"Claudi made one of his sound machines, an elegant little structure with a flat, round, steel plate on which a few steel bullets of various sizes rolled in circles along a circular notch. Underneath the round plate, a perpetually turning steel 'finger' lifted the plate from one point to the next, making the bullets roll and roll in circles. The sound of these rolling bullets was picked up by tiny microphones that transmitted the sound through speakers placed all over the space. A mechanical ROAR filled the place, influencing the atmosphere of the gallery and the works. The object itself was placed in the window and backlit by daylight; it was beautifully fragile in the sunlight, yet simultaneously as monumental as the Catedral de la Santa Creu that formed its backdrop." PB

LOCATION	Barcelona, Spain
CLIENT	Collegi d'Arquitectes de Catalunya
STATUS	Completed
SCOPE	Exhibition and lighting design, installation
MATERIALS	Various
SCALE	ca. 250 m^2
COLLABORATORS	OMA, Groszstadt/Donald van Dansik, Parthesius and de Rijk, Ron Steiner, Herman Helle, Hans Werlemann/Hectic Pictures, Claudi Cornaz, Jos Stoopman
DESCRIPTION	Exhibition, lighting design and installation: we opened up the high windows onto the shopping street, covered the open office spaces with white cloth and closed off the sunken exhibition space from the entrance hall with a temporary, monumental, ceiling-high red wall with a narrow opening. In that way, we created an intriguing gallery space that lies almost hidden to the inside, but totally visible to the outside world. By connecting the gallery floor to the lower edge of the windows on street-level with a sloping plane, we created a "landscape" as base for OMA's "exploded" urban plan models. In this way we established a direct connection between the gallery and the Barcelona street life.
	A large-scale introductory collage was wallpapered to one of the walls; flag-like paper panels of text hung softly down from another. City plans were loosely laid out on the sloping surface and studied with great interest by passers-by. Models placed on high pedestals could be viewed at eye level. A huge construction lamp mounted on the wooden fence of the adjacent building site lit up the entire exhibit from across the street. At night, its miraculous light beam cast exciting urban shadows, a "holy announcement" of the exhibition inside.

The temporary wall we made to create an entrance

Urban plan of Lille, with exploded Congrexpo building, positioned on the sloping plane we created to connect the exhibit to life on the streets

The sound instrument by Claudi Cornasz with the cathedral as backdrop

Rem and I checking the final details

The exhibit lit with one single wide-angle building lamp, placed outside on the adjacent construction fence

1988–1991   **Typical Home**
Nexus World Housing

"When we arrived in Fukuoka on a cold April day, we noticed that the building site was extremely clean and organised. The trucks had to drive through a wide pond to clean their wheels before entering or exiting the site, and all workers wore white gloves. So did we. Inside, all the furniture we had selected had arrived, waiting for us in opened crates. The curtains were there too, each one made to perfection. Used to rolling up my sleeves, I got ready to hang up curtains and unpack furniture. But no way: I was politely requested to only give instructions. When I wanted to make a change to my design of the entrance patio (I no longer liked my own idea for the sculpture and wanted to replace it with another object that I had prepared), the contractor took out my drawing and sternly remarked that the works had been delivered as specified and that nothing was to be changed – the fact that I was the 'artist' didn't matter."   PB

LOCATION	Fukuoka, Japan
CLIENT	Fukuoka Jisho
STATUS	Completed
SCOPE	Interior finishes and furnishing for "typical home," curtains for living room and bedrooms, patio and green roof design for the OMA housing complex
MATERIALS	Living-room curtains in dark-blue velvet, lined with silk; bedroom curtains, natural rough silk (hues of beige); patios with bamboo bench, loose white pebbles and white pebble tiles (path accessing the entrance hall), sculpture, bamboo; roofs with a grass-covered hill; furniture and lighting, from Dutch antique (chairs, chandelier) to European and Japanese modern
SCALE	Living-room curtains, ca. 35 m^2; bedroom 1, 12.5 m^2; bedroom 2, 8.75 m^2; roof gardens, 18 m^2 each; patio gardens, 20 m^2 each
COLLABORATORS	OMA, Keiko Hoshino, Fred Bosschaert, local seamstresses
DESCRIPTION	Working with Kyoko Ohashi from the OMA office, we advised on all interior materials and selected the furniture from the catalogues that we received from the commissioner, in fact several crates full, each with a different theme: antique Japanese / modern Japanese / modern Western. We added some Dutch antiques for welcome contrast. I designed very classical curtains, sent the textiles to the Fukuoka-based seamstresses with instructions in the form of recipe drawings. We had antique Dutch chairs purchased, restored, upholstered and then shipped. We also delivered designs for patio gardens and green roofs.

"This was my first involvement with a private villa – a different scale and level of intima-cy after working on the interiors of the Nederlands Dans Theater, so the project was full of surprises. It was great fun choosing vintage textiles and furniture to counter the mod-ern, Tati-like architecture with its technical tricks and contradictions (e.g., a swimming pool on a glass base) and new materials (e.g., a corrugated plastic kitchen wall). I softened daughter Laure's concrete bedroom by adding the aqua chintz curtains with lively birds and flowers to cover the entire glazed front facade, sewing the widths together random-ly to give it a little alienating effect. The iridescent silk curtain encircles the seating area to create an independent, intimate room within the very modern living space – an expect-ed intervention, of course, but very effective. What comes as a surprise, though, is what happens when the glass facades, forming one corner of the house, are slid open and the curtain billows out into the garden and starts dancing over the bright green lawn. This in-and-out movement, the fluttering and billowing in the wind made all the difference to me: natural conditions that influence the behaviour and therefore add character to a piece of cloth – a well-behaved curtain suddenly comes to life. The choreography of a theatre curtain is controlled by a motorised system, but here the curtain is brought to life by air. A 'living' presence, changing its environment with every move, every change of light, every shift in weather. That is the key."

"We all worked closely with the owners, and for the furnishings Koolhaas and I actually went shopping with them in Paris, choosing funny red armchairs in second-hand shops and looking for fabrics in a few typical chic Parisian fabric boutiques, where classic tex-tile designs and high-quality silks were sold. No doubt as an ode to Mies and Reich, Koolhaas chose an iridescent soft (pinkish-)yellow silk for the living room, whereas I fell for a chintz cotton in aqua green with an exuberant seventeenth-century print of bright-coloured flowers and birds."   PB

LOCATION	Saint-Cloud, Paris, France
CLIENT	Private owner
STATUS	Completed
SCOPE	Interior finishes and furnishing advisory, curtains for living room and bed-rooms, photoshoot production Hectic Pictures
MATERIALS	Yellow-pink changeant silk, chintz cotton with exotic bird and plant design, (re-make of French eighteenth-century design), blue-grey dupioni silk with eggplant-purple satin lining, vintage furniture and light elements
SCALE	Interior and curtains, 1,350 m²
COLLABORATORS	OMA, Maarten van Severen, Yves Brunier, Hans Werlemann/Hectic Pictures, Marc Mimram, Loic Richalet, Robert Coulon
DESCRIPTION	Finishing materials for the floors and the shading screens along the glass facade and general advisory on the colour scope for the house, including those for the curtains of the master bedroom, daughter's bedroom and living room. Sketched a concept for the "style" of furniture to be found. Designed the small green plant carpet on the roof, next to the pool that overlooks the Bois de Boulogne and the Eiffel Tower – with orange safety net.

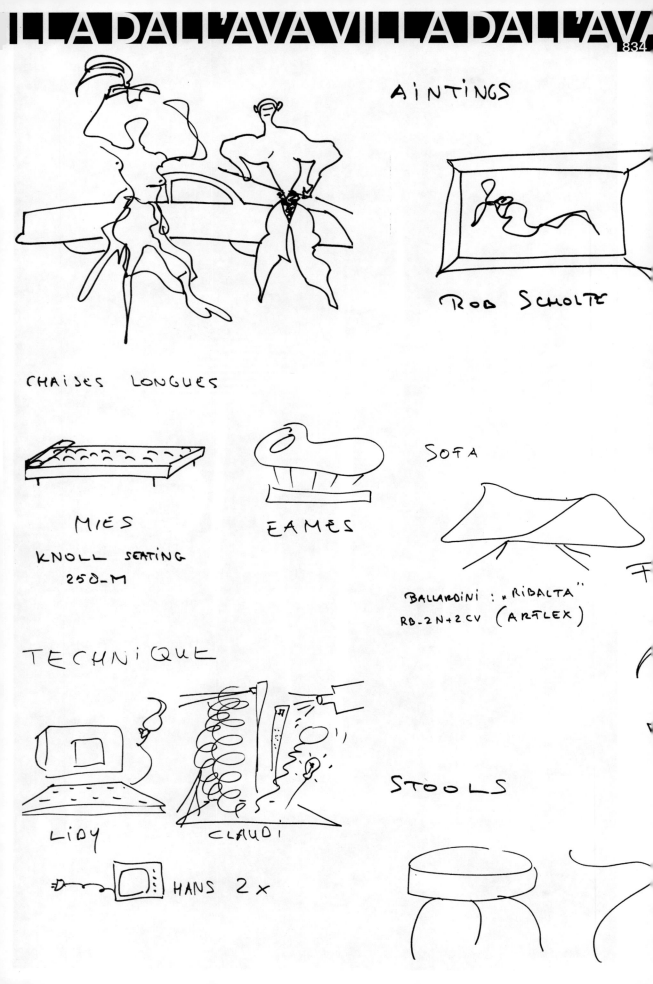

AINTINGS

ROB SCHOLTE

CHAISES LONGUES

MIES

KNOLL SEATING
250-M

EAMES

SOFA

BALLARDINI : "RIBALTA"
RB-2N+2CV (ARTFLEX)

TECHNIQUE

LIDY

CLAUDI

HANS 2x

STOOLS

GARDEN TOOLS

FONTANA

CHEN TOOLS ?

LAMPS

(FONTANA ARTE)
CASA LUCE
A i c
I A _ 2 2 2

STARCK : „LuciFair"
(FLOS)
150 w.
30 × 14 × 24 cm

LAMPADAIRE 3 LUMIÈRE
STEEL BLACK

SERGE MOUILLE
(IDÉE) FORME

JEKS

ANIMALS

GIRAFFE   BOA   WOOLF

PROJECTION

→ CAPI

VIDEO BEAM

TIME BASE CORRECTOR

FILM (CNN) → CLAUDI
HANS

Daughter Laure in her bedroom

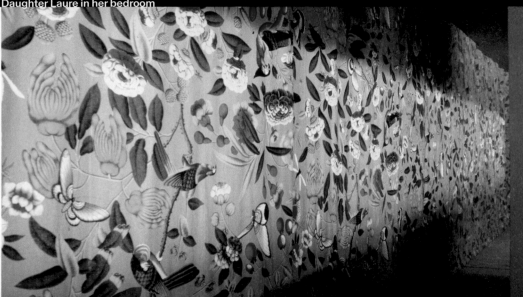

The eighteenth-century print on cotton chintz, sewn together with unmatching seams

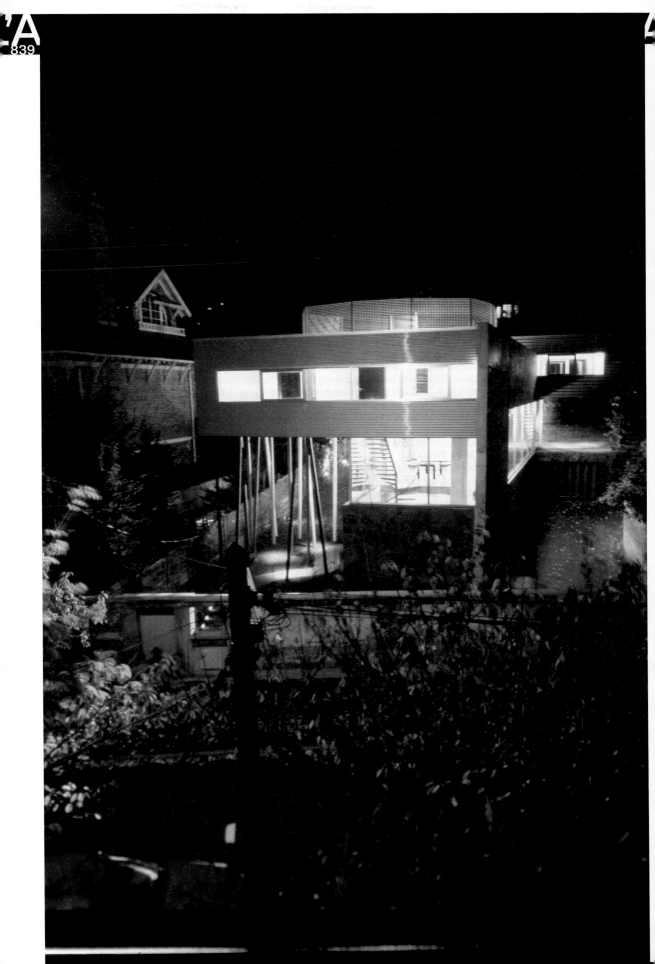

Evening view of front of house, with orange safety net around roof garden

OMA Fin de Siècle
L'Institut Français d'Architecture (IFA)

840

"This is the first installation that included my so-called girl's room collage in which the sources of inspiration for Koolhaas and the OMA team are represented by black-and-white photocopies of keywords, quotes, poems and images, all of which are wallpapered onsite. Artists, film directors and actors, porn stars, poets, writers, politicians, philosophers, scientists, architects, sports heroes, fashion models, cooks and amazing housewives… everyone and everything that meant anything to the architects – their work, their interests, their frames of mind, their sense of humour – was to be represented in an artistic and anarchistic way. That was the goal. The more serious work came with the choice of 'keywords' that were scattered over the collage – and that later would reappear in the *SMLXL* book by Rem and Bruce. This 'word' research was conducted in collaboration with Jennifer Sigler."   PB

LOCATION	Paris, France
CLIENT	L'Institut Français d'Architecture (IFA) – Patrice Goulet, Luciana Ravanel
STATUS	Completed
SCOPE	Exhibition design and installation
MATERIALS	Various
COLLABORATORS	OMA, Hans Werlemann/Hectic Pictures, Jennifer Sigler; Herman Helle, Parthesius & de Rijk, Chiel van Stelt, Het Paleis van Boem, Hard Werken
DESCRIPTION	Rooms of different sizes and shapes meander through this old Parisian building.

Entrance room: black-and-white chequered floor with a composition of thin, tilted iron columns, mimicking the Villa dall'Ava, then in construction. On two walls the "girl's room" collage: black-and-white images and quotes of everything that inspired OMA/Rem Koolhaas at the time, from art to porn, from literature to food to politics. The keywords that we added were later used as the basis for the book *SMLXL*.

Second room/workspace: brightly lit work room, showing the process of debating and designing the Euralille/Lille Grand Palais project.

Third room/horizontal projects: a very small darkened room exhibiting vertical models of the urban plan (Parc de la Villette, Melun-Senart). Blacklight illuminates the texts. A small lamp slowly moves from east to west over a steel cable, mimicking the sun and casting shadows over the models. Sounds of a passing train, a tennis match creates the illusion of boundless space.

Fourth room/vertical projects: a narrow, long room under the roof turned into an exaggeratedly narrow "corridor" by adding one wallpapered wall with information and one wall with enlarged photographs of the "lost" projects: City Hall, The Hague; Sea Terminal, Zeebrugge; National Library of France, Paris; and Media Centre, Karlsruhe. The black-wallpapered wall shows dramatically lit sketches, texts and technical drawings. The models are displayed between these two walls. The sound of steel balls rolling over a metal plate fills the room and enhances the sensation of large scale.

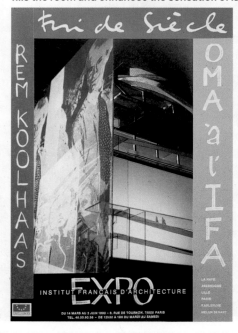

841

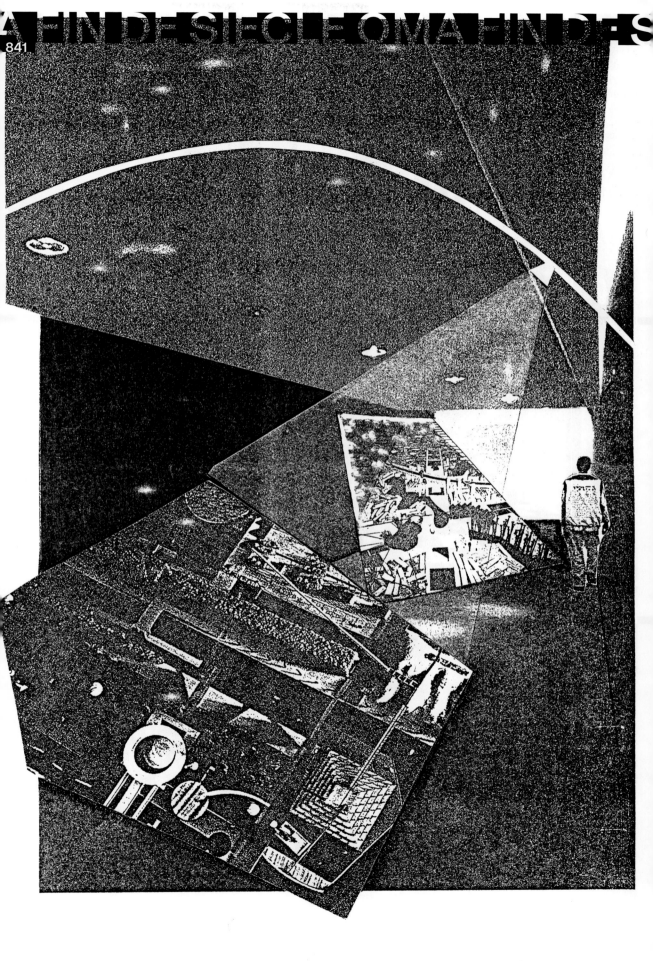

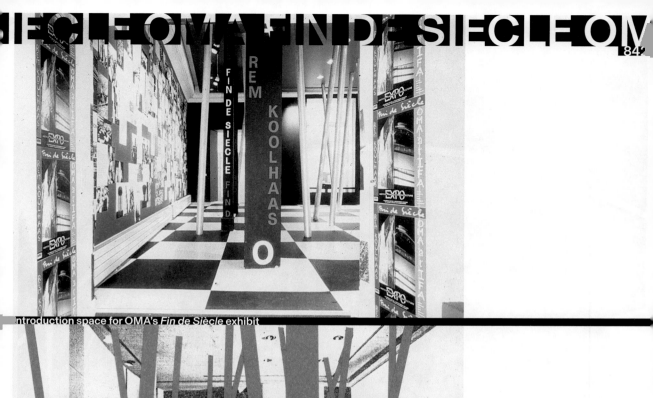

Introduction space for OMA's *Fin de Siècle* exhibit

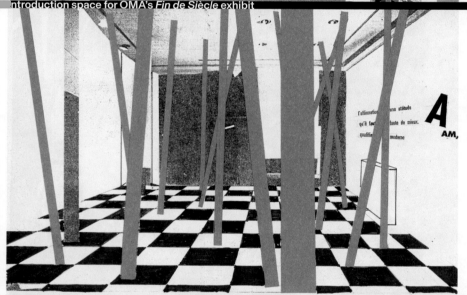

My collage with predictions for that space

One of the 'girl's room' collages in the entry

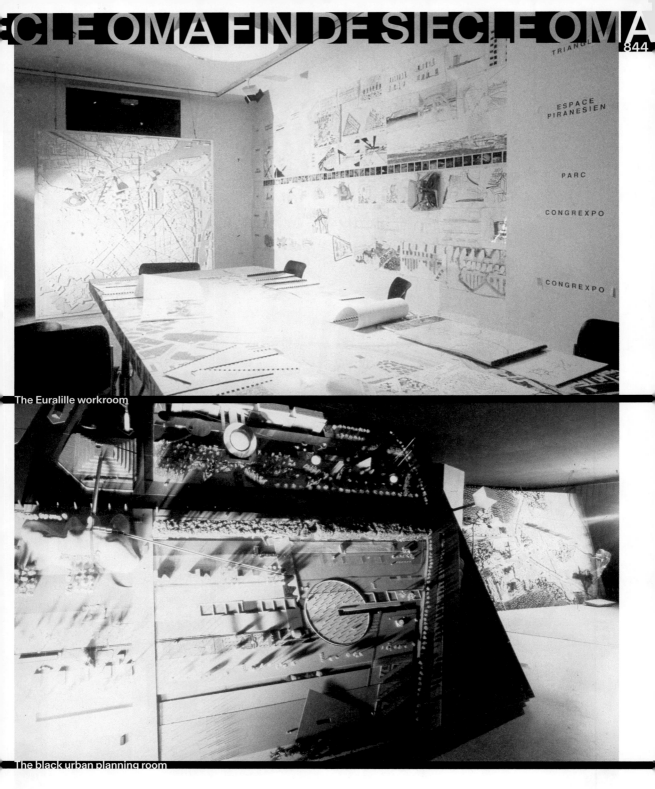

TRIANGL

ESPACE
PIRANESIEN

PARC

CONGREXPO

CONGREXPO

The Euralille workroom

The black urban planning room

Hard Werken's wallpaper of unbuilt projects, created for the attic space

Hans Werlemann's enlarged model pictures on canvas, forming a wall; and gypsum models of unbuilt projects on high pedestals

One of my collages, envisioning the non-built installation in the attic space of the IFA building: narrowing the space down even more with large "paintings" along one wall (Hans Werlemann); and a continuous graphic information board along the other (Hard Werken). Sound and light installations were hidden behind. A row of models on tall socles under dramatic lighting.

OMA The First Decade
Museum Boijmans van Beuningen

"The exhibit took place in two beautifully spacious rooms – one square and one rectangular – with large, floor-to-ceiling windows that bathed the rooms in daylight. I produced a yellow silk curtain (with horizontal seams!) to filter the light of the large window in the first room. A small fan kept the curtain in constant movement, billowing and fluttering. The main hall was so large that the exhibition material got lost in it. We had to provide scale. So, we constructed a large square black tent in the centre of the space for the unbuilt projects, enlarged all the drawing prints and urban planning models to XL in scale and added the 6 m grid of made-to-size rebar-wire tree trunks to give the space strength and rhythm. We filled one trunk with purple silk – something to do with Prince. ;-) The curved introduction wall that marked the entrance to the exhibit was made onsite by two construction workers who had never worked in an indoor environment before: they really suffocated from the heat!"   PB

LOCATION	Rotterdam, the Netherlands
CLIENT	Museum Boijmans van Beuningen – director Wim Crouwel
STATUS	Completed
SCOPE	Exhibition design and installation
MATERIALS	Various
SCALE	450 m²
COLLABORATORS	OMA, Hans Werlemann/Hectic Pictures, Claudi Cornaz, Herman Helle, Parthesius & de Rijk, Ron Steiner
DESCRIPTION	We exhibited in an extension of the Boijmans Museum by architect Alexander Bodon.

Space 1 vertical projects: A grid of daylight lamps mounted on the false ceiling bathed the large, tall room in exaggerated sunny daylight during the rainy Dutch autumn season.

A transparent "introduction wall" of rebar wire (made on site by construction workers) displayed OMA's paintings/silk screens. Spread over the room, a 6-metre grid of "trees" made of rebar wire mimicked the plan of OMA's Architecture Institute design. Models, small screens and drawings were attached to "branches" sticking out of the tree trunks, and large construction drawings – white with black lines for "realised projects" – lined the surrounding walls. A thin, yellow silk curtain covered the large corner window and billowed incessantly thanks to a small fan.

A square black tent was placed in the middle of the room; it was very dark inside with only a narrow slit to admit visitors. Here the unbuilt projects were shown, dramatically illuminated with spotlights and casting their shadows on the milk-white window in the tent's far side. A black-and-white film of the Arnhem Panopticon Prison was projected with a very old and very noisy film projector. On the walls outside the tent 4 × 3 m prints – black with white lines – clad the surrounding walls, showing one key drawing for each "lost" project.

Space 2 horizontal projects: A very large window overlooking the garden bathed the entire space in daylight. One half contained the "Lille office space": sketches, notes and study models spread out on the walls and a large conference table. On the other side of the space, the sculptural model of Melun Senart and other urban models were shown on the walls and on one huge textile "scanachrome" print of La Villette.

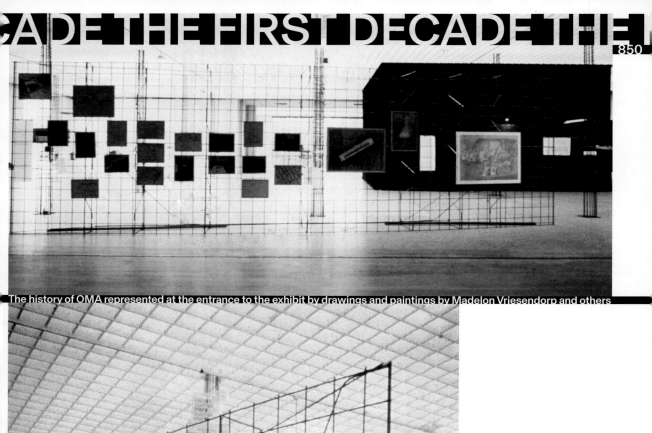

The history of OMA represented at the entrance to the exhibit by drawings and paintings by Madelon Vriesendorp and others

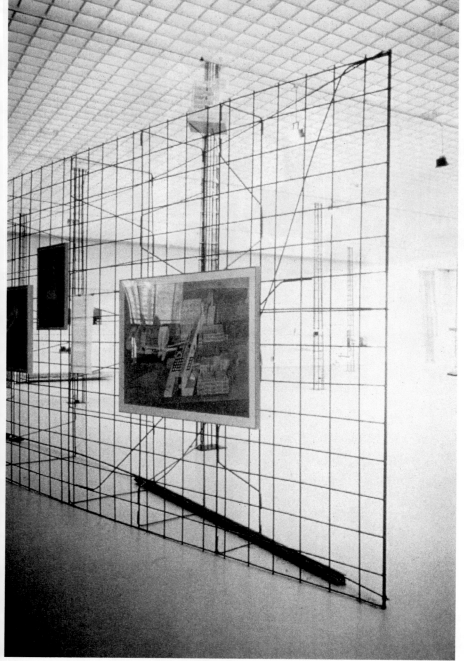

The built projects presented in different media, fixed on the rebar trees

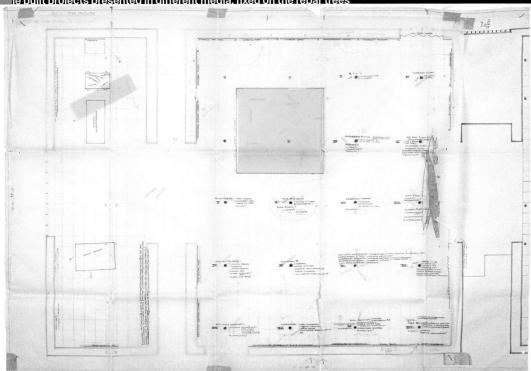

My installation plan for the exhibit

OMA's curved reconstruction of the Mies Pavilion Barcelona (1929) for the Triennale di Milano, 1986 (scale study model hung on rebar tree filled with purple silk)

Yellow silk curtain fluttering in the wind

Black tent with the unbuilt projects

The second room with all the urban plans for Parc de la Villette, Euralille and Melun Senart

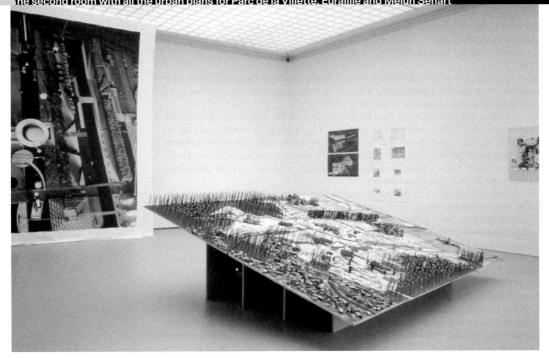

"At first, I designed a more Japanese-like garden with minimal plantings and with a round, pointy mound on one side of the jetty, near the water's edge. I made this mound from sand and fortified it with cement. It was approximately one metre in height by two metres in diameter, and the idea was that its surface would turn green with moss over time. Unfortunately, the mound partially obstructed the view of the creek, where ducks, geese and other waterfowl passed by. This turned out to be a huge problem for the owners. A Dutch landscape needs to be wide open, not three-dimensional. Out it went."

"The owners said that they definitely didn't have green thumbs and wouldn't know what to do in a garden. They wanted to enjoy an attractive view from inside and from the terrace; the garden was to be a space for relaxation and an object of beauty."   PB

LOCATION   Kralingen, Rotterdam, the Netherlands
CLIENT   Private owner
STATUS   Completed
SCOPE   Interior finishes, curtains and garden (for one of the twin houses)
MATERIALS   Silk, wood, plantings
SIZE   Curtains, 266 m²; garden, 500 m²
COLLABORATORS   OMA
DESCRIPTION   The villa lies on a dike and has two floors along the street and one floor that faces a small garden bordered by a creek. To the west, a meadow; to the east, the semi-detached house and garden.
                Along the glass facade that faces south onto the garden, there are two thin, translucent silk curtains, 2/3 white, 2/3 light grey. The widths are sewn together horizontally. When the facade slides open, they catch the breeze, billowing and fluttering in and out. The glass facade consists of different kinds of glass panels that change from neutral to sandy to bluish so that the colour of the curtain changes accordingly.
                The wooden floor of the interior seamlessly connects to the terrace outside. The terrace follows the facade, but the centre stretches out over the lowered garden like a jetty, ending by the water. Thus, the garden is experienced from a slightly higher position, from a distance and at various angles. The southern border of the garden is defined by the creek; a line of bamboo and willow twigs line the west and east borders, respectively. A circle of boxwood slides under the jetty to form a flower bed that changes colour and structure throughout the seasons. A deep-green ivy carpet lies all around, from which bulbous flowers sprout. Two apple trees, planted closely together to form one crown, generate shade for the terrace. Near the creek, a tuft of ornamental grass mimics a fountain, golden in the autumn sun. Along the creek three pollard willows with orange branches form a transparent screen between the garden and the landscape opposite.

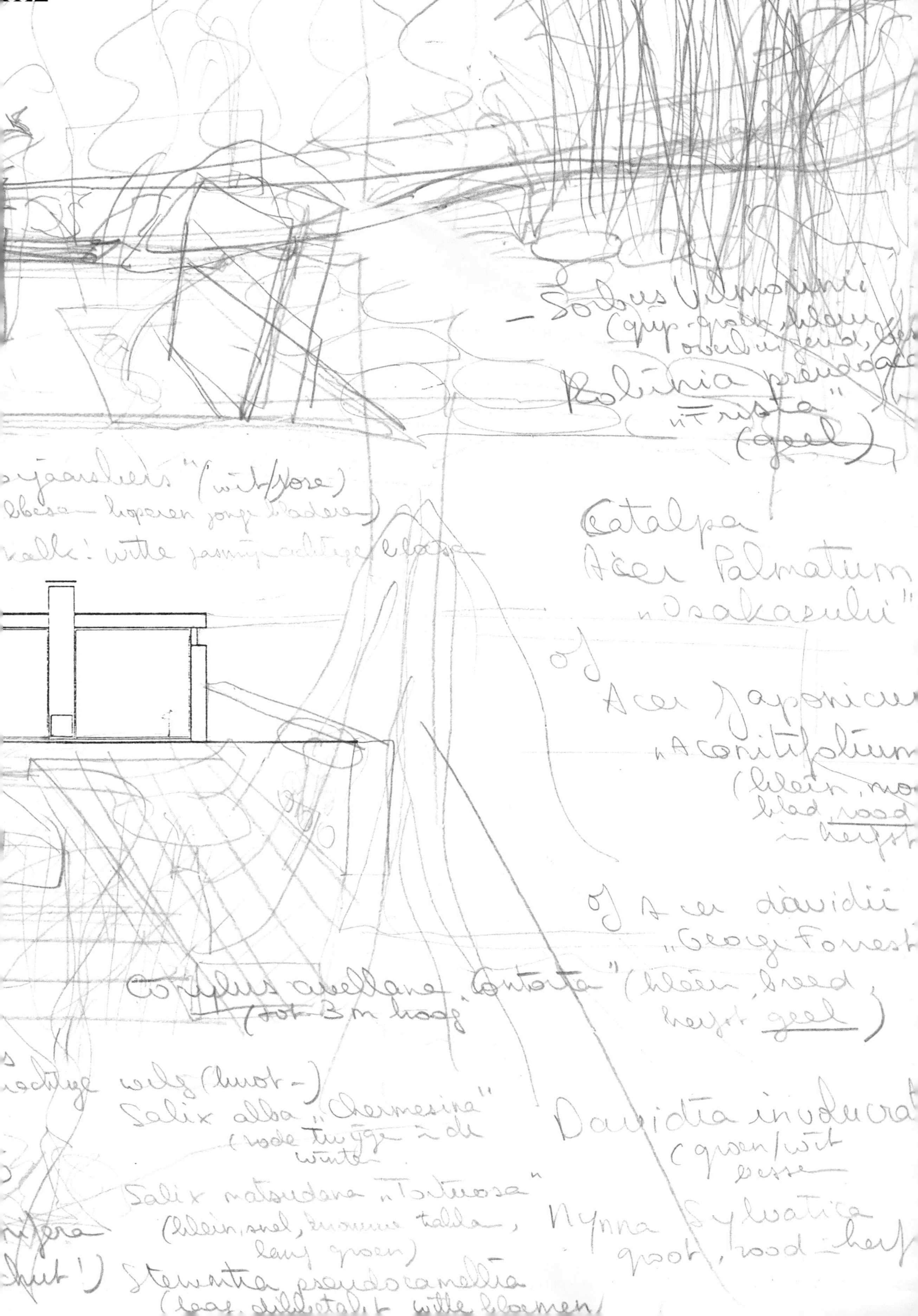

— Sorbus Vilmorinii
(grijp groot, bloeit,
oranjerood, ser...)

Robinia pseudoa...
"Frisia"
(geel)

Catalpa
Acer Palmatum
"Osakasuki"

Acer Japonicum
"Aconitifolium"
(klein, mo...
blad rood
in herfst...

Acer davidii
"George Forrest"
(klein, breed,
herfst geel)

...jaanslers "(wit/rose)
...besa — hopven jonge bladen —)
...ll: witte jammachtige bloem

Corylus avellana "Contorta"
(tot 3m hoog)

...chtige wilg (knot —)
Salix alba "Chermesina"
(rode twijgen in de
winter

Salix matsudana "Tortuosa"
(klein, snel, kronke talla —
lang groen)

...fera
...hut!) Stewartia pseudocamellia
(laat, dikbetak, witte bloemen

Davidia involucrata
(groen/wit
besse

Nynna Sylvatica
groot, rood herfst

First design for this private garden

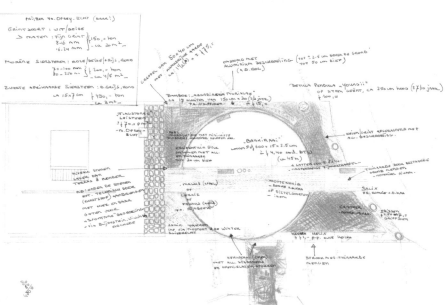

The garden one year after realisation

"We had to open the wooden crates and take out the models on the shopping street in front of the museum because the crates didn't fit through the building's doors. Inside the crates, each model was kept in place and protected by loose Styrofoam flakes that filled the entire crate. When we opened the first one, a gust of wind blew all of the white foam flakes into the air: whirls of flakes danced through the streets, higher and higher, round and round they went like a swarm of birds, catching the light, then settling in each and every corner and crevice. Beautiful."

"The museum, under the direction of Ulrike Jehle Schulte-Strathaus at the time, was very well heated. The Boompjes model had been recently constructed, and its main volume was built of massive wooden blocks. Fresh wood, it turned out. We installed it on a high, bright-red plinth and lit it with a dramatic spotlight. A day later, after a long day's work, we were about to leave the museum when we heard a loud BANG!!!! We ran up to the 'vertical' floor and saw to our dismay that the Boompjes had collapsed with incredible force. Because of the heat, the wooden blocks had become warped and were drooping like a bouquet of flowers in a vase. Ulrike found the best carpenter in town, and he managed to reassemble the model using the dovetailing technique (plus moisture and clamps). Just like the painters, who could imitate the colour of the tiniest material sample that we gave them, their craftsmanship was very impressive – and we felt spoilt by Swiss perfectionism."   PB

LOCATION	Basel, Switzerland
CLIENT	Architekturmuseum Basel – director Ulrike Jehle Schulte-Strathaus
STATUS	Completed
SCOPE	Exhibition design and installation
MATERIALS	Various
COLLABORATORS	OMA, Hans Werlemann/Hectic Pictures, Claudi Cornaz, Herman Helle, Parthesius & de Rijk, Ron Steiner
DESCRIPTION	Introduction floor: dark space with slide projection on translucent "flap" hanging down from ceiling to floor, chairs Vertical project floor: Boompjes, Churchillplein, City Hall Horizontal project floor: La Villette, World expo, Citroenne Cévennes, Melun-Senart, Bijlmermeer. Nederlands Dans Theater floor: complete history, colour and material samples, including stage curtain.

"Through contacts with local politicians and developers, I was able to reserve the Holland America Line building in Kop van Zuid for the Rotterdam '88 project. A beautiful, spacious building from which many Dutch people, my father included, took the ship to America after World War II. Of course, in 1988, travellers still needed to use the building to embark or disembark ships, so a section was reserved for that purpose. I turned the hall into an exhibition space by, among other things, covering the large south-facing windows with white textile screens and by opening up the entire first floor. We organised various exhibits, one in collaboration with OMA with whom we constructed a diagonal wooden floor for the sculptures of Scott Burton (American artist, died 1989). His objects stuck out of the sloped wooden flooring. It was very beautiful, people were climbing up the slope, passing by these strong, angular stone objects – each a different kind of stone and in various colours."

"We also built a long wooden wall with large 'windows' for the Buren installation and I had his pink-white striped cloth made into curtains that hung inside the windows. The 'facade' was painted with black-and-white stripes, of course."

"I worked with Mario Merz to set up his spiral iron vegetable table, bringing everything with me from the food market in beautiful cardboard boxes that I kept to use at home afterwards. Merz was serious but nice. We placed red, green and yellow peppers onto the structure, then we placed the wicker object inside it."

"When we held an exhibition on architecture at the passenger terminal, I wanted to show the models in the open – without protective covers. This made the Coop Himmelb(l)au team very angry, and there was no way to convince them otherwise. The risk of damage to their model – or worse: theft! – was just unacceptable. Pity, I always think those shiny Perspex hoods take away the materiality of things."   PB

LOCATION	Holland America Line, Kop van Zuid, Rotterdam, the Netherlands
CLIENT	Rotterdamse Kunststichting
STATUS	Completed
SCOPE	Selection and preparation of location, organisation and design of a series of fine and applied arts exhibitions throughout 1988
SIZE	ca. 4,500 m²
MATERIALS	Various
COLLABORATORS	OMA, Rotterdamse Kunststichting team
DESCRIPTION	Rotterdam '88 exhibitions: Daniel Buren, Mario Merz, Scott Burton, Zaha Hadid, Coop Himmelb(l)au and more.

Liquid Gold
Nederlands Dans Theater

"I had just left my job as assistant at the Stedelijk Museum's applied arts department when Koolhaas and his OMA team invited me to join the Dans Theater project to influence the building's interior colour and material scheme. The Dans Theater was an artistic, low-budget project financed by savings of the dance company itself and managed by Carel Birnie and creative director Jiří Kylián. Projected on a newly developed square (masterplan by Carel Weeber) and hugging an equally new concert hall, the Dans Theater needed to take up a minimum of built volume. We shared the foyer with the adjacent building to save space – a building that had an 'awful' bluish-pink facade with black diagonal stripes facing 'our' building. So, one of the first decisions was to paint our facade bright RED to warm up the pink. We worked day and night, inventing, researching, designing and physically building, painting, installing lights and placing furniture, coordinating and unpacking deliveries, checking colours and organising food and drink for everyone along the way. Given the limited budget, we all had to be extremely inventive and creative, but this didn't dampen our enthusiasm in the least: we didn't earn anything but we managed to get by, we were used to improvising. After the official opening and theatre festivities, we must have all slept for days on end – exhausted but proud."

"I travelled through the country to find vintage 'design' furniture and discarded building materials such as compressed aluminium pipes – beautiful blocks! – or rubber elements found at waste plants. On one of these trips around the countryside with Hans Werlemann, we spotted a bleached tree trunk on the banks of a river. It had the exact shape of a chaise longue. Hans picked it up with a trailer and took it back to his studio in Rotterdam. There, the trunk came to life: mosquitoes hatched, little beetles crawled out and tiny plants showed their faces. Did we take a picture? No, we forgot. But the image is etched in my memory: moving, precarious, full of promise! In the end and to my regret, we had to gas the trunk to be able to use it as furniture. The chaise longue was placed in the dancer's living room until it was stolen."

"My first thought was to make the curtain from metallic links that would constantly turn and catch every ray of light. But I quickly learnt that a stage curtain needs to be light and soundproof. In other words, massive. Traditionally, wool velvet is used as it is durable and also easy to treat for flame resistance. I contacted the laboratories of Texoprint and Vlisco. They were willing to invest in inventing a technique to attach golden foil onto a wool velvet base according to a specific pattern. They produced a copper roll with the three-dimensional dot-pattern that we provided. Under pressure, this roll flattened the upstanding hairs of the woollen cloth, an ancient technique used for traditional velvet upholstery. A thin glue was developed, fluid enough to be suitable for screen-printing. Once the glue was in place on the flattened areas, the foil sheets were pressed on with heat, after which the sheets were pulled off, leaving the gold behind only on the dot pattern. Although some choreographers found that the curtain competed with the often minimalist dance pieces, the 250 m² of 'liquid gold' became the symbol of the theatre. Point taken." PB

LOCATION	The Hague, the Netherlands
CLIENT	Nederlands Dans Theater / OMA
STATUS	Completed
SCOPE	Design of stage curtain and interior interventions, seating for auditorium, sound reflectors, underside of "flying" champagne foyer; vintage furniture for dancers' lounge and dressing rooms, restaurant
MATERIALS	Wool velvet, mohair velvet, gold foil, gold leaf, tree trunk, bent wood, gold paint, mirror, cord, vintage furniture
SCALE	ca. 4,000 m², auditorium and seating for 1,001 persons; stage curtain, 22 × 11 m; six sound reflectors; gold foil column, 100 × 50 cm
COLLABORATORS	OMA, Hans Werlemann, Utopia, Theatex, Texoprint
DESCRIPTION	Auditorium stage curtain: grey wool velvet with applied gold foil, 22 × 11 m; chairs: 1,001 chairs, upholstered with dark-blue mohair velvet; six sound reflectors: bent plywood panels, golden powder paint, small rectangular mirrors (used for sound tests, left in place).

Flying champagne foyer (underside): flesh-pink velvet, filling, thick cord.

Main foyer: sloping "oyster" ceiling: white irregularly perforated gypsum board with integrated light; floor: black and white terrazzo tiles; concrete columns painted in various colours; smallest concrete column half-covered with gold leaf, lit with construction lamp.

Dancers' lounge: wood floor, coloured gypsum walls, green marble separation wall (an ode to Mies).

Furniture: Noguchi paper floor lamps, vintage furniture with new upholstery, bleached tree trunk as chaise longue (found in nature).

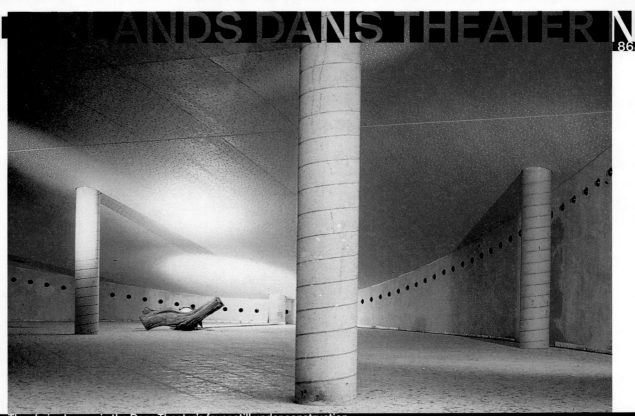

The chaise longue in the Dans Theater's foyer still under construction

Dancers in their lounge with Noguchi lamps and re-upholstered vintage furniture

The suspended champagne bar seen from below, with its flesh-coloured velvet bottom bound with thick rope

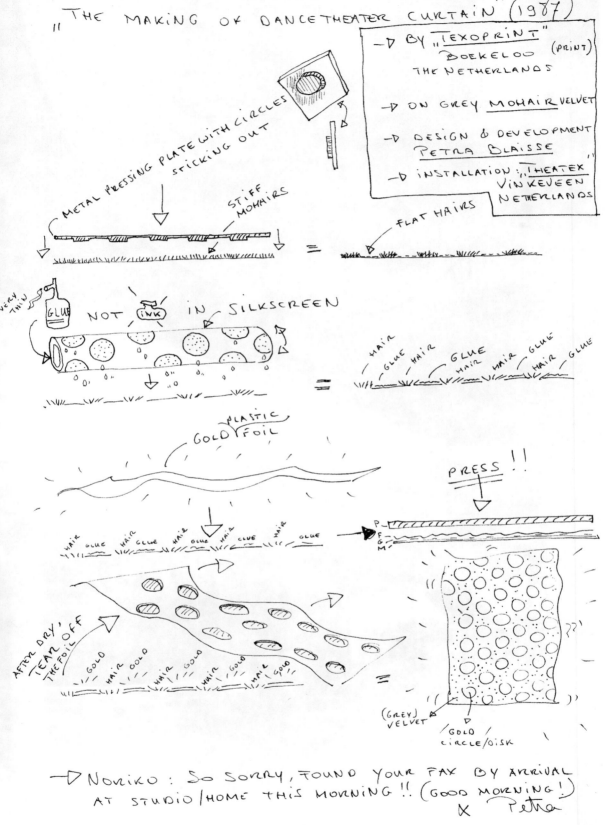

" THE MAKING OF DANCE THEATER CURTAIN " (1987)

—▷ BY "TEXOPRINT" BOEKELOO (PRINT) THE NETHERLANDS

—▷ ON GREY MOHAIR VELVET

—▷ DESIGN & DEVELOPMENT PETRA BLAISSE

—▷ INSTALLATION : "THEATEX" VINKEVEEN NETHERLANDS

METAL PRESSING PLATE WITH CIRCLES STICKING OUT

STIFF MOHAIRS

FLAT HAIRS

VERY THIN GLUE

NOT INK IN SILKSCREEN

HAIR GLUE HAIR GLUE HAIR GLUE HAIR GLUE HAIR GLUE

GOLD PLASTIC FOIL

PRESS !!

HAIR GLUE HAIR GLUE HAIR GLUE HAIR GLUE GLUE

P F G M

AFTER DRY, TEAR OFF THE FOIL

GOLD HAIR GOLD HAIR GOLD HAIR GOLD HAIR GOLD

??

(GREY) VELVET

GOLD CIRCLE/DISK

—▷ NORIKO : SO SORRY, FOUND YOUR FAX BY ARRIVAL AT STUDIO/HOME THIS MORNING !! (GOOD MORNING!)
X Petra

Recipe for gold stage curtain

Three of the six sound reflecting panels, painted in gold, with mini mirrors placed in the centre

Curtain in action for curtain calls

The stage curtain at rest with neutral lighting

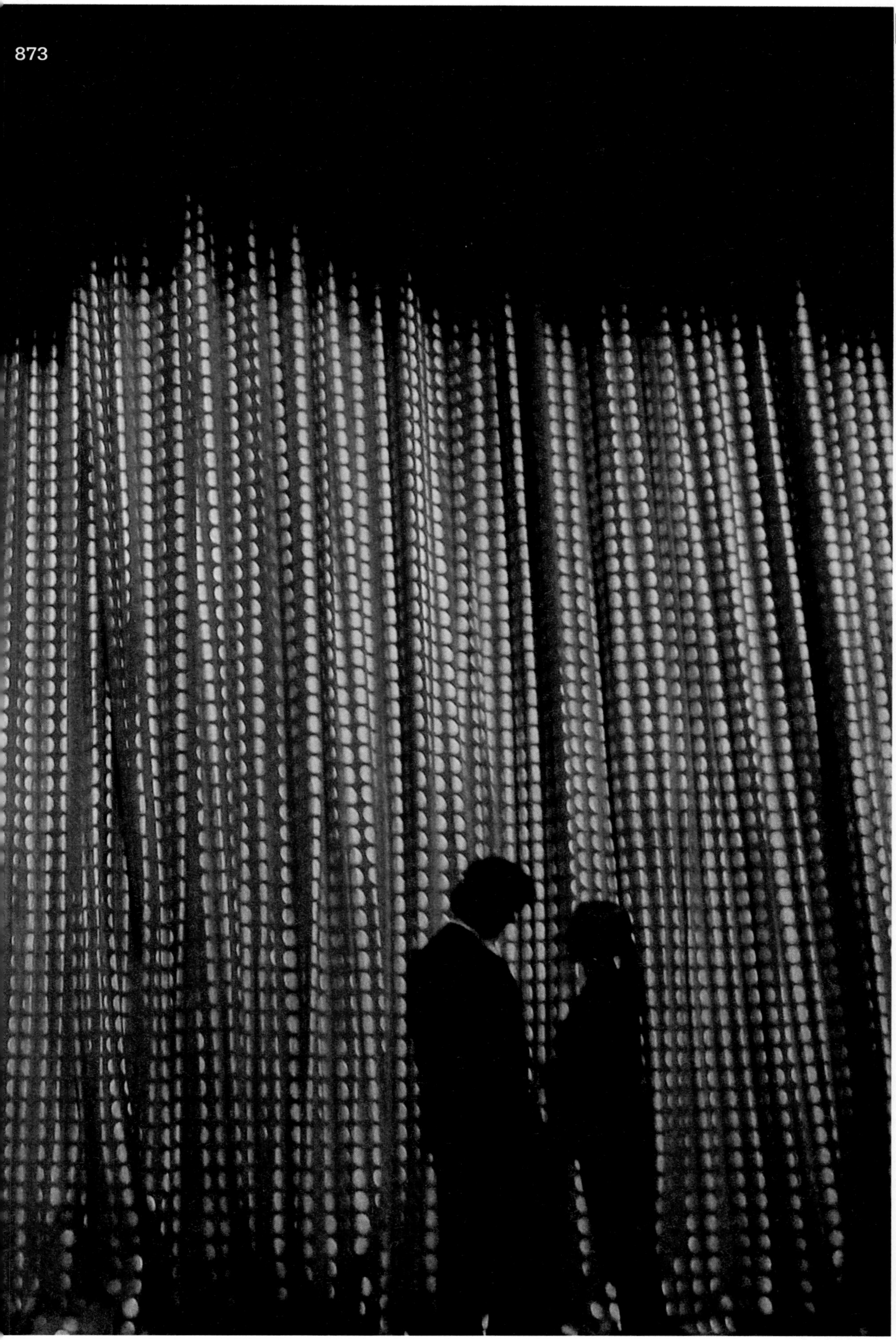

You have to act;

it

radically transf[orm]

And you

do i[t]

all the

VICTOR MALLET — PARIS
SAM FLEMING — BRUSSELS

Emmanuel Macron has urged the creation of a broad "community" of European democracies to include non-EU members amid calls to reform the way the continent is governed following the Russian invasion of Ukraine.

In a speech to the European Parliament yesterday, Macron also joined a push for the rewriting of EU treaties to speed decision-making in the 27-member Union.

"Europe... cannot be in the short term the only means of structuring the European continent."

The proposal comes as EU leaders rethink the way the union handles relations with its close neighbours following the war in Ukraine. One of the key questions is how to manage the aspirations of non-EU countries aspiring to join the bloc.

The new federation would allow European countries adhering to the EU's "core values" to co-operate on...

...organise Europe politically in a broader way than the EU", Macron said in Strasbourg on the anniversary of Robert Schuman's 1950 declaration on European integration. "It's our historic obligation to respond to that today and to create what I would call a European political community."

He added: "The European Union...

membership, but countries aspiring to become members are likely to view his idea with suspicion, given frustrations that the union has been stalling their applications. Macron said the new club was needed because would-be EU members such as Ukraine were waiting for years and even decades before they could join.

Macron also jo[ined]... for the rewriti[ng]...

Trade unions seek pay rises

even as uncertainty from

conflict clouds horizon

MARTIN ARNOLD — FRANKFURT

As Germany's biggest union, IG Metall, begins discussions on demands for a wage increase of up to 8.2 per cent for the country's 85,000 steelworkers in the coming weeks, Birgit Dietze expects reverberations for workers across Europe.

"When companies are making high profits, as they are at the moment, there can and must be compensation for the sharp rise in prices for employees," Dietze, IG Metall's chief negotiator in the east German steel industry, told the Financial Times ahead of a vote by the union's board on Sunday, when members backed the proposed rise.

The IG Metall discussions, which are set to conclude by the summer, are expected to provide a benchmark for negotiation rounds in other industries later in 2022. Esther Lynch, deputy general secretary of the European Trade Union Confederation, said: "Everybody who bargains on wages looks very closely at what these negotiations in German industry are doing."

A bumper pay deal for Germany's steelworkers would also raise eyebrows among policymakers at the European

Central Bank who are increasingly [focused] on raising interest rates in July to tackle record inflation of 7.5 per [cent in] April. Officials fear spiralli[ng] growth will mean price pr[essures] becoming entrenched, risking [a] style "wage-price spiral".

Yet, with a cost of living crisis l[ooming] and unemployment in the 19-c[ountry] bloc falling to a record low of 6.8 p[er cent] in March, demand for better wages is strong. Lynch added: "I'm now hearing from almost every delegate examples of how low-paid workers can't even meet the basics of paying for food and electricity, and they want action now."

Unions across the eurozone have called for rises for the region's worst off. FNV, the biggest Dutch union with...

minimum wage from €9.82 an hour to €12 an hour in October. The country's statistical office said this would affect 7mn workers, mostly women, or about one-sixth of the workforce.

France's minimum wage has risen three times in the past year for a total increase of 5.9 per cent, but unions including the leftwing CGT, which represents more than 700,000 workers...

...cent in 2006 to 16 per cent... said. Union membership in G[ermany] meanwhile, has dropped from... cent after the country's reunification.

do i[t]

all the

— US
— UK
— Eurozone

2015   20   22
Source: OECD

Dietze said IG Metall was "monitori[ng] the economic situation very closely an[d] taking it into account when makin[g]...

Janiform kantharos; a two-handled wine cup with addorsed heads of a male African and a female Greek Ceramic, ca. 480–470 BC, culture: African, Attic, 14.9 × 13.8 × 11.2 cm, diam. rim 9.2 cm

The two subjects may represent a visual exposition of Herodotus's theories of racial difference or a display of slaves and female companions in the service of Greek men – Collection Princeton University Art Museum

IMAGE CREDITS

In some cases, despite efforts to do so, the obtaining of copyright permissions and usage of excerpts of text was not always successful.

INSIDE OUTSIDE COLLABORATORS

PARTNERS
Petra Blaisse
Aura Luz Melis
Jana Crepon

WITH
Peter Niessen

A
Aaron Kop
Akane Moriyama
Alexandra Devaux
Alexandra Pander
Allesandro Macaluso
Allesandro Solci
Agnieszka Zborowska
Amelia Millan
Ana Beja da Costa
Ana Barbara Somaglino
Andrea Mologni
Anky Adriaanse
Anna van Dorp
Anna Madella
Annelies Bloemendaal
Anouk Vogel
Armand Paardekoper
Asmira Salkanovic
Astrid Steegmans
Atir Kahn

B
Barbara Pais
Bella Janssens
Bram de Regt
Brennen Birch

C
Camilla Panzeri
Carlotta Basoli
Carolina Martinho
Carmen Buitenhuis
Cecile-Diama Samb
Céline Baumann
Chantal Vos
Charly Blödel
Che-Yi Shih
Christine Yadlowski
Claire Oude Aarninkhof

D
Daisy Bravo
Daphne Keraudren
Danique Landburg
Daniyal Sherafat
Danyan Liu
Desiree Pierluigi
Diana Lukjanska
Dick Zeeuwe
Domenika Dyminska

E
Egle Kazdailyté
Eirini Trachana
Elena Beri
Eline Holtes
Elisa Boscarato
Esther Bentvelsen
Eunjee Hyun
Eva Radionova
Ewen Le Rouic

F
Farnoosh Bazrafkan
Federica Zatta
Fenna van der Klei
Floris Schiferli
Francesca Porro
Francesca Sartori
Frits Veenis

G
Gabriela Piasta
George Huzum
Giacomo Santoro
Gianluca Tramutola
Guillaume Bordin

H
Henri Comptdaer
Huo Geng
Hans Werlemann
Haruka Maeda

I
Irene Curulli
Isabella Calducci
Isabella Di Mille
Izumi Sato

J
Jaap de Vries
Jacques Abelman
Jaime Macfarlane
James Teng
Jan Geysen
Jaume Vidal Pardo
Jeannette Krusemann
Jennifer Siani
Jeroen Kooistra
Jeroen Langen
Jesscia Minn
Julia Gersten

K
Kanika Pawar
Karin Falkenhage
Kate Armstrong
Katie Kelly
Kim van Beek
Kim Olde Loohuis
Kim Uyting

L
Lalo Gambini
Laura Baird
Laura van Santen
Lieuwe Conradie
Lily Xiaohan Liang
Loes Gieles
Lorenzo Cantoni
Lukasz Bakowski

M
Marcel Musch
Maria-Christine Elsmore-Andersen
Marieke van den Heuvel
Marjolein Schoonewagen
Marleen de Vries
Marnix van den Broek
Marta Galmarini
Martina Prokop
Martina Lucchese
Martyna Rajewska
Mathias Lehner
Mathilde Stubmark
Mees Rijckevorsel
Melody Stein
Merel Haenen
Micha van Rooijen
Michal Jagodzinski
Mikel Orbegozo
Miki Sato

N
Nafsika Efklidou
Nika Jazaei
Nur Zayat

P
Panos Rigopoulos
Patricia Rivero Bartolomé
Peppina Peeman
Pratyusha Suryakant

R
Rabia Zuberi
Reinier Suurenbroek
Remco Swart
Robert Kater
Rosetta Elkin
S
Sam Fu Shi Man
Samantha Kroliczak
Sara Dughetti
Shane van Lunteren
Signe Swarttouw
Simao Fereira
Stephan Willenborg
Sophie Vanwijnsberghe
Susanna Roccucci
Szu-Yi Wang
T
Tania Sanjurjo Fernandez
Theodoris Chalvatzoglou
V
Valentin Frechet
Viola Guarano
Vivi Wei Zeng
W
Wen Klopstra-Jiang
Wim Poppinga
Y
Yasemin Silahtaroglu
Yuting Guan
Yinyin Liu
Yukie Nagasawa
Yukiko Nezu
Z
Zeger Dalenberg

Art Applied
Inside Outside / Petra Blaisse

Petra Blaisse
Jana Crepon
Aura Luz Melis
Peter Niessen

EDITORS   Fredi Fischli and Niels Olsen
gta Exhibitions, ETH Zurich
AUTHORS   Petra Blaisse, Jana Crepon, Penelope Curtis, Nafsika Efklidou, Fredi Fischli,
Christophe Girot, Ann Goldstein, Rem Koolhaas, Charlotte Matter, Aura Luz Melis,
Peter Niessen, Niels Olsen, Fatma Al Sehlawi, Jack Self, Laurent Stalder, Helen Thomas,
Philip Ursprung, Christopher Williams
GRAPHIC DESIGN   Teo Schifferli with Martin Lostis
PRODUCTION   Morgan Crowcroft-Brown
PROJECT EDITOR   Louis Rogers
COPY-EDITING   Catherine Schelbert, Elizabeth MacFadyen
PROOFREADING   Rebecca Bligh
EDITORIAL ASSISTANCE   Elena Bally, Kim van Beek, Lisa Boos, Valentina Ehnimb,
Nafsika Efklidou, Aura Luz Melis, Peter Niessen, Geraldine Tedder
INDEX   Emma Caddy
TYPEFACE   Basel Grotesk, Optimo

This research and publication project was financially supported by

ETH Zurich
Department of Architecture
Institute for the History and Theory of Architecture (gta)

Creative Industries Fund NL
Graham Foundation
Andy Warhol Foundation
Inside Outside
Petra Blaisse
Rem Koolhaas
Gerriets GmbH
HCM 365
Architectura & Natura

First edition published by MACK

Printed in Germany
ISBN 978-1-915743-34-3
mackbooks.co.uk

Acknowledgements by Petra Blaisse

All the works shown in this book would not have been realised without the involvement of the hundreds of collaborators who contributed to the projects of Inside Outside through the years. I wholeheartedly thank them for their creative energy and input.

The realisation of this book would not have been possible without the support of the current Inside Outside team in these past three years. I specifically want to thank my partners Aura Luz Melis and Jana Crepon; project architect Nafsika Efklidou; curtain designer Peter Niessen; PR collaborators Merel Haenen and Kim van Beek (respectively); and our loyal office manager Loes Gieles.

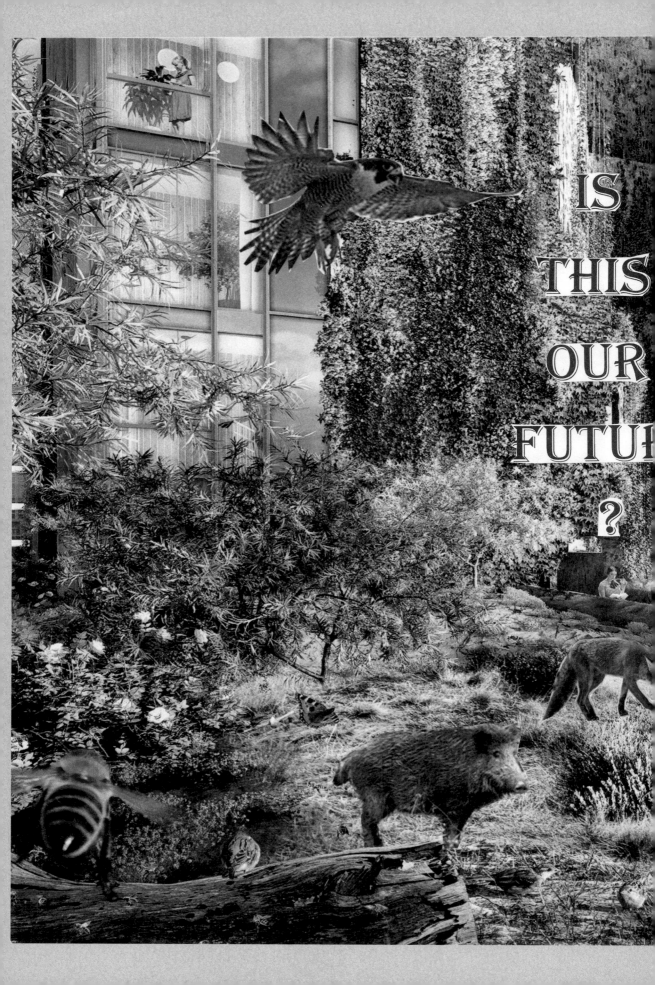